ISSUES IN AMERICAN ECONOMIC HISTORY

Issues

in

AMERICAN

ECONOMIC

HISTORY
SELECTED
READINGS

EDITED BY

Gerald D. Nash

THE UNIVERSITY OF NEW MEXICO

D. C. HEATH AND COMPANY   *Boston*

Preface

The great activity in American Economic History during the last three decades and the bewildering succession of new interpretations provide a justification for this book of readings which is designed to introduce the novice to the subject. The aims of the volume are fourfold. First, it is designed to provide supplementary readings in American Economic History from a variety of secondary sources. Second, it seeks to acquaint its readers with some of the controversial issues in the field. Third, it presents challenging reinterpretations of these problems which have revised accepted views within the past generation. Finally, it can serve as a basis for discussions since selections have also been chosen for their clashing and contrasting opinions.

The readings in this volume are focused upon the theme of economic expansion. Thus, topics and selections relate to the historical development of factors responsible for economic growth. These include ideas, population and labor, government policies, technology, entrepreneurship, and crises. Materials in the book bear upon conflicting assessments of the influence which these forces have had upon the evolution of the American economy. To be sure, this is only one of several strands that could be used to present American Economic History to students but it is hoped that a broad theme will provide some unity for the contents. In their courses instructors are likely to introduce other themes and other emphases. The book is designed to be flexible, and to provide introductions to broad issues while leaving the determination of specific approaches open.

The making of this volume has been a cooperative endeavor. The authors whose selections have been included have made the major contribution. Three master teachers have also generously given their advice and counsel. Professor John D. Hicks of the University of California gave initial encouragement. Professor Thomas A. Bailey of Stanford University gave helpful advice concerning the structure of the work. Professor George R. Taylor of Amherst College made important suggestions for improvements. My students at Stanford University, Northern Illinois University, University of Maryland, and the University of New Mexico have taught me much about their needs for a book which would help them to begin their study of American Economic History. Mrs. Olive Knox of the Department of History at the University of New Mexico provided invaluable typing assistance. The help of all of these individuals is gratefully acknowledged since without them this volume could not have taken shape.

Contents

ISSUES IN AMERICAN ECONOMIC HISTORY

1. The European Background of American Economic History

PROBLEM: *Was puritanism well suited to stimulate economic expansion?*

To trace precisely the complicated web of relationships between religious and economic ideas is not an easy task for any period of history. No wonder, therefore, that more than a half century ago the great German sociologist Max Weber created a lively controversy when he argued, in *The Protestant Ethic and the Spirit of Capitalism,* that the newly emerging Puritan religious doctrines of the sixteenth century were peculiarly favorable to the rapid development of capitalism in western Europe. Other scholars soon criticized this theory, thus giving rise to the problem whether Puritanism was especially stimulating to economic growth. This issue is particularly pertinent in Colonial America where the Puritans sought to establish their ideal society. One of the first scholars to apply Weber's thesis specifically to the United States was A. Whitney Griswold, later the president of Yale, who attempted to demonstrate that certain Puritan doctrines were uniquely suited to encourage business. These included values such as diligence, sobriety, thrift, and a concern with material and worldly success. Such an interpretation is persuasively challenged by E. A. J. Johnson of Johns Hopkins University, an outstanding student of early American economic thought. Johnson finds little evidence in the writings of Puritan leaders to indicate that their attitude was peculiarly inclined toward trade and commerce. In fact, their economic outlook was strongly influenced by concepts drawn from medieval Christian doctrines and contained little that was new. Certainly this was true of their beliefs in the virtue of hard labor, a "just" price, the desirability of wealth, and the primacy of religious values.

1

The following selections illustrate these varying emphases in the interpretation of Puritanism and Capitalism in early America and suggest further problems. Were Catholic, Quaker, or Baptist doctrines less conducive to economic activity? What other influences in Colonial America fostered Puritan values such as industry and thrift? How were religious beliefs reflected in Colonial agriculture and business?

Three Puritans on Prosperity

A. WHITNEY GRISWOLD

I

Since the German economist, Max Weber, first called serious attention to the relationship of Protestantism and capitalism, various scholars have become intrigued with the idea. Some have taken issue with Weber on minor points, but most have accepted his general conclusions. R. H. Tawney, in particular, has elaborated the thesis, and integrated it with the history of the Reformation. Ernst Troeltsch has shown its development in sectarian ethics. Yet so far, no one has sought to demonstrate the forms in which this relationship has manifested itself in American history.

For three centuries, Americans have been taught to admire material success: the "frontier," perhaps, provided the economic basis for the lesson. The growing sense of nationalism, the democratic levelling of social barriers, immense natural resources have combined to make us a nation of "rugged individualists," intent upon getting rich. In addition, we have been harangued, severally and individually, on the virtue of making money by a race of success-prophets indigenous to our soil. It is with three early members of that race that this paper deals.

It is worth while, by way of orientation, to review, in brief, the essence of Weber's theory. Because no one has done this so concisely as Professor Morison, let us borrow from his *Builders of the Bay Colony:*

Max Weber, a German economist of the last century, propounded the interesting theory that Calvinism released the business man from the clutches of the priest, and sprinkled holy water on economic success. According to him, John Calvin defended the taking of interest on loans, which the medieval church had condemned under the name of usury. Since God would not justify reprobates

Reprinted by permission from A. Whitney Griswold, "Three Puritans on Prosperity," *The New England Quarterly*, Vol. VII (September, 1934), pp. 475–493.

by prosperity, so the argument goes, the successful business man was probably one of God's elect; hence the Puritan sought success as evidence of his election to eternal bliss.

This is the theory to which Tawney, Troeltsch, and others have given added currency. Not so Mr. Morison. He rejects it on the grounds that "in none of the scores of funeral sermons which I have read, is it hinted 'Our departed friend was successful, so he must be in Heaven.' " Further, Mr. Morison proceeds to the conclusion of Professor Clive Day that "the economic ideas of the New England Puritans were medieval; and so far as their church had political power, it regulated rather than stimulated business enterprise."

With the economic implications of the criticism of Messrs. Morison and Day, we are not specifically concerned. Yet their suggestion that "the economic ideas of the New England Puritans were medieval" needs considerable qualification. In spite of the evidence offered by Mr. Day in support of this contention, we can not overlook the failure of the collectivist experiment at Plymouth. It is incorrect to deny that at least the seeds of rugged individualism came over on the *Mayflower*. Later they grew so luxuriantly as to shut collectivism completely out of the Puritan sun. In partial proof of this we offer the sermons of our three Puritans.

Mr. Morison's criticism of the rational process suggested by Weber holds more water. Weber would have us believe that the New England farmer of Calvinist persuasion sought to make money not in order to secure the approval of God, but to prove to himself that God already had bestowed His approval, that he was already a member of the elect. The notion is over-subtle. Doubtless it has been entertained by wealthy merchants of the Back Bay and Salem; but, whether through inadvertence or shame, none seems to have committed it to writing. This does not justify the conclusion that Weber is entirely wrong. The fact is that God did "sprinkle holy water on economic success." Only He did it in a much more forthright manner, which the masses could understand, and which neither the Teutonic intellect of Herr Weber nor the sharp wit of Mr. Morison would have missed had they been citizens of that Puritan world. The three Puritans will speak for themselves. They are far from the old-world seats of learning. They address frontier audiences. They have no use for subtleties. They deal in plain truths for plain men.

II

Cotton Mather dealt most specifically with the relationship of business and religion in *Two Brief Discourses, one Directing a Christian in his General Calling; another Directing him in his Personal Calling*, a document of 1701 published in Boston the same year. Mather has become a much-quoted authority for the Weber thesis. Weber himself hastens over this document. It may profit us to turn its pages more leisurely. As its explicit title implies, the work deals with the relation of a man's business to his religion. There is a "calling" for each. The "general calling" is "to serve the Lord Jesus Christ," the "personal calling" "a certain Particular Employment by which his *Usefulness* in his neighborhood is distinguished." Each is a matter of the utmost seriousness. A godly man must worship the Lord punctiliously. At the same time he should contract to do no business he "cannot comfortably venture to pray over." And he must have a business. Worshipping the Lord in prayer and hymn is not enough. Contemplation of the good means nothing without accomplishment of the good. A man must not only be pious; he must be useful.

Now it follows also, that a man must not only be useful but likewise successful. The Lord had made provision for that, too. One should "be careful about the point: *What call from God have I to be in this place and at this work? Am I now where my Lord Jesus Christ would have me to be?*" After assuming this propitious attitude, he might safely trust in God "for the *Success* of all our *Business*, all the day long." But if he refused so to do, failure would be his lot, for "At no time of the Day, may we expect that our Business will succeed without *God's Blessing*." . . .

As worldliness crept into the Puritan religion, occasioning the desperate effort of Jonathan Edwards to revive the fire and brimstone of primitive Calvinism, the social ethics preached by Mather did not die. American Protestants became divided into hostile sects: Methodists, Baptists, Unitarians. Some called themselves Deists. But as a general rule, their business remained a vital part of their religion, a calling. God continued to fill the nets of individual enterprise. Call it rationalization, hypocrisy, inspiration, or what you will, Puritans clung to the doctrine that God would point the way to individual prosperity, and would be pleased at its achievement.

Cotton Mather did not invent this doctrine: he merely gave it expression. His utterances are of interest to us not so much for the persuasive influence they may have had upon his contemporaries, as because they represent the mind of orthodox Puritanism two centuries ago. They indicate that thinking men were casting about in their minds for a moral sanction for money-making, and that they found that sanction in the ethical system originally propounded by Martin Luther and John Calvin. Thus, in a sense, Cotton Mather deserves recognition as one of the first to teach American business men to serve God by making money.

III

One day in 1724 Cotton Mather received a young caller at his home in Boston. It was a sober youth of eighteen years who presented himself. Benjamin Franklin had returned from Philadelphia for a brief visit to his native town, and had stopped to pay his respects to the great Puritan,

whom he much admired. Franklin's later account of the visit indicates that
it made some impression on him. Mather

... received me in his library [he wrote] and on my taking leave showed me a
shorter way out of the house, through a narrow passage, which was crossed
by a beam overhead. We were talking as I withdrew, he accompanying me
behind, and I turning partly towards him, when he said hastily, *"Stoop, stoop!"*
I did not understand him till I felt my head hit against the beam. He was a man
that never missed any occasion of giving instruction, and upon this he said to
me: *"You are young, and have the world before you;* STOOP *as you go through
it, and you will miss many hard thumps."* This advice, thus beat into my head,
has frequently been of use to me, and I often think of it when I see pride
mortified and misfortunes brought upon people by carrying their heads too
high.

Was this all that Mather had to offer his visitor; or was there a real
spiritual bond between the two? ...

It would be interesting to lay the texts of Mather's *Essays* and Franklin's
Autobiography side by side, so much is the former reflected in the latter.
The purpose in recording his own rise "from the poverty and obscurity in
which I was born and bred, to a state of affluence and some degree of
reputation in the world," Franklin declares, is to allow others to profit by
his example. He himself thought it "fit to be imitated" and therefore he
would write a book about it. But first he desired "with all humility to
acknowledge that I owe the mentioned happiness of my past life to
[God's] kind providence, which led me to the means I used and gave
them success." How like a Puritan to attribute to the Lord "a state of
affluence and some degree of reputation in the world." The *Autobiography* is filled with similar professions of humility and piety. To the un-
critical reader, the sermon it preached must have seemed even more convincing than Mather's, for it had received from its author the pragmatic
sanction of successful practice. So he declared, at any rate. He had found
it helpful as a young printer's apprentice to draw up a chart of the virtues
necessary for complete moral perfection, and then to score himself daily
on progress made—or not made. Mather himself could not have improved
the list. It included temperance, silence, order, resolution, frugality, industry, sincerity, justice, moderation, cleanliness, tranquility, chastity, and
humility. Of these, industry was most important. "Lose no time," he said
to himself, "be always employed in something useful; cut off all unnecessary actions."

But it is *Poor Richard* who sings the loudest praise of industry. Luck,
says he, is of no account. Americans need only work hard and never
trouble themselves about luck, for *"Diligence is the Mother of good luck,*
and *God gives all things to industry."* *Poor Richard* likewise knows all
about the calling: *"He that hath a trade hath an estate, and he that hath a
calling hath an office of profit and honor."* In fact the way to wealth was,
in his own words, "as plain as the way to market" to Benjamin Franklin.

It depends chiefly on two words, *industry* and *frugality*—that is, waste neither *time* nor *money*, but make the best use of both. Without industry and frugality nothing will do, and with them everything. He that gets all he can and saves all he can . . . will certainly become rich, if that Being who governs the world, to whom all should look for a blessing on their honest endeavors, doth not, in his wise providence, otherwise determine.

Did Franklin learn all this from Cotton Mather? It is authentic Puritanism. Mather had, at times, stooped low enough to commend charity as a profitable business venture. Franklin certainly knew Mather and read his works. Yet the man who paraphrased classic aphorisms for simple Americans feared no Puritan God. The thunderbolt which was the angry voice of Jehovah to Mather trickled harmlessly off a wet kite-string into Franklin's Leyden jar. *Poor Richard's* wisdom is savory with business acumen. Whence, therefore, the piety? Was it an after-thought?

It makes little difference where Franklin got his Puritanism. Very likely Mather made substantial contributions. Yet the piety, in all probability, was no after-thought. It was put there with deliberate intent. Let us not forget that Benjamin Franklin was a journalist and publisher by trade. *Poor Richard's Almanac*, like most of his other publications, was distinctly a money-making venture. Its shrewd author knew his trade; and what was more, he knew his public. Any publisher knows that catering to a public's taste is profitable, and that is precisely what Franklin did. He understood Puritanism well enough to realize that it offered assurances of material prosperity to all who followed its code of morals. Piety was inexpensive, and so although he himself was worlds apart from orthodoxy, he preached Puritan ethics as good as Mather's. From an unmoral point of view he perceived that the Puritan virtues had immense utilitarian value. And, skeptic though he was, he doubtless thought it wise to be on the safe side, to propitiate whatever God there might be. However that may be, he knew his public would think so.

The popularity of his writings bears witness to Franklin's shrewdness. The *Autobiography* became a famous American success story. Let its author be accused of hypocrisy in affecting the moral austerity of Puritanism. His public must have been delighted to find that he, a scientist, a patriot, a man who had in actuality risen to "a state of affluence and some degree of reputation in the world" endorsed the same democratic virtues as their ministers. It must have relieved them to have such a man turn thumbs down on chance, as it rejoiced them to hear him re-affirm the sanctity of individual prosperity. Benjamin Franklin not only commended prosperity; he dramatized it. . . .

IV

While Cotton Mather represents the mind of orthodox Puritanism, and Franklin a secularized version of the same, Timothy Dwight is the soul of Puritan revivalism. Unlike the other two, Dwight was never really e national figure. His fame and his influence are localized in Connecticut, over the spiritual destinies of which he presided as Congregational "Pope." Although a persevering student and a teacher of some accomplishment, Dwight was scarcely a profound thinker. His preaching is of interest to us because it embodies the latter-day Puritanism revived in the outward form of Congregationalism. In a new age, in a new church, Dwight taught the old ethics of his spiritual fathers; and out of them he evolved a primitive social philosophy which became a national religion. The sermons of Timothy Dwight are Puritan documents. As might be expected, they deplored the seven deadly sins; they dealt uncompromisingly with Satan, and they lauded the Christian virtues. In them we find the same doctrine of good works and the calling, the same especial praise for industry. Only Dwight, being somewhat of a scholar, adduced the wisdom of classical antiquity as well as that of the Old Testament to drive home his points. "The diligent hand maketh rich" he balanced with "Diligentia vincit omnia." And speaking for himself, he declared that idleness was "not only a gross vice in itself, but the highway to all the other vices."

Like Cotton Mather, the man of God, and Benjamin Franklin, the man of the world, Dwight believed that individuals must save their own souls first, the soul of society afterwards. He, too, felt that the Puritan virtues were, and ought to be, individualistic. His exposition of the calling is proof of this. Each man has a soul, he said, and

. . . the value of that soul is inconceivable. It is infinite. The world, nay the universe, weighed against it is nothing. . . . It claims, therefore, it deserves, all your attention, all your labours, all your prayers. . . . At the same time your earthly concerns are not to be forgotten. They, too, have their importance.

So far, we might be listening to Cotton Mather. But in the words which follow a more specific relationship is established between business and religion than any we have yet observed. It shows that Dwight had begun to look at the whole ethical problem objectively, and was trying to find a rational place for it in American life. Spiritual and earthly concerns, he resumed, are not incompatible.

Happily for you the attention which they really demand is in no degree inconsistent with the effectual promotion of your eternal welfare. The same sobriety of mind, which is so useful to the advancement of your heavenly interests, is the direct means of your earthly prosperity.

This was a splendid way to popularize "sobriety of mind" among worldly folk, prosperity among the religious. . . .

V

So spoke three Puritans at various moments in our early history: Cotton Mather from the mysterious universe of Jehovah, Benjamin Franklin from the commercial capital of a new world, Timothy Dwight from the pulpit of revivalism. As their lives overlapped each other, so did their thoughts. And from their several vantage points they came into clear agreement that individual prosperity was a highly desirable thing.

How much influence their teaching may have had it is difficult to say. Possibly it is more than a coincidence that in New England, where business was a calling, and wealth both a sign of heavenly approval and a bulwark of civilization, the Federalists should have their principal strength. When one is told in church that property is sacred, its acquisition a duty, its charitable distribution profitable, it is not strange that he should vote for that same "hedge of law" which Timothy Dwight and Alexander Hamilton thought so essential. Neither is it strange, on the other hand, that a religious gospel promising material success to all who served the Puritans' God should find many adherents among the self-made men who followed Jefferson. One thing is certain, however. Insofar as Cotton Mather, Benjamin Franklin, and Timothy Dwight represent the various facets of American Puritanism, they laid down a code of living the followers of which believed that God desired Americans to be rich.

Economic Ideas of John Winthrop

EDGAR A. J. JOHNSON

How important a role a philosophy plays in men's actions and lives can actually never be determined. A philosophy is never a prime mover, but often an influence so omnipresent and persistent that it becomes worth while to investigate the thoughts as well as the deeds of great men. For this reason, it seems worth while to examine the economic thoughts of John Winthrop. He held definite views about wealth, production, value, communism, colonization, and kindred subjects. He was well equipped in theory before he set out on one of the greatest economic missions of modern times.

There is indeed little that is original in Winthrop's economic thought. But originality is a gift which the gods give reluctantly; and to be great is not necessarily to be original. Winthrop reflected the current beliefs of his age reasonably well. He was not a political economist, but a political and religious leader; and as such, we would not expect him to have more than a reasonable acquaintance with economic speculation. As a devout Christian, economics to him was concerned with what should exist, and with proper relations between citizens of a Christian commonwealth.

Reprinted by permission from Edgar A. J. Johnson, "The Economic Philosophy of John Winthrop," *The New England Quarterly*, Vol. III (April, 1930), pp. 235–250.

This is as much as to say Winthrop's ideas were mediaeval, transmitted to him chiefly through English ecclesiastical sources.

Like his mediaeval predecessors, Winthrop accepted the idea of a blissful state of primitive communism which was presumed to have existed when men (in a state of innocency) had all in common. "The first right to the earth," wrote Winthrop, "was naturall when men held the earth in common every man soweing, and feeding where he pleased." But the fall of man brought an end to this ideal communism (the period analogous to the golden age of the ancient Greeks), and man in his corruption acquired an insatiable acquisitive propensity. "Adam in his first estate," said Winthrop, "was a perfect modell of mankinde," and love was the sole principle of human relations. "But Adam rente himselfe from his Creator" and, as a consequence, "rent all his posterity allsoe one from another." As a result of this moral degradation, "every man is borne with this principle in him to love and seeke himselfe onely, and thus a man continueth till Christ comes and takes possession of the soule and infuseth another principle, love to God and our brother."

Possessed with an economic motive, man seeks wealth. What should be the attitude of the Christian toward this search? That intemperance in the pursuit of riches injures public morals, was clear to Winthrop. It may have been more than a political consideration which led him to castigate Thomas Dudley for building an unnecessarily elaborate house for himself and thereby setting a bad example for the community. For the pursuit of wealth for ostentation's sake was not the mediaeval view which Winthrop had inherited. Wealth was conceived to be a manifestation of God's bounty and God's benevolence, entrusted to men who must husband it as stewards. The Gospel law, according to Winthrop, not only sanctions, but expects men to accumulate wealth. The reader must not be misled. The accumulation of wealth was not idealized as an end. It was lawful and necessary to lay up riches, but not indefinitely, or for their own sake. Nay, the Christian must "lay upp as Joseph did to have ready uppon such occasions, as the Lord, (whose stewards wee are of them) shall call for them from us." Wealth, then, was a gift from a benevolent God, the acquisition of which was necessary for the individual and for the state. The desire for wealth was the result of man's fall from grace and his relinquishment of primitive communism. But even corruptible men must be God's stewards and therefore husband wealth for the glory of God.

Although God's bounty was the first cause of wealth, it was not the sole cause. Man himself was not passive; wealth was the result of labor. This theory had found frequent expression in the mediaeval philosophy, and Winthrop tersely and accurately states the ecclesiastical theory when he says that "whatsoever wee stand in need of is treasured in the earth, by the Creator and is to be fetched thence by the sweat of our Browes." Labor, therefore, was a second, but an indispensable, factor of production made mandatory under the Gospel, and was equivalent to appropriation of a divine bounty. Idleness could not be countenanced in the Christian Commonwealth, because not only would it impair mankind morally, but arrest the very production of necessary wealth. . . .

But in spite of Winthrop's profound respect for property, and in spite of his acceptance of the mediaeval notion of economic classes, he found room in his philosophy for some exceptions. These exceptions proceeded from the Christian doctrines of charity. Pure communism, he believed, could obtain only in a society of ideal men. But a circumstantial communism might become necessary, and to a discussion of this, Winthrop turns in his "Modell." First, he sets forth a theory of social relations. Originally man's relations with his fellow-man were determined by the law of nature. This required that every man should help his fellow-man "in every want or distresse," and "that hee performe this out of the same affection which makes him carefull of his owne goods." The law of nature could have application only in "the estate of innocency." When that blissful period had ended, the law of nature was supplanted by "the lawe of the Gospell" whose obligations upon men are not constant and immutable but vary between "seasons and occasions." Indeed, there are times, said Winthrop, "when a Christian must sell all and give to the poore, as they did in the Apostles times." There are other times when Christians "must give beyond their ability, as they of Macedonia," and "likewise community of perills" calls for extraordinary liberality. The sharing of goods under the "Gospell law" was a requirement of God, although the extent of this enforced communism was dependent upon circumstances. For example, all sharing of goods, Winthrop carefully pointed out, must be subsequent to the provision for one's own family of the "probable meanes of comfortable subsistence." In short, "the Gospel law" requires always circumstantial communism, while a "community of perill" might require almost complete sharing of goods. But what constituted a "community of perill"? Winthrop cites the case of the Primitive Church as an illustration when the early Christians "sold all, had all in Common, neither did any man say that which he possessed was his owne." In like fashion, the return from captivity, with the danger of enemies common to all, demanded a greater sharing of goods than ordinarily was necessary. We see, therefore, that Winthrop's theory of communism converges with his theory of the origin of wealth. The duties of lending, giving, forgiving, and sharing were the consequences of the divine distribution of private property. "The care of the publique must oversway all private respects," wrote Winthrop, and "particular Estates cannott subsist in the ruine of the publique." Private property must be limited by enforced circumstantial communism on occasions of danger; and by public interest, love, and Christian charity at all times. And this is exactly what mediaeval scholars had written. . . .

Such was the economic philosophy of Winthrop. It is a fair example of the economic ideas of the American Puritans. Wealth and wealth-getting were not despised. The Puritan was not truly ascetic. Nor did he idealize wealth-getting as it is the fashion to believe to-day. He attempted to impose the social philosophy of the mediaeval schoolmen on a pioneer community where the temptation to a life of material acquisition was limited only by the opportunity. Herein is another evidence of the immense gulf that separates the Puritan ideals of 1630 from the current social philosophy of New England (and America).

FOR FURTHER READING: Weber's thesis is developed more fully in Max Weber, *The Protestant Ethic and the Spirit of Capitalism* with foreword by R. H. Tawney (New York, 1958). Another interpretation of Protestantism and Capitalism in England is in R. H. Tawney, *Religion and the Rise of Capitalism* (New York, 1926). Weber's ideas are questioned by Samuel E. Morison, *Builders of the Bay Colony* (New York, 1930), and Perry Miller and Thomas H. Johnson, *The Puritans* (New York, 1938). A more general criticism is by H. M. Robertson, *Aspects of the Rise of Economic Individualism: A Criticism of Max Weber and His School* (New York, 1959).

2. *Colonial Agriculture*

PROBLEM: *Was colonial agriculture profitable?*

As the major industry of Colonial America, employing more than 90 per cent of the population, agriculture constituted the basis of economic life in the seventeenth and eighteenth centuries. But was it a profitable venture for most farmers? Students of Colonial agriculture still disagree over this issue. Impressed by the relative decline of farm income in more recent times they have traced contemporary problems such as overproduction, foreign market fluctuations, and falling prices to the Colonial era. Lewis C. Gray, perhaps the foremost agricultural historian of the first half of the twentieth century, expertly traces the problems of Southern tobacco growers in the seventeenth century. Already by 1638 tobacco farmers faced mounting surpluses and declining profits. Gray thus seriously questions the profitability of one of the most important segments of Colonial agriculture. A more optimistic appraisal of the profitability of agriculture in the north during the later eighteenth century is presented by William Sachs. Utilizing sophisticated techniques of economic analysis Sachs notes that despite continuous complaints about hard times by northern farmers, price statistics indicate that they were generally prospering. While the ramifications of agricultural surpluses in the history of American agriculture are complex, these authors introduce important issues that need to be considered in examining the problem. How did foreign market fluctuations affect farmers in the New World? Were the promotional and regulatory policies of colonial legislatures adequate to aid farmers to overcome existent obstacles? Why have American farmers complained about their condition even during times of prosperity?

The Market Surplus Problems of Colonial Tobacco

LEWIS C. GRAY

I have been moved to select the subject of this paper because of the paramount interest of the present problem of market surpluses, and because in the history of colonial tobacco may be found many analogies and parallelisms with the present-day aspects of the problem.

EARLY ARTIFICIAL LEVEL OF PRICES AND ITS COLLAPSE

At the time it first began to be planted by the Virginia colonists in 1610–1611 tobacco in the English market was essentially a luxury product. In the seven years preceding 1622 there had been imported from Spain an annual average of about 60,000 pounds of high-grade tobacco produced in the West Indies, with probably about as much more introduced by smugglers. In 1619 it was stated that the Spanish product customarily sold for eighteen shillings sterling per pound, an enormous price considering the high value of sterling in that period. Virginia tobacco as made in these earlier years was of much poorer quality than the Spanish product, and though it was assessed in the English "Book of Rates" at ten shillings the pound, actually sold at less than half this amount in the latter part of 1619. However, in 1620 it sold as high as eight shillings in the London market. Under these conditions it is not surprising that tobacco was mainly used by the wealthy and was retailed on the London streets by the pipeful.

On the basis of these prices the Virginia Company in 1618 authorized its representatives in the Colony to allow three shillings for the best grades and eighteen pence for that of second quality in trade at the company's warehouse. Naturally such prices stimulated a frenzy of activity in colonial tobacco planting comparable with the feverish spirit of a mining camp. The volume of production and of exports was rapidly expanded. From 1615 when the first colonial shipment reached England until 1622 the exports had increased to 60,000 pounds, and six years later to 500,000 pounds, or more than eight times the amount of official imports of England a little more than a decade earlier. The next decade witnessed a three-fold increase, the annual exports averaging 1,395,063 pounds for the four years, 1637–1640, inclusive.

Prices fell precipitately from their unnatural levels, in spite of frantic efforts by the Crown and the Company to maintain them. By 1630 Governor Harvey was complaining that the merchants were buying tobacco in Virginia for less than a penny per pound.

Reprinted by permission from Lewis C. Gray, "The Market Surplus Problems of Colonial Tobacco," *Agricultural History*, II (January, 1928), pp. 1–34.

From this time forward prices never returned to their original high levels, but until the outbreak of the Revolutionary War ranged between about three pence per pound as a maximum down to a half penny or less. Indeed at times even this minimum price was purely nominal, for tobacco was practically unsalable. It was rarely higher than two pence.

I shall not attempt in this paper to trace the course of prices year by year, but it is desirable to devote some attention to the behavior of prices for longer periods.

The data indicate not only fluctuations from year to year, reflecting the seasonal variations in yield and consequently in volume of production, but also the periodical emergence of long periods of acute depressions. It is desirable to trace briefly the record of these depressions. As already noted, the precipitate fall of prices from the original high levels had brought tobacco by 1630 to what then appeared to be an absurdly low price. For several years thereafter prices were ruinously low, and various legislative attempts were made to deal with the problem.

The crop of 1638 was two and a half times as large as the average for the other years from 1637 to 1640, inclusive, and being thrown into an already sagging market, caused prices again to collapse. In 1638–9 prices were so low that planters could not subsist by them, and there resulted a series of attempts at legislative price-fixing which will be described later. The probability is that in spite of the rather generous official rates placed on tobacco during the next two or three years, prices did not recover until the situation was relieved by the short crop of 1644.

While the outbreak of the civil war in England appears for a short time to have depressed prices, the activity of the illicit trade with the Dutch tended to sustain prices fairly well, with only occasional years of low prices until after the Restoration. In the latter part of the sixth decade there began a period of depression which, excepting a slight improvement in 1663, continued until 1667. It is probable that the acreage planted to tobacco had become excessive by reason of the rapid migration to the colonies induced by the disturbances of the period of the Civil War and the Protectorate. Probably another factor was the extension and more rigid application of the navigation policy in 1660 and the following years and the restrictions on Dutch competition. The situation was further complicated by the unusually large yield of the crop of 1666, and by the demoralization of the market due to the plague in London, which was so severe that in 1665 the tobacco fleet did not go to the colonies at all. The depression was relieved by the great storm of 1667 which destroyed from two-thirds to four-fifths of the crops in Virginia and by the destruction of twenty tobacco ships by the Dutch.

For about a decade conditions appear to have been somewhat improved,

but with a tendency for prices to sag to very unprofitable levels in particular years, as in 1671, 1673, 1678. Apparently throughout this period the tobacco acreage was so large as to permit reasonably good prices only following years of small yield with a constant tendency toward entirely unprofitable prices in years of good crops.

The enormous crop of 1677, said to be in Virginia as large as the total production of three normal years and in Maryland the largest "ever heard of" precipitated another crisis. In 1680 Governor Culpeper, of Virginia, wrote the French authorities that the low price of tobacco "staggered" him and that its continuance would prove "the fatal and speedy ruin of this once noble Colony." The crop of that year, however, proved again unusually large, and added to an already abnormal carry-over so glutted the market that tobacco became practically worthless. For several years the depression continued, leading in 1682 to plant-cutting riots in New Kent, Gloucester, and Middlesex counties, Virginia. As a result of the destruction of about 10,000 hogsheads of tobacco by the rioters, the price of tobacco was improved in 1683.

From this time forward until after the outbreak of the war of the Spanish Succession in 1702 there was a period of generally favorable tobacco prices. It was a period of expanding demand, and years of poor yields occurred with sufficient frequency to prevent the accumulation of an abnormal carry-over.

One of the most desperate periods of depression in the history of the industry began to make its influence felt in 1703 and continued for a decade. The good prices just preceding the war had stimulated production and a gradually increasing carry-over. The war cut off the tobacco trade to Spain, France, Flanders, and part of the Baltic States, leaving only Holland as the principal foreign market. Since the Dutch preferred the brighter variety of Oronoke, the Dutch market had been glutted with the brown type. The depression grew worse as the war continued. In 1704 several thousand hogsheads of consignment tobacco brought the planters no return whatever, and the returns from some of it were not sufficient to pay the freight. In 1705 complaints were made of "the extraordinary low price of tobacco of this year beyond what hath been known for several years past." Conditions continued to get worse. In 1710 it was said that the merchants in Maryland would make no advance on tobacco. In Virginia tobacco was nominally rated at a penny per pound, but large quantities were actually unsalable. Toward the close of the war William Byrd wrote that poor people could not make enough to clothe themselves, while the larger planters were getting deeper and deeper in debt. Many had been forced to sell part of their lands and negroes to meet debts, while still others had emigrated to the Carolinas and elsewhere.

Good prices continued for four years after the close of the war. This relief, however, was but temporary, and merely served to stimulate expansion of production, which again brought low prices in 1720, continuing until 1724, when a crop failure brought temporarily good prices. Then followed a decade of severe depression. Thus the industry appears to have suffered from extreme depression for a period of fourteen years with the exception of one year, and during a period of thirty-two years depression had prevailed except for one interval of four years and another of one year of good prices.

After 1734 there ensued a period of a quarter of a century free from a serious and protracted price depression, although there were occasional years of low prices. Even the War of the Austrian Succession and the Seven Years War did not bring serious price depression, such as had prevailed during the War of the Spanish Succession, for the tobacco trade had become so important both to England and to France that during the two later wars an indirect and informal arrangement was made between England and France whereby tobacco ships, whether British or neutral, engaged in carrying tobacco from England to France were given special passes exempting them from capture, very curious instances of the deliberate continuance of trade relations by belligerent nations. An examination of trade statistics indicates that neither of the later wars seriously affected the volume of the tobacco trade; and prices do not appear to have been abnormally affected, with the exception of the last two years preceding the peace of Paris. The inflation of the Virginia currency which accompanied the course of the war began to manifest itself in a general rise of prices in 1760, which continued until 1764. However, tobacco appears to have lagged behind in the general advance. It appears probable that in spite of the higher nominal prices paid for tobacco there was a period of almost continuous depression from about 1760 or 1761 until about the beginning of the eighth decade, followed in turn by several years of good prices.

I shall not undertake to say how much the behavior of tobacco prices, as revealed by this summary of the experience of a century and a half, is characteristic of the price history of other agricultural products and of other periods, nor to what extent the conditions responsible for it have prevailed elsewhere. To some extent, probably, these conditions are generic in a sense, but to some extent they were peculiar to the production and marketing of colonial tobacco. . . .

ATTEMPTED SOLUTIONS OF THE PROBLEM

Many attempts were made to deal with the problem of marketing the tobacco surplus more effectively so as to bring greater advantages to the producer, including a vast amount of legislation, probably more than has ever been devoted to any other crop, with the possible exception of sugar.

Attempts at monopoly. In an earlier part of this paper it was shown that the first decade of tobacco growing in the American colonies was on the basis of an abnormally high price level. It was an age of monopoly, and, consequently, the attempts to uphold this abnormally high level took the form of a series of monopolistic concessions calculated to maintain unity of control in merchandizing the product. There was also sufficient practical recognition of the laws of supply and demand to lead to provisions in the earlier proposals for restricting the quantity brought to market from the colonies and from Spain, and later to restrict the quantity grown in the colonies.

I shall not undertake to trace in this paper the various negotiations in connection with the proposed contract with Henry Somerscales in 1619; the contract with Sir Thomas Rowe and his associates in the following year; the Jacobs contract arranged in 1621–2; the long negotiations by the Virginia Company itself for an exclusive monopolistic privilege in marketing tobacco, which contract was finally nullified through the factional controversies in the Company itself; the Ditchfield contract of 1625, which failed because of the determined opposition of the Virginia planters; the Anis contract of 1627, which also met the strong opposition of the colonies; and finally the negotiations in 1638 for the Goring contract, in which the proponents attempted to popularize their proposal by suggesting the revival of the Virginia Company, a scheme which did not break down the determined resistance of the colonists.

While the colonists opposed these various attempts at monopolistic concessions, except that of the Virginia Company, which was a matter of controversy both in the Company itself and in the Colony, this opposition was due less to antagonism to the monopolistic solution than to the fact that the various proposals were made largely for the benefit of the Crown and of a persistent group of courtiers who sought to fatten their purses at the expense of the planters. . . .

Legislative price-fixing. In the early decades of the industry some attempts were made at crude legislative price-fixing. Two such acts were passed in 1632, two others in the following year, and other acts in 1639 and 1640. These were acts fixing the general price level for tobacco and prohibiting by penalties its exchange at a lower price. They are to be distinguished from the numerous rating acts, necessitated by the use of tobacco as currency, to determine the ratio of tobacco to sterling in payment of taxes, fees, quitrents, tavern rates, and ferry charges. In 1641 a royal ordinance inspired by the merchants put an end to these attempts at legislative price determination.

Our forefathers are not to be charged with complete ignorance of the laws of economics in the passage of these acts fixing the general price level of tobacco. In the first place, the several acts were associated with attempts at stinting or restricting the volume of production. In the second place, they were more or less justified by the uncertain conditions of marketing and the imperfection of marketing machinery. At a time when no general price level had as yet developed and when the individual planter was largely at the mercy of the merchant who chanced to call for his crop the legislative enactments served to define crudely the limits of bargaining and to supply a price criterion for the application of the laws against engrossing, forestalling, and regrating.

Restriction of volume of production or of exports. As suggested above, from an early period attempts were made to solve the surplus problem by stinting or restricting production, usually by allowing so many plants for each household, for each tithable or other unit of labor. Various arrangements for stinting were included in the later monopolistic contracts, as well as in connection with the price-fixing acts just described. In the legislation of 1639–40 designed to restrict production and fix prices, it became apparent that such legislation would be largely futile without an inter-colonial agreement with Maryland. This was the beginning of a succession of attempts to achieve such agreements.

There is evidence that Virginia legislation for stinting existed in the latter part of the seventeenth century and the early part of the eighteenth. The depression beginning in 1725 resulted in renewed attempts at control of volume of production. Virginia renewed an act in 1727, which had expired in 1725, for improving the staple of tobacco, probably involving destruction of inferior grades and stinting. A stinting act passed at the special session of the Maryland Assembly in 1726 encountered the opposition of the council because of the provision for scaling fees and debts by reason of the expected rise of prices. Another attempt in 1727 in which a compromise was effected on the scaling problem was vetoed by the proprietor. The continuing distress, which culminated in an outbreak of plant-cutting riots in Maryland, finally led to the successful passage of a stinting act in 1730, which, however, lapsed in 1732. The currency act of 1733 provided for the enforced destruction of 150 pounds per taxable during each of the two succeeding years. During this period also negotiations were carried on between Maryland and Virginia looking to mutual legislation for restricting the latest date of planting tobacco, in the interest of curtailing production.

The restriction of volume of production was also intrinsic in numerous acts passed from time to time in both colonies, partly for the purpose of improving quality, such as prohibitions against the packing of ground leaves and suckers, the tending and packing of second growth crops ("seconds"). In some of these acts it was provided that viewers should annually inspect the fields in their respective localities and insure the destruction of second growth tobacco. To some extent restriction of quantity was also achieved by the various acts against packing inferior tobacco and the destruction of such tobacco found in tobacco hogsheads. Restriction of quantity was also involved in the practice of stemming tobacco, which was strongly opposed by the British government because of resulting loss of revenues and prohibited in 1722 by an act of Parliament. However, the act led to vigorous protest by the colonies, Virginia sending John Randolph to London especially to obtain repeal of the act, which he succeeded in achieving.

The aim of restricting the quantity of tobacco was also more or less present in the various acts in the early colonial period requiring the production of food crops (the two-acre acts), acts to exempt new settlers from taxation for a time on condition that they refrain from tobacco cultivation, and certain temporary legislation against the importation of slaves.

ATTEMPTS AT STANDARDIZATION AND IMPROVEMENT OF MARKETABILITY

Probably more effective than the attempts at direct control of price and restriction of output were the efforts to improve the marketability of the product.

Prohibition of shipments in bulk. Among these measures we may include the long struggle to restrict the shipment of tobacco in bulk instead of in the hogshead. The former custom increased greatly in the latter part of the seventeenth century and early decades of the eighteenth by reason of the expansion of the industry into frontier regions where facilities for prizing in hogsheads were lacking, and by reason of the practice of pioneer farmers trading small miscellaneous lots of tobacco at neighborhood stores in exchange for goods brought by the outport ships.

The practice of shipping in bulk, which had increased rapidly with expansion of the industry into the back country, was strongly opposed by the administrative authorities, by the old-time commission merchants, and by the larger planters, because it was favorable to smuggling; because it was an obstacle to the standardization of quality; because a smaller number of ships for transportation were required, which did not appeal to the mercantilist ideals of the period; and because the earlier arrival of the bulk tobacco tended to disorganize the market, besides lending itself to cut-throat competition by small and irregular dealers. We may suspect that in part the opposition grew out of the general resistance of the old-line commercial agencies to the encroachments of the aggressive outport merchants, whose new and vigorous methods were tending to displace them in the trade.

The practice was defended on the ground of smaller cost of transport and because it was essential to the welfare of the poorer classes on the frontier and to the profits of the small outport merchants; and for many years this democratic resistance defeated attempts at prohibition in the colonies. The practice was prohibited by Parliament in 1698, but there was much evasion until the practice was prohibited by the inspection acts hereafter mentioned.

Attempts to regulate size and shape of hogsheads. There was also a long struggle to regulate the size and shape of the hogshead and the time of shipment. Both of these points were of special concern to the merchants, for hogsheads of irregular shape and size were costly to transport because requiring an undue amount of cargo space. Carelessly made hogsheads came to pieces or warped apart in transit. Maryland long held out for a larger hogshead than was specified by Virginia laws on the ground that the character of Maryland tobacco did not admit of such close packing as in Virginia, while the Virginians attributed the difficulty to slovenly methods of packing in Maryland. Even an order by the Queen annulling the Maryland act and requiring that the Maryland specifications be made identical with those of Virginia did not settle the problem. . . .

Provisions for official inspection before shipment. It early became apparent that none of these measures for improvement of quality would be effective without a system of standardization by thorough inspection before shipment. As early as 1619 there was developed the practice of employing sworn viewers to inspect tobacco. From this time forward various temporary or partial measures for inspection were provided for, which cannot be traced in the present paper. No permanently effective system was achieved until the passage of the Virginia act of 1730, which marks an important milestone in the evolution of agricultural marketing machinery and practice.

The foundation for this important measure was laid by the warehouse act of 1712, which provided for the establishment of public warehouses at convenient points not more than one mile from navigable water. Though these warehouses might be privately owned they were made public utilities. The rates and conditions of storage were fixed by law.

An inspection law was also passed in 1713 providing for licensed inspectors to enforce certain minimum standards, issuing warehouse receipts against tobacco. However, the measure excited tremendous opposition, including that of such important merchant planters as William Byrd (II), who reflected the attitude of the conservative consignment merchants, such as Micajah Perry, of London. These influences obtained in 1717 the royal veto of the measure.

Fortunately, the warehouse act, slightly amended in 1720, still remained to serve as a nucleus, and the serious and protracted depression beginning in 1725 brought public sentiment to the support of the act of 1730. Variously amended from time to time, this act and the cognate warehouse act constituted the backbone of the colonial system of marketing until the Revolutionary War.

I cannot undertake here a detailed description of the system. Briefly, it involved several licensed and bonded inspectors stationed at public warehouses. They were authorized to open each hogshead; with the consent of the owner to sort out and destroy inferior tobacco, and lacking his consent to destroy the entire hogshead. The class and grade of the tobacco was then marked on the repacked hogshead. For the purpose of issuing warehouse receipts a distinction was made between "transfer" tobacco and "crop" tobacco. Against the former, general negotiable receipts were issued which did not entitle the owner to any particular hogshead, while the receipts for "crop" tobacco were specific in character, representing largely the consignment tobacco. When the receipts in course of circulation reached the hands of the exporter, he could demand delivery and at that time require a second opening and inspection of the hogshead, and in case the tobacco was found below the standard, could enforce judgment against the inspector for compensation and costs. A scale of allowances for shrinkage was provided, and tobacco stored in public warehouses was publicly insured against loss by fire and other causes.

This was probably the most constructive type of marketing legislation passed in the colonial period, and its influence was profound. It contributed to improving the average quality of exports, standardized the commodity as a medium of exchange and of public payments and as a standard of deferred payments, and improved the system of customs administration. It gave Virginia growers and merchants a great advantage over those of Maryland. In 1743 Daniel Dulaney wrote that Maryland factors were moving to Virginia where they could buy better tobacco, though at a higher price. The French "regie" buyers also were turning more and more to Virginia to obtain their supply. The Council and governor of Maryland informed the proprietor that unless Maryland took similar action the whole trade in tobacco would be lost to Virginia.

Maryland experimented for about a quarter of a century with a vacillating policy comprising acts against tending of seconds, suckers, and ground leaves, and acts imposing heavy penalties for false packing, enforced by the offer of rewards to informers. Finally, in 1747, the colony was forced to adopt the Virginia solution by the adoption of an inspection law closely modelled after that of the sister colony.

Summary. Through more than a century and a half great progress was made in the marketing of tobacco along the lines of more complete commercial organization and greater standardization. It is probable this progress accounts in part for the comparative freedom from protracted depression during the last three or four decades of the colonial period; but the market surplus problem, as we know it today, remained unsolved in spite of the numerous and varied efforts at solution which have been described. It continues as one of the outstanding economic problems of our own time.

Agricultural Conditions in the Northern Colonies Before the Revolution

WILLIAM SACHS

I

Many writers treating the late colonial period have touched upon the subject of economic fluctuations, but no agreement is found as to the duration, intensity, and amplitude of these alterations of good and bad times. Nor has any investigation as yet assembled all the available data necessary to an understanding of this phenomenon. Since agriculture constituted an important aspect of the colonial economy, some light may be shed upon these economic vicissitudes by an examination of Northern agricultural conditions in the two decades preceding the Revolution.

Although contemporaries depicted the period of the French and Indian War as one of great prosperity, the benefits that farmers derived from the war were not strikingly impressive. From 1755 to 1759 inclusive, prices of agricultural products remained almost stationary, while prices of almost all other commodities climbed steadily. Meanwhile, as provincial governments commenced to raise and outfit regiments, taxes began to mount. Thus, while farmers' outlays were unmistakably increasing, the evidence of price data indicates a lag in farm income. Admittedly, an exact computation of agricultural income for this period is impossible, since we do not know how much farmers produced. Nevertheless, price data together with other available information can provide a rough approximation of how the agricultural classes fared.*

In 1759 and 1760, prices of agricultural products exhibited a significant upward movement for the first time since the beginning of the war. This relatively short period of farm prosperity came to an abrupt end in 1761 when a severe drought laid waste the crops. Governor Bernard of Massachusetts proclaimed a day of public prayer to the end that God "would visit us with refreshing showers, as may still preserve the remaining fruits of the earth, and bring forward the withered grass, that there may be fruit for man and beast." The supplications went unanswered, no rains came to moisten the parched earth, and crops withered before they were ripe.

The next year the colonists again suffered from unrelenting droughts

Reprinted by permission from William Sachs, "Agricultural Conditions in the Northern Colonies Before the Revolution," *Journal of Economic History,* XIII (Summer, 1953), pp. 274–290.
* Wholesale prices in Philadelphia for wheat, corn and pork, major staple crops, generally declined until 1758 when they began a steady rise that continued till the end of the Seven Years' War. [Editor's note]

and serious crop failures. Complaints of distress were heard from every quarter—from the lower classes in the cities who found wages out of line with famine prices and from farmers who saw their income shrinking while debts mounted. Frontier communities, especially hard hit, flooded legislatures with petitions for relief. Pontiac's Revolt in 1763 added further hardships to frontier counties, particularly in Pennsylvania. However one may impute material gains made from war, certain it is that farmers, for whom the war years were not years of exceptional prosperity, emerged from the war in serious economic plight.

At about the same time that poor harvests brought economic hardship to the farm population, merchants also were complaining of depressed trade and financial stringency. The agricultural depression contributed directly to this business slump. At a time when English merchants were pressing their American debtors for settlement of balances outstanding, payments from rural areas to urban merchants were not forthcoming; exports of farm products to foreign ports, an important source of remittance for American merchants, were drastically curtailed; and rural buying shrank when other markets also were contracting. On the other hand, the postwar business depression, although aggravating the situation, did not produce any striking effect upon the economic fortunes of agriculture. Following a lively speculation in real estate, land values seem to have been generally depressed by 1763. For most farmers, however, what was derived from the land and what possible improvements could be made upon it were matters of greater significance than the money rating imputed to land. With the first abundant harvest, prices of farm products dropped from their famine peaks. The fundamental question in relation to prices is, however, how severe was the decline?

TABLE 1

AVERAGE PRICES OF THE FOURTH QUARTER OF THE YEAR AT PHILADELPHIA

Product	Unit	1756	1757	1758	1759	1760	1763
Wheat	S—bu.	3.36	3.44	4.10	5.42	5.16	5.42
Flour	S—cwt.	11.33	11.11	12.67	16.31	15.16	14.42
Corn	S—bu.	2.11	1.70	2.13	3.41	3.06	3.69
Beef	S—bbl.	50.00	44.50	47.50	50.00	51.93	68.73
Pork	S—bbl.	60.50	61.63	59.17	69.53	71.17	93.33

By referring to Table 1 . . . , we can compare prices of agricultural commodities in 1763 with those that farmers obtained during the war years. Philadelphia has been selected because it was the most important colonial market for provisions, because price data for that port are most adequate, and because Pennsylvania currency, in which prices are measured, was relatively stable. Since the heaviest trading in farm products took place during the fall months, the last quarter of each year has been selected for comparison.

Excluding the famine years of 1761 and 1762, a period when farm income was much reduced, quarterly averages in 1763 were even slightly above those of the prosperous years of 1759 and 1760, except for flour. In comparison with the remainder of the war years, prices of all important agricultural commodities were substantially higher in 1763.

By the end of 1763, prices of farm produce still hovered at relatively high levels, while shortages, particularly of animal products, made themselves felt. Unable to procure provisions on the Continent for the army garrison at Nova Scotia, John Hancock was forced to turn to Ireland for supplies. Similarly, John Watts ordered a shipment of pork from Ireland, as that commodity was "excessively dear" at New York. In December of 1763 John Van Cortlandt instructed his various agents to remit in wheat to New York as the demand for that article was brisk. On January 14, 1764, John Watts informed his correspondent at Madeira that he would try to ship wheat from Philadelphia, for "here [New York] it is not to be had without an advanc'd price and scarcely then." At Philadelphia, however, the produce market was no more favorable to such operations than at New York. "Corn @ 5/ not 300 Bushels to be got— flour @ 19 to 20/—pork 5 pounds. Few barrels to be had, bought up months past," wrote Thomas Riche of Philadelphia in response to an order for provisions from the West Indies. The new army contractors of the Pittsburgh district, finding themselves unable to secure sufficient provisions for fulfilling the terms of their contracts, effective as of April 13, 1764, requested that the army administration sell them the surplus food supplies obtained from the previous contractors.

Yet in 1764 American merchants complained persistently of poor markets abroad. Why then should prices of provisions in home markets remain at moderate levels when exports constituted the main outlet for farm surpluses? The answer is to be found in trade statistics. With the cessation of privateering, production of large crops, and a fall in freight and insurance rates after the war, the volume of overseas commerce expanded rapidly. American importers found it decidedly more profitable to send out their ships full-freighted than empty while vessels bringing goods to America sought return freight. In turn, the augmented volume of trade created a strong demand for agricultural products.

II

Farmers' difficulties immediately following the termination of war were the result of financial liabilities incurred when crop failures had reduced their income. Debts, both public and private, weighed heavily upon them, while in every province postwar taxes were taking a larger chunk out of farm income than they had before the war.

In New England particularly, postwar taxes were extremely heavy, while public creditors further aggravated the situation by adding their weight to a policy of rapid currency contraction. It is little wonder that in an area of relatively low agricultural productivity, yet experiencing the heaviest taxation and most marked currency appreciation north of the Potomac, debts constituted the one great complaint of farmers. Shortly after the end of the war, however, Connecticut and New Hampshire eased tax burdens considerably by using the Parliamentary grant to liquidate their liabilities, and with the appearance of good harvests both of these colonies realized improved economic conditions more rapidly than elsewhere in New England.

Although rural taxes in New York were higher after 1763 than before the war, it can hardly be said that they were burdensome. In Pennsylvania, taxes on rural real estate were relatively light in the postwar years. Of a total annual assessment of £34,855, about one half came from Philadelphia and Chester Counties and the city of Philadelphia. Although times were hard immediately after the war, farmers of the middle colonies did not seem to have been heavily involved in debt litigation, foreclosures, or in other types of legal action indicating financial disabilities. Quite in contrast with New England, complaints of such a nature were conspicuously absent from newspaper columns, legislative journals, reports of government officials, and other media of public expression. In these colonies, where taxes were relatively low, agricultural productivity high, and currency contraction slow, it did not take farmers long to emerge from hard times once large crop yields succeeded those of the drought years. German farmers, enjoying flourishing conditions, took no part in the agrarian disturbances that occurred in Pennsylvania in 1764. More significant still, the economic grievances of the disaffected western sector pertained mainly to Indian affairs, land speculation, and disbursements of public funds—they did not include complaints of economic distress or demands for debtor relief. Similarly, the tenants' revolt in New York in 1765–1766 was not connected with depressed agricultural conditions; it was essentially an attempt of farmers to extricate themselves from a landholding system that denied them secure tenure. It would be strange indeed that men who so copiously poured forth their economic complaints, real or imagined, and who were ready to secure their demands by force of arms should be so negligent as to omit any reference to hard times if they were suffering from an economic depression.

Not only were crop yields large in the years after 1763, but prices which farmers received were excellent. Students of price history have pointed out the divergence in the movement of imported- and domestic-commodity prices at New York. A similar divergence seems to have taken place at Philadelphia; while domestic-commodity prices moved rather upward, prices of imported commodities seemed to oscillate around a horizontal trend.

With prospects of an abundant harvest, agricultural prices at Philadelphia declined somewhat in 1764. From the last quarter of that year, however, prices of farm products began a steady and uninterrupted rise which was not arrested until the middle of 1768. The price of wheat, Pennsylvania's major crop, rose from a monthly relative of 125 to 230 (1741–1745 = 100), surpassing the famine peak of 1763! In 1769 the price of wheat turned definitely downward but still stood substantially above the price levels of 1764. The average price of the lowest quarter of 1769 was still above the highest quarterly average of 1764, and 28 per cent over the lowest quarterly average. The price movement of flour strongly paralleled that of wheat, while prices of corn, beef, and pork displayed a similar tendency.

On the other hand, prices of salt, rum, and molasses, like those of agricultural commodities, dropped drastically after the war. But unlike farm-commodity prices, prices of this group of products fell well below the base or prewar period and, except for the brief period of nonimportation in 1765–1766, failed to rise much above the depressed price levels of 1764. The lowest quarterly average price of New England rum in 1769 was but 9 per cent above that of 1764, molasses only 8 per cent higher, while salt dipped to 11 per cent below. From evidence of scattered prices—mainly those of osnaburgs, a representative coarse linen fabric—Anne Bezanson and her associates have indicated the course of prices of British imported textiles as falling after the Peace of Paris and fluctuating around a horizontal trend from about 1764 to 1775. Although prices of farm implements and finished metal products are nonexistent for this period, the available evidence affords reasonable ground for belief that this group of products fell in price during the 1760's. For what amounts or in what proportions farmers exchanged their surpluses for salt, molasses, rum, iron products, and dry goods we do not know, since consumption statistics are unavailable. However, since these commodities constituted rather important single items of farmers' budgets in the eighteenth century, the conclusion is almost inescapable that farmers' per unit expenditures decreased in relation to farm revenue per unit of output.

After 1769 merchants once again began to enjoy a period of political calm and generally improved business conditions, at least until the latter part of 1772 or early 1773. Farmers, too, shared in the general prosperity. Prices of agricultural products again began to climb, reaching even higher peaks than before, and not until the eve of the Revolution did any significant decline occur from the new high levels. Meanwhile, prices of salt, molasses, and rum remained fairly constant at the levels of the preceding decade.

III

The prevailing high prices of agricultural produce from 1764 to 1775 were mainly the result of an expansion in demand from abroad. Beginning in 1764, a series of poor crops converted England from a grain exporting to a grain importing nation. European ports formerly supplied with English grain immediately turned to the British colonies in America to supply the deficit. On February 19, 1766, the British Parliament modified its corn laws to allow the importation of American grain duty free. British merchants sought American foodstuffs not only for their home markets but also to fulfill their contracts with foreign mercantile houses. Poor crops in scattered parts of Europe in 1766 and more serious crop failures beyond the Atlantic the next year further augmented the demand for American provisions.

TABLE 2

TONNAGE CLEARED FROM PHILADELPHIA, NEW YORK, AND BOSTON

	Philadelphia		New York		Boston	
Year	West Indies	Southern Europe	West Indies	Southern Europe	West Indies	Southern Europe
1764	—	—	7,340	1,882	—	—
1765	13,494	4,455	8,385	3,190	7,806	1,075
1768	12,019	7,255	6,981	2,360	10,095	1,333
1769	11,114	12,040	5,466	3,278	8,995	1,081
1770	13,842	10,940	7,005	2,920	8,248	813
1771	13,449	7,110	7,708	2,029	9,171	1,113
1772	15,674	8,415	8,076	2,449	10,703	555

Source: Harrington, *The New York Merchant*, pp. 356–68.

Table 2 represents tonnage cleared annually from the three major ports of the Northern colonies to the two most important foreign markets for American agricultural staples. This record, while it does not show particular commodities shipped, provides a rough, over-all indication of quantity change and of the direction of trade to specific areas. The strong demand for American foodstuffs is especially noticeable in the tonnage statistics of Philadelphia, the largest colonial mart for provisions. From 1765 to 1769 tonnage clearing to the West Indies declined absolutely, but that to southern Europe increased almost threefold, surpassing exports to the West Indies for the first time in colonial history. Improved markets in the West Indies after 1769 further augmented the demand for Pennsylvania grain and flour but reversed the movement of exports. For the entire period, however, the major increase in Philadelphia's export trade, as measured by tonnage, was with southern Europe. Exports of New York, ranking next to Philadelphia as a grain-exporting port, followed a somewhat similar course to that of the Quaker City. Boston, however, lacking a highly productive hinterland and a prominent staple having a strong demand abroad, witnessed its foreign-export trade develop in a different direction from that of its sister ports to the south. From 1765 to 1769, tonnage cleared from Boston to southern Europe remained almost stationary, while a 15 per cent increase took place in tonnage cleared to the West Indies. By 1772 exports to the West Indies, on the basis of tonnage, had grown by an additional 19 per cent. But while these markets offered Boston traders strong allurements, exports to southern Europe dwindled to insignificant proportions.

IV

An analysis of the consensus of contemporary opinion reinforces the conclusions drawn from the preceding data. Unfortunately, farmers left no letters, carefully kept diaries, or other written records from which the historian might form some judgment about what they thought their economic position to be. Thus, our conclusions must be based on different types of evidence coming from people who were not tillers of the soil and whose interests were at times diametrically opposed to those of farmers.

During the early political controversies with Great Britain, colonial agitators advanced the argument of the "poverty of the people" and predicted the most dire results for the rural population as a consequence of British legislation. Some even insisted that these grim forebodings were actually taking place. Such contentions had as their purpose the creation of a favorable opinion in order to secure modification of specific Parliamentary legislation regarded by the colonists as inimical to their interests.

After the Sugar Act was modified and the Stamp Act repealed, all utterance on agricultural distress practically ceased. In fact, the complaints came only from urban quarters and were concerned not with farm distress but with soaring prices, food shortages, and rising costs of living. As early as the Stamp Act controversy, "Colbert" argued that a policy of conducting no business without stamps would hurt Britain because large orders of grain were "bought up or shipped by orders from home, and if it should remain here now it will be sold at a cheaper rate to our increasing manufacturers."

With the continuing high prices of food, complaints emanating from the cities mounted. One writer depicted farmers as literally rolling in wealth and urged that more people take up farming in order to increase the supply of wheat and to reduce its price. Another New Yorker accused farmers of getting rich at the expense of city people. "In Consequence of the Scarcity and Dearness of Provisions in Europe . . . upwards of Twenty sail of European ships arrived last Week in different Ports of America, in order to purchase Wheat," he wrote. "This must of Consequence raised the Price of Wheat and other Provisions upon us, already too high for the Poor of this City . . . If those Ships get their Loads of Wheat, it will benefit Farmers that have it to sell, but it must impoverish the Citizens, in advancing the Price of Provisions."

By 1766 a persistent agitation developed in New York City to prohibit the exportation of provisions until prices should fall to "reasonable levels." "Flour has risen to the enormous price of twenty four shillings per [cwt], which . . . is higher than it rose in the last war, and considering the prodigious scarcity of money . . . how can we afford to pay for bread even to the price which it is now risen?" When prices have risen to a point at which people cannot possibly pay, the author argued, "it must demonstrate the strongest reason" to embargo exportation of food supplies. "The price of wheat and provisions are . . . already too high for the poor of this city," claimed another, while advocating similar measures. Colonial legislatures, however, took no effective steps to halt the rising prices of food, and protests from city dwellers continued.

By no means were such protests against high food prices motivated by humanitarianism, or by a purely philanthropic desire to ease the burdens of the "deserving poor." The mercantilist mind, regarding low costs of production as beneficial and wages as directly related to the cost of living or the level of subsistence, naturally viewed with hostility a rise in the price of indispensable necessities. Taxpayers did not relish a rise in poor rates which mounting prices might occasion. Merchants generally looked upon high prices of commodities earmarked for exportation with disfavor, and some exporters were not slow in accusing farmers of cupidity and outright profiteering. Benjamin Fuller, a Philadelphia merchant, informed his correspondent that "wheat is now at 5/6, but its a kind of nominal price—the farmers are Rich and are loth to part with it at that." ". . . tho' the last Crop is said to be a tollerable good one yet the Farmers having been used a long time to great prices the most of them are become wealthy, and therefore will keep back their supply unless they can obtain what they call a good price," another Philadelphia merchant reflected in 1773. Nevertheless, artisans and mechanics, small shopkeepers, and common laborers, finding it ever more difficult to make ends meet, fully supported the publicists who urged legislative action to beat down climbing prices of food. John Woolman's "Conversation between a thrifty Landholder, and a Labouring man" posed the problem confronting the lower urban classes as follows:

Labouring Man: I observe of late years that when I buy a bushel of grain for my family, I must do more work to pay for it than I used to do twenty years past. What is the reason of this change?
Landholder: Towns and villages have a gradual increase in these provinces, and the people now employed in husbandry bear, I believe, a less proportion to the whole inhabitants . . . but the main cause is that of Sending So much grain & flower abroad.

Massachusetts offered bounties for the production of wheat and flour, among other reasons, to free itself of outside dependence for food supplies for its maritime towns. However, it was the city governments which, possessing a large degree of control over local consumption and more amenable to the pressure of a grumbling and resentful citizenry, attempted in many ways to alleviate the disabilities of their consumers. New York City, frustrated in 1763 from assizing provisions in its public markets at rates lower than those current, turned to other stringent regulatory practices aimed at depressing retail prices. Boston followed closely in the footsteps of New York in strengthening its code regulating public markets. Nevertheless, the continuation of a seller's market provided incentives to speculation and temptations for traders to buy up supplies before they ever reached the markets, frequently causing serious food shortages. By 1769 the situation at Boston had become so serious that a town meeting appointed a committee "to investigate and propose methods for the General Court to prevent forestalling of the markets." A petition to the Pennsylvania Assembly in 1772 from the inhabitants of Germantown, made up largely of artisans, claimed that butter and middling flour were being bought up before reaching the public market and requested legislation to prevent "engrossing and forestalling." It is not at all strange that mercantilist regulations regarding prime necessities were strengthened by city administrations at the same time all other types of mercantilist enactments were disintegrating.

The validity of the claims and denials, charges and countercharges, accusations and vindications of those who partook of the heated arguments over food prices, trading practices, and government regulation is of no concern here. What is relative to this study is the fact that complaints of hard times emanated almost wholly from urban groups and did not picture farmers as victims of depressed economic conditions. When it is considered that over 90 per cent of the population made their living directly from agriculture, the years from the Peace of Paris down to the Revolution may be viewed as fairly prosperous for the major body of income receivers.

FOR FURTHER READING: Lewis C. Gray's views are more fully elaborated in his *History of Agriculture in the Southern United States to 1860* (Washington: 1933). Factual surveys are Percy W. Bidwell and John I. Falconer, *History of Agriculture in the Northern United States, 1620–1860* (Washington: 1925), and Philip A. Bruce, *Economic History of Virginia in the Seventeenth Century* (2 vols., New York: 1895). William B. Weeden, *Economic and Social History of New England* (2 vols., Boston: 1891) and Theodore Saloutos, "Efforts at Crop Control in Seventeenth Century America," *Journal of Southern History*, XII (February, 1946), pp 45–66, are enlightening.

3. *Colonial Labor*

PROBLEM: *What were the social origins of the colonial labor force?*

Quite obviously, population is one of the primary factors of economic growth since quality of the labor force helps to determine levels of achievement. No wonder, therefore, that one of the issues over which historians of colonial America have differed concerns the social origins of settlers in seventeenth-century Virginia. Was the early labor force composed of convicts or of yeomen? One of the leading students of early southern history, Professor Thomas J. Wertenbaker, argued that the greater portions of indentured servants in the Old Dominion came from impoverished, but sturdy and honest English peasantry. A somewhat different approach is taken by a younger scholar, Abbot E. Smith, who examined hitherto unnoticed records. On the basis of this new research Smith concluded that a large number of criminals came to Virginia as indentured servants although many of them were eventually integrated with the general populace into a middle class. If not too flattering to ancestral pride, these interpretations raise questions about the social background and skills of Colonial workers. What types of convicts came to the New World? How did the social backgrounds of the colonists affect their economic efficiency? How did the American environment influence the Colonial labor force?

Patrician and Plebeian in Virginia or the Origin and Development of the Social Classes of the Old Dominion

THOMAS J. WERTENBAKER

Many freed servants took up in Virginia unpatented land, trusting that their residence upon it might give to them in time a legal title. Others settled upon tracts that had been deserted. In some instances, where these people, or their descendants, had prospered and had built homes and barns and stables on the property, or had otherwise improved it, their claims to the land were confirmed by law. In other cases, when patents were made out to land already occupied by "squatters," the lowly settlers were forced to leave their farms and to seek homes elsewhere, probably on unclaimed territory in remote parts of the colony. This gave rise to that fringe of rough humanity upon the frontier, that spread continually westward as the colony grew. Many of the servants that escaped from their masters fled to the mountains, seeking refuge among the defiles and woods of the Blue Ridge or the more distant Alleghanies. The descendants of these wretched people still exist in the mountains of Virginia, North Carolina, Tennessee and Kentucky, exhibiting in their ignorance, their disregard for law, their laziness and even in their dialect the lowness of their origin.

The facts presented in the preceding paragraphs lead us inevitably to the conclusion that that portion of the vast body of indentured servants that were brought to Virginia which made its lasting imprint on the character of the population of the eastern countries was composed of men of sterling qualities, and was rather an element of strength than of weakness to the middle class into which they went. That many did rise to places of trust and influence is well established. There are numerous instances of servants, who, after serving their term of indenture, became burgesses, justices, etc. Thus John Trussell, who came over in 1622 as a servant, became a burgess in 1654. The Assembly of 1629 included in its members William Warlick, William Poppleton, Richard Townsend and Anthony Pagett, all of whom had come to the colony under terms of indenture. Garford, a puritanical preacher of the Commonwealth period, wrote that at that time some of the former servants were still filling offices of trust in the colony. The author of Virginia's Cure asserted, in 1662, that the

Reprinted from Thomas J. Wertenbaker, *Patrician and Plebeian in Virginia or the Origin and Development of the Social Classes of the Old Dominion*, pp. 178–86 (Charlottesville, Virginia, 1910. Reprinted in *The Shaping of Colonial Virginia*, New York: Russell and Russell, Inc., 1958.)

burgesses "were usuall such as went over as servants thither, and though by time, and industry, they may have obtained competent estates, yet by reason of their poor and mean condition, were unskilful in judging of a good estate, either of church or Commonwealth." This, however, is undoubtedly an exaggeration. Yet, in 1651, Governor Berkeley, in an address to the Assembly, stated that hundreds of examples testified to the fact that no man in the colony was denied the opportunity to acquire both honor and wealth. . . .

The existence of high wages for so many years accelerated the formation of the middle class, for the hired laborer could, if he were economical, save enough to purchase land and to become an independent farmer. So crude were the agricultural methods then in use in the colony that very little capital was needed by the small planters, and tobacco and corn could be raised by them almost as economically as upon the large plantations. Moreover, since men of the middle class could seldom afford to employ laborers to till their fields, they were in a sense brought into competition with the wage earner. The price of tobacco was dependent in large measure upon the cost of production, and could not, except upon exceptional occasions, fall so low that there could be no profit in bringing servants from England to cultivate it, and this fact reacted favorably upon those that tilled their fields with their own hands. On the other hand this very circumstance made it hard for the small farmer to enlarge the scope of his activities. Unless he had obtained a fair degree of prosperity, it would be impossible for him to purchase servants or hire laborers and the output of his plantation was limited to his own exertions, or those of the members of his family.

By 1660, the middle class was fully formed. From the thousands of indentured servants that had been brought to the colony numerous families had emerged which, though rough and illiterate, proved valuable citizens and played an important rôle in the development of the country. Added to the free immigrants of humble means they formed a large body that needed only organization and leaders to wield a powerful influence in governmental affairs. . . .

The Transportation of Convicts to the American Colonies in the Seventeenth Century

ABBOT E. SMITH

The proportion of convicts among indentured servants during the colonial period is a matter which has attracted the attention of many historians and of some statesmen. It is generally known that after an act of Parliament in 1718 convicts were regularly transported to America. Their numbers have been suggested, and may be reckoned with considerable accuracy from the Treasury Papers. As for the prevalence of the trade before 1718, it has remained an obscure matter, known only from hints in state papers and an occasional mention in private correspondence. It is a fact, however, that the transportation of convicts was a regular and systematic pursuit throughout the seventeenth century as well as the eighteenth. The method and development of the process may be clearly demonstrated.

"But no power on earth," says Blackstone, "except the authority of Parliament, can send any subject of England out of the land against his will; no, not even a criminal. For exile and transportation are punishments at present unknown to the common law; and, whenever the latter is now inflicted, it is either by the choice of the criminal himself to escape a capital punishment, or else by the express direction of some modern act of Parliament." During the seventeenth century there were only two such acts of Parliament which concerned felons, as distinguished from vaga-bonds or political prisoners. One of these was a short-lived act of the year 1666, which permitted justices to take away benefit of clergy, and sentence to transportation notorious thieves and spoilers in Northumber-land and Cumberland. This statute (18 Car. II. c. 3), applying only to special cases in the two border counties, expired after seven years and was not renewed. The other act (22 Car. II. c. 5) was passed in 1670, and permitted justices to transport "such as steal cloth from the rack," or purloin ammunition under certain conditions. This act was invoked at least as late as the year 1763. It is important to realize that with the ex-ception of a few persons condemned under one of these acts, no felons were transported to America in the seventeenth century by reason of a legal sentence.

It is well known that there were in this period some three hundred crimes which were designated as felonies, and that a felony, where clergy could not be pleaded, was punishable with death. The laws were strictly

Reprinted by permission from Abbot E. Smith, "The Transportation of Convicts to the American Colonies in the Seventeenth Century," *The American Historical Re-view*, XXXIX (January, 1934), pp. 232–249.

determinative; the judge had no alternative. He could condemn to death, or he could reprieve the felon for some good reason, but there was no third course open and no lighter penalty which he might impose. But this harsh code was by no means in complete harmony with the best thought of the times. From early days a wholesale slaughter of small thieves was avoided in various ways. The French and Spaniards were accustomed to use convicts for some of their colonizing and exploring expeditions in the sixteenth century. Frobisher took some men from the jails of England. Governor Dale of Virginia suggested in 1611 that felons should be sent to that colony, believing that they would be at least as effective settlers as the disreputable crew which he had brought out with him.

It was not until three years later that anything definite was attempted. On January 24, 1614/1615 the transportation of English convicts was inaugurated by James I., in a commission addressed to a large section of the privy council headed by the archbishop of Canterbury. The commission is worth quoting at length, for it sets forth the motives behind the system as well as the procedure which was to be followed:

. . . Nowe of late wee finde by experience that with our people offences and offenders alsoe are encreased to that number, as besides the severitie of our lawes punishing offenders in felonies to death. It is moste requisite some other speedy remedy be added for ease unto our people. Wherein as in all things els tending to punishment it is our desire that Justice be tempered with mercie, Soe likewise it is our care soe to have our Clemency applied as that greate and notorious malefactors may not be encouraged, and yet the lesser offendors adiuged by lawe to dye may in that manner be corrected, as that in theire punishment some of them may live and yield a profitable service to the Comon Wealth in parts abroad where it shall be found fitt to imploie them. Wee therefore reposing greate trust and confidence in you our said lord Archbishopp . . . doe for us our heires and successors give full power warrant and authoritie by theis presents to you or any six or more of you whereof some of you the said Lord Chauncellor Lord Treasourer lord Chiefe Justice of England, Sir Ralfe Winwood to be twoe, to reprive and stay from execucon such and soe many persons as nowe stand attaynted or convicted of or for any robberie or felonie, (wilful murder rape witchcraft or Burglarie onlie excepted) whoe for strength of bodie or other abilities shall be thought fitt to be ymploied in forraine discoveries or other services beyond the Seas. This to be done after Certificate in Writing made unto you by any one or more of our Judges or Serieants at Lawe before whom such felons have bene tried. . . .

The commission then continues, giving power to the same persons to bestow reprieved felons upon any specific undertaking they may see fit, and for a length of time which they are to fix. If such felons return within the time limit, or refuse to go in the first place, their reprieve is to become void. Finally it is directed that all proceedings in accordance with this commission are to be certified by the principal secretary of state at the time, and "to be entred and enrolled on Record by the Clarke of our Crown in the Office called the Crowne Office" belonging to the court of king's bench.

Two days after the date of this commission the first batch of convicts was reprieved. An open warrant by the privy council recited at length the substance of the commission. It then went on to state that having received a certificate from the recorder of London to the effect that a given list of men were of able body and fit to be employed beyond the seas, the council therefore did reprieve them, and appoint them to be handed over to Sir Thomas Smith, governor of the East India Company. They were to be conveyed by him or his assignees into the East Indies, or other parts beyond the seas where he might direct, with all convenient speed, and were not to return without a warrant under the hands of six of the privy council. Finally, the sheriff of the county where the prisoners were in custody was directed to deliver them to Sir Thomas Smith, or to whom he might appoint to receive them. There were seventeen names in the list. On July 7 in the same year, 1615, three felons were similarly reprieved upon certificate from a judge of admiralty, and three more upon the advice of the recorder of London.

The Commission had authorized the reprieve of "soe many persons as nowe stand attaynted." It is possible that the king intended only a temporary experiment. It is certain that no very satisfactory system for regularly reprieving and transporting convicts was evolved until the middle of the century. A number of different methods were tried with varying success, and convict transportation was a desultory process, reflecting its uncertain career in very mixed and ill-assorted evidence. After the initial commission which the king issued in 1615, there were at least six renewals, when in 1617, 1621, 1622, 1626, 1628, and 1633 similar power was given to the council. These reissues were rendered necessary by the death or removal of persons who had been of the quorum in former commissions. The 1621 document excludes from reprieve criminals guilty of arson or highway robbery, in addition to the murderers and others already placed beyond mercy, but the rest of the renewals show no changes, and it is apparent that an attempt was made to develop a permanent mode of procedure. . . .

Those colonies which granted land upon a headright system kept some account of immigration among the land records. In the records of Jamaica, no enrollment of names had been preserved, but Virginia and Maryland each have registers of headrights. The Virginia Land Books record only the final land patent, together with the names of those immigrants for who it was granted. Groups of servants are thus distinguished, not by the ship upon which they came, but by the importer who paid for their passage and settled them upon the land. The Maryland Books, on the other hands, record the entry of ships, and the passengers on board, for a certif-icate of land was granted to the captain if he imported passengers, and no proof of settlement was required. Consequently the Maryland records are very much more satisfactory for tracing cargoes of convicts. Among the Virginia land patents, under date of July 15, 1669, may be found a grant of six thousand acres to John Pate and William Beverley, in con-sideration of the transportation of one hundred and twenty persons. Among these are the convicts who had been granted to Pate in 1667. These convicts had arrived in Virginia before July 10, 1667, when they were mentioned in the Order Book of the Lancaster County Court. It may be seen from this instance that it is possible to trace convicts arriving in Virginia, albeit with difficulty and uncertainty. An examination of the land books up to 1675 has failed to disclose any other groups which can be identified with a group of Newgate felons.

In Maryland, however, the case is different. A shipload of convicts was there registered intact upon the day they arrived, although the only way of recognizing them is by a comparison of names with lists from the Patent Rolls. The first consignment arrived on February 6, 1671/1672, and consisted of ten felons who had been excluded from Virginia by the act of 1670, and were brought over by Mr. Robert Collis in the sloop *Elizabeth.* Twenty-nine persons from the 1672 pardons also came to Maryland. On May 22, 1674, Captain Benony Eaton proved his right to 2450 acres of land for transporting forty-nine persons, and of this number thirty-five came from Newgate, having been pardoned on October 16, 1673. Similarly Captain Benjamin Cooper, on February 9, 1674/1675 registered seventy-one immigrants, of whom forty-one were from New-gate, being all with the exception of eight from the pardon of July 18, 1674. Thirty-seven more came from the lots pardoned in 1675, after which Maryland passed her law forbidding the further importation of convicts. The registers indicate that this law was respected, with its renewals for the remainder of the century.

There is one further possibility of tracing the actual shipment of con-victs. This is to search for evidence in the records at the Guildhall in London. There should be some traces of the bonds which merchants were required to give for safe conveyance, or some note of shipment in the court books. It is evident that after the market was closed in Virginia and Mary-land the machinery of convict transportation did not work exactly as the law intended. A note in a sessions book at the Guildhall for the year 1681 reads as follows:

Whereas Itt appeareth to this Courte That the Convicted prisoners in New-gate for some yeares past whoe have given Recognizance for transporting themselves upon his Majesties gracious Letters of pardon have not departed this kingdome according to the provisoe in the same express But have remayned

her notwithstanding such Recognizance and committed new felonyes and
offences And likewise increased their numbers As experience sheweth And
alsoe by reason of the insufficiency of their manucators noe advantage can be
taken of them Itt is therefore ordered by this Courte that the provisoe in such
like pardons for Convicts be drawne and made as obligation to his Majesty
with good suretyes in A penalty with a Condicon made according to the same
provisoe And that the same be made and kept by the Towne Clerke of the
City of London or his deputy as antiently hath beene accustomed in whose
hands the pardon is constantly kept. And by whom this Courte is to be informed of any breach of the said pardon Or of the said obligacon And whoe
must certify such obligacon upon the breach of the Condicon thereof And are
answerable for any miscarriage therein.

The security clause in the Newgate pardons was altered to suit this decree.
Christopher Jeaffreson gave a bond of 500 pounds to the recorder in 1684,
but no trace of this or any other similar bond made as a result of the
court's ruling has been preserved.

There are, however, twelve recognizances of earlier dates which may
be seen. They were given between 1666 and 1670, and their general nature
bears out the allegations in the above note. It is recited in each, that whereas
the king has pardoned this list of persons under a condition mentioned in
the pardon, and whereas the above-mentioned individuals have undertaken
to transport them "into the Island of Barbados or some other part of
America now inhabited by the Subject of our said" king, then if this undertaking is fulfilled and the custom of the country, that the bond is null
and void. In each bond appear lists of convicts duly agreeing with the
lists on the patent Rolls.

When any considerable number of felons are named (the longest list is
of forty-five names) the amount of the bond is 500 pounds. As few as ten
are also taken for the same amount. For this reason the bonds seem
slightly suspicious; but there is a further reason for doubting their worth,
which is considerably stronger. It has been mentioned that John Pate
petitioned the king, on March 1, 1666/1667, for the transportation of
twenty-one convicts. These he named from a list given him by the clerk
of Newgate prison, and this list was dated February 25. The petition was
granted, and the pardon was issued on October 25. On the 30th,
Humphrey Taylor of St. Margaret's Lothbury, and Richard Taylor of
Southwark gave a bond of £500 for the transportation of the convicts in
the pardon of October 25, including Pate's men. But we know, beyond
any doubt, that at least eight of Pate's men were in Lancaster County,
Virginia, by July 10, 1667. Not only are some of the names mentioned
more than once in the court record, but Pate's name is connected with
theirs. Thus they had been transported some months before the pardon
was issued. This fact is not surprising, as they were specially granted to
him by the king, but the fact that they are named in the bond given by

the Taylors, seems to indicate that such bonds were written out, as a matter of "common form," soon after the issue of the pardon.

There is no further evidence worth mention respecting shipment. Convicts for transportation may be traced in the Newgate calendars kept at the Guildhall, but there is no regular note of their shipment. They merely disappear from the calendar, with no indication of whether they died, escaped, were set free, or were transported.

A few general points must be noted in conclusion. It is a great mistake to confuse felons with political prisoners. The two classes were perfectly distinct. Our jailbirds were criminals, and their characters do not warrant whitewashing. There was not the slightest need for an aspiring colonist to commit a small crime to assure his transportation to America. Such a man would be joyfully received as an indentured servant. Nor is it true to say that their crimes were negligible according to our modern codes. It will be found that most of them were thieves, but some were convicted of more serious crimes, perhaps on doubtful evidence. It may be remarked here that no accurate idea of the criminal processes of the seventeenth century can be gained without a study of the system of pardons. The printed sessions reports, issued in the later decades of the century, do not indicate the true nature of the sentences passed. For example, in eight assizes held between July, 1684, and June, 1685, ninety-two persons, according to the printed reports, were sentenced to death. An inspection of the Patent Rolls shows that of these ninety-two, thirty-three were pardoned conditionally upon their transportation, and thirteen were pardoned without condition. The same printed reports show that the judges refrained from passing sentence upon forty-four persons, reserving them for transportation, and of these, three were pardoned freely, according to the Patent Roll. It is thus apparent that the lighter offenders were pardoned outright, while those whose crimes were slightly worse were pardoned for transportation. It should also be remarked that few persons could spend any period of time in the Newgate of those days without contamination. Transported convicts were definitely undesirable in the colonies, although their standard probably improved in the eighteenth century, when offenders in clergy began to be shipped.

There is little to be said concerning the convicts in the colonies. Although their exile was fixed at seven years, it does not appear that they were usually expected to remain in the status of bond servants for a time longer than that established by the custom of the country for ordinary servants. The Leeward Islands passed a law requiring eight years' servitude from transported convicts at the time of the Jeaffreson incident, but this did not become firmly established. Jamaica alone passed a law, in 1681, requiring that transported felons should serve for the term of their exile. They were merged in the general population of indentured servants, and each had the opportunity which was vouchsafed to any servant to make his place in the New World.

FOR FURTHER READING: The contributions of labor to the Colonial economy are discussed in Marcus W. Jernegan, *Laboring and Dependent Classes in Colonial America* (Chicago: 1931), and Richard B. Morris, *Government and Labor in Early America* (New York: 1946). Abbot E. Smith's views are presented in fuller detail in *Colonists in Bondage: White Servitude and Convict Labor in America, 1607–1776* (Chapel Hill: 1947). For general orientation on this subject see John R. Commons *et al, History of Labor in the United States* (4 vols., New York: 1918), vol. I, and M. L. Hansen, *The Atlantic Migration, 1607–1860* (Cambridge, Mass., 1940).

4. *Business in Colonial America*

PROBLEM: *Did British administration of mercantile policies impede the American economy?*

For over half a century American historians have argued at great length over the influence of British mercantile regulations upon the economic development of the thirteen colonies. In recent years they have placed less emphasis on the economic impact of Imperial policies than on the political and administrative difficulties which attended their execution. The biographical sketches which are included below illuminate administrative problems of the British Customs Service by describing the character of two very different men in its ranks. Alfred S. Martin analyzes the career of John Swift, collector of customs at Philadelphia, who tried his best to execute British regulations without injuring the prosperity of American merchants. Another type of public servant, Hugh McCulloh, is discussed by Charles G. Sellers, who indicates that McCulloh used his official position in the British bureaucracy to exploit Americans for his own private gain. These two selections represent two divergent views concerning the effect of British economic policies on the colonies. What discrepancies arose between the aims of British commercial policies and their execution? How did the British mercantile system affect the business practices of Americans? How could the British mercantile system have been improved?

The King's Customs: Philadelphia, 1763–1774

ALFRED S. MARTIN

A teasing Custom House and Multiplicity of perplexing regulations
ever have and ever will appear the masterpiece of finance to people
of narrow views.

—BURKE

This is a story with a strange hero. In terms of contemporary American
folklore he should not have been a hero at all but an unsympathetic character, slightly contemptible, slightly sinister, since he was a civil servant,
an administrative official in Britain's bureaucracy. Are not bureaucrats
like that?

John Swift, collector of customs in Philadelphia during the crucial
period before the American Revolution, was, however, of quite different
metal. Intelligent, honest, hard-working, and patriotic, he demands admiration and sympathy. Britain's policy and British navigation laws put
Swift in an impossible situation; but although damned by supervisors and
by taxpaying merchants alike, he continued to enforce the laws as best he
could. The unsuccessful efforts of this customs officer to achieve a balance between official regulations and reasonable practice demonstrate the
problems inherent in a system grown too cumbersome for efficient operation.

The basic principles of the English navigation laws, though far from
universally approved or condoned by the people they affected, were well
understood by the middle of the eighteenth century. Enumerated commodities, direct shipment, British goods and crews, and permanently or temporarily closed trades were legal facts. The day to day operation along
the waterfront of the law in which these legal facts were embodied provides an interesting, at times an amusing, view of the bureaucratic maze in
which the honest port officer sometimes came perilously close to losing
himself.

An account of the operation of bringing a vessel into port will give a
concise picture of the multifarious customs officials and of their functions.
On entering the harbor a ship's master made immediate report to the collector, who, with the comptroller were deputies of men who held office
by royal patent. The master furnished the collector with cockets—sealed
certificates—showing the quantity, description and weight of all the goods
laded in his vessel. These cockets also showed the various brands and
marks of the items in the cargo as well as the names of the consignees. In
the meantime a tidesman was placed aboard the vessel, and no part of the

Reprinted by permission from Alfred S. Martin, "The King's Customs: Philadelphia,
1763–1774," *William and Mary Quarterly*, V, (April, 1948), pp. 201–216.

cargo could be landed until this officer had listed the goods and made a search for hidden or illegal parcels. When this was done, the cargo was landed under the supervision of a waiter, or "landwaiter," who checked the goods as they came from the boat. If the ship could not be unloaded in a single day, or if illegal practices were suspected, a watcher was put aboard to make sure that nothing was landed without supervision. A weigher and gauger checked dutiable goods for customs assessments. If illegal or additional goods were found, they were seized and stored for closer inspection or further action. If the information obtained by the tidesman, collector and waiter checked completely, the customs fee was assessed, and the consignees could claim their goods when the duty was paid or satisfactory arrangements made to pay it. The procedure was almost directly reversed when the vessel cleared.

To carry further the system of checks and balances, or perhaps merely to add to the number of patent offices, a surveyor was appointed to check the collector and comptroller who were already checking each other. In larger ports, such as Philadelphia, the tidesmen and waiters might also have supervisors or surveyors to check their work. Over all the local officials stood the surveyor general. Appointed under Treasury warrant the four North American surveyors general were directly responsible to the London Board of Customs, and might appear anywhere without warning to investigate any or all of the port officers under their jurisdiction.

In addition a host of bonds, sufferances and certificates had to be given or cancelled by master and port officials before a ship was free to sail. If enumerated commodities were shipped to legal destinations, bond had to be given that they would be sent directly to a specified port. A bond also had to be given that non-enumerated goods would be shipped to Europe only south of Cape Finisterre. Shipments of rum were bonded not to go to the Isle of Man. At one time or another certificates had to be given for British coffee, sugars and pimento. Naturally each step in the process required the payment of a fee. In Philadelphia the collector's fee for a ship's clearance was one pound ten shillings; the total fees paid ran to over five pounds.

A strict observance of the laws was almost impossible. Despite instructions and rate books, few men were qualified to understand all the ramifications of the acts. Who was to judge the subtle flavors of the wines imported, or to know accurately the hundreds of different classes of cloths and other goods brought in? The written guides given to local officials were veritable miracles of elaboration, but special exceptions and provisions changed from day to day and the legal niceties involved were exasperating and bewildering. Honest officials were harassed by the multitude of provisions and snowed under by hundreds of quires of bonds and certificate forms. No wonder that John Swift, the collector at Philadelphia, in 1769 included in an order for 128 quires of bond and certificate forms a request "1 Doz. red Tape to tye up the Papers."

The laws were not only involved and forever changing but the statutes if literally interpreted occasionally operated to defeat their original purpose. Under the regulations made in 5 George II. c. 22 the exportation of hats from one colony to another was forbidden under severe penalty. Swift was of the opinion that he would "as soon eat fire as sign a cocket for Hatts," yet what was he to do when a consignment came directly from Manchester to Philadelphia for merchants in New Jersey or Delaware? A shipment of hats came from Bermuda with a certificate from the collector and comptroller there that they were legally imported. Should the shipment be seized? Both Swift and the commissioners were of the opinion that such action would be contrary to the purpose of the act which was designed to promote the English hat industry. Further, were goods subject to duty if they had been shipped before the imposition of a duty but not landed until after it was in effect? Did the new duties imposed in 1764 on the importation of Madeira wine apply to imports of wine of the Azores? When the Crown attorney general and the Board of Customs disagreed on all these points, what was the collector to do? To enforce the law according to its letter left him open to civil action by outraged merchants; non-enforcement might lead to dismissal by the Board of Trade.

The Townshend revenue act brought a host of equally knotty problems to the colonial customs officers. Were empty bottles to be charged a duty if the contents had been consumed during the voyage? Was glass in frames and mirrors dutiable; and if bottles were full and sealed were the officers to break the seal in order to get the empty weight of the bottles? To make matters worse, crated glass had to be unpacked and weighed, and the officers were liable for damages on all breakage. Duty on paper was levied by the ream, but sometimes paper came in boxes and in square feet. Despite the fact that sample books of paper were made up, many varieties were imported that had no classification. How were these to be judged? And in the case of tea and other dutiable commodities, should abatement be allowed for damages before the fee was assessed?

The Sugar Act of 1764, with the taxes it levied on wines, sugar, molasses, and other products, added to the difficulties and to the unpopularity of the colonial officers. Two additional measures dating from almost the same period grated on the nerves of the colonial mercantile classes. The first was the empowering of naval officers stationed on ships off the North American and West Indian coasts to act in suppressing illegal trade. The new officers of enforcement lacked a nice understanding of what, for the sake of efficiency and national advantage, should be ignored and what enforced in the navigation laws. They interpreted the law so literally that the Annual Register found it amazing that "the trade of the colonies, as far as it depended upon these new-fangled customhouse officers, was not

... totally annihilated." The second measure with its proposed re-shuffling of the admiralty courts irked merchants because it might necessitate long journeys for appellate cases, and because the merchant who felt the customs officers had acted wrongly in seizing his goods was no longer allowed redress through the common law, if probable cause for seizure was shown in the admiralty court.

The resentments engendered by these acts had barely simmered down when the Stamp Act set the caldron boiling again. November 1, the day the act was to become effective, came in the middle of the busy season for the merchants and customs officers at Philadelphia. Since no stamps were available, the question as to whether vessels should be allowed to enter or to clear without stamped papers added to the confusion. In Virginia Governor Fauquier ordered the customs officials to abide strictly by the terms of the act, and warned that deviations would be at their own peril. Fortunately the surveyors general were more mindful than were the colonial governors of the administrative problems, and from the beginning leaned toward the position that cockets and clearances should be granted with a certificate showing that stamps were not obtainable. Since no word was received from the London Board of Customs all through the period of the Stamp Act crisis, the tie-up of shipping would have been tremendous had these officers been less realistic in their approach to the problem.

Administration of the customs laws by remote control was obviously becoming impracticable. From Collector John Swift's career comes another example of the difficulties which beset the customs officers because of the thousands of miles which separated them from authority. It had taken the Philadelphia collector six months to learn from London whether duties were to be levied on molasses at every colonial port of importation, or only at the first port entered. Even then the matter was not settled, for some little time later, the Crown attorney general overruled the decision of the Board of Trade, and duties collected on secondary importations had to be returned. When an answer from London was months in coming, it is not surprising that, in cases where infringement of the laws rested on technical interpretations, most officers were chary about making seizures. Moreover, while the customs officials waited for instructions, wines might spoil and other libelled goods deteriorate and leave the officers open to civil suits for damages. Efficiency demanded the creation of a local agency with equivalent powers to the London board.

This was the state of affairs when, as a corollary of the Townshend revenue act of 1767, the American board of customs was set up in Boston. Increased efficiency in the collection of revenue as well as in the administration of the laws at the waterside prompted the measure. The board was to be independent and equal in power to the London commission, and its sphere of jurisdiction ran from "Davis Streights" to the Capes of Florida.

Five commissioners made up the American board: Henry Hulton, formerly Plantation clerk for the London board; John Temple, before his appointment surveyor general of the northern customs district; Charles Paxton, who had been surveyor of the port and marshal of the admiralty court at Boston; John Robinson, a deputy collector in Rhode Island; and William Burch, who seems to have been distinguished for little except for signing his name last on most of the official papers of the new commission. To complete the reorganization of the American customs, the warrants for the four surveyors general then in the colonies under the authority of the London board were revoked, and the Plantation office, where Hulton had been chief clerk, was abolished. Several valuable adjunct offices were created for the new commission. To give the incumbents greater authority, the cashier and the comptroller were henceforth to be appointed under the Great Seal.

Such a board could scarcely escape the odium attached to the laws it was to enforce. A rumor was soon circulated that the members had shown their true colors by refusing to appoint any man to the service who had an American wife or any blood connections in the colonies. A Virginia merchant assured a Boston associate that the new commission was far from a blessing, but rather "one of the Plagues of Aegupt. . . . Swarms of hungry Locusts through all our Coasts, to feed on the Fat of the Land, and annoy, impoverish and perplex us." Others felt that the board's appointees were of such character that they were scarcely to be trusted around a cargo. It must be admitted that much of the early work of the board did smack of petty bureaucratic methods; the old adage of the new broom was never more shockingly exemplified than by this group.

Within two weeks after the Boston board began its meetings, Philadelphia's Collector Swift was in possession of a bewildering array of new forms to be filled out immediately, had been told tartly to number all of his letters, to report on the quality of all the men under him, and to describe the business of the port of Philadelphia. Before these requests could be filled, collector and comptroller were deluged with another batch of instructions. They were charged to prosecute their offices vigorously, to report infringements of the new acts, to dispatch immediately the seals and signatures of their duty, and to make immediate application for writs of assistance.

The impact of all this on a capable and honest official like John Swift can be imagined. His work was doubled at the busiest season of the year, and he was further harassed by the rising tide of resentment that the new restrictions engendered in the mercantile classes. To make matters worse, this outburst of officiousness came from a group of men who were all his juniors in experience, and most of them in status as well, before their recent appointments.

Swift, who was not noted for his tact, replied as promptly as he could

and his answers were more courteous than might have been expected. In the course of his report, he made some sound recommendations. The tidesmen, who received only thirty pounds a year, should have their salaries raised. "An Honest Man" could not live in Philadelphia on that sum. Care must also be taken with the merchants. More revenue was collected in Philadelphia than in any other colonial port, and the merchants were not pleased with that record. There seemed a determination among them not to pay additional duties, "and should they be unanimous not to pay any more Duties, we fear it will not be in our power to compel them." The hat and woolen acts were not violated but certain other acts, such as the one dealing with sailcloth manufacture, had never been enforced. If neglected acts were to be enforced, it would be well to give notice of the intention, otherwise the collector would run the "risk of Losing his ears." Swift continued by remarking that no application had been made for a writ of assistance because the need for one had never arisen and, so far as the collector and the comptroller understood, such a writ was not perpetual, but had to be applied for each time it was needed. Finally, he recommended that the merchants be allowed to pay duties in gold as well as in silver, since the colonial supply of the latter was very limited.

Two new orders, one for enforcing the Greenwich Hospital duty, the other for copying the cockets of all entering ships, brought Swift's temper to the boiling point. To copy the cockets of entering vessels was impossible, he declared. A vessel from London might have as many as fifty cockets, "and some of them . . . not less than a yard square." Frequently almost all the items in the book of rates might be found in one cargo. It was, furthermore, almost impossible to get a completely accurate invoice from a London captain. "You might as well insist upon his giving you the actual tales, weight or measure of Land upon the Sea Shore as the goods in his Ship, & we doubt not he would do the one with as much exactness as the other; for one half of them can scarcely write their own Names." Swift's wrath, once aroused, was mighty. He went on to complain that the books sent for keeping the accounts were smaller than the sample accounts. What did they want him to leave out? Moreover, the books were unruled. Since former commissioners had always ruled the books, and since he was certain that the commissioners had more time than he did, Swift was sure they would not object if he returned the books to be ruled. He ended with an acrimonious reminder that the instructions he received from the board were varied, and never complete.

To add to Swift's irritation, the Boston board usually ignored the recommendations of the Philadelphia officers in making minor appointments to the customs service. The American commissioners, like the London board, took turns in filling customs vacancies, and some conspicuous personnel failures were sent to Philadelphia by this means. Take, for example, the case of William Sheppard, Charles Paxton's first appointee, sent to fill the place of a searcher who had refused the job. From the beginning of his service, Sheppard did nothing but create a generous amount of trouble between the customs officials and the Philadelphia merchants. He also made himself unpopular with his fellow workers when he demanded to share the customs house office with the collector and comptroller and absolutely refused to do anything but supervisory work. Matters reached a climax, however, when Sheppard undertook to increase his private income by requiring a fee for signing sufferances to load a ship.

Since Philadelphia produced nothing that was dutiable on exportation, the sufferances had always been granted orally. Written sufferances would create about five thousand new forms to be filed yearly, and would add nothing to the revenue. At first the merchants flatly refused to pay the new fees, but after a conference with Swift they agreed to them, if the attorney general decided they were legal. Sheppard apparently concurred in this decision. The next day the searcher openly declared that he would abide by no such proposition and, saying that his word was as good as the collector's, he left for Boston to lay his case before the commissioners. The merchants then took a new line of action. They would pay the fees, and sue the port officials at civil law for extortion, if the fees were found illegal. The possibility of such an action before an unfriendly jury did not make pleasant contemplation.

The Boston board upheld Sheppard and demanded that the fees be paid. Meanwhile, three Philadelphia lawyers, Benjamin Chew, Joseph Galloway, and John Dickinson, had decided that the fees were not legal and held the collector liable at common law for any damages sustained by the merchants. The inspector general, sent to investigate the case, agreed with the lawyers. Swift was ready to stand by the decision of the board, if they would indemnify him against damages that might be sustained in the prosecution of his duty. This the commissioners refused to do, and Sheppard was instructed not to take any fees unless the merchants voluntarily granted them. There, after seven months, the matter rested, where it had begun. Nothing had been accomplished except that the irritated merchants who were already considering a non-importation agreement were further antagonized.

Another of Paxton's appointees, David Ross, was likewise a failure. Sent, despite Swift's protests, to command the new customs sloop in the Delaware River, Ross' virtue unfortunately "held but short seige," and he was dismissed in disgrace. Thayer, another Paxton man who succeeded Ross, was honest enough, but equally troublesome. He finally brought about his own downfall by seizing some tea loaded on a wagon headed for the interior. Reporting this valorous action directly to the Boston board instead of to Swift, Thayer mentioned the difficulty of getting draymen to carry the tea back to Philadelphia. The board in reply sarcastically pointed out that the horses and dray were both liable to seizure along with the tea. It was agreed that Thayer thought "of nothing but being a great man, and that to accomplish that thee would sacrifice the whole revenue," and he was consequently dismissed.

Obviously the problem of enforcement hinged squarely on the personnel of the customs service. The most efficient officers could not prevent infringements of the navigation and revenue acts when given dishonest subordinates. Yet it was extremely difficult to obtain honest men for the service, especially when merchants' bribes were infinitely more lucrative than the low salaries the board of customs was willing to pay. Dishonest tidesmen and waiters might let masters enter with more sugar than their cockets called for, and allow the surplus to be landed in the night. The next day the collector would find the cockets and cargo in harmony. It was extremely hard, moreover, to find men who could be trusted with the revenue cutter. Most of the available men were unable to withstand a great deal of temptation. It is worthy of note that Swift had to fight with the Boston board for two years to secure the appointment of one man whose honesty he felt to be unimpeachable.

Instances of friction between board and collector could be multiplied. Swift was unjustly accused of keeping the customs office in his own house because of the profit he derived from the rent. It took two years to get confirmation for the appointment of a needed waiter, who was without salary during that time. The Boston board, on another occasion, waited ten months before acting on a recommendation to reinstate a dismissed tidesman. Only one appointee of the board was eminently satisfactory to Swift, Joshua Loring, the controller. As a matter of fact Swift was entirely too blunt in his dealings with the commissioners, and as early as 1768 he was under the shadow of their displeasure. Charles Stewart, the former surveyor general of the Philadelphia district, managed to smooth matters over, but recommended that Swift be a little more subtle in his dealings. This excellent advice was followed sparingly. Joshua Loring, also advised Swift to be more tactful in his relations with the board: his letters did not have "Flummery eno in them, alas not big eno with respect." Despite the advice, Swift could not bring himself to the point of flattering the commissioners and eventually he lost his place.

The revision and the redistricting of the admiralty courts mentioned earlier, like the establishment of the board of customs, were effected to increase administrative efficiency. Coming as an adjunct of the Townshend duties, this program also aroused a storm of protest in the colonies. The new system, ordered under warrant of the Treasury in July, 1768, provided for four courts. The court at Philadelphia, with Jared Ingersol as judge, had original jurisdiction in New York, Maryland, Pennsylvania, New Jersey, and Delaware. In addition it could take appellate cases from any subordinate court. The salary granted to the judges was to come from penalties and forfeitures, and from the sale of old naval stores. Under no circumstances were they to take any fee or gratuity for a judgment given, or for any other business transacted in their court. Two features in particular opened the courts to trouble. If the admiralty court found probable cause for seizure, the defendant was allowed no action for redress at common law. Quite mistakenly, as it turned out, colonial opinion held that no case would ever arise in which the admiralty judge would not find probable cause. The courts' overlapping spheres of influence in cases of seizure also aroused antagonism. A seizure in one district might be carried to another for trial. Though there was some basis for colonial protest, it is hard to believe that the new courts fairly earned all the calumnies heaped upon them.

Few lawyers in Philadelphia would try cases for the customs service. Even James Allen, the attorney general, did so with reluctance. Informers were likewise exceedingly rare and very unpopular. A third share in the sale of condemned goods did not seem enticing, if it might entail the wrath of an excited mob. Known informers could expect to receive a coat of tar and feathers after assorted beatings, stonings, and duckings. In any case the informer's share was likely to be small, since most of the illegal goods were brought to Philadelphia in small parcels aboard pilot boats. Under such conditions the prosecution fees consumed most of the profits. Generally the customs officers preferred to make the seizures themselves, as the work of informers only brought them a double share of odium.

The geographical position of Philadelphia made smuggling relatively easy in cases where it was profitable. During 1770, a large number of vessels began to enter at New Castle and trans-ship their cargoes to Philadelphia in shallops. Molasses came up with duty paid, but rum was certified as British by the collector at New Castle. In view of the fact that there was not a pair of scales in that port, some suspicion was aroused at Philadelphia. When a weigher and gauger and a pair of scales were sent to assist the New Castle collector, the trade stopped immediately. The favorite method of avoiding the customs, however, was to hold the ship some distance below the port while illegal cargo was transferred to small pilot boats. The master then proceeded to Philadelphia in ballast with false clearances; the pilot boat slipped into one of the many small creeks and inlets where the cargo was unloaded in safety. In such cases there was nothing the collector could do unless he could prove the clearances false. In one instance, Swift knew that a vessel from Fayal was anchored below the city, and sent officers to watch it. After several days, the ship entered port in stone ballast. Despite the fact that it was obviously too light for a sea voyage, and that the top masts had to be struck to keep it upright, there was no basis for legal seizure, since the ship's papers purported to show that it had cleared in ballast. Such procedure was not unusual, and the officers feared the consequences for the revenue, if these methods should become even more fashionable.

There were other ways of evading the law. Customs officers found some illegal wines in Philadelphia and seized them. During the night the warehouse where they had been stored was broken into, and the wines stolen. The next day a group of prominent merchants disowned the act and promised to have the wines returned. This was done, and in due course the wines were libelled in admiralty court, condemned and sold for the appraised value. But the condemned wines were "sad stuff" and sold for only £5 a ton; different wines had been substituted for those originally seized. In other cases, condemned goods were appraised so low by the mercantile body that their sale did not cover the cost of court proceedings.

Colonial customs officers were never entirely safe from bodily harm at the hands of irate mobs. John Hatton, the collector of Salem and Cohansey, and his son were almost killed while attempting to make a seizure. Having observed a ship off the Capes unloading into small pilot boats, they manned two wherries with eight men and started in pursuit. As they neared the ship, the crew stove several casks of claret and threw them overboard. The two wherries were then ordered to stand off under pain of annihilation. Parley availed the customs party nothing, so they set out to capture one of the escaping pilot boats. One was caught and found to have an illegal cargo. Hatton and his son, together with a Negro slave, boarded the prize and set out for port. Unfortunately, the wind failed at this juncture and the seized boat was becalmed. Barges from the ships soon arrived and recaptured it. Hatton and his son were beaten unmercifully and put ashore. As soon as he was able to travel, young Hatton came to Philadelphia to report the incident to Swift. Going to identify the pilot boat while the collector was absent on business, Hatton was seized by a mob, his bandages ripped off, and a coat of tar and feathers applied. After being ducked, pilloried and beaten he was taken across the river and left more dead than alive at Coopers Ferry.

Even the customs house schooner was not immune from attack. Early in the evening of November 23, 1771, Captain Muskett and his crew boarded a suspicious looking pilot boat from Chester. When illegal teas and wine were found, the boat was seized and a prize crew put aboard. Again the wind failed and the officers were forced to anchor off Red Bank. A large group of heavily armed men put out from the shore and surrounded the schooner and her prize. They "attacked Capta. Muskett & his people with such violence that presently laid most of them flat on the deck & threw them, into the Hold & others into the Cabbin of the Custom Ho. Schooner & fastened the hatches upon them." The rigging and sails of the schooner were cut away, the cables and anchors stolen, and the rescued boat carried off in triumph, while the schooner was towed ashore and left marooned in the mud. The mayor and chief justice promised justice if the offenders were caught, but they were not apprehended.

Although the American board of customs, the Treasury, and the English foreign consular service cooperated in a remarkably efficient espionage system for detecting infractions of the navigation laws, their efforts were often of no avail. One voyage of Gregg and Conningham's ship the *Speedwell* offers a case in point. The Treasury reported the suspicious clearance of this ship from Liverpool in ballast. Shortly thereafter, Swift received word that the vessel had taken on a cargo of tea at Gottenberg. A little later the same information was relayed to him from the Boston board. Report was made to the commander of the customs schooner, and to Lieutenant Dudingston, in command of a naval vessel off the Delaware Capes. When the *Speedwell* entered Philadelphia it was immediately seized, despite the master's intention to clear for Charleston without breaking bulk. Ballast of salt and coal was unloaded, but nothing else was found, "the bird had flown before the vessel came up. . . ." In another instance, tidesmen seized a vessel and were carried off to sea for their pains. Likewise the capture of offending pilot boats did little good. Legal penalties, equal to three times the value of the vessel and cargo, were not effective, because the boats were usually put in charge of young boys who had no possible way of paying the fine. For all intents and purposes, the English customs service in the colonies broke down completely with the coming of the Association in 1774. "What can magistrates do unless they are supported by their fellow citizens? What can the King's officers do if they make themselves obnoxious to the people amongst whom they reside?"

Private Profits and British Colonial Policy: The Speculations of Henry McCulloh

CHARLES G. SELLERS, JR.

Why did the once loyal inhabitants of British America become the rebels of 1776? This question—which no simple reply satisfies—remains and will remain the first question asked about the origins of the United States, and any answer which throws light on any aspect of the problem is of value. This paper addresses itself to one feature of the story in one colony—North Carolina—in the hope that the story of Henry McCulloh will help to explain in part why certain North Carolinians were willing to set their feet on the road that led to revolution in 1776.

British officials in their dealings with the American colonies subscribed

Reprinted with permission from "Private Profits and British Colonial Policy: The Speculations of Henry McCulloh," *William and Mary Quarterly*, VIII (October, 1951), pp. 535–551.

heartily to orthodox mercantilist axioms. But there proved to be many a slip between principle and practice. Efforts to explain the inconsistencies of England's colonial policy have emphasized British politics and the problem of administrative organization. Too little attention has been paid to the less obvious influence of the acquisitive Englishman with friends in high places, whose interests were permitted to override the demands of sound colonial administration. Through the four decades preceding the Revolution, the ambitious land speculations of one Henry McCulloh helped keep the politics of the province of North Carolina in turmoil. All the while, in London, McCulloh was giving royal officials advice on colonial problems, advice which was by no means uninfluenced by his personal concerns.

Scottish by descent, McCulloh displayed in his pursuit of profit a full measure of the shrewdness and tirelessness for which his countrymen were becoming unpopular. By the 1730's he was netting an average of £600 a year from his mercantile business and by the end of the decade had accumulated a modest fortune of £5400. Since 1726 he had been supporting a young Scot, Gabriel Johnston, who had come to London as a political publicist and quickly made the acquaintance of influential men. In 1734 Johnston's friends secured for him an appointment as governor of North Carolina.

Just how McCulloh first became connected with Johnston or what part he had in obtaining the governorship for him is not known. But the canny merchant at once planned to use his protege's new position to advantage. He put the governor under further obligations to himself by paying the fees for his commission, freighting a ship to carry him and his retinue to America, buying plate and furniture for his house, and providing him with credit to supply his immediate needs. Johnston's debt to McCulloh amounted to at least £2400.

The land-locked coast of the early settled northern section of North Carolina had helped make the province one of Britain's more backward possessions. But when Governor Johnston arrived in America, the southeastern corner of the colony, where the Cape Fear River afforded an adequate anchorage, was beginning to be settled rapidly. The original promoters of the Cape Fear country, led by Maurice Moore, Roger Moore, and Edward Moseley, were members of a wealthy family connection which had long been the dominant force in provincial politics. Rice, indigo, and naval stores proved to be profitable staples along the Cape Fear, and competition for the engrossment of choice lands in the province's fastest growing section was keen.

Johnston's appointment and McCulloh's early participation in North Carolina affairs seem to have been parts of a scheme, countenanced by Colonel Martin Bladen, leading spirit of the Board of Trade, to contest with the "Family" for supremacy in the rich Cape Fear area. North

Carolina already had a strong anti-Family faction, which included Nathaniel Rice, secretary of the province and son-in-law of Bladen. Others
opposed to the Family were Chief Justice William Smith, who also owed
his appointment to Bladen, and a majority of the Council, including
Robert Halton, Eleazar Allen, and Matthew Rowan. Johnston and Mc-
Culloh could also depend for support on the governor's close friend
Captain Samuel Woodward, Captain James Innes, who seems to have
come to America in Johnston's entourage and who was later a member of
the Council, and another young Scot, James Murray. McCulloh largely
financed Murray's venture to the Cape Fear in 1735 to establish himself
as a merchant. He was soon the largest trader on the river, and later
Johnston was able to get him made a member of the Council and secretary
of the province.

The Family's hopes for engrossing the best Cape Fear lands were based
on "blank patents" which had been fraudulently issued in large numbers
in the late proprietary period. These patents were so carelessly drawn
that they could be laid upon almost any tract and predated to exclude
later grants. The strategy of McCulloh and his allies was to use their
political influence to have the blank patents annulled and then to secure
extensive grants for themselves through the governor and Council and
directly from the Crown.

This struggle tied in with the knottiest problem encountered by British
officials in their efforts to establish the royal government of North Carolina on a firm foundation, the question of land policy and quit rent collection. Quit rent rates and the mode of payment had been such hotly
contested issues that assembly after assembly had refused to pass any law
setting up a regular registration and collection procedure, and the whole
system had fallen into disorder. Complicating the situation was the insistence of the holders of blank patents, principally members and allies
of the Family, that no law be passed unless it recognized their claims.

Johnston brought with him to America instructions, drafted by the
Board of Trade, to insist on a quit rent law requiring payments at a high
rate and invalidating the blank patents. When the assembly, under Family
influence, refused to pass such an act, he announced that he would collect
without a law. The governor and his friends also moved into the Cape
Fear region and began to encourage the development of the little port of
Newton as a rival to the Family's stronghold, Brunswick, which was located farther down the river.

In November, 1735, Johnston informed the Council that

he had lately recd a letter from Mr Dobbs and some ether Gentleman of Distinction in Ireland and Mr Henry McCulloh Mercht in London representing
their intention of sending over to this Province several poor Protestant Familys
with design of raising Flax and Hemp. . . .

Captain Woodward, as agent for the group, had already located a body of good land on the Cape Fear and applied for a grant of 60,000 acres, which the governor announced his intention of issuing. The Council approved this action, notwithstanding the fact that grants were only supposed to be made on the basis of fifty acres for each person actually brought into the province.

This first grant was typical of the McCulloh land-grabbing procedure. The patents for the 54,000 acres finally obtained were made out to "divers persons, then and now unknown," but were actually for the benefit of McCulloh, who had sold rights to most of the lands to his friends in Ireland for around £1,000. Purchaser of 6,000 acres was Arthur Dobbs, engineer-in-chief and surveyor-general of Ireland, who continued to be associated in the McCulloh speculations. This was the one large grant McCulloh secured on which he promised to pay quit rents at once; yet Dobbs was the only grantee who fulfilled this obligation. Not only did McCulloh fail to pay quit rents on the portion he retained, but when he became commissioner of quit rents for the Carolinas, he connived at non-payment by those who had purchased from him.

Almost immediately McCulloh shifted his operations to London and applied to the Privy Council for two grants in North Carolina totalling 132,000 acres, one of 72,000 acres between the Northeast Cape Fear and Black rivers, and the other at the "Haw Fields" on the headwaters of the Northwest Cape Fear. The grants were approved after the persuasive McCulloh had outlined ambitious plans for placing several hundred people on the lands to produce potash, hemp, and naval stores, and to engage in the fur trade. He was also able to convince the Crown officials that, in view of the expense of settling the tracts, he should be exempted from quit rents for ten years. He was required, however, to establish three hundred Protestants on the lands in the ten year periods.

McCulloh sold the 60,000 acre grant on the Northwest Cape Fear to Governor Johnston, and attempted to settle the more valuable lands on the other branch of the river himself, bringing in some 150 Irish and 42 Swiss immigrants. Johnston and Murray received the settlers, and the latter provided them with shelter and provisions through the first winter. But several of them were carried off by Carolina's notorious fevers, and the whole Swiss colony soon departed.

Meanwhile, the Family was fighting back. While Arthur Dobbs was making plans to place Irish settlers on his 6,000 acres, Murray wrote to McCulloh,

I cannot help giving you an instance how much some gentlemen here endeavour to defeat all the Govrs Designs for settling the country. Roger Moore I am told has wrote to Mr Dobbs that it will not be his interest to concern himself in land here or something to that purpose. His view in which is that if the Irish come over here they will be a weight against him in the Assembly and will by Cultivating the land confirm Mr Dobbs right to what he would be content to take the advantage of a lapse of, in case a new Govr should be appoint'd, which all the blank patent gentry are in great hopes of.

But for the moment McCulloh's enemies could do little except continue to block passage of a quit rent law. Newton, in the meantime, with the governor's support, was rapidly outstripping the Family's rival Brunswick. Johnston, Murray, Woodward, Innes, and Rowan all owned lots there, and in 1740, when they finally succeeded in getting a law passed incorporating the town as Wilmington, Murray wrote to McCulloh, "I think I may Venture to say that it is for your Interest to Support that law and get it confirmed if Possible." The speculator was all the while using his influence in other small ways for his North Carolina friends, securing the collectorship of the Cape Fear for Murray by the judicious distribution of 200 pounds.

McCulloh was by no means satisfied with his successes. Possessed of influence at the Board of Trade and having the governor and provincial officials (as he thought) in his vest pocket, he concluded that North Carolina was his for the asking. On May 7, 1736, only eight days after the Privy Council had approved the 60,000 and 72,000 acre grants, two London merchants, James Huey and Murray Crymble, "and Associates," petitioned the Crown for a grant of 1,200,000 acres in the province of North Carolina.

It had best be explained at once that the entire promotion was, as Johnston later testified, "a private Jobb of his (McCulloh's) own and a great imposition upon his Majesty in Council." The truth of the governor's statement is established beyond doubt by an affidavit of Huey and Crymble to the effect that all the lands were for the use of McCulloh. When the patents were finally issued in 1746, some were made out in the names of persons other than McCulloh, but all of them had either purchased rights to the grants from him or were holding in trust for him.

Lengthy discussions of the petition at the Board of Trade, with Huey, Crymble, and McCulloh all appearing, delayed approval of the project, and the necessary order did not pass the Privy Council until May 19, 1737. The surveyor general of North Carolina was ordered to lay off and the governor to grant to Huey, Crymble, and their associates 1,200,-000 acres on the headwaters of the Yadkin, Cape Fear and Neuse rivers. The grantees were to pay the customary fees to the provincial officers, but were to be exempt from quit rents for ten years from the date on which the governor issued the final grants. In this period they were to settle on the lands six thousand Protestants, or one for every two hundred acres.

Though McCulloh was undoubtedly elated by the success of his bold project to this point, ominous signs began to appear on the North

Carolina horizon. The legislative stalemate brought about by the insistence of the blank patent men that their rights be recognized before they would allow the governor to set up an effective quit rent system had continued for session after session of the assembly. Recognizing the danger, McCulloh began to appear at meetings of the Board of Trade as Governor Johnston's agent, explaining the iniquity of blank patents and urging stronger support for the governor. In fact, the Board began to consider McCulloh as an authority on quit rent matters and to seek his advice. But the situation was even more serious than McCulloh realized. For Johnston showed signs of acknowledging obligations other than those to his London ally. Recognizing that continued insistence on his position on quit rents could only keep the province in turmoil, he began to think of compromise. At this juncture, the vast Huey-Crymble grant was authorized, and the governor saw in it opportunities for himself.

The trouble arose over the surveying of the lands. About three months after the order in council was issued, McCulloh sent a copy of it to Governor Johnston, so that he could prevent others from taking up the desired tracts, and informed him that the associates would send an agent later with specific instructions about how the grant was to be laid off. When the copy reached Johnston in the early fall of 1737, he and his North Carolina friends discovered a way to enrich themselves through the fees for surveying and granting this immense domain. The surveyor general of the province had just died, and Johnston now proceeded to give Matthew Rowan an interim appointment to succeed him. At the same time Rowan signed an agreement promising to pay half his salary and fees to Captain Samuel Woodward, the governor's crony. Knowing that a permanent surveyor general would probably be sent over soon from England, Johnston did not wait for McCulloh's instructions, but delivered the Huey-Crymble order at once to Rowan, who started on the survey four days after the above agreement was signed.

McCulloh was enraged when he learned what had happened. His carefully prepared instructions, designating a large tract on the Northeast Cape Fear and other choice lands for survey, had been nullified by the governor's order to Rowan to lay off the grant as far west as possible. One million acres of it were surveyed in a single rectangular tract on the uninhabited waters of the Yadkin, and two other pieces of 100,000 acres each were also located far from the coast, on the waters of the Haw and of the Tar, Flat, and Eno rivers. Rowan did divide the large tract into 100,000 acre parcels, but it had been McCulloh's plan to have him further divide it into 12,500 acre tracts. If this had to be done by a second survey, the surveyor would be entitled to double fees. Complaining that, even so, the North Carolina officials were charging double the fees they were entitled to, McCulloh refused to pay them, and Johnston insisted that the grants would not be issued until the fees were paid. This suited the speculator well enough, since delay would merely increase the value of the lands without endangering his right to them.

McCulloh's influence at Whitehall now afforded him a means of revenging himself upon his erstwhile allies and of rescuing his speculations at the same time. The Board of Trade, which had been in great perplexity over land and quit rent difficulties in both Carolinas, had found in him an able, though interested, adviser on colonial problems. Colonel Martin Bladen, probably acting at McCulloh's instance, now persuaded Sir Robert Walpole of the wisdom of sending the speculator to America as a special commissioner to investigate the situation. After this plan had been approved privately, McCulloh, early in 1738, presented a memorial to the Privy Council setting forth the defects in the land and quit rent system in the Carolinas and suggesting remedies. The Board of Trade endorsed his proposals and recommended that he be given a commission to effect the reforms he had outlined. The appointment was delayed for almost a year, while the Lords of the Treasury, in whose province quit rent problems properly lay, were being persuaded that the mission was necessary; but they finally gave their approval, authorizing a salary of £600 a year with £200 for clerk hire, "payable out of such quit rents in North and South Carolina as shall be recovered and improved by this means." McCulloh's commission, which was finally issued May 16, 1739, gave him very broad powers to investigate conditions, enforce regulations, and recommend further reforms. His effort to get himself made a member extraordinary of the councils of both provinces was defeated only by the spirited objections of Governor Glen of South Carolina, who happened to be in London at the time.

Before the commissioner could leave for America, news arrived that Johnston had at last patched up his quarrel with the North Carolina assembly, abandoning the strict letter of his instructions to get a quit rent law passed. Under this compromise act, 150,000 acres of the blank patents were to be recognized as valid. The connection between the governor's decision and his recent break with McCulloh must be left to conjecture, but there can be no doubt that the new law had the effect of ending the political turmoil which had prevailed in the province. Murray, who was still financially dependent on McCulloh in his trading business, wrote to him in January, 1740, that the new law had brought both the Family and the influential politicians of the Albemarle region to Johnston's support. His letter continued:

I hear Mr. Roger Moore Alledges that he has an old patent (which is now confirmed by the Q.R.L. (Quit Rent Law) that he says is Within your 72,000 acres; and sometimes he says it is Within the Bounds of the Land Sold Vaughan. You'll Observe a Clause in the Quit Rent Law that all Disputes between Proprietors' Patents and those lately issued are Determinable by the Govr. in Council, who I hope will take Care that no injury be done to you.

Moving quickly to protect his interests, McCulloh memorialized the Privy Council to disallow the new law. He obtained the support of a number of London merchants trading to Carolina for his petition, the Board of Trade was persuaded, and the act was disallowed. The politics and revenues of North Carolina were thus thrown once more into confusion. McCulloh's objectives were not only to protect his lands from the blank patents, but also to destroy the new alliance between Governor Johnston and the Family and to prevent any settlement of the quit rent difficulties which might make his mission to America unnecessary.

McCulloh arrived at Charleston early in 1741 and entered upon his duties with great vigor. In South Carolina, however, the opposition of speculating local politicians combined with his own arbitrary and tactless methods to render his efforts largely fruitless. He had even less success in North Carolina, where both the governor's party and the land speculators had special reason to oppose him. Most of his time seems to have been spent trying to establish his own grants and developing a fine plantation on his lands on the Northeast Cape Fear.

McCulloh complained repeatedly to his London superiors of the defiance of the provincial officials, but the Lords of the Treasury, who had never had much enthusiasm for his mission, ignored his pleas for official backing. Auditor General Horatio Walpole even stopped payment of his salary, on the ground that he had not actually improved quit rent collections. This lack of support encouraged the commissioner's North Carolina antagonists to wage war on him. Suits were brought against McCulloh in the provincial courts for nonpayment of fees on his land grants and for slanders he was accused of publishing against the colonial land officers. The legal battles continued for several years, with McCulloh at one time under technical arrest. But he was finally able to repel the attacks of his enemies and move onto the offensive. Obtaining a copy of the collusive Rowan-Woodward agreement of 1738, he held it as a club over the heads of the colonial officials to force them to issue his long-suspended grants. Governor Johnston was even compelled to agree to pay the larger part of the fees himself, in discharge of his old indebtedness to McCulloh.

The speculator had thus secured what amounted to an eight year extension of quit rent exemption and payment of the major portion of the fees out of a debt he was unlikely to collect in any way. Patents for the 1,200,000 acres were finally issued on March 3, 1746, in ninety-six separate grants of 12,500 acres each. Thirty-four of them were made out in McCulloh's name, and sixteen went to Arthur Dobbs in discharge of a mortgage McCulloh had given on 500,000 acres. Rights to sixteen additional grants had been sold to John Selwyn, an Englishman who moved in high circles, and all the rest went to others in trust for McCulloh or to McCulloh's children and agents. Huey and Crymble received not an acre.

McCulloh later induced his friends at the Board of Trade to extend the period of quit rent exemption from 1756 to 1760, and the lands which had not been settled in accordance with the terms of the grant by the latter date were not actually surrendered until 1765. Even then the Board released him from payment of the accrued quit rents, his son informing a friend at this time that "my Father's political Connections, are far from Contemptible."

The Board of Trade also helped McCulloh collect his back salary as commissioner, which by 1752 amounted to some £9,000. The Treasury Board and Auditor General refused at first to make any payment whatever. When, however, he secured a ruling from the Attorney General upholding his claims on all points, they gave him a warrant for £6,200 on the Receiver General of South Carolina, but required him to surrender his commission and all further claims. When McCulloh found it exceedingly difficult to collect from the South Carolina official, it was the Board of Trade which came to the rescue, allowing him to apply £1,035 of the warrant, and later the £2,584 of arrears not covered by the warrant, as a credit against the quit rents he would have to pay in North Carolina after 1760. This credit sufficed to cover all payments on his lands until he lost them at the time of the American Revolution.

The settlement of 1746 between Johnston and McCulloh did not put an end to their mutual hostility. When the Crown had acquired the Carolinas from the Lords Proprietors, one of them, Lord Granville, had refused to sell his share and had been assigned property rights to the unsold portion of the northern half of North Carolina. In 1743 a line setting off the Granville District had been run some distance into the interior. Three years later, only seventeen days after his settlement with McCulloh, the governor issued a commission for the extension of the line about 160 miles farther westward, so as to take in some 480,000 acres of McCulloh's recently granted lands. The speculator was, of course, furious at this perfidy.

But Granville promised at once that McCulloh should enjoy under him the same rights he would have had under the Crown. By a liberal agreement finally reached in 1761, McCulloh was granted a reduced quit rent rate from 1756, the date when his quit rent exemption expired, until two years after the end of the French and Indian War. At that time he was to be allowed to retain 300,000 acres, regardless of settlement, at the regular quit rent rate.

A sudden turn in North Carolina politics a few months after the showdown with Johnston in 1746 gave McCulloh a handle for new attacks on the governor. With the rapid growth of the southern or Cape Fear section of the province during the thirties and forties, a marked sectionalism had begun to be evident. The people on the Cape Fear particularly resented the fact that the older Albemarle counties each had five representatives in the assembly, while only two members had been allowed the newer counties to the south and west. Governor Johnston, having patched up his quarrel with the Family, favored the claims of the Cape Fear region.

In the fall of 1746 the governor initiated the "Great Schism" in North Carolina history by calling the assembly to meet at Wilmington, hoping that the long journey would reduce the Albemarle representation. When the Albemarle members, who were a majority of the assembly, boycotted the session, the rump body went ahead and passed an act reducing the representation of the northern counties to two each. As a result, the northern counties defied the laws and did not appear in the assembly again until 1754, when their extra representation was restored.

Fishing in these troubled waters was Henry McCulloh, and the governor complained to the Board of Trade that "the People in the Northern Counties were by McCulloh's Artifices all in an uproar on account of their five members." Shortly after this conflict broke out, having settled his land business, McCulloh returned to England. There, freed from the harassment of colonial law suits, he took up with renewed vigor his vendetta against the governor. Acting as agent for the Albemarle men, he presented their grievances to the Board of Trade and at the same time joined with Arthur Dobbs and others in an effort to have Johnston removed from office. The governor's enemies succeeded in getting the ever-complaisant Board of Trade to recommend his removal, but Johnston was saved for the moment by the skilful delaying tactics of his agent, James Abercromby.

Immediately after the failure of this move, McCulloh instituted charges against the governor on his own account, accusing Johnston of sundry loose practices in granting lands, recounting his misdeeds in connection with the Huey-Crymble grants, and denouncing his arbitrary procedure in judicial matters, his assent to currency and quit rent laws in violation of his instructions, and other irregular actions. When the Board of Trade authorized the taking of proofs on these allegations, Johnston intimidated McCulloh's agents in North Carolina, and on McCulloh's complaint, the Board gave him permission to take additional proofs. In this way final determination was delayed until 1752, when the governor died.

The direction in which events were tending at the time of Johnston's death was indicated by the appointment of McCulloh's longtime ally in speculation, Arthur Dobbs, to succeed him. The new governor was expressly directed by the Privy Council to restore the extra representation of the northern counties and to support the rights of McCulloh and his associates to their lands.

McCulloh was able to do little toward selling his lands until 1755, when he designated as agents his nephew, Alexander McCulloh, for whom he had earlier secured an appointment as deputy auditor for North Carolina and who was to be a member of Dobbs' Council, and John Campbell, a prominent merchant and the political leader of the Albemarle area. But the French and Indian War soon rendered their efforts ineffectual, and not much was actually done until 1761, when McCulloh's son, Henry Eustace, was sent over as agent. The younger man had the arduous task of surveying the lands to be retained when the unsettled parts were surrendered in 1765, laying them off in small parts, and selling them. As subordinate agents he employed such prominent provincials as Edmund Fanning, John Frohock, and Thomas Polk. Young McCulloh exhibited considerable astuteness and courage in dealing with the violent opposition he and his surveyors encountered in the southern interior part of the province where conditions had long been disturbed because of the unlocated boundary with South Carolina.

The average price at which the McCulloh lands were being sold in 1747 was about 5 pounds per hundred acres. Ten years later, 320 acres brought 25 pounds, while in 1761 Henry Eustace McCulloh settled with a large number of squatters on the lands for from 5 pounds to 12 pounds per hundred acres. The highest price which has come to notice was 30s an acre for a tract sold in 1773. This section of the province filled up rapidly in the twenty-five years preceding the Revolution, and prices increased steadily throughout the period.

Just how much money McCulloh made on his sweeping transactions is difficult to determine. In the forties and fifties he sold 525,000 acres to various speculators. By his agreement with Lord Granville, he surrendered about 175,000 acres, retaining 300,000, while outside the Granville District 339,325 acres were given up to the Crown in 1765, with 129,335 being kept by himself and his children. Some of the lands sold to speculators were included in the acreage surrendered. How much of the lands which he held for disposal to actual settlers had been sold by the time of the Revolution, when all the McCulloh property was confiscated, has not been determined. With the rapid settlement of the backcountry in the last decades of the colonial period and with McCulloh's freedom from quit rents outside the Granville District, it seems likely that the lands produced a considerable profit.

When McCulloh returned to England in 1747 to devote himself to reaping the benefits of his speculations, he also set himself up as an adviser to the government on colonial problems generally. During the next fifteen years he presented his ideas in numerous memorials to the Duke of Bedford, the Earl of Halifax, the Duke of Newcastle, and the Earl of Bute. His proposals were also elaborated to the public in two lengthy, anonymous pamphlets in 1755.

A thoroughgoing mercantilist, McCulloh echoed the conventional demand that the colonies be made more advantageous to the mother country by stricter regulation of their trade. His most frequent complaint, plainly stemming from his difficulty in defending himself from Governor Johnston's attacks, was that the royal officials in the colonies did not obey their instructions and did not keep and transmit promptly to London full records of their proceedings. McCulloh did have some constructive recommendations to make. One of the more interesting of these was that Britain issue a uniform, interest-bearing paper currency for all the colonies, with a fund for redemption to be provided by Parliamentary taxation. Another idea—first elaborated by McCulloh in 1751 and later to bear fruit in the Sugar Act—was that duties on molasses imported into the colonies from the foreign West Indies should be lowered to a more reasonable level, so as to discourage smuggling.

McCulloh's most significant proposal, appearing first in his memorial to the Earl of Halifax in 1751, was that

all Writings, Deeds Instruments or other matters relating to the law in the said Provinces should be on Stamp Paper or Parchment and . . . the Money arising therefrom should be applyed (*sic*) only to the Security and Advantage of the Colonies under the Management of the said Council of Trade, it is conceived that a very large Sum would arise therefrom even so, as under a just Application thereof the colonies would not be much longer Burthensome to this Kingdom in advancing money for their Security and enlargement.

The stamp tax idea was not original with McCulloh, but he was one of its most persistent advocates, reiterating the scheme in his subsequent pamphlets and memorials. It was not until 1763, however, that the British government made up its mind to raise substantial revenues in the colonies, and in July of that year McCulloh addressed a letter to Charles Jenkinson, one of Grenville's secretaries at the Treasury, suggesting that an American stamp tax would yield £60,000 a year. He enclosed a draft of the kind of bill which would be necessary, with a preamble which showed that McCulloh's primary objective was to provide the Crown with funds for controlling the Indians, whose incursions in North Carolina during the recent war had seriously hampered his efforts to sell his lands.

The Grenville government showed great interest in McCulloh's plan, and a Treasury official interviewed him on its details. When, in September and October, the Treasury Board began to discuss the specific provisions which should be embodied in a colonial stamp act, they seem to have used McCulloh's proposals as a starting point. But the actual drafting of a bill was delayed until the following year, and there is no evidence that McCulloh played an important part in the final discussions. When the act was eventually passed in 1765, Doctor William Houston, who had long been one of McCulloh's agents in North Carolina, was appointed stamp master for the province.

McCulloh seems to have been as successful in getting favors from Tory governments as from the Whigs. The instructions to William Tryon, who succeeded Dobbs as governor of North Carolina in 1765, directed him to be friendly to their interests. Two years later, Henry Eustace McCulloh, who had been given a seat on the provincial council under the

Dobbs regime, returned to England to act as agent for North Carolina. He depended mainly on the influence of his father, who was on familiar terms with the counsel to the Board of Trade and who had other connections in the government. The younger man secured an appointment for himself as collector of Port Roanoke in North Carolina and later obtained the transfer of the same post to James Iredell, a young kinsman who had been serving as deputy collector. While in London, Henry Eustace wrote to Iredell that, "I have a friend in a corner with Lord North, who I hope will secure matters for the present, and bring them about hereafter," and on another occasion that, "I have too good a friend in my Lord North to fear any attempts against my office."

The McCullohs were by no means the only deserving Englishmen who continually besieged Whitehall for place and pelf in the American colonies. The provincial governorships, chief justiceships, collectorships, and other offices were filled with men whose main qualification was influence with a member of the Privy Council or a key official of the Treasury or the Colonial Office. Just as McCulloh's pursuit of profits in North Carolina was one of the important factors in the history of that province, so the cumulative impact of the large class of men with similar interests in other colonies must have played a large part in producing the bumbling colonial policy by which Great Britain eventually lost its American possessions. Moreover, the resentment of dominant provincial groups, such as the Family, at the competition of officially backed "foreigners" like McCulloh in the race to engross the wealth of America certainly added bitterness and determination to the growing movement for home rule. In North Carolina it was a group of these native politicians, intent on controlling the colony to the advantage of their own class and impatient of increasing restrictions by the mother country, which furnished the leadership for the Revolution.

FOR FURTHER READING: O. M. Dickerson, in *The Navigation Acts and the American Revolution* (Philadelphia, 1951), argues that difficulties of administration by incompetent officials were a major factor in causing Colonial discontent. See also Lawrence H. Gipson, *The Coming of the Revolution, 1763–1775* (New York, 1954), for another version of this view. For the attitudes of American merchants see Bernard Bailyn, *The New England Merchants in the Seventeenth Century* (Cambridge, 1953), and Arthur M. Schlesinger, Sr., *The Colonial Merchants and the American Revolution, 1763–1776* (New York, 1918). For more favorable estimates of the British system see George L. Beer, *British Colonial Policy, 1754–1765* (New York, 1907) and his *The Old Colonial System, 1660–1754* (2 vols., New York, 1912), and also Lawrence A. Harper, *The English Navigation Laws* (New York, 1939).

5. *Colonial Finance*

PROBLEM: *Did monetary policies of colonial governments stimulate expansion?*

Deficit financing in America is not an innovation of the twentieth century. Over three hundred years ago colonial legislatures embarked on the issuance of paper money to stimulate economic development. Although the practice was quite common, it aroused much controversy, then as later. Contemporaries often clashed over the issue: "Was paper money or hard specie best to promote economic expansion?" Historians too have not agreed on this question. Writing at the close of the nineteenth century, C. J. Bullock attacked the issuance of fiat currency because he believed that it would inevitably depreciate, and so impede growth of the economy. In a more recent and favorable appraisal, perhaps conditioned by theories of deficit spending advocated by the British economist John M. Keynes, Professor E. James Ferguson of the University of Maryland finds that Colonial issues of paper money were not always subject to depreciation, and that they provided needed investment funds for exploitation of the undeveloped economy. Both authors use cogent arguments to sustain their respective views and raise broad questions. Why do advocates of hard money find deficit financing evil? What were the results of cheap money in the Colonial Era? What were some strengths and weaknesses of the paper money policies of colonial legislatures?

Colonial Paper Money

CHARLES J. BULLOCK

Soon after the colonies commenced to advance the ratings of their current coins, there began a series of attempts to establish private banks. It must be remembered that, during the entire colonial period, the word "bank" meant simply a batch of paper money, a conception that has disappeared only gradually during the present century as the functions of deposit and discount have assumed greater importance in modern banking. During the seventeenth century, more especially during its closing decades, public and private credit had been developed in the countries of northern Europe upon a scale that was previously unknown. Naturally enough the real nature and precise limitations of the great agency thus created were not clearly understood. It was perceived that credit increased enormously the control over capital enjoyed by a person or a company; but it was not realized so readily that credit is not the same as capital, and that capital cannot be directly created by credit, although its efficiency may be greatly increased. John Law's projects, the Mississippi Scheme in France, the English Land Bank Scheme, and the South Sea Bubble were no isolated phenomena: many other fallacious enterprises grew out of the misunderstandings that prevailed concerning the nature and proper uses of credit. Theories and plans of a paper currency began to appear in England as early as 1650, when William Potter published "The Key of Wealth, or A new way for Improving of Trade." Other schemes followed, all of which proposed to find some other medium than metallic money for a basis of paper credit. For this purpose deposits of merchandise or pledges of land were commonly suggested. In England the existence of more settled industrial conditions and the possession of a larger supply of capital facilitated the growth of sounder views concerning the true nature and proper basis of credit, but these lessons were not learned until much sad experience had been gained from unsafe banking ventures; while, as late as the period of restriction from 1797 to 1819, all the forces of unreason had to be most vigorously combated before it was generally admitted that the premium on bullion was due to the depreciation of the paper currency, and not to an alleged scarcity of gold. In the American colonies, however, the economic conditions were precisely the reverse of those which prevailed in the mother country; and all circumstances favored the persistence of erroneous ideas.

At some time previous to 1652, "paper bills" seem to have circulated

Reprinted with the permission of the Macmillan Company from *Essays on the Monetary History of the United States* by Charles J. Bullock (New York, 1900), pp. 29–59.

in some parts of Massachusetts, and there is a record of projects "for raiseing a Banke." William Potters's "Key of Wealth," or some similar publication, may have come to the attention of Governor John Winthrop, of Connecticut; for, in 1661, he is found to be entertaining "some proposalls concerning a way of trade and banke without money." A few years later, the Rev. John Woodbridge submitted a project "for erecting a Fund of Land, by Authority, or private Persons, in the Nature of a *Money-Bank* or *Merchandise-Lumber*." In 1671, 1681, and 1686, private banks were actually established in Massachusetts; and bills were issued, probably upon the security of "such Real Estates of Lands, as also personal Estates of goods and Merchandizes not subject to perishing or decay." These projects, however, proved to be short lived. In them can be distinctly traced the influence of theories that were then prevalent in England. In 1690, Massachusetts, followed shortly by other colonies, emitted its first public bills of credit. Such issues soon became so common as to divert attention, in a great measure, from private banking enterprises. Yet in 1700, 1714, 1733, 1739, and 1740, private banks were projected in Massachusetts, and were finally suppressed with great difficulty. In some cases, however, these associations actually placed a considerable quantity of their bills in circulation. The great Land Bank of 1740 issued about £35,000 of notes, and made a most vigorous struggle to maintain its existence. In New Hampshire, Connecticut, and South Carolina, associations were formed, between 1732 and 1738, for the purpose of engaging in similar ventures; and at a later date we hear of other attempts in Pennsylvania and Virginia. But Parliament interfered, in 1741, by extending to the colonies the provisions of the "Bubble Act," which had been passed twenty-one years earlier in order to suppress such swindles as had occurred during the time of the South Sea Company.

The paper money that so long cursed the American colonies was issued by acts of the several legislatures. Massachusetts had led the way, in 1690, with an issue of bills that were used to defray the expenses of a disastrous military expedition. Her example proved contagious; and, by 1712, New Hampshire, Rhode Island, Connecticut, New York, New Jersey, North Carolina, and South Carolina had issued quantities of bills of credit in order to meet the outlays occasioned by Queen Anne's War. In subsequent years bills were emitted as a regular means of defraying the current expenses of government; and, as the volume of paper accumulated, a great depreciation ensued. Sooner or later all the plantations were deeply involved in the mazes of a fluctuating currency, for the burdens attending the various wars of the eighteenth century were so great as to induce even the most conservative colonies to resort to this easy method of meeting public obligations. Virginia succumbed last, in 1755, but made large issues in the ensuing years.

A second excuse for issuing bills of credit was found at an early date.

In 1712, South Carolina created a public loan bank, and issued bills that were loaned to its citizens at interest, upon real or personal security. This expedient was followed sooner or later by nearly all of the other colonies. Rhode Island easily distanced all competitors in the readiness and facility with which she created loan banks; while Pennsylvania, New Jersey, and Delaware followed a more conservative course than most of the other plantations.

The abuses attending both forms of paper currency were usually of the most flagrant sort. Bills were issued for the payment of current expenses or extraordinary outlays, and taxes would be voted for the purpose of redemption. Then subsequent assemblies would extend the period during which the paper money should be current, or would neglect to levy sufficient taxes for its withdrawal. Thus the currency tended always to accumulate, and its depreciation increased. Sometimes a legislature would resolve that the bills in circulation should not exceed a certain sum, but such a declaration would prove utterly worthless. In almost every colony the first issues were to remain current for a short time only, and were to be redeemed speedily by taxes; but the periods were gradually lengthened to twelve, sixteen, or twenty-five years. Laws were often passed providing for the emission of new bills to replace worn or mutilated issues. Then the new money would frequently be placed in circulation without withdrawing and cancelling the old, while bills that had been withdrawn for the original purpose of destroying them would often be reissued for current expenses. In some colonies it happened that paper issued upon loan would not be repaid at the stated periods, and interest payments were commonly in arrears. When this occurred, the legislature would frequently extend the time of the loans, and sometimes a large part of both principal and interest would never be repaid. In this respect Rhode Island was probably the worst offender. Her loan banks were placed in the hands of a few favored persons, called "sharers," who happened to possess the requisite "pull." The "sharers" then proceeded to lend out the money at a rate of interest that was, for the first ten years, five per cent higher than that which they were obliged to pay to the colony. In some cases the fortunate "sharers" would sell their privileges for premiums that sometimes amounted to as much as thirty-five per cent. The results of such performances can readily be imagined.

Although the colonial bills of credit were not always made a legal tender, they were usually given a forced circulation. Most of the advocates of paper money would have agreed with the New York legislature that bills not legal tender were useless. The direct penalties—fines, imprisonment and confiscation—were imposed upon those evil-disposed persons who should dare to discriminate in favor of specie; but such forcing laws were as ineffectual in supporting the credit of the paper money as they have proved in all other cases. When older issues had depreciated hopelessly, "bills of a new tenor" were often emitted; and these were sometimes followed by others of a newer tenor. Thus it happened that issues of the "old tenor," "middle tenor," and "new tenor" circulated concurrently at different rates of depreciation, the legislature usually undertaking to fix the relative values of the three classes of currency. In order to prevent depreciation some of the issues bore interest, but this was a provision that was readily repealed by subsequent assemblies.

As has always been the case, the appetite for paper money increased with the issues of bills of credit. Complaints of the scarcity of money almost invariably followed each emission, and one pretext after another was found for issuing larger quantities of paper. Trade was said to be decaying, public buildings had to be constructed, fortifications were needed, and dozens of other things must be done by setting the printing presses at work. The experience of the colonies demonstrates conclusively the impossibility of satisfying the desire for "more money" by issuing a paper currency. Depreciation commenced at an early date, and tended to increase as time went on. In New England sterling exchange was 133 in 1702, a rate corresponding exactly to the rating of the dollar at 6s. In 1713, it rose to 150, and had reached 550 by the year 1740. The climax was reached in Massachusetts and Connecticut in 1749 and 1750, when exchange was quoted at 1100, indicating a depreciation of nearly 9 : 1. In Rhode Island, the old tenor bills finally sank to 23 for 1. In the middle colonies the depreciation never reached such figures. In Pennsylvania exchange once reached 180, while the par of exchange for specie was not higher than 166½. In Maryland exchange rose from 133 to 250. In North and South Carolina the paper currencies finally sank to one-tenth the value of sterling. Such fluctuations in the standard of value wrought intense hardships. . . .

Currency Finance: An Interpretation of Colonial Monetary Practices

E. JAMES FERGUSON

The accepted view of the financial and monetary history of the American colonies needs revision. It owes too much to the influence of nineteenth-century scholars who were themselves partisans in currency disputes. In

Reprinted by permission from E. James Ferguson, "Currency Finance: An Interpretation of Colonial Monetary Practices," *William and Mary Quarterly*, X (April, 1953), pp. 153–180.

their own day, William G. Sumner, Albert S. Bolles, Charles J. Bullock, and Andrew M. Davis stood for "sound money" against inflationist movements. One of their chief aims was to show the disastrous effects of wandering off the straight line of a sound-money policy.[1] Hence, they studied those colonies whose money depreciated and relied on the opinions of such eighteenth-century controversialists as Dr. William Douglass, Thomas Hutchinson, and others in whose views they concurred.[2] With the notable exception of Andrew M. Davis, who did a scholarly work on Massachusetts,[3] they were interested in the colonies chiefly as background to the financial history of the Revolution. Their works in the latter field incorporated study in primary sources and were generally accepted as authoritative.

The pattern they stamped on historical interpretation still survives in its major outlines. Recent books sometimes modify their harsher judgments and bring in new material, but the interpretation rests largely on the story they told of paper money in Massachusetts, Rhode Island, and the Carolinas. These were the provinces where depreciation created a

[1] See a review by Curtis Nettels of Richard A. Lester, *Monetary Experiments, Early American and Recent Scandinavian* (Princeton, 1939), in *English Historical Review*, LVI (1941), 333.

[2] The treatment of the colonies in William Graham Sumner, *A History of American Currency* (New York, 1874) is hardly a serious effort, and the same can be said of the earlier work of William M. Gouge, *A Short History of Paper Money and Banking in the United States, Including an Account of Provincial and Continental Paper Money*, 2nd ed. (New York, 1835). Of considerably greater merit are two studies of particular colonies: Joseph B. Felt, *An Historical Account of Massachusetts Currency* (Boston, 1839) and Henry Bronson, "An Historical Account of Connecticut Currency, Continental Money. and the Finances of the Revolution," New Haven Historical Society, *Papers*, I (1865), 1–192 (separate pagination following page 170). Early works displaying another bias are Henry Phillips, *Historical Sketches of the Paper Currency of the American Colonies, Prior to the adoption of the Federal Constitution* (Roxbury, Mass., 1865–1866) and John H. Hickcox, *A History of the Bills of Credit or Paper Money Issued by New York from 1709 to 1789* (Albany, 1866). The book by Phillips includes surveys of several colonies, written by different authors.

The case against paper money as drawn by nineteenth-century historians rested heavily on the data and opinions supplied by William Douglass, *A Discourse Concerning the British Plantations in America* (Boston, 1740). This treatise came out of a bitter controversy and was highly partisan. A careful reading shows how deeply the local situation in New England colored Douglass's attitudes and his judgment of the situation in other colonies. Even in the case of New England, he correctly attributed depreciation to the uncontrolled emissions of one province, Rhode Island. His observations on other colonies are not reliable.

[3] Andrew M. Davis, *Currency and Banking in the Province of Massachusetts-Bay*, American Economic Association, *Publications*, 3rd ser., I (1900), no. 4. Davis was a careful and honest scholar, but his main concern was to expose the evils of fiat money. He relied, for example, on the testimony of Thomas Hutchinson and Douglass, although his chapter on sources listed without comment works by Franklin and Thomas Pownall, as well as secondary accounts, which gave quite another view of colonial currency. It must be said, however, that these sources related to provinces outside New England and therefore lay beyond the immediate scope of his study. See *ibid.*, I, 413–435.

The same year that Davis's essay came out, Charles J. Bullock published *Essays in the Monetary History of the United States* (New York, 1900) which included a general survey of colonial currency and more detailed treatment of North Carolina and New Hampshire. The latter studies were based on research in primary sources and are of value.

major problem. Neglect of other colonies whose experiments were more fortunate conveys the impression that paper money typically depreciated and was harmful to the community.

A correlated idea is that paper money was significant mainly as a ground of conflict between colonial debtors and creditors. No doubt this view is more readily accepted because it fits in with the Turner hypothesis. Here again, Massachusetts furnishes the prime example. The land bank controversy of 1740 is portrayed as a struggle of creditors against debtors, coastal merchants against back-country farmers. Other instances can be found in the early history of South Carolina.

While the debtor-creditor thesis has logical probability and a foundation in fact, it is nonetheless inadequate when viewed in a perspective embracing the whole development of the American colonies. Historians generally concede, for example, that in most provinces, a propertied aristocracy dominated the government. The debtor-creditor thesis, broadly considered, affords no sufficient explanation for the fact that in the half century before the Revolution, these aristocratic bodies regularly and persistently issued paper money. The thesis is also at odds with the fact that in the middle provinces, at least, mercantile groups strongly opposed the act of Parliament which prevented the colonies from making paper money a legal tender in private transactions. On the assumption that serious internal conflict existed between debtor and creditor, the stand taken by merchants would be inexplicable.

Several accounts of individual provinces appearing in the last few decades appraise the fiat money methods of the colonies in their setting. As the authors have stayed close to primary sources and have extended their range beyond New England, they depict a more successful use of paper money. The collective influence of these works has not been as great as one might suppose. Curtis P. Nettels has added a general study of monetary affairs; unfortunately, it covers only the period before 1720, when the colonies were just beginning to employ paper currency.

There are signs, however, that the dogmas which have prejudiced research are giving way. Fiat money is now the rule, and most economists have ceased to believe that currency must be convertible into gold or silver. Governments freely manipulate currency, as a means of economic control. In this frame of reference, the ways of the American colonies acquire new significance. An economist, Richard A. Lester, explores their use of paper money in the attempts to curb economic depression. He finds that their tactics were analogous to those of the New Deal and bore some ancestral relationship to present-day Keynesian doctrine. The most promising effort, however, is an unpublished doctoral dissertation by Leslie Van Horn Brock, which displays a grasp of colonial usages and attitudes seldom found in older studies. When such works as these attract more notice, other scholars may be persuaded to explore a field which is rich in implications for social and economic history.

Until more evidence is brought together, any general conclusions must be tentative. The formulations attempted in this paper are, therefore, exploratory and subject to correction. It seems possible, however, to qualify older interpretations and point out the tendency of future research. An effort will be made to show that in the middle colonies, from New York to Maryland, paper money was successful. Secondly, it will be argued that except in New England and the Carolinas, paper money did not engender any great conflict between broad classes of the population. Finally, the system of paper money will be described in general terms and an attempt made to define the essential features of "currency finance."

In judging the success of paper money, the first question is whether it depreciated. The answer cannot always be explicit. Different authors do not mean exactly the same thing by the word depreciation. Older historians were inclined to go by the rate of exchange. If currency passed below its legal rate in trade for hard money or in the purchase of bills of exchange, they considered that it had depreciated and inferred that too much had been issued or that people lacked confidence in fiat money. This was certainly true in colonies like Rhode Island, Massachusetts, and the Carolinas, where currency sank to low levels. In colonies where fluctuations in the value of money were only moderate, however, a discount on currency in exchange for specie or sterling bills did not necessarily imply that the currency was unsound. Historians of such provinces refer to paper money as stable, even though its value sometimes sank in relationship to specie.

It was normal to discount currency somewhat in exchange for hard money. First of all, the colonies sought to attract foreign coin by giving it a high legal value. They fixed such rates that hard money equivalent to £100 British sterling was legally worth from £133 to around £175 in the currency of different provinces. This was the legal rate. But hard money ordinarily commanded a premium beyond this, for it had more uses than paper. It was more negotiable in payments to foreigners and in inter-colonial transactions.

Besides a general preference for hard money, other factors sometimes worked to bring about a further discount on paper money. Detailed information on the processes of colonial trade is lacking, but it appears that most payments to Britain were made in bills of exchange, that is, drafts payable in Britain which the colonists procured largely by shipments of cargoes. The availability of sterling bills in America depended on the condition of trade. When British purchases fell off and the colonies shipped less than would pay for their imports, sterling bills became scarce and expensive, and people sought hard money to make payments abroad. Specie and bills of exchange rose in value relative to paper money.

On the other hand, there were times during the French and Indian War when the colonies enormously increased the volume of their domestic currency, yet the exchange with specie remained constant or even improved because large British expenditures, decreased importations, and a greater supply of specie at hand reduced the need for hard money. Circumstances beyond the control of colonial governments affected the rate of exchange, regardless of how scrupulously the colonies managed their paper money or how good its credit was at home.

The most accurate test of the stability of paper money would be its value in exchange for commodities sold in colonial markets. An adequate price study exists for Pennsylvania, and there is some information for a few other colonies. Unfortunately, this kind of data is fragmentary, and historians usually have to depend on scattered figures and the casual remarks found in contemporary letters.

The weight of evidence suggests, however, that in the middle colonies fluctuations were not great enough to impair the credit or utility of paper money. Historians agree that Pennsylvania "maintained the system without fear of repudiation and to the manifest benefit of the province." It appears that for the half century before the Revolution, the domestic price level was more uniform than in any succeeding period of equal length. The emissions of New Jersey and Delaware are said to have been stable and to have passed usually at par with that of Pennsylvania. New York's currency was highly regarded, and the colony's ability to keep its bills at par was a "subject for special commendation."

Maryland's first emission of 1753 depreciated, even though well-secured, apparently because tobacco remained the primary medium of exchange. Later her bills rose in value and by 1764 were reported "locked up in the Chests of the Wealthy" for the sake of the interest falling due on them. Thereafter, in spite of heavy additions, the bills held their value. "As a colony," writes a modern scholar, "Maryland had solved the problem of a paper currency."

The provinces further south had trouble with their currency. Until 1755, Virginia supplemented the hard money in circulation with tobacco notes, which passed in local exchange and payment of taxes. But the coming of the French and Indian War forced the colony to emit paper money. The bills held their value until 1760, when a sharp break in tobacco prices marked the onset of a long and severe depression. For the next several years, planters could hardly sell their crops, and prices stayed very low. A shortage of the planter balances ordinarily arising from tobacco sales in Britain caused bills of exchange and specie to grow scarce, and their value rose in terms of the currency offered by planters obliged to make payments to British creditors. Virginia currency was discounted as much as 50 per cent to 60 per cent in purchase of bills of exchange. Although specie was extremely scarce, the colony did not put aside its plans to retire war-time paper emissions, and it probably contributed to the easement of conditions that the treasurer of the province, John Robinson, restored some £100,000 to circulation through secret loans to hard-pressed planters. Robinson's defalcations probably occurred in 1765 and 1766. It appears, however, that the decline in Virginia's currency in these and preceding years owed little to Robinson's private emissions, but was rather the result of trade depression. In the last years of the decade, the value rose, and by 1771 it was reported that the British merchants who had formerly complained of paper money were among its warmest advocates.

In the Carolinas, depreciation was severe, though it occurred for the most part early in the eighteenth century, when these colonies were thinly populated and undeveloped. Clearly, however, the legislature of North Carolina did little to sustain its first emissions, and the bills steadily depreciated. In 1748, they were called in to be exchanged for new bills at the rate of 7½ to 1. The new bills fluctuated thereafter around a point considerably below their nominal value, but were rising towards the end of the colonial period, when the British government kept the legislature under close rein.

A different situation prevailed in South Carolina, where all the depreciation occurred before 1731. The infant colony was then under heavy financial strain resulting from war. Debtor elements found the depreciation to their liking, however, and tried to maintain the downward trend. They were overcome after a bitter struggle. The currency was stabilized in 1731 at the rate of 7 to 1 of sterling, which remained unchanged until the Revolution. During its maturity, the province had a stable currency and a record of successful management.

Constancy of value was not, in many minds, the sole test of a currency. Another criterion is suggested by the remark of Thomas Pownall, that in spite of the depreciation in New England, "it was never yet objected that it injured them in trade." Thomas Hancock, one of the greatest merchants in America, seems at one time not to have been altogether convinced that paper money was an unmitigated evil, though he had dealt in a depreciated medium all his life. Of the legislation which placed Massachusetts on a sound money basis, he said: "This d——d Act has turn'd all Trade out of doors and it's Impossible to get debts in, either in Dollars or Province Bills." No study has been made of the economic effects of depreciation in the provinces where it occurred. It is possible that a steady and continuing inflation was not wholly injurious to an expanding country whose people seldom had fixed incomes or large stores of liquid capital.

Even if stability is taken as the sole rule in judging the success of colonial currency, the record is not entirely black. The depreciation in New England was mainly the fault of Rhode Island, whose emissions flooded the unitary economy of that area and undermined the currency of her neighbors. Elsewhere, North Carolina was the leading offender. The colonies, it must be said, did not have complete freedom to act. Each of them felt, in varying degree, the weight of British authority, which was always cast on the side of moderation in the use of currency. Nevertheless, the predominating fact was not the failure of paper money but its success and good credit—in the colonies from New York to Maryland, and in Virginia, as well as in South Carolina during its later development.

Serious conflicts between debtors and creditors did not arise when paper money stayed near par value. Ideally, perhaps, men of property would have preferred a circulation of coin or a currency backed by precious metals. Practically, however, most of them shared the popular belief that there was no alternative to the existing system. "Contrary to the traditions that historians have perpetuated," writes a modern student of economic thought, "a critical analysis of the contemporary literature indicates that the proponents as well as the critics were not poor debtors or agrarians, but for the most part officials, ministers, merchants, and men of substance and learning in general."

Pennsylvania's currency was esteemed by all classes and regarded as having contributed to the growth and prosperity of the colony. In his widely read work on colonial affairs, Thomas Pownall wrote that there "never was a wiser or a better measure, never one better calculated to serve the uses of an encreasing country . . . never a measure more steadily pursued, nor more faithfully executed for forty years together." Merchants and traders of Philadelphia formally opposed the restraining act of 1764 which prevented the colonies from making paper money legal tender. As colonial agent in England, Benjamin Franklin fought the enactment of the law and afterward wrote pamphlets urging its repeal. Franklin joined other colonial representatives and English merchants to argue the case for repeal before British ministers and members of Parliament. By 1767, the American agents planned to secure the introduction of a repealing act into Parliament. They gave up the idea only when it became known that Parliament would very likely insist that the price of such a concession must be the surrender by the colonies of permanent revenues to the crown.

Franklin told the House of Commons that restrictions on paper money were among the leading reasons why the American provinces had become alienated from the mother country. In 1774, the First Continental Congress cited the restraining act among the violations of colonial rights.

New York merchants also protested the restraining act. The assembly appointed a committee of New York county members, whose duties included corresponding with other provinces and the colonial agent with respect to the act. Governor Moore espoused the cause and repeatedly asked the Board of Trade to sanction an emission on the terms desired by the province. The assembly refused aid to British troops unless the crown approved a currency bill, and, according to Carl Becker, opposition to the Townshend Acts had one of its sources in this grievance. Popular unrest was stilled not only by the repeal of the duties, but also by a special act of Parliament which allowed the colony to issue paper money.

Public opinion in Maryland, according to historians of the province, was nearly unanimous in favor of paper money. Among the beneficiaries of the currency system were many of the most prominent men of the colony, who received loans from the government. The list included a "surprising number" of merchants. After Parliamentary restrictions were laid down in 1764, all classes concurred in the need for further emissions, and Maryland's agents in London tried to get the act repealed.

In spite of the notorious depreciation which afflicted North Carolina's emissions, paper money does not seem to have been a major factor in the sectional antagonisms of that colony. Both houses of a legislature presumably dominated by the "court house ring" petitioned the crown in 1768 to approve paper money legislation. At a time when the Regulator Movement in the backcountry had begun to split the colony into warring factions, Governor Tryon added his pleas to those of the legislature. His letters to the Board of Trade repeated familiar arguments, which, coming from less responsible sources, have often been dismissed as the pretence of debtors trying to evade their obligations. He said a larger circulating medium was necessary and that much distress arose from the lack of it.

In South Carolina, the early struggle between debtors and creditors was never quite forgotten, but in time the memory grew so dim that the contemporary historian, David Ramsay, could write: "From New-York to Georgia there had never been in matters relating to money, an instance of a breach of public faith." On the basis of his personal recollection, no doubt, he wrote that the use of paper money "had been similar from the first settlement of the colonies, and under proper restrictions had been found highly advantageous." Another historian of the province, Alexander Hewatt, an extreme foe of paper money at the time he wrote, acknowledged the benefit of currency emissions to a "growing colony" like South Carolina, provided they were kept within bounds.

Virginia's treasurer, Robert Carter Nicholas, expressed the view of a conservative planter. In a public defense of the government's conduct in emitting paper money, he declared that the outbreak of the French and Indian War had made it absolutely necessary. Sufficient funds could be obtained in no other way, and, though hesitant at first, the assembly found no other course open. Nicholas himself knew well the dangers of a paper medium and was conversant with the arguments against it, including the pamphlet of William Douglass, its ardent foe in New England.

But Nicholas believed that the evils discovered in some places did not arise from paper money as such. "They have been chiefly, if not totally owing," he wrote, "either to these Bills of Credit not being established upon proper Funds, or to a Superabundance of them or to some Mismanagement." Granting a risk was involved, Nicholas believed that many countries had derived great benefit from paper money. He thought it had been helpful to Virginia.

Nicholas's opinion was much like that of a conservative New York merchant, John Watts, who was highly critical of the restraining act of 1764. Like many others, Watts thought the act would virtually put an end to paper money. "The use of paper money is abolished as an evil," he complained, "when, properly treated, it is the only medium we have left of commerce and the only expedient in an exigency. Every man of estate here abominates the abuse of paper money, because the consequences fall upon himself, but there is just the same difference in the use and abuse of it as there is in food itself . . ."

The writings of the post-Revolutionary era contain many allusions to the success of paper money in colonial times and the esteem in which it was then held. In 1786, a correspondent to a New York newspaper recalled how easily the provinces had maintained their paper money systems:

Before the commencement of the late war, when public faith was still in possession of vestal chastity, divers of the states, then provinces, had large sums in circulation at full value, depending on funds calculated to redeem only five to ten per centum per annum of the amount issued; consequently it must be from ten to twenty years before the whole would be redeemed; and yet, tho' the money drew no interest . . . it circulated freely and at its full nominal value on a perfect equality with specie . . .

As this article appeared, the New York Chamber of Commerce made the same point in declaring its opposition to a paper money issue contemplated by the legislature. The Chamber of Commerce acknowledged that paper money had worked well in colonial times, but argued that this should not be taken as evidence that it would succeed under changed conditions.

An observation frequently made in these times was put down by David Ramsay in his *History of the American Revolution*. Noting that Continental currency held its value during the first year or two of the war, even though it had no security behind it, Ramsay explained: "This was in some degree owing to a previous confidence, which had been begotten by honesty and fidelity, in discharging the engagements of government." Alluding to the same fact, Financier Robert Morris observed: "There was a time when public confidence was higher in America than in any other country."

The inflation of the Revolution destroyed that confidence, at least among propertied men, for they believed that paper money could never be a reliable instrument in an era when the whims of the people dictated, as they said, the policy of the government. A great proportion of the people, however, never lost the old affection for paper money. "From the earliest settlement of America," declared a petition composed in 1785 for presentation to the Pennsylvania legislature, "most of our improvements have been aided by the medium of paper currency . . . and your petitioners are persuaded that . . . public faith might be restored, and the ancient system revived, to the great ease of the inhabitants and emolument of the community." Such an appeal invoked common knowledge.

It becomes clear that paper money occupied an important place in colonial affairs not because it embodied the aims of a particular class, but because it rendered important services to the community.

The circumstances which led to the adoption of paper money are well known. There was not enough hard money to provide a medium of trade for domestic transactions. Gold and silver coins flowed outward in purchase of British commodities and while in the colonies circulated mainly among merchants. Much business was done on the basis of book credits and debits, but specie was nearly always in short supply. Economic depression intensified the problem, for when cargoes did not raise enough to meet debts owed abroad, specie had to be shipped. Domestic trade became almost wholly barter. People who had specie could get an exorbitant premium, and those forced to make payments in hard money faced difficulty. Provincial governments could not collect taxes. The inhabitants felt the need of a medium of exchange which, unlike specie, would not "make unto itself wings and fly away."

The colonies, therefore, adopted paper money. It was issued by two different processes. The first method, in point of time, was the direct emission of fiat money by the government to pay expenses, particularly the costs of war. The other method, which we shall consider immediately, was the emission of money through a loan-office or "land bank."

The land bank was the primary social legislation of colonial America. It was a method of putting currency into circulation and at the same time affording loans to farmers which they could scarcely obtain from other sources. Provincial governments set up loan offices which advanced currency to farmers at low rates of interest, taking mortgages on real property as security. An individual could usually get only a limited sum. He repaid the loan in annual installments over a period of years. Frequently, though not always, the bills were legal tender in private transactions; in any case, they were almost always accepted in payments to the government for taxes, land, etc. As the annual installments due on the principal came back into the loan office, the bills were cancelled and retired, though they were often reissued, or successive banks established to keep up a continuous flow of loans. The colonies thus developed a medium of exchange out of "solid or real property . . . melted down and made to circulate in paper money or bills of credit."

The land banks of the middle colonies were, from all accounts, markedly successful. Pennsylvania managed one almost continuously after 1723 without mishap. For more than twenty-five years before the French and Indian War, the interest received by the government from money out on loan supported the costs of provincial administration, without the necessity of direct taxes. Relative freedom from taxation probably contributed to Pennsylvania's remarkable growth.

Other middle colonies also obtained good results. New Jersey enacted three separate loans up to 1735, and the interest enabled the government to exist without direct taxation for sixteen years before 1751. Delaware issued land bank notes from 1723 to 1746, with apparent benefit to the province. New York extended its land bank of 1737 until the last installment of the principal fell due in 1768, at which time all classes demanded its renewal. The bank was reinstituted in 1771 by virtue of the special act of Parliament, of which mention has already been made. Governor Tryon's report in 1774 showed that the interest from loans comprised about half the revenue of the province, an amount which nearly matched expenses in time of peace.

The notes which Maryland issued on loan in 1733 fell considerably below par, but later rose to nominal value. A modern historian writes:

Considering the peculiar benefits to grain and tobacco culture, the conveniences offered to trade, the exceptionally high exchange that the bills maintained throughout most of their life, and the faithful redemption of every shilling at face value, it is hardly too much to say that this was the most successful paper money issued by any of the colonies.

A new bank was instituted in 1769, and the notes stayed at par until the Revolution.

Virginia never adopted a land bank. In North and South Carolina, land banks figured in the early depreciation of paper money, and it became the settled policy of the British government to disallow acts for their establishment. Similarly, as is well known, the land banks of the New England colonies, particularly those of Rhode Island, contributed to the decline of currency in that area and brought on the first statutory regulation of paper money by Parliament.

This system of agricultural credit so widely practiced in the colonies would seem to be a subject of considerable importance for social and economic history, yet it has not received the attention it deserves. The economist, Richard A. Lester, offers a general view of the use of land bank emissions to curb depressions, and it may be added that such a background of experience explains why even after the financial chaos of the Revolution, the common people still looked to paper money for relief from hard times. But the subject has further ramifications. Agriculture's need for credit facilities has been a constant factor in American history and a source of political unrest. Banks have served commerce and industry; until lately, agriculture remained at a disadvantage. It should be an interesting fact that colonial governments loaned money to farmers at low rates of interest. But no analysis has been made of the effects of land bank loans in the domestic economy, nor has anyone yet approached the general subject with sufficient breadth of view to place it in its relationship to the main currents of American development.

The revenue problems of colonial governments were lessened by land bank emissions; taxes were more easily collected when citizens had access to money. During the frequent wars of the eighteenth century, however, the provinces developed another use of paper money. They emitted it to pay governmental expenses. The procedure became a rationalized system of public finance.

Provincial revenues were normally small and inflexible. Officials drew fees rather than salaries, and the few public services were performed mainly by local government. Such provinces as Pennsylvania and New York spent no more than £5,000 a year apart from war expenses. Taxation was adjusted to limited needs. Imposts and excise taxes usually afforded a maintaining fund, while direct levies on polls and property raised what else was needed. None of these revenues could be freely expanded. Heavy duties on imports tended to drive off trade or cause smuggling. Direct taxes were often hard to collect and slow coming in.

Colonial governments found it difficult or impossible to borrow money from their own citizens. Private capital was tied up in lands or commodities. No banks or business corporations existed with liquid capital which could be enlisted in the public service. When a war or other emergency required large outlays, colonial governments knew no alternative but to issue paper money. Massachusetts hit upon this device in 1690, and eventually all the colonies took it up. "Currency finance" became the regular mode of financing government during war and often, as well, in time of peace.

Practice varied in details, but over the period in which the colonies experimented, they regularized their procedure in something like a system conducted on the basis of known principles. The one exception was Massachusetts, which went on a sound money basis in the 1750's. Elsewhere, methods fall into a pattern that can be described in general terms.

The essential feature of the system was that it avoided dealing in hard money. During a war, for instance, colonial legislatures printed, from time to time, the money needed to pay their expenses. Usually, the act which authorized the emission also appropriated sufficient taxes to withdraw the money from circulation. If expenses were large, the taxes for several years ahead might be pledged to the redemption of money issued during a single year.

The credit of the bills depended on several interrelated factors. Regardless of any promise on the face of the notes, the basic security was the fund assigned to withdraw the money. The holder had to be certain that all taxes and payments to the government taken together would be enough to create a general use for the bills and ensure a demand for them. He must rest easy in the knowledge that withdrawals would be continuous and that future governments would have the ability and the will to collect taxes. As this money was created and upheld by political acts, confidence in government was essential to its value.

Meanwhile, the value of the money was sustained by its current usages, as in paying fees, buying land from the province, or use in ordinary trade. So long as there was no great reason to question it, the people accepted currency in day-to-day transactions because it was the recognized medium of exchange. Colonial legislators, however, knew something about the quantity theory of money and understood that the amount must not exceed too far the requirements of trade at existing price levels, else depreciation would occur regardless of guarantees.

The system appears to have worked against the accumulation of public debt. The debt at any particular time consisted of bills of credit in circulation; to retire it, the government levied taxes payable in the certificates of indebtedness themselves. If the debt was large, paper money was apt to be correspondingly plentiful and widely distributed. The people were taxed in a medium readily accessible to them. As withdrawals reduced the supply of currency and it became concentrated into fewer hands, the debt was by that token rendered less onerous, until at some point the taxes imposed to cancel it could be discontinued and the remaining currency left in circulation. Under the benign operation of currency finance, the facility with which the public debt could be retired was in rough proportion to its size.

Other means than currency were used to anticipate future income. Colonial governments, and to a much greater extent the state governments of the Revolution, issued various kinds of warrants and certificates which, though often given an extensive circulation, did not serve as a medium of exchange to the same degree as paper money. With certain exceptions, however, these notes were issued and redeemed on the same terms as currency. In spite of variations, therefore, it is possible to trace a basic pattern in the financial methods employed by the colonies. They met expenses by issuing a paper medium, whether currency or certificates, directly to individuals in payment for goods and services. They redeemed this paper not by giving specie to those who held it, but by accepting it for taxes or other payments to the government. This was the system of currency finance.

It was not a system which would stand the strain of a prolonged and expensive war. Nonetheless, it sufficed for the wars in which the colonies engaged. During the French and Indian War, for example, New York emitted £535,000. Pennsylvania, whose currency normally stood at £80,000, issued £540,000. Virginia authorized £440,000. Other colonies made extraordinary contributions. The Board of Trade estimated that the North American provinces spent £2,500,000 sterling beyond their ordinary costs of government. About £800,000 of this represented expenditures of Massachusetts, the sound money colony. The remainder of £1,700,000 sterling consisted almost entirely of currency or certificates issued in the expectation that they would be retired only by acceptance for taxes and other payments to the government. In spite of the volume of this paper, little or no depreciation appears to have resulted in most provinces. The colonies benefited from expenditures of the home government, and from large British subsidies which put specie in their hands.

Debt retirement was rapid after the war. Virginia's currency was down to £206,000 by 1767, according to the treasurer's report, and though two small post-war emissions restored some money to circulation, only £54,391 was afloat in 1773. Pennsylvania, no longer tax free, made regular withdrawals until the Revolution. In New York, an acute shortage of currency existed by 1768. Elsewhere, the provinces quickly freed themselves of their debts. A speaker in the House of Commons observed in 1766 that they had already retired £1,755,000, and that most of the remaining debt of £760,000 could be written off within two years.

How much this happy situation was due to British subsidies is hard to know. During the war, Parliament granted over £150,000 sterling for distribution among the American colonies, a sum which was nearly half of the £2,500,000 estimated as their war expenses. Even so, when one compares their real expenditures during the war with the sums involved in their ordinary fiscal operations, it appears that they made what was for them a most unusual effort, and the ease with which they retired their debts must in some measure be attributed to the peculiar facility offered by the methods of currency finance.

British policy on matters pertaining to colonial currency is a subject which has scarcely been touched. No doubt it was a factor of greater importance in imperial relations than is commonly understood. From the one considerable treatment available, it appears that most of the time the British government acknowledged the necessity of colonial emissions. Before 1740, the Board of Trade was "reluctantly sympathetic and essentially reasonable" in sanctioning both land bank loans and direct emissions. The Board, however, always opposed making currency a legal tender in private transactions, even though it approved laws for this purpose. Generally speaking, the Board tried to regulate colonial issues by ensuring that the amounts were reasonable, that funds for redemption were adequate, and that emissions were withdrawn within a limited period of time. Control was exerted largely through instructions to governors, who were ordered to refuse assent to laws which did not have a clause suspending their execution until approved by the crown.

Supervision was not effective and lapsed almost completely during frequent periods of war. As currency emissions were the only way the provinces could furnish aid, governors were permitted to approve acts without a suspending clause, provided the Board's other stipulations were satisfied. The colonies took advantage of their bargaining position, however, to procure the governors' assent to laws which did not comply with the Board's requirements. Neither governors nor the crown could afford to scrutinize too closely the modes by which assistance was rendered.

War still hindered the enforcement of policy, but British control tightened after 1740. Rhode Island's emissions were a flagrant abuse. The Board also appears to have been more susceptible to complaints of British merchants, some of whom claimed injury from legal tender laws. The same mercantile and creditor interests carried their appeals to Parliament, with the result that after 1750 the standing instructions of the Board of Trade were given statutory effect.

The act of 1751 applied only to New England. It did not abolish the paper money system even in that area, as is sometimes supposed, but merely established rules for carrying it on. Bills already in circulation were to be retired in strict accord with the terms of the issuing acts. When these were withdrawn, no paper money was to be legal tender. The provinces were allowed to emit bills from year to year to pay governmental expenses, provided they committed taxes sufficient to redeem them within two years. This clause was flexible enough to accommodate a moderate expansion of currency. In event of war or other emergency, all curbs were relaxed as to the amount which could be issued, provided enough taxes were appropriated to redeem the bills within five years. The act of 1751 left the colonies outside New England undisturbed. Within New England, its major effect was to prohibit legal tender laws and to rule out land banks.

The restraining act of 1764 came at the end of the French and Indian War, when the colonies had large sums outstanding. As first drafted, it would have placed all the provinces under the curbs imposed on New England. In its final form, it merely prohibited legal tender laws and required that existing legal tender currencies be sunk at their expiration dates. Many colonies protested, in the belief that the legal tender feature was an essential prop to their money. Experience was to show, however, that the restriction did not materially impair the workings of the currency system.

There is more than a hint that by this time Britain's policy as to paper money was subordinated to the larger purpose of securing a permanent civil list, and that attempts were being made to trade approval of colonial emissions for the grant of a fixed revenue to the crown. Even so, the colonies made headway against British restraints, though they could not again pass legal tender laws. New York was permitted to renew its land bank in 1771. After a long struggle, New Jersey exacted consent for the establishment of a land bank in 1774. Pennsylvania continued to emit currency and in 1773 renewed its land bank. Maryland issued £173,733 to pay war debts and over half a million dollars to finance improvements and to establish a land bank. Virginia's council annulled two land bank acts passed by the lower house, but the province emitted £40,000 for other purposes. North Carolina, closely confined by the British government, issued treasury notes and debenture bills, while South Carolina emitted "public orders" and "tax certificates," which were in effect a non-legal tender currency.

Parliament in 1773 legalized colonial monetary practices as carried on under the restrictive acts of 1751 and 1764. A question had arisen as to how far the prohibition of legal tender applied. To clarify the matter, Parliament passed an explanatory act which declared that the prohibition ruled out only those laws which made currency legal tender in private transactions. The colonies were allowed to make it legal tender in payments to the government. In stating the latitude permitted by existing law, Parliament defined the essential workings of the currency finance system. The act is worth quoting because it verifies the general survey given above:

Whereas the want of gold and silver currency in several of his Majesty's colonies and plantations in America may make it necessary, as well for the publick advantage as in justice to those persons who may have demands upon the publick treasuries in the said colonies for services performed, that such publick creditors should be secured in the payment of their just debts and demands, by certificates, notes, bills, or debentures, to be created and issued by the authority of the general assemblies . . . on the securities of any taxes or duties given and granted to his Majesty—for and towards defraying expenses incurred for publick services; and that such certificates, notes, bills, or debentures, should be made chargeable on the publick treasurers of the said colonies and received and taken by them as a legal tender in discharge of any such duties or taxes, or of any debts whatsoever, due to the publick treasuries . . . be it enacted . . . That . . . any certificates, notes, bills or debentures which shall . . . be voluntarily accepted by the creditors of the publick . . . may be made . . . to be a legal tender for the publick treasurers . . . for the discharge of any duties, taxes, or other debts whatsoever . . .

Had the Revolution not occurred, Britain might have reached a solution of colonial monetary problems. As early as 1754, Richard Jackson and Franklin exchanged plans to form one or more land banks based on capital loaned from the Bank of England or subscribed by private investors. It was expected that land bank notes would provide a circulating medium for the continent. Later, when the Stamp Act was under discussion, Franklin and Thomas Pownall broached a similar scheme, as an alternative way of gaining a revenue from the colonies. They envisaged a continental land bank with a branch office in each province, centrally managed in Britain. The bank was to issue legal tender notes on loan at 5 per cent interest, the principal to be repaid over a period of ten years. The notes would circulate as currency throughout the American colonies. Franklin and Pownall pressed this scheme for three or four years.

By 1767, it appears that the Secretary of Trade concurred in the idea that the restraining act of 1764 should be modified to permit the colonies to establish loan offices which would emit legal tender notes valid for all transactions except payment of sterling debts. A bill for this purpose was being prepared and the ground laid for its introduction into the House of Commons, when the colonial agents learned that the Commons would probably seize the opportunity to declare the income arising from the loan offices subject to the appropriation of the crown. As the colonial agents could not risk this outcome, they gave up the project. Saying he had hoped to make better use of his plan for a continental land bank, Pownall published the details of it in the 1768 edition of his Administration of the Colonies.

Any solution of the money problem under British auspices was forestalled by the Revolution. When it was too late, the British government instructed its peace commissioners of 1778 in a number of schemes which might have borne fruit if attempted earlier.

A view of the evidence suggests that generations of historical scholarship have fostered a mistaken impression of the monetary practices of the colonies. The efforts of the American provinces to create a medium of exchange, erect a system of agricultural credit, and equip their governments with the means of incurring and discharging responsibilities, hardly constitute a "dark and disgraceful" picture; nor, on the whole, is the record one of failure. Most of the colonies handled their currency with discretion and were successful in realizing the purposes associated with its use. Except for New England, where depreciation had given it a bad name, paper money was the "ancient system," which had long served well the needs of trade and the ordinary processes of government. Although mindful of its dangers, men of property accepted it as useful and necessary. In time of war, all the colonies but one were fully prepared to adopt the methods of currency finance as the only way of meeting an emergency. Emissions might then be over-large, as the Revolution was to prove, but the common need precluded any nice regard for the effect on contracts.

FOR FURTHER READING: A compact critical survey of Colonial fiscal policies may be found in Davis R. Dewey, *Financial History of the United States* (12th ed., New York, 1939). More favorable appraisals are in Richard A. Lester, *Monetary Experiments: Early American and Recent Scandinavian* (Princeton, 1939), E. J. Ferguson, *Power of the Purse: A History of American Public Finance, 1776–1790* (Chapel Hill, 1961), and Theodore Thayer, "The Land Bank System in the American Colonies," *Journal of Economic History*, XIII (Spring, 1953), pp. 141–159.

6. *Economic Growth and the American Revolution*

PROBLEM: *Did the economic expansion of the American colonies contribute to the outbreak of the Revolution?*

One of the most controversial issues in American Colonial History revolves about the effects of British mercantilism on the economic development of the colonies. Did British regulations restrict American trade and manufacturing? Thus, the Navigation Act of 1660 allowed the shipment of Colonial goods only in British or American bottoms. It also provided for certain enumerated commodities such as sugar and tobacco, which Americans were allowed to sell only in British markets. Manufacturing regulations such as the Woolens Act of 1699, the Hat Act of 1732, and the Iron Act of 1750 were designed to limit the competition of artisans in the colonies with those of the mother country. At the same time the Currency Act of 1751 prohibited the issuance of paper money by New England legislatures. But, while these acts appeared formidable on the statute books, few were enforced consistently or effectively before 1763. Moreover, many Colonial merchants enjoyed increasing prosperity in the eighteenth century. Nor is the evidence conclusive to indicate that British regulations seriously retarded colonial manufacturing. Since the effects of British mercantile legislation are not clearly discernible it is not surprising that historians have disagreed over the impact of British mercantilism on the colonies, and its influence in fomenting Revolutionary sentiment. Representative of one group is Louis Hacker, who finds that British commercial policies restricted economic expansion, and thus constituted one of the underlying causes of the American Revolution. This interpretation has frequently been questioned, as the selection by Professor Lawrence A. Harper of the University of California indicates. On the basis of an intensive study, *The English Navigation Laws,* Harper notes that there is little evidence to prove that British policies actually hampered American economic expansion, and so fomented the Revolution. The arguments presented by these two men form but a brief introduction to one of the major problems concerning public policies in the Colonial Era. Was there a mercantilist "system"? How did British imperial legislation retard or promote the American economy? In what ways did British imperial restrictions promote Revolutionary sentiment?

The First American Revolution

LOUIS M. HACKER

That America has had a revolutionary past is, by this time, common knowledge; but that the first American Revolution, the war of independence against England, in quite every significant particular conformed to the revolutionary outlines of those better-known uprisings, the French Revolution and the Russian Revolution, is not generally understood. It is difficult to find disinterested students who are willing to contend that the French Revolution and the Russian Revolution could have been averted; for it must be apparent, given the character of the existing productive forces and the economic and social relations growing out of them, the shaping class antagonisms, and the onset of crisis, that the revolutionary challenge to authority on the part of the French bourgeoisie in one instance and of the Russian proletariat in the other was as inevitable as the normal progression of human life from birth to death. In both France and Russia, continued existence within the restricting forms of a declining productive system had become impossible; in each case, matters had been brought to a head within a brief and crowded interval by desperate efforts on the part of the ruling classes to continue in control of the corporate agencies of privilege; in each, the revolt was undertaken by underprivileged classes who, forming themselves into extra-legal groups, swept aside the by then dead hand of prerogative authority and erected revolutionary governments.

Such, also, were the broad outlines of the revolutionary process in colonial America, beginning with the last third of the eighteenth century:

Reprinted by permission from *Columbia University Quarterly,* XXVII, Number 3, Part 1 (September, 1935), pp. 259–295.

the general characteristics of contradiction, repression, crisis and thrust for power all were present. All these things we know: there are any number of American scholars who can without difficulty tick off the titles of virtually hundreds of monographs and learned articles that in detail support such an interpretation. And yet, it is one of the curiosities of American scholarship that no effort has been made to unite all these generally accepted facts into a coherent pattern.

Many historians, today, in trying to plumb the mystery of the American Revolution, seem to be quite as ingenuous in their approach as Parson Weems, the redoubtable creator of the Washingtonian myth. To the good preacher the reason for American revolt was altogether simple: the colonies were being plundered to take care of the royal poor relations and to feed the insatiable appetites of the ministers surrounding the English throne. Such an explanation, by personalizing the oppressive forces, undoubtedly serves an important patriotic function when all the issues of the struggle have not been yet resolved, but obviously it will not do long after passions have cooled. Incredible as it may seem, this explanation has not altogether disappeared from history books, although, of course, its present-day guise is surrounded perhaps with an air of greater thoughtfulness. Thus, Professor Channing, writing in 1909, could say that the issue was not forced by the patriots of 1763–1775: "That was the work of selfish placemen in England, whose horizon was bounded by the narrow seas of their own island, and of over-zealous and stubborn officials in America, whose thoughts were ever intent upon places and pensions— Townshend, Hillsborough, and Lord North in England; Hutchinson, Dudingston and Tryon in America."

Also, to see the Revolution simply as a struggle for democratic rights in the political sphere: to build the whole theory of the Revolution around the slogan "No Taxation Without Representation" and to consider it merely as a continuation of "the Englishman's long struggle for political liberty," in the face of the almost immediate repeal by Parliament of the Stamp Tax Act and the Townshend duties and despite the fact that in the colonies themselves (as in England) the great mass of the adult population was disfranchised anyway: this is to make confusion only worse confounded. Nor is it possible to regard the struggle as arising out of a change in English colonial policy: that, beginning with 1763, the doctrine of mercantilism, with its more or less casual relations between mother country and dependencies, was replaced by the more modern concept of imperialism, under which the colonies were to be closely integrated into the political life of the whole empire. We are to believe (at least upon the authority of Professor Van Tyne) that a race of stubborn imperial patriots, originating in the landed classes entirely, had suddenly come into control of affairs with the termination of the Seven Years' War and was bent upon consolidating the empire in the interests of the greater glory of England, the opposition of the home merchant classes to the contrary notwithstanding.

At the basis of these various beliefs is the supposition that if only wiser heads had been guiding the English ship of state, if a beneficent statesmanship and not embittered partisanship had prevailed—if only Burke, Barré and a well Chatham had been the directors of the empire's destinies! —then Americans today, like all good British subjects, would be celebrating the King's Jubilee along with Canadians, Jamaicans and Fiji Islanders. For had not the great Whig leaders continuously pleaded for conciliation: for an end to colonial coercion, for withdrawal of troops, for the abandonment of all those policies whose only effect was to convert contented colonials into disloyal and plotting subjects? In short, accommodation was possible. (This thought, like a minor theme, runs through the writings of all modern American scholars. So, Professor Andrews declares: "We are driven to believe that a little more yielding, a little more of the spirit of friendliness and compromise, and a little less of British ignorance, stubbornness and prejudice would have calmed the troubled waters and stilled the storm that was brewing.") Accommodation was possible: the dispute about trade was a minor matter, the heated controversy over taxation was quickly adjusted in America's favor, the troops were insignificant irritants and could quickly have been removed: for, in effect, the English Whigs were right in assuming that mercantilism could work forever—if there could be only a fair degree of give and take. We shall see— obviously the Revolution can have no meaning otherwise—that the break took place not because of the inauguration by England of a new policy but because the sharpening of the contradictions that lay at the heart of mercantilism had to tear asunder the imperial-colonial relations.

Finally, scholars find refuge in an obscurantism that is difficult to penetrate; and there is nothing more surprising than to see Professor Andrews, who has done so much to clarify the nature of the commercial relations existing between England and its colonies, adopting such a position. The following is Professor Andrews' argument. For one hundred and fifty years, from the very hour of settlement itself, mother country and colonies had been growing farther and farther apart psychologically and institutionally. England was "an old, well-settled, highly organized land"; its social and economic life had hardened into iron-bound molds; its ruling class, seated on its great estates and in firm possession of all the citadels of privilege, was guided by "rigid and sinister ideas of power and government." The colonies, on the other hand, were youthful, growing, and filled with "a frontier people instinct with individualism and possessed of but a rudimentary sense of obligation and duty." Thus, it really was the old, old struggle between aristocracy and democracy, between settled areas, with an ancient culture and a caste tradition, and the frontier with a fluid institutional life and a passionate belief in egalitarianism. The magical concept of the frontier, it seems, will explain everything to American historians. What if class divisions were as sharply drawn in the colonies as in England, that the colonial merchants and their legal spokesmen were as contemptuous of "mobsters" as were their English counterparts, that colonial planters settled on their broad acres in Virginia, Maryland and South Carolina lived as much in the aristocratic tradition as noble lords with estates in Surrey and Kent? All this, apparently, is irrelevant. The frontier made Americans free and out of this individualism was engendered a spirit of liberty.

In the face of these conflicting and implausible theories of learned scholars, bewilderment on the part of the uninformed is only natural. Unless we are prepared to start out with the premise that the economic and social relations flowing out of the prevailing system of the day, that is to say, mercantilism, no longer could be maintained, then the whole history of the critical period that preceded the American Revolution is simply unintelligible. And if the past does not make sense, then we must consign its study over to the pure and simple antiquarians. But because the past has a clear and inevitable logic, our study of this period in America's development is of the greatest contemporary significance because we, today, living as we do also in an era of productive decline, class oppressions and approaching crisis, have much to learn from the ways employed by American patriots of an earlier time in the resolution of their perplexities.

The economic program the rulers of England adopted following the successful termination of the Puritan Revolution of 1641–49 (all the gains of the Revolution were finally consolidated with the establishment of the constitutional monarchy in 1689) we have come to call mercantilism. What mercantilism was, simply, was a policy to assure the continued advance of the English merchant, or preindustrial, capitalism, once the restrictive ties of the absolute and mediaeval state had been cast off. In this sense, therefore, mercantilism had two faces: at home it utilized the agency of the state to strengthen the position of commercial enterprisers in trade, manufacturing and agriculture; and abroad, particularly in the colonial relations, it from the beginning attached the oversea possessions in a subordinate capacity to the economy of the mother country. We shall not understand the character of the American crisis of 1763–1775 unless we are prepared to hold ever in mind the fact that every imperial administrative program, whether in the economic or political realms, was designed to further this end: to utilize the colonies as an economic appanage of the mother country. That the English from the very beginning were fully conscious of the nature of this relationship, there is ample evidence. Thus, as early as 1726, a member of the Board of Trade wrote:

Every act of a dependent provincial government ought therefore to terminate in the advantage of the mother state unto whom it owes its being and protection in all its valuable privileges. Hence it follows that all advantageous projects or commercial gains in any colony which are truly prejudicial to and inconsistent with the interests of the mother state must be understood to be illegal and the practice of them unwarrantable, because they contradict the end for which the colony had a being and are incompatible with the terms on which the people claim both privileges and protection. . . . For such is the end of the colonies, and if this use cannot be made of them it will be much better for the state to be without them.

It is apparent, therefore, that mercantilism was more than a monetary policy, as is so commonly believed. It is true that mercantilism did place a high value on a favorable balance of trade and as a result sought to encourage a flow of the precious metals into the home country. . . .

It has been said that the mercantilist policy of English merchant capitalism demanded that the economic life of the American colonies be kept subservient to that of the mother country. From the very beginning—certainly, at any rate, from the turn of the eighteenth century when merchant capitalism was fully installed in the economy of the empire and in possession of its prerogative power—this was so: and a governmental apparatus was set up whose purpose it was consciously and constantly to maintain the imperial-colonial connection in this relationship. The real significance of all those imperial administrative agencies—the Privy Council, the Board of Trade, the Secretary of State in charge of Colonial Affairs, the Commissioners of Customs, the Treasury, the Admiralty and the royal governors—lay in the fact not that they created political or constitutional ties to unite colonies to the mother country but that they forged the fetters that bound the colonial merchant capitalism to that of England.

An examination of the activities of the imperial administrative agencies will plainly indicate that such an economic policy was consistently pursued: the period after 1763 merely marked its intensification as a result of the sharpening of the contradictions that appeared in mercantilism itself. The Board of Trade had been established in 1696, as O. M. Dickerson points out, largely "to make the colonies commercially profitable to the mother country." And this it sought to do, over a period of more than three-quarters of a century, with a devotion and singleness of purpose that left small room for complaint. The commissioners, of course, made it their business to keep the Privy Council and Parliament informed as to the progress of the oversea possessions; but their powers were more than reportorial, for through four specific devices they were able to direct and supervise closely the economic development of the colonies. The Board of Trade was more or less in charge of preparing the colonial civil list, and it was also its function to supervise the activities of the colonial judiciary: by control over personnel its influence therefore was measurable. But more important were: first, its power to review colonial legislation and, if the purposes of provincial statutes ran counter to the welfare of the mother country, recommend their disallowance by the Privy Council; and second, its power to prepare specific instructions to the governors for their guidance in the exercise of the veto over colonial encroachments on the privileges and prerogatives of English citizens.

There were at least a dozen points at which the Board of Trade (representing English merchant capitalism) and the colonial legislatures (representing colonial merchant capitalism) constantly were in conflict, exactly because of the clash of economic interests. The outstanding of these were: colonial interference with the mother country's hold on foreign trade and shipping; attempts by the colonies to control the traffic in convicts and slaves; and colonial efforts to permit the payment of quit rents in paper money, to lower interest rates, to ease the judicial burdens imposed on debtors and to monopolize the Indian trade for colonials. Most important were the stern checks imposed by the Board of Trade on attempts by the colonial assemblies to encourage native manufacturing and to relieve the oppression of debts (because every section of colonial America, as we have seen, was in a debtor relationship toward England) through the increase of the money supply of the colonies.

In order to maintain the English control over trade and commerce, the Board of Trade recommended and obtained the disallowance by the Privy Council of legislation placing export duties on colonial raw materials needed by English enterprise; it was equally successful in outlawing acts whose purpose it was, through the grant of exemptions, to favor colonial shipowners in the carrying trade; and it ceaselessly moved against measures placing import duties on foreign wines and liquors and on English merchandise. Finally, when this last threatened to become a general practice, the Board issued blanket instructions to the governors ordering them to veto laws placing duties on European goods imported in English vessels (1724) and on the produce or manufactures of Great Britain (1732), and all those laws under which the natives of a province were given preferential treatment over those of Great Britain (1732).

The Privy Council repeatedly was called upon to disallow legislation laying high or prohibitive duties upon the importation of Negro slaves and interfering with the free transport of convicted felons overseas. The colonies for the most part were moving to protect themselves against the growth of undesirable elements in their population; although the motives of revenue and the protection of the quality of the slaves also were present. But the Board and the Privy Council were not unmindful of the great English slave-carrying trade that was bound to be affected by such legislation: its solicitude therefore was plain. Finally, in 1731, when the colonies persisted in their efforts to pass such bills, circular instructions were sent to the governors ordering them to veto legislation interfering with the free importation of Negroes and felons.

. . . The events of 1763–1775 can have no meaning unless we understand that the character of English imperial policy was never changed: that Pitt and his successors at Whitehall were following exactly the same line that Cromwell had laid down more than a century before; that the purpose of the general program was to protect the English capitalist interests which now were being jeopardized as a result of the intensification of colonial capitalist competition; and that English statesmen yielded quickly when a fundamental principle was not at stake and only became more insistent when one was being threatened. If in the raising of a colonial revenue lay the heart of the difficulty, how are we to account for the quick repeal of the Stamp Tax and the Townshend Acts and the lowering of the molasses duty? And, on the other hand, how are we to account for the tightening of enforcement of the Acts of Trade and Navigation at a dozen and one different points, the passage of the Currency Act, the placing of iron on the enumerated list, English seizure of control of the wine trade, and the attempt to give the East India Company a monopoly over the colonial tea business? The struggle was not over high-sounding political and constitutional concepts: over the power of taxation and, in the final analysis, over natural rights: but over colonial manufacturing, wild lands and furs, sugar, wine, tea and currency, all of which meant, simply, the survival or collapse of English merchant capitalism within the imperial-colonial framework of the mercantilist system.

Even before Pitt gave up the French sugar islands in 1763 because of the insistence of the British sugar interest in Parliament, he had already moved to protect the same monopoly group through his orders to the navy to stamp out colonial smugglers operating in the illicit foreign West Indian trade. The colonial courts were directed to issue and recognize the doubtfully legal writs of assistance (general search warrants), as early as 1761. Two years later, the peace-time navy was converted into a patrol fleet with powers of search even on the high seas. In the same year, absentee officials in the customs service were ordered to their colonial posts. A vice-admiralty court was set up for all America in 1764 and the number of local admiralty courts (sitting without juries) was increased. In 1768 a new board of five customs commissioners to be resident in America was created. By statutes, by orders, by instructions, every conceivable weapon was employed to break up a traffic and therefore to weaken a group so dangerous to English capitalist interests. Spying was encouraged by offers to share with informers the sequestered cargoes; customs officials were protected from damage suits for unwarranted seizures when they were declared non-liable personally and when the burden of proof was placed on the owners of vessels and goods; the stricter registration and inspection of vessels were ordered; to protect informers and make possible the easier obtaining of verdicts, it was provided that suits for the seizure of cargoes might be tried directly in the vice-admiralty court and that revenue cases might be heard in the admiralty instead of the local courts; and to further free the courts from local pressure, the payment of the salaries of judges was to be made out of customs revenues.

The revenue acts of 1764 and later were used as a screen behind which the work of compressing within even narrower limits the economy of colonial merchant capitalism and of fastening tighter on it a dependent status was to go on. The Act of 1764 and the Stamp Act of 1765 called for the payment of duties and taxes in specie, thus further draining the colonies of currency and contracting the credit base. To divert colonial capital into raw materials, the first measure increased the bounties paid for the colonial production of hemp and flax, placed high duties on the colonial importation of foreign indigo, and removed the English import duties on colonial whale fins. To cripple the trade with the foreign West Indies a high duty was placed on refined sugar. The importation of foreign rum was forbidden altogether, and lumber was placed on the enumerated list. To give English manufacturers a firmer grip on their raw materials, hides and skins (needed for the boot-and-shoe industry), pig and bar iron (needed in the wrought iron industry), and potash and pearl ashes (used for bleaching cloth and hence needed in the woolen industry), were placed on the enumerated list. To maintain the English monopoly of the colonial finished-goods market in 1764 the entrance into the colonies of certain kinds of French and Oriental drygoods was taxed for the first time; in 1765, the importation of foreign silk stockings, gloves and mitts was altogether forbidden; also the drawbacks of duties paid on foreign goods landed in England and re-exported to the colonies were rescinded. To extend the market of English merchants in Europe, in 1766 Parliament ordered that all remaining non-enumerated articles (largely flour, provisions and fish) bound for European ports north of Cape Finisterre be landed first in England. And to weaken further colonial commercial activity, in 1764 high duties were placed on wines from the wine islands and wine, fruits and oil from Spain and Portugal brought directly to America (in American ships, as a rule), while such articles brought over from England were to pay only nominal duties.

As has been said, the revenue features of these acts were quickly abandoned; the Stamp Act was repealed; and in 1770, three years after their passage, the Townshend duties on paper, paint and glass were lifted. Only the slight tax on tea remained and even this was lightened in 1773 when the new Tea Act provided for a full drawback of English import duties on British tea shipped to the American colonies.

But it was exactly this new Tea Act which clearly revealed the intention of London: that not only was the economic vassalage of the American colonies to be continued but the interest of colonial enterprisers was to be subordinated to every British capitalist group that could gain the ear of Parliament. For, to save the East India Company from collapse, that powerful financial organization was to be permitted to ship in its own vessels and dispose of, through its own merchandising agencies, a surplus stock of 17,000,000 pounds of tea in America: and, in this way, drive out of business those Americans who carried, imported and sold into retail channels British tea (and indeed, foreign tea, for the British tea could be sold cheaper even than the smuggled Holland article). The merchants all over America were not slow to read the correct significance of this measure. Their spokesmen sounded the alarm. As Arthur M. Schlesinger has put it, pamphleteers set out to show "that the present project of the East India Company was the entering wedge for larger and more ambitious undertakings calculated to undermine the colonial mercantile world. Their opinion was based on the fact that, in addition to the article of tea, the East India Company imported into England vast quantities of silks, calicos and other fabrics, spices, drugs and chinaware, all commodities of staple demand; and on their fear that the success of the present venture would result in an extension of the same principle to the sale of the other articles." The result would be, as a Philadelphia pamphleteer signing himself "A Mechanic" warned:

They will send their own factors and creatures, establish houses among us, ship us all other East India goods; and in order to full freight their ships, take in other kinds of goods at under freight, or (more probably) ship them on their own accounts to their own factors, and undersell our merchants, till they monopolize the whole trade. Thus our merchants are ruined, ship building ceases. They will then sell goods at any exorbitant price. Our artificers will be unemployed, and every tradesman will groan under dire oppression.

By 1773, therefore, it was plain that America was to be sacrificed: colonial merchant capitalists were compelled to strike back through the destruction of the tea and the writing and enforcement of the Continental Association.

The blows aimed at colonial merchant capitalism through the strengthening of the Acts of Trade and Navigation, the promulgation of the Proclamation Line of 1763 and the passage of the Currency Act of 1764 precipitated the crisis in the imperial-colonial relations: and merchant capitalists (whether land speculators or traders) were soon converted from contented and loyal subjects into rebellious enemies of the crown.

But, to be successful, the revolutionary host had to be swelled from the ranks of the lower middle-class small farmers and traders and the working-class artisans, mechanics, seamen, fishermen and lumbermen. This was not difficult: for the material well-being of the lower classes was tied to the successful enterprising of the upper, and contraction of economic opportunity in the higher sphere was bound to bring want and suffering in the lower.

The colonies had enjoyed a period of unprecedented prosperity during the Seven Years' War: the expanding market in the West Indies, the great expenditures of the British quartermasters, the illegal and contraband trade with the enemy forces, all had furnished steady employment for workers and lucrative outlets for the produce of small farmers. But with the end of the war and the passage of the restrictive legislation of 1763 and after, depression had set in. With stringency and bankruptcy everywhere confronting merchant capitalists, it was inevitable that mechanics, artisans, seamen and lumbermen should be thrown out of employment, small tradesmen should be compelled to close the doors of their shops, and that small farmers should be confronted with an expanded acreage, a diminished market and heavy fixed charges made even more onerous as a result of currency contraction. Into the bargain, escape into the frontier zones—always the last refuge of the dispossessed—was shut off. Openly abetted by merchants and land speculators, the lower classes moved into the revolutionary host.

It would be a mistake to assume, however, that the working class and lower middle-class groups surrendered up their identities completely and operated only at the behest and with the encouragement of the merchant capitalists. Under the direction of their own leaders in the Sons of Liberty and the Committees of Correspondence, they were able to articulate their own class demands: the result was, the period of revolutionary crisis saw the development of a radical program which merchants and planters regarded with misgivings and dread but with which they dared not interfere lest, in alienating the underprivileged farmers, tradesmen and workers, they lose that mass support upon which their own destiny so completely was dependent. The lower classes began to look upon the revolution as the instrument for attaining their freedom: from the civil disability of almost universal disfranchisement, from the inequalities of entail and primogeniture, from oppression at the hands of engrossing landlords and from the threatened dominance and exactions of an oversea ecclesiastical authority.

For these and similar class reasons, the lower middle classes and the workers of colonial America joined with the merchants and planters in demonstrations against the imperial program: and when peaceful agitation and pressure proved unavailing, they were ready to take up arms when England resorted to coercion and violence. In 1774 and 1775, through the agencies of the Coercive Acts and the Restraining Acts, England, by striking at the economic life of the colonies directly, virtually opened hostilities. The colonists replied with two declarations of freedom. The first, naturally representing the dominant interest of merchant capitalism, was embodied in a series of resolutions passed by the Second Continental Congress, 6 April, 1776; these nullified the Acts of Trade and Navigation and put an end to the colonial slave trade: and with this single blow colonial merchant capitalism smashed the hampering fetters of the imperial-colonial relations. The second, adopted by the Congress, 4 July, 1776, was the Declaration of Independence: written by the radicals, this was a political manifesto which called upon the masses to defend the revolution. The first American Revolution then moved fully into the stage of armed resistance.

Mercantilism and the American Revolution

LAWRENCE A. HARPER

The cynic who declared that history is the process whereby a complex truth becomes a simplified falsehood may have had in mind interpretations of the American Revolution. Even before the Revolution occurred, Vergennes prophesied that France's loss of Canada would eventually bring it about. The very document which made the severance final attributed the blame to George III, a fashion which has been generally followed. . . . These points are called to attention merely to remind us . . . that there are many interpretations. Our immediate task is to concentrate upon one—the relation of English mercantilism to the American Revolution.

The term "mercantilism" is one of those words which have different meanings for different people. On the one hand, George Louis Beer claimed that English mercantilism was a well-balanced system designed for the benefit of the colonies as well as the mother country, and on the other, Sir William Ashley declared that the regulations of English mercantilism were either pious formulas nullified in the actual world of commerce by fraud and evasion, or merely a codification of commercial habits which would have been followed in any case. For reasons which have been explained more fully elsewhere we shall reject Beer's claim that there was no exploitation and accept the statements of the mercantilists themselves that they planned to exploit the colonies for the benefit

Reprinted by permission from Lawrence A. Harper, "Mercantilism and the American Revolution," *Canadian Historical Review*, XXIII, No. 1 (March, 1942), pp. 1–15.

of the mother country. We shall deny the Ashley view that there was no actual regulation and conclude from more recent studies of the evidence that the English laws did regulate trade and commerce.

These two conclusions provide us with a working definition of English mercantilism in its colonial aspects. It had as its purpose, exploitation, and as its means, regulation. Both phases of the problem, exploitation *and* regulation, are important. To understand the relationship of mercantilism and the Revolution we must not only analyse the extent to which the colonists were exploited but also consider the skill with which they were regulated.

An analysis of how the colonists were exploited is no easy task, as any one knows who has struggled with the many statutory ambiguities involved. The calculations involved in estimating the burdens placed upon the colonial economy are complicated. They call for arithmetical computations involving duties, preferences, or drawbacks of such odd amounts as 1s. 10d. and 15 16/75 of a twentieth of a penny per pound of tobacco. They run afoul of complicated analyses of costs and close decisions about the incidence of taxation. The answer required some thousands of hours of WPA and NYA labour in tabulating the necessary data and hundreds more in analysing and correlating them, the details of which have been compressed in thirty-eight rather dull pages. All that can be attempted here is to state the conclusions and indicate the grounds upon which they are based. We can, however, simplify our analysis of the mercantilist code which exploited the colonies by dividing it into four parts: first, the basic provisions concerning the trans-Atlantic trade; second, the supplementary measures restricting manufactures; third, the subsidiary rules with reference to the American trade; and fourth, the much discussed measures enacted after the French and Indian War.

In examining the first part, we find that the basic provisions concerning the trans-Atlantic trade placed a heavy burden upon the colonies. By means of the Navigation Acts England attempted both to keep foreign vessels out of the colonies and to enable English merchants to share in the more profitable parts of the trans-Atlantic trade. The enumeration of key colonial exports in various Acts from 1660 to 1766 and the Staple Act of 1663 hit at colonial trade both coming and going. The Acts required the colonies to allow English middlemen to distribute such crops as tobacco and rice and stipulated that if the colonies would not buy English manufactures, at least they should purchase their European goods in England. The greatest element in the burden laid upon the colonies was not the taxes assessed. It consisted in the increased costs of shipment, transshipment, and middleman's profits arising out of the requirement that England be used as an *entrepôt*.

The burdens were somewhat lightened by legislation favouring the colonies, but not as much as usually alleged. The suppression of tobacco production in England, for example, was comparatively unimportant to the colonies since the great quantities of colonial tobacco re-exported caused its price to be determined by a world rather than an English market. Moreover, the motive was not goodwill for the colonists but fiscal, since the heavy revenues derived from tobacco could be collected more easily at the waterfront than upon the farm. Likewise, although colonial shipbuilders and shipowners approved the clauses of the Navigation Acts which eliminated Dutch rivals, they did not need such protection. They had managed to carry cargoes and to build ships which could be sold in the world market before the laws were enacted and they continued to do so after the Revolution. The fact is that colonial shipowners suffered, directly, and colonial shipbuilders, indirectly, under the Navigation Acts since other clauses enabled English shipowners (as contrasted with American) to carry eighty per cent of the trade between the British Isles and the Thirteen Colonies whereas they carried only twenty per cent after the Revolution.

Similarly the drawbacks, bounties, and tariff preferences, of which we are so often reminded, did not materially offset the burdens placed upon the trans-Atlantic trade. The drawbacks paid by English customs authorities on foreign products re-exported to the colonies should not be listed as a benefit to the colonies. There would have been no duties to be drawn back except for the requirement that the colonists purchase their European goods in England. The portion of the duties which England retained, while less than it might have been, was obviously greater than nothing at all. Likewise, *bounties paid upon English manufactures* exported to the colonies, were of advantage to the English producer, who received them whether his goods were exported to the colonies or anywhere else, rather than of benefit to the colonial consumer who otherwise would, and often did, buy competitive European goods.

On the other hand, however, the bounties paid upon colonial products were of real advantage to the colonies. They sustained the growth of indigo in South Carolina, did much to foster the development of naval stores in North Carolina, encouraged the lumber industry in New England, and at the end of the colonial period averaged more than £65,000 a year for the Thirteen Colonies alone. Similarly the preferences granted colonial products were beneficial in so far as they operated. Although they had no effect upon such commodities as tobacco and rice and their effect upon other commodities is somewhat uncertain, colonial raw silk, naval stores, and lumber definitely benefited. Yet the total sum represented by such preferences was never great and it is doubtful whether the benefit the Thirteen Colonies thus derived amounted to even one-twentieth of that obtained by the British West Indian planters who in the year 1773 alone, pocketed £446,000, thanks to a preferential rate which enabled their sugar to hold the English market despite a five-shilling-per-hundred-weight differential in price.

The uncertainties underlying many of our calculations do not permit an exact statement, but judging from calculations for the year 1773, it would seem that after all proper allowances have been made for bounties and other preferences, the net burden imposed upon the Thirteen Colonies by the restraints upon the trans-Atlantic trade was between two million and seven million dollars a year. In these days of astronomical budgets such figures do not seem especially impressive, but the annual per capita burden represented by the lower estimate would come close to meeting all the expenses of operating the national government during Washington's administration, and an annual per capita tax based upon the higher estimate would, in addition to paying the current expenses of government, have raised in twelve years (from 1790–1801) a sum sufficient to pay both the domestic and foreign debt incurred by the United States government during the Revolutionary War.

When we turn to the second part of our discussion, the supplementary measures restricting manufacture, we find a difference of opinion concerning the effect of English restrictions upon manufacturing wool, hats, and iron. The earlier tendency was to dismiss the regulations as immaterial, but recently some have swung the pendulum to the other extreme and argue that the restraints were very important. Neither extreme appears to accord with the facts. In the case of hats, proximity to the source of supply of furs and the comparatively simple process of manufacturing had led to the development of an industry which appears to have been injured by the legislation, but the hat industry played only a minor part in the total economy. Woollen manufactures were, of course, much more important, but there is much evidence to indicate that the English prohibitions had little material effect. The colonies found that they were handicapped by an inadequate supply of good wool when they tried to develop homespun goods at the time of the Revolution—and even as late as 1791 Hamilton found that an adequate supply of labour was one of the chief stumbling blocks to his programme for encouraging industry. It required an embargo, a war, and a protective tariff before large-scale woollen manufacturing began to develop, and it did not pass beyond the household stage until many years after being freed of English mercantilism—which, incidentally, had never forbidden the manufacture of homespun for domestic use or local distribution.

In the case of iron manufactures the British legislation encouraged the development of pig and bar iron and tried to discourage the manufacture of more advanced forms, but in both respects the influence of the legislation is doubtful. Because of the proximity of iron ore to forests America had a great advantage in producing crude iron, before coke replaced charcoal, and probably did not need legislative encouragement. With such an advantage in producing crude iron it was only natural that some more advanced iron articles would be produced in the colonies, whatever thorough-going mercantilists might dream about having the crude iron sent over to England and having it returned in the form of pots, pans, and other manufactures.

The various disallowances of colonial laws which were intended to foster colonial manufacturing further illustrate the English intention of discouraging it but, despite that intent, English mercantilism as a whole probably had a greater tendency to promote than to hinder colonial industry. The colonies' most dangerous industrial competitors were in many respects, not the English, but the Dutch, the Germans, and other Europeans—to say nothing of the natives of India—against whose competition the provisoes of the Staple Act of 1663 provided a very useful tariff barrier. Moreover, the large sums which mercantilism withheld from the colonies reduced their available cash, and probably forced many colonists to use homespun or other American products instead of buying British.

The third point of our inquiry into colonial exploitation by England should not detain us long. Until the Molasses Act of 1733 the inter-American trade had been left virtually alone except for the requirement that the English colonies trade in English or colonial ships. Even after 1733, the prohibitive duties on foreign sugar, molasses, and rum were usually evaded. Such evasion required bribery, fraud, or concealment which probably served as a mildly protective tariff in favour of the British sugar islands, but the prices quoted in the Thirteen Colonies for sugar, molasses, and rum do not indicate that the legislation had any radical effect upon the trade.

The fourth part of our inquiry—that relating to the period after 1763 —is a different matter. The researches of Schlesinger and others have demonstrated how the British measures of that period aroused the resentment of the merchants who unleashed an avalanche of agitation which soon went beyond their control. The agitation was not directed toward revolution at first, but agitation by its very nature promotes conditions favourable for revolution—and revolution followed as a natural sequence. Yet, conceding all the irritation thus aroused, we must still face the questions: Were the measures unduly exploitive? Did they fundamentally upset the economic equilibrium? Were they fatal ills which would inevitably lead to the death of the Empire, or merely minor upsets from which the Empire might have recovered—granted otherwise favourable conditions and good luck?

In reviewing the period it does not seem fair to blame British mercantilism for prescribing regulations which were demanded by the circumstances of the time. The British currency and land policies seem to fall under this category. The restrictions upon paper money undoubtedly distressed those who lacked funds, but they merely affirmed a truth which Americans had to learn from sad experience—that in the eighteenth century at least, no political alchemy could transmute paper into gold. Similarly the Proclamation of 1763 and the Quebec Act of 1774 essentially concerned imperial problems and American imitation of the policy after independence was not mere flattery but a tribute to its inherent soundness. The measures disappointed those who had hoped to acquire fortunes from land speculation, but what else could the British have done? Neither they nor the United States government after them could allow private individuals to stir up trouble by moving into Indian territory before the way had been prepared for settlement by negotiations which extinguished the Indians' claims to the area. In view of the British debt it was merely good fiscal policy to charge for the land, and the prices and terms of sale proposed by the British mercantilists seem very reasonable when compared with the prices and terms adopted by the federal government after 1787. And what solution did the Thirteen States themselves find for the conflicting claims to the territory west of the Alleghanies except to create a new governmental unit?

To one who frankly does not profess to be an expert on the point, it is difficult to understand how British mercantilism discriminated materially against the colonists. It is true that in the manœuvering for land grants, British interests sometimes clashed with colonial interests, but we hear fully as much about clashes between different colonial groups. Both the small frontiersmen and the big speculators were charged more for land than they were accustomed to pay, but it was not as much as they were to be charged by the United States government thereafter. In the readjustments which accompanied the establishment of the new policies the fur traders of the Thirteen Colonies suffered somewhat because of the machinations of British opponents but their loss was not great, and in any event by the Revolutionary period trade in furs formed only a negligible fraction of the colonial economy.

The pre-Revolutionary taxation measures, however, are a different matter, and one for which British mercantilism must bear full responsibility. Yet in analysing the figures we find that the average annual revenue raised by the Sugar Acts, the Townshend Acts, and all the other taxes collected in the Thirteen Colonies by the British government amounted to only £31,000. This sum barely exceeded the indirect taxes which were collected on colonial merchandise passing through England. Moreover, both the taxes collected indirectly in England and directly in the colonies failed to equal the bounties which the British government was paying to the colonies—to say nothing of the advantages which they were deriving from preferential duties on their shipments to England. More interesting still, calculated on an annual per capita basis, the taxes collected during the Revolutionary period directly in the colonies and indirectly in England, totalled less than one-seventh of the taxes assessed at the beginning of the century.

Yet even though the amount of taxation was not great, we must consider the possibility that the form of its assessment detrimentally affected colonial interests. The Tea Act, for one, definitely injured the illicit trade in tea by so reducing the price of the legal article that it lessened, if it did not eliminate, the profit from smuggling. However unfair smugglers may have thought such tactics, they can hardly be said to have injured the economy of the country—especially since tea was not a pivotal commodity.

Molasses, the rum which was made from it, and the provision trade which accompanied it, however, were vital factors in colonial economy, and historians have often called attention to their importance in such books as *Rum, Romance, and Rebellion.* The Sugar Act of 1764 served notice that the British government intended to make its regulations effective when it lowered the duty on foreign sugar and molasses and prohibited the importation of foreign rum entirely. The provisions concerning sugar and rum were comparatively immaterial since no great quantities were imported, but the duty of 3d. per gallon on molasses was another matter, since literally millions of gallons came from the foreign West Indies. Many feared that the trade could not bear a tax of 3d. per gallon, and in response to their pleas the duty was reduced in 1766 to 1d. per gallon and the tax was assessed on both British and foreign molasses. The excitement aroused by these taxes leads one to look for evidence of the havoc which they wrought in trade, but an examination of the wholesale prices of molasses does not disclose any noticeable change attributable to the legislation. And if we carry our investigations further we find that the tax which the federal government placed and kept upon imports of molasses after 1790 almost equalled the 3d. per gallon placed upon foreign molasses in 1764 and materially exceeded the 1d. duty retained after 1766. In brief, whatever the connection between rum and romance, the statistics of colonial trade disclose no correlation between rum and rebellion.

In so far as the statistics can be followed, the correlation between wine and rebellion is much closer. The Sugar Act of 1764 had also placed a duty upon wines which gave those imported by way of Britain a preferential rate of £3 per ton. The preference was not sufficient to enable the English to capture the trade in Madeira wine, but it enabled them to gain a flourishing trade in port which previously had been negligible. Yet such an infringement of colonial taste hardly seems to justify a revolt—especially when we note that the quantity involved was not large, and that by the post-Revolutionary period Americans preferred port and other wines to Madeira.

Thus, an analysis of the economic effects of British mercantilism fails to establish its exploitive aspects as the proximate cause of the Revolution. The only measures which afforded a sufficient economic grievance were the *entrepôt* provisions of the Navigation Acts, which governed the trans-Atlantic trade. They helped to create a fundamental economic unbalance, but cannot be connected directly with the Revolution. The colonists had lived under them for more than a century without desiring independence and even in the Revolutionary period with few exceptions the *entrepôt* provisions were accepted as the mother country's due for the protection which she afforded. In fact, the official representatives of the colonies were willing to guarantee the British commercial system provided that the measures of political taxation were withdrawn. If there were any inexorable economic forces which were inevitably drawing the colonies toward revolution, they are hard to detect and the colonists were unaware of them.

Anyone who maintains that the Revolution resulted from the inevitable clash of competing capitalisms must reckon with several points: That burdens upon the trans-Atlantic trade were proportionately greater at the beginning of the eighteenth century than in 1776; that the restraints of the land and currency policies were basically the same as those prescribed by the federal government; and that after 1766 the taxes laid on molasses by Britain were less than those imposed by the United States after 1790. He should also explain why the surplus colonial capital alleged to be bursting its confines did not venture into the manufacturing enterprises which the law did not prohibit; why the colonists did not finance their own middlemen in England; and, finally, why they did not pay their debts. If by a clash of expanding capitalism is meant that colonists with money were irritated because their freedom of action was restrained by outside regulation, one must immediately concede that the charge is justified; but such colonial resentment seems more properly classified as a political rather than an economic factor. It is merely an old point dressed in new garb and was better expressed by John Adams when he declared that the American Revolution began when the first plantation was settled.

When we turn, however, from the economic effects of mercantilism to its regulatory aspects, we are faced with a different story. We can establish a direct correlation between mercantilism and the Revolution. Although earlier English regulations had been reasonably satisfactory the regulatory technique of the British government under George III was pitifully defective. As a mother country, Britain had much to learn. Any modern parents' magazine could have told George III's ministers that the one mistake not to make is to take a stand and then to yield to howls of anguish. It was a mistake which the British government made repeatedly. It placed a duty of 3d. per gallon on molasses, and when it encountered opposition, reduced it to 1d. It provided for a Stamp Act and withdrew it in the face of temper tantrums. It provided for external taxes to meet the colonial objections and then yielded again by removing all except one. When finally it attempted to enforce discipline it was too late. Under the circumstances, no self-respecting child—or colonist—would be willing to yield.

Moreover, British reforming zeal came at a very bad time. The colonists were in a particularly sensitive state due to the post-war deflation and the economic distress which accompanied it. The British also attempted to exert unusual control at a time when the removal of the French from Canada had minimized the colonists' dependence upon Britain. Most important of all, the reforms followed one another too rapidly.

In social reform, irritation often is to be measured not so much by what a regulation attempts to achieve as by the extent to which it changes established habits. The early history of English mercantilism itself offers a good illustration of the point. Bitter complaints came from Virginia and Barbados when tobacco and sugar were first enumerated because those colonies had become accustomed to conditions of comparatively free trade, whereas few or no complaints were heard from Jamaica which had developed under the restrictive system. The mercantilist system was geared for leisurely operation and before George III's reign succeeded by virtue of that fact. Its early restraints led to Bacon's rebellion in Virginia but fortunately for the mother country the pressure against New England was deferred until the next decade when it, too, led to an explosion in the form of revolt against Andros. These uprisings were separated both geographically and chronologically so that neither attained dangerous proportions, and both were followed by a reasonably satisfactory settlement of at least some of the colonial grievances.

During the Revolutionary era, however, the tempo of reform was not leisurely. Doubtless all the colonists were not irritated by any one British reform, but each individual had his own feeling of grievance which enabled him to agree fervently with the complaints of others against British policy and thus add to the heated tempers of the time. The politician who objected to the political implications in taxation reforms found an audience in the land speculators and frontiersmen who complained that the colonists were being deprived of the reward of their blood and suffering by the Proclamation of 1763 and the Quebec Act of 1774. Debtors and inflationists chimed in to tell of the iniquities of the Currency Act; lawyers and printers could not forget the threat to their interests in the Stamp Act. On Sundays the preachers thundered against the dangers of popery in Quebec and voiced their fear that Britain planned to establish an Anglican Church in the colonies. The merchant was always ready to explain not merely how harmful British taxes were to colonial economy, but how irksome were the new administrative rules and regulations. Such chronological and geographical barriers as existed were overcome and a community of antagonisms was maintained by the Committees of Correspondence and other agitators, but such revolutionary forces could not have succeeded if the different elements of the colonies had not recently experienced a mutual sense of grievance.

In short, many of the misunderstandings which have arisen in connection with mercantilism and the American Revolution have grown out of the failure to distinguish between the two phases of mercantilism: exploitation and regulation. The fact that the colonists were exploited by English mercantilism does not necessarily mean that mercantilism caused the American Revolution. Economic forces are not magnets which inexorably move men in predetermined patterns. For better or for worse, men try to regulate their economic as well as their political destiny. A large part of governmental activity consists in attempting to mould economic conduct and to minimize the friction which results from clashes or constraints. English mercantilism was such an attempt. It succeeded rather well in minimizing friction until 1764. For the next decade it bungled badly, and the penalty was the loss of the Thirteen Colonies.

FOR FURTHER READING: A favorable appraisal of British mercantile policy is in G. L. Beer, *British Colonial Policy, 1763–1785* (New York, 1907). Critical views include Lawrence H. Gipson, *The Coming of the American Revolution* (New York, 1954), Edmund S. and Helen Morgan, *The Stamp Act Crisis: Prologue to Revolution* (Chapel Hill, 1953), J. Franklin Jameson, *The American Revolution Considered as a Social Movement* (Princeton, 1926), and Louis M. Hacker, *The Triumph of American Capitalism* (New York, 1940).

7. *The Confederation*

PROBLEM: *Was the post-revolutionary decade critical for the American economy?*

One of the persistent controversies in American history has revolved over interpretation of the Confederation period. Was the post-war depression (1783–1787) a truly critical phase in the development of the American Economy? Or was it merely a temporary post-war dislocation such as the United States has experienced after every conflict? John Fiske, one of the widely read popular writers of the late nineteenth century first popularized the view that this era was one of the most critical in the American experience. Fiske emphasized the political weaknesses of the Confederation government, such as the absence of national executive or judicial power, which created confusion in trade, business, and finance. This interpretation, however, has been challenged increasingly during the last two decades. Led by Professor Merrill Jensen of the University of Wisconsin, the newer generation of historians tends to emphasize the positive, rather than the negative economic conditions of the era. Viewing it as a period of post-war readjustment, Jensen points to the slow growth of foreign trade, the increase of manufactures, the payment of national and state debts, and gradual stabilization of the currency. Both writers provide persuasive arguments for their point of view and raise questions about the period. Which economic problems of the Confederation era seemed critical? What economic achievements were made during this period? Do the failures of the Confederation government's economic policies outweigh its accomplishments?

108

The Critical Period

JOHN FISKE

... But for the Navigation Act and the orders in council, it was said, all ships would by and by come to be built in America, and every time a frigate was wanted for the navy the Lords of Admiralty would have to send over to Boston or Philadelphia and order one. Rather than do such a thing as this, it was thought that the British navy should content itself with vessels of inferior workmanship and higher cost, built in British dock-yards. Thirty years after, England gathered an unexpected fruit of this narrow policy, when, to her intense bewilderment, she saw frigate after frigate outsailed and defeated in single combat with American antagonists. Owing to her exclusive measures, the rapid improvement in American shipbuilding had gone on quite beyond her ken, until she was thus rudely awakened to it. With similar short-sighted jealousy, it was argued that the American share in the whale-fishery and in the New-foundland fishery should be curtailed as much as possible. Spermaceti oil was much needed in England: complaints were rife of robbery and murder in the dimly lighted streets of London and other great cities. But it was thought that if American ships could carry oil to England and salt fish to Jamaica, the supply of seamen for the British navy would be diminished; and accordingly such privileges must not be granted the Americans unless valuable privileges could be granted in return. But the government of the United States could grant no privileges because it could impose no restrictions. British-manufactured goods were needed in America, and Congress, which could levy no duties, had no power to keep them out. British merchants and manufacturers, it was argued, already enjoyed all needful privileges in American ports, and accordingly they asked no favours and granted none.

Such were the arguments to which Adams was obliged to listen. The popular feeling was so strong that Pitt could not have stemmed it if he would. It was in vain that Adams threatened reprisals, and urged that the British measures would defeat their own purpose. "The end of the Navigation Act," said he, "as expressed in its own preamble, is to confine the commerce of the colonies to the mother country; but now we are become independent states, instead of confining our trade to Great Britain, it will drive it to other countries"; and he suggested that the Americans might make a navigation act in their turn, admitting to American ports none but American-built ships, owned and commanded by Americans. But under the articles of confederation such a threat was idle, and the

Reprinted from John Fiske, *The Critical Period* (Boston: Houghton Mifflin Company, 1888), pp. 189–205.

British government knew it to be so. Thirteen separate state governments could never be made to adopt any such measure in concert. The weakness of Congress had been fatally revealed in its inability to protect the loyalists or to enforce the payment of debts, and in its failure to raise a revenue for meeting its current expenses. A government thus slighted at home was naturally despised abroad. Great Britain neglected to send a minister to Philadelphia, and while Adams was treated politely, his arguments were unheeded. Whether in this behaviour Pitt's government was influenced or not by political as well as economical reasons, it was certain that a political purpose was entertained by the king and approved by many people. There was an intention of humiliating the Americans, and it was commonly said that under a sufficient weight of commercial distress the states would break up their feeble union and come straggling back, one after another, to their old allegiance. The fiery spirit of Adams could ill brook this contemptuous treatment of the nation which he represented. Though he favoured very liberal commercial relations with the whole world, he could see no escape from the present difficulties save in systematic retaliation. "I should be sorry," he said, "to adopt a monopoly, but, driven to the necessity of it, I would not do things by halves. . . . If monopolies and exclusions are the only arms of defence against monopolies and exclusions, I would venture upon them without fear of offending Dean Tucker or the ghost of Dr. Quesnay." That is to say, certain commercial privileges must be withheld from Great Britain, in order to be offered to her in return for reciprocal privileges. It was a miserable policy to be forced to adopt, for such restrictions upon trade inevitably cut both ways. Like the non-importation agreement of 1768 and the embargo of 1808, such a policy was open to the objections familiarly urged against biting off one's own nose. It was injuring one's self in the hope of injuring somebody else. It was perpetuating in time of peace the obstacles to commerce generated by a state of war. In a certain sense, it was keeping up a warfare by commercial instead of military methods, and there was danger that it might lead to a renewal of armed conflict. Nevertheless, the conduct of the British government seemed to Adams to leave no other course open. But such "means of preserving ourselves," he said, "can never be secured until Congress shall be made supreme in foreign commerce."

It was obvious enough that the separate action of the states upon such a question was only adding to the general uncertainty and confusion. In 1785 New York laid a double duty on all goods whatever imported in British ships. In the same year Pennsylvania passed the first of the infamous series of American tariff acts, designed to tax the whole community for the benefit of a few greedy manufacturers. Massachusetts sought to establish committees of correspondence for the purpose of entering into a new non-importation agreement, and its legislature resolved that "the present powers of the Congress of the United States, as contained in the articles of confederation, are not fully adequate to the great purposes they were originally designed to effect." The Massachusetts delegates in Congress—Gerry, Holton, and King—were instructed to recommend a general convention of the states for the purpose of revising and amending the articles of confederation; but the delegates refused to comply with their instructions, and set forth their reasons in a paper which was approved by Samuel Adams, and caused the legislature to reconsider its actions. It was feared that a call for a convention might seem too much like an open expression of a want of confidence in Congress, and might thereby weaken it still further without accomplishing any good result. For the present, as a temporary expedient, Massachusetts took counsel with New Hampshire, and the two states passed navigation acts, prohibiting British ships from carrying goods out of their harbours, and imposing a fourfold duty upon all such goods as they should bring in. A discriminating tonnage duty was also laid upon all foreign vessels. Rhode Island soon after adopted similar measures. In Congress a scheme for a uniform navigation act, to be concurred in and passed by all the thirteen states, was suggested by one of the Maryland delegates; but it was opposed by Richard Henry Lee and most of the delegates from the far South. The southern states, having no ships or seamen of their own, feared that the exclusion of British competition might enable northern ship-owners to charge exorbitant rates for carrying their rice and tobacco, thus subjecting them to a ruinous monopoly; but the gallant Moultrie, then governor of South Carolina, taking a broader view of the case, wrote to Bowdoin, governor of Massachusetts, asserting the paramount need of harmonious and united action. In the Virginia assembly, a hot-headed member, Rev. Charles Thruston, known as "the warrior parson," declared himself in doubt "whether it would not be better to encourage the British rather than the eastern marine;" but the remark was greeted with hisses and groans. Amid such mutual jealousies and misgivings, during the year 1785 acts were passed by ten states granting to Congress the power of regulating commerce for the ensuing thirteen years. The three states which refrained from acting were Georgia, South Carolina, and Delaware. The acts of the other ten were, as might have been expected, a jumble of incongruities. North Carolina granted all the power that was asked, but stipulated that when all the states should have done likewise their acts should be summed up in a new article of confederation. Connecticut, Pennsylvania, and Maryland had fixed the date at which the grant was to take effect, while Rhode Island provided that it should not expire until after the lapse of twenty-five years. The grant by New Hampshire allowed the power to be used only in one specified way, —by restricting the duties imposable by the several states. The grants of Massachusetts, New York, New Jersey, and Virginia were not to take effect until all the others should go into operation. The only thing which

Congress could do with these acts was to refer them back to the several legislatures, with a polite request to try to reduce them to something like uniformity.

Meanwhile, the different states, with their different tariff and tonnage acts, began to make commercial war upon one another. No sooner had the other three New England states virtually closed their ports to British shipping than Connecticut threw hers wide open, an act which she followed up by laying duties upon imports from Massachusetts. Pennsylvania discriminated against Delaware, and New Jersey, pillaged at once by both her greater neighbours, was compared to a cask tapped at both ends. The conduct of New York became especially selfish and blameworthy. That rapid growth which was so soon to carry the city and the state to a position of primacy in the Union had already begun. After the departure of the British the revival of business went on with leaps and bounds. The feeling of local patriotism waxed strong, and in no one was it more fully manifested than in George Clinton, the Revolutionary general, whom the people elected governor for six successive terms. He was a kinsman of Sir Henry Clinton, the British general; both were descended from Earls of Lincoln. By dint of shrewdness and untiring push, George Clinton had come to be for the moment the most powerful man in the state of New York. He had come to look upon the state almost as if it were his own private manor, and his life was devoted to furthering its interests as he understood them. It was his first article of faith that New York must be the greatest state in the Union. But his conceptions of statesmanship were extremely narrow. In his mind, the welfare of New York meant the pulling down and thrusting aside of all her neighbours and rivals. He was the vigorous and steadfast advocate of every illiberal and exclusive measure, and the most uncompromising enemy to a closer union of the states. His great popular strength and the commercial importance of the community in which he held sway made him at this time the most dangerous man in America. The political victories presently to be won by Hamilton, Schuyler, and Livingston, without which our grand and pacific Federal Union could not have been brought into being, were victories won by most desperate fighting against the dogged opposition of Clinton. Under his guidance, the history of New York, during the five years following the peace of 1783, was a shameful story of greedy monopoly and sectional hate. Of all the thirteen states, none behaved worse except Rhode Island.

A single instance, which occurred early in 1787, may serve as an illustration. The city of New York, with its population of 30,000 souls, had long been supplied with firewood from Connecticut, and with its butter and cheese, chickens and garden vegetables, from the thrifty farms of New Jersey. This trade, it was observed, carried thousands of dollars out of the city and into the pockets of detested Yankees and despised Jerseymen. It was ruinous to domestic industry, said the men of New York. It must be stopped by those effective remedies of the Sangrado school of economic doctors, a navigation act and a protective tariff. Acts were accordingly passed, obliging every Yankee sloop which came down through Hell Gate, and every Jersey market boat which was rowed across from Paulus Hook to Cortlandt Street, to pay entrance fees and obtain clearances at the customhouse, just as was done by ships from London or Hamburg; and not a cart-load of Connecticut firewood could be delivered at the back-door of a country-house in Beekman Street until it should have paid a heavy duty. Great and just was the wrath of the farmers and lumbermen. The New Jersey legislature made up its mind to retaliate. The city of New York had lately bought a small patch of ground on Sandy Hook, and had built a lighthouse there. This lighthouse was the one weak spot in the heel of Achilles where a hostile arrow could strike, and New Jersey gave vent to her indignation by laying a tax of $1,800 a year on it. Connecticut was equally prompt. At a great meeting of business men, held at New London, it was unanimously agreed to suspend all commercial intercourse with New York. Every merchant signed an agreement, under penalty of $250 for the first offence, not to send any goods whatever into the hated state for a period of twelve months. By such retaliatory measures, it was hoped that New York might be compelled to rescind her odious enactment. But such meetings and such resolves bore an ominous likeness to the meetings and resolves which in the years before 1775 had heralded a state of war; and but for the good work done by the federal convention another five years would scarcely have elapsed before shots would have been fired and seeds of perennial hatred sown on the shores that look toward Manhattan Island. . . .

By 1786, under the universal depression and want of confidence, all trade had well-nigh stopped, and political quackery, with its cheap and dirty remedies, had full control of the field. In the very face of miseries so plainly traceable to the deadly paper currency, it may seem strange that people should now have begun to clamour for a renewal of the experiment which had worked so much evil. Yet so it was. As starving men are said to dream of dainty banquets, so now a craze for fictitious wealth in the shape of paper money ran like an epidemic through the country. There was a Barmecide feast of economic vagaries; only now it was the several states that sought to apply the remedy, each in its own way. And when we have threaded the maze of this rash legislation, we shall the better understand that clause in our federal constitution which forbids the making of laws impairing the obligation of contracts. The events of 1786 impressed upon men's minds more forcibly than ever the wretched and disorderly condition of the country, and went far toward calling into existence the needful popular sentiment in favour of an overruling central government.

The disorders assumed very different forms in the different states, and brought out a great diversity of opinion as to the causes of the distress and the efficacy of the proposed remedies. Only two states out of the thirteen—Connecticut and Delaware—escaped the infection, but, on the other hand, it was only in seven states that the paper money party prevailed in the legislatures. North Carolina issued a large amount of paper, and, in order to get it into circulation as quickly as possible, the state government proceeded to buy tobacco with it, paying double the specie value of the tobacco. As a natural consequence, the paper dollar instantly fell to seventy cents, and went on declining. In South Carolina an issue was tried somewhat more cautiously, but the planters soon refused to take the paper at its face value. Coercive measures were then attempted. Planters and merchants were urged to sign a pledge not to discriminate between paper and gold, and if any one dared refuse the fanatics forthwith attempted to make it hot for him. A kind of "Kuklux" society was organized at Charleston, known as the "Hint Club." Its purpose was to hint to such people that they had better look out. If they did not mend their ways, it was unnecessary to inform them more explicitly what they might expect. Houses were combustible then as now, and the use of firearms was well understood. In Georgia the legislature itself attempted coercion. Paper money was made a legal tender in spite of strong opposition, and a law was passed prohibiting any planter or merchant from exporting any produce without taking affidavit that he had never refused to receive this scrip at its full face value. But somehow people found that the more it was sought to keep up the paper by dint of threats and forcing acts, the faster its value fell. Virginia had issued bills of credit during the campaign of 1781, but it was enacted at the same time that they should not be a legal tender after the next January. The influence of Washington, Madison, and Mason was effectively brought to bear in favour of sound currency, and the people of Virginia were but slightly affected by the craze of 1786. In the autumn of that year a proposition from two counties for an issue of paper was defeated in the legislature by a vote of eighty-five to seventeen, and no more was heard of the matter. In Maryland, after a very obstinate fight, a rag money bill was carried in the house of representatives, but the senate threw it out; and the measure was thus postponed until the discussion over the federal constitution superseded it in popular interest. Pennsylvania had warily begun in May, 1785, to issue a million dollars in bills of credit, which were not made a legal tender for the payment of private debts. They were mainly loaned to farmers on mortgage, and were received by the state as an equivalent for specie in the payment of taxes. By August, 1786, even this carefully guarded paper had fallen some twelve cents below par,—not a bad showing for such a year as that. New York moved somewhat less cautiously. A million dollars were issued in bills of credit receivable for the custom-house duties, which were then paid into the state treasury; and these bills were made a legal tender for all money received in lawsuits. At the same time the New Jersey legislature passed a bill for issuing half a million paper dollars, to be a legal tender in all business transactions. The bill was vetoed by the governor in council. The aged Governor Livingston was greatly respected by the people; and so the mob at Elizabethtown, which had duly planted a stake and dragged his effigy up to it, refrained from inflicting the last indignities upon the image, and burned that of one of the members of the council instead. At the next session the governor yielded, and the rag money was issued. But an unforeseen difficulty arose. Most of the dealings of New Jersey people were in the cities of New York and Philadelphia, and in both cities the merchants refused their paper, so that it speedily became worthless.

The business of exchange was thus fast getting into hopeless confusion. It has been said of Bradshaw's Railway Guide, the indispensable companion of the traveller in England, that no man can study it for an hour without qualifying himself for a lunatic asylum. But Bradshaw is pellucid clearness compared with the American tables of exchange in 1786, with their medley of dollars and shillings, moidores, and pistareens. The addition of half a dozen different kinds of paper created such a labyrinth as no human intellect could explore. No wonder that men were counted wise who preferred to take whiskey and pork instead. Nobody who had a yard of cloth to sell could tell how much it was worth. But even worse than all this was the swift and certain renewal of bankruptcy which so many states were preparing for themselves. . . .

The Roots of Recovery:
Growth of Business Enterprise

MERRILL JENSEN

As Americans reopened old trade routes and found new ones after the Revolution, they also developed new opportunities within the United States. They turned to manufacturing as they had never done before, and they began founding banks that were to be relatively permanent. There had been repeated demands for the development of manufacturing during the colonial period. Colonial legislatures from time to time had aided local manufactures by gifts of land and freedom from taxation. But manu-

Reprinted from *The New Nation* by Merrill Jensen, pp. 219–234, 375–399, by permission of Alfred A. Knopf, Inc. Copyright 1950 by Alfred A. Knopf, Inc.

facturing developed slowly, for it was an agricultural society in which labor was high, land was cheap, and ordinarily goods could be brought from England more cheaply than they could be made in the colonies. When successful colonial manufactures did develop, such as beaver hats, finished iron, and woolens, Britain attempted to check them. Some times, as in the case of naval stores, she gave bounties for the development of colonial products needed in England. But in general, the manufactures of the colonies were local in importance and domestic in character: boots, shoes, cloth, nails, and the like, and they were produced in homes and small shops.

The Revolution freed American artisans in many ways. It did away with British restrictions; the war itself acted as a protective tariff; the need for army clothing aided cloth manufactures; the need for powder and guns focused attention of American governments and artisans on that business and helped to expand the development of iron manufactures. The release from old restraints and opportunities born of war turned more and more men to manufacturing. Such a man was Benjamin Gale who declared that he had always been anxious to promote manufactures, and that since the break with Great Britain he was convinced that the only way to win real independence was to develop them. He and his two sons-in-law had erected a furnace for casting hollow ware. They contracted with the United States for sixty tons of shot and shell and were now running the second blast. During the summer of 1780 he erected a pottery factory and hoped to get someone from France who could help him produce "French Delph ware." Barnabas Deane, Jeremiah Wadsworth, and General Nathanael Greene organized a company which dealt in many kinds of business, including the manufacture of rum, salt, and the operation of gristmills.

New industries did not collapse with the end of the war. The flood of imported manufactured goods after the war was slowed up when merchant credit ran short. Thus the commercial panic was probably a boon for local industries. By the time commercial recovery was at hand, the artisan manufacturers in New England and Pennsylvania had gotten protective tariffs which helped them meet the competition of foreign manufactures.

Contemporary sources illustrate the success of the new nation in widening its economic base. In January 1783, John Biddis of Philadelphia was offering white lead "allowed by the best judges in this city to be equal in quality to any imported from Europe." In addition, he offered colors ground in oil, paint brushes, and other necessities for painters. By the end of 1785 Stephen Higginson reported that "to increase our manufactures has become the rage of the day." The farmers were busy making nails during the winter. Boots, shoes, wool cards, coarse woolens, and iron were also produced in Massachusetts and already "very considerable quantities of some of these articles" were being exported to the southern states. But as a merchant, he could not but view with alarm too great an attention to manufactures, for to attempt to produce all a country might need within itself "would be in effect to attempt the destruction of all commerce. . . ." The fears he thus expressed were a reality, not for his, but for a future generation of New England merchants. Such fears could not dampen the new interest in national self-sufficiency. The *Massachusetts Centinel* reported that a factory in New Hampshire was making buttons, thread, and cloth. It declared that the benefits for the United States in the encouragement of local manufactures was obvious and that no one with "one spark of patriotism" should withhold it. In New Haven, Connecticut, a local paper declared "with pleasure and a degree of blameless pride" that over 160,000 silkworms had been raised in New Haven during the season. This was in response to reports in Pennsylvania papers of a family which owned 2,000 silkworms. Such reports are more proof of American persistence than anything else, for Americans had been trying to raise silkworms since early in the seventeenth century. Far more important was the manufacture of nails and this, too, the papers reported with pride. The *Pennsylvania Gazette* and the *New Haven Gazette* within a few days of one another printed an identical report from Providence, Rhode Island. The report declared that "the establishing of manufactories in our young country is a matter of the greatest consequence. . . ." In the east parish of the town of Bridgewater, there was made one morning before nine o'clock, when the workmen usually went to breakfast, "61,500 good tenpenny nails—may success attend industry!" Later in the same year it was stated that the manufacture of nails in Pennsylvania alone would save the country £100,000 sterling annually. The *Pennsylvania Gazette* reported that wool was in greater demand than "was ever known" and that all kinds of woolen and linen manufacturing were going on with great spirit.

The actual production of nails, woolen goods, spinning wheel irons, and the like was more than matched by all sorts of schemes that for the moment did not pan out. During 1784 Samuel Wetherill set forth in Pennsylvania newspapers a prospectus for the creation of a cotton manufacturing establishment. Wetherill had interviewed one Roger Fursdon, who had previously advertised for capital. Fursdon can do what he claims, said Wetherill. All that is needed is yarn. Then, if investors can be found, a building fifty by one hundred feet and five stories high will be built on a constant stream of water. It will house 16,000 spindles. The whole can be built for about £9,000 if they begin with one third of the spindles. To this should be added £11,000 to carry on the business. To run such a plant would take ten men—overseers, mechanics, and clerks, whose wages would average twelve shillings a day apiece. For labor they would need 83 women whose wages would average 3s. 6d. per day, and 134 children from eight to ten years of age whose wages would average 2s. 6d. per day. With such a labor force they could spin a thousand pounds of yarn a day. The "neat profit" could be estimated at £162 14s. 6d. per day or £48,000 a year.

James Wilson, who had come from Scotland and who was to become a justice of the United States Supreme Court, and who died as such while fleeing from sheriffs who wanted to jail him for debts, was equally optimistic during the 1780's. To prospective Dutch investors he described the rolling and slitting mills which he said he and his brother-in-law, Mark Burd, were building on the Delaware near Philadelphia. The names of Robert Morris and Peter John Van Berckel, minister from the States-General of the United Netherlands, were given as references. Wilson claimed that he and his brother-in-law had large fortunes [in land] but that money could not be borrowed in America at the moment. As security he asserted that he had real estate worth 750,000 florins on which he wished to borrow but 500,000 florins.

The interest, the schemes, the hope of the future, and aid by state governments after the Revolution, combined to bring about a rapid expansion of American manufacturing. Within ten years after the Revolution, Brandywine Creek had about sixty mills along the seven or eight miles of its course through Delaware. Household production of cloth was such that the state of New Jersey had forty-one fulling-mills at a time when there were no manufactories of cloth in the state. A few years after the Revolution a shop in Philadelphia sold fifteen hundred sets of spinning wheel irons in a single year. Manufacturing spread rapidly to the frontier. By 1790 the people of Kentucky were producing a greater variety of things than the people of New York had done in 1765. By 1790 American paper mills, developed to supply the rapid increase of newspapers and magazines, were supplying most of the American market. Glass making was firmly established as an American industry. In fact, so substantial was the general increase that Pennsylvania alone was reported to be taking the place of Great Britain in supplying the need for manufactured goods in the southern states.

Tench Coxe of Philadelphia summarized the growth of American manufactures in a speech to a group of men who met in Philadelphia in August 1787. The group had met for the purpose of forming a society for the encouragement of manufactures and the "useful arts." Coxe declared that despite the disadvantages "it must afford the most comfortable reflection to every patriotic mind, to observe their progress in the United States, and particularly in Pennsylvania." For a long time the forefathers' needs were supplied by the work of European hands. "How great—how happy is the change! The list of articles we now make ourselves, if particularly enumerated, would fatigue the ear, and waste your valuable time. Permit me, however, to mention them under their general heads: meal of all kinds, ships and boats, malt liquors, distilled spirits, potash, gun-powder, cordage, loaf-sugar, pasteboard, cards and paper of every kind, books in various languages, snuff, tobacco, starch, cannon, muskets, anchors, nails, and very many other articles of iron, bricks, tiles, potters ware, millstones, and other stone work, cabinet work, trunks and windsor chairs, carriages and harness of all kinds, corn-fans, ploughs and many other implements of husbandry, saddlery and whips, shoes and boots, leather of various kinds, hosiery, hats and gloves, wearing apparel, coarse linens and woolens, and some cotton goods, linseed and fish oil, wares of gold, silver, tin, pewter, lead, brass and copper, clocks and watches, wool and cotton cards, printing types, glass and stoneware, candles, soap, and several other valuable articles, with which the memory cannot furnish us at once. . . ."

THE BALANCE SHEET OF THE CONFEDERATION

Perhaps no clear balance sheet of the Confederation can be created, but the records of the treasury, which have hitherto never been used by men who have written about the finances of the Revolution, offer enough evidence to show that the traditional stories are half truths at best. The achievement of the Confederation government in settling accounts is a partial demonstration of this. The government did not solve all the problems that faced it, but it can be asked, what other government before or since ever did either?

The biggest task of the Confederation government was the liquidation of the national debt. The total war debt of the Revolution was an enormous sum in terms of the paper used, but the vast bulk of it had been cancelled by the end of the war. Perhaps $400,000,000 in paper money, quartermaster, and commissary certificates of the central government, and equally great sums that had been issued by the states, had been wiped out by the middle of 1783. The remaining war debt was small by comparison, although its political significance was enormous.

In the spring of 1783 Congress estimated the remaining domestic debt of the United States at about $34,000,000. This estimate included the loan office debt, the army debt, arrears in interest, and an uncertain amount of unliquidated debt in various forms of certificates scattered throughout the country. The reduction of this estimate to precise figures was the task of the board of treasury and the various commissioners appointed to "liquidate" the accounts of the United States during the 1780's. As the work continued, the treasury reported its progress to Congress. By the end of 1785, $14,578,009 had been liquidated. By the end of 1787, the task was essentially complete. The liquidated loan office debt was

$11,412,285. The certificates issued the army and still in circulation came to $8,932,293. Commissioners settling accounts between the states and the United States had issued $3,614,011. The commissioners settling the accounts of the army departments had issued $817,330. An item of $2,680,429 represented credits on the funding books of the treasury for settled accounts and cancelled certificates issued by commissioners and loan officers. Miscellaneous items brought the total of the liquidated debt to $27,995,242.

Hamilton's first report on the public credit in 1790 is ample evidence of the success of the Confederation in liquidating the debt. His figure for the liquidated domestic debt of the United States was $27,383,917.

In May 1788 the foreign debt of the United States was estimated at $10,271,561. This included money borrowed from the French and Spanish governments, the Farmers General of France, and the bankers of Holland. The foreign debt grew rapidly during the Confederation. French loans were stopped at the end of the war but Dutch bankers began making loans in 1782. Between then and 1789 they loaned the United States $3,600,000. As in the case of the domestic debt, Hamilton was in substantial agreement with Nourse as to the foreign debt. He estimated it to be $10,070,307 in 1790, a smaller figure than Nourse's, but he added to it arrears in interest which he calculated at $1,640,071.

The money borrowed during the Confederation was spent carefully, with the result that excellent credit was maintained in Holland. In the four years from 1784 through 1787, $583,062 was paid in interest, $127,598 was used to pay the expenses of American ministers, $172,087 was spent in the payment of old accounts, and $136,737 was paid in premiums on the loans made. In addition $319,242 was paid by Ferdinand Grand and the American ministers for bills of exchange drawn by Robert Morris and the board of treasury. The failure of a Dutch banking house in which the United States had deposited money accounted for $43,110. The total cash spent was $1,381,836 by the end of 1787.

The United States thus maintained a handsome cash balance on deposit with Dutch and French bankers throughout the Confederation. This was the result of the policy of the board of treasury, of John Adams, and of the cautious Dutch bankers who not only lent money to the government, but who bought up increasing amounts of the domestic debt of the United States during the 1780's. Interest on the Dutch loans was paid regularly. The only interest defaulted was that on a French loan which came due in 1786, whereupon the French government assumed the payments on it until 1790. The faith of the Dutch bankers in the future of the United States was shown in offers to buy the entire debt of the United States to France.

In this they soon found competition from various American speculators and European bankers. It seemed to all the interested parties that the hard-pressed French government might be induced to sell the American debt at a healthy discount, and all of them believed that the United States was a land of opportunity. Interest grew more avid as the Constitution of 1787 was sent to the states for adoption, but it was the unsettled land of the United States that seemed the best justification for speculation in American debt. American land might not always be at the center, but it was always in the near periphery, of even the most cautious banker's hopeful thoughts of the future in the eighteenth century.

When an international combine of French and English bankers and speculators sent Brissot de Warville to America in 1787, one of them told him that the Americans would adopt the new constitution and that thereafter every eye ought to look to America "as being the unfailing road to prosperity" and that Europeans would buy land there. "I know of no period when the spirit of speculation has been so general as at the present," he wrote, "no period which presents a revolution like that of independent America; and no foundation so solid as that which they are about to establish."

When de Warville got to America in 1788 he met Andrew Craigie and William Duer, secretary of the board of treasury. An agreement was soon worked out between de Warville acting for Etienne Claviére, a Swiss banker who had moved to France, and Craigie and Duer. They proposed to buy up the United States debt to France and as much of the domestic debt as they could manage. In addition they hoped to get control of all the loans to be made by the United States. Duer and de Warville were given large shares, in the hope of preventing them from dealing with Robert and Gouverneur Morris, who had similar notions. Duer had as a secret partner Samuel Osgood of the board of treasury, who had indeed traveled far since the days when he had denounced the speculations of Robert Morris.

Duer was not a man to limit his opportunities by loyalty to agreements or partners. Soon he was in touch with Robert Morris and Jeremiah Wadsworth. Then, after Duer "conceived" that Mrs. Henry Knox "had been assailed on the subject," the secretary of war became interested. All these men were aware that the Dutch bankers had the inside track in American finances and that they had offered to buy the debt in 1786. They decided that if the proper man could be sent as minister to Holland, it might help in the competition for the purchase of the American debt to France. Some of them thought that Gouverneur Morris would be the right man, but Knox and Wadsworth suggested Rufus King. Duer therefore approached King. King was coy but interested and said that he was not indisposed to a foreign appointment, and that "if in perfect consistence with the duties and dignity of the office, I could promote the interest of my friends it would be a great satisfaction to me."

The plans of this group of hopeful speculators were frustrated, partly by their own duplicity toward one another, and partly because the Dutch bankers had laid their grounds well through the purchase of large sums of the domestic debt and through loans to the government of the United States. Eventually they did buy the French debt, and they remained the chief bankers of the United States after 1789 as they had been before. The foreign debt of the United States was thus a matter of lively interest to contemporaries, who had much more faith in its ultimate payment than most of the people who have written about it since that time. Interest mounted after the Convention of 1787, but Europe's most cautious bankers had shown their confidence in the United States before anyone knew there would be such a convention.

The domestic debt was a subject of similar interest, although it sold on the market at far less than its face value. The market value was low because the government was able to pay only part of the interest and that part in indents rather than in cash. Furthermore, as it passed from hand to hand and was consolidated in the hands of relatively few men, there was a persistent demand in the states that when the debt was paid, its holders should be paid what they had given for it and not its face value. That was the practice in the payment of some of the state debts during the 1780's and perhaps only the wildest visionaries among the speculators hoped for what Hamilton gave them after 1789. Despite this the debt was a subject of ever-increasing interest. The states began buying it up against the day of final settlement between them and the central government; the Dutch bankers began buying it; and western lands were opened for sale and could be bought with debt certificates. All these things started the market upwards, and after the Convention of 1787 the boom was on.

Meanwhile the Confederation was not a government staggering along without an income, as is so often assumed. The treasury records for the 1780's are full and often confusing, but at the same time illuminating. During the administration of Robert Morris the total receipts of the treasury, from taxes, loans, financial operations, and the like, were $8,177,431. Expenses dropped drastically at the end of the war; and so did income. The treasury records, however, show that the central government continued to have a yearly, if fluctuating, income throughout the Confederation. The receipts of the treasury were the following: 1785, $632,389; 1786, $478,491; 1787, $799,556; 1788, $1,557,179; 1789, $422,897. The money taken in consisted of specie and indents collected by loan office commissioners in the states, sales of bills of exchange, collections from debtors of the government, and treasury warrants issued for salaries and expenses in advance of collections.

The largest share of income came from the states. Between 1 November

1784 and 12 September 1789, the loan office commissioners received $1,488,000 in specie and $2,235,000 in indents, a total of $3,723,000, from the state governments. Of this amount over three quarters of a million dollars in specie and indents was still in the hands of the loan officers at the end of the Confederation. The treasury, however, took in over a million dollars more than it received from the loan officers. A large part of this sum came from bills of exchange drawn against balances in European banks. The bulk of the remainder came from the settlement of old accounts.

Of course the government did not get as much money as it needed. Its biggest problem was the payment of interest on the national debt. The treasury managed to pay most of the interest on the foreign debt, chiefly by means of loans from Dutch bankers. The use of indents to pay interest on the domestic debt was a novel device whose effectiveness was defeated largely because of the concentration of the national debt in the North in the hands of a relatively few men. The big holders of the national debt got far more indents than they could use to pay state taxes; hence their market value declined. If the debt had been widely held among the people the indents would have served a useful purpose as a circulating medium and carried the debt until the sale of western lands got under way.

However, the rough balance sheet of the Confederation does show certain positive things. It shows that the new nation had a cash income from the states; that it had sound credit with Dutch bankers; that it paid most of the interest on the foreign debt and part of the interest on the domestic debt; and finally, that it had arrived at a position where it could begin to pay the principal as well as the interest on the domestic debt through the sale of western lands. It was "deficit financing," of course, but it can be argued that the Confederation perhaps came as close to making means match needs as many a twentieth century government has been able to do. These have kept going by enormous increases in national debts, whereas the Confederation actually managed to reduce the principal of its debt. Its methods were not "sound" finance by modern standards, but we have yet to see how "sound" the national debts of the twentieth century will be.

The lack of an independent income was the great political as well as the great economic weakness of the Confederation government. This lack, perhaps more than any other single fact, brought about its downfall. If the government had been able to acquire an income of its own, the strongest argument against it would have been shattered. Even so the problem of the national debt was being solved in a different fashion. One state after another during the Confederation assumed the national debt owned by its citizens. This process was the result of the joint pressure of public creditors who demanded better returns on their holdings, and of politicians who feared that national payment of the debt would mean a powerful central government.

FOR FURTHER READING: A good, general recent survey is Edmund S. Morgan, *The Birth of the Republic, 1763–1789* (Chicago, 1956). Emphasis on discontent during the period is placed by Allan Nevins in *The American States During and After the Revolution* (New York, 1924), Robert J. Taylor, *Western Massachusetts in the Revolution* (Providence, 1954), and E. W. Spaulding, *New York in the Critical Period, 1783–1789* (New York, 1932). A more optimistic approach is by Jackson T. Main, *The Anti-Federalist, Critics of the Constitution, 1781–1788* (Chapel Hill, 1961).

8. *Economic Growth and the Constitution*

PROBLEM: *Was the Constitution framed mainly to protect moneyed interests?*

Perhaps one of the most famous and most widely read works of American History ever published was Charles A. Beard's *An Economic Interpretation of the Constitution of the United States*. Half a century after its first appearance (1913) historians still debate many of the questions which it raised. Breaking new ground, and diverging from the political approach of previous students of the Constitutional Convention, Beard raised the issue: "Were members of the Constitutional Convention motivated primarily by economic considerations?" Beard himself strongly implied the affirmative. Four groups of men, he wrote, concerned mainly with the protection of their private property had prime influence in the drafting of the Constitution. They represented owners of personal property, real estate, slaves, and government securities. Since three-fourths of all eligible voters in 1787 were disfranchised by property qualifications, and never had an opportunity to express their opposition to the Constitution at the ballot box, these interests were also able to secure its adoption by ratifying conventions. This provocative interpretation has called forth hundreds of rebuttals. Towering above many is Forrest MacDonald's *We, the People*. Following Beard's suggestion that his own hypotheses be further tested, McDonald challenged Beard's underlying premise that mere possession of property was evidence of a desire to protect personal interests. In fact, he concluded that the evidence does not show property interests to have had a decisive voice either in the Philadelphia convention or in the ratifying bodies. Both of these writers raise important queries. Have political institutions in America been established mainly to protect private property? What interest groups were protected by the Constitution? How did the Constitution affect the national economy?

An Economic Interpretation of the Constitution

CHARLES A. BEARD

THE ECONOMIC INTERESTS OF THE MEMBERS
OF THE CONVENTION

A survey of the economic interests of the members of the Convention presents certain conclusions:

A majority of the members were lawyers by profession.

Most of the members came from towns, on or near the coast, that is, from the regions in which personalty was largely concentrated.

Not one member represented in his immediate personal economic interests the small farming or mechanic classes.

The overwhelming majority of members, at least five-sixths, were immediately, directly, and personally interested in the outcome of their labors at Philadelphia, and were to a greater or less extent economic beneficiaries from the adoption of the Constitution.

1. Public security interests were extensively represented in the Convention. Of the fifty-five members who attended no less than forty appear on the Records of the Treasury Department for sums varying from a few dollars up to more than one hundred thousand dollars. Among the minor holders were Bassett, Blount, Brearley, Broom, Butler, Carroll, Few, Hamilton, L. Martin, Mason, Mercer, Mifflin, Read, Spaight, Wilson, and Wythe. Among the larger holders (taking the sum of about $5000 as the criterion) were Baldwin, Blair, Clymer, Dayton, Ellsworth, Fitzsimons, Gilman, Gerry, Gorham, Jenifer, Johnson, King, Langdon, Lansing, Livingston, McClurg, R. Morris, C. C. Pinckney, C. Pinckney, Randolph, Sherman, Strong, Washington, and Williamson.

It is interesting to note that, with the exception of New York, and possibly Delaware, each state had one or more prominent representatives in the Convention who held more than a negligible amount of securities, and who could therefore speak with feeling and authority on the question of providing in the new Constitution for the full discharge of the public debt:

Langdon and Gilman, of New Hampshire.

Gerry, Strong, and King, of Massachusetts.

Ellsworth, Sherman, and Johnson, of Connecticut.

Hamilton, of New York. Although he held no large amount personally, he was the special pleader for the holders of public securities and the maintenance of public faith.

Dayton, of New Jersey.

Robert Morris, Clymer, and Fitzsimons, of Pennsylvania.

Mercer and Carroll, of Maryland.

Blair, McClurg, and Randolph, of Virginia.

Williamson, of North Carolina.

The two Pinckneys, of South Carolina.

Few and Baldwin, of Georgia.

2. Personalty invested in lands for speculation was represented by at least fourteen members: Blount, Dayton, Few, Fitzsimons, Franklin, Gilman, Gerry, Gorham, Hamilton, Mason, R. Morris, Washington, Williamson, and Wilson.

3. Personalty in the form of money loaned at interest was represented by at least twenty-four members: Bassett, Broom, Butler, Carroll, Clymer, Davie, Dickinson, Ellsworth, Few, Fitzsimons, Franklin, Gilman, Ingersoll, Johnson, King, Langdon, Mason, McHenry, C. C. Pinckney, C. Pinckney, Randolph, Read, Washington, and Williamson.

4. Personalty in mercantile, manufacturing, and shipping lines was represented by at least eleven members: Broom, Clymer, Ellsworth, Fitzsimons, Gerry, King, Langdon, McHenry, Mifflin, G. Morris, and R. Morris.

5. Personalty in slaves was represented by at least fifteen members: Butler, Davie, Jenifer, A. Martin, L. Martin, Mason, Mercer, C. C. Pinckney, C. Pinckney, Randolph, Reed, Rutledge, Spaight, Washington, and Wythe.

It cannot be said, therefore, that the members of the Convention were "disinterested." On the contrary, we are forced to accept the profoundly significant conclusion that they knew through their personal experiences in economic affairs the precise results which the new government that they were setting up was designed to attain. As a group of doctrinaires, like the Frankfort assembly of 1848, they would have failed miserably; but as practical men they were able to build the new government upon the only foundations which could be stable: fundamental economic interests.

THE POLITICAL DOCTRINES OF THE MEMBERS
OF THE CONVENTION

It is now interesting to inquire whether the members of the Convention at large entertained substantially identical views as to the political science of the system. There are several difficulties in the way of such an investigation. Not all of the delegates, indeed not all of the most influential, were speech makers or writers or philosophers. As intensely practical men they were concerned with tangible results, not with the manner in which political scientists might view the details of their operations. There is, accordingly, a considerable danger of attempting too much in making generalizations, and to obviate this as far as possible, the method of taking the members in alphabetical order is adopted, and the evidence of the views entertained by each is fully documented.

The leaders in politics and political philosophy in the eighteenth century were not far removed from that frank recognition of class rights which characterized English society, and they were not under the necessity of obscuring—at least to the same extent as modern partisan writers —the essential economic antagonisms featuring in law and constitution making. Their clarity of thought was greatly facilitated by the disfranchisement of the propertyless, which made it unnecessary for political writers to address themselves to the proletariat and to explain dominant group interests in such a manner as to make them appear in the garb of "public policy."

There does not appear, of course, in the writings of American political scientists in the eighteenth century, that sharp recognition of class rights which characterizes the feudal legists, because within the propertied interests politically represented in the government, there were divisions which had to be glossed over; and there were also mutterings of unrest on the part of the disfranchised which later broke out in the storm that swept away the property qualifications on voters and introduced political equalitarianism. Under these circumstances the supporters of the Constitution had to be somewhat circumspect in the expression of their views; but, happily for science, the proceedings at Philadelphia during the drafting of the Constitution were secret, and they were able to discuss with utmost frankness the actual politico-economic results which they desired to reach. Fortunately, also, fragmentary reports of these proceedings have come down to us, and have been put in a definitive form by Professor Farrand.

Abraham Baldwin, of Georgia, did not indulge in any lengthy disquisitions on government in the Convention, and his literary remains are apparently very meagre. However, his view that the Senate of the United States ought to represent property came out in the debate on June 29, over a motion by Ellsworth to the effect that the "rule of suffrage in the second branch be the same as that established by the Articles of Confederation." Baldwin immediately opposed the proposition, saying, "He thought the second branch ought to be the representation of property, and that in forming it therefore some reference ought to be had to the relative wealth of their constituents, and to the principles on which the senate of Massachusetts was constituted." At the time the senate of that commonwealth rested upon special freehold and personalty qualifications, and the members were apportioned among the several districts on the basis of the amount of taxes paid by each. It is thus apparent that Baldwin wished the Senate of the new government to be based frankly upon property.

Gunning Bedford, of Delaware, did not participate extensively in the debates of the Convention, but it seems from the character of the few remarks that he made that he favored a more democratic form than was finally adopted, although he signed the Constitution. This inference is drawn from a brief notice of his objection to the establishment of a council of revision composed of the executive and a certain number of the judiciary to exercise a sort of censorship over the acts of Congress. Madison records as follows:

Mr. Bedford was opposed to every check on the Legislative, even the Council of Revision first proposed. He thought it would be sufficient to mark out in the Constitution the boundaries to the Legislative Authority, which would give all the requisite security to the rights of the other departments. The Representatives of the People were the best judges of what was for their interest, and ought to be under no external controul whatever. The two branches would produce a sufficient controul within the Legislature itself.

Jacob Broom was among those who wished to "lessen the dependence of the general government on the people," to use Jefferson's phrase, by lengthening the terms of public officers. He seconded Read's motion to increase the term of Senators to nine years; he opposed the election of the executive by popular vote, and supported Luther Martin's resolution in favor of election by electors appointed by the legislatures of the several states; he wished to give life tenure to the executive, that is, during good behavior, and he favored the suggestion that Congress should be given a negative over state legislatures. Broom seldom spoke in the Convention, but there is no doubt that he believed in a restricted and well "balanced" democracy.

Pierce Butler, of South Carolina, on more than one occasion urged the desirability of making property at least one of the elements in the distribution of representation. On June 6, when Charles Pinckney moved that the lower house of the national legislature should be chosen by the state legislatures and not by the people, Butler said:

I am against determining the mode of election until the ratio of representation is fixed—if that proceeds on a principle favorable to wealth as well as numbers of free inhabitants, I am content to unite with Delaware (Mr. Read) in abolishing the state legislatures and becoming one nation instead of a confederation of republics.

In connection with a discussion of the Senate, "he urged that the second branch ought to represent the states according to their property." Later in the sessions of the Convention he again "warmly urged the justice and necessity of regarding wealth in the apportionment of representation." He was also particularly solicitous about slave property, and he declared that "the security which the southern states want is that their negroes may not be taken from them."

Daniel Carroll favored the popular election of the executive, but he advocated a three-fourths vote in Congress to overcome the executive veto. Speaking on this point, "He remarked that as a majority was now to be the quorum, seventeen in the larger and eight in the smaller house might carry points. The advantage that might be taken of this seemed to call for greater impediments to improper laws." Carroll did not indulge in any philosophic reflections in the Convention so that his "political science," if he had worked out any definite system, is not apparent in the records.

George Clymer entertained the notions of government which were common to the Federalists of his time. He held that "a representative of the people is appointed to think *for* and not *with* his constituents"; and invariably, during the course of his career, he "showed a total disregard to the opinions of his constituents when opposed to the matured decisions of his own mind." It was on these principles that he "warmly opposed the proposition introducing a clause in the Constitution which conferred upon the people the unalienable right of instructing their representatives."

W. R. Davie, although he is reputed to have been an accomplished orator and profound student, does not figure extensively in Madison's meagre records. At no point does he expound any philosophy of government. His views were always practical. On the proposition to count slaves in apportioning representation, he threw down the gauntlet to the Convention, and declared that if the rate was not at least three-fifths, North Carolina would not federate. As to the basis of government Davie "seemed to think that wealth or property ought to be represented in the second branch; and numbers in the first branch."

Davie fully understood the significance of the obligation of contract clause which was designed as a check on the propensities of popular legislatures to assault private rights in property, particularly personalty. Speaking in the convention of North Carolina on this clause, he said: "That section is the best in the Constitution. It is founded on the strongest principles of justice. It is a section, in short, which I thought would have endeared the Constitution to this country." Davie undoubtedly understood and approved the doctrines of balanced classes in the government, as expounded in Adams' *Defence of American Constitutions*.

At no time does Davie appear to have courted popular favor in his native state, for a writer speaking of his candidacy for the legislature in 1798 says:

The "true Whigs," as they styled themselves, dined together under the oaks and toasted Mr. Jefferson. The other party, who were called "aristocrats," ate and drank in the house on entirely different principles. General Davie dined in the house with the "aristocrats." The "true Whigs" took offence at this and resolved to oppose his selection, and it was only with much address that they were kept quiet. . . . If any person had had the impudence to dispute the election, General Davie would certainly not have been returned. The rabble, which in all places is the majority, would have voted against him.

John Dickinson, of Delaware, frankly joined that minority which was outspoken in its belief in a monarchy—an action that comported with his refusal to sign the Declaration of Independence and his reluctance to embark upon the stormy sea of Revolution. At the very opening of the Convention, on June 2, he expressed his preference for a regal government, although he admitted that the existing state of affairs would not permit its establishment in America. Madison records him as saying:

A limited Monarchy he considered as one of the best Governments in the world. It was not certain that the same blessings were derivable from any other form. It was certain that equal blessings had never yet been derived from any of the republican form. A limited monarchy, however, was out of the question.

Dickinson was also among the members of the Convention who wished to establish a property qualification for voters because he thought no other foundation for government would be secure. In the debate on this subject on August 7, according to Madison's notes:

Mr. Dickinson had a very different idea of the tendency of vesting the right of suffrage in the freeholders of the Country. He considered them as the best guardians of liberty; And the restriction of the right to them as a necessary defence agst. the dangerous influence of those multitudes without property & without principle, with which our Country like all others, will in time abound. As to the unpopularity of the innovation it was in his opinion chimerical. The great mass of our Citizens is composed at this time of freeholders, and will be pleased with it.

According to King's notes:

Dickinson—It is said yr. restraining by ye Constitution the rights of Election to Freeholders, is a step towards aristocracy—is this true, No. —we are safe by trusting the owners of the soil—the Owners of the Country—it will not be unpopular—because the Freeholders are the most numerous at this Time—The Danger to Free Governments has not been from Freeholders, but those who are not Freeholders—there is no Danger—because our Laws favor the Division of property—The Freehold will be parcelled among all the worthy men in the State—The Merchants & Mechanicks are safe—They may become Freeholders besides they are represented in ye State Legislatures, which elect the Senate of the U.S.

No member of the Convention distrusted anything savoring of "levelling democracy" more than *Oliver Ellsworth*. Later as Chief Justice he denounced from the bench Jefferson and the French party as "the apostles of anarchy, bloodshed, and atheism." In the Convention, he opposed the popular election of the President and favored associating the judges with the executive in the exercise of a veto power over acts of Congress. He believed in the restriction of the suffrage to those who paid taxes. He was a warm advocate of judicial control, in general, and thoroughly understood the political significance of the system.

Thomas Fitzsimons, the wealthy merchant and stockbroker from Pennsylvania, was, after his kind, not a loquacious man, but rather a man of action—a practical man; and the records of the Convention contain no lengthy speech by him. When Gouverneur Morris, on August 7, proposed to restrain the right to vote to freeholders, Fitzsimons seconded the motion, apparently without saying anything on the point. While he thus sympathized with the movement to set the Constitution frankly on a property basis, Fitzsimons was naturally more interested in such matters as protection to manufactures and harbor improvements.

Benjamin Franklin, who at the time of the Convention was so advanced in years as to be of little real weight in the formation of the Constitution, seems to have entertained a more hopeful view of democracy than any other member of that famous group. He favored a single-chambered legislature, opposed an absolute veto in the executive, and resisted the attempt to place property qualifications on the suffrage. He signed the Constitution when it was finished, but he was accounted by his contemporaries among the doubters, and was put forward by the opponents of ratification in Pennsylvania as a candidate for the state convention, but was defeated.

Elbridge Gerry, of Massachusetts, participated extensively in the debates of the Convention, but his general view of government was doubtless stated in his speech on May 31, when he expressed himself as not liking the election of members of the lower house by popular vote. He said on this point:

The evils we experience flow from the excess of democracy. The people do not want virtue; but are the dupes of pretended patriots. In Massts. it has been fully confirmed by experience that they are daily misled into the most baneful measures and opinions by the false reports circulated by designing men, and which no one on the spot can refute. One principal evil arises from the want of due provision for those employed in the administration of Governnt. It would seem to be a maxim of democracy to starve the public servants. He mentioned the popular clamour in Massts. for the reduction of salaries and the attack made on that of the Govr. though secured by the spirit of the Constitution itself. He had, he said, been too republican heretofore: he was still, however, republican, but had been taught by experience the danger of the levelling spirit.

When the proposition that Senators should be elected by the state legislatures was up for consideration,

Mr. Gerry insisted that the commercial and monied interest wd. be more secure in hands of the State Legislatures, than of the people at large. The former have more sense of character, and will be restrained by that from injustice. The people are for paper money when the Legislatures are agst. it. Massts. the County Conventions had declared a wish for a depreciating paper that wd. sink itself. Besides, in some States there are two Branches in the Legislature, one of which is somewhat aristocratic. There wd. therefore be so far a better chance of refinement in the choice.

Nicholas Gilman was by temper and interest a man of affairs, more concerned with the stability of public securities and the development of western land schemes than with political theorizing. From Madison's record he does not appear to have said anything in the Convention.

Nathaniel Gorham was opposed to property qualifications on the suffrage in the federal Constitution and the association of the judiciary with the executive in the exercise of the veto power. Speaking on the latter point, however, he said,

All agree that a check on the legislature is necessary. But there are two objections against admitting the judges to share in it which no observations on the other side seem to obviate. The 1st is that the judges ought to carry into the exposition of the laws no prepossessions with regard to them; 2d that as the judges will outnumber the executive, the revisionary check would be thrown entirely out of the executive hands, and instead of enabling him to defend himself would enable the judges to sacrifice him.

Alexander Hamilton had a profound admiration for the British constitution. "The House of Lords," he said in the Convention, "is a noble institution. Having nothing to hope for by a change and a sufficient interest by means of their property, in being faithful to the national interest, they form a permanent barrier against every pernicious innovation whether attempted on the part of the Crown or of the Commons." Doubtless his maturely considered system of government was summed up in the following words:

All communities divide themselves into the few and the many. The first are the rich and well born, the other the mass of the people. The voice of the people has been said to be the voice of God; and however generally this maxim has been quoted and believed, it is not true in fact. The people are turbulent and changing; they seldom judge or determine right. Give therefore to the first class a distinct, permanent share in the government. They will check the unsteadiness of the second, and as they cannot receive any advantage by a change, they therefore will ever maintain good government. Can a democratic assembly who annually revolve in the mass of the people, be supposed steadily to pursue the public good? Nothing but a permanent body can check the imprudence of democracy. . . . It is admitted that you cannot have a good executive upon a democratic plan.

In consonance with these principles Hamilton outlined his scheme of government which included an assembly to consist of persons elected for three years by popular vote, a senate chosen for life or during good behavior by electors chosen by the voters, and a president also elected for life or during good behavior by electors chosen by the voters. The Convention failed to adopt his programme, and he entertained a rather uncertain view of the Constitution as it was finally drafted, doubting its stability and permanency.

William Houstoun, of Georgia, seems to have spoken only once or twice; but he gave an indication of his political science in a remark which he made to the effect that the Georgia constitution "was a very bad one, and he hoped it would be revised and amended." The constitution to which he alludes was the radical instrument made in 1777, which provided for a legislature with a single chamber and an unusually wide extension of the suffrage.

Jared Ingersoll, in spite of his great abilities as a student and lawyer, seems to have taken no part at all in the debates of the Convention. Such at least is the view to which Madison's records lead. Something is known, however, of the political principles which he entertained. Though he became intimately associated with President Reed on his migration to Philadelphia in 1778, he never accepted the extreme democratic principles embodied in the constitution of that state in 1776. His biographer, after making an exception of Ingersoll's services in the Convention, says:

I am not aware that he held or sought a position in any popular or representative body whatever. He was what is called conservative in politics; that is to say, he was not by constitutional temper a rebuilder or reconstructor of anything that had been once reasonably well built; nor was his favorite order of political architecture, the democratic. After the great subversion in 1801 he was found as rarely as anybody in Pennsylvania on the side of the majority. He was known to be inclined to the contrary, so far that with or without his consent he was selected in that state, in the year 1812, as the opposition or anti-Madisonian candidate for the office of Vice-President of the United States.

Rufus King correctly understood the idea of a balanced government independent of "popular whims" and endowed with plenty of strength. He favored a long term for the President, and speaking on the executive department in the Convention he

expressed his apprehensions that an extreme caution in favor of liberty might enervate the government we were forming. He wished the house to recur to the primitive axiom that the three great departments of governments should be separate and independent: that the executive and the judiciary should be so, as well as the legislative: that the executive should be equally so with the judiciary. . . . He [the executive] ought not to be impeachable unless he hold his office during good behavior, a tenure which would be most agreeable to him; provided an independent and effectual forum could be devised; But under no circumstances ought he to be impeachable by the legislature. This would be destructive of his independence and of the principles of the constitution. He relied on the vigor of the executive as a great security for the public liberties.

King also believed in the principle of judicial control—that most effective check on the popular attacks on property through legislatures.

It was largely on King's initiative that the prohibition against interference with contracts was placed in the Constitution.

William Livingston took a middle ground between the "high-toned" system of John Adams and the simple democracy of such writers as "Centinel" of Pennsylvania. *The Defence of the Constitutions* he impatiently characterized as "rubbage"; and a "Humiliating and mortifying acknowledgement that a man is incapable of governing himself." But for the opposite party that would set up a simple democratic government through legislative majorities, Livingston had just as little patience.

The security of the liberties of a people or state depends wholly on a proper delegation of power. The several component powers of government should be so distributed that no one man, or body of men, should possess a larger share thereof than what is absolutely necessary for the administration of government. . . . The people ever have been and ever will be unfit to retain the exercise of power in their own hands; they must of necessity delegate it somewhere. . . . But it has been found from experience that a government by representation, consisting of a single house of representatives, is in some degree liable to the same inconveniences which attend a pure democracy; a few leading men influence the majority to pass laws calculated not for the public good, but to promote some sinister views of their own. To prevent this, another representative branch is added: these two separate houses form mutual checks upon each other; but this expedient has not been found to be altogether effectual. If the legislative power, even tho' vested in two distinct houses is left without any controul, they will inevitably encroach upon the executive and judicial; . . . But further, as prejudices always prevail, more or less, in all popular governments, it is necessary that a check be placed somewhere in the hands of a power not immediately dependent upon the breath of the people, in order to stem the torrent, and prevent the mischiefs which blind passions and rancorous prejudices might otherwise occasion. The executive and judicial powers should of course then be vested with this check or controul on the legislature; and that they may be enabled fully to effect this beneficial purpose, they should be rendered as independent as possible. . . . Tho' it is so short a time since our governments have been put in motion, yet examples have not been wanting of the prevalence of this dangerous thirst after more power in some of our legislatures; a negative therefore lodged in the hands of the executive and judicial powers, is absolutely necessary in order that they may be able to defend themselves from the encroachments of the legislature.

Livingston thought that there were some grave defects in the Constitution as drafted at Philadelphia and proposed some emendations. He believed that the President should enjoy the appointing power without any control by the Senate; he thought the Chief Justice should hold office during good behavior and be empowered to appoint his colleagues; and he further held that the President, the Chief Justice, and a Superintendent of Finance should be organized into a council of revision to pass upon the acts of Congress.

James McClurg, of Virginia, left the Convention during the early part of August, and was silent on most of the questions before that body. On July 17th, he proposed that the term of the executive should be changed from seven years to "good behavior"; and he was particularly anxious to have the executive independent of the legislature. He said that he

was not so much afraid of the shadow of monarchy as to be unwilling to approach it; nor so wedded to republican government as not to be sensible of the tyrannies that had been and may be exercised under that form. It was an essential object with him to make the executive independent of the legislature; and the only mode left for effecting it, after the vote destroying his ineligibility the second time, was to appoint him during good behavior.

That McClurg had small respect for legislatures in general is shown by a letter which he wrote to Madison from Virginia on August 7, 1787, in which he said:

The necessity of some independent power to controul the Assembly by a negative, seems now to be admitted by the most zealous Republicans—they only differ about the mode of constituting such a power. B. Randolph seems to think that a magistrate annually elected by the people might exercise such a controul as independently as the King of G. B. I hope that our representative, Marshall, will be a powerful aid to Mason in the next Assembly. He has observ'd the continual depravation of Mens manners, under the corrupting influence of our Legislature; & is convinc'd that nothing but the adoption of some efficient plan from the Convention can prevent Anarchy first, & civil convulsions afterwards.

James McHenry belonged to the conservative party of his state and opposed "radical alterations" in the constitution of that commonwealth as it stood in November, 1791.

Writing in February, 1787, on the property qualifications placed on voters and representatives in Maryland, McHenry explained that "These disabilities, exclusions, and qualifications have for their object an upright legislature, endowed with faculties to judge of the things most proper to promote the public good." He was warmly opposed to the doctrine that the people had a right to instruct their representatives. Democracy was, in his opinion, synonymous with "confusion and licentiousness."

James Madison was the systematic philosopher of the Convention and set forth his views with such cogency and consistency on so many different topics that no short quotations will suffice to state his doctrines. His general scheme of political science was, however, embodied in the tenth number of *The Federalist* which has been discussed above and need not be reconsidered here.

Alexander Martin was among the silent members of the Convention, for Madison records only an occasional and incidental participation by him in the proceedings.

Luther Martin was the champion of the extreme states' rights' view, and entertained rather democratic notions for his time, although, in arguing against the clause prohibiting Congress to issue paper money, he held that, "considering the administration of the government would be principally in the hands of the wealthy," there could be little danger from an abuse of this power. Martin was in fact a champion of paper money in his state, and he opposed that part of the Constitution which prohibited the emission of bills of credit. As a representative of the more radical section of his community, he was against the clauses restricting the states to the use of the gold and silver coin of the United States, and was opposed to the clause forbidding the impairment of the obligation of contract. Speaking on the latter point he said:

There might be times of such great public calamities and distress, and of such extreme scarcity of specie, as should render it the duty of a government for the preservation of even the most valuable part of its citizens in some measure to interfere in their favor, by passing laws totally or partially stopping the courts of justice, or authorizing the debtor to pay by installments, or by delivering up his property to his creditors at a reasonable and honest valuation. The times have been such as to render regulations of this kind necessary in most or all of the states, to prevent the wealthy creditor and the moneyed man from totally destroying the poor, though even industrious debtor. Such times may again arrive. . . . I apprehend, Sir, the principal cause of complaint among the people at large, is the public and private debt with which they are oppressed, and which in the present scarcity of cash threatens them with destruction, unless they can obtain so much indulgence in point of time that by industry and frugality they may extricate themselves.

As might have been expected, a man entertaining such radical notions about the power and duty of a government to interfere with the rights of personalty in behalf of the debtor could not have accepted the instrument framed at Philadelphia. In fact, Martin refused to sign the Constitution; he wrote a vehement protest against it to the legislature of his state; he worked assiduously against its ratification; and as a member of the state convention, he voted against its approval by his commonwealth —but in vain.

George Mason thoroughly understood the doctrine of a balanced government. Speaking in the Convention on the function of the upper house, he said:

One important object in constituting the senate was to secure the rights of property. To give them weight and firmness for this purpose a considerable duration in office was thought necessary. But a longer term than six years would be of no avail in this respect, if needy persons should be appointed. He suggested therefore the propriety of annexing to the office a qualification of property. He thought this would be very practicable; as the rules of taxation would supply a scale for measuring the degree of wealth possessed by every man.

On another occasion, he presented a motion requiring "certain qualifications of landed property, in members of the legislature." Although Mason refused to sign the Constitution, his reasons were based on personal economic interests, not on any objections to its checks on democratic legislatures.

J. F. Mercer, of Maryland, who opposed the Constitution in its final form and became the belligerent anti-federalist leader in that state, does not appear to have been so warmly devoted to the "people's cause," behind the closed doors of the Convention, for he took exceptions to the proposition that the determination of the qualifications of voters should be left to the several states. But his particular objection was "to the mode of election by the people. The people cannot know and judge of the characters of candidates. The worst possible choice will be made."

Thomas Mifflin took no part worthy of mention in the proceedings of the Convention, and expounded no views of government during the debates.

Gouverneur Morris, of Pennsylvania, was the leader of those who wanted to base the new system upon a freehold suffrage qualification; and, on August 7, he made a motion to this effect. In the course of the discussion which followed, Morris said:

He had long learned not to be the dupe of words. The sound of Aristocracy, therefore, had no effect on him. It was the thing, not the name, to which he was opposed, and one of his principal objections to the Constitution as it is now before us, is that it threatens this Country with an Aristocracy. The Aristocracy will grow out of the House of Representatives. Give the votes to people who have no property, and they will sell them to the rich who will be able to buy them. We should not confine our attention to the present moment. The time is not distant when this Country will abound with mechanics & manufacturers who will receive their bread from their employers. Will such men be the secure & faithful Guardians of liberty? Will they be the impregnable barrier agst. aristocracy?—He was as little duped by the association of the words, "taxation & Representation"—The man who does not give his vote freely is not represented. It is the man who dictates the vote. Children do not vote. Why? because they want prudence, because they have no will of their own. The ignorant & the dependent can be as little trusted with the public interest. He did not conceive the difficulty of defining "freeholders" to be insuperable. Still less that the restriction could be unpopular. 9/10 of the people are at present freeholders and these will certainly be pleased with it. As to Merchts. &c. if they have wealth & value the right they can acquire it. If not they don't deserve it.

In all the proceedings of the Convention, Morris took a deep interest and expressed his views freely, always showing his thorough distrust of democratic institutions. As his biographer, Mr. Roosevelt, puts it,

He throughout appears as the *advocatus diaboli;* he puts the lowest interpretation upon every act, and frankly avows his disbelief in all generous and unselfish motives. His continual allusions to the overpowering influence of the baser passions, and to their mastery of the human race at all times, drew from Madison, although the two men generally acted together, a protest against his "forever inculcating the utter political depravity of men, and the necessity of opposing one vice and interest as the only possible check to another vice and interest."

This protest from Madison, however, betrays inconsistency, for on more than one occasion in the Convention he expounded principles substantially identical with those which he reprobated in Morris. Indeed, what appeared to be cynical eccentricity on the part of the latter was nothing more than unusual bluntness in setting forth Federalist doctrines.

Robert Morris, the merchant prince and speculator of Pennsylvania, seems to have broken his rule of absolute silence only two or three times in the Convention, and he apparently made no speech at all. He nominated Washington as president of the assembly, and seconded Read's motion that Senators should hold office during good behavior. There is no doubt that Morris appreciated the relative weight of speeches and private negotiations.

In the proceedings of the Convention, *William Paterson* was chiefly concerned with protecting the rights of small states; but he signed the Constitution, and after its adoption became an ardent Federalist, serving as an associate justice of the Supreme Court. On the bench he was one of the most scholarly and eminent supporters of the doctrine of judicial control over legislation.

William Pierce took little part in the proceedings of the Convention. On the question of states' rights he held a broad view, saying,

state distinctions must be sacrificed so far as the general government shall render it necessary—without, however, destroying them altogether. Although I am here as a representative from a small state, I consider myself as a citizen of the United States, whose general interest I will always support.

On no occasion, apparently, did Pierce indulge in any general reflections on the basis of all government. He did not sign the Constitution, but he explained this fact by saying,

I was absent in New York on a piece of business so necessary that it became unavoidable. I approve of its principles and would have signed it with all my heart had I been present. To say, however, that I consider it as perfect would be to make an acknowledgement immediately opposed to my judgment.

Charles Pinckney was among the members of the Convention who thought that it was desirable to fix the property qualifications of members of the national legislature firmly in the Constitution. Speaking on the subject of property and government he said:

The Committee as he had conceived were instructed to report the proper qualifications of property for the members of the Natl. Legislature; instead of which they have referred the task to the Natl. Legislature itself. Should it be left on this footing, the first Legislature will meet without any particular qualifications of property; and if it should happen to consist of rich men they might fix such qualifications as may be too favorable to the rich; if of poor men, an opposite extreme might be run into. He was opposed to the establishment of an undue aristocratic influence in the Constitution, but he thought it essential that the members of the Legislature, the Executive, and the Judges—should be possessed of competent property to make them independent & respectable. It was prudent when such great powers were to be trusted to connect the tie of property with that of reputation in securing a faithful administration. The Legislature would have the fate of the Nation put into their hands. The President would also have a very great influence on it. The Judges would have not only important causes between Citizen & Citizen but also where foreigners were concerned. They will even be the Umpires between the U. States and individual States as well as between one State & another. Were he to fix the quantum of property which should be required, he should not think of less than one hundred thousand dollars for the President, half of that sum for each of the Judges, and in like proportion for the members of the Natl. Legislature. He would however leave the sum blank. His motion was that the President of the U. S., the Judges, and members of the Legislature should be required to swear that they were respectively possessed of a clear unincumbered Estate to the amount of ———— in the case of the President, &c &c —

Pinckney, in fact, had no confidence in popular government, for on March 28, 1788, he wrote to Madison:

Are you not . . . abundantly impressed that the theoretical nonsense of an election of Congress by the people in the first instance is clearly and practically wrong, that it will in the end be the means of bringing our councils into contempt.

General Charles Cotesworth Pinckney entertained views with regard to the special position that should be enjoyed by property, which were substantially identical with those held by his cousin. He proposed that no salary should be paid to members of the Senate. As this branch, he said, "was meant to represent the wealth of the country, it ought to be composed of persons of wealth; and if no allowance was to be made the wealthy alone would undertake the service." General Pinckney also wished to extend property qualifications not only to members of the legislature, but also to the executive and judicial departments.

Edmund Randolph was not only fully aware of the distress to which property had been put under the Articles of Confederation, but he also understood the elements of a "balanced" government. Speaking on the subject of the structure of the Senate, he said:

If he was to give an opinion as to the number of the second branch, he should say that it ought to be much smaller than that of the first, so small as to be exempt from the passionate proceedings to which numerous assemblies are liable. He observed that the general object was to provide a cure for the evils under which the U. S. Laboured; that in tracing these evils to their origin every man had found it in the turbulence and follies of democracy: that some check therefore was to be sought for agst. this tendency of our governments: and that a good Senate seemed most likely to answer the purpose. . . . Mr. Randolph was for the term of 7 years. The Democratic licentiousness of the State Legislatures proved the necessity of a firm Senate. The object of this 2d. branch is to controul the democratic branch of the Natl. Legislature. If it be not a firm body, the other branch being more numerous, and coming immediately from the people, will overwhelm it. The Senate of Maryland constituted on like principles had been scarcely able to stem the popular torrent. No mischief can be apprehended, as the concurrence of the other branch, and in some measure, of the Executive, will in all cases be necessary. A firmness & independence may be the more necessary also in this branch, as it ought to guard the Constitution agst. encroachments of the Executive who will be apt to form combinations with the demagogues of the popular branch.

George Read was most outspoken in his desire to see the Articles of Confederation completely discarded. He said that

he was against patching up the old federal system: he hoped the idea would be dismissed. It would be like putting new cloth on an old garment. The Confederation was founded on temporary principles. It cannot last; it cannot be amended.

He favored vesting an absolute veto power in the executive; and he proposed that Senators should hold office during good behavior.

John Rutledge held that the apportionment of representatives should be on a basis of wealth and population. He favored a property qualification for the legislative, executive, and judicial departments; and he thought that Senators should not be paid. In fact, he was one of the most ardent champions of the rights of property in government in the Convention. He was strictly opposed to the introduction of sentimental considerations in politics, for, speaking on an aspect of slavery and the Constitution, he said:

Religion & humanity had nothing to do with this question—Interest alone is the governing principle with Nations—The true question at present is whether the Southn. States shall or shall not be parties to the Union. If the Northern States consult their interests they will not oppose the increase of Slaves which will increase the commodities of which they will become the carriers.

Roger Sherman believed in reducing the popular influence in the new government to the minimum. When it was proposed that the members of the first branch of the national legislature should be elected, Sherman said that he was "opposed to the election by the people," insisting that it ought to be by the state legislatures. "The people," he said, "immediately should have as little to do as may be about the government. They want information and are constantly liable to be misled."

Richard Dobbs Spaight does not seem to have made any very lengthy speeches in the Convention, but his occasional motions show that he was not among those who believed in "frequent recurrence to the people." On September 6, he moved that the length of the President's term be increased to seven years, and finding this lost he attempted to substitute six years for four. Spaight was the one member of the Convention, however, who came out clearly and denounced judicial control; but he nevertheless proved a stout champion of the Constitution in North Carolina—defending it warmly against charges to the effect that it was aristocratic in character.

Caleb Strong carried into the Convention the old Massachusetts tradition in favor of frequent elections. He favored a one year term for representatives, voted against a seven year term for President, and also opposed a seven year term for Senators. He supported the Constitution, however, in his native state, and was a member of the convention that ratified it.

George Washington's part in the proceedings of the Convention was almost negligible, and it does not appear that in public document or private letter he ever set forth any coherent theory of government. When he had occasion to dwell upon the nature of the new system he indulged in the general language of the bench rather than that of the penetrating observer. For example, in his Farewell Address, which was written largely by Hamilton, he spoke of the government's being "the offspring of our own choice, uninfluenced and unawed, adopted upon full investigation, and mature deliberation, completely free in its principles, in the distribution of its powers, uniting security with energy." He feared, however, the type of politics represented by the Democratic Societies which sprang up during his administration, and looked upon criticism of the government as akin to sedition. Like Jefferson, he also viewed with apprehension the growth of an urban population, for in a letter to La Fayette at the time of the French Revolution, he said, "The tumultuous populace of large cities are ever to be dreaded. Their indiscriminate violence prostrates for the time all public authority."

Hugh Williamson was against placing property qualifications on voters for members of Congress; and he was opposed to the association of the judges with the executive in the exercise of the veto power. He preferred to insert a provision requiring a two-thirds vote for every "effective act of the legislature." He was, however, an opponent of the paper money party in North Carolina and in the Convention he supported a proposition forbidding the states to pass ex post facto laws, on the ground that "the judges can take hold of it."

James Wilson was among the philosophers of the period who had seriously pondered on politics in its historical and practical aspects. In the Convention he took a democratic view on several matters. He favored the annual election of representatives by the people, he advocated the popular election of United States Senators, and he believed also in the popular election of the President. He furthermore opposed the proposition to place property qualifications on voters. His check on popular legislation was to be found in judicial control, at first in the association of the judges with the executive in its exercise, and later in its simple, direct form. In fact, Wilson shared the apprehensions of his colleagues as to the dangers of democratic legislatures, though he did not frankly advocate direct property checks. He doubtless believed that judicial control would be sufficient.

George Wythe was a representative of the old school of lawyers in Virginia, and he was a profound student of historical jurisprudence, although he apparently made no attempt to apply his learning to any of the general political questions before the Convention. He was a warm advocate of the doctrine of judicial control and gave practical effect to principles while on the bench in Virginia.

The conclusion seems warranted that the authors of *The Federalist* generalized the political doctrines of the members of the Convention with a high degree of precision, in spite of the great diversity of opinion which prevailed on many matters.

Charles A. Beard's Pioneer Interpretation of the Making of the Constitution

FORREST MCDONALD

The day was Monday, September 17, 1787, the place, Philadelphia. The long and, as tradition has it, steaming hot summer was finally ending. Throughout the city, serenely unaware that historians were one day to know this as the Critical Period of American history, Philadelphians were busy preparing a record wheat crop for export. Inside a crowded room in the State House (later to be rechristened Independence Hall) thirty-odd men penned their signatures to a document they had styled a "Constitution for the United States of America."

Reprinted from *We the People* by Forrest McDonald (Chicago, 1958), pp. 3–6, 349–357, by permission of The University of Chicago Press. Copyright 1958 by The University of Chicago Press.

There was no exuberance, no display of enthusiasm, and very little reverential solemnity. Fourteen members of the body had previously walked out for one reason or another, most of them because they had personal business they considered more deserving of attention or because the hot clash of personalities had been too much for them. Even now, at the very end, a half dozen men were wrangling about minor details, and three others flatly refused to sign the instrument. Another group was already worrying about and planning for the strenuous campaign for ratification which lay ahead. Mostly, however, the atmosphere pervading the room was one of exhaustion and a sense of relief that the four-month ordeal was over.

The importance of the event insured that the making of the Constitution of the United States would become the subject of debate, study, and writing for many years to come. In addition the actors in the drama helped to fan the flames of debate and to provoke perhaps even more writing than the subject itself warranted. Almost as if to vex future scholars, the members of the Philadelphia Convention kept their proceedings secret and passed down to historians only the most fragmentary of notes; the Constitution was deliberately couched in ambiguous language; the disputants in the contest over ratification clouded both the contest and the conditions that shaped it by publishing reams of misleading, often fantastic propaganda. Partly because of the nature of the event, partly because of the chaotic record left by the participants, the mountains of historical writings on the subject have often been colored by emotionalism and shrouded in confusion. The men in the Convention have been depicted as a group of demigods, a band of ruthless conspirators, and virtually every intermediate brand of humanity. The document has been characterized at one extreme as scarcely less sacred than the Holy Bible, at the other as the greatest single barrier to the progress of social justice. Interpretation of the ratification has run the gamut from the noblest act of a free people under divine guidance to an unprincipled *coup d'état*.

Early in 1913 there emerged from this historiographical maze a work that was destined to become a classic. In that year Charles A. Beard, then a young professor of politics at Columbia University, published his *An Economic Interpretation of the Constitution of the United States*, a brilliant, challenging, and provocative study that has towered over everything else written on the subject, before or since. No other work on the making or the nature of the Constitution has been so much debated, so widely known, and ultimately so widely accepted.

The central points in the thesis advanced by Professor Beard were these: "Large and important groups of economic interests were adversely affected by the system of government under the Articles of Confederation, namely, those of public securities, shipping and manufacturing, money at interest; in short, capital as opposed to land." After failing to safeguard their rights, "particularly those of the public creditors," through the regular legal channels, these groups called a convention in the hope of obtaining "the adoption of a revolutionary programme." In other words, the movement for the Constitution originated with and was pushed through by "a small and active group of men immediately interested through their personal possessions in the outcome of their labors. . . . The propertyless masses were . . . excluded at the outset from participation (through representatives) in the work of framing the Constitution. The members of the Philadelphia Convention which drafted the Constitution were, with a few exceptions, immediately, directly, and personally interested in, and derived economic advantage from, the establishment of the new system."

In essence, then, the Constitution was "an economic document drawn with superb skill by men whose property interests were immediately at stake; and as such it appealed directly and unerringly to identical interests in the country at large." It was based "upon the concept that the fundamental private rights of property are anterior to government and morally beyond the reach of popular majorities."

The system "consisted of two fundamental parts—one positive, the other negative." The positive part comprised four great powers conferred on the new government: "taxation, war, commercial control, and disposition of western lands." This meant for the manufacturers a protective tariff; for trade and shipping groups, tariffs and other legislation against foreign shipping; for money interests the prevention of "renewed attempts of 'desperate debtors' like Shays"; and for public creditors, ample revenues for the payment of their claims. The negative portion placed restrictions on the states: "Two small clauses embody the chief demands of personalty against agrarianism: the emission of paper money is prohibited and the states are forbidden to impair the obligation of contract."

In the contest over ratification, Beard concluded, only about a fourth of the adult males were eligible—or interested enough—to vote on the question, and the Constitution was ratified by no more than a sixth of the adult males. In five states it was "questionable whether a majority of the voters participating . . . actually approved the ratification." "The leaders who supported the Constitution in the ratifying conventions represented the same economic groups as the members of the Philadelphia Convention; and in a large number of instances they were also directly and personally interested in the outcome of their efforts." Of the voters on ratification, those favoring the Constitution were "centred particularly in the regions in which mercantile, manufacturing, security, and personalty interests generally had their greatest strength." The holders of public securities "formed a very considerable dynamic element, if not the preponderating element, in bringing about the adoption of the new system." The opposition, on the other hand, came almost exclusively from the

agricultural regions and from the areas in which debtors had been formulating paper-money and other depreciatory schemes. In short, "the line of
cleavage for and against the Constitution was between substantial personalty interests on the one hand and the small farming and debtor interests on the other."

*   *   *

Professor Beard interpreted the making of the Constitution as a simple,
clear-cut series of events. When all the groups that became Federalists are
brought together and analyzed, he asserted, and all the anti-Federalists are
brought together and analyzed, the events can be seen as mere manifestations of a fundamentally simple economic conflict. His analysis led him to
formulate three basic propositions, one regarding the Philadelphia Convention and two regarding the contest over ratification. In the light of
the data in the foregoing chapters, we may now focus our attention upon
these three key propositions of Beard's economic interpretation of the
Constitution.

THE PHILADELPHIA CONVENTION

From his analysis of the Philadelphia Convention, Beard concluded that
the Constitution was essentially "an economic document drawn with
superb skill" by a "consolidated economic group . . . whose property
interests were immediately at stake"; that these interests "knew no state
boundaries but were truly national in their scope."

From a thorough reconsideration of the Philadelphia Convention, however, the following facts emerge. Fully a fourth of the delegates in the
convention had voted in their state legislatures for paper-money and/or
debtor-relief laws. These were the very kinds of laws which, according
to Beard's thesis, the delegates had convened to prevent. Another fourth
of the delegates had important economic interests that were adversely
affected, directly and immediately, by the Constitution they helped write.
The most common and by far the most important property holdings of
the delegates were not, as Beard has asserted, mercantile, manufacturing,
and public security investments, but agricultural property. Finally, it is
abundantly evident that the delegates, once inside the Convention, behaved as anything but a consolidated economic group.

In the light of these and other facts presented in the foregoing chapters, it is impossible to justify Beard's interpretation of the Constitution
as "an economic document" drawn by a "consolidated economic group
whose property interests were immediately at stake."

THE CONTEST OVER RATIFICATION, FIRST PROPOSITION

Beard asserted that the ultimate test of the validity of an economic interpretation of the Constitution would rest upon a comparative analysis

of the economic interests of all the persons voting for and all the persons voting against ratification. He made an analysis of the economic interests of some of the leaders in the movement for ratification and concluded that "in the ratification, it became manifest that the line of cleavage for and against the Constitution was between substantial personalty interests on the one hand and the small farming and debtor interests on the other."

For the purpose of analyzing this proposition it is necessary to employ Beard's own definitions of interest groups. In the paragraphs that follow, as in the foregoing chapters, the term "men of personalty interests" is used to mean those groups which Beard himself had in mind when he used the term, namely, money, public securities, manufacturing and shipping, and western lands held for speculation.

From a thorough reconsideration of the contests over ratification the following facts emerge.

1. In three states (Delaware, New Jersey, and Georgia) the decisions of the ratifying conventions were unanimous, and it is therefore impossible to compare the interests of contending parties. The following analyses of the conventions in these three states may be made, however.

In Delaware almost 77 per cent of the delegates were farmers, more than two-thirds of them small farmers with incomes ranging from 75 cents to $5.00 a week. Slightly more than 23 per cent of the delegates were professional men—doctors, judges, and lawyers. None of the delegates was a merchant, manufacturer, banker, or speculator in western lands.

In New Jersey 64.1 per cent of the delegates were farmers, 23.1 per cent were professional men (physicians, lawyers, and college presidents), and only 12.8 per cent were men having personalty interests (one merchant, three iron manufacturers, and one capitalist with diversified investments).

In Georgia 50 per cent of the delegates were farmers (38.5 per cent slave-owning planters and 11.5 per cent small farmers), 11.5 per cent were frontiersmen whose economic interests were primarily agrarian, 19.2 per cent were professional men (lawyers, physicians, and professional officeholders), and only 11.5 per cent had personalty interests (all merchants). The interests of 7.7 per cent of the delegates were not ascertained.

Beard assumed that ratification in these states was pushed through by personalty interest groups before agrarian and paper-money groups could organize their forces. The opposite is true. In each of these three states agrarian interests dominated the conventions. In each state there were approximately equal numbers of delegates who had voted earlier for and against paper money.

2. In two states in which the decision was contested (Virginia and North Carolina) the great majority of the delegates on both sides of the question were farmers. In both states the delegates who voted for and the

delegates who voted against ratification had substantially the same amounts of the same kinds of property, most commonly land and slaves. A large number of the delegates in the Virginia convention had voted on the question of repudiation of debts due British merchants, and the majority of the delegates who had favored such repudiation voted for ratification of the Constitution. Large numbers of delegates in both North Carolina conventions were speculating in western lands. In the first convention a great majority of these land speculators opposed the Constitution; in the second a substantial majority of them favored ratification.

Beard assumed that ratification in these states represented the victory of wealthy planters, especially those who were rich in personalty other than slaves, over the small slaveless farmers and debtors. The opposite is true. In both states the wealthy planters—those with personalty interests as well as those without personalty interests—were divided approximately equally on the issue of ratification. In North Carolina small farmers and debtors were likewise equally divided, and in Virginia the great mass of the small farmers and a large majority of the debtors favored ratification.

3. In four states (Connecticut, Maryland, South Carolina, and New Hampshire) agrarian interests were dominant, but large minorities of delegates had personalty interests.

In Connecticut 57.8 per cent of the delegates who favored ratification and 67.5 per cent of those who opposed ratification were farmers. Ratification was approved by 76.2 per cent of all the delegates, by 81.8 per cent of the delegates having personalty interests, and by 73.3 per cent of the farmers in the convention. Here, then, four delegates out of five having substantial personalty interests favored the Constitution. On the other hand, three of every four farmers also favored the Constitution.

In Maryland 85.8 per cent of the delegates who voted for ratification were farmers, almost all of them wealthy slave-owning planters; 27.3 per cent of the opponents of ratification were farmers, all of them substantial slave-owning planters. The opponents of ratification included from three to six times as large a proportion of merchants, lawyers, and investors in shipping, confiscated estates, and manufacturing as did the delegates who favored ratification. It is to be observed, however, that because the vote in the Maryland ratifying convention was almost unanimous (63 to 11), statistics on the attitudes of the various interest groups would show that every major interest group except manufacturers favored the Constitution. A majority of the areas and of the delegates that had advocated paper money also favored the Constitution.

In South Carolina 59 per cent of the delegates who voted for ratification were large slave-owning planters and 10.7 per cent were lesser planters and farmers. Of the delegates who voted against ratification, 41.7 per cent were large slave-owning planters and 34.2 per cent were lesser planters and farmers. Merchants, factors, and mariners favored ratification, 70 per cent to 30 per cent, a margin almost identical to the vote of the entire convention—67 per cent for, 33 per cent against—and manufacturers, artisans, and mechanics were unanimous in support of the Constitution. On the other hand, 35.7 per cent of the delegates who favored ratification were debtors who were in a desperate plight or had borrowed paper money from the state. Only 15.1 per cent of those who voted against ratification were debtors or had borrowed paper money from the state. No fewer than 82 per cent of the debtors and borrowers of paper money in the convention voted for ratification.

As respects New Hampshire, comparisons are difficult because of the lack of adequate information concerning 28.2 per cent of the delegates. Of the delegates whose interests are known, 36.9 per cent of those favoring the Constitution and 25 per cent of those opposing it were farmers; of the known farmers in the convention 68.7 per cent favored ratification. If it is assumed, however, that all the delegates whose interests are not ascertainable were farmers (as in all likelihood most of them were), then 49.1 per cent of the delegates favoring ratification were farmers, 54.3 per cent of those opposing ratification were farmers, and 52.8 per cent of the farmers in the convention voted for ratification. Delegates whose interests were primarily in personalty (merchants, tradesmen, manufacturers, and shipbuilders) voted in favor of ratification, 60.9 per cent to 39.1 per cent. Delegates from the towns which had voted for and against paper money divided almost equally on the question of ratification: 42 per cent of the towns that had voted for paper money and 54 per cent of those that had voted against paper money sent delegates who voted for the Constitution.

Beard assumed that in these states ratification was the outcome of class struggles between commercial and other personalty groups (Federalists) on the one hand and farmers and advocates of paper money (anti-Federalists) on the other. This generalization is groundless. In each of these states a majority of the men having personalty interests favored ratification, but in each of them a similar majority of the farmers also favored ratification. In one of these states there was no great demand for paper money, in another a large majority of the friends of paper money favored ratification, and in the other two the advocates of paper money were divided almost equally on the question of ratification.

4. In four states (Massachusetts, Pennsylvania, New York, and Rhode Island) men having personalty interests were in a majority in the ratifying conventions.

In Massachusetts, in the popular vote (excluding that of Maine) men whose interests were primarily non-agrarian favored the Constitution by about three to two, and men whose interests were primarily agrarian opposed the Constitution by about 55 per cent to 45 per cent. In the ratifying convention 80 per cent of the merchants and shippers engaged in water-borne commerce, 77 per cent of the artisans and mechanics, and 64 per cent of the farmers favored ratification. About 83 per cent of the retail storekeepers, 85 per cent of the manufacturers, and 64 per cent of the miscellaneous capitalists opposed ratification. One-fourth of those favoring and one-sixth of those opposing the Constitution were farmers. Of the personalty groups combined, 57.5 per cent opposed and 42.5 per cent favored ratification. The realty groups combined, including artisans and mechanics, favored ratification by 67 per cent to 33 per cent.

In Pennsylvania only 34.8 per cent of the delegates favoring ratification were farmers, and only 26.1 per cent of the opponents were farmers. Almost three-fourths—72.7 per cent—of the farmers in the convention favored ratification. The great majority of the delegates on both sides, however, 84.7 per cent of those favoring and 91.3 per cent of those opposing the Constitution, had substantial investments in one or more of Professor Beard's four forms of personalty.

New York delegates are difficult to classify as farmers because almost all farmers in the convention were also landlords with tenants. Delegates to the state's convention may be classified as elected Federalists, converts from anti-Federalism, delegates who abstained from voting, and anti-Federalists. Of the delegates about whom there is sufficient data on which to generalize, fewer than 20 per cent of each group consisted of farmers who had no tenants and who owned none of Beard's four forms of personalty.

Rhode Island delegates do not lend themselves to occupational classification because almost everyone in the state normally combined in his own economic activities several kinds of functions. Only 11.8 per cent of the delegates favoring ratification and only one of the delegates opposing ratification were found to have no interests except farming. The early opponents of paper money formed the original core of those favoring ratification, yet in the final vote 62 per cent of the delegates voting for ratification and 63 per cent of those opposing ratification were men who had borrowed paper money from the state.

Beard's thesis—that the line of cleavage as regards the Constitution was between substantial personalty interests on the one hand and small farming and debtor interests on the other—is entirely incompatible with the facts.

THE CONTEST OVER RATIFICATION, SECOND PROPOSITION

Beard was less certain of the foregoing point, however, than he was of this next one:

Inasmuch as so many leaders in the movement for ratification were large security holders, and inasmuch as securities constituted such a large proportion of personalty, this economic interest must have formed a very considerable dynamic element, if not the preponderating element, in bringing about the adoption of the new system. . . . Some holders of public securities are found among the opponents of the Constitution, but they are not numerous.

This proposition may be analyzed in the same manner that Beard's more general personalty-agrarian conclusion was analyzed. To repeat, Beard asserted that public securities were the dynamic element within the dynamic element in the ratification. This assertion is incompatible with the facts. The facts are these:

1. In three states (Delaware, New Jersey, and Georgia) there were no votes against the Constitution in the ratifying conventions, and hence no comparisons can be made. If public securities were the dynamic element in the ratification, however, it would be reasonable to expect that the great majority of the delegates in these states which supported the Constitution so unreservedly should have been security holders. But the fact is that in Delaware only one delegate in six owned securities, in New Jersey 34 per cent of the delegates, and in Georgia only one delegate.

2. In two states (New Hampshire and North Carolina) the numbers of security holders among the delegates were very small. In New Hampshire only 10.5 per cent of those who voted for and only 2.2 per cent of those who voted against ratification held securities. In the first North Carolina convention only 2.4 per cent of the friends and only 1.1 per cent of the opponents of ratification held securities. In the second convention only 2.0 per cent of those favoring and only 3.9 per cent of those opposing the Constitution were security holders. Superficially these facts tend to substantiate Beard's thesis, for these virtually security-less states were slow to ratify the Constitution. It has been shown, however, that actually the reluctance of these states to adopt the Constitution and their vulnerability to raids on their securities by outsiders were both merely surface manifestations of the same underlying conditions—the isolation, the lack of information, and the lethargy of the majority of the inhabitants of North Carolina and New Hampshire.

3. In three states (Rhode Island, Maryland, and Virginia) where there were contests and considerable numbers of security holders, the advocates and the opponents of ratification included approximately the same percentages of security holders: in Rhode Island, 50 per cent of the advocates and 47 per cent of the opponents; in Virginia, 40.5 per cent of the advocates and 34.2 per cent of the opponents; and in Maryland, 17.4 per cent and 27.3 per cent respectively. The facts relative to these three states clearly contradict Beard's thesis.

4. In two states (Massachusetts and Connecticut) the advocates of ratification included a considerably larger percentage of holders of securities than did the opponents. In Massachusetts 31 per cent of the ratificationists and only 10.1 per cent of the anti-ratificationists were security

owners, and in Connecticut 36.7 per cent and 15 per cent respectively. The situations in these two states, and in these two states alone, tend strongly to support Beard's thesis.

5. In three states (Pennsylvania, South Carolina, and New York) a considerably larger percentage of the delegates opposing ratification than of the Federalist delegates held public securities. In Pennsylvania 73.9 per cent of the opponents and 50 per cent of the supporters of ratification were security owners, in South Carolina 71 and 43 per cent respectively, and in New York 63 and 50 per cent respectively. The facts pertaining to these states not only fail to harmonize with Beard's thesis but indicate that there the precise opposite of his thesis is true.

In the light of the foregoing facts it is abundantly evident that there are no more grounds for considering the holding of public securities the dynamic element in the ratification than for considering this economic interest the dynamic element in the opposition. There were, indeed, some holders of public securities among the opponents of the Constitution and, contrary to Beard's assertion, they were as numerous as the security holders among the supporters of the Constitution.

On all counts, then, Beard's thesis is entirely incompatible with the facts. Beard's essential error was in attempting to formulate a single set of generalizations that would apply to all the states. Any such effort is necessarily futile, for the various interest groups operated under different conditions in the several states, and their attitudes toward the Constitution varied with the internal conditions in their states.

FOR FURTHER READING: Old but still provocative is O. G. Libby, *The Geographical Distribution of the Vote of the Thirteen States on the Federal Constitution, 1787–88* (Madison, 1894). Of the critics, see Robert E. Brown *Charles A. Beard and the Constitution: A Critical Analysis of "An Economic Interpretation of the Constitution"* (Princeton, 1956). Elaborating on Beard's position is Merrill Jensen, *The New Nation, A History of the United States During the Confederation, 1781–1789* (New York, 1950).

9. *Jeffersonian Economic Theory*

PROBLEM: *What were the basic elements in Jefferson's economic thought?*

It is well known that Jefferson never developed a comprehensive, compact system to expound either his political, social, or economic views. Instead, he scattered his ideas in a vast multitude of writings throughout various stages of his career. No wonder, therefore, that later students of his works came to stress different aspects of his thought, and to disagree over the nature of his beliefs, including those concerning the economy. Joseph Dorfman, author of a majestic five-volume history of American economic thought, has emphasized that agrarianism constituted a basic premise of all of Jefferson's economic ideas. Agrarianism to Jefferson meant encouraging the establishment of a nation of small farmers whose prosperity would be enhanced by government's abstention from interference. As Dorfman elaborates this theory, it comprised emphasis on economy in government, low taxes, opposition to high tariffs, self-sufficiency, and a laissez-faire policy toward industry. Such an interpretation of Jefferson's economic theories has by no means been accepted by other students of his thought. Economist William Grampp has challenged this view and instead has pointed to the changing nature of the great Virginian's outlook. According to Grampp, Jefferson's economic ideas passed through three stages, from agrarianism, to laissez-faire, to protectionism. It is true, this author notes, that Jefferson may have been an agrarian to 1776, advocating a mixed commercial and agricultural economy operating with a minimum of governmental interference. But from 1776 until 1805 he espoused laissez-faire doctrines, until, in the nineteenth century, he was converted to protectionism, as now he envisioned a balanced economy with agriculture, commerce, and manufacturing each receiving a fair share of government protection and encouragement. As these contrasting appraisals indicate, Jefferson was a complex thinker, and agreement on fundamental assumptions of his thought is no simple matter. Moreover, these selections leave other questions unanswered. Was Jefferson's economic thought self-contradictory? Was Jefferson opportunistic? What elements of Jefferson's ideas on economy have relevance to modern times?

The Economic Philosophy of Thomas Jefferson

JOSEPH DORFMAN

Doubtless the most notable thinker ever to become President of the United States was Thomas Jefferson. The dominant American economic and political philosophy has run in his idiom ever since his administration. Radicals, liberals and conservatives have constantly based their arguments on what they conceived to be his social philosophy. Further adding to the confusion has been the futile habit of contrasting sharply the Jeffersonian scheme with that of his great adversary, Alexander Hamilton. The latter, it is agreed, believed that the mass was turbulent, ignorant and poverty stricken, that with the growth of wealth, inequality and class antithesis must increase. Therefore the stability of the social order and the security of person and property could only be maintained by a strong government in the hands of the wealthy and intelligent. To these classes, government at all times should render financial aid, for the sake of attaching them to the government by the strongest bond, that of interest, thus increasing national wealth and maintaining the employment of the mass.

Jefferson, like the other enlightened minds of the eighteenth century, held that republican government was best because it prevented governmental restraints on the free acquisition of wealth. Thereby all men had an equal opportunity to acquire a comfortable livelihood. Government should be limited, lest those in power, animated like all men, by self-interest, deprive the industrious of the fruits of their labor. In the absence of privileges granted by government, wealth would be acquired by industry rather than by law. With government limited, opportunity available to all, and the habits of thought of the despotic past, surely though slowly disintegrated by education, mankind's progress, material and intellectual, was illimitable.

Jefferson's career was full of shifts and contradictions. These, however,

Reprinted from the *Political Science Quarterly*, Vol. LV (March, 1940), pp. 98–121.

were grounded on his fundamental premise that republican government would endure only as long as opportunities and resources for the acquisition of property were available to an ever increasing population. His was the planter's logic. Under it wealth meant landed possessions, but specie, credit, markets and more lands were necessary for its maintenance and increase. The consequences of these premises were the expansion of empire and the correlative development of the money economy. The process can be seen in the Virginian's own career.

Jefferson had eminently respectable antecedents. He was the son of a Virginia planter, and a student at the royal College of William and Mary. Since the law was the road to political preferment, he became, in the accepted Southern tradition, a lawyer as well as a planter. He absorbed the regnant "common sense" philosophy which maintained that accepted beliefs embodied in the dominant institutions were self-evident or "common sense" truths. The philosophy did not disallow changes in policy. A primordial moral sense dominated men's actions, but worked itself out through the calculus of utility which nature made the test of virtue. Whether an act was useful, and thus virtuous, depended on the habits and circumstances of the people. But utility to Jefferson was not a matter of strict empirical determination. Rather it was what common sense found useful. Foremost among Jefferson's common sense truths was that property was founded "in our natural wants, in the means with which we are endowed to satisfy these wants, and the right to what we acquire by those means without violating the similar rights of other sensible beings." His academic and legal training impressed upon him the "commercial principles which bring wealth into our country and the constitutional security . . . for the enjoyment of that wealth." Consequently, he opposed parliamentary restrictions on the trade and industry of the colonies and defended trade with the enemy. Appealing to the great principles of right and wrong which were "legible to every reader," he declared that property was held by absolute tenure. Since the original settlers conquered the country with their fortunes and their lives, their heirs owned the country. This worked no hardship, because the institutions and resources insured the acquisition of property by the poor but enterprising of all nations. Therefore the colonies took up arms, to defend their natural freedom and property "acquired solely by the honest industry of our forefathers and ourselves." . . .

Only the abolition of the feudal remnants was secured, but still the scheme of things, at least for the consumption of foreigners, was, according to Jefferson, rather ideal. Hardly any poverty existed because lands were available. The few beggars were foreigners in the towns. But such a happy state of affairs, under a government formed on the principles of natural reason, could continue only as long as the country remained agricultural.

This agrarian basis was sound on both economic and political grounds. The agricultural people were God's chosen people. They were incorruptible because they were not dependent on the caprices of customers. Manufacturers, by creating dependence, were responsible for mobs, corruption, servility and ambition.

European economists such as Adam Smith, said Jefferson, taught that every nation should supply its own manufactures, but overlooked the fact that the same immutable principles of political economy gave different conclusions in this country because circumstances were different. Europe, having no available lands, must turn to manufactures to employ the surplus labor. Therefore let the workshops remain in Europe, and the agricultural surplus here be exchanged for manufactures.

Dependence on markets for the agricultural surplus might be an afterthought in Jefferson's philosophic meditations on the agricultural state, but he was aware of its reality. His primary occupation as minister to France from 1784 to 1789 was to acquire markets. He informed the French authorities that France was wise to prohibit foreign manufactures, but American goods were non-competitive raw materials and foodstuffs. France would even find it profitable to subsidize manufactures in order to increase employment in both countries. . . .

Jefferson still retained his commercial-agrarian ideal. The people would remain virtuous only as long as the principal object was agriculture, and lands were available, for the moderate, sure income of husbandry begot permanent improvement and orderly conduct in private and public life. When the population should mass in the cities, then the people would become corrupt and eat one another as in Europe. Fortunately, said Jefferson, manufactures would not get a foothold in his generation.

Merchants and commerce were also not altogether desirable. Merchants were weak in virtue and *amor patriae*. Commerce, beyond that needed to export the surplus produce, fostered a gambling spirit in society. But eventually agricultural production would exceed both the foreign and domestic demand; the surplus population should then enter navigation and commerce. Furthermore, since a good proportion of the people were by habit and taste addicted to these occupations, a faithful representative must follow not what was sound in "theory" but what was practicable and protect these interests. . . .

He approved or disapproved financial policies in accordance with what he conceived to be the interests of agriculture. But he still believed that those interests were subserved by policies which strengthened the national credit, and brought in specie. Thus, at first, he approved Hamilton's funding measure for full payment of the public debt, and felt that funds should be kept at Amsterdam to purchase the stock, when it fell below par. Later he asserted that Hamilton's other great measures threatened the agricultural interest and republican government. The National Bank

Act providing for a privately managed national bank, with its capital primarily in funded debt, and with its bank notes exclusively receivable for government dues, in addition to specie, placed the circulating medium of the country under the control of the speculative interests. The agricultural interest would be at the mercy of the Bank, and since agriculture was the only productive interest, the profits of the Bank would be at the expense of agriculture. . . .

Jefferson's agricultural economics was slowly modified by the changing circumstances. He did not abandon, at least formally, his view that the agricultural state was the ideal state, if only Europeans would grant free access to markets. He praised highly Malthus' *Essay on Population,* which attributed England's distress to redundant population, but he said that Malthus' conclusions did not apply to the United States because the circumstances were not the same. By employing all laborers here in agriculture, the surplus produce could be exchanged for the manufactures of the excessive population of Europe. Moral duty and interest were thus in harmony. But he felt that his early strictures on manufactures were misunderstood. Here manufacturers were as comfortable and independent as the agriculturists, because they could turn to agriculture, if the other classes attempted to reduce them to the minimum of subsistence. . . .

A Re-examination of Jeffersonian Economics

WILLIAM D. GRAMPP

> In so complicated a science as political economy, no one axiom can be laid down as wise and expedient for all times and circumstances, and for their contraries.
>
> —JEFFERSON, 1816

It is with some hesitancy and not a few misgivings that one must approach the economic writings of Thomas Jefferson. So much has been written about Jefferson in the past century and a half, so diverse are these expressions, and so overlaid has his thought become with the views of his interpreters, that any addition to this grand depository can be justified only as a departure from past efforts. The student of economic doctrine cannot but be a little bewildered upon comparing what Jefferson wrote on economic matters with what he is reputed to have believed. The purpose of this paper is mainly the negative one of demonstrating that the

Reprinted by permission from *The Southern Economic Journal,* XII (January, 1946), pp. 363–382. [Portions of this article have been deleted by the editor of this volume.]

prevalent notions of Jeffersonian economics cannot be substantiated by reference to his works, and it would not be offered, at least in its present form, if these notions had not such general currency. To serve this end, I shall attempt (1) to show that there was not one system of Jeffersonian economics, but three, corresponding to three periods in his public life; (2) to set down the sources of this thesis and to show its development in Jefferson's hands; and (3) to show the relation between Jefferson's economic doctrine and that prevailing concurrently in Europe, and the inter-relations between his economic and political thought, the last because of the intimacy of the connection and its importance for understanding the man's doctrine. The method adopted in this study is a genetic one. Because of the significant changes in his thought, it can be examined most fruitfully by tracing its evolution in some detail.

To the mystification of students in the economic field, Jefferson has been fixed, variously, as a Physiocrat, an advocate of agrarian self-sufficiency, as an apologist for agrarian capitalism (a kind of bucolic Hamilton), as a protectionist, single-taxer, disciple of Adam Smith, forerunner of Marx, "democratic collectivist,"—to say nothing of the more esoteric interpretations that have been laid upon his work. It is obvious that he could not have been all of these, or even many of them, and it is equally true that, however valid some of these interpretations are for a particular period of Jefferson's life, each is in error to the extent that it purports to describe any doctrine as held throughout his entire career.

Neither the political nor economic principles of Jefferson's thought ranked as presuppositions, but were as sides of a coin minted from his conception of human nature. This conception was drawn from the systems of Helvétius and Holbach, who, however much they may have antagonized Jefferson by their materialistic bias, influenced him by their utilitarian doctrine. Human nature, to Jefferson, was not to be taken as given (as it was to Hamilton) but as subject to restraint and improvement at the hands of a government that would be subject to the same forces in the hands of the people. Neither governors nor governed could be trusted, nor could a system of checks and balances be relied upon to achieve an equilibrium of interests and thereby maintain peace and liberty. Elementary caution, he believed, demanded that governmental powers be few and extremely limited. He believed individuals should not be permitted to acquire wealth enough to give them great influence, and, that government should not be given significant powers to control economic behavior. Jefferson was at one with Hamilton's dictum, that power over a man's subsistence is power over his will, but, unlike Hamilton, he did not believe that men were capable of looking after their own interests by creating a governmental structure in which an equilibrium between opposing interests would be established and departures from it would be largely self-correcting. Rather than give each individual and group the power to advance its own ends and to protect itself against incursions by others—which was the rationale of the tri-partite structure of government —Jefferson believed that the sources of conflict had to be removed before "right" social relations could be established. The source of most evil was, he maintained, men's material interests. Hence the kind of economic behavior men engaged in was of fundamental importance to a government that wished to preserve order and liberty. If men were to be turned to the true path of social righteousness, they must be turned away from the mainsprings of corruption, and the great and leading principle of economic policy then became the cultivation of an economic environment that would be conducive to the realization of the ends of government.

Given these primary considerations, it is possible, I believe, to explain the great political and economic struggles of the years from the Constitution to the rise of Jacksonian democracy and to discover the essential differences that separated the first two parties and their successors to the year 1829. Though the convenient categories of "aristocrat and democrat," or "nationalist and states-righter," "mercantilist and Physiocrat" may serve for some purposes, they help but little in fixing clear-cut distinctions; and for purposes of discovering differences in economic doctrine they are of no help at all. Here it must be noted, that to speak of Jeffersonian *economics* is somewhat misleading, for neither Jefferson nor his followers pretended to develop a theoretical system embracing value, distribution, finance, and economic policy, as the British and French economists of the period were doing. No one in America attempted such a system until the third decade of the nineteenth century when Daniel Raymond wrote his *Thoughts on Political Economy*. "Jeffersonian economics" is really a set of ideas concerning the economic role of the state together with a few, and cursory, remarks concerning value and money. This is not to say that the early Americans were unaware of the totality of prevailing economic thought but that they were most concerned with those aspects relevant to the problem of government.

I

Jefferson's earliest expression of doctrinal importance was made in 1774 when he wrote in *The Summary View of the Rights of British America* that the exercise of free trade was "possessed by the American colonists, as of a natural right," and he described the act of George II forbidding Americans to make fur products as "an instance of despotism to which no parallel can be produced in the most arbitrary ages of British history." He declared that freedom in the disposition of property was one aspect of the total endowment of freedom that man derived from the Creator.

Although the reference in this tract is to real property, or economic goods, Jefferson usually meant much more by the term "property" and most often used it as his spiritual forebear, John Locke, did, to comprehend man's "life, liberty and estates." Jefferson believed with Locke that men form societies in order to protect their "property," and he meant by this, not that government exists to secure wealth and vested interests (as is so often claimed), but to guarantee each man's birth-right to liberty.

Jefferson's next work of importance was the famous *Notes on Virginia* in which he described in encyclopedic fashion the most important agricultural state and one of the two or three most important economic regions in America, and appended sundry observations on man and the material with which he worked. These notes, from which Jefferson's reputation as a Physiocrat is largely derived, were written before 1781 and hence before he left America to become ambassador to France. They grew out of observations made over a number of years preceding his departure, and they were by no means intended to be exhaustive nor even to represent satisfactorily Jefferson's views on the limited subjects treated. They were published about 1785 with some hesitation, and then privately circulated. The original edition, published in French, was, in Jefferson's words, "interverted, abridged, mutilated, and often reversing the sense of the original." A partially corrected English edition was published later, but was not completely accurate. Yet it is this admittedly tentative and not completely reliable publication that first gave Jefferson his reputation as a Physiocrat.

In the English edition the *Notes* are still replete with panegyrics over the agriculturist. Agriculture begets self-sufficiency; it creates a stalwart yeomanry that is the bulwark of liberty and bearer of an elevated moral code. "Those who labor in the earth are the chosen people of God." This agrarian strain runs throughout Jefferson's life. In 1804, he wrote to J. B. Say, the French classicist, that the agriculturist possessed a "moral and physical preference" over the laborer of the cities. In 1816, after he had become a protectionist, he still clung to the supremacy of agriculture and maintained that it produced a value greater than an equal application of labor and capital to manufacturing because of "the spontaneous energies of the earth." Jefferson's agrarianism was infectious, and superiority of farming became a byword among those who were opposed to the industrialization of America. The protectionists were forever confronted with a kind of moral superciliousness on the part of the agrarians. Matthew Carey, inveterate champion of a high tariff and prolific pamphleteer on its behalf, blamed this hauteur upon Jefferson and added querulously: "His Arcadia must have been sought, not in Virginia or Maryland, but in Virgil's or Pope's pastorals, or Thomson's seasons."

Yet Jefferson's preference for agriculture does not necessarily make of him a Physiocrat any more than a forerunner of the Congressional farm bloc. Even in the years before 1790 when his agrarianism was most pronounced, it was not a system of true Physiocracy. Although Jefferson commended at various times throughout his life the work of Les Économistes and noted particularly du Pont de Nemours, Quesnay, Gournay, Le Trosne, Turgot, and Destutt de Tracy, he was also familiar with the doctrines of Say, Malthus, Sismondi, Hume, John Law, and Smith. Of the last, he declared: "In political economy, I think Smith's *Wealth of Nations* the best book extant." Because he possessed an almost religious devotion to the soil, Jefferson usually has been called a Physiocrat, the assumption apparently being that such devotion was the essence of Physiocracy and the direct tangible proof deriving from Jefferson's residence in France and his mention of the doctrine. Yet in his works there not only is no definitive exposition of Physiocratic doctrine but there is not even any evidence that he was more influenced by it than by British classicism. In point of formal respect paid to contemporary doctrine, Jefferson is much more of a British classicist than a follower of the French economists; even his rent theory is in no way inconsistent with that of Smith. . . .

II

When Jefferson returned from France and became Secretary of State in Washington's first cabinet in 1790, his economic policy began to change, and in the succeeding years, until 1805, the ideas which he expressed were markedly different from those of his early life. This period reveals two significant departures from his early position: the idea of self-sufficient economic units, in any *explicit* form, disappears, and his program of free trade is modified by a policy of reciprocity. In this period one can observe an intimate relation between Jefferson's political doctrine and his domestic economic policy. He pursued a policy that was largely in harmony with that of the British classicists; the elements of agrarianism were subsumed in the kind of synthesis made by Joseph Priestley between British classicism and Physiocracy. Priestley, who is better known as the discoverer of oxygen, wrote considerably on political and economic matters, and was a close friend of Jefferson. (He fled to America in 1794, when the British government fell on sympathizers of the French Revolution and after Burke did him the honor of execration in his *Reflections*.) Priestley's *Lectures on History and General Policy* constitute an important liberal testament of the late eighteenth century and are especially relevant for the economic doctrine they expound. He adapted French notions of the supremacy of agriculture to a mixed—agricultural and manufacturing—economy, by declaring that the earth was the ultimate source of all wealth (suggestive of Ricardo's original and indestructible powers of the soil). Manufacturing, however, must be "excited," for it furnishes a market for agricultural products. Where Turgot posited the labor of the husbandman as the only productive factor, Priestley extended the labor theory of value to all productive activity (in the sense of labor as the source of all value). . . .

III

Beginning in 1805 there was a pronounced change in Jefferson's economic policy. Both the early objective of agrarianism and the free trade which supplanted it were given over for a system of protection. The continued hostility of England and the Continental System of Napoleon forced a new assertion of national power from the United States at a time when the Republicans were in office. In his second inaugural address (1805) Jefferson revealed the progress that Federalist ideas had made within his own system and within the Republican party. Gone were the proclamations of a revolution in public polity that had ushered in the regime in 1801. In the first administration, Gallatin had attempted to execute a policy of strict economy in governmental expenditures, and Jefferson had attempted to relegate the state to the rank of a wise and tolerant overseer of economic behavior. Gallatin's policy of economy had effected a reduction in the size of the army and navy, instituted savings in the diplomatic and customs services, and reduced the national debt. The Jeffersonian administration between 1801 and 1804 was much more conducive to *laissez faire* than the preceding administrations, simply because the government exercised so few economic powers. But such an administration was destined for a short life. Even had there been no opposition within the nation, the turmoil of Europe would have forced a change.

Jefferson began his second administration by looking forward to the time when the public revenue would be freed from debt service in order that it might be applied "to rivers, canals, roads, arts, manufactures, education, and other great objects w[i]thin each state." Such a policy would first have to be legitimated by a constitutional amendment and probably would have to be executed in co-operation with the governments of the states. The promotion of American manufactures, however, did not wait for a constitutional amendment, any more than did the Louisiana Purchase. The embargo and non-intercourse policy after 1807 furnished more assistance to American manufacturing than the entire Federalist policy had been able to offer. Although the intent was to preserve American neutrality in the Napoleonic Wars, the effect was not out of harmony with Jefferson's new economic position.

In these later days, Jefferson devised an economic policy which he thought would establish a "national equilibrium" between agriculture, manufactures, and commerce; such a policy would "simplify" the economic organization of the United States and restrict economic activity to meeting simple needs, and it would make the United States self-sufficient and removed from the turmoil which international economic relations engender. He declared that the embargo and related policies had promoted domestic manufactures:

They will have hastened the day when a equilibrium between the occupations of agriculture, manufactures, and commerce, shall simplify our foreign concerns to the exchange only of that surplus which we cannot consume for those articles of reasonable comfort or convenience which we cannot produce.

Jefferson also proposed that all raw materials produced in the United States be worked into manufactured commodities rather than be exported, in order to lessen the nation's dependence on the rest of the world. His opponents charged that this was a "Chinese" policy of commerce, which indeed it was. To avoid the embarrassment of advocating that which he had once decried—a manufacturing system—Jefferson urged that Americans concentrate on household fabrications as a complement to their agricultural pursuits. Indicating that he was aware of the dilemma, his letters between 1810 and 1815 reiterate the virtues of household manufactures. These, he said, would beget diligence and self-reliance among the citizenry and remove them from the caprices of the market, and would make the United States economically independent of the rest of the world. He repeatedly urged that all foreign (particularly British) goods imported into the United States be boycotted (with the exception of extreme necessities). Jefferson himself established an extensive spinning mill at Monticello. . . .

Over the years Jefferson gradually abandoned his categorical opposition to monopoly. He had written in 1785 that monopoly was "contrary to the spirit of trade, and to the dispositions of merchants," yet even then he recognized that governmental grants of monopoly privileges could be of advantage. He remarked on the question again in 1787 in considering the problem of exclusive rights in patents. Government interposition in such matters was of great value, he wrote, but "in practice so inseparable from abuse that it is best to leave citizens free in their pursuits with neither aid nor hindrance." A few years later he declared that the constitutional provision for exclusive patent rights had "given a spring to invention beyond my imagination." Eventually Jefferson settled upon the compromise of giving the inventor an exclusive grant but prohibited him from imposing any conditions upon the user of the invention. What he wanted essentially was the increased incentive resulting from monopoly grants without the ill effects of monopoly. In conditions where free enterprise was unable to function, Jefferson approved of exclusive grants of trade. An instance of this was his approval of John Jacob Astor's plan to open fur trade in the Columbia River territory. He wrote to Astor, the founder of the famous family, "Your name will be handed down with that of Columbus and Raleigh, as the father of the establishment and founder of such an empire," (which would arise from commerce). And while Astor was providing for future generations, Jefferson hoped that he might "find a present account in the just profits you are entitled to expect from the enterprise." The generous tone of the letter is remarkable in view of Jefferson's ill-concealed dislike of "millionary merchants."

IV

In recapitulation, an examination of Jefferson's papers and their relation to the economic problems of the United States between 1774 and 1816 reveals not one Jeffersonian system of economic policy but three. Until about 1790 he was dominated by agrarianism, and his expressions of policy most often took the form of advocating self-sufficient agrarian units. From 1790 to 1805, Jefferson formally adopted *laissez faire* as an objective but his expressions were still tinged with the earlier form of agrarianism. After 1805, he proposed measures that were consistent with the objectives established by Hamilton, though his methods differed from those of Hamilton in revealing a greater concern with constitutional legitimacy. That these periods in Jefferson's policy have not been distinguished and that he is most often categorized as a Physiocrat (for which, as we have seen, the evidence is unsatisfactory) is not difficult to understand. His stature as a statesman and political thinker makes him vulnerable to wilful interpretations. No little violence has been done to his ideas in the past century or so. Even after his declaration of 1816 in favor of protection, the Southern free traders continued to claim him as their own. Nor could the protectionists agree on what he said or what he meant. Matthew Carey castigated him for romantic agrarianism while Friederich List set him at one with Hamilton.

This three-fold development in Jeffersonian economics might suggest fundamental inconsistencies in his system of thought, and in one important aspect it does. Before 1805 he could very easily harmonize his minimum state with his economic policy, for the policy required no great concentration of power. After 1805 serious difficulties arose, however, over the compatibility of state and individual power in relation to the avowed economic functions of government. Because the international economic policy of the state cannot be separated from its domestic policy, the problem of protection cannot be viewed differently from the question of internal improvements. Here Jefferson's logic was impaled. He was alarmed by Federal power over internal improvements, even though he admitted the power of protection. In the constitutional controversy of the 'twenties, he submitted to Madison a "Solemn Declaration and Protest of the Commonwealth of Virginia, on the Principles of the Constitution of the United States of America, and on the Violations of Them," which condemned internal improvements under direct or indirect Federal auspices but said not one word on protection. This artificial separation was forgotten in the resolutions actually passed by Virginia. However anomalous this declaration is in a political sense, it is significant as Jefferson's last pronouncement on economic policy, revealing that he maintained his advocacy of protection to the end.

FOR FURTHER READING: Vernon L. Parrington, *Main Currents in American Thought* (3 vols., New York, 1927), volume I, emphasizes physiocratic tendencies of Jefferson. An essay by Joseph Spengler, "The Political Economy of Jefferson, Madison, and Adams," in David K. Jackson (ed.), *American Studies in Honor of William Kenneth Boyd* (Durham, 1940), 3–59, stresses laissez-faire aspects, while William A. Williams, "The Age of Mercantilism: An Interpretation of the American Political Economy, 1763–1828," *William and Mary Quarterly*, XV (October, 1958), pp. 419–437 shows Jefferson as a mercantilist.

10. *Commerce, 1790–1860*

PROBLEM: *Did tariffs promote American manufacturing?*

Although Congress provided for federal customs duties as early as 1789, and although Alexander Hamilton advocated them in his *Report on Manufactures* two years later, the first truly protective tariff for the benefit of the emerging textile and iron industries was not adopted until 1816. In succeeding years businessmen demanded increasingly higher rates and Congress responded with the enactment of the tariffs of 1824 and 1828 and 1832. But the pressures of Southerners in Congress resulted in the lowering of rates in 1833, 1846, and 1857. Thus by 1860 many northern Republicans were aroused and favored increasing the schedules, a stand on which they were openly challenged by most southern Democrats who felt that tariffs were detrimental to the South, an exporting section with few factories of its own. While both sides assumed that the tariff had an important effect in promoting the growth of northern industry, later students have been less sure about its precise impact. Whether the tariff was an important means of stimulating economic development during the first half of the nineteenth century is thus an issue. D. G. Harriman, a passionate advocate of protection, in the selection below argues that tariffs brought positive benefits to American manufacturers, mainly the exclusion of competing foreign goods, and the encouragement of new industries in the United States. This widely held and popular belief was seriously doubted by Frank W. Taussig, a distinguished Harvard economist and author of *American Tariff History*, who concluded that in actual operation the tariff had very little impact either in promoting or hindering economic expansion. Taussig noted that some industries prospered without protection while others were already well established by the time that tariffs were applied. Both authors point to prominent arguments that need to be con-

166

sidered in an appraisal of protectionism, and they raise further questions. In what ways did tariffs encourage specific industries? What evidence supports the validity of the two opposing arguments? Why were tariffs such an important element of political dispute among contemporaries of the nineteenth century?

The Benefits of Protection

D. G. HARRIMAN

. . . At the close of the war between the United States and Great Britain, England and English manufacturers made two discoveries which were very startling and disagreeable to them. First, That having been deprived by the Embargo Act and the subsequent war of the American markets, the British manufacturers found their warehouses at the close of the war full to bursting with unsold productions of various kinds, for which they were very anxious, but unable, to find a market. Second, That the Americans, compelled by the same reasons to rely upon themselves instead of the English manufacturers for their supplies during this period, had established successfully a large number of home industries, and were, by this means, able to a great degree to supply their own market.

In this dilemma, England saw that she must act promptly and crush out these young American industries, or her American market would be forever lost, and her manufacturing industries permanently crippled. So she resolved to flood this country with her goods then on hand, many of which were old and out of fashion, far below cost. It was a matter of so much importance that it was discussed in Parliament, and Mr. (afterward Lord) Brougham declared in the House of Commons in 1816: "It is well worth while to incur a loss upon the first exportation, in order, by the glut, to stifle in the cradle those infant manufactures in the United States, which the war has forced into existence."

This policy was decided upon, and Great Britain poured her fabrics and acculmulated [sic] stocks of goods into our markets in an overwhelming torrent and far below cost. The tariff of 1816 was intended as a barrier against this inundation, and under ordinary circumstances would have proved such. But it was a matter of life or death with the English manufacturers, and so they continued to pour in their goods

From D. G. Harriman, *American Tariffs from Plymouth Rock to McKinley, A Complete and Impartial History* (New York: The American Protective Tariff League, 1892), pp. 23–27.

upon us at prices far lower than we could make them; and true to British custom they perservered [*sic*] in this policy till our own industries were very nearly ruined.

The foreign goods imported at this period were more than twice the quantity that could be consumed. Niles, in his history, says: "It is notorious that great sums of money were expended by the British to destroy our flocks of sheep, that they might thereby ruin our manufactories. They bought up and immediately slaughtered great numbers of sheep; they bought our best machinery and sent it off to England, and hired our best mechanics and most skillful workmen to go to England, simply to get them out of this country, and so hinder and destroy our existing and prospective manufactures."

Results of the Repeal.—Then great depression in all branches of business at once followed. Bankruptcy soon became general, and financial ruin was everywhere present. It could not be otherwise. Carey, Greeley, Clay, Benton and others show that this was one of the most distressful periods of our national existence. "No price for property; no sales except those of the sheriff and the marshal; no purchasers at execution sales except the creditor, or some hoarder of money; no employment for industry; no demand for labor; no sale for the products of the farm; no sound of the hammer, except that of the auctioneer knocking down property. Distress was the universal cry of the people; relief, the universal demand, was thundered at the doors of all Legislatures, State and Federal." (Benton).

Horace Greeley says of this period: "At the close of the second war with England, Peace found this country dotted with furnaces and factories which had sprung up under the precarious shelter of embargo and war. These not yet firmly established found themselves suddenly exposed to a relentless and determined foreign competition. Great Britain poured her fabrics, far below cost, upon our markets in a perfect deluge. Our manufactures went down like grass before the mower, and our agriculture and the wages of labor speedily followed. Financial prostration was general, and the presence of debt was universal. In New England, fully one-fourth of the property went through the sheriff's mill, and the prostration was scarcely less general elsewhere. In Kentucky the presence of debt was simply intolerable. In New York, the leading merchants, in 1817, united in a memorial to Congress to save our commerce as well as our manufactures from utter ruin, by increasing the tariff duties."

Henry Clay declared that the average depression in the value of property, under that state of things, was not less than fifty per cent.

1818.—The Tariff Act of 1818 was simply an amendment by which tariff duty was imposed upon a few articles which, prior thereto, were free.

It thus appears that the Tariff Acts of 1816 and 1818 were no exception to the rule that protective tariffs conduce to national prosperity, and very low tariff rates to national adversity; for though they were "moderately protective," in name, yet, under the outrageous and disgracefully selfish policy of Great Britain—a policy which we could not then have anticipated—those tariffs afforded insufficient protection; and insufficient protection is, practically, as bad as tariff for revenue only.

SECOND PROTECTION PERIOD—1824–1833

1824.—Protection again Restored.—The disastrous state of affairs described in Chapter III continued for several years, until our people, with a mighty effort, resolved to endure it no longer; and in 1824 Congress gave us a new tariff, far in advance of that of 1789, and our first protective tariff that gave us real protection.

This tariff was passed in response to a general demand of the country; and upon the urgent recommendation of President Monroe to give "additional protection to those articles which we are prepared to manufacture," etc. Everybody, except a few free traders, had become disgusted with a tariff that was nominally "moderately protective," while in fact, it afforded no real protection; and the Congress of that year was largely in favor of a strong protective tariff, in fact as well as in name.

The advocates of this Tariff Act insisted upon its passage, in order to give to the country that strength and power which arise from possessing within itself the means of defense, and to rescue it from the dangers and disgrace of habitual dependence upon foreign nations for the common daily necessaries of life.

The enemies of the bill were no less determined in their opposition. No denunciation of it could be too severe; no prophecy of evil to come from it could be too doleful.

Soon after the tariff bill of 1824 was reported, a New York evening newspaper, now, as then, one of the ablest and most uncompromising advocates of free trade, said, editorially:

"Pass the tariff as reported by the committee and you palsy the Nation. Pass it, and where will you any longer find occupants for your costly piles of stores and dwelling-houses? Pass it, and who will be exempt from its grinding operation?

"The poorer classes, especially, must feel its effect in paying an additional price for every article of clothing they and their families wear, and every mouthful they eat or drink, save cold water; and to that will they ere long be reduced."—New York *Evening Post*, July, 1824.

Major McKinley, commenting on this, says: "None of these awful prophecies were fulfilled; none of these dire results ensued. The nation was not palsied, but quickened into new life. The merchants did not move out of their costly piles of stores and dwelling-houses, they remained only to require larger and finer and more costly ones; the poorer classes were not driven to cold water as their only food and diet, but their labor was in greater demand and their wages advanced in price. The entire country under the tariff moved on to higher triumphs in industrial progress, and to a higher and better destiny for all of its people."

John Randolph, one of the ablest of Democrats, fiercely opposed the bill, and in a speech in Congress, after showing the great advantages of Great Britain in manufacturing, added: "It is in such a climate only that the human animal can bear, without extirpation, the corrupted air, the noisome exhalations, the incessant labor of these accursed manufactories. Yes, sir, accursed, for I say it is an accursed thing. We should have the yellow fever from June to January, and January to June. The climate of this country alone, were there no other natural obstacles to it, says aloud—You shall not manufacture."

One of its strongest advocates and supporters was Andrew Jackson, then United States Senator, and now the patron saint of the Democratic Party. Let us see what he thought of protection in 1824: "Providence," said he, "has filled our mountains and our plains with minerals—with lead, iron and copper—and given us a climate and soil for the growing of hemp and wool. These being the greatest materials of our national defense, they ought to have extended to them adequate and fair protection, that our manufacturers and laborers may be placed in a fair competition with those of Europe; and that we may have within our country a supply of those leading and important articles so essential in war. We have been too long subject to the policy of British merchants. It is time we should become a little more Americanized; and, instead of feeding the paupers and laborers of England, feed our own; or else in a short time by continuing our present policy (that under tariff of 1816) we shall all be rendered paupers ourselves. It is my opinion therefore that a careful and judicious tariff is much wanted."

Results Quick and Helpful.—The Bill was passed, and again, and at once, an era of great financial prosperity set in. So marked and helpful was the improvement that in 1828 the duties were raised still higher; and yet business improved; new industries were started, and prosperity gladdened the people.

Hear what President Andrew Jackson said in his annual message, in December, 1832, concerning the results and benefits of eight years of protection under the Tariffs of 1824 and 1828: "Our country presents, on every side, marks of prosperity and happiness, unequalled, perhaps, in any other portion of the world."

The relief to the country, attained through these Tariffs of 1824 and 1828, "was profound and general, reaching all classes—the farmer, the manufacturer, the ship-owner, the mechanic, and the day laborer. The change was as great as was wrought when Hamilton smote the rock of public credit and abundant streams of revenue gushed forth." (Webster.)

Henry Clay, speaking in the United States Senate in 1832 about this period, said: "On a general survey we behold cultivation extended; the arts flourishing; the face of the country improved; our people fully and profitably employed; the public countenance exhibiting tranquility, contentment and happiness; its public debt of two wars nearly redeemed; and, to crown all, the public treasury overflowing. If the term of seven years were to be selected of the greatest prosperity which this people has enjoyed since the establishment of their present Constitution, it would be exactly that period of seven years which immediately followed the passage of the Tariff of 1824."

This view is sustained by the best writers concerning that period, who all agree that our manufactures were flourishing, that our currency was good, our crops abundant, and our commerce prosperous. These combined influences invariably enhance the demand for labor, increase its value, establish a general prosperity for the country and contentment for the people.

President John Quincy Adams, who succeeded Mr. Monroe, was also a strong friend of protection, and in his fourth annual message discusses at some length our agricultural, commercial and manufacturing interests, and shows that "all these interests are alike under the protecting power of the legislative authority," and proceeds to make himself clear and explicit in his defense of the principles of protection.

1832.—Tariff of 1828 Amended.—The Tariff Act of 1832 was really nothing but some slight amendments to the Act of 1828. Southern feeling against the Tariff of 1828 was exceedingly bitter, and they were determined to have actual free trade, if possible. They demanded, through the Committee of Ways and Means, that the protective system be "utterly and absolutely abandoned"; and declared that "congress should adopt no half-way measures, no temporary expedients, but 'reform it altogether.'"

But the country, as a whole, had never been so prosperous as under the policy of the Tariff of 1828, and they were in no mood to yield to this foolish demand of the South. But, for the sake of peace and of conciliating the South, they were willing to make some concessions to this free trade prejudice, and, therefore, certain coarse wools were put upon the free list, and some reduction was granted upon articles made from those wools. But the protective principle of the Act of 1828 was still retained on the expressed ground that it was necessary for building up and sustaining our own manufactures as one of the essential means of increasing and maintaining our national greatness.

Protection to Young Industries

F. W. TAUSSIG

THE COTTON MANUFACTURE

When . . . the period of restriction began, in 1808, the importation of foreign [cotton] goods was first impeded, and soon entirely prevented. The domestic manufacture accordingly extended with prodigious rapidity. Already during the years 1804–8 greater activity must have prevailed; for in the latter year fifteen mills had been built, running 8,000 spindles. In 1809 the number of mills built shot up to 62, with 31,000 spindles, and while 25 more mills were in course of erection. In 1812 there were 50 factories within thirty miles of Providence, operating nearly 60,000 spindles, and capable of operating 100,000. During the war the same rapid growth continued, rendered possible as it was by the increasing supply of raw cotton from the South. The number of spindles was said to be 80,000 in 1811, and 500,000 in 1815. In 1800, 500 bales of cotton had been used; in 1805, 1,000 bales. In 1810 the number consumed rose to 10,000; in 1815, it was 90,000. These figures cannot be supposed to be at all accurate; but they indicate clearly an enormously rapid development of the manufacture of cotton.

The machinery in almost all these new factories was for spinning yarn only. Weaving was still carried on by the hand-loom, usually by weavers working in considerable numbers on account for manufacturers. Toward the end of the war, however, a change began to be made almost as important in the history of textile manufactures as the use of the spinning-jenny and mule: namely, the substitution of the power-loom for the hand-loom. The introduction of the power-loom took place in England at about the same time, and some intimation of its use seems to have reached the inventor in this country, Francis C. Lowell. He perfected the machine, however, without any use of English models, in the course of the year 1814. In the same year it was put in operation at a factory at Waltham, Mass. There for the first time the entire process of converting cotton into cloth took place under one roof. The last important step in giving textile manufactures their present form was thus taken.

When peace was made in 1815, and imports began again, the newly established factories, most of which were badly equipped and loosely managed, met with serious embarrassment. Many were entirely abandoned. The manufacturers petitioned Congress for assistance; and they received, in 1816, that measure of help which the public was then disposed

From F. W. Taussig, *The Tariff History of the United States* (New York: G. P. Putnam's Sons, 1892) pp. 25–59.

to grant. The tariff of 1816 levied a duty of 25 per cent. on cotton goods for three years, a duty considered sufficiently protective in those days of inexperience in protective legislation. At the same time it was provided that all cotton cloths, costing less than 25 cents a yard, should be considered to have cost 25 cents and be charged with duty accordingly; that is, should be charged 25 per cent. of 25 cents, or 6¼ cents a yard, whatever their real value or cost. This was the first of the minimum valuation provisos which played so considerable a part in later tariff legislation, and which have been maintained in large part to the present time. A similar minimum duty was imposed on cotton-yarns. At the time when these measures were passed, the minimum provisos hardly served to increase appreciably the weight of the duty of 25 per cent. Coarse cotton cloths were then worth from 25 cents to 30 cents, and, even without the provisos, would have paid little, if anything, less than the minimum duty. But, after 1818, the use of the power-loom, and the fall in the price of raw cotton, combined greatly to reduce the prices of cotton goods. The price of coarse cottons fell to 19 cents in 1819, 13 cents in 1826, and 8½ cents in 1829. The minimum duty became proportionately heavier as the price decreased, and, in a few years after its enactment, had become prohibitive of the importation of the coarser kinds of cotton cloths.

During the years immediately after the war, the aid given in the tariff of 1816 was not sufficient to prevent severe depression in the cotton manufacture. Reference has already been made to the disadvantages which, under the circumstances of the years 1815–18, existed for all manufacturers who had to meet competition from abroad. But when the crisis of 1818–19 had brought about a rearrangement of prices more advantageous for manufacturers, matters began to mend. The minimum duty became more effective in handicapping foreign competitors. At the same time the power-loom was generally introduced. Looms made after an English model were introduced in the factories of Rhode Island, the first going into operation in 1817; while in Massachusetts and New Hampshire the loom invented by Lowell was generally adopted after 1816. From these various causes the manufacture soon became profitable. There is abundant evidence to show that shortly after the crisis the cotton manufacture had fully recovered from the depression that followed the war. The profits made were such as to cause a rapid extension of the industry. The beginning of those manufacturing villages which now form the characteristic economic feature of New England falls in this period. Nashua was founded in 1823. Fall River, which had grown into some importance during the war of 1814, grew rapidly from 1820 to 1830. By far the most important and the best known of the new ventures in cotton manufacturing was the foundation of the town of Lowell, which was undertaken by the same persons who had been engaged in the establishment of the first power-loom factory at Waltham. The new town was named after the inventor of the power-loom. The scheme of utilizing the falls of the Merrimac, at the point where Lowell now stands, had been suggested as early as 1821, and in the following year the Merrimac Manufacturing Company was incorporated. In 1823 manufacturing began, and was profitable from the beginning; and in 1824 the future growth of Lowell was clearly foreseen.

From this sketch of the early history of the cotton manufacture we may draw some conclusions. Before 1808 the difficulties in the way of the introduction of this branch of industry were such that it made little progress. These difficulties were largely artificial; and though the obstacles arising from ignorance of the new processes and from the absence of experienced workmen, were partly removed by the appearance of Slater, they were sufficient, when combined with the stimulus which the condition of foreign trade gave to agriculture and the carrying trade, to prevent any appreciable development. Had this period come to an end without any accompanying political change—had there been no embargo, no non-intercourse act, and no war with England—the growth of the cotton manufacture, however certain to have taken place in the end, might have been subject to much friction and loss. Conjecture as to what might have been is dangerous, especially in economic history, but it seems reasonable to suppose that if the period before 1808 had come to an end without a jar, the eager competition of well-established English manufacturers, the lack of familiarity with the processes, and the long-continued habit, especially in New England, of almost exclusive attention to agriculture, commerce, and the carrying trade, might have rendered slow and difficult the change, however inevitable it may have been, to greater attention to manufactures. Under such circumstances there might have been room for the legitimate application of protection to the cotton manufacture as a young industry. But this period, in fact, came to an end with a violent shock, which threw industry out of its accustomed grooves, and caused the striking growth of the cotton manufacture from 1808 to 1815. The transition caused much suffering, but it took place sharply and quickly. The interruption of trade was equivalent to a rude but vigorous application of protection, which did its work thoroughly. When peace came, in 1815, it found a large number of persons and a great amount of capital engaged in the cotton manufacture, and the new processes of manufacture introduced on an extensive scale. Under such circumstances the industry was certain to be maintained if it was for the economic interest of the country that it should be carried on.

The duties of the tariff of 1816, therefore, can hardly be said to have been necessary. Nevertheless, they may have been of service. The assistance they gave was, it is true, insignificant in comparison with the shelter from all foreign competition during the war. Indeed, most manufacturers desired much higher duties than were granted. It is true, also, that the minimum duty on cottons was least effective during the years immediately after the war, when the price of cottons was higher, and the duty was therefore proportionately less high. But these years between the close of the war and the general fall of prices in 1819 were trying for the manufacturers. The normal economic state, more favorable for them, was not reached till the crisis of 1818–19 was well over. During the intervening years the minimum duty may have assisted the manufacturers without causing any permanent charge on the people. The fact that careful and self-reliant men, like the founders of the Waltham and Lowell enterprises, were most urgent in advising the adoption of the rates of 1816—at a time, too, when the practice of appealing to Congress for assistance when in distress had not yet become common among manufacturers—may indicate that those rates were of service in encouraging the continuance of the manufacture. How seriously its progress would have been impeded or retarded by the absence of duties, cannot be said. On the whole, although the great impulse to the industry was given during the war, the duties on cottons in the tariff of 1816 may be considered a judicious application of the principle of protection to young industries.

Before 1824, the manufacture, as we have seen, was securely established. The further application of protection in that and in the following years was needless, and, so far as it had any effect, was harmful. The minimum valuation was raised in 1824 to 30 cents, and in 1828 to 35 cents. The minimum duties were thereby raised to $7\frac{1}{2}$ and $8\frac{3}{4}$ cents respectively. By 1824 the manufacture had so firm a hold that its further extension should have been left to individual enterprise, which by that time might have been relied on to carry the industry as far as it was for the economic interest of the country that it should be carried. . . .

THE WOOLLEN MANUFACTURE

The sudden and striking growth of the cotton manufacture in the last hundred years has caused its history, in this country as in others, to be written with comparative fullness. Of the early history of the manufacture of woollen goods in the United States we have but scanty accounts; but these are sufficient to show that the general course of events was similar to that in cotton manufacturing. During the colonial period and the years immediately after the Revolution, such woollen cloths as were not spun and woven in households for personal use were imported from England. The goods of household manufacture, however, formed, and for many years after the introduction of machinery continued to form, by far the greater part of those in use. The first attempt at making woollens in large quantities is said to have been made at Ipswich, Mass., in 1792; but no machinery seems to have been used in this undertaking. In 1794 the new machinery was for the first time applied to the manufacture of wool, and it is noteworthy that, as in the case of the cotton manufacture, the machinery was introduced by English workmen. These were the brothers Arthur and John Scholfield, who came to the United States in 1793, and in the next year established a factory at Byfield, Mass. Their machinery, however, was exclusively for carding wool, and for dressing (fulling) woollen goods; and for the latter purpose it was probably in no way different from that of the numerous fulling-mills which were scattered over the country during colonial times. Spinning and weaving were done, as before, on the spinning-wheel and the hand-loom. The Scholfields introduced carding-machinery in place of the hand-cards, and seem to have carried on their business in several places with success. A Scotchman, James Saunderson, who emigrated in 1794, also introduced carding-machines at New Ipswich, N. H., in 1801. Their example, however, was followed by few. Carding-machines were introduced in a few other places between 1800 and 1808; but no development of the business of systematically making cloth, or preparing wool for sale, took place. The application of machinery for spinning does not seem to have been made at all. One great difficulty in the way of the woollen manufacture was the deficient supply and poor quality of wool. The means of overcoming this were supplied when in 1802 a large flock of fine merino sheep was imported from Spain, followed in 1809 and 1810 by several thousand pure merinos from the same country. But imports from England continued to be large, and those woollen cloths that were not homespun were obtained almost exclusively from the mother country.

When the period of restriction began in 1808, the woollen manufacture received, like all other industries in the same position, a powerful stimulus. The prices of broadcloth, then the chief cloth worn besides homespun, rose enormously, as did those of flannels, blankets, and other goods, which had previously been obtained almost exclusively by importation. We have no such detailed statements as are given of the rise of the cotton manufacture. It is clear, however, that the manufacture of woollen goods, which had had no real existence before, began, and was considerably extended. The spinning of wool by machinery was introduced, and goods were made for sale on a large scale. As early as 1810 the carding and spinning of wool by machinery was begun in some of the cotton mills in Rhode Island. In Northampton, Mass., Oriskany, N. Y., and other places, large establishments for the manufacture of woollen goods and of satinets (mixed cotton and woollen goods) sprang up. The value of woollen goods made in factories is said to have risen from $4,000,000 in 1810 to $19,000,000 in 1815.

After 1815 the makers of woollens naturally encountered great difficulties in face of the renewed and heavy importations of English goods. The tariff of 1816 gave them the same duty that was levied on cottons,

25 per cent., to be reduced in three years to 20 per cent. The reduction of the duty to 20 per cent., which was to have taken place in 1819, was then postponed, and in the end never took place. No minimum valuation was fixed for woollen goods; hence there was not, as for cotton goods, a minimum duty. Wool was admitted at a duty of 15 per cent. The scheme of duties, under the tariff of 1816, thus afforded no very vigorous protection. Nor did the provisions of the act of 1824 materially improve the position of the woollen manufacturers. The duty on woollen goods was in that act raised to 30 per cent. in the first instance, and to 33⅓ per cent. after 1825. At the same time the duty on wool (except that costing ten cents a pound or less) was raised to 20 per cent. in the first place, to 25 per cent. after 1825, and to 30 per cent. after 1826. If foreign wools had to be imported to supplement the domestic supply,—and such a necessity has constantly existed in this country since 1816,—the increased price of wool in this country, as compared with other countries which admitted wool free or at a lower duty, would tend to make the effectual protection to woollen manufacturers far from excessive.

Notwithstanding the very moderate encouragement given from 1816 to 1828, the woollen manufacture steadily progressed after the crisis of 1819, and in 1828 was securely established. During the years from the close of the war till 1819 much embarrassment was felt, and many establishments were given up; but others tided over this trying time. After 1819 the industry gradually responded to the more favorable influences which then set in for manufactures, and made good progress. During 1821 and 1822 large investments were made in factories for making woollen cloths, especially in New England. In 1823 the manufacturers of woollens in Boston were sufficiently numerous to form an independent organization for the promotion of their interests, which were, in that case, to secure higher protective duties. The best evidence which we have of the condition of the industry during these years is to be found in the testimony given in 1828 by various woollen manufacturers before the Committee of the House of Representatives on Manufactures. This testimony shows clearly that the industry was established in 1828 on such a scale that the difficulties arising from lack of skill and experience, unfamiliarity with machinery and methods, and other such temporary obstacles, no longer had influence in preventing its growth. The capital invested by the thirteen manufacturers who testified before this committee varied from $20,000 to $200,000, the average being $85,000. The quantity of wool used by each averaged about 62,000 pounds per year. These figures indicate a scale of operation very considerable for those days. Six of the factories referred to had been established between 1809 and 1815. With the possible exception of one, in regard to which the date of foundation was not stated, none had been established in the years between 1815 and 1820; the remaining six had been built after 1820. Spinning-machinery was in use in all. Some used power-looms, others hand-looms. The application of the power-loom to weaving woollens, said one manufacturer, had been made in the United States earlier than in England. An indication, similar to this, of the point reached by the American producers in the use of machinery, was afforded by the difference of opinion in regard to the comparative merits of the jenny, and of the "Brewster," a spinning-machine of recent invention. Goods of various kinds were made—broadcloths, cassimeres, flannels, satinets, and kerseys. The opinion was expressed by several that the mere cost of manufacturing was not greater in the United States than in England; that the American manufacturer could produce, at as low prices as the English, if he could obtain his wool at as low prices as his foreign competitor. This testimony seems to show conclusively that at the time when it was given the woollen manufacture had reached that point at which it might be left to sustain itself; at which accidental or artificial obstacles no longer stood in the way of its growth. That many of the manufacturers themselves wanted higher duties, is, for obvious reasons, not inconsistent with this conclusion. Progress had been less certain and rapid than in the case of the kindred cotton manufacture, for the conditions of production were less distinctly favorable. The displacement of the household products by those of the factory was necessarily a gradual process, and made the advance of the woollen manufacture normally more slow than that of the kindred industry. But the growth of the cotton manufacture, so similar to that of wool, of itself removed many of the obstacles arising from the recent origin of the latter. The use of machinery became common, and, when the first great steps had been taken, was transferred with comparative ease from one branch of textile production to another. In 1828, when for the first time heavy protection was given by a complicated system of minimum duties, and when the actual rates rose, in some cases, to over 100 per cent., this aid was no longer needed to sustain the woollen manufacture. The period of youth had then been past.

It appears that direct protective legislation had even less influence in promoting the introduction and early growth of the woollen than of the cotton manufacture. The events of the period of restriction, from 1808 to 1815, led to the first introduction of the industry, and gave it the first strong impulse. Those events may indeed be considered to have been equivalent to effective, though crude and wasteful, protective legislation, and it may be that their effect, as compared with the absence of growth before 1808, shows that protection in some form was needed to stimulate the early growth of the woollen manufacture. But, by 1815, the work of establishing the manufacture had been done. The moderate duties of the period from 1816 to 1828, partly neutralized by the duties on wool, may have something to sustain it; but the position gained in 1815 would hardly have been lost in the absence of these duties. By 1828, when strong protection was first given, a secure position had certainly been reached. . . .

CONCLUDING REMARKS

. . . It has appeared that the introduction of the cotton manufacture took place before the era of protection, and that—looking aside from the anomalous conditions of the period of restriction from 1808 to 1815—its early progress, though perhaps somewhat promoted by the minimum duty of 1816, would hardly have been much retarded in the absence of protective duties. The manufacture of woollens received little direct assistance before it reached that stage at which it could maintain itself without help, if it were for the advantage of the country that it should be maintained. In the iron manufacture twenty years of heavy protection did not materially alter the proportion of home and foreign supply, and brought about no change in methods of production. It is not possible, and hardly necessary, to carry the inquiry much further. Detailed accounts cannot be obtained of other industries to which protection was applied; but so far as can be seen, the same course of events took place in them as in the three whose history we have followed. The same general conditions affected the manufactures of glass, earthenware, paper, cotton-bagging, sail-duck, cordage, and other articles to which protection was applied during this time with more or less vigor. We may assume that the same general effect, or absence of effect, followed in these as in the other cases. It is not intended to speak of the production of agricultural commodities like sugar, wool, hemp, and flax, to which also protection was applied. In the production of these the natural advantages of one country over another tell more decidedly and surely than in the case of most manufactures, and it has not often been supposed that they come within the scope of the argument we are considering.

Although, therefore, the conditions existed under which it is most likely that protection to young industries may be advantageously applied —a young and undeveloped country in a stage of transition from a purely agricultural to a more diversified industrial condition; this transition, moreover, coinciding in time with great changes in the arts, which made the establishment of new industries peculiarly difficult—notwithstanding the presence of these conditions, little, if anything, was gained by the protection which the United States maintained in the first part of this century. Two causes account for this. On the one hand, the character of the people rendered the transition of productive forces to manufactures comparatively easy; on the other hand, the shock to economic habits during the restrictive period from 1808 to 1815 effectually prepared the way for such a transition. The genius of the people for mechanical arts showed itself early. Naturally it appeared with most striking results in those fields in which the circumstances of the country gave the richest opportunities; as in the application of steam-power to navigation, in the invention and improvement of tools, and especially of agricultural implements, and in the cotton manufacture. The ingenuity and inventiveness of American mechanics have become traditional, and the names of Whitney and Fulton need only be mentioned to show that these qualities were not lacking at the time we are considering. The presence of such men rendered it more easy to remove the obstacles arising from want of skill and experience in manufactures. The political institutions, the high average of intelligence, the habitual freedom of movement from place to place and from occupation to occupation, also made the rise of the existing system of manufacturing production at once more easy and less dangerous than the same change in other countries. At the same time it so happened that the embargo, the non-intercourse acts, and the war of 1812 rudely shook the country out of the grooves in which it was running, and brought about a state of confusion from which the new industrial system could emerge more easily than from a well-settled organization of industry. The restrictive period may indeed be considered to have been one of extreme protection. The stimulus which it gave to some manufactures perhaps shows that the first steps in these were not taken without some artificial help. The intrinsic soundness of the argument for protection to young industries therefore may not be touched by the conclusions drawn from the history of its trial in the United States, which shows only that the intentional protection of the tariffs of 1816, 1824, and 1828 had little effect. The period from 1808 till the financial crisis of 1818–19 was a disturbed and chaotic one, from which the country settled down, with little assistance from protective legislation, into a new arrangement of its productive forces.

FOR FURTHER READING: Importance is assigned to tariffs by Edward Stanwood, *American Tariff Controversies in the Nineteenth Century* (2 vols., New York, 1903). Minimizing the impact of tariffs is Frank W. Taussig, *The Tariff History of the United States* (7th ed., New York, 1923). See also George R. Taylor (ed.), *The Great Tariff Debate, 1820–1830* (Boston, 1953).

11. *Agriculture in the Nineteenth Century*

PROBLEM: *Was nineteenth-century land speculation profitable?*

Land was a major source of wealth in nineteenth-century America and land speculation one of the principal means for acquiring wealth on the frontier. But whether such speculation was remunerative is still an unsettled issue among historians. The federal land acts of 1800 and 1820 allowed the sale of tracts at $2 and $1.25 per acre, respectively, and the Preemption Act of 1841 allowed squatters to secure titles to tracts which they had occupied without legal rights. All of these laws were designed to distribute large portions of the public domain to private ownership. In this process of transfer, speculators played an important role. Whether their speculations were remunerative, however, is still debatable. Professor Paul W. Gates of Cornell University, a distinguished authority on American land policies, has concluded, on the basis of a number of his own specialized studies, that frequently it was a profitable endeavor. He notes that, despite ups and downs, individual land jobbers often made great profits. A somewhat different conclusion was reached by Professor Allan Bogue of the University of Iowa. In studying the business transactions of selected land dealers he found that some received smaller returns than from other forms of investment. Bogue feels that the evidence does not allow definitive conclusions. Both selections raise questions about the influence of land distribution on economic expansion. What factors explain the rise of land speculators? What functions did middlemen perform in the process of land transfers? What factors need to be considered in determining the profitability of land investments in nineteenth-century America?

The Role of the Land Speculator in Western Development

PAUL W. GATES

The land use pattern of the twenty-nine public land states of the South, the Middle West and the Far West is the result of a long process of development and adaptation in which such factors as speculation, absentee ownership, credit, usury, farm mechanization, transportation and government controls have played important roles. Only recently has the United States come to realize the errors it permitted to develop in this land use pattern. Land laws that were designed to meet a particular set of conditions at one time were permitted to remain in operation when circumstances were very different and the laws, once beneficial, now became subject to major abuse and the cause of much harm. Other laws proved full of loopholes seemingly impossible of being plugged by the incompetent and sometimes dishonest administrative officials. All this and the refusal to place restrictions on land accumulation until the best lands were gone permitted engrossment of great bodies of land by speculatively inclined individuals and groups of capitalists.

Wishful thinking, unwillingness to face the facts and political oratory combined to obscure the appearance of ominous signs that the land system was not working in the ideal way Jefferson had hoped it would in assuring a democratic pattern of farm ownership. A few notable spokesmen protested against policies which permitted concentration of land ownership; but Americans, big and little, were too much concerned with the accumulation of wealth through land speculation to listen to their Cassandra-like predictions. . . .

The term "land speculator" meant different things to different people and different sections. To a frontiersman it meant an eastern capitalist who bought large quantities of newly offered land in anticipation of settlers to come; or it meant a railroad or canal construction company to which had been given alternate sections of land in a strip ten or twenty miles wide paralleling the line of the improvement; or it meant a pineland baron who acquired 5,000, 10,000 or 50,000 acres of rich timberland. The frontiersman distinguished between resident and absentee speculators. Only non-resident owners of land who were not contributing to the development of the West by making improvements upon their lands were regarded by him as speculators and were the object of his resentment. Land grants for internal improvements were strongly favored by the

Reprinted from Paul Wallace Gates, "The Role of the Land Speculator in Western Development," *The Pennsylvania Magazine of History and Biography*, LXVI (July, 1942), pp. 314–333.

frontier which thirsted for connections with the outside world but the frontiersman expected these lands to be sold promptly and on the pre-emption system.

To an urban worker the term "speculator" meant someone who laid out towns or additions to them, donated lots of churches and schools, attracted industries or state institutions to the new communities and peddled out building lots at high prices to newcomers. To Horace Greeley the term meant, in addition, the thousands of persons settling the West who sought a stake in the land greater than they could expect to use personally. Greeley also applied it scornfully to those westerners of means who purchased wild lands as an investment, as did their eastern associates. All were speculators; all contributed their share to the pattern of ownership which exists today.

Although frontiersmen, as a rule, possessed little or no capital they were anxious to own as much land as possible. The first wave of settlers who followed the fur trader squatted upon choice locations, made rude improvements, and, when new arrivals came in, sold their claims and moved on to a new frontier before the government auction took place. These squatters were in a sense speculators. They sought to engross a half section or more and established claim associations to protect their rights. Henceforth these quasi-legal claims were bought and sold just like patent titles.

The second wave of settlers remained on the land until the auction sale on which occasion they borrowed to the hilt to buy as much land as possible. The more successful, who had brought considerable money with them, or who had accumulated something from the land and barter exchanges on the frontier, might have sufficient credit at the western banks to enable them to purchase 320, 480, or 640 acres. Loose banking policies made credit easy to secure and everyone attempted to borrow for land speculation. Rosy dreams of profits to be made distracted the attention of frontiersmen from the business of making farms in the wilderness. An English observer shrewdly remarked:

Speculation in real estate . . . has been the ruling idea and occupation of the Western mind. Clerks, labourers, farmers, storekeepers, merely followed their callings for a living, while they were speculating for their fortunes. . . . The people of the West became dealers in land, rather than its cultivators.

Calvin Fletcher, an Indianapolis banker and large landlord, deplored the granting of credit for speculative purchases of land. "The consequence is," he said in 1838, "that for the last 4 years say 6 years there has scarcely been the extension of a farm. No new fields opened & at the same time an enormous increase of consumers—What Son will go to work or what farmer will draw out the energies of his family where they can dress them, clothe them & feed them on the glorious anticipation of a year's accidents which may or may not pay the debt without an effort."

On every frontier the settler-speculator was present. He rarely learned from experience. By claiming 320 acres instead of 160 he separated himself that much more from his neighbor. He had to bear a heavier proportion of the cost of road construction and maintenance; his school costs were increased or the establishment of schools was delayed and his children were denied educational opportunities; the expense of county and state government, in a period when the land tax was the principal source of government income, was burdensome. Other social institutions like churches, granges, and libraries came more slowly because the population was so dispersed. Furthermore, railroads, which all settlers wanted in their vicinity, could not be pushed into sparsely settled areas without large subsidies. State and county subsidies required special assessments upon the already overburdened taxpaying farmers, and land grants, whether by federal or state governments, created a near land monopoly. Careful observers like Greeley saw many of these results and urged settlers to be content with smaller tracts which they could conveniently cultivate.

The chance of making a fortune in wild lands or town lots in the rapidly expanding communities of the West was an allurement difficult to resist. Fantastic stories of the profits others had won were printed in the newspapers and retold in letters from the West. Here, in 1818–1819, 1835–1837, or 1850–1857 was the lodestone to quick wealth. Touched by the fever of land speculation, excited people throughout the country borrowed to the extent of their credit for such investments. Men from all walks of life permitted their dreams to overcome their better judgment. Politicians, bankers, writers, ministers, planters and poets, everyone, it seemed, who had any resources at all undertook to invest in western lands. Levi Beardsley, a prominent New Yorker who went West in 1836 to invest some $20,000 in wild land, has left an interesting description of the speculative excitement of that year:

Every one was imbued with a reckless spirit of speculation. The mania, for such it undoubtedly was, did not confine itself to one particular class, but extended to all. Even the reverend clergy doffed their sacerdotals, and eagerly entered into competition with mammon's votaries, for the acquisition of this world's goods, and tested their sagacity against the shrewdness and more practiced skill of the professed sharper.

The existence of a class of professional land agents facilitated land purchases by absentee capitalists. Eastern papers with a wide circulation among the wealthy contained numerous advertisements of these land agents during the years from 1830 to 1857. In every enterprising community on the frontier were found agents who were prepared to buy or enter land for others with cash or warrants. For a commission of five per cent or a share in the transaction, generally from a third to a quarter, they would select land, sometimes by personal investigation, sometimes by a superficial search of the entry books and make purchases for their principals.

Some of the more important of these land agents were Henry W. Ellsworth of Lafayette, Indiana, Cook and Sargent of Davenport, Iowa, and Henry C. Putnam of Eau Claire, Wisconsin. Ellsworth published a booklet, *Valley of the Upper Wabash*, to attract attention to western Indiana and eastern Illinois and he and his father, Henry L. Ellsworth, Federal Commissioner of Patents, were able to induce hundreds of easterners, mostly New Englanders, to invest in the West. Cook and Sargent maintained offices in each of the eight land-office towns in Iowa where they entered nearly 200,000 acres. Putnam's entries in Wisconsin exceeded a half million acres.

These western land agents rank with the registers and receivers of the land offices as among the most important people on the frontier. They dealt in land warrants and scrip, ran a local note-shaving business, purchased exchange, sometimes operated a bank of issue with funds provided by eastern capitalists, loaned eastern funds to squatters at frontier rates ranging from twenty to sixty per cent, bought and sold land, paid taxes for absentee owners and undertook to protect their lands against depredations. At a later date, they arranged for renting land, made collections, and sold produce received in payment of rent. Small investors in the East were obliged to work through these agents, to submit to their exactions, and to suffer from their inefficiency and could not effectually protest against their obvious neglect. The agent could take his commission from rents or sales before any money was remitted to the owner, could sell his own land to prospective purchasers, rather than that of the owners he represented, could neglect tax payments and get the title involved, or could pay taxes on the wrong land. In numerous cases western agents took advantage of their clients, used the prestige which their contacts provided for personal interests, and constantly minimized the value of the land they represented in order to increase sales and thereby commissions. In this way absentee investors whose eastern responsibilities did not permit them to give personal attention to their possessions in the West were imposed upon and victimized.

A case in point is that of Senator Henry H. Hubbard of New Hampshire who, in association with Daniel Webster and other Yankees, invested well over $50,000 in western lands. Hubbard sent Moses B. Strong of Vermont to Wisconsin Territory in 1836 to invest a part of this money. Land was acquired and some sales were made by Strong before the crash of 1837 put a stop to the business. Thereafter the investment went from bad to worse. Strong's charges for the slight services rendered after the actual purchase were so heavy that Hubbard was forced to sell part of the land at distress prices. When sales declined Strong neglected the business for politics and Hubbard was obliged to supplant him.

An analogous case is that of Cyrus Woodman who represented a group of New England capitalists organized as the Boston and Western Land Company. This company invested $100,000 in 60,000 acres of wild land and in numerous embryo towns in Illinois, Wisconsin and Missouri in 1835 and 1836. The crash of 1837 broke the market; lands could scarcely be sold at any price and interest, taxes, and agents' costs further discouraged the Boston promoters. Woodman, who was sent to the West to retrieve something from the wreck of the company's once ambitious scheme, made no effort to put the investment in its best light but, from the first, filled his letters with pessimistic forebodings of ever greater contraction in prices accompanied by rising taxes. It is small wonder then that the owners became discouraged and sold their property to Woodman for a fraction of its cost. The land was that good prairie and timberland which in the fifties was to bring prices that almost justified the optimistic hopes of the thirties; but the original purchasers were not to share in the prosperity.

One of the most successful agent-speculator relationships was that of William A. Woodward and Henry C. Putnam who were natives of New York State. Both were shrewd judges of land values and both knew thoroughly the techniques of the land business. Putnam went to Wisconsin in the fifties where he invested funds of Woodward and other New Yorkers in short term loans to settlers and in timber and prairie land. The fees Putnam received for the numerous services performed for his eastern principals made him a leading businessman in the rising town of Eau Claire. He aided in selecting the university, school and swamp land, became land agent for a land-grant railroad, was elected register of deeds and county surveyor, and appointed Deputy United States Assessor, and with others founded the leading bank in Eau Claire. When Ezra Cornell was looking for someone to help him locate the million acres in land scrip which New York State had received under the Agricultural College Act, Woodward and Putnam persuaded him to let them make the selections in the Chippewa Valley where, Cornell was assured, Putnam virtually controlled all land entries by means of his position in the United States land office at Eau Claire. Cornell gave them the agency and from it they both made substantial profits.

A great impetus was given to land speculation in the mid-thirties by federal and state banking policies. The failure to recharter the Second Bank of the United States removed the curbs on state bank policy while the lure of federal deposits led to a scramble for such easy funds and to a mushroomlike growth of new banks in the South and West. Loans on real estate at inflated valuations were easily secured. Rising land values and easy credit attracted unprecedented quantities of capital from the

East for investment in wild lands and corner lots. The federal surplus produced by increased land sales was distributed among the states, thereby providing funds for elaborate schemes of internal improvements. Canals, railroads, highways were projected throughout the newer states, regardless of their feasibility. This combination of an easy banking policy with large government expenditures on public works came at a time when emigration to the western country was greatly accelerated. The total purchases of the hordes of immigrants and the speculators who were attempting to anticipate settler's needs made the public land sales of these years the largest in American history.

Between 1835 and 1837, 38,000,000 acres of public lands were sold, 29,000,000 of which were acquired for speculation. A minimum speculative investment of $36,000,000—exclusive of agents' costs, interest and taxes—was thus tied up in unimproved lands. To this figure should be added perhaps as large an amount for investments in town and city lots.

Much of this land purchasing was done by banks or bankers. For example, Isaac Bronson and his sons Frederick and Arthur, prominent bankers of New York, together with Charles Butler, brother of the attorney general of the United States, and a group of New York capitalists, used funds of the New York Life Insurance & Trust Company and other banks with which they had connections to buy a third of a million acres in eight states and territories. The prominence of the promoters and the fact that some of them were closely identified with an administration which favored land reform and denounced land speculators gave the Whigs an opportunity of showing how hollow were the pretensions of some Jacksonians.

Another group whose purchases of land were made with credit of banks it controlled consisted of such well-known Massachusetts financiers as John Tillson, Jr., John Shaw Hayward, Charles Holmes, Jr., Winthrop Gilman, and Griggs, Weld & Company. These men controlled the state bank of Illinois from which they were able to borrow for their extensive land speculations. When the bank itself undertook to loan funds to squatters and to buy large quantities of land it came to be regarded as the great financial octopus of Illinois and Iowa against which numerous anti-monopoly tirades were directed.

A group whose operations in banks, land and railroads was scarcely to be matched consisted of Alvah Buckingham and Solomon Sturges of Zanesville, Ohio, and their numerous children. They acquired or established banks of issue in Ohio, Indiana and Illinois, some of which received federal deposits. The banks made it possible for them to pyramid their land purchases until they ultimately reached 275,000 acres, or the equivalent of 1,760 quarter section farms. Railroads, grain elevators and lumber yards were added to this princely estate. Neither the Panic of 1837 nor that of 1857 destroyed the economic power of Buckingham and Sturges and for a generation their names were widely known from Ohio to Nebraska.

Throughout the East and, indeed, to a somewhat less degree in the old South, other banks, directors and customers of banks were using the credit to buy public lands. For years thereafter these banks or their receivers were engaged in disposing of quantities of wild land they had bought directly or acquired through mortgage foreclosures.

Squatters upon the public lands did not benefit from the easy banking policies of the thirties. Since they had no property to mortgage, credit was available to them only on the most usurious terms.

When newly surveyed lands were first announced for sale the squatters had to arrange for the purchase of their lands—made valuable by their improvements—before the opening of the auction or run the risk of losing them to speculators. Claim clubs and special preemption laws gave them protection against speculators only to the date of the sale. Squatters were inclined to put their meager capital into stock, housing, fencing and clearing which seemed the most essential for the moment and to hope that the land sale would be postponed until they could accumulate money with which to purchase their claims. The sale, although announced in advance by advertisement, seemed always to catch the settlers unprepared and obliged them to borrow from the "loan shark."

These moneylenders were the representatives of western banks and eastern capitalists. Their charges were five per cent for arranging loans and from two and one-half to five per cent for making collections. Such eminent westerners as William B. Ogden, James W. Grimes and Lucius Lyon, later to become, respectively, president of the Chicago and Northwestern Railroad, and United States Senators from Iowa and Michigan, made their start by lending eastern funds on such a basis.

Loan sharks were present at every public land auction and their agents were stationed in every land-office town, prepared to buy claims for squatters. The ten or twelve per cent allowed by the usury laws did not satisfy these moneylenders who found it possible to evade such restrictions. They would buy claims on which squatters had their improvements, according to previous agreements, and would then resell the land to them for an advance of $30 above cost on a quarter section. The squatter would agree to pay at the end of one or two years the maximum interest allowed by law. If the legal interest was twelve per cent and the debt was paid in one year the lender would net twenty-eight per cent upon his investment. The loan agents always denied that they were violating the usury laws but they were exceedingly loath to have cases involving their transactions taken into the courts. Thousands of desperate squatters throughout the West snatched at the aid offered by the moneylenders who personally or through land agents invested many millions of dollars in this lucrative business. When later the squatters had difficulty in meeting their obligations they turned against their creditors and raised the cry of usury.

Jackson's specie circular of 1836 struck squarely at the rapidly expanding volume of land purchases. It showed that the chief executive, unlike many of his followers such as Butler, Kendall, Walker, and Ellsworth, did not approve of the operations of land speculators and moneylenders. The president's purpose in issuing the circular was to "repress alleged frauds, and to withhold any countenance or facilities in the power of the Government from the monopoly of the public lands in the hands of speculators and capitalists, to the injury of the actual settlers in the new States, and of emigrants in search of new homes. . . ." Jackson further explained his purpose in his annual message of December, 1836, wherein he said the circular was intended to "save the new States from a non-resident proprietorship, one of the greatest obstacles to the advancement of a new country and the prosperity of an old one." Except for Jefferson, Jackson was the only American president who seriously deplored that feature of public land policy which permitted speculators to buy land in unlimited amounts.

The specie circular required that only gold or silver be accepted from purchasers of land, except actual settlers who were permitted to use bank notes for the remainder of the year. The order brought down the whole bloated structure which had been erected by unsound banking practices, the deposit of federal funds in the state banks, and the elaborate programs of internal improvements undertaken by the states. Land purchases by speculators stopped immediately; only the business of lending money to squatters remained.

The federal government's need of revenue caused the moneylending business to thrive for a time after the crash of 1837. Quantities of land were ordered into the market when it was clear that squatters could raise the purchase price of their claims only with the greatest difficulty. Despite pleas for postponement the sales were held. Western banks were now closed, only gold or silver was accepted at the sales and only eastern bankers could furnish it. In 1838 and 1839 Ogden found it possible to loan eastern funds to squatters to net thirty per cent a year before the deduction of commissions. Such usurious interest rates continued into the forties and, indeed, were increased in the fifties when it was possible for brokers to use in place of cash the military land warrants then in wide circulation at prices ranging downward to fifty cents an acre. By this means returns of forty, fifty and even sixty per cent could be secured from squatters.

Ogden, Grimes and Lyon had assured their principals that there was no risk in lending money to squatters to buy their claims since their improvements had already raised the value of the land above the government minimum price and since they would make every possible effort to pay their debts and secure title to land on which they had expended years of toil. These men did not foresee the deplorable situation into which the West was plunged after 1837. Squatters, now attempting to meet their payments under the most trying circumstances, fought a losing battle. Payments were delayed and then completely suspended. Many settlers became discouraged and moved on to another frontier to try once more to gain ownership of a piece of land.

Moneylenders, land speculators and gamblers in town lots now found themselves loaded with financial burdens which they could not carry. Their land was unsaleable, yet their taxes continued to mount as did also the interest on the money they had borrowed. Having invested everything in property not easily liquidated, they now were forced to surrender much of their land to the banks when these institutions began to call in their loans. The abstracts of conveyances for the years following the Panic of 1837 show a tremendous volume of mortgage foreclosures of large estates.

These foreclosures, the suspension of most of the wildcat banks and the bankruptcy of many financial institutions in the East all combined to keep land titles in the West in a state of chaos. Taxes were paid tardily, if at all, tax titles of a dubious nature were annually issued and the difficulties of an already complex situation were thereby increased. During the period of stress settlers accumulated grievances against the absentee owners which seemed to justify stealing their timber, despoiling their fences and buildings and using their land for pasture. New settlers moved on the absentee-owned land, sometimes bought a tax title and set up a claim of ownership by right of possession and the tax deed. Absentee owners were powerless to deal with such a problem unless their property investment was sufficiently large to enable them to maintain a local agent employed on a full-time basis to watch over their interests.

During the bleak years of the early forties the equity of absentees was gradually eaten up by tax titles, agents' costs, interest and depredation. Ultimately the burden became too great and many sold their holdings for less than the original cost, disregarding interests, fees and taxes. It was this situation that induced Dr. Joseph Schafer, for years a careful student of land problems and policies, to conclude that land speculation was on the whole an unprofitable business.

The career of Calvin Fletcher, a cautious Hoosier from New England and reared in an atmosphere of conservative finance, sheds much light on this era of unbridled land speculation. The craze for speculation overcame Fletcher's better judgment and with Nicholas McCarty, likewise a Hoosier, he engaged in a joint speculation with $40,000 borrowed from the state bank of Indiana of which Fletcher was a director. The mental torture Fletcher went through during the following years as a result of this "hazardous" investment is recorded in his diary. Unlike the majority of settler-speculators who lost their land when the depression years set in, Fletcher was able to carry his investment until it began to produce returns. In 1846, when the banks had foreclosed many mortgages and thousands of farmers having lost their homes had either gone elsewhere to make another attempt at securing ownership of land or had sunk to the position of tenants upon their old claims, Fletcher stated that one third of the voters of Indiana were then "tenants or day laborers or young men who have acquired no property."

On the frontier the fog of depression is quickly dissipated by rising commodity prices, quickened immigration, and a new influx of capital. In the middle forties these factors were again at work and there followed a new era of land speculation in which old residents and new settlers participated equally. The curve of land purchases shot upward as people in all occupations once more neglected their routine work to buy raw prairie land or corner lots in newly platted cities. Eastern capitalists again established banks of issue in the West and South under the lax systems still prevailing there and used the funds to purchase land. Land agents, professional locators, loan sharks, town-site promoters flourished. Few seemed to have learned from experience.

The peak years of speculative purchasing were 1854 to 1858, when a total of 65,000,000 acres of public domain were disposed of to purchasers or holders of land warrants. To this figure should be added an equal or greater amount of land which was granted to the states for canals, railroads, swamp drainage and education and by them sold, mostly to speculators, large and small. A comparison of the census figures of land in farms with the land-office figures of land sold shows a tremendous concentration of speculator-owned land in all public land states, especially in the newer states like Iowa, Wisconsin, Illinois, Missouri and Arkansas.

The speculators' contributions to the present day pattern of land ownership and land use are most important. For a generation agricultural economists have said that tenancy was an inevitable result of the commercialization of farming and rising land values. This is true but tenancy got its start in the Middle West as a result of the activities of land speculators and moneylenders. Squatters who could not meet their usurious demands had their contracts cancelled and their equity confiscated. They might, however, remain on their old claims as tenants and pay rent for the land or they might make a new contract for the land but at a higher valuation. In either case, the farmer found ownership difficult to attain. Elsewhere speculators dismayed at the cost of carrying their projects, sought relief by inducing land seekers to settle on their holdings, the sole condition being that they must pay taxes. If land was scarce it was not difficult to persuade immigrants to settle upon speculators' tracts, perhaps with the understanding that they might be able to buy later. The farmers' improvements raised the value of the property but did not bring in immediate cash income sufficient to enable them to make payments upon the land. As the value went up the owners' price increased; ownership proved unattainable to many. Tenancy thus had come to stay in the first generation of settlement in Illinois, Indiana, Iowa, Kansas and Nebraska. Furthermore, owners of small farms had borrowed heavily to secure title and from their debts many were never to be free. Some were ultimately depressed to the state of tenancy.

Speculator ownership and tenancy did not always result in the best use of the land. It has already been seen that speculator ownership forced widespread dispersion of population and placed heavy tax burdens upon farmers whose improved lands could be more heavily assessed than the speculators' unimproved land. Furthermore, speculators were slow to pay taxes. They resisted increased levies, secured injunctions against expenditures for buildings and roads, and sometimes simply refused to pay taxes. Heavy interest penalties and tax titles did not trouble them particularly since they knew they could later make a compromise settlement with the hard-pressed county boards, or could have the tax titles set aside by the courts. All this meant that the tillers of the soil, if they were to enjoy the benefits of schools, roads and local railroads had to dig down into their own jeans more deeply because the speculators were not carrying their share of the burden. Taxes continued to climb and rarely or never declined, even in a period of depression. They are one of the rigid costs which trouble the farmers deeply when their own income is sharply declining. Heavy tax burdens forced farm practices which depleted the soil, produced erosion and diminished land values.

Speculators left their mark on the West in other ways than in land ownership. The nationalizing influence of their investments in western lands should not be neglected. Speculators were naturally inclined to favor internal improvements in the vicinity of their land. The Wabash Canal, the Illinois and Michigan Canal, the Des Moines River Navigation and Improvement Company and the Fox and Wisconsin Canal were all the work of speculators who sought to increase the value of their holdings by bringing transportation facilities to them at government expense. The investments of Daniel Webster of Massachusetts and John Rockwell of Connecticut in central Illinois made them keenly aware of the need for internal improvements in the prairie state and led them to support the movement for railroad land grants for that area.

The land and town lot speculators were also influential in securing state, county and municipal subsidies for local railroads. Many railroad enterprises were in themselves as much land speculations as transportation developments. The pinery railroads of northern Wisconsin promised few or no profits from operations but the land grants included valuable stands of white pine from which large returns might be secured. Some of the railroads for which there now seems little justification were doubtless chartered for the sake of the land grant.

Land and town lot speculators had much to do with railroad strategy in the West. During the territorial period of Kansas and in the first decade of statehood the struggle between the supporters of rival routes for land grants for their railroad enterprises is one of the chief issues, transcending in importance the slavery and union issues. Out of the melee certain groups emerged triumphant such as that which revolved around one of the most notorious corruptionists in American history, Samuel C. Pomeroy. Two railroads of which he was an officer and stockholder received land grants, one was permitted to buy a valuable ceded Indian reservation for less than its current value and three were required to converge on his own town of Atchison. The struggle over the location of the eastern terminus of the Union Pacific Railroad, the efforts of Cairo, Illinois, promoters to require the Illinois Central to locate its southern terminus at that point, the desire of the Northern Pacific to build up its own town on Puget Sound are illustrations of how speculators, whether operating within or without the railroad companies, have influenced the location of railroad routes and their terminal points. Another factor which tended to prevent railroads from selecting the shortest line between two points was the desire of their promoters to secure the largest possible land grants.

The petty fights over the location of county seats, territorial and state capitals, land offices, state universities, agricultural colleges and normal schools, and institutions for the insane, the blind and the criminal comprise no small part of the political controversies of the time. That some of these institutions were located in remote, inaccessible places wholly unsuited to the functions they were to perform may be blamed upon speculators who succeeded in having them established in the vicinity of their lands.

Westerners were united in their demand that the federal government should donate to the states the land within their boundaries. This demand was never attained in full but it was achieved in part through a piecemeal system of securing special grants for education, canals, river improvements and the drainage of swamp lands. As successive states entered the union they were given larger proportions of their land, the proportion running as high as one third in the case of Arkansas, Louisiana, Michigan, and Minnesota, to two thirds in the case of Florida. The states were expected to sell these lands for the best possible price and the proceeds, if derived from education grants, were to provide endowments. Speculator influence in the state capitals and county seats tended to break down the effective utilization of these grants.

Numerous scandals marked the sale of state lands and indicate that state and local governments were even more subject to speculator influence than was Congress and the General Land office. The two-township grant for state universities brought little in return, the common school sections were in many cases wastefully administered, the agricultural college lands or their scrip equivalent were sold for a pittance by Rhode Island, Massachusetts, Indiana, Ohio and other states and the river improvement grants were wasted away. Worst managed of all were the swamp lands, of which 64,000,000 acres were patented to the states. Some were sold for as low as ten cents an acre; others were given to railroad companies to aid in construction; still others were granted to drainage companies for the improvements they contracted to make. Little or no security was ever required by the local officials for the performance of the contracts and in few cases were the improvements actually made. One prairie county of Illinois permitted its judge to contract 47,000 acres to a Utica, New York, resident on the understanding that he would drain the lands. The latter were conveyed but no improvements were made; later it was found that the judge had an interest in the business.

Indian lands were fair game for speculators who used both legal and illegal means to secure them. Traders and speculators devised a method by which treaties of cession would include 640 acre allotments of the choicer lands to chiefs and half-breeds. They could easily be induced to sign away their allotments for an extra potion of whisky. By this means most of the desirable land along the upper Wabash Valley in Indiana and other valuable tracts in Illinois, Mississippi, Alabama and Wisconsin passed into the hands of speculators including the great trading firm of W. G. & G. W. Ewing of Fort Wayne, Senator John Tipton of Indiana and Simon Cameron of Pennsylvania.

In Kansas speculator influence carried this method of land acquisition even farther. Here Indian tribes such as the Potawatomi (whose members had already been victimized by the Wabash traders), the Kickapoo, the Delawares, the Cherokees, and the Osage were induced to cede over 9,000,000 acres of land in trust, to be sold for their benefit. Such lands were not to become part of the public domain and were, therefore, not subject to the general laws. Until Congress woke up to what was going on these tracts were being rapidly conveyed to groups and individuals close to the Indian Office for distinctly less than their actual market value at the time.

Speculators pressed for the general allotment system which was adopted in 1887. They also cooperated with the lumbermen of Wisconsin and Minnesota in securing the opening of reservations containing valuable stands of white pine.

To gain their objectives the speculators were forced to enter politics. Whether from the East or West, they opposed a free homestead policy which, they feared, would reduce the value of their holdings. They favored grants for railroads and measures to make easier land accumulation. They were influential in local and state governments which they warped to suit their interests. Thus one sees Wisconsin in the seventies and eighties controlled by a tight little group of lumbermen-speculators including Cadwallader Washburn, Jim Thorp, Nelson Luddington, Philetus Sawyer, William Price, and Isaac Stephenson. Elsewhere the story is the same. These men opposed land reform, fought other agrarian legislation, championed protective tariff duties, and condemned monetary heresies. They represented the creditor, the large property owners, the railroads and the rising industrialists. Not until 1888 and 1889, by which time the best of the public land was gone, were they ready to abandon their long struggle to prevent the public domain from being reserved for actual settlers only, a recommendation long since made by Jefferson and Jackson.

The successful land dealer of one generation became the banker, the local political oracle and office holder or the country squire of the next. Scarcely a city or country town in the West but had its first family whose fortune had been made by shrewd selection of lands and their subsequent sale or rental to later comers. Wealth which had come easily to them through their speculations had become a vested interest which they sought to protect against the demagogues who demanded the ten hour day in the sawmills, or the imposition of an income tax, or the regulation of railroads.

The influence of the speculator may also be noted in the cultural field. The owners of western lands were not only responsible for a flood of pamphlets, booklets, guidebooks and emigrant gazettes advertising their projects, but also for many travel books published for the same purpose. It is well known that Samuel Augustus Mitchell's *Illinois in 1837*, was published to aid the sale of the 124,000 acres of land purchased in 1836 and 1837 by John Grigg, Mitchell and other Philadelphians. Similarly, none can doubt that Henry W. Ellsworth's *Valley of the Upper Wabash*, is a real estate advertisement and not a careful appraisal of the Grand Prairie of Indiana and Illinois. William Ferguson, J. G. Kohl, and Richard Cobden also wrote accounts primarily to aid the sale of lands in Illinois. James Caird, an English agricultural journalist, on the other hand, disguised his land promotion propaganda so effectively that reputable historians have continued to borrow from his *Prairie Farming in America*, little realizing how prejudiced and distorted it is. Even Charles Dickens, whose investment in Cairo real estate proved disastrous to him, was attracted to America, in part, out of curiosity to see the investment which had repaid him so poorly. The productions of numerous other writers who were interested in western lands were widely read at the time of their publication and for years were drawn upon by subsequent travelers and compilers of guide books.

For better or for worse the speculator, whether absentee or resident, squatter or banker, local politician or eastern senator, was present on every frontier. He affected every phase of western development and left in all places his indelible mark. His motives and his deeds one may deplore but so characteristically American was he, so dynamic a part did he play in shaping land and cultural patterns that it is difficult to imagine an American frontier without him.

"Profits" and the Frontier Land Speculator

ALLAN AND MARGARET BOGUE

From the days of the confederation through the nineteenth century, the frontier land speculator was a familiar figure in the United States. Perambulating foreigners recorded the activities of this gentleman, and land speculation was discussed in both Congress and in the editorial columns of Western newspapers. Many twentieth-century students of America's political and economic development have dealt in one way or another with frontier land speculation. They have depicted the land speculator at times as a sinister figure, corroding the morals of national or state legislators as the lawmakers endeavored to formulate land policy. Writers have sketched the antagonism between speculator and "actual settler." Nor have they ignored the effect which the speculator had upon the social and economic development of the region in which he operated. Such commentators have contributed to a literature that has its share of colorful characters and even displays the occasional symbol: star-crossed Robert Morris entering debtors' prison; the desperate debtors of the Holland Land Company advancing upon the Batavia land office; the little spade that William Scully lashed to his saddle as he set out to transplant Irish tenancy to the Illinois prairies.

There are, however, a number of overlapping and interdependent questions concerning frontier land speculation to which the answers are as yet far from complete. How and to what extent, for example, did land speculators affect the economic development of the United States? To what degree did Western land speculation contribute to the concentration of capital in America during the nineteenth century? How, if at all, did this alternative avenue of investment affect the policy decisions of the American businessman? Did the land speculators actually get something for nothing, as some writers seem to suggest? What rate of return did speculators in the raw lands of the frontier actually derive from their

Reprinted by permission from *The Journal of Economic History*, XVII, No. 1 (March, 1957), pp. 1–24.

capital? The answers to the first four questions obviously are closely related to the one given to the fifth; this article will be primarily concerned with the answer to the last question.

Land speculation was a recurrent theme in Joseph Schafer's careful analysis of the settlement process in Wisconsin. In two volumes of the Wisconsin Domesday series Schafer considered the profits of specific land speculators, and he generalized his findings to some extent in *The Social History of American Agriculture.* He concluded that the state lands in Wisconsin provided better speculations than did Federal government land and that pine-bearing Federal land was more remunerative than farm land. When speculators bought land shortly before settlers arrived "they of course made money fast." But in "their expectations of profit from holding farm lands speculators were often disappointed. For in numerous instances the holding period was long, and when the lands came to be wanted by farmers it was difficult to sell, in competition with land-office sales of Congress land, at prices that would recoup the speculators for both principal and interest, to say nothing of such taxes as they had to pay in the interim."

Schafer based his conclusions on the cost and sale data of a number of speculators, but in several instances he did little more than compare sale and cost figures in impressionistic fashion without resorting to careful calculation. When he did present a more elaborate analysis of the returns obtained from 20,000 acres purchased on behalf of Sir Charles A. Murray during the 1830's, he was to be criticized for mishandling the item of sales commissions and for neglecting the possibility that the speculator might have received some returns from rent prior to sale. More serious, however, were the defects in his method of calculating returns. In brief, Schafer compounded interest at an arbitrary 5 per cent on Murray's cost until 1880 when the last tract was sold. Similarly, he compounded interest at 5 per cent against the receipts from sales to the same year and then compared the two totals at his terminal date, concluding that Murray had met a small loss because the accumulated costs of $266,000 outweighed the compounded receipts by $6,000. But much of Murray's land was actually sold during the 1850's and 1860's, and it was highly misleading to continue compounding interest against the investment in land which was sold long prior to the terminal date. Similarly it was confusing to compound the receipts since such returns actually signified that the speculation from which they were derived was closed.

During the early 1940's two graduate students at the University of Mississippi, Mattie Russell and Edwin W. Chapman, undertook intensive study of speculation in two Mississippi counties between 1836 and 1861 with the express purpose of determining whether or not investors in wild land realized profits. Subsequently their graduate director summarized their findings in *The Journal of Southern History.* Both Russell and

Chapman defined speculators as all land companies, individuals, and partnerships purchasing 2,000 acres or more, "unless a large amount of the land was held by an individual at the time of his death." Using this yardstick the researchers compiled lists of large owners from the deed records and abstracted all their individual purchases and sales. Then the authors calculated both total and average purchase and sale prices for the entire acreage purchased by each speculator. They presented the difference between these purchase and sale figures as profit. If an investor's transactions covered a span of fifteen years, then total profit divided by fifteen was taken as the yearly profit on the investment. Both students concluded that speculators as a group did not realize "large returns" on their investments. Their method of calculating profit, however, hardly inspires confidence. They made no effort to compound interest; they did not consider costs of ownership other than the original purchase price of the land; and they failed to take into consideration the fact that speculators usually liquidated their investment at an uneven rate.

In the writings of Paul W. Gates may be found a more optimistic evaluation of the profitability of land speculation for at least some investors. He has referred to the commonplace of "first families" in Middle Western communities whose financial strength grew from "shrewd dealings in real estate." In the *Wisconsin Pine Lands of Cornell University* this author went beyond such generalizations and presented an analysis of expenditures and income arising from Cornell's speculation in some 512,400 acres of land in Wisconsin, Minnesota, and Kansas. Subtracting from all income the items of expense incurred by ownership of the land including taxes, interest, location fees, legal expenses, salaries, commissions, and the cost of land scrip, he found that the venture returned a net profit of approximately $5,000,000 to the university. All expenses totaled $1,728,596. Gates concluded: "The Cornell land business was one of the outstandingly successful land speculations in American history. . . ." The preservation of university records relating to the land business made possible so concrete an answer to the question of whether this speculation was or was not profitable, but Professor Gates did not consider it feasible to reduce his net profit to a per cent per annum basis. . . .

Although there are notable exceptions to this point of view, one can hardly study the body of literature bearing on speculator profits without concluding that speculation in Western lands was usually a losing business. James Silver reflected this prevailing point of view in his summary of the work of Russell and Chapman when he wrote, "An occasional bonanza proved to be the exception to the rule," and claimed that the work of his students added "confirmatory evidence that many buoyant hopes and expectations of speculators in frontier farm lands faded into disillusionment under the harsh light of reality." If historians accept such generalizations they are forced by logic to a rather unflattering evaluation of the perspicacity of American businessmen during the nineteenth century. Many of them were gamblers indeed who persisted in buying land on speculation, although the returns were consistently low and although, to borrow Professor Silver's phrasing, "greater success with much less risk could have been secured in commercial enterprises in the more settled Eastern communities." Or perhaps we should conclude that there was an obtuse element among American capitalists whose members stubbornly diverted capital from more remunerative uses into frontier land speculation although its wide and continuing prevalence must have demonstrated that the "bonanza" was exceptional. Actually the evidence is so scattered and so unsatisfactory that historians are hardly justified in generalizing upon the losses and gains of the frontier speculator.

Because the evidence bearing upon the profits from frontier land speculation is inadequate at this point, we have ventured to work up and present relevant material which we accumulated in the course of other research. We have calculated the returns obtained by land speculators from the purchase and sale of some three townships of agricultural land in the Middle West between 1835 and 1904. Stated differently, these figures picture the returns obtained from 77,529 acres of land divided into 946 tracts which were held for periods of time varying from but a few months to some thirty-five years.

These data can be summarized most easily by presenting them in two parts; one section is devoted to some speculative ventures in the Grand Prairie of Illinois and a second describes the operations of the Davenport brothers of Bath, New York, in eastern Nebraska. Both groups obtained and sold greater acreages than are treated here. In order to be certain, however, that the calculations involved only land which had not been improved at the owner's expense prior to resale, considerable acreage was discarded. In the case of the Davenports another major criterion of selection was applied as well; since it was wished to have one portion of the study stand as a clear-cut illustration of the speculative opportunities presented by Federal land policy, land which the brothers purchased from grantors other than the Federal government, the state government, or the land grant railroads was discarded. The cost, sale, and tax figures for the Illinois lands were derived from the Federal land entry books, county records, and a collection of business papers belonging to one of the speculators. The land account book and business correspondence of the Davenports provided the basic data for the Nebraska study. In neither case, as shall be pointed out in greater detail later, were the sources completely free from defects.

The method of calculating returns on the investments of the speculators was not complicated. For each parcel of land that was sold as a unit, a schedule was prepared showing the initial investment and yearly taxes. Some of the Davenport schedules were more complicated than others because the brothers paid for some of their land in installments, and revenue was obtained prior to sale from rents and abortive sales. For each tract of land the rate of interest was found which, when compounded against the original investment and subsequent costs, gave a total investment at the date of sale equal to the sale price. This was called the rate of return on invested capital. When rents or the occasional down payment from a canceled sale were obtained from a tract of land, such income was subtracted from the total investment in the tract at the date when it was received. This procedure, of course, raised the rate of return. The various rates of return on tracts sold in the same year were combined into weighted means, showing the average rate of return per dollar invested. Second, the total investment and the average rate of return per dollar invested at five-year intervals for both the Illinois and the Nebraska lands have been shown. It has been assumed in this last calculation that each tract returned year by year the rate which its ultimate sale price revealed. Knowledge of these rates was, of course, denied to the speculators themselves, prior to the sale of any given tract. . . .

Chosen for study here are some 43,229 acres of raw land which John and Ira Davenport acquired in six counties, located in the rolling prairie of eastern Nebraska, during the years 1870, 1871, and 1880 and sold during their lifetimes. The brothers purchased this acreage in part directly from the Federal government and in part obtained it from major land-distribution agencies which had acquired the land from the Federal government. Neither speculator nor hopeful farmer had intervened in the chain of title prior to the Davenports. Nor did the brothers endeavor to enhance the value of this land in any way by adding improvements at their own expense.

Of this acreage, the New Yorkers purchased 16,521 acres in Dodge County from the Union Pacific Railroad Company during 1870 and 1871, at prices ranging from $4.00 to $7.00 per acre. In making this purchase the brothers took advantage of the five-year credit plan offered by the railroad and cut their outlay by tendering in payment the company's land-grant bonds which they could buy at a considerable discount during the early 1870's. Both of these circumstances have been taken into consideration in calculating the return of the Dodge County lands. In 1880 John and Ira Davenport acquired another 4,817 acres of railroad lands in the Nebraska grant of the Burlington line. These holdings lay in Madison County and cost on the average $2.40 per acre.

From those lands given by the Federal government to finance the construction of a state penitentiary in Nebraska, the New Yorkers purchased 5,285 acres in Lancaster and Seward counties during 1871. The price of individual tracts in this purchase varied from $3.50 to $5.00 per acre. During the same year the Davenport brothers located 16,606 acres of government land by private entry in Wayne and Pierce counties, using military bounty warrants which they had acquired at a cost of approximately $1.15 per acre through brokers in New York and Chicago. Land-office fees, purchase of settler locations, and the services of an agent at Omaha combined to raise the initial cost of these lands to an estimated $1.25 per acre.

L. D. Richards of the firm of Richards, Keene and Company, located at Fremont, Nebraska, supervised the administration and sale of all the Davenport land in the six counties, although he selected local representatives in several counties with whom he split commissions. These amounted to approximately 3½ per cent of the sale price. Consistently the Davenports urged that their lands be sold to actual farmers on adjacent lands, and that the sale price be fully equal to the actual use value of the land so that speculators would not be attracted. Detailed study of individuals who purchased the Dodge County lands showed that Richards heeded these admonitions in that county at least. For some 22,500 acres of Davenport land almost complete tax lists could be prepared. For the remainder, specific information was generally available for more than half the years. The gaps in the tax series were filled in with estimates which were placed at as high a figure as seemed credible in the light of the yearly payments of which definite record was found. Undoubtedly there were additional petty expenses chargeable to land account which were not discovered but they could not have been very important. The Davenports began to offer their Dodge County lands in 1877, and over the next ten years also opened the lands in the other five counties to sale. Between 1878 and the death of the surviving brother, Ira, in 1904, the brothers sold land from their Nebraska holdings every year.

When the average returns on these Nebraska lands by year of sale are considered, it is found that they ranged from 9 to 12 per cent over the first four years of sales. Then followed a number of years in which the rate of return did not fall below 11 per cent per annum and in one year stood slightly above 19 per cent. With 1887 the returns dropped back to nearly the level of the first years, holding fairly steady between 10 and 12 per cent. The year 1893 marked a sharp break and thereafter returns held between 6.9 and 9 per cent until 1901, when 2,803 acres of land yielded an average return of 5.7 per cent on the investment. In the following three years the returns held at 6 and 7 per cent with the exception of one 40-acre tract in Dodge County which had been rented since the early 1880's and on which rental payments raised the rate of return up to 12 per cent.

When the calculation of the total investment of the Davenports in their Nebraska land at five-year intervals along with the average return per dollar invested was made, the results appeared less striking than the year-by-year analysis. Returns on the investment fund dropped steadily from just under 11 per cent on the $267,974 invested in 1880 down to 6.5 per cent on the $93,946 invested in the year 1900.

Some of the variations in return become more understandable when the county averages that underlie the aggregate averages are discussed. The relatively high returns of the early 1880's reflect a real-estate killing which John and Ira Davenport made on the lands purchased from the Burlington Railroad in Madison County. The brothers bought these lands in 1880 and sold them in short order on a rising land market. Although the return on individual tracts ran still higher, of course, some 4,000 acres of these lands averaged 39.5 per cent on the investment when sold in 1882. By 1885 the stimulating effect of the Madison lands had disappeared from the averages. In general through the 1880's the yearly rate of return on the Union Pacific land and on the acreage obtained by locating land warrants held between 10 and 12 per cent, but the returns on penitentiary land pulled the over-all average downward. When Western real-estate prices fell generally in 1893, and returns on the Davenport lands fell across the board, the penitentiary lands still stood as the least remunerative among these investments. On 800 acres of Lancaster land that were sold in 1901, the Davenport brothers realized but 3 per cent on the funds invested.

Contrary to the case in Illinois, the survey reports describing Nebraska soils are sufficiently detailed that discussion of the relation between speculator returns and soil productivity is possible. We must remember, however, that most of the Davenport lands were located and sold before the characteristics of eastern Nebraska soils were known in more than a general way. Nor were the pioneer farmers fully aware of the variations in rainfall which, along with topography, are important in determining the productivity of agricultural land in eastern Nebraska. The Davenport lands comprised a percentage of the choicer soil types that equaled or was greater than the equivalent county percentage with the exception only of the holdings in Lancaster County. There, soil types now considered unsuitable for cropping made up 32 per cent of the Davenport lands, while the county as a whole contained but 6 per cent of the same soils. Taking soils, rainfall, and topography into consideration, the most desirable Davenport lands lay in Dodge, Wayne, and Madison counties, and it is significant that the brothers realized their highest returns in those counties. Despite the fact, however, that the farmer works under more favorable conditions in Dodge and Wayne counties, the lands in Madison County produced the highest rate of return to the speculator. Obviously productivity was not the only factor affecting proceeds.

The initial cost of the Davenport land varied from county to county as did the tax rate. So did the length of time which the land was held, but, as was explained in the discussion of the Illinois lands, such variation is most properly considered a reflection of other factors. In Madison

County, productive land, a relatively low purchase price, a low tax rate, and fast turnover on a buoyant market produced a high rate of return even though the sale prices, ranging usually between $5.50 and $8.00, were little greater than those which the Davenports paid for their Union Pacific and penitentiary lands. Much of the penitentiary land in Lancaster County, on the other hand, was held for more than twenty years. When the tax rate in Madison County was but five cents per acre, it stood at more than twenty cents per acre in Lancaster County, and there the quality of much of the Davenport land was inferior. Undoubtedly the Davenports misjudged the future in Lancaster County, but their mistake is not difficult to understand. The capital was located in this county, and a seat of government, speculators generally assumed, was a guarantee of rising land values. In this case it seems rather to have guaranteed a high tax rate. Parcels of Lancaster land commanded prices ranging from $20 to $30 per acre during the 1890's, but the per cent return was disappointing.

The initial cost per acre of the Union Pacific lands in Dodge County was on the average higher than that of the other types of land purchased by the New Yorkers, but these lands proved to be a satisfactory investment. The tax rate was moderate and most of the Dodge lands were sold prior to the depression of 1893. Reflecting the fact that Dodge was to emerge as one of the state's most productive counties, land values were checked in their upward surge only briefly during the 1890's. In one sale after 1900 in this county the purchaser paid $75 per acre to Ira Davenport, a price, however, which would have represented only 8 per cent per annum on the investment had not the land brought in revenue in rent. Much of the land located with military bounty warrants during 1871 was held into the 1890's. But the initial cost of this land was low and the rate of return on the Wayne holdings was slightly more satisfactory than that derived from the railroad land in Dodge County, although few tracts brought more than $25 per acre. The sandy soils of Pierce County no doubt largely account for returns in that county which were significantly lower than those obtained in adjacent Wayne County.

In conclusion it should be emphasized that the tables undoubtedly do not exactly mirror the returns obtained by the speculators whose operations were studied. In the process of analysis sins of omission and estimation were committed. Yet the work was based on the actual cost and sale figures of the Illinois and Nebraska lands, and it is believed that the estimates are close to actual fact. Neither the amount of the location fees paid by the Illinois speculators nor the rate of commission which they paid to real-estate agents for selling their lands was known. In the case of the Davenports these costs were known, but the rates of return would not have been significantly higher had they been ignored. Such charges were of little moment in comparison to the cost price of the land, the accumulation of interest, and to a lesser extent the tax payments, although it was discovered that a year more or less of taxes seldom made much difference in the rate of return. Had interest been compounded semi-annually the rates of return would have been lowered slightly. The rate of return, of course, does not stand as a synonym for profit. Some, perhaps, would prefer to substitute the term "yield" for "rate of return" and to this there is no great objection, although it should be obvious that yield in its usual sense does not involve our type of calculations. If the reader desires a figure which he can call profit, he must allocate an interest rate to the invested capital and subtract this from the rate of return. To go one step further and subtract an allowance for the time spent by the speculators in supervision of their holdings, thereby isolating a figure which could be called net profit, would involve estimation of a factor—administration cost—which undoubtedly varied widely among speculators.

It is reasonable to say that a well-informed resident of east-central Illinois could have purchased unimproved land in his neighborhood with his own funds, given the land his personal supervision, and earned something from his investment. If he bought during the mid-1830's and sold the land twenty to thirty years later, the money might have earned 6 to 8 per cent. Had he purchased land from the United States for about $1.10 per acre in the early 1850's, he might have realized 16 per cent upon his investment if he sold the land during the 1860's and 1870's. Or real estate bought during the mid-1860's at low figures and sold rapidly between 1867 and 1870 might have returned very large earnings.

Were residents of Illinois well advised to divert their funds into land speculation in preference to other uses? If the earnings from every alternative opportunity were known, a more meaningful answer could be given. The rates of return obtained by our Illinois speculators can be compared with the rate realized by moneylenders on real-estate mortgages in the same region. The usual rate on such loans down to the mid-1870's was at least 10 per cent. Those who put their money into unimproved land in the 1830's might have done better, therefore, had they financed the land purchases of others. Having lent their money, however, they quite possibly would have found themselves owners of unimproved land by foreclosure. Those who paid cash for tracts of raw prairie in the 1850's and 1860's and later sold them perhaps fared better than the moneylender. Each alternative presented elements of risk. Yet none could predict the future with complete accuracy, and the optimism of boom times in the 1830's and 1850's tinged the judgment of the most clairvoyant.

From their Nebraska lands the Davenport brothers received handsome returns on a sizable investment. As it happened, they were also lending funds on the security of farm real estate in the same region. Although the mortgage rate stood at more than 12 per cent during the early 1870's, it had dropped by the end of the decade to the vicinity of 8 per cent, while the average rate of return per dollar invested in the Nebraska lands at the close of 1880 stood at 10.9 per cent. Although the gap had been closed considerably by 1890, the rate of return on real estate stayed above the mortgage rate until the death of Ira Davenport. Had the brothers turned their funds during the early 1870's into railroad bonds, or had they enjoyed the "average experience" of those investing in common stocks between 1871 and 1904, they would have done less well than they did by turning to the trans-Missouri prairies.

In this article we have endeavored to make some contribution to the literature bearing on the returns derived from frontier land speculation as well as to stimulate historians toward a greater precision of method in calculating such returns. There were, evidently, a considerable number of factors which, interacting over time, might bring either losses or munificent returns to the land speculator; particular attention has been called to some of these in recounting the experiences and in calculating the returns of half-a-dozen individuals or groups who hazarded funds on the assumption that the raw lands of Illinois and Nebraska would rise sufficiently in value after purchase that a lucrative return might be won by resale. Their experience does not prove either that frontier land speculation in the United States during the nineteenth century was generally well rewarded or generally unremunerative. Despite the assumptions of a number of historians, perhaps neither alternative is correct, and the speculative losses of some real-estate plungers were canceled by the speculative gains of others. When careful studies of the returns from frontier land speculation on an area basis are available, historians will be in a better position to suggest answers to all of the questions posed in the introductory remarks and at the same time will have a much clearer understanding of the economic development of our frontier regions.

FOR FURTHER READING: Ray A. Billington, "The Origin of the Land Speculator as a Frontier Type," *Agricultural History*, XIX (October, 1945), pp. 204–211, Shaw Livermore, *Early American Land Companies* (Princeton, 1939), and Roy Robbins, *Our Landed Heritage* (Princeton, 1936), imply that land speculation was profitable.

12. *Finance in the National Period*

PROBLEM: *Were Andrew Jackson's bank policies desirable?*

For over a century a dispute raged in the United States between the advocates of a decentralized as opposed to a centralized banking system. The defenders of the former argued that a national bank was dangerous because it concentrated power over loans and currency expansion in a relatively small group of men who would follow their own selfish interests. But a large number of small banks would prevent the concentration of such powers, and the dangers of abuse. On the other hand, the proponents of a centralized bank system stressed its useful functions, especially of providing needed investment capital and credit, and of keeping the amount of currency in circulation flexible. Only a centralized institution could provide such services. Whether a centralized or decentralized banking system was best suited to promote American economic expansion thus became an issue. It came out clearly in Andrew Jackson's struggle against the Second Bank of the United States. Arthur M. Schlesinger, Jr., a brilliant young historian, formerly of Harvard University, found that the menace to representative government by the Second Bank of the United States under its aggressive president, Nicholas Biddle, fully justified its destruction at the hands of Andrew Jackson. Schlesinger believed that directors of the Bank wielded unwarranted political and economic power to the detriment of farmer-debtors and Eastern workingmen. As a monopoly, its political power provided numerous opportunities for abuse and undermined the principle of equality in American society. This evoked a strong rebuttal from Bray Hammond, formerly assistant secretary of the Federal Reserve Board, who emphasized the economic advantages of the

206

Bank for the economy. Hammond stressed the efficiency of the Bank in performing its functions of maintaining a sound and uniform currency and serving as a depository for the government. Both authors point out significant arguments that were used in the dispute over the advantages of a centralized banking system. What methods did the Second Bank of the United States use to promote and regulate economic activity? How did businessmen and also farmers benefit from central banking? How did politics affect the economic functions of the Bank?

The Bank War

ARTHUR M. SCHLESINGER, JR.

BEGINNINGS OF THE BANK WAR

In 1836 the charter of the Second Bank of the United States was to expire. This institution was not in the later sense a national bank. It was a banking corporation, located in Philadelphia, privately controlled, but possessing unique and profitable relations with the government. To its capital of thirty-five million dollars, the government had subscribed one fifth. It served as repository of the public funds, which it could use for its own banking purposes without payment of interest. It could issue bank notes up to the physical ability of the president and cashier to sign them; after 1827 it evaded this limitation by the invention of "branch drafts," which looked and circulated like notes but were actually bills of exchange. The Bank was not to be taxed by the states and no similar institution was to be chartered by Congress. In return for these privileges the Bank paid a bonus of one and a half million dollars, transferred public funds and made public payments without charge, and allowed the government to appoint five out of the twenty-five directors. The Secretary of the Treasury could remove the government deposits provided he laid the reasons before Congress.

I

Even advocates of the Bank conceded that this charter bestowed too much power. That staunch conservative Hezekiah Niles, writing in the heat of the fight for renewal, declared he "would not have the present

From *The Age of Jackson*, pp. 115–131, by Arthur M. Schlesinger, Jr., copyright 1945 by Arthur M. Schlesinger, Jr. Reprinted by permission of Little, Brown and Company.

bank re-chartered, with its present power . . . for the reason that the bank has more power than we would grant to any set of men, unless responsible to the people" (though he ultimately supported the Bank). Nathan Appleton, who had tried vainly to modify the charter in 1832, wrote carefully but emphatically in 1841: "A great central power, independent of the general or state governments, is an anomaly in our system. Such a power over the currency is the most tremendous which can be established. Without the assurance that it will be managed by men, free from the common imperfections of human nature, we are safer without it."

There could be no question about the reality of the Bank's power. It enjoyed a virtual monopoly of the currency and practically complete control over credit and the price level. Biddle's own testimony disclosed its extent:

> Q. Has the bank at any time oppressed any of the State banks?
> A. Never. There are very few banks which might not have been destroyed by an exertion of the powers of the bank. None have ever been injured.

To radical Democrats like Taney, Biddle's tone implied that he thought himself entitled to credit for his forbearance. "It is this power concentrated in the hands of a few individuals," Taney declared, "—exercised in secret and unseen although constantly felt—irresponsible and above the control of the people or the Government for the 20 years of its charter, that is sufficient to awaken any man in the country if the danger is brought distinctly to his view."

There could be no question either about the Bank's pretensions to complete independence of popular control. Biddle brooked no opposition from within, and the government representatives sat through the directors' meetings baffled and indignant. "I never saw such a Board of *directors*," raged Henry D. Gilpin, "—it is a misuse of terms of *directed*. . . . We know absolutely nothing. There is no consultation, no exchanges of sentiments, no production of correspondence, but merely a rapid, superficial, general statement, or a reference to a Committee which will probably never report." He added, "We are perfect cyphers."

Biddle not only suppressed all internal dissent but insisted flatly that the Bank was not accountable to the government or the people. In 1824 the president of the Washington branch had written Biddle, "As . . . there are other interests to be attended to [besides those of the Bank], especially that of the Government, I have deemed it proper to see and consult with the President." Biddle hotly replied, "If . . . you think that there are other interests to be attended to besides those with which you are charged by the administration of the bank, we deem it right to correct what is a total misapprehension. . . . The moment this appointment [of the five government directors] takes place the Executive has completely fulfilled its functions. The entire responsibility is thenceforward in the directors, and no officer of the Government, from the President downwards, has the least right, the least authority, the least pretence, for interference in the concerns of the bank. . . . This invocation of the Government, therefore . . . is totally inconsistent with the temper and spirit which belong to the officers of the bank, who should regard only the rights of the bank and the instructions of those who govern it, and who should be at all times prepared to execute the orders of the board, in direct opposition, if need be, to the personal interests and wishes of the President and every officer of the Government."

In Biddle's eyes the Bank was thus an independent corporation, on a level with the state, and not responsible to it except as the narrowest interpretation of the charter compelled. Biddle tried to strengthen this position by flourishing a theory that the Bank was beyond political good or evil, but Alexander Hamilton had written with far more candor that "such a bank is not a mere matter of private property, but a political machine of the greatest importance to the State." The Second Bank of the United States was, in fact, as Hamilton had intended such a bank should be, the keystone in the alliance between the government and the business community.

II

Though conservative Jeffersonians, led by Madison and Gallatin, had come to accept Hamilton's Bank as necessary, John Taylor's dialectics and Randolph's invective kept anti-Bank feeling alive, and men in the old radical tradition remained profoundly convinced of the evil of paper money. Jackson's hard-money views prompted his opposition to the Tennessee relief system in 1820. "Every one that knows me," as he told Polk in 1833, "does know, that I have been always opposed to the U. States Bank, nay all Banks." Benton, from talks with Macon and Randolph and his observations of the collapse of the paper system in 1819, similarly concluded that the only safeguard against future disaster lay in restricting the system; and that, to this end, the government should deal only in gold and silver, thus withdrawing support from the issues of privately owned banks. Van Buren, Cambreleng, Taney and Polk more or less shared these views.

The ordinary follower of Jackson in the West also regarded the Bank with strong latent antagonism, but for very different reasons. Its policy in 1819 of recalling specie and checking the note issue of state banks had gained it few friends in any class, and, in Kentucky especially, the Relief War kept resentments alive. But this anti-Bank feeling owed little to reasoned distrust of paper money or to a Jeffersonian desire for specie. As a debtor section the West naturally preferred cheap money; and Kentucky, for example, which most vociferously opposed the United States Bank, also resorted most ardently to wildcat banking of its own. The crux of the Kentucky fight against the Bank was not the paper system, but outside control: the Bank's sin lay not in circulating paper money itself, but in restraining its circulation by Kentucky banks. Almost nowhere, apart from doctrinaires like Jackson and Benton, did Westerners object to state banks under local control.

Indeed, during the eighteen-twenties, even the Philadelphia Bank to a considerable degree overcame the Western prejudices against it. In Tennessee, for example, until 1829 "both [Governor William] Carroll and the legislature favored federal as well as state banks, nor does anything in the history of the state indicate that there was any general feeling against such institutions before Jackson became President." Caleb Atwater, a lusty Jackson man from Ohio and something of a professional Westerner, expressed a widespread feeling when he wrote in 1831, "Refuse to recharter the bank, and Pittsburgh, Cincinnati, Louisville, St. Louis, Nashville, and New Orleans, will be crushed at one blow." Even Frank Blair's first large-scale blast against the Bank in the *Argus of Western America* after Jackson's election did not come until December 23, 1829, many months after Eastern groups had begun to agitate the question. This editorial—actually prefaced by an anti-Bank quote from a Van Buren paper in New York—appealed to the Kentucky fear of Eastern control; and all through 1830 the *Argus* continued to focus on the power and privileges of the Bank and the consequent peril to the Commonwealth Bank of Kentucky, never on the general implications of the paper system.

Some writers have talked of frontier life as if it bred traits of "individualism" and equality which made Westerners mystically opposed to banks. Actually, like all other groups in the population, Westerners favored banks when they thought they could profit by them and fought them when they thought others were profiting at their expense. The Western enthusiasm for an assault on the Bank came, not from an intuitive democratic *Weltschmerz* born in the American forest, nor from a Jeffersonian dislike of banks, but from a farmer-debtor desire to throw off restraints on the local issue of paper money.

Similar objections to control from Philadelphia ranged many Easterners against the Bank. State institutions hoped, by falling heir to the government deposits, to enlarge their banking capital, at no expense to themselves. Special grievances multiplied the motives. The state banks of New York, for example, envied the United States Bank because its loan operations were not restricted by Van Buren's safety-fund system. New York City had long resented the choice of Philadelphia as the nation's financial capital. Thus in a fight against the Bank Jackson could expect the backing of a decent minority of the local banking interests.

But there was still another and more reliable source of support. In March, 1829, after the grim depression winter, a group of Philadelphia workingmen, under the very shadow of the Bank, called a meeting "opposed to the chartering of any more new banks." The hard times were blamed upon the "too great extension of paper credit," and the gathering concluded by appointing a committee, "without confining ourselves to the working classes," to draw up a report on the banking system. The committee, which was dominated by intellectuals, included two leading economists, William M. Gouge, editor of the *Philadelphia Gazette*, and Condy Raguet, editor of the *Free Trade Advocate*, as well as William Duane, the famous old Jeffersonian journalist, his son William J. Duane, a lawyer, Roberts Vaux, the philanthropist, Reuben M. Whitney, a disgruntled businessman and former director of the Bank, and William English and James Ronaldson, two trade-union leaders. A week later the committee pronounced its verdict on the paper system:

That banks are useful as offices of deposit and transfer, we readily admit; but we cannot see that the benefits they confer in this way are so great as to compensate for the evils they produce, in . . . laying the foundation of *artificial* inequality of wealth, and, thereby, of *artificial* inequality of power. . . . If the present system of banking and paper money be extended and perpetuated, the great body of the working people must give over all hopes of ever acquiring any property.

This view was spreading rapidly through the Middle and Northern states of the East in the late eighteen-twenties. The working class was no more affected by an instinctive antipathy toward banking than the backwoodsmen beyond the Alleghenies; but they never enjoyed the Western opportunity of having banks under their own control. Their opposition, instead of remaining fitful and capricious, began slowly to harden into formal anti-banking principle. Their bitter collective experience with paper money brought them to the same doctrines which Jackson and Benton gained from the Jeffersonian inheritance.

III

The war against the Bank thus enlisted the enthusiastic support of two basically antagonistic groups: on the one hand, debtor interests of the West and local banking interests of the East; on the other, Eastern workingmen and champions of the radical Jeffersonian tradition. The essential incompatibility between cheap money and hard could be somewhat concealed in the clamor of the crusade. Yet that incompatibility remained, and it came to represent increasingly a difference between the Western and Eastern wings of the party, as the state banking group gradually abandoned the Jackson ranks. It was, indeed, a new form of the distinction between Western and Eastern readings of "equality." The West, in its quest for political democracy and home rule, did not object to paper money under local control, while the submerged classes of the East, seeking economic democracy, fought the whole banking swindle, as it seemed to them, root and branch.

The administration took care not to offend its cheap-money adherents by openly avowing hard-money ideas. Yet, the drift was unmistakable, and it rendered ineffective some of Jackson's Western followers for whom the battle was being pressed on lines they could not understand. Richard M. Johnson, for example, a staunch relief man and ancient foe of the Bank, served on the House committee which investigated the Bank in 1832; but he could take no real part in a hearing dominated by Cambreleng's hard-money views, and, though he signed Cambreleng's report, he confessed later that he had not asked a question or looked at a Bank book. In general, the Western politicians, torn between the hard-money leanings of the White House and the cheap-money preferences of the folks back home, tended to pursue an erratic course.

Only the intellectuals, who did not have to think about re-election, effected a quick adjustment. Amos Kendall, who had been originally a hard-money man, perhaps from his Eastern upbringing, found no difficulty in reverting to his earlier opinions. Frank Blair also rapidly shifted his ground after coming to Washington. These were not basic reversals of position. Their allegiance, after all, had been primarily to a social class, not to a set of financial theories. The experience of the Kentucky relief system taught that salvation was not to be bought so cheaply: however much inflation might temporarily benefit a frontier state with a large debtor element, it was at best a risky expedient, imposed by political necessity; it never could serve as the basis of a national economic policy. Kendall and Blair, liberated from their local obligations, naturally turned to hard-money ideas as affording the only permanent solutions for the financial problems in favor of the non-business classes.

Thomas Hart Benton had long awaited the opportunity to fight for this solution. In the eighteen-twenties, when he fumed about the paper system, Nathaniel Macon would remark that it was useless to attempt reform unless the administration was with you. Now, at last, the administration seemed to be with him. Jackson's first message had expressed grave doubts about the constitutionality and expediency of the Bank. In 1830 the President continued to make ominous allusions to the subject of recharter. But the administration position was still not clear. Jackson's views were widely regarded as the expressions of private prejudice, not of party policy. Few people interpreted the Maysville veto as opening a campaign which might end by involving the Bank. Even now, the Bank was confidently conducting backstairs negotiations with Secretary McLane to work out a formula for recharter, and it had inspired an effective press campaign to counteract Jackson's pronouncements. Benton, watching impatiently, concluded that someone (who else but Benton?) would have to set forth the hard-money case.

He tried several times to get the floor in the Senate, but the friends of the Bank succeeded always in silencing him by parliamentary technicalities. Finally, on February 2, 1831, he outmaneuvered the opposition and launched his comprehensive indictment:

First: Mr. President, I object to the renewal of the charter . . . because I look upon the bank as an institution too great and powerful to be tolerated in a Government of free and equal laws. . . .
Secondly, I object . . . because its tendencies are dangerous and pernicious to the Government and the people. . . . It tends to aggravate the inequality of fortunes; to make the rich richer, and the poor poorer; to multiply nabobs and paupers. . . .
Thirdly, I object . . . on account of the exclusive privileges, and anti-republican monopoly, which it gives to the stockholders.

And his own policy? "Gold and silver is the best currency for a republic," he thundered; "it suits the men of middle property and the working people best; and if I was going to establish a working man's party, it should be on the basis of hard money; a hard money party against a paper party." The words reverberated through the hall—"a hard money party against a paper party"—as Mr. Webster of Massachusetts hastily rose to call for a vote which defeated Benton's resolution against recharter.

But the words also reverberated through the country. The *Globe* speedily reprinted the speech, the party press took it up, and pamphlets carried it through the land, to be read excitedly by oil lamp and candlelight, talked over heatedly in taverns and around fireplaces, on steamboats and stagecoaches, along the crooked ways of Boston and the busy streets of New York and on isolated farms in New Hampshire, Missouri, Iowa, Michigan, Arkansas. Nathaniel Macon read it with deep pleasure in North Carolina. "You deserve the thanks of every man, who lives by the sweat of his face," he told Benton, adding with sturdy candor, ". . . I observe some bad grammar,—you must pardon my freedom." . . .

IV

. . . In their nature as corporations, banks gave rise to one set of objections, springing from their monopoly of financial prerogative through special charter. Indeed, they provided so much the most flagrant instances of abuse of corporate privilege that they were mainly responsible for fixing national attention on the problem.

Their power over the currency was viewed as an especially grave encroachment on the domain of government. The regulation of the currency, in the words of Benton, was "one of the highest and most delicate acts of sovereign power . . . precisely equivalent to the power to create currency"; and he considered it "too great a power to be trusted to any banking company whatever, or to any authority but the highest and most responsible which was known to our form of Government." Commercial credit was another matter, "an affair of trade," as Cambreleng put it, "and not of government"; and the logic of this position pointed to the abolition of banks of note issue, on the one hand, and the establishment of free competition among banks of discount and deposit, on the other. The crucial error of the federal government, according to the hard-money advocates, lay in accepting bank notes in the payment of federal dues, by which it thus extended and virtually underwrote the credit of the banks. The remedy was to exclude bank notes from government payments.

The behavior of banks in practice, moreover, violated the national faith in popular rule. The most powerful argument against Biddle's Bank was always its calm assumption of independence. "The Bank of the United States," Jackson charged, "is in itself a Government which has gradually increased in strength from the day of its establishment. The question between it and the people has become one of power." Biddle's conduct, in 1834, in refusing to allow a House committee to investigate the Bank records or examine the Bank officers, was simply the climax of his oft-expressed theory of the Bank's independence. "This powerful corporation, and those who defend it," as Taney said, without much exaggeration, "seem to regard it as an independent sovereignty, and to have forgotten that it owes any duties to the People, or is bound by any laws but its own will."

But Biddle was simply exhibiting on a larger scale habits long established in banking experience. William Graham Sumner concisely summed up the pretensions of the banks:

The bankers had methods of doing things which were customary and conventional, but . . . contrary both to ordinary morality and to law as applied to similar matters outside of banks. . . . The banks also disregarded law so habitually that it became a commonplace that law could not bind them. . . . We search almost in vain through the law reports for any decisions on the rights or authority of the State over banks or the duties of banks to the State. It may be said that no attempts were made to test or enforce the right of the State against banks, and that, as a matter of practice, it had none. The banks were almost irresponsible. Such decisions as bear at all on the authority of the State over banks proceed from the attempts of the banks to resist the exercise of any authority whatever.

Such a situation obviously could not be long borne. As Theophilus Fisk put it, "Either the State is sovereign, or the Banks are."

V

The social argument—the battle against domination by "the rich and powerful"—represented the culmination of the hard-money doctrine. The economic and political arguments, though capable of standing by themselves, were ultimately directed at conditions preliminary to the question: who shall rule in the state? The recurrent economic crises were evil, not only in themselves, but because they facilitated a redistribution of wealth that built up the moneyed aristocracy. The irresponsible political sovereignties were evil, not only in themselves, but because they provided the aristocracy with instruments of power and places of refuge.

The Bank War compelled people to speculate once again about the conflict of class. "There are but two parties," exclaimed Thomas Hart Benton, giving the period its keynote; "there never has been but two parties . . . founded in the radical question, whether PEOPLE, or PROPERTY, shall govern? Democracy implies a government by the people. . . . Aristocracy implies a government of the rich . . . and in these words are contained the sum of party distinction."

The paper banking system was considered to play a leading role in this everlasting struggle. Men living by the issue and circulation of paper money produced nothing; they added nothing to the national income; yet, they flourished and grew wealthy. Their prosperity, it was argued, must be stolen from the proceeds of productive labor—in other words, from the honest but defenseless "humble members of society"; and Gouge extensively annotated the modes of plunder.

The system was further important in the strategy of the warfare. Taney described the big Bank as "the centre, and the citadel of the moneyed power." "A national bank," declared the Massachusetts Democratic convention of 1837, "is the bulwark of the aristocracy; its outpost, and its rallying point. It is the bond of union for those who hold that Government should rest on property." To a lesser degree all banks acted as strongholds of conservatism. They provided the funds and often the initiative for combat. Their lawyers, lobbyists and newspapers were eternally active. Politicians would gather in their board rooms and consult their presidents and accept gifts of stock. More than any other kind of corporate enterprise, banks boldly intervened in politics when they felt their interests menaced.

The hard-money policy attacked both the techniques of plunder and the general strategy of warfare. By doing away with paper money, it proposed to restrict the steady transfer of wealth from the farmer and laborer to the business community. By limiting banks to commercial credit and denying them control over the currency, it proposed to lessen their influence and power. By reducing the proportion of paper money, it proposed to moderate the business cycle, and order the economy to the advantage of the worker rather than the speculator. It was a coherent policy, based on the best economic thought of the day, and formulated on a higher intellectual level than the alternative of the opposition.

By origin and interest, it was a policy which appealed mainly to the submerged classes of the East and to the farmers of the South rather than to the frontier. Historians have too long been misled by the tableau of Jackson, the wild backwoodsman, erupting into the White House. In fact, the hard-money doctrine, which was not at all a frontier doctrine, was the controlling policy of the administration from the winter of 1833 on; and for some time it had been the secret goal of a small group, led by Jackson, Taney, Benton and Kendall, and passively encouraged by Van Buren. From the removal of the deposits to the end of Van Buren's presidency in 1840 this clique of radical Democrats sought to carry out the policy in its full implications. As soon as the hard-money program was divorced from the glamour of the Hero of New Orleans and had to rest on its inherent appeal, it did very badly in the West.

Andrew Jackson ably summed up its broad aims. "The planter, the farmer, the mechanic, and the laborer," he wrote, "all know that their success depends upon their own industry and economy, and that they must not expect to become suddenly rich by the fruits of their toil." These classes "form the great body of the people of the United States; they are the bone and sinew of the country." Yet "they are in constant danger of losing their fair influence in the Government." Why? "The mischief springs from the power which the money interest derives from a paper currency, which they are able to control, from the multitude of corporations with exclusive privileges which they have succeeded in obtaining in the different States." His warning to his people was solemn. "Unless you become more watchful . . . you will in the end find that the most important powers of Government have been given or bartered away, and the control over your dearest interests has passed into the hands of these corporations."

VI

Taney and Benton worked out the details of the immediate hard-money measures. They proposed to increase the metallic basis of the currency in two directions: by the restoration of gold to circulation, and by the suppression of small notes. The first measure had been for many years close to Benton's heart. Gold had long been undervalued, at the ratio of 15 to 1, with the result that no gold eagles and only a scattering of other gold coins had been minted since 1805, and most of these rapidly left the country. Benton argued that, if the gold were not thus expelled, the amount of specie derivable from foreign commerce, added to the amount obtained from American mines, could supply all financial needs without recourse to small notes or "shinplasters." In June, 1834, his bill to revise the valuation to 16 to 1 passed Congress. As an expression of the strictly economic intentions of the hard-money policy, it made a broad appeal to all men of good will, winning the support of John Quincy Adams, Webster and Calhoun. Only diehards like Clay and Horace Binney opposed it.

Public Policy and National Banks

BRAY HAMMOND

Mr. Schlesinger's book is important and abounds in excellences: it deals with a significant period, it is comprehensive in its interest, and it is entertainingly written. Mr. Schlesinger has a fine talent for peopling an epoch vividly. But his book is marred by two faults. One is a Manichaean naïveté with respect to the nobility of all things Jacksonian and the sordidness of all things opposed. The other is a fumbling treatment of economic matters and particularly of the Bank of the United States.

Mr. Schlesinger's vocabulary purrs over his friends. The landscapes at the Hermitage and Kinderhook smile in a fashion not noticeable where Whigs and Federalists live. The Jacksonian leaders have a "pervading insight," their wrath is "magnificent," one or another of them is "handsome," "grave," "masterly," "erudite," "thoughtful," "quiet," "intelligent," "brilliant," etc., etc., and the old hero himself is touchingly fond of children. The opposition is a sorry outfit. They are Bank "lackeys," they "roar" and "snarl," they deal in "hullabaloo," they are "phony," they have "fantasies," they work "backstairs," their best minds are "opaque," and one gets the impression that Mr. Schlesinger never thinks of them as loving little children at all. Jackson's trick of evading awkward questions by simulating an apoplectic rage that filled his visitors with fear lest the aged president burst a blood vessel on their account is described with affectionate amusement and admiration. The immense services of Hamilton to his country are disregarded. The reader is allowed to look at Van Buren only through high-powered magnifying glasses. Marshall and Story are written down with casual finality, and Taney is promoted as if no dissent existed; Webster is about the only member of Mr. Schlesinger's flock of goats whose defense he bothers to notice.

The Bank war is properly very important in Mr. Schlesinger's account, and yet he does not make the Bank of the United States a clearly func-

This review of Schlesinger's *The Age of Jackson* is reprinted with permission from *The Journal of Economic History*, VI (May, 1946), pp. 79-84.

tioning financial institution nor Nicholas Biddle a central banker with specific monetary policies and programs that can be appraised. Instead he makes the Bank a dim sort of moneyed monstrosity and Biddle a vague, sinister figure, "drunk with power," whose career is a darkened background for Jackson's gleaming achievements. This makes poor history. The Bank of the United States was a central bank and should be discussed as such. But Mr. Schlesinger never uses the term, never mentions the purposes for which the Bank was set up, and never but casually speaks of its functions as public in their nature. He says it was "privately controlled"; but so was the Bank of England and so was practically every other similar institution till recent times. He speaks of the Bank's "profitable relations with the government" as if they were one-sided. He even says the Bank "allowed the government to appoint" five directors—a preposterous statement that may be intended for sarcasm but will be taken by most readers at face value. One might as well assert that the Treasury, for example, or any other government department "allows" the President and Congress to say who shall be at its head; for it was by authority of an act of Congress creating the Bank that the government directors were appointed by the President, with confirmation by the Senate.

That the Bank was a public institution formed at the instance of the government and for its convenience, that under Biddle's management it performed its depository services efficiently, furnished a sound and uniform currency, and regulated the state banks, and that the state banks and their borrowers resented its restraint upon credit—these are facts that the Jacksonians liked to ignore. It is less excusable to ignore them now, for they are facts that Gallatin, Dunbar, Catterall, Dewey, and other scholars, on the basis of known information, long ago put outside the field of intelligent controversy. Mr. Schlesinger does not wholly ignore them, but he mentions them in an offhand way as if they had no special significance. "In destroying the Bank," he says, "Jackson had removed a valuable brake on credit expansion; and in sponsoring the system of deposit in state banks he had accelerated the tendencies toward inflation." Mr. Schlesinger glides over startling facts like these, unstartled; and recognizes no need to reconcile them with his general picture of the Bank as an outlaw institution, obscurely dangerous because it "had too much power."

As to the reality of this power, "there could be no question," he says; and he goes clear out on the limb to say that the Bank "enjoyed a virtual monopoly of the currency and practically complete control over credit and the price level." This is sheer romance. Mr. Schlesinger contradicts himself to indulge in it, for he often speaks elsewhere of the currency issues of the local banks, clearly implying thereby that no "monopoly" existed. In reality, of course, the Bank furnished about a quarter of the total paper circulation. As for "practically complete control over credit," the Bank had nothing of the sort, nor has any central bank ever achieved it, even though it should. As for "practically complete" control of the price level, the idea is ridiculous; it would be hard to surpass its utter detachment from the findings of price analysts and historians, to say nothing of common sense. But Mr. Schlesinger leaves the solid earth frequently, in little things as well as big. For example, he speaks of the Bank's "alacrity in opening new offices" in 1831 and 1832 while renewal of the charter was pending, as conclusive evidence, in Taney's words, of its determination to fasten itself on the country. R. C. H. Catterall found "not a grain of evidence" to support such charges, and no one has produced any since. Far from showing "alacrity" in opening new offices, the Bank established none after 1830, in which year it established the last four of the twenty-nine it had in all; of these, all but ten had been set up during the Bank's initial organization in 1817.

Mr. Schlesinger's failure to make proper use of the work of scholars who have written authoritatively on the Bank seems to me inexplicable. I found reference to Mr. Catterall on only one point of fact, and the whole body of Catterall's judicious and thorough work is neglected for a superficial presentation scarcely above the level of Mr. Marquis James's unpenetrating account in his *Life of Jackson*. I had rather Mr. Schlesinger had shown no knowledge of [the Bank] whatever; for then he would have spared a reviewer the painful effort to understand how he could revive Benton's pomposities. . . . [Gallatin's] unimpeachable contemporary testimony clearly indicates the public nature of the Bank, Biddle's good performance before Jackson's attack, the want of justification for that attack, and the degeneration of Biddle after his failure to withstand the attack.

Mr. Schlesinger makes much of the distinction that although the Jacksonians were understood to be opposed to all banks, they really opposed only the note-issue function and not the deposit function. He devotes an appendix to this point and seems to consider it creditable to the Jacksonians, as if it showed how well they understood banking. The opposite is what it shows. For the differences between note and deposit liabilities are only those of form, and one is as capable of mischief as the other. When Mr. Schlesinger quotes Gallatin to show that banking in the United States was universally understood to mean note issue, he should quote the same authority to the effect that there was not "the slightest difference" between note and deposit liabilities—and incidentally he should enjoy making Webster contradict himself by saying not only that note issue was the essential function of banking but also that it was "not an indispensable ingredient" of banking. Mr. Schlesinger has loyally picked up the Jacksonian confusion on this matter. The actual result of the program he praises was to free both the note and deposit functions from regulation —a blunder that the National Bank Act in 1863 and the Federal Reserve Act fifty years later both purposed to undo.

Mr. Schlesinger properly emphasizes the fact that Jacksonian democracy reflected eastern as well as frontier influences, but it seems to me that he errs in associating the eastern influence with labor alone and not with business enterprise. There was no more important factor in the Jacksonian movement than the democratization of business, which ceased thenceforth to be the *métier* of a predominantly mercantile, exclusive group, or commercial aristocracy, as it was in the days of Hamilton, and became an interest of the common man. This process of democratization went hand in hand with the rise of laissez faire. Mr. Schlesinger appears to see no break in the business tradition, and makes Hamilton represent it as much in 1840 as he did in 1790. But to identify business enterprise of 1840 with business enterprise of 1790, it is necessary to slur over too much—for example, the appeal of Jackson's politics to money-makers like Alexander Hamilton's own son, who was one of Jackson's supporters and advisers, and like Henshaw, who frankly wanted the United States Bank overthrown so that he and his friends might have room for a big bank of their own. It is also necessary to slur over the more general fact that the speculation which mounted to the panic of 1837 was a great popular phenomenon and reflected the current interests of Americans no less than did the labor and utopian movements of the time. Authentic and American as the latter were, they still were typical not of American behavior as a whole but rather of the idealistic rebellion of minorities against the rising spirit of free enterprise. For a brief period all the diverse dissatisfactions with the old order of things united behind the picturesque intransigence of Andrew Jackson, with this new, un-Hamiltonian spirit of free enterprise prominent and powerful among them. The honeymoon was brief, and in 1840 enterprise eloped with the Whigs. But while it was supporting Jackson, it had separated the corporate form of organization from monopoly and put forth the promise that anyone could be a capitalist, an investor, or a speculator; and it had made banking a form of business "free" and open to all. Business had become the citadel of rugged individualism, and American conservatism had become rooted not so much in Wall Street as in the breasts of rural capitalists and village entrepreneurs—to the recurring embarrassment of liberal and radical causes ever since.

In Hamilton's day business had been strongly federal, but it was now beginning to see advantages in states' rights—a ground of opposition to the Bank that it seems to me Mr. Schlesinger neglects. The states'-rights argument had vigorously survived the Supreme Court's vindication of the Bank's constitutionality, thanks partly to strongly held principle, no doubt, but much more to selfish interest. Hence, in destroying the Bank, Mr. Schlesinger's hard-money horses played directly into the hands of the state banks and of the speculators they abominated. The local banks always called the regulatory measures of the Bank of the United States "coercion" and "oppression," and it was notorious that they wanted it out of the way. In state after state, as its end neared, the legislatures were jammed with charter applications. Benton's words, quoted by Mr. Schlesinger, sound pathetic: "I did not join in putting down the Bank of the United States to put up a wilderness of local banks." He might disavow the purpose but not the deed.

The situation in the United States, with a rapidly growing and acquisitive population pressing to exploit immense resources, was one where the public interest required an extremely powerful restraint upon inflation. The Bank under the direction of Nicholas Biddle was applying that restraint. Jackson, since he abhorred speculation, should have corrected and fostered the Bank. Instead he identified it with the evil it was contending against, a bank being simply a bank to him, destroyed it, and delivered the country to the excesses of a disordered currency and unregulated credit expansion. I do not find fault with him for attacking economic privilege; I find fault with him for *thinking* he was attacking it when in fact he was attacking a semigovernmental institution that restrained speculation. His action was calamitous for a people who were entering a fierce and trampling struggle for conversion of the virgin earth into private property and erection of still more property upon it— a lasting struggle in which the objects of Jacksonian concern have had the most to suffer. Nor should I be fond enough to believe that a central bank or any other governmental instrumentality could have prevented that struggle; but it might have tempered it. And it is significant that today the party interests to which Mr. Schlesinger is allegiant turn to central banking as a first means of accomplishing their social aims. To suggest that the Jacksonians might have sought to nationalize the Bank of the United States as the Bank of England and the Bank of France have recently been would be historically fantastic, but one may question the sagacity of those who went so far in the opposite direction as to destroy the central bank just when it began to be needed most. That action may be excused but cannot properly be praised.

Mr. Schlesinger's book will be widely read; and because its documentation is profuse it will be considered authoritative by most of its readers. I do not think it should be so considered. It represents the age of Jackson as one of triumphant liberalism when it was as much or more an age of triumphant exploitation; it fosters a simplistic notion of continuing problems of human welfare; and it thickens the myths around a political leader who had more capacity for action than for accomplishment.

FOR FURTHER READING: Among works emphasizing the constructive functions of the Bank see Ralph C. H. Catterall, *The Second Bank of the United States* (Chicago, 1903), Fritz Redlich, *The Molding of American Banking: Men and Ideas* (New York, 1947), and Walter B. Smith, *Economic Aspects of the Second Bank of the*

United States (Cambridge, 1953). A severe condemnation of the Bank by a contemporary is Thomas Hart Benton, *Thirty Years' View* (2 vols., New York, 1854–56). Sharply critical too is Claude Bowers, *The Party Battles of the Jacksonian Period* (Boston, 1922). A fine historiographical appraisal is provided by Charles G. Sellers, "Andrew Jackson versus the Historians," *Mississippi Valley Historical Review*, XLIV (March, 1958), pp. 615–648.

13. *Labor During the Nineteenth Century*

PROBLEM: *Was the West a safety valve for labor?*

"Go West, young man," said Horace Greeley to one of his friends in 1859, offering what many of his contemporaries considered to be good advice for those dissatisfied with their economic status in the East. But whether the West really served as an outlet for the discontented laboring men in Eastern cities is still a controversial issue. Joseph Schafer, for many years a leading student of the Middle West, took an affirmative stand on this question. A devoted student of Frederick Jackson Turner, Schafer believed with his mentor that the West had exercised a profound influence upon various aspects of development in the older Eastern sections, also in serving as an outlet for the disaffected. To support his views, Schafer adduced contemporary accounts of New England laborers who moved westwards in search of better opportunities. He also pointed to the absence of violent revolutions in the United States in contrast to other nations. But this viewpoint, seemingly so plausible, was severely challenged by another Middle Western historian, Professor Fred A. Shannon of the University of Illinois. Shannon gathered evidence to indicate that the West played a negligible role in serving as an escape hatch for poverty burdened Eastern laborers. He argued that statistics reflecting the increase in the number of farms during the nineteenth century do not indicate that the West was a haven for the discouraged. Moreover, many of the new settlers in the West were foreign immigrants, not Eastern migrants. Even more striking, a larger group of Easterners moved to cities than to farms. Both men offer persuasive arguments with which to evaluate the relation of the West and the rise of the American labor movement in

223

the nineteenth century. How did the West affect the formation of labor unions before the Civil War? What influences did the West exert upon Eastern workingmen? How did the existence of the West stifle radicalism in the United States?

Was the West a Safety Valve for Labor?

JOSEPH SCHAFER

The late Graham Wallas once remarked: "Social events have obstinately refused to follow the path predicted by the nineteenth century political economy; and few economists outside of Moscow now speak with certainty of any economic laws." Notwithstanding the authority of so great a name and so incisive a thinker, some provisional respect should be paid to economic writers whose announced principles grow out of personal experience and observation; such are men like Benjamin Franklin, Thomas Jefferson, and Alexander Hamilton, who laid down for the American people the easily accepted doctrine that an open, partially settled country like the United States was especially advantageous to labor because cheap lands guaranteed high wages.

In his *Observations Concerning the Peopling of Countries,* written at Philadelphia in 1751, Franklin wrote: "So vast is the territory of North America, that it will require many ages to settle it fully; and till it is fully settled, labor will never be cheap here, where no man continues long a laborer for others, but gets a plantation of his own, no man continues long a journeyman to a trade, but goes among those new settlers, and sets up for himself, &c. Hence labor is no cheaper now in Pennsylvania, than it was thirty years ago, though so many thousand laboring people have been imported."

Franklin also saw, what Turner elucidated in a later day, that the American colonies were a "frontier" for Europe; that the cheap lands overseas maintained the level of laborers' wages in England on a higher plane than in continental Europe. "This salutary effect," said Franklin, "will be produced even without emigration, and will result from the mere possibility of emigrating. . . . But the rise of wages will not be equally felt by the different nations of Europe. It will be more or less considerable, in proportion to the greater or less facilities for emigration, which each affords."

The above was written after the French and Indian War but prior to

Reprinted by permission from *The Mississippi Valley Historical Review,* XXIV (December, 1937), pp. 299–314.

the Revolution. The venerable philosopher returned to the same subject again and again, significantly in a discussion of who should emigrate to America, which can be dated after the completion of the Articles of Confederation, probably 1783–1785. Europeans need not look to the confederation government to foster manufactures with bounties, etc. Nor, in general, can such favors be expected from the separate states. Where tried, the results have usually been disappointing, "labor being generally too dear there, and hands difficult to be kept together, everyone desiring to be a master, and the cheapness of lands inclining many to leave trades for agriculture."

In the same article Franklin stated:

Insomuch that the propriety of an hundred acres of fertile soil full of wood may be obtained near the frontiers in many places for eight to ten guineas, hearty young laboring men, who understand the husbandry of corn and cattle, which is nearly the same in that country as in Europe, may easily establish themselves there. A little money saved of the good wages they receive there, while they work for others, enables them to buy the land and begin their plantation, in which they are assisted by the good will of their neighbors, and some credit. Multitudes of poor people from England, Ireland, Scotland, and Germany have by this means in a few years, become wealthy farmers who, in their own countries, where all the lands are fully occupied and the wages of labor low, could never have emerged from the poor condition wherein they were born.

This shows how Franklin's economic theory grew directly out of his observation of the course of social development in Pennsylvania and elsewhere in America.

About the same time Jefferson, in penning for the benefit of European friends his *Notes on Virginia*, had something to say about the desirability of keeping the population of the American communities as little mixed as practicable, an idea heartily shared by Franklin. He had serious doubts about the wisdom of promoting rapid immigration from foreign countries. But, he noted: "I mean not that these doubts should be extended to the importation of useful artificers. The policy of that measure depends on very different considerations. Spare no expense in obtaining them. They will after a while go to the plow and the hoe; but, in the meantime they will teach us something we do not know."

There is, however, an even more authoritative voice among the "founding fathers" than those mentioned above. This country's industrial system has as its classic literary background Hamilton's *Report on Manufactures*. That remarkable exposition of the country's opportunity to diversify and increase its productions recognized the primacy of agriculture and pointed out means of supplementing farm production with a variety of manufactures for which the country was suited and for which necessary labor could be found without drawing it away from the farms. Hamilton had the idea that a vast unused labor source resided in the women and children, a conception which is less popular today than it was in 1790. He believed also that the labor of adult males was only partly utilized in farming operations—largely suspended in winter.

But the great secretary envisioned also another source of labor supply independent of the farms and the women and children, when he wrote: "The desire of being an independent proprietor of land is founded on such strong principles in the human breast, that where the opportunity of becoming so is as great as it is in the United States, the proportion will be small of those whose situations would otherwise lead to it, who would be diverted from it to manufactures. And it is highly probable . . . that the accessions of foreigners who, originally drawn over by manufacturing views, would afterwards abandon them for agricultural, would be more than an equivalent for those of our citizens who might happen to be detached from them."

Implicit in this statement is the full round of concepts that enter into the safety valve theory. Hamilton assumed that land would generally outbid in attractiveness other wealth producing opportunities, and that therefore special inducements would have to be provided in order to toll a reasonable proportion of the laboring classes into industry. The tariff for protection would enable American manufacturers to add extraordinarily high wages to cheap food as inducements to foreign laborers to come over to this country to seek employment. These, together with Americans who were still at loose ends, the surplus help from the farms, and a heavy draft upon woman and child labor could equip a large number of special industries. Cheap land would not only provide an outlet for those native laborers who from time to time should become able to take advantage of it, but it would act as a magnet to draw to American shores the foreign workmen whom he expected to attract into industry in the first instance but who would ultimately, as Jefferson put it, "go to the plow and the hoe."

Hamilton counted heavily on the overseas source of manufacturing labor, and some facts indicate that his expectations were not disappointed. It happened that the colony of Pennsylvania, as early as 1727, alarmed at the rapid influx of Germans, enacted a law requiring all shipmasters bringing aliens to Philadelphia to provide a list of the names for permanent registration. Various changes in the law were made from time to time as additional requirements were imposed upon immigrants—to pass the medical inspection, to take the oath of allegiance, etc. It does not appear that shipmasters were actually in duty bound to do more than supply a careful list of names. But, in the course of a long experience, some of them got into the habit of noting additional facts. Some gave the place of birth, a few recorded the ages of the children in the families, others the ages of old and young alike, a few went so far as to describe the persons—

height, complexion, color of hair and of eyes; two stated the number of persons in each family, and one gave the contract under which the passengers were carried from Amsterdam. Finally, what is even more important, ten captains named the occupations of the adult male immigrants.

These precious glimpses of the character of the German influx happen to fall in the period 1796 to 1807, therefore fitting admirably into this inquiry as to how far the immigration of that time may have favored Hamilton's views. Summarizing the ten lists one finds that those described as "farmers" numbered 155, while the craftsmen, under the various classifications, were just under twice as numerous, or 309. From this it would seem that, as far as the immigration from Germany was concerned, Hamilton's expectations were fully justified. . . .

The foreign travelers in America, decade after decade, saw mechanics and laborers going west to find favorable farming opportunities. Shirreff saw them in motion on the roads of New England. Morris Birkbeck met a party near Zanesville, Ohio, traveling afoot to view the West, stopping to work when necessity dictated that course. Harriet Martineau speaks of Irish, Germans, and Dutch "working their way into the back country and glad to be employed for awhile at Detroit to earn money to carry them farther."

Of special interest in this connection was the testimony of Lieutenant James Allen, in charge of harbor work at Chicago in 1835. Writing to his chief, General Charles Gratiot, on September 30, 1835, Allen said, speaking of "laborers and mechanics": "The influx of this class of emigrants has been great, too; but the apparent facilities offered them of securing valuable portions of public land, by settling on it . . . have encouraged mechanics and laborers, on arriving, or soon after, to abandon their appropriate trades and occupations for a bright hope of soon making their fortunes under the preëmption laws—Some of my best workmen; and who had been on the works since their commencement have, since the sales at this place, refused to continue at a rate of wages from $1.50 to $2.00 per day, and have gone to Milwaukee and elsewhere to make locations on public land in the confident expectation of securing it at the minimum price when it shall be brought into market. The constant changes of workmen, thus made, has been embarrassing and expensive to the work."

Craftsmen and laborers, metamorphosed into prosperous farmers, were actually met with by some of the foreign travelers and were particularly mentioned, notwithstanding that personal references are infrequent in their books.

Familiarity with the local history of any western state will reveal how laborers and craftsmen are embedded in the social complex. For example, a group of English weavers formed a colony in Racine County, Wisconsin; English factory workers from Liverpool settled numerously in Dane

County; Staffordshire potters established a farming community in Columbia and Marquette counties; Cornish miners settled some of the best farm lands of Iowa, Grant, and Lafayette counties. Irish laborers, after helping to build the early Wisconsin railroads, bought land and settled on farms in half a dozen or more widely scattered colonies. Swiss laborers and poor peasants founded the famous colony of New Glarus in Green County. Farming colonies of Welsh, Scotch, Dutch, Belgians, Bohemians, Poles, and Italians doubtless contained their proportionate numbers of laborers and craftsmen, as the Germans did, while native Americans of similar antecedents are to be found in every farming district of the state where available evidence is studied.

Some of the travelers noted that, during a severe depression, mechanics and laborers thrown out of work in the cities were "taking to the woods" along the frontier where they could at least make their living by farming. This, so far as it goes, negatives the contention of some recent writers who believe it was impossible for laborers by reason of destitution even to reach the frontier, much less equip themselves for farming. There usually existed, or were created, agencies to aid persons in such circumstances. Public charity could not be expended more economically than in placing the indigent in a position to become self supporting. But doubtless the most common, as well as the most substantial, aid to emigrants came from members of their own families, or from personal friends concerned about the welfare of those who had fallen upon evil times. At all events, it is known that many went west during depressions.

The real wages paid to American laborers and craftsmen were high enough so that, during prosperous times, it was possible for them if they were thrifty, to lay by a fund to be used for the purchase of land or other property, and when bad times came on, such savings could be converted into frontier farms. A considerable proportion of the laborers in every leading industry have generally owned their homes and some have had cash on hand. A break in employment continuity was a sharp reminder to make a change to farming which may have been contemplated earlier but postponed.

There is direct and unequivocal evidence of movement from the factories to the frontier, and whether the exodus from industry took place in good times or in bad made no difference to the men who were left there. The thinning of the ranks of labor was the important fact: it was the "safety valve." "A great portion of the wages thus monthly received," wrote Mackay, telling a story of the girls and women employed about 1848 in the Lowell mills, "is deposited in the Savings Bank, particularly by the females, who make their work in Lowell a stepping-stone to a better state of existence. After labouring there for a few years they amass several hundred dollars, marry, and go off with their husbands to the

West, buy land, and enjoy more than a competency for the remainder of their days."

Mackay's statement obviously requires qualification. It cannot be supposed that all the young New England girls followed the course he outlined. No doubt, however, many of them did so, or he would not have brought away from his visit to Lowell that information—about which, it may be added, the newspapers were silent. But, if even a moderate proportion of the Lowell girls were earning for the purpose of marrying and moving west to buy land, how can one doubt that a certain proportion of the male artisans also, not only in those mills but in mills and factories everywhere in the East, were similarly motivated! America was country bred. The farms of New England, from early in the century, became static in population through the steady flowing off of young people to new farming areas. "There is hardly a family engaged in the cultivation of the soil," said Stuart, "who do not send out emigrants to distant parts of the same state, or to other states, to clear lots of the forest, and make new settlements."

Did these people go direct from old farm to new? Certainly not in all cases. They engaged for a few years or seasons in the fisheries, worked in the ship yards and lumber mills, made long voyages on whaling ships, peddled tin-ware and "Yankee notions," and also worked in factories and mills—all as means of procuring the wherewithal for a good start as landed proprietors in the West. The character maintained by the metropolitan and village "operative classes," as English travelers called them, is the best testimony to the decent rural sources from which the native portion were derived. . . .

Critics of the safety valve theory have hitherto seemed loath to recognize such evidence as an answer to their contention that the frontier did not significantly affect the labor problem. In fact, some of them make such heavy demands upon the "safety valve" that there would be no possibility of satisfying them. They ask: "Did enough persons leave city employment or were enough diverted from it to prevent explosive unrest?" They find plenty of unrest in industrial labor circles and therefore object that the safety valve, if it existed at all, often failed to work. Well, there was unrest at times even among frontier farmers. Yet, if the doctrine of relativity applies, as it must, to "explosions" as well as to other human affairs, then it would seem that the frontier safety valve was not only a reality but a notable success. There was in America no actual revolution like those of the 1830's and the 1840's in continental Europe, in which laborers and mechanics were deeply involved; also there was no such oppression of the laboring classes as they suffered in England, and no such labor disturbances as that country experienced. Wrote Michel Chevalier: "In America as in Europe, competition among the head-workmen [in factories] tends to reduce their wages; but the tendency is not increased in America, as in Europe, by the competition among the labourers, that is, by an excess of hands wanting employ, for the West stands open as a refuge to all who are unemployed. In Europe, a coalition of workmen can only signify one of these two things; raise our wages or we shall die of hunger with our wives and children, which is an absurdity; or raise our wages, if you do not, we shall take up arms, which is civil war, in Europe there is no other possible construction to be put upon it. But in America, on the contrary, such a coalition means, raise our wages, or we go to the West."

The proof that craftsmen and laborers earned farms for themselves, easily as it may escape those who rely on newspaper evidence, can be amassed, from local sources, to any desired extent. The first source is the one which Carter Goodrich and Sol Davison deliberately rejected as unavailable, namely, the manuscript federal census. That should, in fact, be regarded as the ultimate and most nearly universal basis for the study of such phases of social history as population complexes, population changes, interior migration, and occupational changes. The censuses are not yet in condition for facile use, the work of indexing being merely well begun. But if the current program of the WPA organization for indexing censuses by counties shall be continued, the time will soon come when a plea in avoidance of its use will identify the arm-chair researcher.

The censuses were, of course, always available to those who were willing to perform heavy labor in order to win definite results. By using that source for the study of individuals in Wisconsin towns it was possible to show that men who were laborers and craftsmen at the time of an earlier census had become land-owning farmers some years later; men who were farmers at a later census were identified in an earlier census as laborers and craftsmen. The test was applied in a sufficient number of different towns in different sections of the state to make the results representative. They show that, among the farmers of 1880, from 25 to 60 per cent had been laborers and craftsmen thirty years earlier.

The second source was local biographies as contained in county histories, biographical records, or so-called biographical albums prepared by counties. The county histories for Wisconsin are primarily those edited by C. W. Butterfield which, for the present purpose, are of the right vintage, in and near the year 1880. The biographies in those books, however, except in the cases of a very few towns where the work of collecting data seems to have been ably sponsored, are sadly lacking in the background economic data necessary to show how the subjects acquired the means to become farm owners.

A much better series of county histories, from the point of view of this inquiry, were those of about the same period for Minnesota counties which were edited by Doctor Edward D. Neill. His biographies, useful for genealogy equally with Butterfield's, are usually useful also for the study of economic phases of the subject's personal history. From them it was easy to determine what proportion of the farmers of a given county or a given town had actually earned the beginnings of their farms, and by what means—whether as craftsmen, as common laborers, factory hands, farm hands, farm renters or a combination of several methods. To illustrate, Dakota County, Minnesota, in 1880 had 1,977 farms. Neill's history, 1881, sketches the careers of 355 farmers, or 17.9 per cent of all in the county. Of that number 179, or just over 50 per cent, earned their farm beginnings, 55 of them as craftsmen, 56 as farm hands and renters, 68 as common workers at varied labor. Similar conditions, though not quite so striking, were revealed by the local records for portions of a county in Iowa, another in Nebraska, a third in Kansas, and two in Illinois.

From the results of these studies, it becomes probable that about one-third of the middle western farmers, around 1880, had earned their farms as laborers or craftsmen. The proportion was lower at later periods when second generation settlers had inherited from pioneer parents. The proportions varied also in respect to the population, foreign born settlers being earners in more cases, native born in fewer cases. But seemingly, the labor element was nowhere absent from farming communities. While the research could have been made much more complete, it justifies this much of a generalization.

Did this representation of laborers and craftsmen among the owning farmers of the western states affect the situation of industrial and other labor? To ask this question is to answer it in the spirit of Benjamin Franklin writing 186 years ago: until the land was fully settled, labor could not be cheap in the European sense. And if, as Goodrich and Davison very properly concede, the frontier "tended to hold up the level of industrial wages," the safety valve for labor was a reality whatever research may show as to the comparative fewness of the actual industrial laborers who became western farmers.

The condition of American industrial labor has been by no means ideal. Differences of real wages between America and Europe may not have been as great as American tariff lobbyists claimed, yet that they were substantial the entire history of immigration conclusively proves. Still, despite the disruptive effects of the successive immigrations and the near disasters incident to recurring depressions, a gradual if irregular advance in wages and in working conditions has been achieved latterly, of course, principally through effective organization. Were it not for the safety valve, which operated from the beginning of the nation's history, it is permissible to ask if American employers, served during many years by such a strong and steady influx of cheap labor from abroad, would have been more considerate of their employees than were the employing classes in France, Germany, and England. Here is another question that statistics cannot answer. It is certain, however, that the effect of what has been called the safety valve has been largely psychological, operating alike upon laborers, employers, and the general public. Goodrich and Davison found the belief in it general among politicians, editors, industrialists and, in fact, all classes. Were all mistaken?

A Post Mortem on the Labor-Safety-Valve Theory

FRED A. SHANNON

Since 1935 there has been a growing suspicion among historians that the venerable theory of free land as a safety valve for industrial labor is dead. Out of respect for the departed one even the newer textbooks on American history have begun to maintain silence on the subject. For generations the hypothesis had such a remarkable vitality that a dwindling remnant of the old guard still profess that they observe some stirrings of life in the assumed cadaver. Consequently, it seems that the time has arrived for the reluctant pathologists to don his gas mask and, regardless of the mephitis, analyze the contents of the internal organs. Are the stirrings in the body an evidence of continued animation, or merely of gaseous and helminthic activity? Before the corpse is given a respectable burial this fact must be ascertained beyond any possible doubt.

There can be no question as to the venerable age of the decedent. Thomas Skidmore foretold him as early as 1829 in *The Rights of Man to Property*. George Henry Evans and his fellow agrarians of the 1840s labored often and long in eulogy of the virtues of the safety valve they were trying to bring into existence. The *Working Man's Advocate* of July 6, 1844, demanded the realization of "the right of the people to the soil" and said:

That once effected, let an outlet be formed that will carry off our superabundant labor to the salubrious and fertile West. In those regions thousands, and tens of thousands, who are now languishing in hopeless poverty, will find a certain and a speedy independence. The labor market will be thus eased of the present distressing competition; and those who remain, as well as those who emigrate, will have the opportunity of realizing a comfortable living.

Long before Frederick Jackson Turner tacitly admitted the validity of the theory, even the name "safety valve" had become a middle-class

Reprinted by permission from *Agricultural History*, XIX (January, 1945), pp. 31–37.

aphorism. The idea was so old and so generally held that it was commonly repeated without question. The Republican Party had so long made political capital of the Homestead Act and its feeble accomplishments that the benefit to the industrial laborer had become an axiom of American thought. Turner, himself, made only incidental use of the theory as a further illustration of his general philosophy concerning the West. Apparently he made no effort to examine the basis of the safety-valve assumption. Had he done so, no doubt the theory would have been declared dead forty or fifty years ago, and the present autopsy would have been made unnecessary. It was some of the followers of Turner who made a fetish of the assumption, but in recent years few if any have gone so far as to say that Eastern laborers in large numbers actually succeeded as homesteaders.

The approach has been shifted. An early variation of the theme was that the West as a whole, if not free land alone, provided the safety valve. This, as will be seen, was no more valid than the original theory. Another idea, sometimes expressed but apparently not yet reduced to a reasoned hypothesis, is that land, in its widest definition (that is, total natural resources), constituted a safety valve. This is merely one way of begging the question by proposing a new one. Besides, it is easy to demonstrate that as new natural resources were discovered the world population multiplied to take advantage of them and that the old problems were quickly transplanted to a new locality. It can readily be shown that the monopolization of these resources prevented their widest social utilization and that the pressure of labor difficulties was no less intense in new communities than in the old. Witness the Coeur de'Alene strike in Idaho in the same year as the Homestead strike in Pennsylvania. But the natural-resources-safety-valve theory will require a thorough statement and exposition by one of its adherents before an examination can be made. The manufacture of such a hypothesis will be a tough problem, in view of the fact that, ever since the development of the factory system in America, labor unrest has resulted in violently explosive strikes rather than a gentle pop-off of steam through any supposed safety valve. The question will have to be answered: If any safety valve existed why did it not work? Since it did not work, how can it by any twist of the imagination be called a valve at all?

Another turn of the argument is a revival of the supposition of Carter Goodrich and Sol Davidson (further expounded) that while no great number of industrial laborers became homesteaders, yet the safety valve existed, because it drained off the surplus of the Eastern farm population that otherwise would have gone to the cities for factory jobs. So, free land was a safety valve because it drew *potential* industrial labor to the west.

Again, the question immediately arises: Why did this potential safety valve not work? Was it really a safety valve at all or was it merely a "whistle on a peanut roaster"? There can be no confusion of definitions involved. There is only one definition of the term: "An automatic escape or relief valve for a steam boiler, hydraulic system, etc." Under the catch-all "etc." one may just as well include "labor unrest." Obviously the safety valve is not for the benefit of the steam, water, or labor that escapes from the boiler, hydraulic system, or factory. It is to prevent the accumulation of pressure that might cause an explosion.

A safety valve is of use only when pressure reaches the danger point. This is where the trouble comes with the labor safety valve in all of its interpretations. It certainly was not working at the time of the Panic of 1837, or in the depression following the Panic of 1873, when over a million unemployed workmen paced the streets and knew that free lands were beyond their reach. It was rusted solid and immovable during the bloody railroad strikes of 1877 and the great labor upheaval of the 1880s. When the old-time Mississippi River steamboat captain "hung a nigger" on the arm of a safety valve when running a race, it can be positively asserted that his safety valve as such did not exist. This belief would doubtless be shared by the possible lone survivor picked maimed and scalded off a sycamore limb after the explosion.

No responsible person has ever tried to deny that at all times in America some few of the more fortunate laborers could and did take up land. But this seepage of steam which went on almost constantly did not prevent the pressure from rising when too much fuel was put under the boiler, and the seepage almost stopped entirely whenever the pressure got dangerously high. It was not till the 1830s, when the factory system in America began to bloom and the labor gangs were recruited for the building of canals and railroads, that any situation arose which would call for a safety valve. The shoemaker or carpenter of colonial days who turned to farming did not do so as a release from an ironclad wage system, as millions between 1830 and 1900 would have liked to do if they could. It was an era of slipshod economy and easy readjustment, where no great obstacle was put in the way of misfits. Even if one admits that a scarcity of free labor for hire was one of the minor reasons for the late development of a factory system, and that the choice of close and cheap land kept down the supply, yet a far greater reason was the scarcity of manufacturing capital. When the factory system began, it was easy to import shiploads of immigrant laborers. The same could have been done a generation or two earlier if there had been the demand.

But perhaps a more substantial argument is needed to answer so attractive a hypothesis as that of the potential safety valve. At first glance this new idea has some charm. Certainly the Western farms did not create their own population by spontaneous generation. If not Eastern industrial laborers, then undoubtedly Eastern farmers must have supplied the initial impulse, and each Eastern farmer who went west drained the Eastern potential labor market by one. But the question is: Did *all* the migration from East to West amount to enough to constitute a safety valve for Eastern labor? Did not the promise of free land, and such migration as actually occurred, simply lure millions of Europeans to American shores, seeking farms or industrial jobs, the bulk of the newcomers remaining in the East to make possible a worse labor congestion than would have existed if everything west of the Mississippi River had been nonexistent? The answer is so simple that it can be evolved from census data alone. The post mortem can now be held. If a sufficient domestic migration did take place with the desired results, then there *was* a safety valve, and there is no corpse of a theory to examine. If not, then the theory is dead and the body can be laid to rest.

The first question to be answered is: How large a surplus of farm population developed and where did it settle between 1860 (just before the Homestead Act) and 1900 (by which date the last gasp of steam is admitted to have escaped from the safety valve)? Here close estimates must substitute for an actual count, for before 1920 the census did not distinguish between actual farm and nonfarm residence. But the census officials did gather and publish figures on the numbers of persons employed for gain in the different occupations, and, wherever comparisons can be made, it is noticeable that the ratio of farm workers to all other persons receiving incomes has always been relatively close to the ratio between total farm and nonfarm population. On this basis of calculation (the only one available and accurate enough for all ordinary needs), in forty years the farm population only expanded from 19,000,000 to 28,000,000, while the nonfarm element grew from somewhat over 12,000,-000 to 48,000,000, or almost fourfold. Villages, towns, and cities gained about 18,000,000 above the average rate of growth for the Nation as a whole, while the farm increase lagged by the same amount below the average. These figures are derived from a careful analytical study of occupations, based on census reports, which shows the number of income receivers engaged in agriculture creeping from 6,287,000 to 10,699,000, while those in nonfarm occupations soared from 4,244,000 to 18,374,-000. . . .

These incontestable facts and figures play havoc with the assumption that "perhaps most" of the Eastern boys who left their "ancestral acres" migrated "to the West to acquire and develop a tract of virgin soil." There just was not that much of an increase in the number of farms between 1860 and 1900. Only 3,737,000 units were added to the 2,000,000 of the earlier year, and 2,000,000 of the total in 1900 were tenant-operated. How large a proportion of the Eastern boys who left their fathers' farms could have become by any possibility the owners of the fraction of the increase in farms that lay in the West?

Here the potential-safety-valve advocates spoil their own argument. One of them stresses the great fecundity of Eastern farmers, "a dozen children being hardly exceptional." At only the average rate of breeding for the whole Nation, the 19,000,000 farm population of 1860, with their descendants and immigrant additions, would have numbered about 46,-000,000 by 1900. But barely 60 per cent of that number were on farms anywhere in the country at the later date, and only 7,000,000 could have been on farms owned by themselves or their families. If farmers were as philoprogenitive as just quoted, then by 1900 the number of persons of farm ancestry must have been closer to 60,000,000 than 46,000,000, and the increase alone would amount to at least 40,000,000. But the growth of farm population was only 9,000,000, and, of these, little more than 2,000,000 could have been on farms owned by their families. If it could be assumed that all the augmentation in farm population had been by migrating native farmers, by 1900 there would have been 31,000,000 of farm background (as of 1860) residing in the villages, towns, and cities; 9,000,000 would have been on new farms or subdivisions of old ones; of these, nearly 7,000,000 would have been tenants or hired laborers and their families, depressing industrial labor by their threat of competition; and about 2,000,000 would have been on their own farms, whether "virgin soil" of the West or marginal tracts in the East. But it would be taking advantage of the opponent's slip of the pen to trace this phantasy further. The law of averages is enough in itself to annihilate the safety valvers' contention. By the use of this conservative tool alone it will be realized that at least twenty farmers moved to town for each industrial laborer who moved to the land, and ten sons of farmers went to the city for each one who became the owner of a new farm anywhere in the Nation.

As to the farms west of the Mississippi River, it is well known that many of them were settled by aliens (witness the West North Central States with their large numbers of Scandinavians). Here is a theme that might well be expanded. The latest exponent of the potential-labor-safety-valve theory declares that "potential labor was drained out of the country, and to secure it for his fast expanding industrial enterprise, the manufacturer must import labor from Europe." Anyone must admit that a fraction of the surplus farm labor of the East went on new farms. But how does this additional immigrant stream into the cities affect the safety valve? The immigrants may not really have increased the industrial population. It has often been contended that, instead, the resulting competition restricted the native birth rate in equal proportion to the numbers of the newcomers. Apparently this must remain in the realm of speculation. Be this as it may, the immigrants, with their background of cheap living, acted as a drag on wages, thus making the lot of the city laborer all the harder. This is not the way that even a *potential* safety valve should work.

But, returning to the West, there is a further fact to be considered. The total population west of the Mississippi River in 1860 was about 4,500,000. In 1900 it was just under 21,000,000. Surely the "fecund" Westerners must have multiplied their own stock to about 12,000,000 by the latter date. In the same forty years some 14,000,000 immigrants came to America. By 1900, with their descendants, they must have numbered half again as many, or 21,000,000, for it has not been contended that immigrant competition lowered the immigrant birth rate. On this point the census data are not altogether satisfying. Foreign-born persons and their American-born children (counting only half of the children of mixed American and alien parentage) numbered 23,673,000. No doubt the survivors of the foreign-born counted in the Census of 1860, together with their later children, would reduce the alien accretion since 1860 to the 21,000,000 estimate. If anyone can prove that this should be cut still a few more million, he will not greatly change the estimates that follow.

The Western States, in proportion to their total population, had proved amazingly attractive to the immigrants. Though over 19,087,000 of the 1900 count (including those with only one foreign-born parent) lived east of the Mississippi River, 7,112,000 were in the States (including Louisiana and Minnesota) to the west of the same line. In the eleven Mountain and Pacific States they were 47.6 per cent of the total population, the figure reaching 61.2 in Utah, 57.3 in Montana, and 54.9 in California. Nevada also had a majority. Kansas and Missouri alone of the West North Central group had less than 40 per cent of alien parentage, while the percentage in North Dakota was 77.5, in Minnesota 74.9, and in South Dakota 61.1. In round numbers Minnesota had 1,312,000, Iowa 958,000, California 815,000, Missouri 741,000, Nebraska 503,000, Texas 472,000, and Kansas 403,000. Aside from Texas the numbers, as well as the percentages, in the West South Central States were low.

In 1860 the trans-Mississippi West contained 653,000 persons of foreign birth, but the number of their American-born children was not given. Even if the survivors and the children numbered over a million, by 1900 those twenty-two States still had 6,000,000 of post-1860 immigrant stock. If the estimate for the increase of the pre-1860 element is too low, so, it can be countered, were the totals of the Census of 1900. Grandchildren were not counted, and mature immigrants of the 1860s could have had a lot of grandchildren by 1900. All the descendants of the pre-1860 immigrants were included in the estimate of 12,000,000 for the increase of the inhabitants of 1860, whereas all after the first descent are excluded from the post-1860 immigrant posterity. On the other hand let it be conceded that 12,000,000 by internal expansion and 6,000,000 by immigration, or 18,000,000 in all, is too much. This would leave only 3,000,000 of the West in 1900, or one-seventh of the total, accounted for by migration from the Eastern States. The calculator can afford to be generous. Subtract two million from the internal expansion and another million from the alien stock, and add these to the migrants from the Eastern States. Suppose, then, that 6,000,000 of the West's population of 1900 was of pre-1860 Eastern United States origin, and three times that many foreigners and their children had come into the East to replace them. It all simmers down to the fact that the West acted as a lure to prospective European immigrants, either to take up lands, to occupy vacated city jobs, or to supply the demands of a growing industry. In any case the effect was just exactly the opposite of a safety valve, actual or potential.

Now the question is in order as to how many of those Eastern boys who left their "ancestral acres" and migrated "to the West" actually were able "to acquire and develop a tract of virgin soil." As will soon be demonstrated, only 47.1 per cent of the Western population of 1900 lived on farms. By the same ratio, a mere 2,826,000 of the exaggerated number of the Eastern stock (as listed above) were farm residents. There were barely more than 2,000,000 farms west of the Mississippi in 1900. If two-sevenths of the population was Eastern in origin, it may be assumed that the same proportion of the farming was done by them. This would give them less than 572,000 units to operate as owners, managers, tenants, or hired laborers. But in the West, as in the Nation as a whole, the ratio of tenants and hired laborers to all farmers was very high. A full 35 per cent of all Western farms were occupied by tenants. The high ratio in the West South Central region affects the average for all somewhat, but there were several other States that approximated the worst conditions. The percentage in Nebraska was 35.5, in Kansas 33.9, in Iowa 33.6, in Missouri 30.6, and in South Dakota 21.9. But also, slightly over 40 per cent of all Western farm-income receivers were wage laborers. If these same ratios apply to total population on the farms, then well over 1,130,000 of the Eastern element in the West were wage laborers' families; more than 989,000 were on tenant holdings; and less than 707,000 occupied farms owned by themselves. This means that there was only one person on such a family possession for each twenty-five who left the farms of the Nation in the preceding forty years. But perhaps this number is a little too small. No doubt a good number of the hired laborers were also the sons of the owners. Also, though many of the wage workers in the West lived with their families in separate huts on the farms, another considerable number were single men (or detached from their families) who boarded with the owner. How much this situation affected the given figures is uncertain. But here is something more substantial. Only 65 per cent of the farms, or less than 372,000 in all, were owner-operated. Here, then, is the number of those tracts of "virgin soil" taken up and kept—one for each forty-eight persons who left their "ancestral acres" in the East, or possibly one family farm for each ten families. What a showing for the potential safety valve!

One point remains: Urban development in its relation to safety-valve theories. Between 1790 and 1860 the percentage of persons in cities of 8,000 or more inhabitants grew from 3.3 to 16.1; the number of such places from 6 to 141; and their population from 131,000 to 5,000,000. Over half of this growth took place after 1840. The city was already draining the country. But this was only the curtain raiser for the act to follow. In the next forty years the number of cities was multiplied to 547, their inhabitants to 25,000,000, and their percentage of the total population to 32.9. They had grown more than twice as fast as the Nation at large. The same rule applies to all municipalities of 2,500 and over, as their population expanded from 6,500,000 to 30,400,000. The cities may have bred pestilence, poverty, crime, and corruption, but there is no evidence that they bred population that rapidly. Immigration alone cannot explain the phenomenon, for, if the entire number of immigrants after 1860 is subtracted from the nonfarm population of 1900, the remainder still represents twice the rate of growth of farm population.

It is conceded that the bulk of the immigrants settled in urban localities, and it has been demonstrated that the great bulk of the surplus of farm population did the same. For that matter, outside the Cotton Belt, the majority of the westward-moving population did not settle on farms. When the Eastern city laborer managed to pay his fare or "ride the rods" westward, he, like the migrating farmer, was likely to establish himself in a mining camp, town, or city, where, as in the Coeur d'Alene region of Idaho, he found that he had exchanged drudgery in an Eastern factory for equally ill-paid drudgery (considering living costs) in a Western

PERSONS TEN YEARS OF AGE AND OVER GAINFULLY EMPLOYED IN THE WEST

	1870 TOTAL Thou-sands	AGRICULTURE Thou-sands	Percent	1890 TOTAL Thou-sands	AGRICULTURE Thou-sands	Percent	1900 TOTAL Thou-sands	AGRICULTURE Thou-sands	Percent
United States	12,506	5,922	47.4	22,736	8,466	37.2	29,286	10,438	35.7
Trans-Miss. West	2,199	1,170	53.2	5,811	2,703	46.5	7,717	3,642	47.1
W. N. Central	1,157	648	56.0	2,988	1,432	47.9	3,693	1,707	46.2
W. S. Central	628	417	66.4	1,487	933	62.7	2,322	1,472	63.4
Mountain	134	50	29.9	501	127	25.3	663	192	28.8
Pacific	280	65	23.2	836	212	25.4	1,039	271	26.1

factory or mine. The urbanized proportion of the population west of the Mississippi River, where 1,725,000 new farms had been created, very nearly kept pace with the national average. In 1900, when almost half (47.1 per cent) of America's people were living in incorporated towns and cities, the ratio west of the Mississippi River was over three-eighths (38.1 per cent). Minnesota exceeded, while Missouri, Iowa, and Nebraska nearly equaled the national ratio. The combined eleven Mountain and

Pacific States rated even higher than Minnesota, with 50.6 per cent of their population in incorporated places. It was only the Dakotas and the West South Central States that were so overwhelmingly rural as to keep the trans-Mississippi West below the national ratio. On the basis of the gainfully employed, always a better measure, the West showed a still higher proportion of nonfarm population. The census figures for 1870, 1890, and 1900 are used in the accompanying table to illustrate this point.

In each decade, the Far-Western regions were well below the national ratio of agricultural to town and city labor, and to 1890 they were far below. In 1870, outside the West South Central States and Iowa, the figure averaged 44.3 per cent for seventeen Western States compared with 47.4 per cent for the United States. In the next twenty years, when free land was presumed to be the greatest lure of the West, the towns gained on the farms till the latter included only 46.5 per cent of the Western total in spite of the still preponderantly rural character of the West South Central division. Then in 1890, according to the legend, the gate to free land flew shut with a bang, and the urban-labor safety valve rusted tight forever. Yet, the increase in agricultural population in the next ten years was nearly a fourth larger than the average for the preceding decades. Whereas the city had been draining labor from the farm before 1890, now that the theoretical safety valve was gone the Western farm was gaining on the Western city. Good land—free, cheap, or at speculators' prices—undoubtedly was more abundant before 1890 than afterward. Before that date, without cavil, this land had helped to keep down *rural* discontent and unrest. A small percentage of surplus farmers, and a few other discontented ones in periods of hard times, had been able to go west and take up new farms, but many times that number had sought refuges, however tenuous, in the cities. Whether this cityward migration left the more intelligent and energetic or the duller and more indolent back on the farm is relatively immaterial so far as the release of pressure is concerned. Such evidence as has been uncovered shows no decided weight one way or the other.

This much is certain. The industrial labor troubles of the 1870s and 1880s, when this *potential* safety valve was supposed to be working, were among the most violent ever experienced in the Nation's history. Steam escaped by explosion and not through a safety valve of free land. On the other hand, down to 1890 the flow of excess farmers to the industrial centers was incessant and accelerated. When hard times settled down on the farms of the Middle West, as in the 1870s, Grangers could organize, antimonopoly parties arise, and greenbackers flourish; but the pressure was eased largely by the flow of excess population to the towns. No doubt the migrants would have done better to stay at home and create an explosion. Instead, they went to town to add to the explosive force there. Farm agitation died down when a few reforms were secured, and the continued cityward movement retarded its revival.

However, after 1890 this release for rural discontent began to fail. The cities were approaching a static condition and were losing their attraction for farmers. This condition continued until between 1930 and 1940 there was virtually no net shift of population between town and country. In the 1890s when the city safety valve for rural discontent was beginning to fail, the baffled farmer was at bay. Drought in the farther West and congestion in the cities left him no direction to go. He must stay on his freehold or tenant farm and fight. Populism in the 1890s was not to be as easily diverted or sidetracked by feeble concessions as had been Grangerism in the 1870s. In the forty years after 1890, the farmers, balked increasingly in their cityward yearnings, began to take far greater risks than ever before in their efforts to conquer the arid regions. Four times as much land was homesteaded as in the preceding decades. Great things were accomplished in the way of irrigation and dry farming; but also great distress was encountered, great dust bowls were created, and great national problems of farm relief were fostered.

Generalization alone does not establish a thesis, but already there is a substantial body of facts to support an argument for the city safety valve for rural discontent. Nevertheless old stereotypes of thought die hard. Quite often they expire only with their devotees. It has been proved time after time that since 1880, at least, the old idea of the agricultural ladder has worked in reverse. Instead of tenancy being a ladder up which workers could climb to farm ownership, in reality the freeholder more often climbed down the ladder to tenancy. Yet there are people in abundance who still nourish the illusion that their old friend remains alive. There is no reason for assuming that in the present instance the truth will be any more welcome than it has proved to be in the past. There never was a free-land or even a Western safety valve for industrial labor. There never was one even of the potential sort. So far did such a valve fail to exist that the exact opposite is seen. The rapid growth of industry and commerce in the cities provided a release from surplus farm population. The safety valve that actually existed worked in entirely the opposite direction from the one so often extolled. Perhaps the growth of urban economy also, on occasion, was rapid and smooth enough to absorb most of the growing population without explosive effect. Once the people concentrated in the cities, there was no safety valve whatever that could prevent violent eruptions in depression periods. Of this, the diehards also will remain unconvinced. The persons who mournfully sing that "The old gray mare, she ain't what she used to be" seldom are ready to admit that she never did amount to much.

The post mortem on the theory of a free-land safety valve for industrial labor is at an end. For a century it was fed on nothing more sustaining than unsupported rationalization. Its ethereal body was able to survive on this slender nourishment as long as the supply lasted. But when the food was diluted to a "potential" consistency, it was no longer strong enough to maintain life. Death came from inanition. The body may now be sealed in its coffin and laid to rest. Let those who will consult the spirit rappers to bring forth its ghost.

FOR FURTHER READING: Malfunctioning of the safety valve is treated in Clarence Danhof, "Farm-Making Costs and the Safety Valve, 1850–1860," *Journal of Political Economy*, XLIX (June, 1941), pp. 317–359, Helene Zahler, *Eastern Workingmen and Land Policy, 1829–1862* (New York, 1941), Carter Goodrich and Sol Davidson, "The Wage Earner in the Westward Movement," *Political Science Quarterly*, L (June, 1935), pp. 161–185. An excellent and comprehensive review of varying perspectives on the safety valve is in Ellen von Nardroff, "The American Frontier as a Safety Valve—the Life, Death, Reincarnation and Justification of a Theory," *Agricultural History*, XXXVI (July, 1962), pp. 123–142.

14. *The Economy of the Ante-Bellum South*

PROBLEM: *Was slavery profitable?*

For over a century historians, not unlike former plantation owners and abolitionists, have disagreed whether or not slavery as a labor system was profitable for the master class. One group, for whom Ulrich B. Phillips, a leading historian of the South, was a spokesman has contended that it was essentially unremunerative, that it contained within itself the seeds of its own destruction. Phillips noted that the overcapitalization of slaves due to rising prices, the expense of maintaining the ill and aged, and the inefficiency of forced labor made slavery unprofitable. But this viewpoint has been challenged vigorously by others who find that slavery was indeed profitable for the owners. Perhaps the most sophisticated expression of this stand was taken by two young economists, Alfred Conrad and John Meyer of Harvard University, who dealt with the issue by utilizing economic theories. Analyzing slavery from the perspective of modern capital investment theory they concluded that the annual returns from human property were not less than those from other forms of investment. Most likely this controversy has not yet ended, but the following selections contain arguments frequently used on both sides of the issue. What factors need to be considered in assessing the profitability of slavery, or any labor system? How did non-economic factors affect the profitability of slavery? Have moral considerations affected the views of writers about the economics of slavery?

The Economic Cost of Slaveholding
in the Cotton Belt

ULRICH B. PHILLIPS

Apart from mere surface politics, the ante-bellum South is largely an un-known country to American historians. The conditions, the life, the spirit of its people were so different from those which prevailed and still prevail in the North that it is difficult for northern investigators to interpret correctly the facts which they are able to find. From the South itself they have received little assistance; for before the war Southerners were content, as a rule, to transmit traditions without writing books, and since the war they have been too seriously engrossed in adapting themselves to new conditions to feel any strong impulse towards a scientific recon-struction of the former environment. When the South shall have been interpreted to the world by its own writers, it will be highly useful for students of other sections and other countries to criticize and correct, utilize and supplement the southern historical literature. At the present time, however, the great need seems to be that of interpretation of devel-opments in the South by men who have inherited Southern traditions. This consideration will perhaps justify the following incomplete study.

Whether negro slavery was an advantage in the early colonies and whether it became a burden in the later period, and, if so, how the change occurred, and why the people did not relieve themselves of the incubus—these are a few of the fundamental problems to which the student must address himself. The present essay, based on a study of slave prices, deals with the general economic conditions of slaveholding, and shows the great transformation caused by the opening of the cotton belt and the closing of the African slave trade.

As regards the labor supply, the conditions at the outset in the new world of America were unlike those of modern Europe, but similar to those of Asia and Europe in primitive times. The ancient labor problem rose afresh in the plantation colonies, for land was plentiful and free, and men would not work as voluntary wage-earners in other men's employ when they might as readily work for themselves in independence. There was a great demand for labor upon the colonial estates, and when it be-came clear that freemen would not come and work for hire, a demand developed for servile labor. At first, recourse was had to white men and women who bound themselves to serve three or four years to pay for their transportation across the sea, and to English criminals who were sent to the colonies and bound to labor for longer terms, frequently for five

Reprinted from the *Political Science Quarterly*, XX (June, 1905), pp. 257–275.

or seven years. Indian slaves were tried, but proved useless. Finally the negroes were discovered to be cheap and useful laborers for domestic service and plantation work.

For above half a century after the first negroes were brought to Virginia in 1620, this labor was considered a doubtful experiment; and their numbers increased very slowly until after the beginning of the golden age of the colony toward the end of the reign of Charles II. But the planters learned at length that the negroes could be employed to very good advantage in the plantation system; and after about 1680 the import of slaves grew steadily larger.

In the West Indies the system of plantations worked by slaves had been borrowed by the English settlers from the Spaniards; and when the South Carolina coast was colonized, some of the West India planters immigrated and brought this system with them. In view of the climate and the crops on the Carolina coast, negro slave labor was thought to be a *sine qua non* of successful colonizing. The use of the slaves was confined always to the lowlands, until after Whitney invented the cotton gin; but in the early years of the nineteenth century the rapid opening of the great inland cotton belt created a new and very strong demand for labor. The white farming population already in the uplands was by far too small to do the work; the lowland planters began to move thither with their slaves; the northern and European laboring classes were not attracted by the prospect of working alongside the negroes; and accordingly the demand for labor in the cotton belt was translated into an unprecedented demand for negro slave labor.

Negro slavery was established in the South, as elsewhere, because the white people were seeking their own welfare and comfort. It was maintained for the same economic reason, and also because it was thought to be essential for safety. As soon as the negroes were on hand in large numbers, the problem was to keep their savage instincts from breaking forth, and to utilize them in civilized industry. The plantation system solved the problem of organization, while the discipline and control obtained through the institution of slavery were considered necessary to preserve the peace and to secure the welfare of both races. Private gain and public safety were secured for the time being; but in the long run, as we shall see, these ends were attained at the expense of private and public wealth and of progress.

This peculiar labor system failed to gain strength in the North, because there was no work which negro slaves could perform with notable profit to their masters. In certain parts of the South the system flourished because the work required was simple, the returns were large, and the shortcomings of negro slave labor were partially offset by the ease with which it could be organized.

Once developed, the system was of course maintained so long as it appeared profitable to any important part of the community. Wherever the immediate profits from slave labor were found to be large, the number of slaves tended to increase, not only through the birth of children, but by importations. Thus the staple-producing areas became "black belts," where most of the labor was done by slaves. With large amounts of capital invested in slaves, the system would be maintained even in times of depression, when the plantations were running at something of a loss; for, just as in a factory, the capital was fixed, and operations could not be stopped without a still greater loss. When property in slaves had become important, the conservative element in politics became devoted, as a rule, to the preservation of this vested interest. The very force of inertia tended to maintain the established system, and a convulsion or crisis of some sort was necessary for its disestablishment in any region.

As a matter of fact, it was only in special industries, and only in times of special prosperity, that negro slave labor was of such decided profit as to escape condemnation for its inherent disadvantages. But at certain periods in Virginia and in the lower South, the conditions were unusual: all labor was profitable; hired labor was not to be had so long as land was free; indentured white servants were in various ways unsatisfactory, and negro slaves were therefore found to be of decided profit to their masters. The price of Africans in colonial times was so low that, when crops and prices were good, the labor of those imported repaid their original cost in a few years, and the planters felt a constant temptation to increase their holdings of land and of slaves in the hope of still greater profits.

Thus in Virginia there was a vicious circle: planters bought fresh lands and more slaves to make more tobacco, and with the profits from tobacco they bought more land and slaves to make more tobacco with which to buy yet more land and slaves. The situation in the lower South was similar to that in Virginia, with rice and indigo, or sugar, or in latter times cotton, substituted for tobacco. In either case the process involved a heavy export of wealth in the acquisition of every new laborer. The Yankee skipper had a corresponding circle of his own: he carried rum to Guinea to exchange for slaves, slaves to the plantation colonies to exchange for molasses, molasses to New England to exchange for more rum, and this rum again to Guinea to exchange for more slaves. The difference was that the Yankee made a genuine profit on every exchange and thriftily laid up his savings, while the Southern planter, as a rule, invested all his profit in a fictitious form of wealth and never accumulated a surplus for any other sort of investment.

From an economic point of view the American system of slavery was a system of firmly controlling the unintelligent negro laborers, and of capitalizing the prospective value of the labor of each workman for the whole of his life. An essential feature of that system was the practice of buying and selling the control over the slave's labor, and one of the indexes to the economic situation at any time may be found in the quotations of slave prices.

The slave trade had no particular local home or "exchange," but it extended throughout all the slaveholding districts of America. Though the number and frequency of slave sales was relatively small, the traffic when once developed had many of the features of modern stock or produce markets. It cannot be forgotten, of course, that the slave trade involved questions of humanity and social organization, as well as the mere money problem; but from the financial point of view the slave traffic constituted simply an extensive commodity market, where the article dealt in was lifetime labor. As in any other market, the operations in the slave trade were controlled by economic laws or tendencies. There were bull influences and bear influences, and occasional speculative campaigns. And when at times the supply was subjected to monopoly control, the prices tended to go wild and disturb the general system of finance in the whole region.

In the general slave market there was constant competition among those wishing to sell, and among those wishing to buy. The volume of the colonial slave trade and the rate of slave prices tended to fluctuate to some extent with the tides of prosperity in the respective staple-producing areas; but during the colonial period the plantations in the different regions were of such varied interests, producing tobacco, rice, indigo, cotton, sugar, and coffee, that depression in one of these industries was usually offset, so far as concerned the slave-trader, by high profits in another. Barbados was the information station. The slave ships touched there and gathered news of where their "ebony" was to be sold the highest. The Royal African Company had the best system of intelligence, and about 1770 and 1780 it sold its cargoes at a fairly uniform price of £18 to £22 per head, while the independent traders appear to have obtained from £15 to £25, according to the chances of the market. American-born slaves, when sold, brought higher prices than fresh Africans, because their training in plantation labor and domestic service rendered them more valuable. The prices of the home-raised slaves varied considerably, but so long as the African trade was kept open the price of field hands of all sorts was kept reasonably near to the price of the savage African imports.

In the very early period the sellers in the slave markets were more eager than the buyers, and the prices ranged nearly as low as the cost of purchasing slaves in Africa and transporting them to America; but great prosperity in all the different groups of plantations at the same period soon greatly increased the demand, and the ships in the traffic proving too few, prices rapidly advanced. After this, however, there came a decline in tobacco profits; then the war of revolt from Great Britain depressed all the staple industries simultaneously, and following that the

American production of indigo was ruined by foreign competition. Thus in 1790–95 slave prices reached the bottom of a twenty years' decline.

The developments following Whitney's invention of the cotton gin revolutionized the situation. Slave prices entered upon a steady advance, which was quickened by the prohibition of the African trade in 1808. They were then held stationary by the restrictions upon commerce, and were thrown backward by the outbreak of war in 1812. But with the peace of Ghent the results of the new cotton industry and of the cessation of African imports became strikingly manifest. The inland fields of the lower South proved to be peculiarly adapted for the production of cotton. The simplicity of the work and the even distribution of the tasks through the seasons made negro slave labor peculiarly available. With the increasing demand of the world for cotton, there was built up in the South perhaps the greatest staple monopoly the world had ever seen. The result was an enormous demand for slaves in the cotton belt. American ports, however, were now closed to the foreign slave trade. The number of slaves available in America was now fixed, the rate of increase was limited, and the old "tobacco South" had a monopoly of the only supply which could meet the demand of the new "cotton South."

Till 1815 "colonial" conditions prevailed and the market for slave labor was relatively quiet and steady. In 1815 began the "ante-bellum" régime, in which the whole economy of the South was governed by the apparently capricious play of the compound monopoly of cotton and slave labor. The price of cotton was governed by the American output and its relation to the European demand. And the price of slaves was governed by the profits in cotton and the relation of the labor demand to the monopolized labor supply.

For an understanding of slaveholding economics, a careful study of the history of slave prices is essential. Prior to the middle of the eighteenth century, the scarcity of data, the changing value of gold, the multiplicity of coinage systems and the use of paper money with irregular depreciations unfortunately present so many obstacles that any effort to determine the fluctuation of slave prices would be of very doubtful success. For the following periods the study is feasible, although under the best of existing circumstances slave prices are hard to collect and hard to compare. The proportion of the slave population on the market at any time was very much smaller than the student could wish for the purpose of his study; and many of the sales which were made are not to be found in the records. The market classification of the slaves was flexible and irregular; and, except in Louisiana, most of the documents in the public archives do not indicate the classification. To make thoroughly accurate comparison of slave prices at different times and places, we should need to know, among other things, the sex, age, strength and nativity of the slaves; the purity or mixture of blood of the negroes, mulattoes, quadroons, mestizos, etc.; and their special training or lack of it. For such statistical purposes, however, the records have many shortcomings. In many cases they state simply that the slave Matt or Congo or Martha, belonging to the estate of William Jones, deceased, was sold on the date given to Thomas Smith, for, say, $300, on twelve months' credit. Such an item indicates the sex and states the price, but gives little else. In other instances the slaves are classed as infants, boys, men (or fellows) and old men; girls, wenches and old women. Whole families were often sold as a lot, with no individual quotations given. Women were hardly ever sold separate from their young children. In the dearth of separate sale quotations, any study of the prices of female slaves would have to be based chiefly upon appraisal values, which of course were much less accurate than actual market prices.

The sales made by the professional slave traders were generally recorded each in a bill of sale; but in most of the localities these were not transcribed into the formal books of record, and the originals have mostly disappeared. The majority of the sales of which records are to be found were those of the slaves in the estates of deceased persons. These sales were at auction; and except in abnormal cases, which may often be distinguished, they may be taken as fairly representative of slave prices for the time and place.

There was always a great difference between the values of individual slaves. When the average price of negroes ranged about $500, prime field hands brought, say, $1,000, and skilled artisans still more. At that rate, an infant would be valued at about $100, a boy of twelve years and a man of fifty at about $500 each, and a prime wench for field work at $800 or $900.

The most feasible comparison of prices is that of prime field hands, who may be defined as well-grown, able-bodied fellows, with average training and between eighteen and thirty years of age. To find the current price of prime field hands in lists where no classification is given, we take the average of the highest ordinary prices. We ignore any scattering extreme quotations, as applying probably to specially valuable artisans, overseers of domestic servants, and not to field hands. Where ages are given, we take the average of the prices paid for grown fellows too young to have received special training. We leave aside, on the other hand, the exceptionally low quotations as being due to infirmities which exclude the slave from the prime grade. The professional slave traders in the domestic traffic dealt mostly in "likely young fellows and wenches." In the quotations of the sales of these traders, when no details are recorded, we may assume that the average, except for children, will range just a little below the current rate for prime field hands.

In view of all the hindrances, the production of a perfectly accurate table of prices cannot be hoped for, even from the exercise of the utmost care and discrimination. The table which follows is simply an approximation of averages made in a careful study of several thousand quotations in the state of Georgia.[1]

The parallel quotations of cotton prices[2] afford a basis for the study of slave-labor capitalization. In examining these quotations it will be noticed that during many brief periods the prices of slaves and cotton rose and fell somewhat in harmony; but that in the whole period under review the price of cotton underwent a heavy net decline, while slave prices had an extremely strong upward movement. The change which took place in the relative slave and cotton prices was really astonishing. In 1800 a prime field hand was worth in the market about 1500 pounds of ginned cotton; in 1809, about 3000 pounds; in 1818, about 3500; in 1826, about 5400; in 1837, about 10,000; in 1845, about 12,000; in 1860, 15,000 to 18,000. In his capacity for work, a prime negro in 1800 was worth nearly or quite as much as a similar slave in 1860; and a pound of cotton in 1860 was not essentially different from a pound of cotton in 1800. But our table shows that within that epoch of three-score years there was an advance of some 1000 or 1200 per cent in the price of slaves as measured in cotton.

The decline in the price of cotton was due in some measure to a lessening of cost, through improvements in cultivating, ginning and marketing. The advance in slave prices was due in part to the increasing intelligence and ability of the negroes and to improvements in the system of directing their work on the plantations, and also in part to the decline in the value of money. But the ten-fold or twelve-fold multiplication of the price of slaves, when quoted in terms of the product of their labor, was too great to be explained except by references to the severe competition of the planters in selling cotton and in buying slaves. Their system of capitalized labor was out of place in the modern competitive world; and burdened with that system all the competition of the cotton planters was bound to be of a cut-throat nature. In other words, when capital and labor were combined, as in the American slaveholding system, there was an irresistible tendency to overvalue and overcapitalize slave labor, and to carry it to the point where the financial equilibrium was unsafe, and any crisis threatened complete bankruptcy.

Aside from the expense of food, clothing, and shelter, the cost of slave labor for any given period of time was made up of several elements:

[1] The sources used for this tabulation are the documents in the Georgia state archives and the records of Baldwin, Oglethorpe, Clarke, and Troup counties, all lying in the Georgia cotton belt, together with bills of sale in private hands, travelers' accounts, and articles in the newspapers of the period. Instances of sudden rise or fall in slave prices and sales of large and noted estates were often reported in the local press with comments. There is no printed collection of any large number of slave-price quotations.

[2] The cotton price averages are made from the tables given by E. J. Donnell in his *Chronological and Statistical History of Cotton*, New York, 1872, with the aid of the summaries published by G. L. Watkins, *Production and Price of Cotton for One Hundred Years*, U.S. Department of Agriculture, Washington, 1895.

SLAVE AND COTTON PRICES IN GEORGIA

Year	Average Price of Prime Field Hands	Economic Situation and the Chief Determinant Factors	Average N.Y. Price of Upland Cotton	Years
1755......	£55			
1773......	60			
1776–1783.	......	War and depression in industry and commerce.		
1784......	70	Peace and returning prosperity.		
1792......	$300	Depression due to Great Britain's attitude toward American commerce.		
1793......	......	Cotton gin invented.		
1800......	450	....	30 cents.	1795–1805
1808......	......	African slave trade prohibited.		
1809......	600	Embargo moderates rise in prices.................	19 cents.	1805–1810
1813......	450	War with Great Britain....	12 cents.	1813
1818......	1000	Inflation.	29 cents.	1816–1818
1819......	......	Financial crisis............	16 cents.	1819
1821......	700	Recovery from panic......	14 cents.	1821
1826......	800	Moderate prosperity.......	15 cents.	1824–1827
1827......	......	Depression.		
1828......	700	....	10 cents.	1827–1828
1835......	900	Flush times...............	17½ cents.	1835
1837......	1300	Inflation—crash...........	13½ cents.	1837
1839......	1000	Cotton crisis.............	13½ cents.	1839
1840......	700	Cotton crisis; acute distress.	9 cents.	1840
1844......	600	Depression...............	7½ cents.	1844
1845......	......	Severe depression.........	5½ cents.	1845
1848......	900	Recovery in cotton prices. Texas demand for slaves.	9½ cents.	1847–1848
1851......	1050	Prosperity	12 cents.	1851
1853......	1200	Expansion of cotton industry and simultaneous rise in tobacco prices..........	11 cents.	1850–1860
1859......	1650			
1860......	1800			

(1) Interest upon the capital invested in the slave.

(2) Economic insurange against (a) his death, (b) his illness or accidental injury, and (c) his flight from service.[3] Of course insurance poli-

[3] Physicians' and attorneys' fees should perhaps be included under the head of insurance. It may be noted that doctors' charges were generally the same for slaves as for white persons. To illustrate how expensive this charge often was, we may cite an instance given in the records of Troup county, Georgia, where Dr. Ware collected from Col. Truitt's estate $130.50 for medicine and daily visits to a negro child, from November 29, 1858, to January 5, 1859.

cies were seldom taken out to cover these risks, but the cost of insurance against them must be reckoned in the cost of slave labor for any given period.

(3) The diminishing value of every mature slave by reason of increasing age. Because of the "wear and tear" of his years and his diminishing prospect of life and usefulness, the average slave of fifty-five years of age would be worth only half as much as one of twenty-five years, and after fifty-five the valuation decreased still more rapidly. In computing the cost of any group of slaves it will be necessary to set over against this depreciation the value of the children born; but, on the other hand, the cost by groups would be increased by the need of supporting the disabled negroes who were not in the working gangs.

(4) Taxation assessed upon the capitalized value of the slaves. In the slaveholding region as a whole, in the later ante-bellum period, the total assessed value of slave property was at least as great as that of all the other sorts of property combined.

The rate of slave hire would furnish a good index of the current price of slave labor year by year, if sufficient quotations on a stable basis could be obtained. But on account of the special needs or wishes of the parties to the individual bargains, there were such opportunities for higgling the rate in individual cases that the current rate is very elusive. The following averages, computed from a limited number of quotations for the hire of men slaves in middle Georgia, are illustrative: In 1800, $100 per year; in 1816, $110; in 1818, $140; in 1833, $140; in 1836, $155; in 1841, $140; in 1860, $150. These were in most cases the years of maximum quotations in the respective periods. The local fluctuations in short periods were often very pronounced; but in the long run the rate followed a gradual upward movement.

The relation between the price of slaves and the rate of their hire should theoretically have borne, in quiet periods, a definite relation to the rate of interest upon capital; but the truth is that in the matter of slave prices there was, through the whole period after the closing of the African trade, a tendency to "frenzied finance" in the cotton belt. Slave prices were largely controlled by speculation, while slave hire was regulated more largely by the current rate of wages for labor in general. The whole subject of these relations is one for which authentic data are perhaps too scanty to permit of thorough analysis.

Negro slave labor was expensive, not so much because it was unwilling as because it was overcapitalized and inelastic. The negro of himself, by reason of his inherited inaptitude, was inefficient as a self-directing laborer in civilized industry. The whole system of civilized life was novel and artificial to him; and to make him play a valuable part in it, strict guidance and supervision were essential. Without the plantation system, the mass of the negroes would have been an unbearable burden in America; and except in slavery they could never have been utilized, in the beginning, for plantation work. The negro had no love of work for work's sake; and he had little appreciation of future goods when set over against present exemption from toil. That is to say, he lacked the economic motive without which voluntary civilized industry is impossible. It is a mistake to apply the general philosophy of slavery to the American situation without very serious modification.[4] A slave among the Greeks or Romans was generally a relatively civilized person, whose voluntary labor would have been far more productive than his labor under compulsion. But the negro slave was a negro first, last, and always, and a slave incidentally. Mr. Cairnes and others make a great mistake when they attribute his inefficiency and expensiveness altogether to the one incident of regulation. Regulation actually remedied in large degree the disadvantages of using negro labor, though it failed to make it as cheap, in most employments, as free white labor would have been. The cotton planter found the negro already a part of the situation. To render him useful, firm regulation was necessary. The forcible control of the negro was in the beginning a necessity, and was not of itself a burden at any time.[5]

In American slaveholding, however, the capitalization of labor-value and the sale and purchase of labor-control were permanent features; and when the supply was "cornered" it was unavoidable that the price should be bid up to the point of overvaluation. And this brings us to the main economic disadvantage of the system.

In employing free labor, wages are paid from time to time as the work is done, and the employer can count upon receiving from the products of that labor an income which will enable him to continue to pay its wages in the future, while his working capital is left free for other uses. He may invest a portion of his capital in lands and buildings, and use most of the remainder as circulating capital for special purposes, retaining only a small percentage as a reserve fund. But to secure a working force of slaves, the ante-bellum planter had to invest all the capital that he owned or could borrow in the purchase of slaves and lands; for the larger his plantation was, within certain limits, the more economies he could introduce. The temptation was very strong for him to trim down to the lowest possible limit the fund for supplies and reserve. The slaveholding system thus absorbed the planter's earnings; and for such absorption it had unlimited capacity, for the greater the profits of the planters the more slaves

[4] Palgrave's *Dictionary of Political Economy* contains an excellent article upon slavery, in which it is indicated that harshness and compulsion were not always essential in slave labor; that the motive force was often a sort of feudal devotion to the master; and, further, the negro slave labor was practically essential for developing the resources of the hot malarial swamp regions.

[5] The current rate of hire today for negro workmen in agriculture in Georgia is from $8 to $12 per month; but for the year 1904, the state of Georgia leased out its able-bodied convicts at an average rate of $225 per year. When under strict discipline, the average negro even today, it appears, is worth twice as much as when left to his own devices.

they wanted and the higher the slave prices mounted. Individual profits, as fast as made, went into the purchase of labor, and not into modern implements or land improvements. Circulating capital was at once converted into fixed capital; while for their annual supplies of food, implements and luxuries the planters continued to rely upon their credit with the local merchants, and the local merchants to rely upon their credit with northern merchants and bankers.

Thus there was a never-ending private loss through the continual payment of interest and the enhancement of prices; and, further, there was a continuous public loss by the draining of wealth out of the cotton belt by the slave trade. With the stopping of the African slave trade, the drain of wealth from the lower South was not checked at all, but merely diverted from England and New England to the upper tier of the Southern states; and there it did little but demoralize industry and postpone to a later generation the agricultural revival.

The capitalization of labor lessened its elasticity and its versatility; it tended to fix labor rigidly in one line of employment. There was little or no floating labor in the plantation districts, and the planter was obliged to plan in detail a whole year's work before the year began. If he should plant a larger acreage than his "force" could cultivate and harvest, a part of the crop would have to be abandoned, unless by chance some free negro or stray Irishman could be found for the odd job. As an illustration of the financial hardships which might befall the slaveholder, it may be noted that in 1839 William Lowndes Yancey happened to lose his whole force of slaves through poisoning in the midst of the working season. The disaster involved his absolute ruin as a planter, and forced him to seek some other opening which did not require the possession of capital.

In the operation of cotton production, where fluctuating and highly uncertain returns demanded the greatest flexibility, the slaveholding system was rigid. When by overproduction the price of cotton was depressed, it could be raised again only by curtailing the output in the American cotton belt, which had the monopoly. But the planter, owning cotton lands and slaves trained in the cotton field alone, found it hard to devote his fields with success to other crops or to sell or lease his negroes to anyone else, for no one else wanted them for any other purpose than cotton production. In fact, the proportion of the Southern resources devoted to cotton production tended always to increase. To diminish the cotton output required the most heroic efforts. As a rule, the chances of heavy gains from cotton planting outweighed those of loss, in the popular estimation; and the strong and constant tendency was to spoil the market by over-supply.

There were uncertain returns in cotton-raising, and great risks in slave-owning. The crop might be heavy or light in any year, according to the acreage and the weather, and prices might be away up or away down.

A prime slave might be killed by a rattlesnake or crippled in a log-rolling or hanged for murder or spirited away by the underground railroad. All these uncertainties fostered extravagance and speculation.

In the cotton belt, inflation and depression followed each other in rapid succession; but the times of prosperity brought less real advantage and periods of depression caused greater hardship in the slaveholding South than in any normally organized community. For by the capitalizing of labor, profits were generally absorbed through the purchasing of additional slaves at higher prices, while in time of need the cotton-planter found it impossible to realize upon his investment because his neighbors were involved in the same difficulties which embarrassed him and when he would sell they could not buy.

When after the peace in 1815 the system of industry and finance of the ante-bellum South had fully developed itself, the South and its leaders were seized in the grip of social and economic forces which were rendered irresistible by the imperious laws of monopoly. The cotton-planters controlled the South, and for some decades they dominated the policy of the federal government; but the cotton-planters themselves were hurried hither and thither by their two inanimate but arbitrary masters, cotton and slavery.

Cotton and slavery were peculiar to the South, and their requirements were often in conflict with the interests and ideas prevailing in the other parts of the United States. As that conflict of interests and sentiments was accentuated, it became apparent that the South was in a congressional minority, likely to be overridden at any time by a northern majority. Ruin was threatening the vested interests and the social order in the South, and the force of circumstances drove the southern politicians into the policy of resistance. To the leaders in the South, with their ever-present view of the possibility of negro uprisings, the regulations of slavery seemed essential for safety and prosperity. And when they found themselves about to become powerless to check any legislation hostile to the established order in the South, they adopted the policy of secession-seeking, as they saw it, the lesser of the evils confronting them.

Because they were blinded by the abolition agitation in the North and other historical developments which we cannot here discuss, most of the later generation of ante-bellum planters could not see that slaveholding was essentially burdensome. But that which was partly hidden from their vision is clear to us to-day. In the great system of southern industry and commerce, working with seeming smoothness, the negro laborers were inefficient in spite of discipline, and slavery was an obstacle to all progress. The system may be likened to an engine, with slavery as its great fly-wheel—a fly-wheel indispensable for safe running at first, perhaps, but later rendered less useful by improvements in the machinery, and finally becoming a burden instead of a benefit. Yet it was retained, because it was still considered essential in securing the adjustment and regular working of the complex mechanism. This great rigid wheel of slavery was so awkward and burdensome that it absorbed the momentum and retarded the movement of the whole machine without rendering any service of great value. The capitalization of labor and the export of earnings in exchange for more workmen, always of a low degree of efficiency, together with the extreme lack of versatility, deprived the South of the natural advantage which the cotton monopoly should have given. To be rid of the capitalization of labor as a part of the slaveholding system was a great requisite for the material progress of the South.

The Economics of Slavery in the Ante-Bellum South

ALFRED H. CONRAD AND JOHN R. MEYER

OBJECTIVES AND METHODS

The outstanding economic characteristics of southern agriculture before the Civil War were a high degree of specialization and virtually exclusive reliance on a slave labor force. The large-scale, commercial dependence upon slave labor was to distinguish the ante bellum South not only from other regions in its own time but from all regions at all other times in American agricultural history. Because of this unique historical status, ante bellum southern agriculture has been a subject for special historical attention. Above all else, attention has been focused upon the proposition that, even without external intervention, slavery would have toppled of its own weight. This allegation has its source in the assertions of slave inefficiency to be found in the writings of men who lived with slavery: American or English liberals like G. M. Weston, H. R. Helper, or J. E. Cairnes and southern slaveowners who, in a religious, self-righteous age, could find every motive for the protection of the slave system except that it was personally profitable. The argument is to be found most strongly stated in the work of later southern historians, especially C. W. Ramsdell and U. B. Phillips, who take the position that the Civil War, far from being an irrepressible conflict, was an unnecessary blood bath. They argue that slavery had reached its natural limits and that it was cumbersome and inefficient and, probably within less than a generation, would have destroyed itself. To the question why emancipa-

Reprinted from *The Journal of Political Economy*, LXVI, No. 2 (April, 1958), pp. 95–122, 440–443. By permission of the University of Chicago Press. Copyright 1958 by University of Chicago Press.

tion was not resorted to, they reply that slavery was for the southerners an important (and evidently expensive) duty, part of their "unending task of race discipline." On the other side, Lewis Gray and Kenneth Stampp have strongly contested this view, contending that southern plantation agriculture was at least as remunerative an economic activity as most other business enterprises in the young republic.

The evidence employed in this debate has been provided by the few, usually fragmentary, accounting records that have come down to us from early plantation activities. The opposing parties have arranged and re-arranged the data in accordance with various standard and sometimes imaginary accounting conventions. Indeed, the debate over the value of the different constituent pieces of information reconstructs in embryo much of the historical development of American accounting practices. For example, virtually all the accounting valuation problems have been discussed with relation to the slave question, including the role and meaning of depreciation, the nature and accountability of interest charges, and the validity of distinctions between profits and payments of managerial wages. But, despite the fact that the problem is ostensibly one in economic history, no attempt has ever been made to measure the profitability of slavery according to the economic (as opposed to accounting) concept of profitability. This paper is an attempt to fill this void.

Thus this paper is devoted to establishing methodological as well as historical points. Specifically, we shall attempt to measure the profitability of southern slave operations in terms of modern capital theory. In doing so, we shall illustrate the ways in which economic theory might be used in ordering and organizing historical facts. An additional methodological point is also made evident by this exercise, namely, how the very simple statistical concepts of range and central tendency as applied to frequency distributions of data can be employed in interpreting or moderating inferences from historical facts.

In executing these tasks, we must ask first what it is we are talking about and, second, whether we can say anything that can be proved or disproved. For example, we must ask what the slave economy was. Was it cotton culture? Was it cotton and sugar and tobacco? Was it all of ante bellum southern agriculture? In answering, we shall define slavery in terms of two production functions. One function relates inputs of Negro slaves (and the materials required to maintain the slaves) to the production of the southern staple crops, particularly cotton. The second function describes the production of the intermediate good, slave labor— slave-breeding, to use an emotionally charged term which has colored, even determined, most of the conclusions about this problem.

What do we mean by "efficiency"? Essentially, we shall mean a comparison of the return from the use of this form of capital—Negro slaves —with the returns being earned on other capital assets at the time. Thus we mean to consider whether the slave system was being dragged down of its own weight; whether the allocation of resources was impaired by the rigidity of capitalized labor supply; whether southern capital was misused or indeed drawn away to the North; and, finally, whether slavery must inevitably have declined from an inability of the slave force to reproduce itself.

The hypothesis that slavery was an efficient, maintainable form of economic organization is not a new one, of course. Nor are we, by one hundred years, at least, among the first to conclude that Negro slavery was profitable in the ante bellum South. What we do feel to be novel, however, is our approach. Postulating that American Negro slavery was characterized by two production functions, we argue that an efficient system developed in which those regions best suited to the production of cotton (and the other important staples) specialized in agricultural production, while the less productive land continued to produce slaves, exporting the increase to the staple-crop areas. It is this structure that we are examining.

We propose to test the hypothesis by putting appropriate values on the variables in the production functions and computing the rate of return over cost, the stream of income over the lifetime of the slave. This rate of return, the marginal efficiency of slave capital, must, in turn, be shown to be at least equal to the rate of interest currently available in the American capital markets. It is further necessary to show that appropriate markets existed to make this regional specialization possible and that slavery did not necessarily imply the disappearance or misallocation of capital. Evidence on the ability of the slave force to maintain itself numerically will be had as a corollary result. For these purposes it is necessary to obtain data on slave prices and cotton prices, the average output of male field hands and field wenches, the life-expectancy of Negroes born in slavery, the cost of maintaining slaves during infancy and other nonproductive periods, and, finally, the net reproduction rate and the demographic composition of the slave population in the breeding and using areas.

Looked upon simply as a staple-commodity agriculture, the southern system must appear to have been burdened—possibly even to have been on the verge of collapse—under the weight of areas of inefficient, unprofitable farming. We submit that this view is in error and that the error arises from the failure to recognize that an agricultural system dependent upon slavery can be defined operationally only in terms of the production function for both the final good—in our case, cotton—and the production function for the intermediate good—Negro slaves. Considered operationally, in terms of a neoclassical two-region, two-commodity trade system, it must be seen that a slave system produces labor as an intermediate good. The profitability of the system cannot be decided without considering the system's ability to produce chattel labor efficiently.

There are also non-historical reasons for taking up once again the economics of ante bellum southern slavery. A detailed re-evaluation of the profits of plantation slavery in the American South might help us evaluate the possibilities, first, that the near-slavery existing today in many highly agricultural, underindustrialized lands is an institution that can be expected to disappear automatically or, second, that dislodging it will require substantial governmental pressure or interference. These are, of course, often key policy questions in former colonial countries that are just beginning to develop modern industrial economics.

The possible relevance of the American experience in this connection increases, moreover, as the underlying economic motivations of a slave system are analyzed and established. This happens primarily because, once these motives are recognized, it becomes possible better to understand and predict the political structures that will accompany slavery. In other words, the interrelationships between certain economic and political goals of slavery can be better understood once the underlying economic factors are understood. . . .

REPRODUCTION, ALLOCATION, AND
SLAVE MARKETS

It thus remains to be determined whether an efficient supply mechanism —efficient in both its generative and its allocative functions—existed in the ante bellum South. That the slave force might reproduce itself was not sufficient; there must also have been a capital market capable of getting the labor to the areas where production was expanding if slavery was to be profitable. It will be useful to introduce the secondary propositions by stating several arguments which together form the orthodox opposition to the present hypothesis. The arguments follow, in every case accompanied by a citation as a talisman against any possible charge that we are setting up straw men: (i) slaves are notoriously inefficient and unwilling workers; (ii) slave property, unlike wage labor, must be supported in the years before and after the slave is economically productive; (iii) slaveholding absorbed plantation earnings; (iv) slave economies are constantly threatened by decline because they cannot in general maintain the number of slaves; and (v) capitalization of the labor force inhibits the efficient allocation of labor.

The first and second of these arguments are implicitly tested in the computation of the rate of return on slave capital. We are not concerned with efficiency per se, however that might be measured, or with the efficiency of slaves as opposed to free white laborers. The more sophisticated version of this efficiency argument—that slave ineptness forced the planters to use a particularly wasteful form of agriculture—is probably untestable because of the difficulties of identification where impetus or motives are being considered. It might be suggested as a partial answer, however, that extensive farming was not peculiarly a characteristic of slave agriculture or even of plantation cotton culture. It was common to all North American colonial agriculture and, as late as the end of the nineteenth century, was reputed to be characteristic of farming in the Northwest wheat lands. It is, generally, a salient feature of agriculture where labor is scarce relative to land. But, insofar as slaves were inefficient, the inefficiency must be reflected in the returns computed in our model. Similarly, the costs of maintaining slaves in infancy and dotage are accounted for in our cost of production.

The third argument—that the South lost from the payment of interest and the constant enhancement of prices (and, therefore, overcapitalization of the labor force)—rests in part upon two misapprehensions, attributable to U. B. Phillips: (1) that capitalization involves a net loss through the payment of interest and (2) that slaves were, somehow, a fictitious form of wealth. We have already shown that slave capital earned returns at least equal to those earned by other contemporary forms of capital. For the overcapitalization part of the argument, it remains to be shown that slave prices did not run away from cotton values.

The last two of the assertions state the negative of our principal secondary hypothesis, which is that an efficient market system existed for the supply of slaves to the rapidly growing cotton industry of the Southwest from the exhausted land of the Old South. It will be shown below that the slave population, in all but the Louisiana sugar area, more than reproduced itself. It will be further shown that the border states were not being depleted to provide for western needs but that only the natural increase was being exported. Finally, avoiding the emotion-wracked testimony of the time, we will attempt to demonstrate the existence of regional specialization and an efficient market by comparing the demographic composition of the cotton and border states and by examining the price behavior in the market for Negro slaves.

A. THE REPRODUCTION OF THE SLAVE
LABOR FORCE

The history of slavery is full of examples of slave economies which could not reproduce their population and collapsed because of a failure of supply. Frequently, as in the Roman case, the supply was dependent upon a steady flow of military prisoners. The Augustan peace and the stabilization of the borders of the empire are credited with the decline of Roman slavery for this reason. Similarly, the labor supply in the Caribbean sugar islands could be maintained only by importation. It is generally argued that slavery disappeared from Jamaica because of the inability of the slave population to reproduce itself once the slave trade had been closed and not because of abolition in 1834.

By contrast, the ante bellum cotton-slave economy of the southern states managed to maintain and allocate its labor supply by a system of regional specialization which produced slaves on the worn-out land of the Old South and the border states for export to the high-yield cotton land of the Mississippi and Red River valleys. For the whole nation the Negro rate of increase in the six decades before the Civil War was only slightly below the rate for the white population; for most of the period, the slave rate was very much above that for free Negroes. In the South the disparity between Negro and white rates of increase is in favor of the

TABLE 12
PERCENTAGE DECENNIAL INCREASE IN WHITE AND NEGRO POPULATION, 1790–1860

INCREASE DURING PRECEDING TEN YEARS

Census Year	Total	White	Negro		
			Total	Slave	Free
1800....	35.1	35.8	32.3	28.1	82.2
1810....	36.4	36.1	37.5	33.1	71.9
1820....	33.1	34.2	28.6	29.1	25.3
1830....	33.5	33.9	31.4	30.6	36.8
1840....	32.7	34.7	23.4	23.8	20.9
1850....	35.9	37.7	26.6	28.8	12.5
1860....	35.6	37.7	22.1	23.4	12.3

Source: Bureau of the Census, *Negro Population in the United States, 1790–1915* (Washington, D.C., 1918), Tables 2 (chap. ii) and 1 (chap. v) and pp. 25 and 53. The sharp declines in the rate of increase for slaves in the decades ending in 1840 and 1860 probably reflect the generation cycle following the increase in importations, mostly of mature Negroes, in the years just prior to 1808.

Negro rate; considering the relative rates of immigration of whites and Negroes after the first decade of the nineteenth century, the discrepancy in natural increase is even more striking. The evidence in Table 12 does not admit of any doubt that the slave population was capable of producing a steady supply of labor for the plantation economy.

B. SLAVE MARKETS AND ALLOCATION

The more important issue, however, is whether or not the slave force could be allocated efficiently. The natural rate of increase was more than sufficient in the Old South to meet the needs of agriculture in the region, but in the West it was less than sufficient to meet the demands for increased cotton production. By direct export and by the migration of planters with their work forces, the eastern areas supplied the needs of the Southwest. In every decade before the Civil War, the increase of slaves in the cotton states was much above and in the Atlantic and border states much below the rate of increase for the whole slave population. Indeed, in the decades ending in 1840 and 1860, the net rate of population increase in the Old South was only slightly above the level sufficient to maintain the population at a constant level, 4.5 per cent and 7.1 per cent (see Table 13). From 1790 to 1850 the increase of slaves in the Atlantic states was just 2 per cent per annum, while in the Gulf states (including Florida), Arkansas, and Tennessee the rate was 18 per cent per annum. A rough but probably conservative estimate of the export from the selling states between 1820 and 1860 is given by W. H. Collins. Taking the difference between the average natural increase and the actual rate in the selling states, Collins arrived at the following estimates:

1820–30	124,000
1830–40	265,000
1840–50	146,000
1850–60	207,000

Collins estimated that at least three-fifths of the removals from the border states were due to emigration to the Southwest rather than to export. While this has little bearing upon the issue of allocative efficiency, it does have significance for the corollary assertion that the slaveowners of the border states, consciously or unconsciously, were engaged in a specialized breeding operation, producing chattel labor for the growing Southwest. In 1836 the *Virginia Times* estimated that, "of the number of slaves exported [from Virginia], not more than one-third have been sold, the others being carried by their masters, who have removed." Ruffin supposed that the annual sales in 1859 "already exceed in number all the increase in slaves in Virginia by procreation." Bancroft goes beyond these estimates and states that "in the 'fifties, when the extreme prejudice against the interstate traders had abated and their inadequate supplies were eagerly purchased, fully 70 per cent of the slaves removed from the Atlantic and the border slave states to the Southwest were taken after purchase or with a view to sale, that is, were the objects of slave-trading." Whatever the accuracy of these several estimates, which range from two-fifths to four-fifths of total exports of slaves from the border and the Atlantic states, it is clear that sales of slaves provided an important capital gain for the exporting states. There is ample documentary evidence that planters in the Old South were aware of this, that some welcomed it and depended upon it, and that others were fearful of its effect upon the agriculture of the area and upon the tenability of slavery. Some spoke frankly about Virginia as a "breeding state," though the reply to such allegations was generally an indignant denial. Whether systematically bred or

TABLE 13

PERCENTAGE RATE OF POPULATION INCREASE, BY RACE, IN THE COTTON AND BORDER STATES, 1790–1860

Decade Ending	Cotton States* White	Cotton States* Negro	Border States† White	Border States† Negro
1800....	42.9	47.4	27.9	24.4
1810....	37.5	61.3	23.5	23.4
1820....	38.8	48.0	19.5	15.5
1830....	40.0	46.8	19.0	14.0
1840....	31.3	37.6	21.1	4.5
1850....	34.1	35.6	34.5	11.0
1860....	27.6	29.0	39.2	7.1

Source: Ernst von Halle, *Baumwollproduktion und Pflanzungswirtschaft in den Nordamerikanischen Sudstaaten* (Leipzig, 1897), p. 132. His sources were Tucker, *Progress of the United States* (to 1840), *Census of Population* (1850 and after), and H. Gannett, *Statistics of the Negroes in the United States.*

* North Carolina, South Carolina, Georgia, Florida, Alabama, Mississippi, Louisiana, Texas, Arkansas, and Tennessee.

† Delaware, Maryland, District of Columbia, Virginia, West Virginia, Kentucky, and Missouri.

not, the natural increase of the slave force was an important, probably the most important, product of the more exhausted soil of the Old South.

The existence of such specialization is evident in the demographic composition of the cotton and breeding areas and in the price behavior in the markets for slaves. Table 14 demonstrates that the selling states

TABLE 14

SLAVE POPULATION BY AGE
(Per Cent)

Age (Years)	1860 Total	1860 Selling States*	1860 Buying States†	1850 Total	1850 Selling States*	1850 Buying States†
Under 15	44.8	45.6	43.8	44.9	45.6	44.3
15–19	11.4	11.5	11.4	11.1	11.3	11.0
20–29	17.6	16.5	18.9	18.0	17.0	18.9
30–39	11.7	10.7	11.8	11.3	10.5	12.1
20–49	36.4	34.4	38.1	36.4	34.6	38.1
50 and over	7.5	8.5	6.7	7.5	8.5	6.6

Source: J. C. G. Kennedy, *Population of the United States in 1860* (Washington, D.C., 1864), "Classified Population," Tables No. 1, by state; J. D. B. DeBow, *Statistical View of the United States, . . . Being a Compendium of the Seventh Census* (Washington, D.C., 1854), Part II, Table LXXXII, pp. 89–90.

* Virginia, Maryland, Delaware, South Carolina, Missouri, Kentucky, District of Columbia.

† Georgia, Alabama, Mississippi, Florida, Texas, Louisiana.

contained, in 1850 and 1860, a greater proportion of children under fifteen years and a substantially greater proportion of slaves above the age of fifty than did the buying states. While the disproportions are not great enough to characterize the selling states as a great nursery, the age composition is in the direction which our hypothesis would lead one to expect. The relationship between the prices of men and women in the slave market, when compared with the ratio of hiring rates for male and female field hands, gives an even stronger indication that the superior usefulness of females of breeding age was economically recognized. The relative hiring rates for men and women in 1860, shown in Table 15, can be taken as a measure of their relative values in the field.

TABLE 15

ANNUAL HIRING RATES FOR MALE AND FEMALE SLAVES (INCLUDING RATIONS AND CLOTHING), BY STATES, 1860

State	Men	Women	Ratio (Men : Women)
Virginia	$105	$ 46	2.28
North Carolina	110	49	2.25
South Carolina	103	55	1.87
Georgia	124	75	1.65
Florida	139	80	1.74
Alabama	138	89	1.55
Mississippi	166	100	1.66
Louisiana	171	120	1.43
Texas	166	109	1.52
Arkansas	170	108	1.57
Tennessee	121	63	1.92

To compare to these rates, we have purchase prices of male and female slaves, in the same markets, in 1859 and 1860. The purchase prices should reflect the relative usefulness of the sexes for field work. More than this, however, if there is any additional value to slave women—for breeding purposes, presumably—there should be a premium in the form of a narrower price differential than is found in the hiring rates. The prices shown in Table 16 are taken from Table A in the Appendix. Whenever possible, 1860 is used; wherever necessary, 1859. Table 16 includes age designations and, when available, a description of the grade or class represented in the average price. This evidence is a striking confirmation of the validity of the model. In every case but one, the purchase-price differential is narrower than the hiring-rate differential. The price structure clearly reflects the added value of females due to their ability to generate capital gains. It is especially interesting in this regard to note that the price ratios in Virginia and South Carolina, the two breeding states represented in the list, show practically no differential. This evidence

TABLE 16

SELECTED PRICES OF MALE AND FEMALE SLAVES, 1859 AND 1860

State (Year)	Age	Condition	Male Price	Female Price	Ratio
Virginia (1859)	17–20	Best	$1,350–$1,425	$1,275–$1,325	1.07
South Carolina	....	Prime	$1,325	..........⎫	1.03
	....	Wench	......	$1,283 ⎭	
South Carolina (1859)	....	Field hand	$1,555	...... ⎱	.91
	....	Girl	......	$1,705 ⎰	
Georgia	21	Best field hand	$1,900	...... ⎱	.88
	17	(9 mo. inf.)	......	[$2,150] ⎰	
Georgia (1859)	....	Prime, young	$1,300	...... ⎫	1.04
		Cotton hand			
	....	houseservant	......	$1,250 ⎭	
Alabama (1859)	19	....	$1,635	...... ⎱	1.37
	18, 18, 8	....	......	$1,193 ⎰	
Mississippi	....	No. 1 field hand	$1,625	$1,450	1.12
Texas	21, 15	....	$2,015	$1,635	1.23
Texas (1859)	17, 14	....	$1,527	$1,403	1.09

clearly shows that the Old South recognized in the market the value of its function as the slave-breeding area for the cotton-raising West.

C. THE "OVERCAPITALIZATION" OF
THE LABOR FORCE

The aspect of slave economics that causes the most confusion and out-right error is that which relates to the capitalization, and, in the ante bellum southern case, the presumed overcapitalization, of slave labor. Phillips speaks of an "irresistible tendency to overvalue and overcapitalize" and argues that slaveholding had an unlimited capacity for absorbing the planters' earnings through the continual payment of interest and the en-hancement of prices. For the Cotton Belt this was presumably aggregated into a continuous public drain of wealth, first, to England and New England and, later, to the upper South. Moreover, a series of writers from Max Weber down to the most recent theorists of economic growth have argued that capitalization tends to rigidify the pattern of employment. "Free labor is necessary to make free transfers of labor possible. A pro-duction organization cannot be very flexible if it has to engage in the purchase or sale of slaves every time it changes its output." But this is really a question of how good the market is; no one, after all, claims that manufacturing is made suicidally inflexible by the fact that expanding sectors must buy the capitalized future earnings of machinery. There are three issues to be distinguished in this argument: first, the alleged tend-ency toward overcapitalization; second, the inflexibility of chattel labor and the difficulty of allocating it, geographically and industrially; and, third, the loss of wealth.

First, was the southerner his own victim in an endless speculative inflation of slave prices? The assertion of an irresistible tendency to overvalue and overcapitalize must mean that he was so trapped, if it means anything. Phillips answered the question by comparing the price of cotton with the price of prime field hands, year by year. He found, or believed he found, a permanent movement toward overcapitalization inherent in American slaveholding. But speculative overexpansion is capable of reversal: from the inflation of 1837 to the bottom of the depression in 1845, slave prices fell as sharply as cotton prices. If the rise from that lower turning point is a demonstration of speculative mania, it was a mania solidly based on the increase in the value of the crop per hand, owing to the concentration of production in more fertile areas, the greater efficiency of the American-born slaves, lowered transportation costs, and the development of new high-yield varieties of cotton from the fourth decade of the century on. Finally, the choice of the initial period in Phillips' analysis exaggerates the decline in cotton prices relative to the price of slaves: at the turn of the century the demand for cotton was increasing rapidly, supporting remarkably high prices, while the unrestricted African slave trade kept domestic slave prices well below the level that might be expected in view of the level of profits. Table 17 clearly demonstrates the relationship among slave prices, cotton prices, and the value of cotton output per slave (of field work age, ten to fifty-four). Several things become clear in this comparison. To begin, the relationship between slave and cotton prices is significant for Phillips' purposes only if there is no increase in productivity. While he is struck by the fact that slave prices rise more rapidly than cotton prices in the long upswing starting in the early 1840's, it is equally striking to observe that (New Orleans) slave prices rose about one and one-half times between the low point in 1843–45 to 1860, while values of cotton production per hand rose more than three times from the low in 1842. This was recognized in the *New Orleans Daily Crescent* in 1860, as follows:

> Nor do we agree with our contemporaries who argue that a speculative demand is the unsubstantial basis of the advance in the price of slaves. . . . It is our impression that the great demand for slaves in the Southwest will keep up the prices as it caused their advance in the first place, and that the rates are not a cent above the real value of the laborer who is to be engaged in tilling the fertile lands of a section of the country which yields the planter nearly double the crop that the fields of the Atlantic States do.

Furthermore, it would appear that slave prices fluctuate less than do cotton prices. This and the less clear-cut lag of the slave prices make it difficult to accept the image of unwary planters helplessly exposing themselves in a market dominated by speculators. It would make more sense to argue simply that the rising trend of slave prices coupled with a growing slave population is in and of itself strong evidence of the profitability of slavery.

D. THE EFFICIENCY OF ALLOCATION

The second point relates to geographic allocation and, to a lesser extent, to the mobility of the slave labor force among crops. The slave prices in all regions move very closely with cotton prices and products per hand. It is clear, too, that the eastern prices move directly with the cotton-area slave prices, although in the last two decades the rate of increase of prices fell behind in the breeding area. If the market were extremely imperfect and the transfer between the breeding and consuming states inefficient, in contradiction to our hypothesis, then there should be much less evidence of regional arbitrage than is found here. In response to the western demand, Virginia and the other eastern states shipped their natural increase to the cotton areas. Indeed, it is frequently argued that the transfer was too efficient and that the Old South was being continuously depressed by the high price of labor occasioned by western demand. Edmund Ruffin, particularly, took this position and argued that slave trade could not bring profits to Virginia but could result only in the paralysis of her industry. If true, this argument would be supported empirically by increasing real estate values on the western lands and decreasing values in the Atlantic and border states. That is, the chain of high cotton profits–high slave prices–increased cost of farming in the Old South should have depressed land prices in that area. Emigration, by reducing demand, should have meant more downward pressure. The only influence which operated in the direction of maintaining the value of land in the older states was the profit to be had from the increase and sale of slaves. Indeed, in 1850 and 1860, the value per acre of farm land and buildings in the border states was $7.18 and $12.33, and, in the Lower South for the same two census years, $4.99 and $8.54. Undoubtedly, the western cotton land earned a considerable rent in farming over the older land. It was this rent which maintained the flow of migration to the Cotton Belt. But that migration depended upon and supported the prosperity of the breeding states. It is not clear that slavery was able to continue only by skinning the topsoil and moving on, leaving exhausted land and low slave and land value in its wake. Quite the contrary, the evidence can plausibly be interpreted as indicating a unified, specialized economy in which the settlers on the naturally superior western lands (superior even before the deterioration of the older regions by single-crop cultivation of tobacco and cotton) were able to bid slave labor

T<small>ABLE</small> 17

VALUE OF COTTON PRODUCTION AND
SLAVE POPULATION, 1802–60, NEW ORLEANS PRICES

Year	Crop (Thousands of Pounds)	Average Price (Cents per Pound)	Value (Thousands)	No. of Slaves Aged 10–54 Years*	Crop Value per Slave	Price of Prime Field Hand	Crop Value per Hand per Dollar Slave Price
1802....	55,000	0.147	$ 8,085	550,708	$ 14.68	$ 600	.02
1803....	60,000	.150	9,000	568,932	15.82	600	.03
1804....	65,000	.196	12,740	587,157	21.70	600	.04
1805....	70,000	.233	16,310	605,381	26.94	600	.05
1806....	80,000	.218	17,440	623,606	27.97	600	.05
1807....	80,000	.164	13,120	641,831	20.44	600	.03
1808....	75,000	.136	10,200	660,055	15.45	640	.02
1809....	82,000	.136	11,152	678,280	16.44	780	.02
1810....	85,000	.147	12,495	696,505	17.94	900	.02
1811....	80,000	.089	7,120	717,376	9.93	860	.01
1813....	75,000	.155	11,625	759,118	15.31	600	.03
1814....	70,000	.169	11,830	779,989	15.17	650	.02
1815....	100,000	.273	27,300	800,860	34.09	765	.05
1816....	124,000	.254	31,496	821,731	38.33	880	.04
1817....	130,000	.298	38,740	842,602	45.98	1,000	.05
1818....	125,000	.215	26,875	863,473	31.12	1,050	.03
1819....	167,000	.143	23,881	884,344	27.00	1,100	.03
1820....	160,000	.152	24,320	905,215	26.88	970	.03
1821....	180,000	.174	31,320	933,517	33.55	810	.04
1822....	210,000	.115	24,150	961,818	25.11	700	.04
1823....	185,000	.145	26,825	990,120	27.04	670	.04
1824....	215,000	.179	38,485	1,018,421	37.99	700	.05
1825....	255,000	.119	30,345	1,046,723	28.99	800	.04
1826....	350,000	.093	32,550	1,075,024	30.28	840	.04
1827....	316,900	.097	30,739	1,103,326	27.86	770	.04
1828....	241,399	.098	23,657	1,131,627	20.91	770	.03
1829....	296,812	.089	26,416	1,159,929	22.77	770	.03
1830....	331,150	.084	27,817	1,208,034	23.03	810	.03
1831....	354,247	.090	31,882	1,247,489	25.56	860	.03
1832....	355,492	.100	35,549	1,275,061	27.88	900	.03
1833....	374,653	.112	41,961	1,302,633	32.21	960	.03
1834....	437,558	.155	67,821	1,330,206	50.99	1,000	.05
1835....	460,338	.152	69,971	1,357,778	51.53	1,150	.05
1836....	507,550	.133	67,504	1,385,350	46.79	1,250	.04
1837....	539,669	.090	48,510	1,412,923	34.38	1,300	.03
1838....	682,767	.124	84,663	1,440,495	58.77	1,220	.05
1839....	501,708	.079	39,635	1,468,067	27.00	1,240	.02
1840....	834,111	.091	75,904	1,507,779	50.34	1,020	.05
1841....	644,172	.078	50,245	1,568,022	32.04	870	.04
1842....	668,379	.057	38,098	1,611,269	23.65	750	.03
1843....	972,960	.075	72,972	1,654,516	44.11	700	.06
1844....	836,529	.055	46,009	1,697,762	27.10	700	.04
1845....	993,719	.068	67,573	1,741,009	38.81	700	.06
1846....	863,321	.099	85,469	1,784,256	47.90	750	.06

1847....	766,599	.070	53,662	1,827,503	29.36	850	.04
1848....	1,017,391	.058	59,009	1,870,750	31.54	950	.03
1849....	1,249,985	.108	134,998	1,913,996	70.53	1,030	.07
1850....	1,001,165	.117	117,136	1,979,059	59.19	1,100	.05
1851....	1,021,048	.074	75,558	2,034,482	37.14	1,150	.03
1852....	1,338,061	.091	121,764	2,080,554	58.53	1,200	.05
1853....	1,496,302	.088	131,675	2,126,626	61.92	1,250	.05
1854....	1,322,241	.084	111,068	2,172,698	51.12	1,310	.04
1855....	1,294,463	.091	117,796	2,218,770	53.09	1,350	.04
1856....	1,535,334	.124	190,381	2,264,843	84.06	1,420	.06
1857....	1,373,619	.112	153,845	2,310,915	66.57	1,490	.05
1858....	1,439,744	.115	165,571	2,356,988	70.25	1,580	.04
1859....	1,796,455	.108	194,017	2,403,060	80.74	1,690	.05
1860....	2,241,056	0.111	$248,757	2,460,648	$101.09	$1,800	.06

Source: *Crops:* Computed from the data on number of bales and average weight of bales in James L. Watkins, *Production and Price of Cotton* for One Hundred Years (U.S. Department of Agriculture, Miscellaneous Series, Bull. 9 (Washington, D.C., 1895). *Price:* Gray, op. cit., Table 41 "Weighted Yearly Averages and Monthly Prices in Cents per Pound of Short-Staple Cotton at New Orleans for the Crop Years 1802–1860." *Slaves:* Bureau of Census, Negro Population in the United States, 1790–1915, "Slave and Free Colored Population at Each Census by Sections and Southern Divisions: 1790–1860," p. 55, and "Negro Population in Years Specified Classified by Sex and Age Periods; 1830–1910," p. 166. *Slave Prices:* Estimated visually from the chart "Approximate Prices of Prime Field Hands in Hundreds of Dollars per Head: . . . at New Orleans. . . ," in V. B. Phillips, *Life and Labor in the Old South* (Boston, 1935), p. 177.

To estimate the slave population in the intercensal years, the increase over each decade was divided into equal parts and assigned to each year in the decade. The proportion of Negroes in the field-work age brackets (between the ages of ten and fifty-four) was .641 in 1863, .635 in 1850, .621 in 1840 and .610 in 1830. The census-year proportions at the beginning and end of each decade were averaged for use in intervening years. For the years before 1830, an estimate of .60 was used. There is no implication that we have measured the number of field hands, but it should be noted that the range .60–.65 brackets several contemporary estimates of the slave population employed in cotton agriculture (see, e.g., P. A. Morse, Southern Slavery and the Cotton Trade," *De Bow's Review*, XXIII [1857], 475–82.)

away from general farming and to make wholesale removal unnecessary, if indeed there had ever been such a necessity.

E. SLAVERY AND SOUTHERN ECONOMIC GROWTH

Finally, there are two economic arguments about slavery and potential southern growth to be considered. The assertion that slavery per se was inimical to economic growth rests in part upon the alleged inefficiency of slave labor in industrial pursuits and in part upon the loss of capital that might otherwise have gone into industrialization and diversification.

The inefficiency argument is not supported very securely. There were slaves employed in cotton factories throughout the South. Slaves were used in the coal mines and in the North Carolina lumbering operations. In the ironworks at Richmond and on the Cumberland River, slaves comprised a majority of the labor force. Southern railroads were largely built by southern slaves. Crop diversification, or the failure to achieve diversification, appears to have been a problem of entrepreneurship rather than of the difficulties of training slaves. In the face of the demand for cotton and the profits to be had from specializing in this single crop, it is hardly difficult to explain the single-minded concentration of the planter.

In what ways was slavery allegedly responsible for the drain of capital from the South? The lack of diversification, to the extent of a failure even to provide basic supplies, made necessary the import of much food and virtually all manufactured articles from the North. But half of this assertion, the argument that laid the responsibility for the single-crop culture upon slavery, has been found questionable already.

The major avenues by which wealth is said to have been drained from the cotton states were the excessive use of credit (through dependence upon factors' services) and the "absorption" of capital in slaves. The dependence upon advances was, in effect, a dependence upon the New York or London money market and was, therefore, an impediment to the accumulation of capital in the South. Good crop years bring the temptation to expand production; bad years do not bring any release from the factors. But resort to factoring is characteristic of speculative, commercial agriculture, whether or not the labor force is organized in slavery. It is also frequently argued that slavery gave southern planters a taste for extravagant, wasteful display, causing the notorious lack of thrift and the relative lack of economic development, compared to that experienced in the North and West. This is a doubtful inference, at best. Slavery did not make the Cavalier any more than slavery invented speculation in cotton. However, insofar as successful slave management required military posture and discipline, the southerner's expensive image of himself as a *grand seigneur* was encouraged. It is beyond the scope of this paper to offer hypotheses about the reasons for the relative degrees of entrepreneurship in Charleston and Boston; in this context it is sufficient to state that slavery per se does not seem to have been responsible for the excessive reliance upon factoring and external sources of credit.

There remains only the absorption of capital in slaves to set the responsibility for lack of growth in the South upon the peculiar institution. Earnings that might have gone out of the South to bring in investment goods were fixed in the form of chattel labor. For the early years, during the external slave trade, there is some plausibility to this argument, though it is difficult to see how the capitalization of an income stream, excellent by contemporary standards, can be said to count as a loss of wealth. In the later years there was, except to the extent that northern or English bankers drew off the interest, a redistribution of wealth only within the slave states: from the cotton lands back to the less profitable field agriculture of the older section. And, to the extent that the old planting aristocracy used the profits to maintain the real or fancied magnificence of the preceding century, capital was absorbed. Slavery made this possible, so long as the natural increase could be shipped off. But, as Russel pointed out, slavery also made the profits in the cotton fields and the resultant demand for eastern hands. We are left with the conclusion that, except insofar as it made speculation in cotton possible on a grander scale than would otherwise have been the case and thereby weakened whatever pressure there might have been for diversification, capitalization of the labor force did not of itself operate against southern development.

IV. CONCLUSION

In sum, it seems doubtful that the South was forced by bad statesmanship into an unnecessary war to protect a system which must soon have disappeared because it was economically unsound. This is a romantic hypothesis which will not stand against the facts.

On the basis of the computation of the returns to capital in our model of the ante bellum southern economy and the demonstration of the efficiency of the regional specialization, the following conclusions are offered:

1. Slavery was profitable to the whole South, the continuing demand for labor in the Cotton Belt insuring returns to the breeding operation on the less productive land in the seaboard and border states. The breeding returns were necessary, however, to make the plantation operations on the poorer lands as profitable as alternative contemporary economic activities in the United States. The failure of southern agriculture on these poorer lands in the post bellum period is probably attributable, in the main, to the loss of these capital gains on breeding and not, as is so often suggested, to either the relative inefficiency of the tenant system that replaced the plantations or the soil damage resulting from war operations. These factors were unquestionably contributing elements to the difficulties of post bellum southern agriculture, but they were of relatively small quantitative importance compared with the elimination of slave-breeding returns.

2. There was nothing necessarily self-destructive about the profits of the slave economy. Neither the overcapitalization argument nor the assertion that slavery must have collapsed because the slaves would not reproduce themselves is tenable. Slave prices did not outpace productivity, and the regional slave price structure would imply a workable transfer mechanism rather than the contrary.

3. Continued expansion of slave territory was both possible and, to some extent, necessary. The maintenance of profits in the Old South depended upon the expansion, extensive or intensive, of slave agriculture into the Southwest. This is sufficient to explain the interest of the Old South in secession and does away with the necessity to fall back upon arguments of statesmanship or quixotism to explain the willingness to fight for the peculiar institution.

4. The available productive surplus from slavery might have been used

for economic development or, as in totalitarian regimes in this century, for militarism. In spite of this good omen for development, southern investment and industrialization lagged. It is hard to explain this except on the social ground that entrepreneurship could not take root in the South or on the economic ground that the South did not really own the system but merely operated it. Furthermore, the American experience clearly suggests that slavery is not, from the strict economic standpoint, a deterrent to industrial development and that its elimination may take more than the workings of "inexorable economic forces." Although profitability cannot be offered as a sufficient guaranty of the continuity of southern slavery, the converse argument that slavery must have destroyed itself can no longer rest upon allegations of unprofitability or upon assumptions about the impossibility of maintaining and allocating a slave labor force. To the extent, moreover, that profitability is a necessary condition for the continuation of a private business institution in a free-enterprise society, slavery was not untenable in the ante bellum American South. Indeed, economic forces often may work toward the continuation of a slave system, so that the elimination of slavery may depend upon the adoption of harsh political measures. Certainly that was the American experience.

FOR FURTHER READING: For negative estimates see Thomas P. Govan, "Was Plantation Slavery Profitable?" *Journal of Southern History*, VIII (November, 1942), pp. 513–535, Robert W. Smith, "Was Slavery Unprofitable in the Ante-Bellum South?" *Agricultural History*, XX (January, 1946), pp. 62–64, Robert R. Russel, "The General Effects of Slavery Upon Southern Economic Progress," *Journal of Southern History*, IV (February, 1938). Per contra, consult Kenneth Stampp, *The Peculiar Institution* (New York, 1956), and Albert V. House, *Planter Management and Capitalism in Ante-Bellum Georgia—The Journal of Hugh Fraser Grant, Ricegrower* (New York, 1954).

15. *Economic Antecedents of the Civil War*

PROBLEM: *Did Northern business interests seek war?*

Amid various explanations offered by historians to explain the outbreak of war in 1861 the economic interpretation has loomed large. But the exact nature of the economic forces which brought on the conflict has long been a controversial issue. The theory that economic factors were most important in provoking sectional strife was presented in its most challenging form by Charles and Mary A. Beard who viewed the war as a Second American Revolution in which an oligarchy of northern capitalists secured control of the national government in order to promote its own selfish interests. The Beards elaborated this startling thesis by pointing to the aims of the Republican Party. In 1860 its national platform contained demands for a homestead law, a transcontinental railroad, and also a protective tariff. As long as Southerners exercised great influence in Congress, the Presidency and the Democratic Party, the Beards argued, Northern businessmen could secure none of these desirable objectives. New England textile manufacturers and Pennsylvania iron makers especially desired protection against foreign competition. In their agitation for a high tariff, therefore, Northern businessmen reflected a desire mainly to achieve their economic ends. This interpretation influenced a large number of scholars but was strikingly challenged by Richard Hofstadter of Columbia, soon to become one of America's leading historians. In subjecting the Beard thesis to closer scrutiny, with special reference to the tariff, he found that there was little unity among Northern business groups such as the Pennsylvania iron manufacturers. Some of them favored a lower tariff. Also woolen manufacturers disputed with wool growers over

273

a high tariff. Many merchants in New England as well as in New York were opposed to it lest it diminish trade with the South. Both of these authors raise significant questions concerning the role of economic factors in the outbreak of the war. How were the economic issues of sectional controversy related to politics? Which economic policies created unity within the North and South? Which created dissent? What advantages did the protective tariff bring to Northern business groups?

The Tariff as a Cause of Sectional Strife and the Civil War

CHARLES AND MARY BEARD

. . . In this clash of sectional interests, the outstanding issue of the middle period was the tariff. From it sprang nullification in South Carolina and South Carolina finally led the way into secession. In general it was the representatives of the manufacturing group who fostered the demand for protection and showed the greatest facility in gathering recruits for that cause in national elections. On the whole, opposition to protection and support for free trade, or at all events low rates of duty, came from the agricultural and importing interests.

Yet the matter, as already indicated, was by no means simple. Every revenue law imposing taxes on goods coming into the United States was a complex of many items arranged under several separate schedules—a complex which in practice reflected the demands of many groups and factions, sometimes even conciliating opposing interests by compensatory favors of real or dubious utility. In these circumstances, American political society presented revolving kaleidoscopic patterns whenever the revenue question was up for controversy. Woolen manufacturers and sheep raisers might be united by a tariff that protected both cloth and raw wool but sent flying asunder by hardware schedules. Hemp and flax growers burned brown under blazing suns might be made to feel a common cause with steel and iron magnates bleached white in shaded offices. Nevertheless two powerful agricultural groups, cotton and tobacco growers, supplemented by corn raisers, provided a fairly con-

Reprinted with permission of The Macmillan Company from *The Rise of American Civilization*, I, pp. 678–682, II, pp. 34–38, by Charles and Mary Beard. Copyright 1927, 1930, 1933 by The Macmillan Company, Renewed 1955, 1958 by Mary Beard.

sistent leadership for a relentless war against the general principle of protection for manufactures.

Five times between 1830 and 1860 the tariff was revised, showing on the whole a downward tendency. A sliding-scale cut was made in 1833, as we have seen, under a threat of revolution on the part of South Carolina's planters, and when, nearly ten years later, the Whigs with aid from the opposition forced the duties upward again, the champions of low tariffs swept the polls in the election of 1844. Then the tide definitely turned, the Democratic party under southern leadership driving the country steadily in the direction of free trade until the grand climax of 1860. By the tariff act of 1846, Congress struck a smashing blow at the protective system, the members of the South and West being in the vanguard of the majority that did the terrible execution; of the ninety-three votes against the measure in the House, New England and the Middle States furnished sixty-three.

As this law soon brought a surplus into the Treasury, triumphant Democracy delivered another savage thrust in 1857 making the rates still lower—in actual operation below the figure set in the famous compromise of 1833. Though the vote on this bill in the House seemed to reveal a confused state of public opinion in the large, it betrayed unmistakable tendencies. Members from the South and Southwest cast sixty votes for the measure and but two against it. More salient still was the fact that the West and Northwest furnished thirty-three votes against tariff reduction and only fourteen for it. The South was now almost solid; the West was evidently swinging away from its old moorings and was in a mood for a new political combination—one so adroitly effected at Chicago in 1860.

In the course of the long conflict over the tariff, statesmen from the South worked out a positive theory as to its practical effect on the distribution of wealth. The creed was perfectly formulated in a logical fashion by Senator McDuffie of South Carolina as early as 1830, all elaborations by those who followed in his footsteps being merely fine glosses on his protocol. In the Senator's own words, the argument ran as follows: "Owing to the federative character of our Government, the great geographical extent of our territory, and the diversity of the pursuits of our citizens in different parts of the Union, it has so happened that two great interests have sprung up, standing directly opposed to each other." The first of these interests embraces the manufacturers who cannot thrive in the face of European competition without protection and subsidies from the government; the second is composed of the producers of agricultural staples in the South—staples that can find a market only in foreign countries and can be advantageously sold "only in exchange for the foreign manufactures which come into competition with those of the Northern and Middle States. . . . These interests then stand diametrically and irreconcilably opposed to each other. The interest, the pecuniary interest, of the Northern manufacturer is directly promoted by every increase of the taxes imposed on Southern commerce; and it is unnecessary to add that the interest of the Southern planter is promoted by every diminution of the taxes imposed on the productions of his industry."

Thus the southern statesman reduced this phase of the political struggle of the middle period to its final terms: a conflict over the distribution of wealth. The planter desired a public policy that put money into his pocket, or, to use his customary language, enabled him to keep it there; the manufacturer of the North clamored for a policy that transferred it into his own. In McDuffie's mind it was the old and simple plan of getting and keeping; no political litany could obscure the issue for the initiates. Within two decades, practically all the statesmen of the planting interest were unreservedly committed to the Senator's faith.

No mere academic theory was this concept of the political battle. Statisticians of the South even tried to visualize it in terms of dollars and cents by figuring out the exact amount of "tribute" paid by the planting class to the capitalists of the North. In that calculation they estimated that forty million dollars in round numbers had been poured into the coffers of northern shipowners by 1850 in the form of freight rates. Finding that southern exports amounted to about one hundred millions annually, they came to the conclusion that this enormous sum was in fact lent without interest to northern merchants for use in the manipulation of foreign and domestic exchanges. The toll levied on the South by machine industry, they thought, was especially burdensome. "Were she to work up her 2,500,000 bales of cotton," exclaimed a southern economist, "and receive the profit of $40 each, she would realize 70 to 100 millions annually." To cap the climax, the calculators estimated that the southern people spent fifteen millions in the North traveling for health and pleasure.

If the figures sometimes missed the mark, the thesis was at least plain: through all the economic processes of trade, manufacture, exchange, merchandizing, and luxury, the South was taxed and exploited—in stark reality, brought down to the status of a tribute bearer to northern capitalism. "The South," lamented one orator, "stands in the attitude of feeding upon her own bosom a vast population of merchants, shipowners, capitalists, and others who, without the claims of her progeny, drink up the life blood of her trade. It cannot be here asserted that a deduction should be allowed for that portion of the southern crop which is shipped directly from the southern ports to foreign countries. The tonnage register will show that nine-tenths of the shipping employed belong to northern capitalists. . . . Where then goes the value of our labor but to those who, taking advantage of our folly, ship for us, buy for us, sell to us, and after turning our own capital to their profitable account return laden with our money, to enjoy their easily earned opulence at home?"

From this point of view the task before the planting states was, therefore, emancipation from the dominion of northern capitalism. "We confidently affirm," declared McDuffie, "that the people of the southern and southwestern states are invoked by considerations of the most enlightened patriotism, as well as of an enlightened self-interest, to apply a speedy and effective remedy. The means of achieving our commercial independence are abundant." ...

Extraordinary measures on behalf of slavery were accompanied by others that touched far more vitally economic interests in the North. In 1859, the last of the subsidies for trans-Atlantic steamship companies was ordered discontinued by Congress. In 1857, the tariff was again reduced, betraying an unmistakable drift of the nation toward free trade. In support of this action, the representatives of the South and Southwest were almost unanimous and they gathered into their fold a large number of New England congressmen on condition that no material reductions should be made in duties on cotton goods. On the other hand, the Middle States and the West offered a large majority against tariff reduction so that the division was symptomatic.

Immediately after the new revenue law went into effect an industrial panic burst upon the country, spreading distress among business men and free laborers. While that tempest was running high, the paper money anarchy let loose by the Democrats reached the acme of virulence as the notes of wildcat banks flooded the West and South and financial institutions crashed in every direction, fifty-one failing in Indiana alone within a period of five years. Since all hope of reviving Hamilton's system of finance had been buried, those who believed that a sound currency was essential to national prosperity were driven to the verge of desperation. On top of these economic calamities came Buchanan's veto of the Homestead bill which the impatient agrarians had succeeded in getting through Congress in a compromise form—an act of presidential independence which angered the farmers and mechanics who regarded the national domain as their own inheritance. . . .

During the confusion in the Democratic ranks [1860], the Republicans, in high glee over the quarrels of the opposition, held their convention in Chicago—a sectional gathering except for representatives from five slave states. Among its delegates the spirit of opposition to slavery extension, which had inspired the party assembly four years before, was still evident but enthusiasm on that ticklish subject was neutralized by the prudence of the practical politicians who, sniffing victory in the air, had rushed to the new tent. Whigs, whose affections were centered on Hamilton's program rather than on Garrison's scheme of salvation, were to be seen on the floor. Advocates of a high protective tariff and friends of free homesteads for mechanics and farmers now mingled with the ardent opponents of slavery in the territories. With their minds fixed on the substance of things sought for, the partisans of caution were almost able to prevent the convention from indorsing the Declaration of Independence. Still they were in favor of restricting the area of slavery; they had no love for the institution and its spread helped to fasten the grip of the planting interest on the government at Washington. So the Republican convention went on record in favor of liberty for the territories, free homesteads for farmers, a protective tariff, and a Pacific railway. As the platform was read, the cheering became especially loud and prolonged when the homestead and tariff planks were reached. Such at least is the testimony of the stenographic report.

Since this declaration of principles was well fitted to work a union of forces, it was essential that the candidate should not divide them. The protective plank would doubtless line up the good old Whigs of the East but tender consideration had to be shown to the Ohio Valley, original home of Jacksonian Democracy, where national banks, tariffs, and other "abominations" still frightened the wary. Without Ohio, Indiana, and Illinois, the Republican managers could not hope to win and they knew that the lower counties of these states were filled with settlers from the slave belt who had no love for the "money power," abolition, or anything that savored of them. In such circumstances Seward, idol of the Whig wing, was no man to offer that section; he was too radical on the slavery issue and too closely associated with "high finance" in addition. "If you do not nominate Seward, where will you get your money?" was the blunt question put by Seward's loyal supporters at Chicago. The question was pertinent but not fatal.

Given this confluence of problems, a man close to the soil of the West was better suited to the requirements of the hour than a New York lawyer with somewhat fastidious tastes, obviously backed by fat purses. The available candidate was Abraham Lincoln of Illinois. Born in Kentucky, he was of southern origin. A son of poor frontier parents, self-educated, a pioneer who in his youth had labored in field and forest, he appealed to the voters of the backwoods. Still by an uncanny genius for practical affairs, he had forged his way to the front as a shrewd lawyer and politician. In his debates with Douglas he had shown himself able to cope with one of the foremost leaders in the Democratic party. On the tariff, bank, currency, and homestead issues he was sound. A local railway attorney, he was trusted among business men. . . .

A spirited campaign followed the nomination of the four candidates for the presidency on four different platforms. Huge campaign funds were raised and spent. Besides pursuing the usual strategy of education, the Republicans resorted to parades and the other spectacular features that had distinguished the log-cabin crusade of General Harrison's year. Emulating the discretion of the Hero of Tippecanoe, Lincoln maintained a judicious silence at Springfield while his champions waged his battles for him, naturally tempering their orations to the requirements of diverse interests. They were fully conscious, as a Republican paper in Philadelphia put it, that "Frémont had tried running on the slavery issue and lost." So while they laid stress on it in many sections, they widened their appeal.

In the West, a particular emphasis was placed on free homesteads and the Pacific railway. With a keen eye for competent strategy, Carl Schurz carried the campaign into Missouri where he protested with eloquence against the action of the slave power in denying "the laboring man the right to acquire property in the soil by his labor" and made a special plea for the German vote on the ground that the free land was to be opened to aliens who declared their intention of becoming American citizens. Discovering that the homestead question was "the greatest issue in the West," Horace Greeley used it to win votes in the East. Agrarians and labor reformers renewed the slogan: "Vote yourself a farm."

In Pennsylvania and New Jersey, protection for iron and steel was the great subject of discussion. Curtin, the Republican candidate for governor in the former state, said not a word about abolishing slavery in his ratification speech but spoke with feeling on "the vast heavings of the heart of Pennsylvania whose sons are pining for protection to their labor and their dearest interests." Warming to his theme, he exclaimed: "This is a contest involving protection and the rights of labor. . . . If you desire to become vast and great, protect the manufactures of Philadelphia. . . . All hail, liberty! All hail, freedom! freedom to the white man! All hail freedom general as the air we breathe!" In a fashion after Curtin's own heart, the editor of the *Philadelphia American and Gazette*, surveying the canvass at the finish, repudiated the idea that "any sectional aspect of the slavery question" was up for decision and declared that the great issues were protection for industry, "economy in the conduct of the government, homesteads for settlers on the public domain, retrenchment and accountability in the public expenditures, appropriation for rivers and harbors, a Pacific railroad, the admission of Kansas, and a radical reform in the government." . . .

From what has just been said it must be apparent that the forces which produced the irrepressible conflict were very complex in nature and yet the momentous struggle has been so often reduced by historians to simple terms that a reëxamination of the traditional thesis has become one of the tasks of the modern age. On the part of northern writers it was long the fashion to declare that slavery was the cause of the conflict between the states. Such for example was the position taken by James Ford Rhodes and made the starting point of his monumental work.

Assuming for the moment that this assertion is correct in a general sense, it will be easily observed even on a superficial investigation that "slavery" was no simple, isolated phenomenon. In itself it was intricate and it had filaments through the whole body economic. It was a labor system, the basis of planting, and the foundation of the southern aristocracy. That aristocracy, in turn, owing to the nature of its economic operations, resorted to public policies that were opposed to capitalism, sought to dominate the federal government, and, with the help of free farmers also engaged in agriculture, did at last dominate it. In the course of that political conquest, all the plans of commerce and industry for federal protection and subvention were overborne. It took more than a finite eye to discern where slavery as an ethical question left off and economics—the struggle over the distribution of wealth—began.

On the other hand, the early historians of the southern school, chagrined by defeat and compelled to face the adverse judgment of brutal fact, made the "rights of states"—something nobler than economics or the enslavement of Negroes—the issue for which the Confederacy fought and bled. That too like slavery seems simple until subjected to a little scrutiny. What is a state? At bottom it is a majority or perhaps a mere plurality of persons engaged in the quest of something supposed to be beneficial, or at all events not injurious, to the pursuers. And what are rights? Abstract, intangible moral values having neither substance nor form? The party debates over the economic issues of the middle period answer with an emphatic negative. If the southern planters had been content to grant tariffs, bounties, subsidies, and preferences to northern commerce and industry, it is not probable that they would have been molested in their most imperious proclamations of sovereignty.

But their theories and their acts involved interests more ponderable than political rhetoric. They threatened the country with secession first in defying the tariff of abominations and when they did secede thirty years later it was in response to the victory of a tariff and homestead party that proposed nothing more dangerous to slavery itself than the mere exclusion of the institution from the territories. It took more than a finite eye to discern where their opposition to the economic system of Hamilton left off and their affection for the rights of states began. The modern reader tossed about in a contrariety of opinions can only take his bearings by examining a few indubitable realities. . . .

The Tariff Issue on the Eve of the Civil War

RICHARD HOFSTADTER

One of the outstanding features of Dr. and Mrs. Charles A. Beard's interpretation of the Civil War is its emphasis upon the tariff as a causal factor. In *The Rise of American Civilization* they stress the enthusiasm

Reprinted by permission from *The American Historical Review*, XLIV (October, 1938), pp. 50–55.

shown for the tariff platform at the Republican convention in Chicago and the crucial role that the tariff played in the Pennsylvania and New Jersey elections. There can be little doubt that the condition of the iron and coal industries, always a great power in Pennsylvania politics, influenced the Republican platform on the tariff. That platform carried the state for Lincoln, and the presence of Pennsylvania in the Republican column was necessary to his election. This raises the question whether Pennsylvania and its industries represented an attitude prevailing in the North.

The tariff of 1857 was the lowest tariff enacted by Congress since 1816. The attitude of manufacturers toward that bill should serve as an index of the vitality of the tariff issue in the North. The record reveals that outside of Pennsylvania Northern industry offered no serious opposition to reduction. On the contrary, the reductions were welcomed. This was not because manufacturers were reductionists in principle, but because political exigencies led them to seek lowered duties on raw materials as a substitute for direct protection. Thus we find Senator Wilson of Massachusetts declaring during the debates that in his state the "merchants, manufacturers, mechanics and business men in all the departments of a various industry . . . are for the reduction of the revenues to the actual wants of an economical administration of the government." He said that he had received a note from Samuel Lawrence, in which the latter declared that "a reduction of the revenue alone would save the country from a commercial crisis . . . and that the manufacturers of Massachusetts were prepared to share with other interests in the reduction which the exigencies of the country now impose upon the American people." Sherman of Ohio later spoke of the tariff of 1857 as "the manufacturers' bill," a characterization which was also expressed at the time of its passage by Stanton of Ohio and Letcher of Virginia.

Certainly the majority of votes from the manufacturing states (other than Pennsylvania) was not cast against the reductions in the Hunter amendment of 1857. The roll call in the Senate shows every vote from Massachusetts, Connecticut, and Rhode Island cast for the bill; New York split its vote, Fish standing for and Seward against; the only vote cast from New Hampshire was favorable. In the House the votes from Massachusetts, Connecticut, and Rhode Island were fourteen to one in favor of the measure. While Pennsylvania voted quite solidly against it, New York stood sixteen to eleven and New Jersey two to one in favor.

Although the Hunter amendment, providing for a general reduction in all schedules, brought forth a sectional vote and a sectional controversy, the sections involved were not the North and the South. Nor was there a quarrel between manufactures and cotton. In the House all but three votes from the South, including Maryland, were in favor of reduction, but with this solid Southern front were allied the Northern states of

Massachusetts, Connecticut, and Maine, and three fifths of New York. Outside of Pennsylvania the bulk of the opposition was drawn not from the manufacturing areas but from the agricultural and sheep-raising states of Vermont, Illinois, Ohio, Indiana, and Michigan. It was this alignment which led one Ohio representative to speak of "the coalition of extreme sections of the country against the Northwest."

The real conflict in 1857 was between the woolen manufacturers and the wool growers, both of whom had been in bad straits since the tariff of 1846. During the decade following 1850 the domestic wool producer had steadily lost ground in the face of foreign competition; by 1860 two-thirds of all the wool consumed in the country was foreign. The House ways and means committee in 1856 had ascribed the depression in wool growing and woolen manufactures to the tariff of 1846, which had raised the duties on raw wools to thirty per cent ad valorem and reduced that on flannels and blankets to twenty per cent. Previously all wool priced at seven cents a pound or under had been taxed five per cent, and wools over seven cents had been taxed three cents a pound and thirty per cent. This increase in the cost of his raw material, as well as other factors unrelated to the tariff, had so handicapped the manufacturer that his extensive business in blankets and broadcloth had been destroyed. "The business was prostrated," the report declared, "by the premium which that act in effect offered to the foreign manufacturer, and the nominal protection of the wool grower resulted in the ruin of his business, as in that of the clothmaker. The home market was destroyed for the farmer; in the foreign he could not compete, and the flocks were sent to the slaughter because the woolen factories had been sold at auction or converted to other services." The wool growers would be crushed if raw wools were admitted free of duty, it was held, and seriously harmed as consumers if manufacturers were protected and increased their prices. On the other hand, if woolen goods were not protected, domestic manufactures would be ruined and the growers deprived of their only market. To meet this dilemma the committee advocated the exemption of all foreign wools costing less than fifteen and more than fifty cents a pound, the retention of duties on intermediate grades such as were produced at home, and the raising of duties on manufactures to adequate protection. The effect of this would be to lower the manufacturers' costs in those wools which did not compete with domestic production, protect their finished product from foreign competition, and compensate the wool growers by retaining the existing thirty per cent duties on competing foreign wools.

A less satisfactory solution was set before the Senate in 1857 by Senator Hunter of Virginia in his amendment to the House revenue bill. The proposal to scale down duties on woolens from thirty to twenty-three per cent and on raw wool from thirty to eight per cent was strenuously resisted by Senator Pugh of Ohio, then the leading wool-growing state, and by Collamer of Vermont. It was charged that the disproportionate reduction was a scheme of woolen manufacturers in New England and New York to sacrifice the wool growers for their own aggrandizement. Wilson attempted to answer them by showing how seriously the tariff of 1846 had affected the woolen manufacturers; the making of finer woolens had all but ceased, he said, and thousands of dollars had been invested and lost in the manufacture of coarser cloth. The only remedy was general reduction; in this the manufacturers were willing to share.

Hunter's argument had been that if the wool growers needed protection that was a sure sign that they could not sell abroad. Therefore they needed the domestic market and were dependent upon the prosperity of home manufacturers; whatever would help the manufacturer would be to the interest of the wool grower in the long run. The opposition, however, could not be convinced of the practicability of what they regarded as a plan to enable the sellers of wool to sell dear and the buyers to buy cheap. Collamer's amendment to strike out the provision including wool in the eight per cent schedule was passed by the Senate by a 26–23 vote. In order that this measure might be passed it was necessary to swing the votes of some of the reductionists in the Senate. It is interesting to note that this willingness to compromise came largely from the South, while the representatives of manufacturing constituencies were generally adamant. Of eighteen Southern senators who were to vote for the Hunter amendment, seven stood for the Collamer proposal, while only one of nine northeastern senators made the same concession. It was finally agreed to admit free of duty cheap wools costing twenty cents a pound or less and to levy a tariff of twenty-four per cent on better wools, which were likely to compete with domestic produce.

It is obvious why the manufacturers urged a general reduction. It was impossible to get direct protection because of the hostility of the South and the indifference of many interests in the North. They chose, therefore, to obtain a reduction in costs as a substitute for protection by scaling down the duties of their raw materials. This policy applied not only to wools but also to Manila hemp, flax, raw silk, lead, tin, brass, hides, linseed, and other articles. So eager were the woolen manufacturers to get reductions that one concern in Lowell, Massachusetts, spent $87,000 in promoting the passage of the bill.

This explains the fact that manufacturers were not deeply averse to the raising of schedules after the South seceded. What is most significant with respect to the causation of the Civil War is the fact that there was no open hostility on this issue at the time between these manufacturers and the South that might have been exploited for a partisan purpose. Whatever latent hostility may have existed was kept from active expression by the admission of cheap raw wool free of duty. Unsatisfactory as this was to the wool growers, it had the desired effect upon the manufacturers. The industry revived, and Senator Hunter was later able to point triumphantly to the absence of a strong demand by manufacturers for a change in schedules.

It was not such a demand which prompted the upward revision proposed by Morrill in 1860 and passed in 1861 after the first bloc of Southern states had seceded. The most important direct changes in the act, the increased duties on iron and wool, were plainly written with an eye on the coming elections, "to attach to the Republican party Pennsylvania and some of the western states." In Pennsylvania the tariff issue did its work, but elsewhere manufacturers were aloof. Rice of Massachusetts declared that they asked for no additional protection; Sherman said that they had "asked over and over again to be let alone"; and Morrill himself admitted in later years that his tariff "was not asked for and but coldly welcomed by the manufacturers."

In February, 1861, the Senate was petitioned by the Chamber of Commerce of New York not to pass the Morrill Bill. It was argued that it would seriously affect commerce and the revenue, and that the growing sentiment for its repeal would deter manufacturers from erecting new mills and buying new machinery. An equally important objection was that the passage of the bill would widen the existing breach between the North and the South.

It is well known that commercial and financial capital in the North was, on the whole, strongly opposed to Lincoln's election. Merchants were apprehensive that it might result in cancellation of orders from the South, and bankers expected the repudiation of Southern debts amounting to over $200,000,000, if the South should secede. The opposition press made a concerted effort to frighten business and financial interests. Merchants contributed so lavishly to the Fusion ticket in New York that Lincoln was disturbed. When panic broke out in Wall Street during the latter days of October, the Republican press claimed that it had been fostered by heavy stock sales on the part of the Fusionists and Southern bankers and stockjobbers. The *New York Daily Tribune* charged Secretary of the Treasury Cobb with complicity in the scheme on the ground that he withheld the sale of government loans. After the election Horace Greeley complained of the intensity and unanimity of the "commercial furor" against the Republican party and compared it to that aroused by the bank controversy of 1832–38.

The fears of the mercantile interests were shared by many manufacturers, whose concern for Southern markets was much greater than their interest in tariffs. Early in 1860 a group of Connecticut manufacturers had censured the spirit of sectionalism associated with the Republican party. Manufacturers in Newark and New York City attempted to induce their workers to vote the Fusion ticket. On the eve of the election the *New York Herald* reported that eleven hundred mill workers in one

Connecticut town had been discharged because of a dearth of orders from the South. When the election returns were in, one Newark paper, disappointed at the fact that New Jersey was the only free state which failed to cast its entire electoral vote for Lincoln, attributed this defection to the manufacturers, who "simply desire to know what would be gratifying to those Southern traders who seek to buy their principles with their goods."

While Pennsylvania capital provided the dynamic element in the movement for a higher tariff, manufacturers elsewhere were divided. If the votes and statements of congressional representatives of manufacturing constituencies are conceived to have any close relation to their interests, the majority of the manufacturers appear to have desired reduction in 1857. The example of the woolen manufacturers offers a clue to the strategy of this group. Adversely affected by the tariff of 1846, they had the alternative of working for greater protection or lowering costs through reduced duties on their raw materials. In choosing the latter course, they chose to do parliamentary battle with the Western wool growers rather than the Southern planters. Their satisfaction with the effect of the tariff of 1857 left them indifferent, or actually hostile, to any further changes in 1860.

FOR FURTHER READING: Economic factors are highlighted in Robert R. Russel, *Economic Aspects of Southern Sectionalism* (New York, 1924), and H. K. Beale, "Causes of the Civil War," in Social Science Research Council, *Bulletin* #54 (New York, 1953). They are minimized in A. O. Craven, *The Coming of the Civil War* (Chicago, 1942). T. M. Pitkin, "Western Republicans and the Tariff in 1860," *Mississippi Valley Historical Review*, XXVII (1940), pp. 401 ff. shows their discontent with the high tariff policy of the party. Read also Malcolm R. Eiselen, *Rise of Pennsylvania Protectionism* (Philadelphia, 1932).

16. *Economic Effects of the Civil War*

PROBLEM: *Did the Civil War promote industrial expansion?*

The assumption that the Civil War was a prime factor in stimulating industrialization after 1865 has been widely held by economists as well as by historians, but rarely subjected to the test of historical or statistical evidence. Not until 1961 did a leading economic historian, Thomas C. Cochran, openly take issue with this view. Utilizing statistics and stressing long-term trends he sought to demonstrate that instead of promoting economic development, the war actually may have retarded it. Nevertheless, production trends are only one indicator of economic growth, critic Stephen Salsbury points out in assessing Professor Cochran's thesis. Salsbury questions Cochran's selection of 1840 as the year signifying the beginning of industrial expansion. If, instead, the decade prior to the Civil War is compared with the one immediately following, great increases in selected areas of industrial production are noticeable. Moreover, Salsbury also underscores important political and social effects of the conflict which may have hastened industrialization, although their impact has not as yet been assessed precisely. If neither author presents conclusive proof concerning the effect of the war upon American economic development, both point to important elements that need to be considered in the appraisal of the problem, and raise questions. Why did the war have little influence on production trends in some important basic industries? What other factors need to be considered in determining the influence of the war on the economy? What forms of military organization and techniques were adaptable to private business after the war?

Did the Civil War Retard Industrialization?

THOMAS C. COCHRAN

In most textbook and interpretative histories of the United States the Civil War has been assigned a major role in bringing about the American Industrial Revolution. Colorful business developments in the North—adoption of new machines, the quick spread of war contracting, the boost given to profits by inflation, and the creation of a group of war millionaires—make the war years seem not only a period of rapid economic change but also one that created important forces for future growth. The superficial qualitative evidence is so persuasive that apparently few writers have examined the available long-run statistical series before adding their endorsement to the conventional interpretation. The following quotations taken from the books of two generations of leading scholars illustrate the popular view.

"The so-called Civil War," wrote Charles A. and Mary R. Beard in 1927, ". . . was a social war . . . making *vast changes* in the arrangement of classes, in the accumulation and distribution of wealth, *in the course of industrial development.*" Midway between 1927 and the present, Arthur M. Schlesinger, Sr., wrote: "On these tender industrial growths the Civil War *had the effect of a hothouse.* For reasons already clear . . . nearly every branch of industry grew lustily." Harold U. Faulkner, whose textbook sales have ranked near or at the top, said in 1954: "In the economic history of the United States the Civil War was extremely important. . . . In the North *it speeded the Industrial Revolution* and the development of capitalism by the prosperity which it brought to industry." The leading new text of 1957, by Richard Hofstadter, William Miller, and Daniel Aaron, showed no weakening of this interpretation: "The growing demand for farm machinery as well as for the 'sinews of war' led to American industrial expansion. . . . Of necessity, *iron, coal, and copper* production boomed during the war years." A sophisticated but still essentially misleading view is presented by Gilbert C. Fite and Jim E. Reese in a text of 1959: "The Civil War proved to be a boon to Northern economic development. . . . Industry, for example, was not created by the war, but wartime demands *greatly stimulated and encouraged industrial development* which already had a good start." In a reappraisal of the Civil War, in *Harper's Magazine* for April, 1960, Denis W. Brogan, a specialist in American institutions, wrote: "It may have been only a catalyst but the War *precipitated the entry* of the United States *into the modern industrial world,* made 'the take-off' (to use Professor W. W. Rostow's brilliant metaphor) come sooner."

Reprinted by permission from *The Mississippi Valley Historical Review,* XLVIII (September, 1961), pp. 197–210.

In all of these reiterations of the effect of the Civil War on industrialism, statistical series seem to have been largely neglected. None of the authors cited reinforce their interpretations by setting the war period in the context of important long-run indexes of industrial growth. Since 1949, series for the period 1840 to 1890 that would cast doubt on the conventional generalizations have been available in *Historical Statistics of the United States, 1789–1945*. In 1960 a new edition of *Historical Statistics* and the report of the Conference on Research in Income and Wealth on *Trends in the American Economy in the Nineteenth Century* have provided additional material to support the argument that the Civil War retarded American industrial development. These volumes give data for many growth curves for the two decades before and after the war decade—in other words, the long-run trends before and after the event in question. The pattern of these trends is a mixed one which shows no uniform type of change during the Civil War decade, but on balance for the more important series the trend is toward retardation in *rates* of growth rather than toward acceleration. This fact is evident in many series which economists would regard as basic to economic growth, but in order to keep the discussion within reasonable limits only a few can be considered here.

Robert E. Gallman has compiled new and more accurate series for both "total commodity output," including agriculture, and "value added by manufacture," the two most general measures of economic growth available for this period. He writes: "Between 1839 and 1899 total commodity output increased elevenfold, or at an average decade rate of slightly less than 50 per cent. . . . Actual rates varied fairly widely, high rates appearing during the decades ending with 1854 and 1884, and a very low rate during the decade ending with 1869." From the over-all standpoint this statement indicates the immediately retarding effect of the Civil War on American economic growth, but since most of the misleading statements are made in regard to industrial growth, or particular elements in industrial growth, it is necessary to look in more detail at "value added by manufacture" and some special series. Gallman's series for value added in constant dollars of the purchasing power of 1879 shows a rise of 157 per cent from 1839 to 1849; 76 per cent from 1849 to 1859; and only 25 per cent from 1859 to 1869.[1] By the 1870's the more favorable prewar

---

[1] *Historical Statistics* (1960 ed.), 402. "Constant" or "real" means dollars adjusted to eliminate price changes. It should be remembered that all series expressed in current dollars need to be corrected for rather violent price movements during these fifty years. Precise adjustments would vary with every series, and would involve many problems, but the movement of wholesale prices in general (Warren-Pearson Index) may be roughly summarized as follows. In 1850 prices were 12 per cent lower than in 1840, but by 1860 they were 11 per cent higher than in 1850. From 1860 to 1865 prices rose 99 per cent, but by 1870 the increase for the decade was only 46 per cent. By 1880 the decline for the decade was 26 per cent, and for the decade ending in 1890 it was 18 per cent. *Ibid.*, 115. In other words, current dollars are a very unreliable indicator, particularly as applied to wholesale prices.

rates were resumed, with an increase of 82 per cent for 1869–1879, and 112 per cent for 1879–1889. Thus two decades of very rapid advance, the 1840's and the 1880's, are separated by thirty years of slower growth which falls to the lowest level in the decade that embraces the Civil War.

Pig-iron production in tons, perhaps the most significant commodity index of nineteenth-century American industrial growth, is available year-by-year from 1854 on. Taking total production for five-year periods, output increased 9 per cent between the block of years from 1856 to 1860 and the block from 1861 to 1865. That even this slight increase might not have been registered except for the fact that 1857 to 1860 were years of intermittent depression is indicated by an 81 per cent increase over the war years in the block of years from 1866 to 1870. If annual production is taken at five-year intervals, starting in 1850, the increase is 24 per cent from 1850 to 1855; 17 per cent from 1855 to 1860; 1 per cent from 1860 to 1865; and 100 per cent from 1865 to 1870. While there is no figure available for 1845, the period from 1840 to 1850 shows 97 per cent increase in shipments, while for the period 1870 to 1880 the increase was 130 per cent. To sum up, depression and war appear to have retarded a curve of production that was tending to rise at a high rate.

Bituminous coal production may be regarded as the next most essential commodity series. After a gain of 199 per cent from 1840 to 1850 this series shows a rather steady pattern of increase at rates varying from 119 to 148 per cent each decade from 1850 to 1890. The war does not appear to have markedly affected the rate of growth.

In the mid-nineteenth century copper production was not a basic series for recording American growth, but since three distinguished authors have singled it out as one of the indexes of the effect of the war on industry it is best to cite the statistics. Before 1845 production of domestic copper was negligible. By 1850 the "annual recoverable content" of copper from United States mines was 728 tons, by 1860 it was 8,064 tons, by 1865 it was 9,520 tons, and by 1870 it was 14,112 tons. In this series of very small quantities, therefore, the increase from 1850 to 1860 was just over 1,000 per cent, from 1860 to 1865 it was 18 per cent, and from 1865 to 1870 it was 48 per cent.

Railroad track, particularly in the United States, was an essential for industrialization. Here both the depression and the war retarded the rate of growth. From 1851 through 1855 a total of 11,627 miles of new track was laid, from 1856 through 1860, only 8,721 miles, and from 1861 through 1865, only 4,076 miles. After the war the rate of growth of the early 1850's was resumed, with 16,174 miles constructed from 1866 through 1870. Looked at by decades, a rate of over 200 per cent increase per decade in the twenty years before the war was slowed to 70 per cent for the period from 1860 to 1870, with only a 15 per cent increase during the war years. In the next two decades the rate averaged about 75 per cent.

Next to food, cotton textiles may be taken as the most representative consumer-goods industry in the nineteenth century. Interference with the flow of southern cotton had a depressing effect. The number of bales of cotton consumed in United States manufacturing rose 143 per cent from 1840 to 1850 and 47 per cent from 1850 to 1860, but *fell* by 6 per cent from 1860 to 1870. From then on consumption increased at a little higher rate than in the 1850's.

While woolen textile production is not an important series in the over-all picture of industrial growth, it should be noted that, helped by protection and military needs, consumption of wool for manufacturing more than doubled during the war, and then *fell* somewhat from 1865 to 1870. But Arthur H. Cole, the historian of the woolen industry, character-izes the years from 1830 to 1870 as a period of growth "not so striking as in the decades before or afterwards."

Immigration to a nation essentially short of labor was unquestionably a stimulant to economic growth. Another country had paid for the im-migrant's unproductive youthful years, and he came to the United States ready to contribute his labor at a low cost. The pattern of the curve for annual immigration shows the retarding effect of both depression and war. In the first five years of the 1850's an average of 349,685 immigrants a year came to the United States. From 1856 through 1860 the annual average fell to 169,958, and for the war years of 1861 to 1865 it fell further to 160,345. In the first five postwar years the average rose to 302,620, but not until the first half of the 1870's did the rate equal that of the early 1850's. Had there been a return to prosperity instead of war in 1861, it seems reasonable to suppose that several hundred thousand addi-tional immigrants would have arrived before 1865. . . .

Much American business expansion was financed by short-term bank loans continuously renewed. Thus major increases in business activity should be mirrored in increases in bank loans, both for financing short-term transactions and for additions to plant and working capital that would, in fact, be paid off gradually. If there was a really great Civil War boom in business activity it should be indicated in the series "total loans" of all banks. But it is not. In constant dollars, bank loans fell slightly between 1840 and 1850, and rose nearly 50 per cent by 1860. It should be noted that none of these three decadal years were periods of high prosperity. During the war Confederate banking statistics were not reported by the comptroller of the currency, but by 1866 there is a com-parable figure for the nation as a whole, and in constant dollars it is some 35 per cent below that of 1860. Even by 1870 the constant dollar value of all loans was more than 15 per cent lower than just before the war. If instead of examining loans one looks at total assets of all banks the decline in constant dollars from 1860 to 1870 is reduced to 10 per cent, the difference arising from a larger cash position and more investment in government bonds.[2]

Net capital formation would be a more proper index of economic growth than bank loans or assets. Unfortunately, neither the teams of the National Bureau of Economic Research nor those of the Census Bureau have been able to carry any reliable series back of 1868. From colonial times to 1960, however, the chief single form of American capital formation has undoubtedly been building construction. Farm houses, city homes, public buildings, stores, warehouses, and factories have year-by-year constituted, in monetary value, the leading type of capital growth. Gallman has drawn up series for such construction based on estimating the flow of construction materials and adding what appear to be appropriate mark-ups. Admittedly the process is inexact, but because of the importance of construction in reflecting general trends in capital formation it is interesting to see the results. The rate of change for the ten-year period ending in 1854 is about 140 per cent; for the one ending in 1859 it is 90 per cent; for 1869 it is 40 per cent; and for 1879 it is 46 per cent. Taking a long view, from 1839 to 1859 the average decennial rate of increase was about 70 per cent, and from 1869 to 1899 it was about 40 per cent.[3] The *rate* of advance in construction was declining and the war decade added a further dip to the decline.

Since the decline in rate is for the decade, the exact effect of the war years can only be estimated, but the logic of the situation, reinforced by the record of sharp cut-backs in railroad building, seems inescapable: the Civil War, like all modern wars, checked civilian construction. The first year of war was a period of depression and tight credit in the Middle West, which checked residential and farm construction in the area that grew most rapidly before and after the war. In both the East and the West the last two years of the war were a period of rapid inflation which was regarded by businessmen as a temporary wartime phenomenon. The logical result would be to postpone construction for long-term use until after the anticipated deflation. The decline in private railroad construction to a small fraction of the normal rate exemplifies the situation.

Lavish expenditure and speculation by a small group of war contractors and market operators gambling on the inflation seem to have created a legend of high prosperity during the war years. But the general series on fluctuations in the volume of business do not bear this out. Leonard P. Ayres's estimates of business activity place the average for 1861 through 1865 below normal, and Norman J. Silberling's business index is below its normal line for all years of the war. Silberling also has an intermediate

[2] The reader is again warned that deflation of current dollar values for this early period is an inexact process.
[3] Gallman has two alternate series which I have averaged. For the purposes of this paper either series leads to the same conclusions.

trend line for business, which smooths out annual fluctuations. This line falls steadily from 1860 to 1869. Much of Silberling's discussion in his chapter "Business Activity, Prices, and Wars" is in answer to his question: "Why does it seem to be true that despite a temporary stimulating effect of war upon some industries, wars are generally associated with a long-term retarding of business growth . . . ?" He puts the Civil War in this general category.

Collectively these statistical estimates support a conclusion that the Civil War retarded American industrial growth. Presentation of this view has been the chief purpose of this article. To try to judge the non-measurable or indirect effects of the war is extremely difficult. But since further discussion of the conventional qualitative factors may help to explain the prevailing evaluation in American texts, it seems appropriate to add some conjectural obiter dicta.

Experience with the apparently stimulating effects of twentieth-century wars on production makes the conclusion that victorious war may retard the growth of an industrial state seem paradoxical, and no doubt accounts in part for the use of detached bits of quantitative data to emphasize the Civil War's industrial importance.[4] The resolution of the paradox may be found in contemporary conditions in the United States and in the nature of the wartime demand. The essential wastefulness of war from the stand-point of economic growth was obscured by the accident that both of the great European wars of the twentieth century began when the United States had a high level of unemployment. The immediate effect of each, therefore, was to put men to work, to increase the national product, and to create an aura of prosperity. Presumably, the United States of the mid-nineteenth century tended to operate close enough to full employment in average years that any wasteful labor-consuming activities were a burden rather than a stimulant.

By modern standards the Civil War was still unmechanized. It was fought with rifles, bayonets, and sabers by men on foot or horseback. Artillery was more used than in previous wars, but was still a relatively minor consumer of iron and steel. The railroad was also brought into use, but the building of military lines offset only a small percentage of the over-all drop from the prewar level of civilian railroad construction. Had all of these things not been true, the Confederacy with its small industrial development could never have fought through four years of increasingly effective blockade.

In spite of the failure of direct quantitative evidence to show accelerat-ing effects of the war on rates of economic growth, there could be long-run effects of a qualitative type that would gradually foster a more rapid

---

[4] Ayres, Silberling, and some other students of economic activity such as Herbert Hoover, however, blame the breakdown of the 1930's on the dislocations caused by World War I. *Ibid.*, 65–66. See also *The Memoirs of Herbert Hoover: The Great Depression, 1929–1941* (New York, 1952), 105.

rate of economic growth. The most obvious place to look for such in-direct effects would be in the results of freeing the slaves. Marxists con-tended that elimination of slavery was a necessary precursor of the bourgeois industrialism which would lead to the socialist revolution. The creation of a free Negro labor force was, of course, of great long-run importance. In the twentieth century it has led to readjustment of Negro population between the deep South and the northern industrial areas, and to changes in the use of southern land.

But economically the effects of war and emancipation over the period 1840 to 1880 were negative. Richard A. Easterlin writes: "In every southern state, the 1880 level of per capita income originating in com-modity production and distribution was below, or at best only slightly above that of 1840. . . . [This] attests strikingly to the impact of that war and the subsequent disruption on the southern economy." In general the Negroes became sharecroppers or wage laborers, often cultivating the same land and the same crops as before the war. In qualification of the argument that free Negro labor led to more rapid industrialization it should be noted that the South did not keep up with the national pace in the growth of nonagricultural wealth until after 1900. . . .

To sum up this part of the obiter dictum, those who write of the war creating a national market tied together by railroads underestimate both the achievements of the two decades before the war and the ongoing trends of the economy. The nation's business in 1855 was nearly as inter-sectional as in 1870. Regional animosities did not interfere with trade, nor did these feelings diminish after the war. By the late 1850's the United States was a rapidly maturing industrial state with its major cities con-nected by rail, its major industries selling in a national market, and blessed or cursed with financiers, security flotations, stock markets, and all the other appurtenances of industrial capitalism.

But when all specific factors of change attributable to the war have been deflated, there is still the possibility that northern victory had en-hanced the capitalist spirit, that as a consequence the atmosphere of gov-ernment in Washington among members of both parties was more friendly to industrial enterprise and to northern-based national business operations than had formerly been the rule. It can be argued that in spite of Greenbackers and discontented farmers legislation presumably favor-able to industry could be more readily enacted. The Fourteenth Amend-ment, for example, had as a by-product greater security for interstate business against state regulation, although it was to be almost two decades before the Supreme Court would give force to this protection. By 1876, a year of deep depression, the two major parties were trying to outdo each other in promises of stimulating economic growth. This highly general-ized type of argument is difficult to evaluate, but in qualification of any theory of a sharp change in attitude we should remember that industrialism was growing rapidly from general causes and that by the 1870's it was to be expected that major-party politics would be conforming to this change in American life.

Massive changes in physical environment such as those accompanying the rise of trade at the close of the Middle Ages or the gradual growth of industrialism from the seventeenth century on do not lend themselves readily to exact or brief periodization. If factory industry and mechanized transportation be taken as the chief indexes of early industrialism, its spread in the United States was continuous and rapid during the entire nineteenth century, but in general, advance was greater during periods of prosperity than in depressions. The first long period without a major depression, after railroads, canals, and steamboats had opened a national market, was from 1843 to 1857. Many economic historians interested in quantitative calculations would regard these years as marking the appearance of an integrated industrial society. Walter W. Rostow, incidentally, starts his "take-off" period in the 1840's and calls it completed by 1860. Others might prefer to avoid any narrow span of years. Few, however, would see a major stimulation to economic growth in the events of the Civil War.

Finally, one may speculate as to why this exaggerated conception of the role of the Civil War in industrialization gained so firm a place in American historiography. The idea fits, of course, into the Marxian frame of revolutionary changes, but it seems initially to have gained acceptance quite independently of Marxian influences. More concentrated study of the war years than of any other four-year span in the nineteenth century called attention to technological and business events usually overlooked. Isolated facts were seized upon without comparing them with similar data for other decades. The desire of teachers for neat periodization was probably a strong factor in quickly placing the interpretation in textbooks; thus, up to 1860 the nation was agricultural, after 1865 it was industrial. Recent study of American cultural themes suggests still another reason. From most standpoints the Civil War was a national disaster, but Americans like to see their history in terms of optimism and progress. Perhaps the war was put in a perspective suited to the culture by seeing it as good because in addition to achieving freedom for the Negro it brought about industrial progress.

The Effect of the Civil War on American Industrial Development

STEPHEN SALSBURY

Much has been written about the Civil War. Until quite recently, however, historians were concerned mainly with its cause and they largely ignored the economic effects of the War. In the nineteenth century most northerners simply blamed the War on slavery. In the same period southerners merely accused politicians of being irresponsible and claimed that fanatical abolitionists ignited the conflict. But to Charles A. Beard, writing in the 1920's, these old statements seemed unconvincing.

Beard viewed America's history as a great movement away from Jefferson's agrarian type of society to the capitalistic, industrial, mechanized, and urban society that we have now. In his view, the forces that moved people were economic ones and not idealistic concerns over states' rights or over the immorality of slavery. Beard's pre-Civil War America consisted of a northern, capitalistic, industrial economy with, opposing it, the southern agricultural system. He saw the economic interest and political power of the South, in the Electoral College, the Senate, House of Representatives, and Supreme Court, as frustrating the economic needs of the rapidly growing industrial north.

Professor Louis Hacker stated the Beard thesis in its most extreme and naked form in his book, *The Triumph of American Capitalism*. "By 1860," he summarized,

a critical situation had arisen in American affairs. Because the southern planter capitalists were in control of the instrumentalities of the national state and, as a result, were thwarting the advance of the (too slowly) growing northern industrial capitalism, their claims to power had to be challenged. This the newly formed Republican party did. The partial success of the Republican party at the polls in 1860 drove the southern leaders—pushed on by extremists in their midst who were under heavy economic pressures—into secession. The Civil War broke out. The Union government, after the departure of the southern legislators, was now wholly possessed by the Republican party.

In Beard's words, the Civil War was the "social cataclysm in which the capitalists, laborers, and farmers of the North and West drove from power in the national government the planting aristocracy of the South. Viewed under the light of universal history, the fighting was a fleeting incident; the social revolution was the essential portentous outcome."

Reprinted by permission from Stephen Salsbury, "The Effect of the Civil War on American Industrial Development," in Ralph Andreano (ed.), *The Economic Impact of the American Civil War*, pp. 161–168 (Schenkman Publishing Co.: Cambridge, Mass., 1962).

This explanation of the causes of the Civil War led Beard and Hacker to the conclusion that the conflict spurred economic growth in the United States:

The Second American Revolution (Civil War), while destroying the economic foundation of the slave-owning aristocracy, assured the triumph of business enterprise. As if to add irony to defeat, the very war which the planters precipitated in an effort to avoid their doom augmented the fortunes of the capitalist class from whose jurisdiction they had tried to escape. Through financing the federal government and furnishing supplies to its armies, northern leaders in banking and industry reaped profits far greater than they had ever yet gathered during four years of peace. When the long military struggle came to an end they had accumulated huge masses of capital and were ready to march resolutely forward to the conquest of the continent —to the exploitation of the most marvelous natural endowment ever bestowed by fortune on any nation.

But Beard made no systematic use of statistical evidence in trying to analyze the War's effect.

Prior to 1860 southern planters successfully used their power in the national government to oppose measures such as the tariff, the Homestead Bill, national banking, etc., favored by the northern industrialists and western farmers. Beard, however, made no attempt truly to evaluate the importance of such measures in economic terms and merely assumed that because northern capitalists could not get their way, their plans for expansion and profits were hindered and that economic growth was thus retarded. Starting with this assumption, Beard saw the War as aiding industrialism. He argued that the transference of power from the Democratic to the Republican party (a condition which lasted, with two short exceptions, from the 1860's until 1932) enabled businessmen to shape government policies in ways that were most helpful to their plans for profit and expansion.

Beard cited the policies and legislation which, he claimed, specifically aided economic growth. He considered as most important the direct federal aid to the vast transcontinental railroad projects; it started with the subsidy and land grant to the Union Pacific and Central Pacific railroads in 1862 and included federal land grants in the following years to the Northern Pacific, Kansas Pacific, Santa Fe (Atlantic and Pacific), and Southern Pacific routes. The protective tariff was named as specifically aiding economic growth. He named also the acts designed to make easy the removal of land (whether farmland, timberland, or mineral land) from the public domain to private hands, the Immigration Act of 1864 which gave federal blessing to the importation of workingmen under contracts "analogous to the indentured servitude of colonial times," and the national banking laws and many others.

But more important than any specific legislative act, according to

Beard's interpretation, was the ascendancy of the Republican party in Washington; this created a climate that tolerated no interference with the private capitalists. Gone were the Jacksonian ideas that opposed the concentration of economic power in the hands of large corporations. After 1860, Leland Stanford, Collis P. Huntington, John D. Rockefeller, John M. Forbes, Jay Gould, and Mark Hanna had almost unlimited freedom to do as they pleased. And when men such as these ran into trouble with labor, their control of the government assured them that federal power would be used to smash opposition.

Charles Beard's main effort was to explain why the United States in the period between 1860 and 1910 became the world's most productive and powerful industrial nation. In giving his explanation, he made only a random use of statistics. But while he was perfectly content to make almost totally undocumented assertions, such as that which attributed the post-Civil War boom to "huge masses of capital made available by war profits far greater than . . . [capitalists] had ever yet gathered," Louis Hacker attempted to support this argument by statistical evidence. He used, for instance, an analysis of the census data to substantiate the thesis that "industrial capitalism (more particularly, *heavy* industry) benefited from the Civil War and it continued to make great forward strides (despite a severe depression) after the political victory was firmly secured."

Lately, the role of the Civil War in positively contributing to the American Industrial Revolution has been questioned. Among the most recent and able of these questioning re-evaluations is Thomas C. Cochran's *"Did the Civil War Retard Industrialization?"* In "reiterations of the effect of the Civil War on industrialism," he writes, giving examples, "statistical series seem to have been largely neglected." Cochran's conclusion, after an examination of statistics (available mainly in the 1949 and 1960 editions of *Historical Statistics of the United States* and in the report of the Conference of Research on Income and Wealth in *Trends in the American Economy in the Nineteenth Century*), strongly suggests that the Civil War slowed industrial growth.

Cochran observes that generally during the two decades preceding the Civil War (1840–1860) and the two decades (1870–1890) following the ten-year census period in which the war occurred, the rate of growth exceeded that of the "war decade" (1860–1870). In short, he points to rapid expansion between 1840 and 1860, then actual stagnation in some areas, and but slight increases in most others during the war period (1861–1865), which caused a slower growth rate for the decade 1860–1870, and finally a resumption of rapid growth in the decades between 1870 and 1890.

Behind Cochran's conclusion that the Civil War retarded industrial growth lies the very unstatistical and also partly unsubstantiated assumption that by 1840 all the ingredients favorable to fast industrial growth were overwhelmingly present in the American society. This implies that by the end of the Van Buren administration, the ground was laid for an almost continuous and uninterrupted expansion. This expansion, however, did not occur and the assumption is made that disruptive effects of the Civil War removed vital capital building goods and services from the economy between 1861 and 1865, making the growth after 1865 less rapid than it otherwise would have been.

Now, available statistics do indicate certain American economic reverses during the War. Cotton production almost ended, cotton textile manufacturing in the North fell sharply, and so did the construction of new railroad tracks. Yet, despite this, other segments such as bituminous coal, Pennsylvania anthracite, pig iron, and railroad rails continued to expand, although some at a slightly reduced rate. From this point of view, statistics show that the economy grew less rapidly during the five Civil War years than at other times. We might fairly conclude that war disruption was partially, at least, responsible for this.

Yet the conclusions of Beard, Hacker, and the other historians who claim that the Civil War speeded the Industrial Revolution do not stand or fall on an analysis of the short run, immediate effects which the War had upon the economy. Rather, these conclusions, which see the War as assuring the "triumph of capitalism," and as producing a long term surge of industrial production, rest on longer range analyses.

Professor Cochran's arguments may be met by comparing the post-Civil War growth rate with prewar activity. If one does this, some surprising results present themselves. Let us, for example, instead of comparing the three decades 1850–1860, 1860–1870, 1870–1880, as Cochran does, compare the decade preceding the Civil War (1850–1860), with that immediately following it (1865–1875). Pig iron production in tons, which he considers as "the most significant commodity index of nineteenth century American industrial growth," increased about 50 per cent between 1850 and 1860, but more than doubled between 1865 and 1873 before it fell, due to the depression which started in 1873. Bituminous coal, "the second most essential commodity series," tells a similar story: here production increased slightly less than 100 per cent during the decade of 1850–1860, while during the years 1865–1875 it increased by about 145 per cent. Railroad track construction, which he deems "essential for industrialization," tell an even more striking story: during the period 1850–1860 about 20,000 miles of track were laid down, compared to roughly 40,000 during the decade 1865–1875. Clearly then, in these three areas which Cochran considers the most important indicators of nineteenth century economic growth, the postwar decade evidences a substantial boom with growth rates much above those of the pre-Civil War era.

Although this kind of analysis tends to cast doubt on the argument and could be used to support Hacker's assertion that "industrial capitalism (more particularly, heavy industry) benefited from the Civil War," such a conclusion would have the weakness which plagues any attempt to assess the economic effects of the Civil War by reference to growth rates, and industrial or agricultural output. Such statistics tell us only how much was produced, or how much the growth rate declined or increased, but they do not tell us why. This returns us to the nonstatistical explanation of Beard which conflicts dramatically with Cochran's underlying assumption that all the ingredients for rapid economic growth dominated the American society by the beginning of William Harrison's administration.

Professor Cochran recognizes that what he calls "indirect effects" may have had some influence upon post-Civil War economic development. For purposes of analysis we can put these "indirect effects" into two categories. First, there were the changes in the political and social system which the War produced; and second there were the stimulants, such as inflation and the creation of a substantial federal debt, which resulted directly from the War itself. Relative to the second category, Cochran admits that "sharp wartime inflation had the usual effect of transferring income from wage, salary, and interest receivers to those making profits, ... (which) meant concentration of savings in the hands of entrepreneurs who would invest in new activities." He also points out that inflation "eased the burdens of those railroads which had excessive mortgage debts." But Cochran seems willing to dismiss these effects of the War with the casual statement that "a great deal of new research would be needed to establish causal connections between the inflationary reallocation of wealth, 1863 to 1865, and the high rate of industrial progress in the late 1870's and 1880's." With this sentiment one can only agree. We add that until such attempts are made one must be careful about characterizing the Civil War as a retarder of industrialization.

Cochran's analysis is similar in his statements about the effect of expanded and superior credit resulting from the establishment of national banks and the increase of the national debt from $64,000,000 in 1860 to over $2,700,000,000 in 1866. He gives no statistics which would indicate the impact of the new banking system and the enormous federal debt, but merely states that "since 1800 a multiplication of banks had made credit relatively easy to obtain in the United States, and in the North this continued to be the situation." Further, he observes that the War destroyed southern banking, and that by 1875 some 40 per cent of the banks were still outside the national banking system. With these statements there can be little disagreement, yet it is difficult to see how they prove or disprove the thesis that the War retarded economic growth. In precise terms, how easy was credit to obtain before 1860? Was there ample credit for large scale ventures? Was there any change in this picture after 1865? If there was, did it result from the War? These questions still remain to be answered. And the fact that some "40 per cent of the banks" in 1875 were outside the national banking system seems almost irrelevant without a great deal of additional analysis which is not supplied.

Finally, Cochran recognizes that he must meet the argument which asserts that the Civil War changed the social structure of the nation. He agrees that there is a "possibility that the northern victory had enhanced the capitalist spirit"; but he maintains that this "highly generalized argument is difficult to evaluate." This is undoubtedly true (and the same statement could be made about most attempts to explain human behavior). But the Beard thesis is not so vague but what it is subject to some trenchant criticism. It is possible to analyze in detail the measures which the Republican Party enacted, and to determine how they affected economic growth. It has already been suggested that it may be feasible to measure the amount of investment capital made available by the creation of the national banking system, and the large national debt. There might also be a thorough quantitative study of government aid to internal improvements. While it is true that "federal and state administrations preceding the Civil War could . . . be regarded as friendly to business," it might be well to compare, as Professor Cochran suggests, federal and state aid during and after the Civil War with that in other periods. This should include an attempt to determine the precise amount in constant dollars made available to transportation enterprises by the various state and local governments and the national Congress. We do have readily available information on federal land granted for such purposes. Some idea of the new Republican attitude can be gained from the fact that, in the single year 1865, the national government granted more land for internal improvements than in all years prior to 1861.

There can be no doubt that the exodus from Washington of southern congressmen speeded by ten years or more the building of our entire transcontinental railroad network. Mr. Cochran suggests that such ventures were "built for speculative purposes uneconomically ahead of demand . . ." and thus concludes without supplying any evidence that they may "for a decade or even two have consumed more capital than their transportation services were then worth to the economy." Although this judgment is not necessarily wrong, it will take much research to prove it one way or the other. Certain it is that the building of our vast transcontinental railway systems, which is partially reflected in 40,000 miles of track laid down between 1865 and 1875, had enormous economic effects both from the point of view of consuming (thus stimulating) the products of heavy industry, and of opening up agricultural land in California, Kansas, Nebraska, Wyoming, Colorado, Utah, Idaho, Montana, Washington, Oregon, Arizona, Nevada, and New Mexico. Here it must be noted that since the first transcontinental road was not finished until May,

1869, the statistical impact of these roads on agriculture would not be seen until the decade 1870–1880.

Professor Cochran's assertion that the Union Pacific, during its first decade, was a drain on the economy has been sharply challenged by Robert Fogel. Fogel not only analyzes the rate of return on the Union Pacific's cash expenditures; he also presents estimates of the line's "social return," that is, the increased national income due to the railroad but not reflected in the company's earnings. In both respects Professor Fogel finds the Union Pacific a success, returning an average of 11.6 per cent on its cash expenditures for the first decade of its operation, and an average social return of 29.9 per cent for the same period. While it must be conceded that the social return statistics as yet mean little since we have few comparable figures for other railroads or other kinds of investments, it is only by this type of investigation that we will finally be able, through the aid of numbers, to shed light upon the question of the economic effect of the Civil War on the railroads.

Finally, however, we must face the inherent limits of statistics. Cochran's argument that the Civil War's contribution to the "spirit of capitalism" is difficult to measure is all too correct. Such actions as those of the Republican-appointed Supreme Court, which interpreted the Fourteenth Amendment to the Constitution to insure the sanctity of corporate property and to protect it from attacks by hostile state legislatures, are not subject to statistical measurement. Yet they vitally affected industrial development, at least the industrialism which characterized nineteenth century America.

In summary, historians must not discard or avoid statistics; they can prove invaluable in drawing a clear picture of what happened. Numbers may even answer questions such as, was the Union Pacific a stimulant to economic growth? and if so how? and in what areas of the economy? Yet the broader question—did the Civil War accelerate industrialism by placing in undisputed power men of business?—is only partially susceptible to statistical analysis. We can gain insight into the impact of some measures (tariffs, aid to railroads, land distributed under the Homestead Act, etc.) through numerical data, yet historians must never fail to integrate such information with interpretations based upon nonstatistical social, political, and psychological analysis.

FOR FURTHER READING: W. M. Persons, "Business and Financial Conditions Following the Civil War," *Review of Economics and Statistics* (1920), II, Supplement; Louis Hacker, *The Triumph of American Capitalism* (New York, 1940); and Ralph Andreano (ed.), *The Economic Impact of the American Civil War* (Cambridge, 1962) present views about the effects of the war upon the national economy.

17. *Economic Aspects of Reconstruction*

PROBLEM: *Was the radical Reconstruction program designed for economic exploitation of the South?*

One hundred years after Reconstruction, when emotions have subsided, scholars still debate over the economic impact of the Northern Reconstruction program on the South. Was the Congressional program of the Republicans in 1865 designed to wreak vengeance on the South? Or was it a conscientious attempt to rebuild the economy of the demolished region? Professor William Hesseltine of the University of Wisconsin appraised the measures dictated by a Northern majority in Congress between 1865 and 1877 as a cold-blooded effort by Eastern capitalists to exploit the prostrate South. He indicates that commercial newspapers advertised economic opportunities in the South and the need to establish peace and order there to restore prosperity. The desire to increase Southern tax revenues was equally important. More recently some younger historians like Stanley Coben have challenged such an economic interpretation of Reconstruction by pointing to the great diversity of aims and lack of unity among a great multitude of Northern business groups. Coben points to disagreements over high and low tariffs and over currency questions. Such an approach focuses on the multiplicity of political, social, and economic interests during Reconstruction. Each of these authors points to pertinent questions. Was there a comprehensive Reconstruction program? Can the actions of Northern business interests be defended? How did non-economic issues affect Northern plans for rebuilding of the South?

302

Economic Factors in the Abandonment of Reconstruction

WILLIAM B. HESSELTINE

By common consent, President Rutherford B. Hayes's withdrawal of the federal troops from the South has been accepted as the end of reconstruction. The President's action, however, was but the outward and visible symbol of an already accomplished revolution in northern sentiment. For a number of years the northern voters had been coming to realize that the effort to force the South into the northern political mold was both costly and futile.

Commentators on the politics of the Reconstruction period have ascribed this reversal of opinion to the rise of new interests among the northern electorate, or have dismissed it with a remark that the people had grown tired of the southern question in politics. Such an interpretation fails to consider that reconstruction itself was an economic as well as a political problem, and that it was not until the political program failed to bring economic results that the control of the South was returned to the southern white man.

Fundamentally, reconstruction was the method by which the "Masters of Capital" sought to secure their victory over the vanquished "Lords of the Manor," and through which they expected to exploit the resources of the southern states. Long before the war was over cotton speculators, acting as the vanguard of an economic army, followed the advancing federal armies and annoyed commanders from the Red River to the Potomac by their persistent efforts to carry on trade with the South. Behind the lines, less mobile entrepreneurs calculated the possibility of carrying the northern economic system into the South at the close of hostilities. In the first months after Appomattox, business men in the North looked for immediate profits from the return of peace and endorsed General Ulysses S. Grant's leniency and President Andrew Johnson's plans for a speedy restoration of the southern states. One of Grant's aides-de-camp found that in the summer of 1865 "all the sober, substantial men" of New York, St. Louis, and Washington were in favor of Johnson's policy. Impressed with the necessity for southern industrial rehabilitation, the New York *Commercial and Financial Chronicle* ingratiatingly assured the South that the northern people contemplated no oppression but would accord the southern states an early readmission to the Union.

Totally ignoring the psychoses of the conquered southerners, northern

Reprinted by permission from *The Mississippi Valley Historical Review*, *XXII* (September, 1935), pp. 191–220.

financial circles seemed to believe that the South would "treat political questions as secondary" until industrial recuperation had been accomplished. This recovery, of course, would be the result of northern capital, in the hands of northern men, flowing into the South. "There can be no way so sure to make the late rebels of the South loyal men and good citizens," declared the New York organ of the financiers, "as to turn their energies to the pursuits of peace, and the accumulation of wealth." When goods from southern factories appeared in the New York markets, they caused this journal to remember that in 1860 there had been 350 woolen mills and 180 cotton mills in the South and that the total value of southern manufactured goods had been over $238,000,000! "Now," proclaimed the hopeful editor, "Northern men, accustomed to business, have gone South and will give a new impetus" to industrial development.

In order to encourage northern men to migrate to the South, commercial newspapers began to advertise the South as the nation's new land of opportunity. The abundance of land, the manufacturing possibilities, the climate, soil, water-power, and timber of the South came in for extensive exposition, and the figures of the South's exports in 1860—over two hundred million dollars—were dangled before the eyes of the northern people. The South was assured that an immigration of new and energetic people would begin as soon as the Johnsonian governments were fully established.

Such roseate dreams of a golden harvest in the South were rudely shattered when the southerners began to take stock of their own position. In the first days after the war planters welcomed ex-officers of the Union armies who came to purchase cotton plantations, but few of these adventurers were successful either in handling Negroes or in living harmoniously with their white neighbors. Political differences which engendered social ostracism and even physical violence soon developed, and the northerners returned to their homes none the richer for their experience. Instead of welcoming immigrants and making provisions to receive migrating capitalists, the provisional governments under Johnson's program showed more interest in attempting to solve the economic problems of an agrarian area. . . .

The passage of the Reconstruction Act of March 2, 1867, renewed the hope of a migration of capital and labor to the South. Union men in Virginia looked forward to the migration of "Northern men with capital and enterprise to develop the resources of our fields and forests." Moreover a political purpose would be served, for such people, wrote a citizen of Richmond, "by their social intercourse and votes . . . would do much to neutralize the prejudices and influence of parties inimical to the Government." When General James A. Longstreet renounced his Confederate heresies in favor of southern prosperity, Massachusetts' Ben Butler hastened to welcome him to the radical fold. If all southerners would take

Longstreet's views, Butler foresaw that "harmony of feeling, community of interest, unity of action as well as homogeneity of institutions" would follow to produce national well being.

But Longstreet was almost alone in his decision to "accept the results of the war" and the military governments in the South could do little to further the North's exploitation of its southern colony. Men who had gone South for economic reasons took advantage of the changed situation to recoup their losses in politics, and others came from the North solely for the plums of office. But the Union men and northerners in the South continued to find themselves at a disadvantage. The property of loyalists was not safe in the courts, and Ben Butler soon heard appeals from the Unionists to turn the courts over to loyal men. "The Northern man will not come here unless his capital is safe," declared one of Butler's Georgia informants. From Texas it was reported that rebel leaders were growing rich but that there was no hope for Union men. On the advice of the "best financiers" Butler decided to abandon his own extensive investments in the South, although he contemplated, according to one newspaper, a bill which would prevent disfranchised rebels from holding office on railroads or chartered companies.

The New York *Commercial and Financial Chronicle,* a consistent supporter of Johnson's policy, soon found that Congressional Reconstruction was paralyzing business and unnecessarily prolonging southern industrial prostration. If Negro majorities controlled the state legislatures, the paper warned, capital would stay out of the section. Despite this analysis, the Radicals pursued their course and blamed bad conditions on President Johnson. When the Tennessee legislature met in December, 1867, Governor William G. Brownlow, the "Fighting Parson," reported that "men of capital and enterprise" had not come into the state in the expected numbers. This was due to Andrew Johnson's "insane policy" of holding out to "pestilential disloyalists" the hope that they would be restored to power. Butler agreed with this contention and declared that only a new president could insure the property rights of northerners in the South. . . .

After the election of 1868 Horace Greeley had become the principal exponent of northern infiltration into the South. In much the same manner that he had formerly urged the male youth to seek the West, he now devoted the columns of the powerful New York *Tribune* to urging groups to settle in the South. Southern land which had been worth twenty dollars an acre before the war and would soon be worth that again could be bought for one or two dollars an acre. Advising settlement in colonies, Greeley estimated that three thousand colonists in Florida, five thousand each in Alabama, Louisiana, Arkansas, and Mississippi, and ten thousand each in Virginia, North Carolina, and Texas would make the South Republican and deliver it from "the nightmare which now oppresses . . . politics and industry." Within the South, said Greeley, there was a division between two classes on the issues of reconstruction. The "land-holders, merchants and men of property, with all who are inclined to industry and thrift" were opposed by a "decreasing faction of sore-heads and malignants." In issue after issue of his paper, the expansionist editor carried articles by the first class of southerners setting forth the advantages of various sections of the South for immigrants and for capital investments. As the Virginia question arose, Greeley reiterated that the South was begging for immigrants and for northern capital, and a *Tribune* correspondent wandered through the South gathering details of the wealth awaiting northern enterprise. North Carolina offered cheap land, docile laborers, ample timber resources, and political peace. In South Carolina there were woolen mills and cotton factories. Tennessee had blast furnaces already established by northern capital and there were rich opportunities for investment in mines of iron, coal, zinc, and copper. The South, editorialized the *Tribune*, had shown a general willingness to come back into the Union on the Greeley platform of "universal amnesty and universal suffrage."

The fundamental issues between the politicians and the business men were clearly brought out in an open letter from Greeley to Butler. Appealing to Butler's practical sense, the editor showed that the Radical program of proscription and disfranchisement had retarded business. In reply, Butler declared that Greeley's course had encouraged the rebels so that they had gained the upper hand in Tennessee and Georgia. In these states, the people had deceived the Republican party. Conditions would have been better if a half dozen leading rebels had been hung at the end of the war. . . .

The congressional elections of 1874 marked the abandonment of political reconstruction by the northern voters. The repudiated Radicals continued their course until after they had delivered the presidency to Hayes, but the popular vote in the North was cast in 1876 for Tilden and for a different method of exploiting the South. With the withdrawal of the federal troops from the South, the masters of capital embarked upon a policy of conciliating their former enemies and of slow infiltration into their conquered but stubborn provinces.

A single glimpse at the situation a decade later will suffice to illustrate the new technique which the North came to employ in dealing with the South. In 1885 young William McKinley went to plead with the people of Virginia to send a protectionist to the Senate. "Do you imagine that anybody is coming to Virginia with his money to build a mill, or a factory, or a furnace, and develop your coal and your ore, bring his money down here, when you vote every time against his interests. . . . ?" he asked. "If you think so, you might just as well be undeceived now, for they will not come. . . . Be assured that the Republicans of the North harbor no resentments—only ask for the results of the war. They wish you the highest prosperity and the greatest development." The change from the method of coercion to that of appeal was great, but the hope was still alive that in spite of the abandonment of political reconstruction the South would receive the master of capital with his promises of prosperity.

Northeastern Business and Radical Reconstruction: A Re-examination

STANLEY COBEN

Historians have generally accepted the view that Radical Reconstruction "was a successful attempt by northeastern business, acting through the Republican party, to control the national government for its own economic ends: notably, the protective tariff, the national banks [and] a 'sound' currency." The Radical program is also said to have been "the method by which the 'Masters of Capital' . . . expected to exploit the resources of the southern states" behind federal protection. Western hostility to these eastern business designs was avoided by large appropriations for rivers, harbors, railroads, free land, and pensions, and by use of the ever-potent "bloody shirt." This is supposed to have been prevented by a union of western and southern agrarian opposition to the industrial and financial masters of the East.

This thesis has met with little serious challenge and has been subjected to only occasional qualification. It continues to influence studies of the political and economic history of the post-Civil War era. Yet a closer examination of the important economic legislation and congressional battles of the period, and of the attitudes of businessmen and influential business groups, reveals serious divisions on economic issues among Radical legislators and northeastern businessmen alike. Certainly neither business leaders nor Radicals were united in support of any specific set of economic aims. Considerable evidence also suggests that the divisions among businessmen often cut across sectional as well as industrial lines. Furthermore, evidence indicates that few northeastern business groups were interested in southern investments in the early postwar years, and that these few were hostile to Radical Reconstruction.

The evident need for new interpretations of the motivation of northern Radicals and of the economic history of the entire period is demonstrated

Reprinted by permission from *The Mississippi Valley Historical Review*, XLVI (June, 1959), pp. 67-90.

by a re-examination of the most important of the "economic ends"
usually agreed upon as motives for Radical Reconstruction: the tariff and
the currency issues, and the charge that northern business interests sought
federal protection for the exploitation of the South.

The tariff split northeastern businessmen more than any other issue. So
fierce was business competition in this era, and so eager were the antagonists to use every possible means of winning an advantage, that almost
all important tariff schedules became battlegrounds between industries,
as well as between firms within the same industry. The copper, iron,
linseed, and woolen textile industries, for example, were bitterly divided
on crucial tariff schedules. The most significant split, however, was between certain high protectionist Pennsylvania interests on one side and influential low-tariff groups in New England and New York on the other.
Pennsylvania coal mine operators feared the competition of rich Nova
Scotia deposits, mined by low-wage labor, close to major American
markets. Iron and steel manufacturers, the largest highly protected interest, were faced with the competition of long-established, technologically
advanced English producers, whose wage scale was only a fraction of that
of the Americans. Pennsylvania carpet, glass, and wool industries demanded protection for similar reasons. The Keystone State was the largest
extractor of iron and steel, of carpets, glass, and chemicals. On the other
hand, powerful opposition to the tariff objectives of the Pennsylvanians
came from the cotton and many of the woolen textile manufacturers of
New England, and from the intertwined importing, financial, and railroad
interests of New York.

New Englanders had become strong advocates of lower tariffs in the
1850's. The sharp tariff reductions of 1857 were accomplished chiefly by
southern and New England votes. New England manufacturers, especially textile producers, desired cheap imported raw materials in order
to lower the price of their finished goods on the international market.
Furthermore, they agreed to reduced rates on manufactured goods to
discourage the growth of domestic competition. Among American manufacturers, New England producers as a group were farthest from domestic sources of raw materials, closest to sources of cheap foreign commodities. Cheap supplies of coal, lumber, flaxseed, building stone, fine
wool, and other commodities were available in nearby Canada and Nova
Scotia. Scottish and British iron, Indian linseed, and Russian and Philip-
pine hemp were imported into Boston in large quantities for the benefit
of manufacturers. Hardly any wool for the finer grades of cloth was
produced in America, either before or after the War; nor were the rough,
lowest grades, used in carpets and blankets, available at home. By the end
of the War, northeastern cotton manufacturers were importing the cheap
Indian Surat cotton already widely used in England.

English textile manufacturers, rivals of the New Englanders both in world markets and in America, obtained their raw materials free of duty. There were good reasons for northeastern producers to believe that only the American system of imposts kept them from equaling the British in world trade. By the 1850's, many American mills had been in operation for three generations. They had experienced managers and weavers, cheap and abundant credit, modern machinery and production methods. In cotton cloth manufacturing, for which machinery could be used most extensively. New England labor was the most productive in the world. By 1860, the average number of looms per weaver was four in America, two in Great Britain. French and German manufacturers lagged even farther behind in methods and machinery.

In addition to high productivity which made their goods competitive in the world markets, and the need to import cheap raw materials, many New England manufacturers preferred low tariffs from a fear that high textile duties would foster the growth of new competitors at home. New producers might bring cutthroat competition and periodic chaos to the industry by their poor judgment of market conditions. A special committee of the Boston Board of Trade acknowledged in 1858 that New England textile manufacturers had potentially dangerous rivals, especially in Pennsylvania; but the committee concluded that the tariff reduction of 1857 removed any immediate threat. "Under the impulse of a high protective tariff they accomplished so little, that now, under a change of policy, there seems no present cause of alarm." When the higher Morrill duties came before the House in 1860, Representative Alexander H. Rice of Massachusetts, speaking for the manufacturers of his state, declared that "excessive protection" would stimulate "ruinous and irresponsible competition at home." In the Senate, textile manufacturer Henry Wilson proclaimed: "A high protective policy . . . is calculated to raise up rivals at home, and is more injurious to us than foreign competition."

After the War, fear of the growth of protected competition continued to influence New England tariff sentiment. Edward Atkinson, president of the Cotton Spinners of New England, and a director of the Boston Board of Trade, wrote to Henry Wilson in 1866: "The strongest men in the trade are more afraid of the unskillful competition built up at home by high duties than they are of foreign competition." Enoch R. Mudge, one of the most influential New England textile men, told the organizing meeting of the National Association of Cotton Manufacturers and Planters in 1868: "When we speak of protection, I think it should be given only at the point where the cotton manufacturer requires it." For well-established, efficient New England producers, of course, there were comparatively few points at which protection was necessary. They had seen evidence of the success of their low tariff theories in the few years the 1857 schedules were in force. "The operation of the tariff of 1857 has contributed largely to the prosperity of our woolen manufactures," one of Boston's largest wool dealers reported in 1859. Exports of cotton cloth had risen steadily, from an average of $7,000,000 in the years 1851 through 1856, to almost $11,000,000 in 1860.

The government's need for revenue allowed protectionists an almost unchallenged ascendancy during the Civil War, but the battle between northeastern business groups over tariff schedules was resumed after Appomattox. For example, when a resolution for lower tariffs was placed before the National Board of Trade convention in 1869, delegates from the Boston Board of Trade and Boston Corn Exchange voted 6 to 1 for the resolution; Philadelphia delegates voted 7 to 0 against it. The Boston Board of Trade also worked unsuccessfully to prevent abrogation of the reciprocity treaty with Canada; Philadelphia's Board joined western agricultural interests in demanding an end to reciprocity.

These divisions within the business community were likewise reflected in the congressional debates and voting on important tariff schedules. Cotton manufacturers resumed their prewar demands for lower schedules, even for cotton textiles. Senator William Sprague, whose sprawling Rhode Island mills were relatively inefficient, protested against the 25 per cent cut in cotton textile duties proposed in 1867. He was answered by Senator William P. Fessenden of Maine, sponsor of the measure: "I am informed by the commissioner [Revenue Commissioner David A. Wells] that these duties were fixed at a rate perfectly satisfactory to those engaged in the manufacture of cottons, who appeared before him. . . . The cotton interest of this country has got so that it can stand of itself pretty much."

Schedules on coal similarly came under attack. As power looms replaced hand looms, and steam power replaced water power, New England manufacturers became increasingly interested in lower coal duties. Under reciprocity and the low tariff of 1857, imports of coal into Boston rose steadily from 88,531 tons in 1858, to 209,225 tons in 1865, most of this being cheap Nova Scotia fuel. Representative George S. Boutwell and Senator Charles Sumner of Massachusetts tried in vain to prevent higher coal schedules from being placed in the proposed tariffs of 1866 and 1867. Sumner acknowledged that there was a lot of coal in Pennsylvania, West Virginia, and the West. "But why," he asked, "should New England, which has a natural resource comparatively near at home, be compelled at a great sacrifice to drag her coal from these distant supplies?" Sumner's amendment was defeated 11 to 25, with eight New Englanders, both New Yorkers, and one senator from Oregon comprising those favoring lower duties on coal.

Many other schedules in the proposed bills of 1866 and 1867 were fought out by competing or conflicting business interests. Manufacturers, especially New Englanders, dependent upon cheap imported raw materials, were continually in opposition to the combined efforts of raw material producers and competing manufacturers closer to these native sources of supply. When Senator Benjamin F. Wade of Ohio moved to raise the duty on linseed, largely grown in the West, Fessenden of Maine accused him of asking the higher rate "for this simple selfish reason: that the trade of crushing seed and manufacturing oil on the sea-coast may be utterly destroyed for the benefit of crushers of seed and manufacturers of oil in the West.

Rolling mills, chiefly eastern, which controlled the American Iron and Steel Association, almost forced through an extremely low duty on scrap iron. Such a duty would allow the mills to import huge quantities of cheap European used rails, and to re-roll them in lieu of using domestic pig iron for new rails. Senator Zachariah Chandler, from the iron producing state of Michigan, demanded that the proposed duty on wrought scrap iron be quadrupled, and the duty on cast iron be almost tripled. Lower schedules, he declared, would close the iron mines, put out every blast furnace, and mean "total ruin to the iron interests of the United States. . . . It is a bill gotten up to suit the railroad rolling-mills, and to sacrifice every other iron interest in the United States." The rolling mills won one Senate vote, but Chandler forced another, which was won by those sympathetic with the mine operators and pig iron producers. Almost all the western senators and both Pennsylvanians voted for higher duties on scrap metal. All but one senator from New England and New York voted for the low schedule.

The only tariff adjustment besides the wool and woolens bill to become law in the early postwar years was a measure passed in 1869, greatly increasing the duties on copper. Eastern smelters, who used a combination of eastern and cheap South American ores, were forced out of business by this bill, passed for the benefit of Lake Superior mine operators, whose domestic ores did not require smelting. The Lake Superior mine owners, some of whom were eastern financiers, were thus given a monopoly of the American market. They were thereby enabled to charge much higher than world prices at home and to dump their surplus abroad at much lower prices. Similar conflicts among business interests developed on tariff schedules for salt (used for scouring wool), zinc, lead, nickel, and building stones.

The wool and woolens bill of 1867, which considerably raised most schedules, has been cited as a prime example of the cooperation of business interests, because it was devised in a conference between a committee of wool growers and representatives of the National Association of Wool Manufacturers. What has generally been overlooked is the fact that the manufacturers' association, like the American Iron and Steel Association, was dominated by a well-organized segment of the industry, in this case by worsted and carpet manufacturers, whose interests conflicted with those of other important groups within the woolen industry.

Most influential of the men who negotiated the agreement for the manufacturers were Erastus B. Bigelow, president and founder of the Association, and America's leading carpet manufacturer; John L. Hayes, permanent secretary of the Association; and J. Wiley Edmonds, treasurer of
the giant Pacific Mills, a leading worsted producer. Hayes reported to the
membership that "for six months Mr. Bigelow gave himself unremittingly
to the great work . . . [and to him they] must attribute the happy results
of the conference." Before this "happy" conclusion, Hayes conceded,
most woolen manufacturers "were becoming more and more disposed to
look abroad for the chief supply of raw material . . . and were inclined
to advocate the British policy of free trade in raw materials, including
wool." Certainly the results of the conference were not so happy for
manufacturers of woolen cloth, the largest item of domestic woolen
output. These producers would be forced to pay much higher rates
for imported raw wool than the worsted manufacturers with whom they
competed. Carpet and blanket manufacturers would pay by far the lowest
rates.

The largest manufacturer of wool cloth taking part in the negotiations
with the growers was Edward Harris of the Harris Manufacturing Company, Woonsocket, Rhode Island. Harris later declared that he had no
part in deciding the schedules, and that his name had been appended to
the agreement without his knowledge or consent. Senator Henry Wilson
of Massachusetts, a manufacturer of fine woolen cloth, told the Senate
Finance Committee that if the new schedules were put into effect, he
would have to close his factory. He subsequently declared in the Senate:
"Some of the very ablest men in Massachusetts and in New England
earnestly believe that this bill, so far as it concerns two thirds of the
woolen manufacturers of the country, is not so good as the present
tariff. [Only] the carpet manufacturers are abundantly satisfied." Wilson's statement was reinforced by other New England senators. William
Sprague of Rhode Island, William P. Fessenden of Maine, and Lot M.
Morrill of Maine reported similar opinions of the wool and woolens bill
among the cloth manufacturers in their constituencies. Nevertheless, there
was no organized opposition in Washington to the energetic Hayes or to
the large number of western congressmen who were anxious to honor
an agreement which gave protection to wool growers. The wool and
woolens bill passed easily despite adverse votes from men like Wilson,
Sumner, and Sprague who had close associations with the New England
woolen industry.

Northeastern opposition to the cloth schedules continued after the
passage of the bill, and in the winter of 1869–1870, Edward Harris and 43
other New England woolen manufacturers petitioned Congress to reduce
the duties on wool for cloth as low as carpet wool duties, which were one
fifth as high. On reaching Washington with this petition, Harris was in-

formed that the wool growers and John Hayes, who said he represented 300 companies and individuals associated with the woolen industry, had first claim on congressmen's votes. In 1889, the woolen cloth manufacturers obtained 530 signatures from wool manufacturers and dealers asking for lower duties—and again failed. Finally, in 1909, the cloth manufacturers formed a separate organization to do permanent battle in Washington with the worsted and carpet interests.

For somewhat different reasons a low-tariff sentiment similar to that in New England was also strong in New York City, by far the largest importing and financial center in the country. New York merchants, shippers, and those who financed their activities opposed tariffs which might restrict imports, while the railroad financiers protested that under the proposed tariff of 1866 the Erie and the New York Central systems alone would have to pay out annually about two million dollars by way of protection." The New York Chamber of Commerce had opposed the Morrill bill of 1861 as "a radical change in the tariff policy of the country," but had patriotically refrained from strenuous protests as tariff rates steadily rose during the War. In listing the organization's postwar objectives, however, Secretary John Austin Stevens declared: "The principles of free, unshackled trade, which it has ever upheld, must be reaffirmed." A few months after the War's end, the *Commercial and Financial Chronicle* observed: "Signs are not wanting that the subject of Free Trade will be made the text of the next political agitation in this country." The *Journal of Commerce* also began agitating for lower tariffs soon after the War; and the introduction of the first postwar tariff bill, providing for generally increased rates, naturally brought a strong protest from the New York Chamber of Commerce.

Clearly, then, New England cotton manufacturers and many wool and other manufacturers preferred and worked for lower tariff schedules—as did most of New York's financial and mercantile community. This fact was obvious to contemporary protectionists, especially the fervent Pennsylvanians. They recognized the role New Yorkers and New Englanders played in reducing many schedules, and in defeating, by obstructionist tactics, bills of which they disapproved. A delegate from Philadelphia's Board of Trade complained to the National Board of Trade in 1869 that New England's industries had been built up behind tariff walls. "Now they are marked disciples of free trade. . . . They overlook the interests yet in their infancy. . . . Is this right? Is this just?" Henry C. Carey, leading spokesman for Pennsylvania iron, coal, and other protected interests, charged in 1867 that for 20 years, on tariff questions, "It has pleased the representatives of Massachusetts to array themselves on the side of cotton planters, slave owners, railroad monopolists."

Northeastern businessmen were thus far from united in support of high tariffs after the Civil War. Leading business interests of New England

and New York believed that they lost more than they gained from high postwar tariffs. Had reconstruction politics allowed them a choice, it seems likely that these important groups would have preferred a return to the coalition which had produced the low tariff of 1857—a coalition which included the South. Certainly they would not have opposed the return of southern representatives in order to retain high imposts.

The business interests of the Northeast were divided into fiercely competing groups not only by the tariff issue, but by currency questions as well. These conflicts were brought into the open shortly after the Civil War by attempts to contract the swollen wartime currency. Secretary of the Treasury Hugh McCulloch's proposals for contraction, designed for quick resumption of specie payments, won a cordial response from many importers and financiers, who would gain materially from the elimination of the premium on gold and a consequent rise in the market value of government bonds. Many businessmen longed for the currency stability they believed resumption would bring. But McCulloch met with warnings and protests from other important northeastern business groups. The Philadelphia Board of Trade immediately warned against hasty action, "lest by injudicious measures and rapid contraction," the people's interests should be sacrificed. A few weeks later, the *Commercial and Financial Chronicle,* a firm advocate of hard money, was forced to admit: "There is little doubt that the depression in public confidence, of which a proof will be found in our account of the week's fluctuation in the Stock Market, is closely connected with the anticipated effects of the contraction movement of the Secretary of the Treasury."

Although only a moderate amount of currency was taken out of circulation, businessmen continued to fear that goods bought at high prices with inflated Greenbacks might have to be sold at much lower prices if McCulloch were allowed to proceed with contraction. Wholesale prices fell sharply after January, 1866, confirming their fears. As general price depreciation continued through 1866 and 1867, businessmen's objections to contraction became increasingly loud and widespread. The Commercial Exchange of Philadelphia adopted a resolution in January, 1867, "That premature resumption will prove a curse and not a blessing." A vice president of the New York Chamber of Commerce, who approved contraction, recalled "living in the midst of the clamor against that process, where almost every man I met was denouncing the Secretary and predicting ruin upon all the interests of the country unless the policy was discontinued."

Opposition to McCulloch's policy spread to Congress, where Representative William D. Kelley of Pennsylvania called it the "road to bankruptcy." Finally, in January, 1868, Senator John Sherman of Ohio introduced legislation to end contraction. "We hear the complaint from all parts of the country," he said, "from all branches of industry . . . that industry for some reason is paralyzed and that trade and enterprise are not so well rewarded as they were. Many, perhaps erroneously, attribute all this to the contraction of the currency."

Passage of Sherman's measure, however, did not end the conflict among northeastern businessmen over currency. Most seem to have favored a stable money supply, and to have opposed currency expansion and quick resumption alike. Many of the more conservative bankers, importers, and merchants, however, continued to support an early return to specie payments. There was also an influential and vocal group of businessmen which persistently called for currency inflation. This last group found adherents among those manufacturers and merchants who sought to take advantage of great postwar demand for their products, but who had difficulty obtaining capital for plant and inventory expansion, even at extremely high interest rates. Many of those who borrowed large sums for investments in factories, mines, and railroads, were apt to favor currency expansion, which they believed would lower interest rates, raise prices, and make debts easier to pay. Radical Senator Sprague, for example, in control of a Rhode Island empire of factories, real estate, utilities, and banks, complained to the Senate that "The interest paid by the borrower today is just double what it was at the close of the War." He placed the blame on "the power centralized in New York."

It is significant that Jay Cooke, once an ardent hard money man, became something of an inflationist after he borrowed millions to build the Northern Pacific, and saw his corporation become a huge land speculator through government grants. In a letter to his brother and partner, written in 1868, Cooke called for moderate currency expansion which would keep pace "with the new habits and enlarged area of Country." "Why," he asked, "should this Grand and Glorious Country be stunted and dwarfed—its activities chilled and its very life blood curdled by these miserable 'hard coin' theories—the musty theories of a bygone age?"

Pennsylvania iron and steel men, through their representatives and periodicals, led eastern demands for an increased supply of currency. Their industry was expanding rapidly behind high tariff walls, stimulated by the postwar spurt in railroad building. Iron manufacturer Thaddeus Stevens was a leader in congressional schemes to inflate the currency. Both Stevens and Kelley of Pennsylvania supported textile manufacturer Benjamin F. Butler's resolution to pay the wartime bonds in paper rather than gold. Representative Daniel J. Morrell, a bank president as well as former general manager of the giant Cambria Iron Works in Pennsylvania, called for more circulation, and contended that under a program of inflation "Capital would be less valuable, and a larger share of the increase in wealth would go to the enterprise and labor which created it." Pennsylvania iron and steel periodicals took up the fight against the bankers. "In the seaboard cities," said *Iron Age* in 1867, "the money power seeks to attain a position of irresistible control, and to subdue and subordinate to itself all the interests of industry." The lines of battle were perhaps drawn more succinctly and cogently in a speech by Representative Kelley in January, 1867. "The contest," he said, "is between the creditor and the debtor class—the men of investments and the men of enterprise."

The issue, however, was not as simple as Kelley put it. Most foreign goods were paid for with gold, not Greenbacks. Customs duties were also payable in gold. As long as specie payments could be postponed, the premium on gold would remain. In the early postwar years, the premium fluctuated between 30 and 40 per cent. The effect was to raise the cost of foreign goods about one third above what their cost would be if specie resumption should occur. Monetary inflation would tend to raise the premium and consequently the price of imports even higher. This fact was not lost on the Pennsylvanians. As early as 1863, the Philadelphia Board of Trade noted that the "premium on foreign exchange adds greatly to tariff and transportation costs." In 1864, Samuel J. Reeves, iron manufacturer and chairman of the executive committee of the American Iron and Steel Association, wrote the Commissioner of Internal Revenue: "The constant advance in the price of gold has acted as so much protection to the home manufacturer above the duty. . . . The iron manufacture now finds its safety only in the high cost of gold; what is to become of it when there will be no premium on gold?" The answer, so far as many iron manufacturers were concerned, was to retain the premium on gold.

The significance of the Pennsylvanians' currency policies was obvious to importers, financiers, and many manufacturers in New York and New England. Most of these favored hard money and low tariffs. The Boston Board of Trade's "Wool Report" for 1863 noted the effect of the gold premium on the price of wool. New York merchants protested that the high price of gold seriously discouraged imports, and the city's Chamber of Commerce adopted a resolution charging that "Powerful interests are striving to perpetuate the existing depreciation of the currency."

When contraction was abruptly ended and tariff reform failed, in 1867–1868, some businessmen in New York and New England felt that the government's policies were falling under the control of high tariff and paper money men. On the other hand, Henry C. Carey, spokesman for Pennsylvania protectionists, charged that New England, aided by New Yorkers, was attempting to create a monopoly in money and manufacturing. One instrument of the monopolists, said Carey, was a low tariff, which New England manufacturers could afford because of their low interest charges and modern machinery, and which they used to ruin domestic competition and to obtain cheap foreign raw materials to aid New England producers. A second instrument, he continued, was the banking system—"a great money monopoly for the especial benefit of the

Trading States." Even with this monopoly, Carey complained, the traders wished to contract the currency, further reducing the pittance allowed Pennsylvania and further raising interest charges manufacturers would have to pay. Either the New Englanders would change their ways, he warned, or they would be compelled to do so by a combination of southern, western, and middle states, in which Pennsylvania would take the lead. In reply, cotton manufacturer Edward Atkinson "rejoiced" at this analysis of New England's advantage, and assured Carey that henceforth the New England representatives would support the low tariff and hard money policies even more strongly. Instead of fearing the threatened combination of sections under Pennsylvania's leadership against those policies, he prophesied that New England would join with the South and the West in promoting them.

Both Carey and Atkinson overstated the unity of New England manufacturers, oversimplified the varied and conflicting interests in the West, and conjectured about the probable political and economic alignments of the postwar South. Nevertheless, both were more realistic than historians who have explained northeastern leadership of Radical Reconstruction in terms of a unified northeastern business interest anxious to keep the South out of the Union in order to protect high tariffs and hard money.

Nor can the direction and support which northeastern representatives gave to Radical Reconstruction be accurately explained as an attempt to "make easy the road for northern economic penetration and exploitation of the South." Few important northeastern capitalists had any desire to place their money in a war-torn, unsettled region. Eventually, northerners invested huge sums in southern factories, mines, railroads, and real estate; but it is significant that only a small number did so as long as Radicals controlled southern state legislatures.

Many southern leaders and periodicals recognized the need for northern capital after the Civil War, and numerous cordial invitations were extended. That such invitations were futile was obvious to businessmen, North and South. "We want capital attracted to the South," said the *Commercial and Financial Chronicle* of New York City, "and this cannot be, so long as the States are under semi-military rule." And from the South *De Bow's Review* echoed, "It is idle to ask capital to venture until order is restored." South Carolina exempted manufacturers from all state and local taxation, but failed to attract northern capital partly because of the uncertainties of Reconstruction. Thomas W. Conway, a former Freedmen's Bureau official, who toured the North in 1866 trying to induce businessmen to make southern investments, reported to the New York Chamber of Commerce, which had encouraged his mission: "The substantial men met by me in all parts of the country are sick of the delay in regard to the settlement of our national political difficulties." Until such settlement occurred, he predicted, there would be continued uncertainty and violence in the South, and poor prospects for northern investment.

Even Pennsylvania's Representative William D. Kelley, who was both a Radical leader and an enthusiastic advocate of northern investments in the postwar South, soon found that Radical Reconstruction interfered with southern industrial growth. In March, 1868, Kelley demanded immediate readmission of Alabama—a potential economic paradise, he said, whose wealth was "paralyzed" while Reconstruction ran its violent course. Thaddeus Stevens, less interested in southern industrial development than was Kelley, fought against his colleague's haste, insisting that Alabama must first guarantee the suffrage rights of Negroes.

New England cotton manufacturers, dealers, and shippers feared that northerners' refusal to send their capital south would result in an insufficient cotton crop. Edward S. Tobey, Boston cotton merchant and manufacturer, recommended that the Freedmen's Bureau be authorized to take over the role of private capital in organizing Negro labor for cotton cultivation. The South's deficiency of capital, Tobey told the Boston Board of Trade in a famous speech in November, 1865, was proved by "frequent applications from Southern men to Northern capitalists to invest in cotton lands at low prices." It would be ideal if private investors could supply this want; but capital, Tobey observed, "is seldom placed by its possessors where society is disorganized and life and property comparatively unprotected by a stable and efficient government." The Board approved Tobey's suggestion.

A few months after Tobey's speech, however, the New Englanders' plans were changed by a sudden shift in the cotton market. The southern cotton crop was larger than expected. Furthermore, the English, with new machinery and methods for manufacturing with cheap Indian Surat cotton, had become increasingly less dependent upon American producers. New England manufacturers and dealers were caught with large supplies of cotton as the price dropped almost 40 per cent in the first four months of 1866. The momentary interest New England businessmen had shown in reconstruction legislation dropped with the price of cotton. The Boston Board of Trade's "Review of the Boston Market for the Year 1867," declared: "Business men, generally, are loud in their complaints against the course of legislation for two years past. Important interests have been neglected by Congress, and too much time has been wasted on questions which only led to discord and bad feeling in the different branches of the Government.

Most large northern investors, instead of being concerned over the difficulties of investing in the South, turned their attention to the many lucrative opportunities elsewhere—in Minnesota timberlands, Michigan iron and copper mines, Pennsylvania coal and oil, and railroads in almost every state. Significantly, the Pennsylvania Railroad, with abundant capital and great influence in Congress, did not attempt to create its "Southern empire" until Radical Reconstruction was nearing its conclusion. Until 1871, the Pennsylvania preferred to take advantage of investment opportunities in the Northwest. When Thomas A. Scott, who guided the railroad's expansion, decided to move south, he dealt with Conservative governors and legislators in the South as successfully as he had with Democrats and Republicans in the North and West.

Only one important northeastern business group was strongly attracted by investment opportunities in the South immediately after the War: New York financiers, the true "masters of capital," who had long-standing commercial ties with the South, and had sufficient funds to risk large amounts in a turbulent area. New York merchants, shippers, and financiers were as interested as Bostonians in large postwar cotton crops, but they emphatically disagreed with the Boston proposal to use the Freedmen's Bureau to grow cotton. When Tobey's plan was put before the executive committee of the New York Chamber of Commerce, the committee reported: "Our best reliance for attaining the desired end is to present to capitalists this most inviting field."

Insofar as northern capital was invested in southern railroads, both before and immediately after the War, most of it was provided by New Yorkers. A recent study shows, for example, that of some 280 directors of 25 major southern lines in 1867–1868 only 11 were northerners, and 10 of these were from New York. Two important New York investors in southern railroads were elected to Congress and were thus in a position to speak publicly about reconstruction legislation. One of the two was William E. Dodge, metal importer, iron manufacturer, land speculator, railroad investor, and president of the New York Chamber of Commerce; the other was William W. Phelps, director of four large banks and eight railroads. The evidence suggests that the opinions these men expressed of Radical Reconstruction were typical of those held by New York's financial leaders.

When Thaddeus Stevens's bill for dividing the South into military districts reached the floor of the House in January, 1867, Dodge voted against it; and in explaining his vote he told his Republican colleagues: "I claim to be as loyal as any other man . . . [but] if these southern states are still to be kept year after year in this state of disquietude we at the North, sympathizing with them in our social and business relations, must to a certain extent suffer with them." Furthermore, said Dodge, businessmen believed that this bill would result in continued high taxation to support an army of occupation in 10 states. And in the debate on Butler's civil rights bill in 1875, Phelps—one of three Republicans to vote against it in the House—expressed sentiments long held in the New York financial community. "You are trying to do," he said, "what it seems to me this House everlastingly tries in one form or another to do—to legislate against human nature. You are trying to legislate against human prejudice, and you cannot do it. . . . Let us end this cruel policy."

Many New York financiers made public their support of President Andrew Johnson in his battle against the Radicals. When Johnson vetoed the bill for the continuation of the Freedmen's Bureau, in February, 1866, a mass meeting to celebrate the veto was arranged by the city's business leaders, and a committee was sent to Washington to offer the President New York's aid. Among those on the committee were Moses Taylor, dean of New York bankers, and William B. Astor, known as the "landlord of New York." Six months later, when Johnson visited New York as part of his "swing around the circle," a grand dinner was given for him at Delmonico's. Chairman of arrangements was Alexander T. Stewart, the "dry goods king"; treasurer for the dinner was Henry Clews, probably second only to Jay Cooke as a dealer in government bonds, and second to none as a dealer in southern railroad securities. A large number of New York's leading businessmen attended the dinner. This was followed on September 17, 1866, by a giant National Union celebration to demonstrate the city's support of the President at the height of his crucial campaign against the Radicals. The reception committee for this impressive meeting included Stewart, Taylor, Clews, Edwards Pierrepont, and August Belmont. Among those who gave public notice of their approval of Johnson's policies by allowing their names to be listed as vice presidents of the meeting were such well-known financiers as William H. Aspinwall, Cornelius Vanderbilt, John J. Cisco, and Henry Grinnell, as well as numerous important merchants and manufacturers.

Similar indications of support or approval of the presidential reconstruction program rather than that of Congress also came from the New York Chamber of Commerce and from the financial press. In 1866 the Chamber of Commerce adopted a resolution, introduced by the banker brother of Radical leader Roscoe Conkling, which expressed the hope that Reconstruction "may be everywhere signalized by magnanimity and clemency and that it may nowhere be stained by a single act which will be condemned as needlessly harsh or revengeful." A copy of this resolution was sent to Washington as encouragement to the President. As early as July, 1865, *Hunt's Merchants' Magazine* and the *Commercial and Financial Chronicle*—two of the leading business journals of the period— had applauded Johnson's program for the speedy restoration of the seceded states. As the Radicals gathered their forces in the fall of 1865, the *American Railroad Journal* announced that Reconstruction "is going on as well as could be hoped. The President . . . sets the example of kindness and benignity and a large majority of both parties . . . are evidently disposed to support his policy." And in January, 1866, the *Journal of Commerce* proclaimed its support of Johnson.

From evidence such as this, the reconstruction program of the Radicals cannot be explained as an organized attempt by the business interests of the Northeast either to preserve and promote their own economic advantages or to obtain protection for economic exploitation of the South. Actually, northeastern businessmen had no unified economic program to promote. Important business groups within the region opposed each other on almost every significant economic question, and this lack of a common interest was likewise reflected in the economic views of Radical congressmen. Thaddeus Stevens, for example, dominant Radical leader in the House, was a fervent protectionist and a proponent of paper money inflation; Charles Sumner, Senate Radical leader, spoke and voted for lower tariff schedules and for resumption of specie payments. With both the businessmen and the legislators thus divided on economic issues, and with the New York merchants and financiers—who were in a position to gain most from economic exploitation of the South—definitely critical of the Radicals' program, it seems clear that factors other than the economic interests of the Northeast must be used to explain the motivation and aims of Radical Reconstruction.

FOR FURTHER READING: The prevalence of economic motives among Northerners engaged in the Reconstruction of the South is stressed in Howard K. Beale, *The Critical Year. A Study of Andrew Johnson and Reconstruction* (Cambridge, 1930), C. Vann Woodward, *Reunion and Reaction, the Compromise of 1877 and the End of Reconstruction* (New York, 1951), and George R. Bentley, *A History of the Freedmen's Bureau* (Philadelphia, 1955). Greater emphasis on non-economic factors during Reconstruction is placed by Francis Simkins and Robert H. Woody, *South Carolina during Reconstruction* (Chapel Hill, 1932), Francis Simkins, *The South, Old and New* (New York, 1947), and E. Merton Coulter, *The South During Reconstruction* (Baton Rouge, 1947).

18. *Transportation, 1865–1914*

PROBLEM: *Was the Federal policy of land grants to railroads desirable?*

Few economic issues aroused as much controversy in the half century after the Civil War as public policy toward railroads. Especially acrimonious was the dispute over land grants to the carriers made by local, state, and national governments. Some historians, and many railway officials, argued persistently that the effects of such aid have been exaggerated. Colonel Robert S. Henry, an official of the Association of American Railroads, argues persuasively for this point of view. Henry notes that the amount of land actually conveyed by various governmental authorities has been greatly overestimated in amount as well as in value. Moreover, many of the carriers performed valuable services in return, while others received no land grants at all. Yet, a large group of economic historians, of whom David M. Ellis is representative, takes issue with these assertions. Ellis feels that Federal aid to railways was far in excess of actual construction costs, and only enriched a few favored individuals and corporations. Certainly the two selections below delineate some of the most important arguments that need to be considered in relation to this problem. They also raise broader questions. What were the advantages of Federal land grants to railways? What alternatives were available to Congress to encourage extension of the rail network? What are the proper functions of government in relation to the transportation system?

The Railroad Land Grant Legend in American History Texts

ROBERT S. HENRY

In 1850, the United States government had a public domain of approximately 1,400,000,000 acres, vacant, unoccupied, and, for lack of transportation, largely unusable and unsalable. Between that year and the end of 1871, the government undertook to use a portion of this land to encourage and assist the building of railroads in vacant or sparsely settled sections, in the same way in which previously it had aided the building of wagon roads and canals. The resulting series of transactions came to be known as the Federal railroad land grants, a subject frequently mentioned in high school and college texts which are the first, last, and only works on the history of their country read by many, if not most, Americans. This paper is the result of an examination of the treatment of the Federal land grant transactions in thirty-seven representative texts.

Since the treatment of a subject of this sort in such works must be brief, and even, in a sense, incidental, accuracy both as to the essential facts themselves and as to their place and proportion in the whole setting becomes all the more important. This inquiry is directed, therefore, to these facts and the manner of their treatment. It is limited to the Federal land grants because those are the grants, which, for the most part, are discussed in the works examined, and are the grants about which the most complete information has been compiled, published, and made available.

A balanced story of the Federal land grant transactions requires reasonably correct answers to these questions, at the very least:

How much land was granted to railroads, and what proportion was this of the whole public domain?

What proportion of the railroad mileage of the country received land grants from the government?

What was this land worth?

What were the terms and conditions of the grants? Were they gifts, or did the government get as well as give?

HOW MUCH LAND?

The first of these questions, purely a matter of recorded fact, deals with the amount of land granted to railroads by the United States government. In the standard general work on the subject, Donaldson's *Public Domain*, published by the government in 1884, the total amount of land

Reprinted by permission from *The Mississippi Valley Historical Review*, XXXII (September, 1945), pp. 171–194.

that would be necessary to fulfill all the acts granting lands to railroads was estimated at 155,504,994 acres. The amount of land actually patented to railroads, however, fell substantially short of this acreage, for a variety of reasons—noncompletion of the lines or other failure to comply with the conditions of the grants, or lack of sufficient acreage within the designated limits to fulfill the terms of the grants. The acreage to which the railroads actually received title appears in the annual reports of the Commissioner of the General Land Office, the latest such report showing a total of 131,350,534.

Of the thirty-seven American history textbooks examined, twenty-four make specific reference to the area granted to railroads by the Federal government. Of these twenty-four, one gives clear and approximately correct figures as to the whole area granted, while one other comes within 10 per cent of the correct figure. Two others which do not state the area as a whole, give correct partial figures. In seven works, a substantially correct statement at one place is contradicted elsewhere, either by another larger figure or by a graphic presentation which greatly exaggerates the area granted. Eight others show the area granted, either graphically or in text, or both, as anywhere from nearly one-fifth more than it was, up to about four times the correct area. Five give partial figures only, which either are incorrect or are so presented as to give a misleading impression. Others make neither arithmetical nor graphic presentation of the area granted, but rely entirely on adjectives. In most of the books, in fact, such adjectives as "huge," "vast," "enormous," "staggering," and "breath-taking" are parts of the treatment of the subject of area. . . .

HOW MUCH RAILROAD WAS BUILT WITH THE AID OF LAND GRANTS?

The second, and equally simple, question deals with the extent of railroad mileage, the construction of which was aided by the government's land grants. Such grants were made in aid of a total of 18,738 miles of railroad line—less than 8 per cent of the total mileage of railroads built in the United States. The fact that more than 92 per cent of all the railroad mileage in the United States was built without the aid of an acre of Federal land grants is nowhere brought out in the texts examined— an omission which tends to throw the land grant transaction out of all proportion as a factor in the development of the national network of railroads.

The same tendency to exaggerate the government's financial part in railroad building appears in the treatment of the bond aid extended to six of the companies chartered to build the pioneer "Pacific" railroads. The government made a loan of its bonds of these railroads, in the total amount of $64,623,512. The roads were to pay 6 per cent interest on the bonds and to pay them off. During the long period of development and light traffic they were not always able to meet these charges, but in the final settlement in 1898 and 1899 the government collected $63,023,512 of principal plus $104,722,978 in interest—a total repayment of $167,746,490 on an initial loan of $64,623,512. Professor Hugo R. Meyer of Harvard was well justified in saying that "for the government the whole outcome has been financially not less than brilliant"—but none of this appears in the treatment of the transaction in the texts. Thirty-four of the thirty-seven texts examined mention the bond aid to these Pacific roads. In one-third of the works, it is not made clear whether the financial assistance referred to was a loan or a gift. Three describe the aid definitely as gifts—which they were not. Twenty-one refer to the transactions as loans, but only four mention the fact that the loans were repaid, while three make the positively erroneous statement that the loans were never repaid.

WHAT WERE THE LAND GRANTS WORTH?

One measure of the value of the lands granted—though no one would contend that it is the correct one—would be the cost to the government of acquiring them, which, according to Donaldson, was an average of 23.3 cents an acre. On that basis, the 131,351,000 acres which the railroads received could be said to be worth less than $31,000,000.

Another possible measure is the standard "minimum" price at which the government offered the public domain for sale in the land grant period. This price was $1.25 an acre, though the government was never able to realize even this figure as an average selling price. But if the new railroad companies had bought from the government the 131,350,534 acres actually received, and had paid the full established price, the lands would have cost them $164,188,167.

Still another measure of the value of the lands during the period of the grants is to be found in the Graduation Act, under which the price of lands long on the market and unsold was graduated downward, starting with a price of $1 an acre after ten years, and ending with a price of 12½ cents an acre for lands unsold after thirty years. Total sales in the years 1854–1862, during which the Act was in effect, even under such price arrangements as these, were only 25,696,420 acres.

A more correct measure of value is the one applied in all ordinary transfers between buyer and seller—the worth of the land granted and received at the time of sale. During the period in which the land grants were being made to the railroads, the average sale price of government lands in the land grant states was less than $1 an acre. Applying that price to the lands granted to the railroads gives a value as of the time of the grants, of less than $130,000,000.

It is sometimes contended that the measure of value in this case should be the amount finally realized by the railroads on their lands, after the roads had been built and after years of colonizing, advertising, sales effort, and development costs had been put upon them. There is no more basis for setting up such a measure of value than there would be for putting it at the 23 cents an acre which it cost the government to acquire the lands in the first place, but because the point is raised in some of the works examined, it may be noted that the average realizations of the railroads from their Federal land grants, plus the estimated value of the lands remaining unsold, was put at $3.38 an acre according to one government study, while in another report, including both state and Federal grants, the average is $2.81 an acre. . . .

THE MAJOR FACT

The net result of the treatment of the land grant transaction as a whole is to present to the student a picture of a wastrel Uncle Sam scattering his substance with reckless extravagance, instead of the much more nearly correct picture of a canny landowner using part of his holdings to increase immeasurably the value of the rest, not as a gift but on terms which constituted a bargain shrewder than he realized. As far back as 1859, indeed, Charles Russell Lowell wrote that with the continued movement of troops and military supplies into the West "it may be found that even with the most liberal construction of the grant, the government has not been so 'munificent' as sharp." The same observer noted, about the same time, "that he who buildeth a railroad west of the Mississippi must also find a population and build up business."

purpose of land grants

The "best and highest interests of the people of the United States in regard to this domain," said William H. Seward in the Senate debate on the passage of the first land grant bill, "is not to derive from it the highest amount of current revenue" from the sales of lands, "[b]ut it is to bring them into cultivation and settlement in the shortest space of time and under the most favorable auspices."

To that end, the land grant device was adopted. Its adoption was sought not only by the people of the West and the newer parts of the South, but also by the people of the manufacturing East. In its administration there were errors and abuses, both on the part of government authorities and on the part of railroads, as revealed, for example, in connection with the movement for forfeiture of land grants which reached its height in the 1880's. But the essential thing is that through the use of land grants, the result sought was accomplished. It may not have been the wisest way to achieve these results, though no one even yet has suggested a better way by which a nation long on land and short on cash and credit could have enlisted the driving forces, which, in the short space of less than a generation, laced the West with rails. It may not have been the wisest way, but it worked. The job was done. . . .

The Railroads and Their Federal Land Grants: A Critical Review

DAVID M. ELLIS

A reappraisal of our land grant policy is long overdue. Unfortunately Colonel Henry's article if allowed to stand unchallenged would create a new legend. Certainly his findings as to the total acreage involved, the value of the land grants, and the amount of rate reductions are debatable and warrant careful analysis.

Historians will welcome Colonel Henry's pleas for a more critical use of the land grant map and greater care in the use of statistics. It is good to have underscored the fact that the railroads actually received a total of 131,350,534 acres from the federal government up to 1943. But this figure is far from complete and taken by itself is quite misleading. It merely states the acreage received from the federal government and does not give the total amount of land granted to the railroads.

A comprehensive survey must also include the grants made by the states. Nine states granted 48,883,372 acres to aid railroad construction. These states, with the exception of Maine and Texas, which gave lands from their own public domain, turned over lands (mainly swamp lands) which the federal government had previously transferred to them. To ignore these grants on the ground that the railroads receiving them were not obliged to extend rate concessions would be to subordinate an integral part of our land grant history to the current controversy over repeal of land grant rates.

Furthermore, the amount of land granted by the federal government itself was much greater than the amount of land actually received by the railroads. For example, those lands granted to encourage railroad construction, but subsequently forfeited because of repeated failure to build any railroad mileage, must also be included. These grants to a score of defaulting roads totalled approximately 35,000,000 acres. To be sure, the companies never gained absolute title, but the government offer of free land stood sometimes as long as thirty years.

The Transportation Act of 1940 encouraged many land grant railroads to give up their claims to unpatented lands still in the process of adjustment. In return for the release of their claims, the carriers were permitted to discontinue preferential reduced rates on government traffic except military or naval property and military personnel when traveling on official duty. With minor exceptions the railroads hastened to qualify

Reprinted by permission from *The Mississippi Valley Historical Review*, XXXII (March, 1946), pp. 557–563.

for this privilege. As a result, approximately 8,000,000 acres were restored to the public domain. For more than seventy-five years the railroads enjoyed valid claims to this land. Only the hope of securing greater revenues from the growing non-military traffic of the government induced them to give up their claims.

In short, the railroads were granted lands well in excess of 223,000,000 acres.

Colonel Henry's discussion of land grant rate reductions warrants careful analysis. He quotes with approval the figure of $900,000,000 advanced by a House report of March 26, 1945. Probably that estimate is as tenable as any that could be drawn up for that date.

The student must realize quite clearly that this figure includes concessions from a much broader category than the original land grant roads. The government derives a greater saving in rates from those carriers which received no land grants, but which have signed so-called equalization agreements, than from the land grant railroads. These railroads have agreed to apply to government shipments moving over their lines the lowest net land grant charges available to the government via any route between the same points. The pressure to secure traffic has been so compelling for our railroads, burdened as they are with heavy fixed costs and unutilized capacity, that they have eagerly bargained for government traffic even though it might barely cover out-of-pocket costs. As a result practically all railroads carry government freight at reduced rates.

Any attempt to estimate the total savings from rate concessions runs into serious difficulties. The records of both railroads and the government are incomplete and scattered. Furthermore, the government and the railroads are in serious disagreement as to what constitutes "military and naval property" for "military or naval use." Most controversial of all is the basis of computation. Shall the savings derived from equalization agreements be included in the total? Colonel Henry answers affirmatively, presumably arguing that the equalized rate concessions are as real as those received from the land grant roads themselves.

The fact remains, however, the equalization rates were voluntarily entered into for the sake of profit. The fact that the Great Northern Railroad accepted lower rates in order to share in government traffic did not make the 39,000,000 acre grant to the Northern Pacific less valuable. It does no good to argue that the railroad industry as a whole has necessarily assumed a heavier burden because lower rates have been extended through land grant and equalization rates. The carriers and the government have never considered these rate concessions as compromising in any way their right to earn a reasonable return on the fair value of their property.

To determine precisely how much of the total savings should be attributed to the land grant railroads and to those railroads which have voluntarily equalized their rates is an impossible task. Certainly an even division would be more than generous to the land grant roads. If one-half of the total savings up to April 1 of 1945 is assigned to the original land grant roads, the figure of $500,000,000 emerges. To this amount there should be added about $10,000,000 a month to September 1, 1945 and perhaps $5,000,000 a month thereafter to October 1, 1946 when the special rate reductions end. Admittedly, these figures on current savings are mere guesswork. Rate savings from land grant railroads, assuming always that they supplied one-half of the total rate reductions, thus will pass the $600,000,000 mark. This figure compares roughly with the proceeds which the railroads derived from the land.

Few will deny Colonel Henry's closing argument that the real importance of the land grants must be found in their effect upon the construction of the railroad net and the colonization of the West. The work of the Illinois Central, the Burlington, the Sante Fe, and the Northern Pacific bears eloquent testimony to the vital role played by the railroads in promoting immigration to our undeveloped areas. But this writer, even though prepared to admit that the land grants were no more abused than other forms of public aid or more ineptly administered than most of our land laws, is not persuaded that Uncle Sam was a "canny landlord" and not a wastrel of his public domain. The long list of delinquent roads, the delays in adjusting grants, the establishment of large timber holdings, the endless controversies between railroads and homesteaders, bona fide and otherwise, and the unfortunate results of awarding alternate sections in the semi-arid and forest regions certainly counterbalance many of the indirect benefits of the land grant policy. The inescapable fact remains that the generation which witnessed the operation of the land grants considered that the evils outweighed the benefits. The historian must therefore focus his major attention upon the contemporary effectiveness of land grants in promoting construction and settlement. The financial "bargain," although pertinent and indubitably important, should not be overemphasized.

FOR FURTHER READING: A cautious approval of federal land grant policies is in Robert F. Fogel, *The Union Pacific: A Case Study of Premature Enterprise* (Baltimore, 1960). Less favorable to the railroads are Paul W. Gates, "The Railroad Land Grant Legend," *Journal of Economic History*, XIV (Spring, 1954), pp. 143–146, and Roy Robbins, *Our Landed Heritage, 1776–1936* (Princeton, 1942). A summary of the various viewpoints is in William S. Greever, "A Comparison of Railroad Land Grant Policies," *Agricultural History*, XXV (April, 1951), pp. 83–90. General factual background for the subject is in J. B. Sanborn, *Congressional Grants in Aid of Railways* (Madison, 1899).

19. *Agriculture After 1865*

PROBLEM: *What were the causes of agricultural unrest between 1865 and 1900?*

One of the most prominent public issues during the later nineteenth century was the dispute over causes of agricultural unrest. Farm groups like the Grangers, a political and social farm organization especially strong in the Middle West during the Seventies, placed the blame on alleged exploitations of middlemen such as railroads, money lenders, and mortgage companies. The Greenbackers, who advocated the issuance of paper money by the federal government to overcome the exactions of private financiers, made a similar analysis. During the hard times of the 1890's another farmer's movement, the Populists, also sought in their party's platform to remedy what they believed to be an underlying reason for the farm depression. The complaints of agricultural reformers found a sympathetic ear among later historians, of whom Hallie Farmer was representative. Farmer indicated that, among other reasons, the difficulty of securing credit, and its high cost, were responsible for the farmer's plight. More recently, however, historians like Allan Bogue have doubted whether excessive charges of middlemen contributed to farm crisis. As an example Bogue examined the detailed history of a Kansas mortgage company and found that its charges were generally not excessive. Whether high interest rates were a cause of the farmer's woes, therefore, is open to question. Both of these selections, however, pave the way for further examination of agricultural unrest during the later nineteenth century. What were the most important reasons for agricultural depression? Why did the farmer's relative share of the national income decline? Were the reform programs of the Grangers, Greenbackers, and Populists well adapted to meet existing agricultural problems?

330

The Economic Background of
Frontier Populism

HALLIE FARMER   *1924*

I. THE BOOM PERIOD

"It is a peculiar fact that in spite of the great increase of population of continental United States from 1890 to 1900 the unsettled area has also increased, principally in the Western States. . . . Extensive, but sparsely settled areas in the western part of Kansas, Nebraska, and South Dakota show a decline in population." In these two sentences one chapter of man's conquest of the American continent is told. It is not a cheerful chapter. It is a story of temporary defeat at the hands of nature, of broken fortunes and disappointed hopes. It is a story, too, of the growing bitterness and discontent of men who, year after year, saw the fruits of their labors swept from them. And, finally, it is the story of a blind, frantic, and often foolish search for a way of escape from the certain destruction which seemed to be upon them.

The period of depression which followed the panic of 1873 served to call the attention of the discontented once more to the millions of acres of land available for settlement in the west. The west needed the population which the panic had made useless and burdensome in the east. The railroads which had built out across the uninhabited prairies were eager for the coming of settlers whose crops would pay freight rates which could be translated into dividends. The speculators were dependent upon the coming of these same settlers for the transformation of acres of buffalo grass into town lots which would multiply their small investments many times. To the widely scattered inhabitants of the prairies new settlers implied neighbors, better roads, more schools, good government, and many other things which would be possible with a larger population to share the burden of taxation. . . .

[An] important result of the advertising which the western states received was the rush of eastern capital into this region. With the return of prosperity after the panic of 1873 the supply of money in the east once more became equal to the demand and interest rates declined. Eastern capitalists seeking greater returns upon their investments found a fertile field in the west, where there was a crying need for money. Every new farmer required money to stock his farm and put in his crops. Every new county must have a courthouse and a jail. Every new school district must have a new schoolhouse and the old districts must have

Reprinted by permission from *The Mississippi Valley Historical Review*, X (March, 1924), pp. 406–427.

larger schools to accommodate the increased population. Cities must have sewers, paved streets, water plants, and electric plants. There must be roads and bridges and, above all, there must be railroads over which the ever-increasing harvests might find their way to the eastern markets. It was to meet these needs that eastern capital turned to the three most productive lines of investment—mortgages, municipal bonds, and railroad securities.

Mortgages offered a field for the small investor. They could be had in small amounts and the interest rates were high, from six to ten per cent on real estate and from ten to eighteen per cent on chattel mortgages. Into this field the eastern people with small means poured their scanty savings. Massachusetts loans to western farmers amounted to eight or twelve million dollars annually. New Hampshire had $25,000,000 invested in western mortgages in 1889. Eastern states found it necessary to pass laws for the examining and licensing of western investment companies in order to protect individuals who were being induced to withdraw their deposits from savings banks and invest them in western securities. In spite of these precautions much eastern money found its way to the west. Competition existed not between borrowers but between lenders. "I found drafts, money orders, and currency heaped on my desk every morning," said the secretary of a western loan company. "I could not loan the money as fast as it came in." The manager of another company stated that "during many months of 1886 and 1887 we were unable to get enough mortgages for the people of the East who wished to invest in that kind of security. My desk was piled high every morning with hundreds of letters each enclosing a draft and asking me to send a farm mortgage from Kansas or Nebraska." . . .

By 1887 the boom had reached its height. The west was overpopulated. Capital had been invested there far beyond the amount upon which immediate return could be expected. The burden of debt, private and public, was heavy. Furthermore, eastern capital, suffering from losses due to fraud which was becoming more and more common in the west, was growing increasingly distrustful of western investment. All evidence pointed to the fact that the day of reckoning was at hand.

II. THE COLLAPSE OF THE BOOM

The break which was inevitable in view of conditions in the west came in 1887. In Kansas the reaction was sudden and violent. In Nebraska and Dakota the disappearance of prosperity was more gradual, but in all the states prosperity vanished and did not return for a decade.

The immediate cause of the collapse of the boom was drought, which resulted in widespread crop failure. The western halves of Kansas, Nebraska, and South Dakota lie within the semiarid belt. In this region rainfall is uncertain and hot winds burn up the crops when rainfall is meager. To produce a crop the rainfall must be from eighteen to twenty inches, well distributed throughout the growing season. . . .

With the loss of his crops year after year and the impossibility of marketing what he did produce at a living profit, starvation seemed imminent for the western farmer. When he turned to the loan companies which had been so eager to force money upon him a few years earlier the farmer found that money was difficult to secure. The number of farm mortgages placed in Nebraska between 1884 and 1887 was 6,000 and their value was $5,467,362. In the next three years only 500 such mortgages were placed with a total value of $663,889. Only twenty-six per cent of the farm mortgages in South Dakota in 1892 had been contracted after 1887. Eastern investors refused to place more money in the west and much of the money already invested was withdrawn as the lenders became frightened over the agitation of the debtors for relief in the form of stay laws.

Finding it impossible to secure aid through real estate mortgages, the farmer was forced to resort to chattel loans, securing such money as he could upon his livestock and farm machinery. These loans bore higher interest rates than the farm mortgages—many of them from twenty to thirty-six per cent—and made the burden of debt under which the farmer struggled still heavier. During the five years ending May 31, 1895, 539,323 chattel mortgages were recorded by the state auditor of Nebraska. Many Dakota families were prevented from leaving the state when crops failed because their horses and wagons were mortgaged and could not be taken from the state.

The mortgages contracted so lightly during the boom period also added to the farmer's burden. It was only after 1887, when the interest payments were hard to meet and foreclosures began, that the west realized how great was the burden which it had assumed. The mortgage debt of these states equaled one-fourth of the value of the farm land. The debt of Kansas, if divided equally among the inhabitants of the state, would have fastened a debt of $170 upon each citizen. In Nebraska the per capita mortgage indebtedness was $126 and in Dakota it was $110. There were counties in Kansas and in South Dakota in which ninety per cent of the farm land was mortgaged.

As times grew harder the farmers who could not meet the interest payments on their mortgages lost their farms. In Kansas, 11,122 farm mortgages were foreclosed between 1889 and 1893. Much of the land passed into the hands of loan companies without going through foreclosure proceedings, since the contracts provided that the land was forfeited without that formality. There were fifteen counties in Kansas in which from seventy-five to ninety per cent of the land was owned by loan companies in 1895. . . .

III. THE REACTION OF THE FARMER

The turn of fortune's wheel which had given the western farmer poverty for prosperity filled him with bewilderment and indignation. He was bewildered by the suddenness of the change and indignant because there was, to his mind, no just cause for the situation in which he found himself. Losses due to drought had to be borne philosophically, but that his suffering should be as great in the years in which nature rewarded his toil with bountiful harvests as it was in the years of drought was a state of affairs which seemed not only unjust, but unreasonable.

"Who is to blame for this state of affairs?" inquired the *Dakota Farmer* in 1896. "The Republicans say that it is the tariff. The Democrats say that it is the silver question. The Pops tell us it is the banking system. And the poor farmer . . . hears the jumble of opposing arguments and grows confused and uncertain. He is certain that something is wrong, but he cannot locate the trouble. He searches the agricultural papers but they do not discuss politics and he gets no light there. So he concludes that it must be because he does not raise enough and he falls to work with redoubled energy only to be nonplussed with the declaration that it is overproduction that ails the country."

Eventually the farmer worked his way through the labyrinth and fixed the blame. His conclusion, however small the element of truth it contained, formed the working hypothesis which determined elections and shaped legislation in Kansas, Nebraska, and South Dakota so long as the depression lasted. The eastern capitalist, reasoned the farmer, was the cause of all his troubles—the capitalist who invested in mortgages and bonds and railroad stocks, the capitalist who fixed the price the farmer paid for his purchases and the price he received for his grain. It was to the greedy eastern capitalist that he paid the interest on his mortgage year after year. It was to this same capitalist that his taxes went in the shape of interest on bonds. Railroad rates were high that the eastern capitalist might receive dividends. Farm prices were low that the eastern capitalist might reap a larger profit. . . .

"Finance, land, and transportation"—these were three fields which the farmer believed that he must control if he were to live. The capitalist was the enemy he faced. His weapon was the ballot and he fought for free silver, stay laws, and legislation hostile to railroads with a zeal born of desperation. The history of the peoples' party is the history of the farmer's struggle to save himself by political means from the penalty for his failure to adjust himself to economic conditions.

[handwritten margin note:] blamed middlemen

The Land Mortgage Company in the Early Plains States

ALLAN G. BOGUE   *1951*

"The whole trouble with Western Mortgages comes from the loan agents. . . . These fellows are the vampires that has brot [sic] all the discredit on Kansas." So wrote the Speaker of the Kansas House of Representatives in 1891. Twenty-three years later a New Englander remarked before a meeting of farm mortgage brokers, "Of course, in New England, we have a great deal of conservatism. New England is very skeptical about Western investments, because twenty-five or thirty years ago . . . (New Englanders) were severely swindled. . . ." Damned by both chagrined investors and indignant agrarians, the promoters of the western farm mortgage business in the late nineteenth century have been allowed by historians to stand guilty as charged.

The business of lending money on farms in the States beyond the Missouri River was as old as the settlers' title to the land. Settlers found that their private resources must be supplemented by borrowed capital as they labored to obtain title to their farms and then to equip and stock them. In the twenty-five years which followed the conclusion of the Civil War, the business of purveying mortgages to investors situated in the Eastern States and abroad became an increasingly important one. Fed by the rapid rush of settlement into the Plains States, and by the accumulation of capital in the hands of eager investors throughout northeastern America and in Europe, the mortgage business reached a peak of activity in the 1870s and 1880s when land mortgage companies were organized.

To estimate the number of these companies exactly is an unrewarding if not impossible task. More than 150 of them came under the surveillance of the fiscal officials of Connecticut, Massachusetts, New York, and Vermont during the years between 1888 and 1895. Most of the companies were organized in the States lying west of the Mississippi River, but some were incorporated in the central and northern States of the eastern seaboard and a few found their genesis abroad. When drought and low prices combined to spread acute depression over the Plains States after 1887, the mortgage companies fared badly. For the most part they acquired imperial domains through foreclosure and then slipped into receivership. Only a handful survived.

At the University of Kansas there are preserved today many of the

Reprinted by permission from *Agricultural History*, XXV (January, 1951), pp. 20–33.

business records of the J. B. Watkins Land Mortgage Company. Although not entirely complete the collection allows the student to reconstruct the history of one land mortgage company. This article is devoted to a brief summary of the company's history and to a more detailed consideration of the experience and policy of its officials in those aspects of the mortgage business which were most bitterly criticized by the farmer radicals of the Plains States.

THE J. B. WATKINS LAND MORTGAGE COMPANY

After teaching school in Virginia, Pennsylvania, Illinois, and Wisconsin, and graduating from the law department of the University of Michigan, Jabez Watkins established himself at Champaign, Illinois, in 1870. In his efforts to work up a lucrative legal practice Watkins acted as local agent for several firms and individuals lending money to farmers in central Illinois. As he gained experience in money lending he made direct contacts with investors and began building up an organization of local agents for himself.

In August 1873, Watkins transferred his base of operations to Lawrence, Kansas. Although he became a member of the Kansas bar his legal business was subordinated to money lending. In Kansas he found the competition among lending agencies to be less severe than in Illinois; money brought a higher rate of interest; and the lender had a larger number of applicants from which to choose. Watkins began a vigorous advertising campaign in the eastern press to solicit funds. At frequent intervals he visited the New England and central seaboard States to back up his advertising with personal appeals. His efforts were so well rewarded that in 1876 he established an eastern office in New York. Two years later he entered the European field and set up an agency in London, England. Especially fortuitous was his contact with the Quakers. . . .

J. B. Watkins incorporated his loan business under the laws of Colorado with a capitalization of $750,000. For the stock representing this sum he traded 52,000 acres of land, which he had acquired in his northern lending field through foreclosure, deeding, or purchase, along with complete control of the business and its assets at offices located in Lawrence, Dallas, New York, and London. His business, Watkins claimed, was returning a net income of over $77,000 annually. He quoted Jay Gould and James Gordon Bennett to prove that the value of a business with such an income should not be less than $770,000. After its organization the new company still had no liquid working capital, but Watkins placed $100,000 at its disposal. Since he did not endeavor to unload large blocks of stock on the eastern market, he was evidently not interested in promoters' profits. Watkins maintained that he would never sell more than a third of the stock and actually did not sell more than a tenth. He never broke away completely from his original method of selling mortgages, but early in 1887 his company began to sell debenture bonds backed by mortgage paper deposited with the Farmers' Loan and Trust Company of New York as trustee.

In Kansas Watkins at first confined his lending activities to the eastern portion of the State, entering the adjacent counties of Missouri as well. By the mid-seventies he was lending funds on farms in western Iowa. During 1880 and 1881 business was extended into Nebraska and the Territory of Dakota. In the fall of 1881 a branch office was established at Dallas, Texas. Henceforth most of the lending business done by Watkins, and later by the J. B. Watkins Land Mortgage Company, was carried on in Kansas and Texas. During the late 1880s mortgage paper was also obtained in Louisiana, drawn in part on farm and plantation land, but mainly on the unimproved lands which Watkins himself owned.

By 1893 J. B. Watkins had supervised the sale of obligations totaling over $18,000,000. It is impossible to apportion this sum exactly, but some two-thirds of the total was loaned in Kansas and Texas. The greater portion of the remainder was lent in Missouri and Louisiana, while relatively smaller sums were advanced on the security of farm land in Iowa, Nebraska, and the Territory of Dakota. Over $5,000,000 of the total was represented by debenture bonds supported by various types of mortgage paper. During the period of the company's greatest activity some twenty-five full-time employees administered its affairs. The local western agents who, at one time or another, represented Watkins or the company undoubtedly totaled several hundred. By no means the largest of the western mortgage companies, the volume of its business entitled the J. B. Watkins Land Mortgage Company to rank well up among the major corporations of its kind.

Until 1891 the company returned an annual dividend of 10 per cent and by 1893 a surplus of over $500,000 had been set aside. But there were elements of weakness in the business. Profits and surplus were derived in part by constantly revising the value of the company's land upward to parallel the highly speculative rise in land values which was general in the Plains States during the 1880s. Much of the company's operating capital was derived from bank loans. Withdrawal of support by the banks in a period of depression could be painful. In the years after 1887 over 250,000 acres of land were taken by foreclosure as the western "boom" came to an end. Utter collapse in the real estate market made it impossible to realize on the funds tied up in this land. Other companies, faced with the same problem, began to fail as early as 1888. Panicky investors withdrew their funds, thereby reducing the income from commissions. Watkins had borrowed large amounts on his unimproved land in Louisiana and fed the obligations into the paper behind the company's debenture bonds in the expectation that migration into the southwest would soon allow him to sell the land at a profit. Such hope proved chimerical. In the meantime, Watkins, the debtor, was paying large amounts of interest to his company, which stood as the agent of eastern and English investors. The recession of 1891 found Watkins' financial lines dangerously extended. Renewed depression in 1893 forced him to place the mortgage company in receivership in April 1894. Most of its rivals had already preceded it into the same unhappy situation.

By 1893 Watkins was a man of many business interests. In Kansas he owned a newspaper and controlled a canning factory and a national bank, in addition to the J. B. Watkins Land Mortgage Company. In Louisiana he owned, controlled, or managed several development companies, a railroad, and a private banking house. Since Watkins linked his enterprises in Louisiana closely to the business of the mortgage company, it is fair to question whether or not the company can be considered a representative example of the incorporated western loan agency. If we are to believe the Massachusetts Commissioner of Foreign Mortgage Corporations, many of the western mortgage promoters dabbled in other fields. Certainly the operating problems of the J. B. Watkins Land Mortgage Company with which we are primarily concerned in this article were the same as those faced by its rivals.

The Agrarian Indictment of Money Lenders. It is easy to reconstruct the case which the agrarian radicals of the late nineteenth century made against the money lender by consulting a few files of Midwestern newspapers and periodicals.

The Populist and his predecessors considered the mortgage to be a sign of distress. There were few among them who dared suggest that a mortgage might fulfill a useful or productive function for the debtor. But if the mortgage indicated that the borrower was in distress, it represented profit to the money lender. A memorial of the National Farmers' Alliance, printed in the Alliance of Lincoln, Nebraska, in June 1889, pictured the growing indebtedness of the citizens of the country while in the meantime, ". . . there are two classes of men who seem above the reach of adverse financial fortune; money lenders and railroad owners. Of these the former are reaping a harvest of wealth unprecedented in the history of the world."

Agrarian writers devoted much of their energy to proving that the interest rate was high. Occasionally correspondents described rates of interest as high as 36 per cent. Generally they confined themselves to arguing that the use of money was bought too dearly. In extreme cases they asked why the security which was good for a loan at 10 or 12 per cent was not equally good for a loan bearing 5 or 6 per cent.

The money lenders were able to maintain high rates of interest because a highly organized money power had risen in the United States after the termination of the Civil War. The way in which this money power was organized and the tactics which its members followed made it virtually "a conspiracy against the people." The association which the farmers regarded as most synonymous with the organized money power was the American Bankers' Association. In hazy fashion the agrarians believed that the money power was composed of eastern capitalists who employed western agents as their tools. Occasionally a real estate agent or lawyer was admitted to be his own master, but the western bankers and money lenders were regarded alike as proven agents of the money power. The price which the farmer paid for his borrowed money was a monopoly price.

When the representatives of an aroused people attempted to check the onslaught of the money power its agents rallied to corrupt the legislatures. The will of the majority was perverted by the lobbying activities of the few. The editor of the *Kansas Farmer* wrote in 1889: "What was settled by the last legislature was that the combined forces of a corrupt lobby in the interests of money lenders were able to override the representatives of the people and defeat the execution of the popular will." Writing three years later the correspondent of a Nebraska newspaper, the Farmers' Alliance, described the money lenders' lobby as "the largest, best organized, and most shrewdly managed lobby that infested the capital the past session."

As in many lands and at many times the money lender was painted as an unlovely figure. He was a "hyena-faced Shylock" with a singularly unattractive personality. He inveigled the innocent into borrowing money when they really had no need for funds. In the process of making a loan the mortgage agent carried out an investigation of the farmer's personal life and business standing that was little short of a personal insult. Once the loan was made, the money lender busied himself in plotting the downfall of the debtor. In this he was merciless. As one editor put it, "A money lender assuming the role of a philanthropist in his business transactions is about equal to a rum seller preaching temperance."

Shylock was eager to assume ownership of the security if at all possible since he obtained the land for a mere fraction of its value. He was, therefore, little better than a thief. But not content with obtaining debtors' farms at figures well below their true value, Shylock often took a personal judgment against the unfortunates whom he had dispossessed. The borrower might eventually lose much more than his farm.

Operating Practices of the Watkins Company. The history of the J. B. Watkins Land Mortgage Company contributes to a fuller understanding of the catalog of grievances which the agrarian radicals presented. It is often pointed out that Kansas among the Plains States was most severely burdened with debt. The remainder of this article applies specifically to that State unless otherwise noted, but it has obvious application to the other Plains States as well.

It is difficult to arrive at the price which the western farmer paid for borrowed capital. The county records generally show the rate of interest which was specified in the note and mortgage. But in addition to the interest paid to the mortgagee both the mortgage company and the local agent received a commission. Sometimes these commissions were included in the interest rate; at other times they were paid by the mortgagor in cash or possibly by a second note and mortgage. At times the mortgage company paid the local agent his commission; more often the local agent obtained his fee from the borrower. It became customary also to offer the borrower a choice between a high rate of interest and a small commission and a low rate of interest and a large commission. In addition to commission and interest the western farmer paid recording fees and was expected to provide an abstract of title, but such charges were minor ones. If one goes no farther than to the county records it is often impossible to determine which of two farmers was actually paying the most for his borrowed funds.

At no time during twenty years of business in Kansas did J. B. Watkins and his associates charge a uniform rate of interest throughout the lending field. In general the rates rose from east to west as the money lender progressed into areas but newly opened to settlement. The size of the loan, the quality of the security, and the character of the borrower all entered into the determination of lending rates.

In 1874 borrowers were paying a maximum fee of 16 or 17 per cent annually on funds borrowed from Watkins. This payment was made up of the 12 per cent interest allowed under the usury law of Kansas and service charges or commission amounting to another 4 or 5 per cent. Until 1879 Watkins usually reimbursed the local agent, a practise which he never completely abandoned. For a time in the mid 1870s he shared a portion of the commission with some of his eastern investors and until the late eighties paid a commission on the investment funds which eastern agents procured for him.

In October 1881, farmers borrowing from J. B. Watkins and Company in Kingman County, Kansas, on the ninety-eighth meridian, were paying total charges amounting to slightly over 11 per cent annually. These charges were made up of an interest rate of 8 per cent and service charges of 10 per cent. Since the mortgages ran from 3 to 5 years, it was standard procedure to calculate 1 per cent of annual interest as equivalent to a commission of 3 per cent.

Stevens County, Kansas, is located on the Oklahoma border in the second tier of counties east of the Colorado boundary. Here the agent of the J. B. Watkins Land Mortgage Company was attempting to lend money at 11 per cent in March 1887. If he was content with a commission of 3 per cent for his services, borrowers were obtaining money from him for about 12 per cent interest. Two tiers to the east in Kiowa

County the equivalent rate was 10 per cent. Rates were dropping swiftly in southwestern Kansas during the spring and early summer of 1887, but they rallied and began to climb as the season proved to be one of drought. The total charges on the type of security desired by Watkins stood at 11 or 12 per cent in the extreme southwestern corner of Kansas as the year ended. By April 1888, officials of the company had decided that the future of agriculture in western Kansas was highly uncertain. Further business in the region was confined to servicing the loans already made.

There was a drop of 4 or 5 per cent in the maximum charges which borrowers paid to Watkins between 1874 and 1881. In 1887 the maximum rate was approximately the same as in 1881, but it had been held up by lending on lands which were less well improved and more recently settled than had been the case in the 1870s and early 1880s. Some companies had made other concessions as well. Borrowers were allowed to pay off the principal in installments or even to pay off the loan completely if notice was given a few months in advance. Such maximum rates were of course obtained on only a portion of the loans made by Watkins' agency. In the central third of Kansas, where Populism was to develop its greatest strength, the farmer with good security could obtain funds in 1886 and 1887 at 6 or 7 per cent, which with commission amounted to 8 or 9 per cent annually.

Certainly the charges which borrowers in Kansas paid to Watkins' company in the 1880s appear high by present-day standards. But we must remember that the loans were usually small. More than $500 was seldom loaned on quarter sections west of the hundredth meridian. The service charge was usually included by the Populist orator as part of the rate. The same procedure has been followed in this article, but it is not customary to do so when giving interest rates. When comparing modern rates with the rates cited by the agrarians, one should remember that the service charge has not yet completely disappeared from the field of farm financing.

Nor can the factor of risk be overlooked. The population in newly settled areas was notoriously fiddlefooted. The possibility that the lender might become an unwilling landowner was ever present. Without doubt many an investor who acquired title to land in the western third of Kansas during the 1880s and '90s remained unconvinced that the rate of interest had been commensurate with the risk involved in his loans.

Finally we distort the perspective of history if we consider the lending rates of the 1880s by themselves. In the territorial period money was lent on landed security in Kansas and Nebraska at rates that were in excess of 36 per cent per annum. By the mid-seventies the borrower in Kansas with good security was paying between 12 and 16 per cent. By 1891 mortgage companies were hard put to find a safe market for funds in

Kansas at 8 or 9 per cent. Undoubtedly the interest rate lagged behind the falling price level, but this was a normal economic phenomenon. . . .

What of the influence which the mortgage brokers exerted upon the elected representatives of the people in the Plains States? Unquestionably the mortgage men did attempt to influence the legislators. In 1886, one of Watkins' investors inquired nervously whether the legislature of Kansas might not levy a tax upon mortgages held by eastern investors. The attorney of the mortgage company, W. J. Patterson, soothed the easterner by pointing out that there was a large and influential element engaged in the mortgage business throughout the State, whose influence would be thrown solidly against any bill levying on the investments of non-residents.

As the legislative session of 1889 opened in Kansas, numerous members of the House of Representatives announced that they would introduce bills dealing with the credit question. Stirred into action, the representatives of the loan companies met at Kansas City and organized. T. B. Sweet was given authority to take any steps which he thought necessary to check or amend legislation on farm credit. According to Patterson the representatives of the loan agencies generally believed that it would be easy to defeat any adverse legislation in the Senate. Only a Republican-sponsored amendment to the interest law was passed during the session.

Nor was such activity among the mortgage companies confined to Kansas. The files of the Dallas office of the Watkins Company reveal the situation in Texas. In December 1890, Samuel Kerr, of the British and American Mortgage Company, wrote to Watkins' manager in Dallas:

. . . the usual number of harassing measures aimed at money lenders will it appears be introduced at the coming session of the legislature. We were able by employing parties in the swim to defeat or shelve many of those brought forward in previous legislatures.

My own Company . . . have agreed to give their usual subscription of $100 (or more if needed) to secure the services of a good man—or men—to watch the interests at stake and keep us advised. My friends representing other companies have asked me to take charge of any funds subscribed as in former years and to write you asking you to aid the cause. The money will be judiciously expended and an account rendered at the close of the session showing what has been done with it. I hope you will send me your cheque payable to me as treasurer of this fund, for such sum as you may think fit . . .

Although there was an organized effort on the part of the mortgage agencies to influence the course of legislation, there is little evidence to show that this influence was exerted on a major scale. The contribution of the companies in Texas could hardly have amounted to more than $3,000 in 1891. A little entertaining or discreet pressure on key figures is obviously all that could be expected from such a sum. Nor is lobbying in itself prima facie proof of dishonesty or predatory intentions. Some of the money lenders, at least, believed that capital was necessary to develop the Plains States and that a revision of the credit laws would cause investors to withdraw their funds. The mortgage companies were attempting to maintain the status quo; they were not lobbying for severer credit laws.

The mortgage companies were charged with enticing farmers into borrowing money. The activities of J. B. Watkins and his subordinates shed some light upon this charge. During the 1870s when Watkins was endeavoring to build a business, he had examined the assessment rolls of the counties lying in the eastern third of Kansas. From the rolls were taken the names of all farmers whose property appeared sufficient security for a loan. Such farmers soon received circulars advertising the money-lending service of J. B. Watkins and Company. As Watkins' business expanded he discontinued this type of advertising. But only farmers who showed a reasonable chance of repaying their loans had been contacted. Nor were applications for loans ever accepted indiscriminately. At times the number of applications rejected by the Lawrence agency fell little short of half of the total submitted. As the eighties wore on it became less easy to exercise discrimination, but there was still a definite effort to obtain adequate security.

Does the policy of Watkins bear out the charge that the money lender was a "heartless grasping Shylock" ever eager to take his debtor's land? Possibly in the first years of his business at Lawrence, Watkins was not averse to acquiring some real estate by foreclosure. But in the early 1880s his firm wrestled for the first time with the problems posed by foreclosure on a large scale. Drought along the ninety-eighth meridian in 1879 and 1880 forced Watkins to assume title to some 45,000 acres of land between 1881 and 1883. Experience proved that land could be a detriment as well as a source of profit. It was not readily saleable in times of depression and taxes were an ever-present cost. The farms were scattered and therefore difficult to supervise. Since Watkins had pledged himself to assume delinquent loans the interest and principal on loans in foreclosure must be sent to the investors despite the default. Watkins' lieutenants expressed grave concern as the number of foreclosures mounted, and Watkins urged them to take great care that such a situation might not occur again. To the small local lender, exemplified by Hamlin Garland's Jim Butler, foreclosure may well have provided a cheap means of acquiring real estate; to the mortgage agency a large number of foreclosures brought grave problems of financial policy. . . .

The Mortgage Business in Perspective. Important aspects of the western mortgage business have received too little attention as yet.

In the first instance it becomes necessary to make a distinction among money lenders. Few of the land mortgage companies centered their interest on the chattel mortgage business. The chattel mortgage was often used to guarantee the payment of rents on farms owned by the mortgage companies or to furnish additional security when extensions were given to hard-pressed borrowers, but such use was incidental to the main business of lending on real estate security. The chattel mortgage business was carried on mainly by banks or individuals and bore a bad reputation even among the brokers who lent eastern funds on western farms. In 1886 a mortgage broker from New Haven, Connecticut, wrote to his son who was establishing a law office at Topeka: "I do not advise having . . . any Chattel Mortgage man in with you. It would prejudice people against you, that business as done in Topeka is too malodorous." Defending himself against the charge that he was a money lender in the "offensive political sense," L. D. Richards, the defeated Republican candidate for the governorship of Nebraska and president of a loan company, maintained in 1890: "I have never been engaged in the chattel mortgage business and have no mortgages of any kind of my own, but am doing a legitimate loaning business for which no apologies need be made."

The borrower who dealt with the chattel mortgage man was often in dire financial straits and therefore in a weaker bargaining position than was the borrower who dealt with the land mortgage companies. Sometimes of course the chattel mortgage represented an effort to meet the interest on long-term obligations. In some cases the local agents of the mortgage companies dabbled in the field of short-term credit in addition to their work in the long-term field. To their extreme annoyance staff members of the J. B. Watkins Land Mortgage Company discovered that some of the local agents were managing to delay the passage of company funds through their hands sufficiently to use them in the chattel mortgage business. It is unfair to lump the land mortgage companies with the short-term credit agencies when evaluating the credit system of the Plains States. Sometimes contemporary critics did make the necessary distinction, but all too often money lenders were indicted as one.

The key position of the local agent in the mortgage business should not be overlooked. The agent who transacted the local business of the mortgage companies was frequently a jack-of-all-trades. He might constitute any combination of lawyer, real estate dealer, banker, and loan agent. The towns of the Plains States overflowed with gentlemen of this type, endeavoring to secure a foothold and to grow up with the country. Such was the pressure of competition among them that they were frequently very hungry indeed. Originally Watkins attempted to keep their appetites in check by paying their commissions himself, but as competition among the companies for agents became keener he was forced to let them collect their own fees. Suspicion was strong in the minds of the officials of Watkins' company that the charges levied by the local agents were at times exorbitant. The secretary of the company summed up his opinion of local agents when he wrote: ". . . a commission will warp the integrity and judgement of the best of them."

Significant from the standpoint of the mortgage companies' financial welfare was the danger that the local agents in an effort to work up a large volume of business would negotiate loans on inadequate security. Despite the use of traveling inspectors it was impossible to check all of the loans, and in some cases the damage was done before mortgage company officials became aware of the situation. D. M. Sprankle, the secretary of the J. B. Watkins Land Mortgage Company, claimed that control of the business in western Kansas during 1886 and 1887 was completely out of the hands of the mortgage companies. All of the lending agencies had large amounts of funds on hand for investment and were forced to give their local agents full leeway lest they should switch their services to a rival company. Between them the local agents and the borrowers set the terms. It was during these years that the loans were made which resulted in the large volume of foreclosures in the Plains States between 1888 and 1892. When officials of Watkins' agency considered the possibility of expanding business in Kansas in July 1891, they agreed that henceforth all loans must be closed by a full-time employee of the company. While the overburdened debtor blamed eastern capitalists for his plight, the real villain of the piece was often in residence at the local county seat.

One must also examine the motivation of the western settler. Inherent in agrarian philosophy was the tenet that the settler went to the frontier in a sincere attempt to establish a home which would belong to his family from generation to generation. Agricultural distress resulted when selfish interests strove to wrest this American birthright away from the common man. But did the settler actually look forward to long years of happy residence on a western farm? No doubt foreign settlers, who regarded the land from the standpoint of the European peasant, did hope to establish a farm which would remain in their family for generations. But many settlers of American origin had very different motives.

In 1855 the editor of the Atchison Squatter Sovereign gave one of the texts for land settlement in Kansas when he wrote:

We have never known it to fail that when a claim was taken, and a cabin erected that the pre-emptor could at any time sell his rights for a handsome sum, —more than enough to pay him for his own labor. So there is a speculation to be made in lands here by those with a limited capital.

Nor did petty speculation die out with the coming of the homestead law. It is a recurrent theme in the western press.

It is impossible of course to segregate the genuine settler from the settler speculator. No doubt where circumstances altered cases the one was merged into the other, but undoubtedly the settler speculator was common in pioneer areas. Some years ago Professor James C. Malin used detailed census data in an attempt to turn the spotlight of quantitative research on the behavior of farm operators in selected Kansas townships. Had the settlers been dominated solely by their desire to establish a home for themselves, the exodus of farm operators from pioneer townships should have been greatest in periods of economic depression. He found, however, little difference in the rate of turnover between periods of relative prosperity and periods of economic distress. In good times the settlers were evidently seizing the opportunity to turn their bit of the national heritage into cash and to realize a profit from the rising value of land. . . .

FOR FURTHER READING: The validity of agricultural complaints is stressed by Solon J. Buck, *The Granger Movement* (Cambridge, 1913), W. A. Anderson, "The Granger Movement in the Middle West," *Iowa Journal of History and Politics*, XXII (1924), pp. 3–51, and Herebert S. Schell, "The Grange and Credit Problems in North Dakota," *Agricultural History*, X (April, 1936), pp. 59–83. More skeptical are George W. Miller, "Origins of the Iowa Granger Law," *Mississippi Valley Historical Review*, XL (March, 1954), pp. 657–680, Gerald D. Nash, "The Reformer Reformed: John H. Reagan and Railroad Regulation," *Business History Review*, XXIX (June, 1955), pp. 189–195, and Robert F. Severson, Jr., "The Source of Mortgage Credit for Champaign County, 1865–1880," *Agricultural History*, XXXVI (July, 1962), pp. 150–155.

20. *The Rise of Big Business*

PROBLEM: *Were John D. Rockefeller's contributions to the petroleum industry constructive or destructive?*

Few captains of industry in the later nineteenth century aroused as much admiration as well as hostility as the undisputed lord of petroleum, John D. Rockefeller. More than most of his colleagues, he became a symbol embodying the virtues and the vices of the Big Business leader of his era. Viewed by contemporaries as having qualities of either saint or sinner, it was not surprising that later historians also differed in their appraisals of his career. Was he a pioneer builder of a great new enterprise, or was he a destroyer of free and healthy competition? In a critical estimate of Rockefeller, journalist Matthew Josephson judged him harshly for his destructive influence. Without denying his contributions to the growth of the oil industry, Josephson points to his ruthlessness in suppressing competition, his use of espionage and violence to gain competitive advantages, his establishment of monopoly, and his general neglect of the public interest. Josephson wrote during the great depression of the Thirties, but in more recent years historians have appraised Rockefeller more favorably. A representative view is presented by Professors Ralph and Muriel Hidy of the Harvard Business School—leading exponents of the relatively new field of business history—who stress the oil magnate's positive and constructive achievements. The Hidys describe Rockefeller's extraordinary mind, his capacity for detail, his decisiveness, and his foresight and vision. They also point to his ability to select outstanding subordinates such as Henry Flagler, or the useful William Rockefeller. But, above all, they dwell on his achievement in creating a large, integrated industrial corporation, on standardization of products and methods, and on the development of new business procedures. The ultimate

achievement was to create order in the hitherto chaotic petroleum industry. Whether one agrees with Josephson or the
Hidys, both provide arguments that can form a basis for evaluating the work of Rockefeller and Big Business leaders in the
later nineteenth century. What were some major reasons for
Rockefeller's success? Do Rockefeller's constructive accomplishments outweigh his destructive impulses? What are the
underlying assumptions of the authors?

The Robber Barons

MATTHEW JOSEPHSON — *1934*

John Rockefeller, who grew up in western New York and later near
Cleveland, as one of a struggling family of five children, recalls with satisfaction the excellent practical training he had received and how quickly
he put it to use. His childhood seemed to have been darkened by the misdeeds of his father, a wandering vendor of quack medicines who rarely
supported his family, and was sometimes a fugitive from the law; yet the
son invariably spoke of his parent's instructions with gratitude. He said:

> . . . He himself trained me in practical ways. He was engaged in different
> enterprises; he used to tell me about these things . . . and he taught me the
> principles and methods of business. . . . I knew what a cord of good solid
> beech and maple wood was. My father told me to select only solid wood . . .
> and not to put any limbs in it or any punky wood. That was a good training
> for me.

But the elder Rockefeller went further than this in his sage instructions,
according to John T. Flynn, who attributes to him the statement:

> I cheat my boys every chance I get, I want to make 'em sharp. I trade with
> the boys and skin 'em and I just beat 'em every time I can. I want to make 'em
> sharp.

If at times the young Rockefeller absorbed a certain shiftiness and
trading sharpness from his restless father, it was also true that his father
was absent so often and so long as to cast shame and poverty upon his
home. Thus he must have been subject far more often to the stern supervision of his mother, whom he has recalled in several stories. His mother
would punish him, as he related, with a birch switch to "uphold the

From *The Robber Barons*, pp. 45–49, 114–120, 265–280, by Matthew Josephson, copyright 1934 © 1962, by Matthew Josephson. Reprinted by permission of Harcourt,
Brace & World, Inc.

standard of the family when it showed a tendency to deteriorate." Once when she found out that she was punishing him for a misdeed at school of which he was innocent, she said, "Never mind, we have started in on this whipping and it will do for the next time." The normal outcome of such disciplinary cruelty would be deception and stealthiness in the boy, as a defense.

But his mother, who reared her children with the rigid piety of an Evangelist, also started him in his first business enterprise. When he was seven years old she encouraged him to raise turkeys, and gave him for this purpose the family's surplus milk curds. There are legends of Rockefeller as a boy, stalking a turkey with the most patient stealth in order to seize her eggs.

This harshly disciplined boy, quiet, shy, reserved, serious, received but a few years' poor schooling, and worked for neighboring farmers in all his spare time. His whole youth suggests only abstinence, prudence and the growth of parsimony in his soul. The pennies he earned he would save steadily in a blue bowl that stood on a chest in his room, and accumulated until there was a small heap of gold coins. He would work, by his own account, hoeing potatoes for a neighboring farmer from morning to night for 37 cents a day. At a time when he was still very young he had fifty dollars saved, which upon invitation he one day loaned to the farmer who employed him.

"And as I was saving those little sums," he relates, "I soon learned that I could get as much interest for $50 loaned at seven per cent—then the legal rate of interest—as I could earn by digging potatoes for ten days." Thereafter, he tells us, he resolved that it was better "to let the money be my slave than to be the slave of money."

In Cleveland whither the family removed in 1854, Rockefeller went to the Central High School and studied bookkeeping for a year. This delighted him. Most of the conquering types in the coming order were to be men trained early in life in the calculations of the bookkeeper, Cooke, Huntington, Gould, Henry Frick and especially Rockefeller of whom it was said afterward: "He had the soul of a bookkeeper."

In his first position as bookkeeper to a produce merchant at the Cleveland docks, when he was sixteen, he distinguished himself by his composed orderly habits. Very carefully he examined each item on each bill before he approved it for payment. Out of a salary which began at $15 a month and advanced ultimately to $50 a month, he saved $800 in three years, the lion's share of his total earnings! This was fantastic parsimony.

He spent little money for clothing, though he was always neat; he never went to the theater, had no amusements, and few friends. But he attended his Baptist Church in Cleveland as devoutly as he attended his accounts. And to the cause of the church alone, to its parish fund and mission funds, he demonstrated his only generosity by gifts that were large for him then—first of ten cents, then later of twenty-five cents at a time.

In the young Rockefeller the traits which his mother had bred in him, of piety and the economic virtue—worship of the "lean goddess of Abstinence"— were of one cloth. The pale, bony, small-eyed young Baptist served the Lord and pursued his own business unremittingly. His composed manner, which had a certain languor, hid a feverish calculation, a sleepy strength, cruel, intense, terribly alert.

As a schoolboy John Rockefeller had once announced to a companion, as they walked by a rich man's ample house along their way: "When I grow up I want to be worth $100,000. And I'm going to be too." In almost the same words, Rockefeller in Cleveland, Cooke in Philadelphia, Carnegie in Pittsburgh, or a James Hill in the Northwestern frontier could be found voicing the same hope. And Rockefeller, the bookkeeper, "not slothful in business . . . serving the Lord," as John T. Flynn describes him, watched his chances closely, learned every detail of the produce business which engaged him, until finally in 1858 he made bold to open a business of his own in partnership with a young Englishman named Clark (who was destined to be left far behind). Rockefeller's grimly accumulated savings of $800, in addition to a loan from his father at the usurious rate of 10 per cent, yielded the capital which launched him, and he was soon "gathering gear" quietly. He knew the art of using loan credit to expand his operations. His first bank loan against warehouse receipts gave him a thrill of pleasure. He now bought grain and produce of all kinds in carload lots rather than in small consignments. Prosperous, he said nothing, but began to dress his part, wearing a high silk hat, frock coat and striped trousers like other merchants of the time. His head was handsome, his eyes small, birdlike; on his pale bony cheeks were the proverbial side-whiskers, reddish in color.

At night, in his room, he read the Bible, and retiring had the queer habit of talking to his pillow about his business adventures. In his autobiography he says that "these intimate conversations with myself had a great influence upon my life." He told himself "not to get puffed up with any foolish notions" and never to be deceived about actual conditions. "Look out or you will lose your head—go steady."

He was given to secrecy; he loathed all display. When he married, a few years afterward, he lost not a day from his business. His wife, Laura Spelman, proved an excellent mate. She encouraged his furtiveness, he relates, advising him always to be silent, to say as little as possible. His composure, his self-possession was excessive. Those Clevelanders to whom Miss Ida Tarbell addressed herself in her investigations of Rockefeller, told her that he was a hard man to best in a trade, that he rarely smiled, and almost never laughed, save when he struck a good bargain. Then he might clap his hands with delight, or he might even, if the occasion warranted,

throw up his hat, kick his heels and hug his informer. One time he was so
overjoyed at a favorable piece of news that he burst out: "I'm bound to
be rich! *Bound to be rich!*" . . .

In the life of every conquering soul there is a "turning point," a moment when a deep understanding of the self coincides with an equally
deep sense of one's immediate mission in the tangible world. For Rockefeller, brooding, secretive, uneasily scenting his fortune, this moment came
but a few years after his entrance into the oil trade, and at the age of
thirty. He had looked upon the disorganized conditions of the Pennsylvania oil fields, the only source then known, and found them not good:
the guerilla fighting of drillers, of refining firms, of rival railroad lines, the
mercurial changes in supply and market value—very alarming in 1870—
offended his orderly and methodical spirit. But one could see that petroleum was to be the light of the world. From the source, from the chaotic
oil fields where thousands of drillers toiled, the grimy stream of the precious commodity, petroleum, flowed along many diverse channels to
narrow into the hands of several hundred refineries, then to issue once
more in a continuous stream to consumers throughout the world. Owner
with Flagler and Harkness of the largest refining company in the country,
Rockefeller had a strongly entrenched position at the narrows of this
stream. Now what if the Standard Oil Company should by further steps
of organization possess itself wholly of the narrows? In this period of
anarchic individual competition, the idea of such a movement of rationalization must have come to Rockefeller forcibly, as it had recently come to
others.

Even as early as 1868 the first plan of industrial combination in the
shape of the pool had been originated in the Michigan Salt Association.
Desiring to correct chaotic market conditions, declaring that "in union
there is strength," the salt-producers of Saginaw Bay had banded together
to control the output and sale of nearly all the salt in their region, a large
part of the vital national supply. Secret agreements had been executed
for each year, allotting the sales and fixing the price at almost twice what
it had been immediately prior to the appearance of the pool. And though
the inevitable greed and self-seeking of the individual salt-producers had
tended to weaken the pool, the new economic invention was launched in
its infantile form. Rockefeller's partners, Flagler and Harkness, had themselves participated in the historic Michigan Salt Association.

This grand idea of industrial rationalization owed its swift, ruthless,
methodical execution no doubt to the firmness of character we sense in
Rockefeller, who had the temper of a great, unconscionable military
captain, combining audacity with thoroughness and shrewd judgment.
His plan seemed to take account of no one's feelings in the matter. Indeed

there was something revolutionary in it; it seemed to fly in the face of human liberties and deep-rooted custom and common law. The notorious "South Improvement Company," with its strange charter, ingeniously instrumenting the scheme of combination, was to be unraveled amid profound secrecy. By conspiring with the railroads (which also hungered for economic order), it would be terribly armed with the power of the freight rebate which garrotted all opposition systematically. This plan of combination, this unifying conception Rockefeller took as his ruling idea; he breathed life into it, clung to it grimly in the face of the most menacing attacks of legislatures, courts, rival captains, and, at moments, even of rebellious mobs. His view of men and events justified him, and despite many official and innocent denials, he is believed to have said once in confidence, as Flynn relates:

> I had our plan clearly in mind. It was right. I knew it as a matter of conscience. It was right between me and my God. If I had to do it tomorrow I would do it again in the same way—do it a hundred times.

The broad purpose was to control and direct the flow of crude petroleum into the hands of a narrowed group of refiners. The refiners would be supported by the combined railroad trunk lines which shipped the oil; while the producers' phase of the stream would be left unorganized— *but with power over their outlet to market* henceforth to be concentrated into the few hands of the refiners. . . .

In John D. Rockefeller, economists and historians have often seen the classic example of the modern monopolist of industry. It is true that he worked with an indomitable will, and a faith in his star à la Napoleon, to organize his industry under his own dictatorship. He was moreover a great innovator. Though not the first to attempt the plan of the pool— there were pools even in the time of Cicero—his South Improvement Company was the most impressive instance in history of such an organism. But when others had reached the stage of the pool, he was building the solid framework of a monopoly.

Rockefeller's problems were far more difficult than those for instance of Carnegie, who quickly won special economies through constructing a very costly, well-integrated, technically superior plant upon a favored site. In the oil-refining business, a small still could be thrown up in the '70's for manufacturing kerosene or lubricating oil at a tenth the cost of the Edgar Thomson steel works. The petroleum market was mercurial compared to iron, steel and even coal; there were thousands of petty capitalists competing for advantage in it. Hence the tactics of Rockefeller, the bold architecture of the industrial edifice he reared, have always aroused the liveliest interest, and he himself appeals to us for many reasons as the greatest of the American industrialists. In no small degree this interest is owing to the legend of "Machiavellian" guile and relentlessness which has always clung to this prince of oil.

After the dissolution of the South Improvement Company, Rockefeller and Flagler had come to a conference of the irate diggers of petroleum with mild proposals of peaceful cooperation, under the heading of the "Pittsburgh Plan." The two elements in the trade, those who produced the raw material from the earth and those who refined it, were to combine forces harmoniously. "You misunderstand us," Rockefeller and Flagler said. "Let us see what combination will do."

There was much suspicion. One of Titusville's independent refiners (one of those whom Standard Oil tried to erase from the scene) made a rather warlike speech against the plan, and he recalls that Rockefeller, who had been softly swinging back and forth in a rocking chair, his hands over his face, through the conference, suddenly stopped rocking, lowered his hands and looked straight at his enemy. His glance was fairly terrifying. — *alert, perceptive?*

You never saw such eyes. He took me all in, saw just how much fight he could expect from me, and then up went his hands and back and forth went his chair. . . .

Where a "deal" across the table could not be effected, Rockefeller might try a variety of methods of expropriation. With his measured spirit, with his organized might, he tested men and things. There were men and women of all sorts who passed under his implacable rod, and their tale, gathered together reverently by Miss Tarbell, has contributed to the legend of the "white devil" who came to rule over American industry.

A certain widow, a Mrs. Backus of Cleveland, who had inherited an oil-refinery, had appealed to Mr. Rockefeller to preserve her, "the mother of fatherless children." And he had promised "with tears in his eyes that he would stand by her." But in the end he offered her only $79,000 for a *why?* property which had cost $200,000. The whole story of the defenseless widow and her orphans, the stern command, the confiscation of two-thirds of her property, when it came out made a deep stir and moved many hearts.

In another instance a manufacturer of improved lubricating oils set himself up innocently in Cleveland, and became a client of the Standard Oil for his whole supply of residuum oils. The Rockefeller company encouraged him at first, and sold him 85 barrels a day according to a contract. He prospered for three years, then suddenly when the monopoly was well launched in 1874, his supply was cut down to 12 barrels a day, the price was increased on some pretense, and the shipping cost over the railroads similarly increased. It became impossible to supply his trade. He offered to buy of Rockefeller 5,000 barrels and store it so that he might assure himself of a future supply. This was refused.

"I saw readily what that meant," the man Morehouse related to the Hepburn Committee in 1879. *"That meant squeeze you out—Buy out your works. . . .* They paid $15,000 for what cost me $41,000. He [Rockefeller] said that he had facilities for freighting and that the coal-oil business belonged to them; and any concern that would start in that business, they had sufficient money to lay aside a fund and wipe them out—these are the words."

In the field of retail distribution, Rockefeller sought to create a great marketing machine delivering directly from the Standard Oil's tank wagons to stores in towns and villages throughout the United States. But in the laudable endeavor to wipe out wasteful wholesalers or middlemen, he would meet with resistance again, as in the producing fields. Where unexpectedly stout resistance from competing marketing agencies was met, the Standard Oil would simply apply harsher weapons. To cut off the supplies of the rebel dealer, the secret aid of the railroads and the espionage of their freight agents would be invoked again and again. A message such as the following would pass between Standard Oil officials:

We are glad to know you are on such good terms with the railroad people that Mr. Clem [handling *independent* oil] gains nothing by marking his shipments by numbers instead of by names.

Or again:

Wilkerson and Company received car of oil Monday 13th—70 barrels which we suspect slipped through at the usual fifth class rate—in fact we might say we know it did—paying only $41.50 freight from here. Charges $57.40. Please turn another screw.

The process of "Turning the Screw" has been well described by Henry D. Lloyd. One example is that of a merchant in Nashville, Tennessee, who refused to come to terms and buy from Standard Oil; he first found that all his shipments were reported secretly to the enemy; then by a mysterious coincidence his freight rates on shipments of all kinds were raised 50 per cent, then doubled, even tripled, and he felt himself under fire from all parts of the field. He attempted to move his merchandise by a great roundabout route, using the Baltimore & Ohio and several other connecting roads, but was soon "tracked down," his shipments lost, spoiled. The documents show that the independent oil-dealers' clients were menaced in every way by the Standard Oil marketing agency; it threatened to open competing grocery stores, to sell oats, meat, sugar, coffee at lower prices. "If you do not buy our oil we will start a grocery store and sell goods at cost and put you out of business."

By this means, opponents in the country at large were soon "mopped up"; small refiners and small wholesalers who attempted to exploit a given district were routed at the appearance of the familiar red-and-green tank wagons, which were equal to charging drastically reduced rates for oil in one town, and twice as much in an adjacent town where the nuisance of competition no longer existed. There were, to be sure, embittered protests from the victims, but the marketing methods of Standard Oil were magnificently efficient and centralized; waste and delay were overcome; immense savings were brought directly to the refining monopoly.

But where the Standard Oil could not carry on its expansion by peaceful means, it was ready with violence; its faithful servants knew even how to apply the modern weapon of dynamite.

In Buffalo, the Vacuum Oil Company, one of the "dummy" creatures of the Standard Oil system, became disturbed one day by the advent of a vigorous competitor who built a sizable refinery and located it favorably upon the water front. The offices of Vacuum conducted at first a furtive campaign of intimidation. Then emboldened or more desperate, they approached the chief mechanic of the enemy refinery, holding whispered conferences with him in a rowboat on Lake Erie. He was asked to "do something." He was urged to "go back to Buffalo and construct the machinery so it would bust up . . . or smash up," to fix the pipes and stills "so they cannot make a good oil. . . . And then if you would give them a little scare, they not knowing anything about the business. You know how. . . ." In return the foreman would have a life annuity which he might enjoy in another part of the country.

So in due time a small explosion took place in the independent plant, as Lloyd and Miss Tarbell tell the tale, from the records of the trial held several years later, in 1887. The mechanic, though on the payrolls of the Vacuum Oil Company, led a cursed existence, forever wandering without home or country, until in complete hysteria he returned to make a clean breast of the whole affair. The criminal suit against high officials of the Standard Oil monopoly included Henry Rogers and John Archbold, but the evil was laid by them to the "overenthusiasm" of underlings. Evidence of conspiracy was not found by the court, but heavy damages were awarded to the plaintiff, who thereafter plainly dreaded to reenter the dangerous business.

These and many other anecdotes, multiplied, varied or even distorted, spread through the Oil Regions of Pennsylvania and elsewhere through the country (as ogre-tales are fed to children), and were accumulated to make a strange picture of Mr. Rockefeller, the baron of oil. Miss Tarbell in her "History," written in her "muckraking" days, has dwelt upon them with love. She has recorded them in rending tones with a heart bleeding for the petty capitalists for whom alone "life ran swift and ruddy and joyous" before the "great villain" arrived, and with his "big hand reached out from nobody knew where to steal their conquest and throttle their future."

But if truth must be told, the smaller capitalists, in the producing field especially, were themselves not lacking in predatory or greedy qualities;

as Miss Tarbell herself admits, they were capable of hurrying away from church on Sundays to tap enemy tanks or set fire to their stores of oil. What they lacked was the discipline to maintain a producers' combination equal in strength to that of the refiners. The other factors in the industry engaged in individualistic marketing or refining ventures were very possibly "mossbacks," as one of the Standard Oil chieftains growled, "left in the lurch by progress." . . .

Up to 1881 the forty-odd companies controlled by Rockefeller and his partners formed a kind of *entente cordiale* bound by interchange of stock. This form of union being found inadequate or impermanent, the counsel of the Standard Oil Company, Samuel C. T. Dodd, came forward with his idea of the Trust. By a secret agreement of 1882, all the existing thirty-seven stockholders in the divers enterprises of refining, piping, buying or selling oil conveyed their shares "in trust" to nine Trustees: John and William Rockefeller, O. H. Payne, Charles Pratt, Henry Flagler, John Archbold, W. G. Warden, Jabez Bostwick and Benjamin Brewster. The various stockholders then received "trust certificates" in denominations of $100 in return for the shares they had deposited; while the Trustees, controlling two-thirds of all the shares, became the direct stockholders of all the companies in the system, empowered to serve as directors thereof, holding in their hands final control of all the properties. The Trustees could dissolve any corporations within the system and organize new ones in each state, such as the Standard Oil of New Jersey, or the Standard Oil of New York. Nor could any outsiders or newly arrived stockholders have any voice in the affairs of the various companies. The Trustees formed a kind of supreme council giving a centralized direction to their industry. Such was the first great Trust; thus was evolved the harmonious management of huge aggregations of capital, and the technique for large-scale industry.

Dodd, the resourceful philosopher of monopoly, defended his beautiful legal structure of the "Standard Oil Trust" both in a pamphlet of 1888 and in an argument before a Congressional committee of that year. It was but the outcome of a crying need for centralized control of the oil business, he argued. Out of disastrous conditions had come "cooperation and association among the refiners, resulting eventually in the Standard Oil Trust [which] enabled the refiners so cooperating to reduce the price of petroleum products, and thus benefit the public to a very marked degree." In these arguments, learned economists of the time, such as Professor Hadley, supported Dodd. The Trust, as perfected monopoly, pointed the way to the future organization of all industry, and abolished "ruinous competition."

From their headquarters in the small old-fashioned building at 140 Pearl Street the supreme council of an economic empire sat together in conference like princes of the Roman Church. Here in utmost privacy confidential news brought by agents or informers throughout the world was discussed, and business policies determined. The management and responsibility was skillfully divided among committees: there was a committee on Crude Oil, a committee on Marketing, on Transportation, and numerous other departments. By these new processes markets or developments everywhere in everybody's business were followed or acted upon.

Every day the astute leaders rounded together by Rockefeller lunched together in Pearl Street, and later in a large and famous office building known as 26 Broadway. No one questioned the preeminence of John D. Rockefeller, though Charles Pratt usually sat at the head of the table. The aggressive Archbold was closest to John D. Rockefeller. His brother, William Rockefeller, an amiable mediocrity, but immensely rich as well, and long trained in the use of money, depended most upon Henry H. Rogers. Rogers took a more dominant place in the management with the passing years. He is described by Thomas Lawson as "one of the most distinguished-looking men of the time, a great actor, a great fighter, an intriguer, an implacable foe."

These, together with Brewster, Barstow, J. H. Alexander and Bostwick, were the leaders who carried on their industrial operations throughout the world like a band of conspiratorial revolutionists. But "there was not a lazy bone nor a stupid head" in the whole organization, as Miss Tarbell has said. Behind them were the active captains, lieutenants, followers and workers, all laboring with the pride, the loyalty, the discipline and the enthusiasm born of the knowledge that "they can do no better for themselves" anywhere than under the "collar" of the Standard Oil. Freed of all moral scruples, curiously informed of everything, they were prompted by a sense of the world's realities which differed strangely from that of the man in the street. They were a major staff engaged in an eternal fight; now they scrapped unprofitable plants, acquiring and locating others; or now they gathered themselves for tremendous mobilizing feats during emergencies in trade. They found ways of effecting enormous economies; and always their profits mounted to grotesque figures: in 1879, on an invested capital of $3,500,000, dividends of $3,150,000 were paid; the value of the congeries of oil companies was then estimated at $55,000,000. Profits were overwhelmingly reinvested in new "capital goods" and with the formation of the Trust capitalization was set at $70,000,000. By 1886 net earnings had risen to $15,000,000 per annum.

"Hide the profits and say nothing!" was the slogan here. To the public, prices had been reduced, it was claimed. But after 1875, and more notably after 1881, despite the fluctuations of crude oil a firm tendency set in for the markets of refined oil products. Upon the charts of prices the rugged hills and valleys of oil markets turn into a nearly level plain between 1881 and 1891. Though raw materials declined greatly in value, and volume increased, the margin of profit was consistently controlled by the monopoly; for the services of gathering and transporting oil, the price was not lowered in twenty years, despite the superb technology possessed

by the Standard Oil. Questioned on this, that "frank pirate" Rogers replied, laughing: "*We are not in business for our health, but are out for the
dollar*."

While the policy of the monopoly, as economists have shown, might
be for many reasons to avoid *maximum* price levels—such as invited the
entrance of competition in the field—it was clearly directed toward
keeping the profit margin stable during a rising trend in consumption and
falling "curve" in production cost. Similarly in perfecting its technology
the Trust was guided by purely pecuniary motives, as Veblen points out,
and it remains always a matter of doubt if the mightier industrial combinations improved their service to society at large in the highest possible degree. As often as not it happened that technical improvements
were actually long delayed until, after a decade or more, as in the case
of Van Syckel's pipe line of 1865, their commercial value was proved
beyond a doubt. It was only after rivals, in desperation, contrived the
pumping of oil in a two-hundred-mile-long pipe line that Rockefeller
followed suit. So it was with the development of various by-products, the
introduction of tank cars, etc.

The end in sight was always, as Veblen said, increase of ownership, and
of course pecuniary gain rather than technical progress in the shape of improved workmanship or increased service to the community. These latter
effects were also obtained. But to a surprising degree they seem accidental
by-products of the long-drawn-out struggles, the revolutionary upheavals
whence the great industrial coalitions sprang.

The greatest service of the industrial baron to business enterprise
seemed to lie elsewhere, as Veblen contended. "The heroic role of the
captain of industry is that of a deliverer from an excess of business management." It is a "sweeping retirement of business men as a class from
service . . . a casting out of business men by the chief of business men."

John D. Rockefeller said that he wanted in his organization "only the
big ones, those who have already proved they can do a big business. As
for the others, unfortunately they will have to die."

Pioneering in Big Business

RALPH HIDY AND MURIEL HIDY — *1955*

During the years from 1882 to 1911 the leaders of the Standard Oil group
of companies, including the Standard Oil Company (New Jersey), carried out an extraordinary experiment in the management of a business.

From *Pioneering in Big Business, 1882–1911*, pp. 3–5, 24–39, by Ralph W. Hidy and
Muriel E. Hidy. Copyright © 1955 by the Business History Foundation, Inc. Reprinted with the permission of Harper and Row, Publishers, Incorporated.

John D. Rockefeller and his associates successfully created and applied a system for operating a large, integrated industrial enterprise which was one of the earliest representatives of Big Business, to use the phrase popular in the United States. As executives of the large combination those men contributed greatly to the rapid development of the American petroleum industry and through it to the growth of the economy as a whole. Being innovators, however, they also made numerous mistakes and learned only slowly that large size and concentrated economic power in a democratic society required conduct conforming to new rules set by popular demand.

The early life of the Standard Oil Company (New Jersey), generally referred to as Jersey Standard, was marked by rapid growth from infancy to early parenthood. Organized as one of the units of the Standard Oil Trust in August, 1882, for its first ten years the corporation existed primarily as the owner of a refinery and other manufacturing establishments at Bayonne; late in the decade the company acquired a few wholesaling facilities in the same northern New Jersey area. As a consequence of a court decision in Ohio in 1892, Standard Oil executives reorganized their enterprise under twenty corporations of which Jersey Standard was one of the three largest; top managers vested this company with direct ownership of extensive additional manufacturing and marketing properties and also made it one of the holding companies within the group of sister corporations. The Jersey Company continued to perform operating functions after it had become the parent of the entire combination in 1899.

As the apex of a pyramid of companies dominating the American petroleum industry, Jersey Standard naturally became the symbol of the much-distrusted Standard Oil "monopoly" in the public mind. In 1911 the Supreme Court of the United States, affirming that general conviction, broke up the combination by divesting the Standard Oil Company (New Jersey) of thirty-three affiliates, thus bringing to a close one eventful and significant phase of the corporation's history. . . .

By 1881 the Standard Oil alliance had brought into its fold a large segment of the American petroleum industry. Within that industry, previously characterized by excessive competition and harassed by depressed conditions, Rockefeller and his associates had created a giant combination. Beginning in 1872–1873 they had proceeded simultaneously to enhance their shareholdings in firms owning gathering lines, refineries, and domestic marketing facilities. Standard Oil had dominance in gathering and refining petroleum, but the influence of the alliance in marketing was distinctly limited, in producing was relatively slight, and in trunk pipelines was only beginning. This general situation of the Standard Oil group of companies on the eve of the birth of Jersey Standard was the result, by and large, of the policies pursued by the team of men who had formed the combination.

As an early corporate product of the Standard Oil combination, Jersey Standard fell heir to the policies and practices of the men who created the alliance. In the course of working together before 1882, this group of executives had set precedents for the management of the Standard Oil family of firms which were to influence vitally the life of the new company.

The Standard Oil alliance in 1881 was the creation of a team of men. As one man paraphrased John D. Rockefeller's own statement, the "secret of the success of the Standard Oil Company was that there had come together a body of men who from beginning to end worked in single-minded co-operation, who all believed in each other and had perfect confidence in the integrity of each other, who reached all their decisions after fair consideration with magnanimity toward each other" in order to assure "absolute harmony."

As an instrument for carrying out the ideas of those men, the combination necessarily took its character from those who made it and managed it. When they chose to create a new corporation, such as Jersey Standard, it became part of the mechanism for pursuing their policies. Extremely significant, therefore, for understanding the history of the company is acquaintance with the individuals who created and directed both the Standard Oil family of companies and the Jersey Company itself. Scores of men made material contributions to the early development of the combination but only a relatively few ranked as outstanding.

John D. Rockefeller (1839–1937) was captain of the team. By all odds the largest holder of shares, he probably would have been chosen the head for that reason alone. Although not the only person to have the conviction in the 1870's that the petroleum industry should be stabilized, he first formulated the idea that the only satisfactory means was to organize a commonly owned unit on a national scale. Allan Nevins has characterized Rockefeller as careful, patient, cautious, methodical, quick to observe and to learn, grave, pious, aloof, secretive, reticent, inscrutable, and taciturn. Rockefeller considered work a duty, loved simplicity, believed in discipline, and possessed little social warmth except with his family and intimate friends. He had a mind of extraordinary force, great power of concentration, and almost infinite capacity for detail. Although he was willing to make decisions and to act forcefully, he possessed not only remarkable foresight, broad vision, and cool judgment, but also willingness to consider the ideas of others.

In the early 1870's Rockefeller began to delegate most details of management to subordinates and thereafter devoted himself primarily to formulation of broad policy. His greatest contribution, beyond the concept of the Standard Oil combination itself, was the persuasion of strong men to join the alliance and to work together effectively in its management. The remarkable fact was that Rockefeller, while still in his thirties, impressed a group of men, almost all older than himself, with his qualities of leadership. His most arduous task later was to preside over meetings of strongly individualistic, positive executives, while they discussed and determined, usually unanimously, strategy and tactics for the combination as a whole.

During the 1860's and 1870's the closest and strongest associate of John D. Rockefeller was Henry M. Flagler (1830–1913). Of average height, slight build, erect figure, unobtrusive and dignified manner, Flagler was an ambitious, patient, and shrewd man of business. It is difficult to determine where the ideas of Rockefeller stop and those of Flagler begin. They were warm personal friends; they talked over their business before, during, and after office hours. Flagler liked to build new things and possessed a faculty for reducing complex problems to their simplest components. His constructive imagination was as broad and as vivid as Rockefeller's. It was caught by a desire to develop Florida, and into its hotels, railroads, and other enterprises he put some $50,000,000, and more of his energy than into Standard Oil, during the 1880's and later. Yet he left his mark on the combination. Having an aptitude for legal affairs, he was a master in drawing up clear, concise contracts. The incorporation of Ohio Standard appears to have been his brain child, and he helped in the later organization of the Trust. Flagler also participated in many negotiations leading to entry of other firms into the Standard Oil family. His special function was the handling of all affairs concerning transportation of both raw materials and finished products, and he drove hard bargains with railroad managers. Gifted with a keen sense of humor and a feeling of personal responsibility to employees, he won the warm respect and loyal support of most subordinates. Not the least important of Flagler's executive positions was the presidency of Jersey Standard during eight of its first seventeen years.

William Rockefeller (1841–1922) was an organizer, a financier, and a marketer. Some of his selling was done in domestic trade east of Ohio, but after 1865 he was the expert in sales for export. Since these accounted later for more than half of the kerosene sales of the combination, they played a dramatic role in its growth, particularly in that of such specialists in manufacturing for export as Jersey Standard. William Rockefeller was also instrumental in persuading Charles Pratt, H. H. Rogers, and other New Yorkers to join the Standard Oil family. From the middle seventies he was the chief representative of the group in all dealings with New York banks and helped to acquire the short-term capital needed during the early days of the combination's development. As significant as any other of William's efforts was his creation of an efficient administrative staff in New York prior to 1882. At that date he became president of the Standard Oil Company of New York, whose central position in the development of the combination will be discussed later. Unwilling to

limit his interests to Standard Oil, William collaborated with James Still-
man of the National City Bank and H. H. Rogers in promotional and
speculative activities in copper, railroads, and gas companies. Less pious
than his older brother, more lavish in his living and less in his giving,
William also amassed a smaller fortune and has been somewhat over-
shadowed by John. It is certain that William was an able organizer, that
his joviality and good humor made him both an excellent marketer and
warmly liked by his fellow workers, and that the history of Standard
Oil would have been vastly different without his activities. . . .

Policies and practices pursued by Standard Oil executives during the
years prior to 1882 emerged in a variety of ways. Some policies were
evidenced by votes of directors of components of the alliance and gradually won more general acceptance among its members. In other instances
precedents and practices developed into policies over time; no formalized
statement ever indicated the direction in which the leaders were traveling, but in a succession of separate steps they evolved a significant behavior pattern.

Many of the concepts and procedures adopted by executives of the
alliance stemmed from their early experience as small businessmen. Probably at no other time during the nineteenth century was economic activity more freely competitive than in the period from 1840 to 1865. The
customs and mores of the small individual enterpriser became the accepted pattern for almost all men. Naturally enough, therefore, Rockefeller and his associates learned in their youth to believe in freedom of
entry into any occupation, in the sanctity of private property, in the
obligation of the owner to manage his own operations, and in the right
to keep his business affairs secret, a concept dating from time immemorial.
As a corollary of that idea, in courts or legislative investigative chambers
a businessman testified to the legal truth, and no more, a practice still
honored by general observance in spite of critical charges of evasiveness
and ambiguity. Since most markets were local, every businessman could
observe his competitors with relative ease, and did. His habit was to use
any competitive device not clearly prohibited by law. Bargaining in the
market place was almost universal, whether for products or for such
services as the transportation of freight. Posted prices were a point of departure for haggling, and price reductions were the most widely utilized
of competitive techniques.

In response to the chaotic and depressed years of the 1870's, however,
Standard Oil men drastically modified some of their socially inherited
concepts about competition. They apparently desired at first to bring all
gatherers of crude oil and refiners of light petroleum fractions into one
commonly owned unit—to create a monopoly. Late in the decade they
added lubricating oil specialists and trunk pipelines to their list of components to be unified. By means of common ownership in an association

of specializing firms, Rockefeller and his associates created a great horizontal and vertical combination, which, on the eve of the birth of Jersey Standard, maintained overwhelming dominance in gathering, storing, and processing petroleum and its derivatives.

Either by design or through pressure of circumstances, the Standard Oil group of executives had not achieved monopoly in any function by 1881. Strong minority interests in many domestic marketing companies within the alliance, and limited coverage of the market by them, set definite limits to the influence of top managers in that field of operations. In almost all sales for export foreign merchants bought oil from companies in the Standard Oil family and carried on marketing in foreign lands. The combination owned few producing properties. United Pipe Lines men failed to keep pace with expansion in Bradford production, and competing gathering and storing facilities kept appearing. Tide-Water Pipe had thrown the first trunk pipeline over the mountains toward the sea and remained a belligerent competitor. Under the agreement with the producers in 1880 the price of crude oil was set on the oil exchanges, not by Standard Oil. In manufacturing, the area of initial intent for monopoly, the top managers of the alliance had stopped short of their goal. They had refused to pay the prices asked by owners of some plants. Others had sprung up in response to inducements offered by the Pennsylvania Railroad, and in 1882 the editor of *Mineral Resources* noted that the combination had "for some reason" not renewed leases on a number of refineries, several of which were doing "a good trade" and "assuming considerable importance." Thus, by that year some of the firms classified by H. H. Rogers in 1879 as being "in harmony" with Standard Oil had gone their independent ways.

Standard Oil executives employed a variety of tactics in carrying out the expansionist program during the 1870's. After the consolidation in Cleveland and the disastrous South Improvement episode, Rockefeller and his associates first won the confidence of competitors through comprehensive voluntary association. They then brought into the alliance the strongest men and firms in specific areas or functions, a policy pursued, with some exceptions, until 1911. Exchange of stock in the different companies by individuals and guarantee of equality in management provided the final assurance needed to convince such strong individualists as Lockhart, Warden, Pratt, and Rogers that combination was to their advantage. All then co-operated eagerly in trying to unify the remaining firms in refining by bringing them into The Central Association, by buying plants whenever feasible, and by leasing other works. If a seller personally chose not to enter the combination, he usually signed an agreement not to engage in the petroleum business for a period of years. In any case, evidence in extant records substantiates the point that Standard Oil men completely and carefully inventoried all properties and paid "good," though not high, prices for them, including compensation for patents, trade-marks, brands, good-will, and volume of business. In many instances prices for properties reflected the desire of Standard Oil officials to enlist the inventive capacities or administrative abilities of the owners in the service of the alliance. The preponderance of the evidence indicates that Rockefeller and his fellow executives preferred to buy out rather than fight out competitors.

At the same time, when Standard Oil men felt it necessary to apply pressure as a means of persuading a rival to lease or sell his plant, they showed no hesitancy in utilizing the usual sharp competitive practices prevailing in the oil industry during the 1870's. On one occasion or another they pre-empted all available staves and barrels, restricted as completely as possible the available tank cars to their own business, and indulged in local price cutting. They meticulously watched and checked on competitive shipments and sales, sometimes in co-operation with railroad men, and diligently negotiated advantageous freight rates on railways, even to the point of receiving rebates or drawbacks on rivals' shipments. All acts were kept secret as long as possible. The size and resources of the alliance gave it overwhelming power, which was sometimes used ruthlessly, though it is worthy of note that numerous oilmen successfully resisted the pressure.

Within the alliance itself executives also retained many of their competitive habits. Although price competition almost completely disappeared within the combination, men and firms raced with each other in reducing costs, devising new techniques, developing products, improving their quality, and showing profits. Top managers believed in competition but not in the undisciplined variety.

In building the alliance the leaders of Standard Oil adopted a long-range view with emphasis on planning, even before they had achieved an organization to carry such an approach into successful operation. They showed a profound faith in the permanence of the industry, a belief not generally held in years when the petroleum business was characterized by instability, rapid exhaustion of producing fields, and doubts about the appearance of new ones. They wanted to plan and to have reasonable assurance that they were taking no more than calculated risks in pushing toward their objectives. A necessary requirement of planning was centralized policy formulation.

That responsibility devolved not upon one man but on a group of executives. The evolution of Standard Oil's committee system, the hallmark of its administrative methods, started early in the seventies. The original bylaws of Ohio Standard provided for an Executive Committee. Its first membership of two, John D. Rockefeller and Flagler, was increased to three during the consecutive terms of Samuel Andrews and O. H. Payne. Archbold replaced the latter in 1879. William Rockefeller, Pratt, Warden, and Bostwick had joined the three Cleveland members the previous year. At that time the Executive Committee absorbed the "Advisory Committee," which had been established as early as 1873 to act in the New York area. William Rockefeller and Bostwick, its first members, had been joined by Pratt and Warden soon after they entered the alliance. The enlarged Executive Committee of 1878 held many of its almost daily meetings at 140 Pearl Street, New York, and two years later made four a quorum because of the geographic split in membership between Cleveland and New York. Members of other committees . . . started consultations before 1882. If the making of decisions as a synthesis of opinion of a group after discussion is a characteristic of modern business, as a recent commentator has implied, then Standard Oil was modern in the 1870's.

In order to have easily available the best data and advice for making decisions, the Rockefellers and their associates built up staffs in Cleveland, New York, and other points. For the use of executives they collected, evaluated, and digested information on crude oil supplies, costs of manufacture, and markets all over the world. The practice of watching and reporting on marketing by competitors everywhere in the United States, not merely locally, was already inaugurated, though not yet systematized. S. C. T. Dodd was engaged as legal navigator; Standard Oil officials desired to operate within the law. A beginning was made in standardizing accounting procedures.

As the emergence of the Executive Committee and the formation of staffs indicated, the creation of the combination permitted a division of labor or specialization within the organization. As Archbold expressed the development in 1888, the grouping of talents within the alliance permitted "various individuals to take up the different features of the business as a specialty and accomplish greater efficiency than can possibly be accomplished by an individual who attempts to cover all in a business."

In the matter of finance, as in other aspects of operations, Ohio Standard set precedents on reporting and central review. In 1877 the directors of that company resolved that all persons responsible for different aspects of the business should make quarterly reports in writing to the board. Two years later, its members unanimously agreed that annual financial statements should be presented. In 1875 the directors had voted that expenditures for new construction in manufacturing exceeding $2,500 should be undertaken only with written consent of seven members of the board, but that resolution was repealed five years later and the company's Executive Committee was given full charge of all matters relating to repairs and new construction.

Since the goal of the members of the alliance was to maximize profits in the long run, they adopted practices to that end. Emphasis was placed on reducing costs, improving and standardizing the quality of products, and striving for new methods of refining, including the engaging of specialists. Stories about John D. Rockefeller's penchant for eliminating waste and effecting economies have been told and retold. As president of the Acme Oil Company in the Oil Regions, Archbold achieved substantial savings through buying supplies in quantity and by making annual contracts regarding the repairing of boilers and barrels for all plants under his jurisdiction. When he purchased a lubricating oil patent in 1879, Archbold guaranteed the owner, Eli E. Hendrick, a salary of $10,000 per year for ten years in return for the devotion of his inventive talents to Acme. Duplicating pipelines were removed, inefficient plants dismantled, strategically located refineries enlarged, and auxiliary manufacturing units developed, all in the name of economy and reduction of costs. By consistently stressing that practice in every function Standard Oil men moved gradually but inevitably toward mass manufacturing and, more slowly, toward mass marketing.

Gathering information, consultation, planning, and experimentation did not always lead to quick action, but the leaders of Standard Oil early indicated flexibility in adopting new methods and thoroughness in carrying them out. Critics voiced the opinion in the late 1870's that Standard Oil, having invested so much in refineries in the Oil Regions, could not take advantage of the pipeline revolution to establish large manufacturing units at the coast. Almost as soon as others had demonstrated the feasibility of building long trunk pipelines the Standard Oil group took action in 1879. It already possessed a system of gathering lines through the United Pipe Lines. After its organization in 1881, the National Transit Company pushed trunk pipeline building vigorously. By the next year it owned 1,062 miles of trunk lines, only 48 of which had been bought from firms outside the alliance. Its policies, enlarged upon in later chapters, illustrate the fact that Standard Oil was not always the earliest to initiate an innovation, but, once launched on a policy, the combination pushed it with a vigor and fervor made possible by efficient organization and ample financial resources.

Standard Oil's financial policy itself was an important element in the successful life of the combination and its components. Not only were the risks spread by the breadth of the alliance's activities, but profits made in one company or phase of the business flowed into development of another when desired. Early in the history of Standard Oil units short-term loans were often obtained from commercial banks, and temporary aid had to be obtained when the properties of The Empire Transportation Company were purchased. A conservative ratio of dividends to net income, however, was soon to permit the accumulation of funds for self-financing.

Ohio Standard furnished an example for the companies in the alliance on the matter of insurance against fire. On the assumption that loss by fire was a normal expense of the petroleum industry and could be carried by a large unit, the directors of the Ohio Company agreed in January,

1877, to insure property in any one place only on the excess of its valuation above $100,000.

As directors of The Standard Oil Company (Ohio), executives of the alliance also set a precedent regarding the ownership of producing properties. In April, 1878, apparently as a result of a suit by H. L. Taylor & Company against John D. Rockefeller and others for breach of contract in a joint producing operation, the directors unanimously voted not to invest any more money in the purchase of crude oil lands. Six months later they resolved to discontinue all activity in producing petroleum and instructed the Executive Committee to dispose of its properties. This point of view had an influence upon the Standard Oil alliance for a decade.

Quite the contrary was the action adopted in regard to pipelines. By 1881 the Standard Oil group was definitely launched on a program for large-scale expansion of its pipeline facilities and soon exercised a greater measure of control over the function. The combination poured an increasing quantity of capital into building lines; the profits from them provided a cushion for all operations of the alliance. The speculatively minded can ask whether the development of the oil industry would have been more rapid or socially beneficial had parallel pipelines competed with each other during the formative years of the industry, and whether the development would have been as efficient, or more so, had the railroad systems controlled competing lines, as had seemed possible in the 1870's. The point remains that the top managers of Standard Oil determined to keep this function in their own hands to the extent possible . . .

The roots of Standard Oil's policies went deep into the personalities and early experiences of Rockefeller and his associates. Though few of their practices had been satisfactorily systematized by 1881, precedents had been established for many later policies of Jersey Standard and other members of the combination.

By the end of 1881 the general public was hard put to make an accurate estimate of Standard Oil's behavior. Legislative investigations and several legal cases had already elicited an enormous amount of conflicting testimony as to the relations of the combination with both railroads and competitors. Rockefeller and his associates had heightened uncertainty and speculation about their activities by their secrecy in building the alliance and by their evasive, often ambiguous, consistently legally accurate testimony on the witness stand. The very newness, size, dominance, and efficiency of the combination, not to mention its absorption of small competitors in adversity and its avid search for the lowest possible railroad rates, all tended to arouse antagonism. In 1882 S. H. Stowell closed his comments on Standard Oil in *Mineral Resources* with an unbiased observer's puzzlement: "There seems to be little doubt that the company has done a great work, and that through its instrumentality oil refining has been reduced to a business, and transportation has been greatly simplified; but as to how much evil has been mixed with this good, it is not practicable to make a definite statement." It was certain that through combination managers of Standard Oil had brought a measure of order to a formerly confused industry, though they thought that the administration of the alliance itself needed further systematization.

FOR FURTHER READING: Matthew Josephson in *The Robber Barons* (New York, 1934), further develops his criticism of Rockefeller, and similar to Josephson in their outlook are Henry Demarest Lloyd, *Wealth Against Commonwealth* (New York, 1922), Ida Tarbell, *History of the Standard Oil Company* (2 vols., New York, 1904), and John T. Flynn, *God's Gold* (New York, 1932). Allan Nevins' *John D. Rockefeller* (Rev. ed., 2 vols., New York, 1953) is a generally favorable judgment. Studies concentrating primarily on the constructive achievements of the Standard Oil Company include Ralph and Muriel Hidy, *Pioneering in Big Business, A History of the Standard Oil Company of New Jersey, 1882–1911* (New York, 1955), Paul H. Giddens, *Standard Oil Company (Indiana), Oil Pioneer of the Middle West* (New York, 1955), and Gerald T. White, *Formative Years in the Far West: A History of Standard Oil of California and Predecessors through 1919* (New York, 1962).

21. *Internal Commerce After 1865*

PROBLEM: *Have distribution costs become excessive?*

During the last thirty years economic historians have recognized increasingly that their undue emphasis on changes in the production of goods has obscured the no less important process of distribution. Such an awareness raised the problem whether the cost of distribution in the American economy after 1865 was excessive, and so diminished many efficiencies of production. While there is general agreement that an increased fraction of the labor force since 1865 has been engaged in distribution, there is less unanimity concerning its efficiency and cost. J. Frederick Dewhurst and Paul Stewart, prominent students of business administration, found that distribution costs have steadily increased, partaking of a larger and, they feel, excessive share of the consumer's dollar. On the other hand, Harold Barger, a Columbia University economist, on the basis of his statistical investigations, concluded that after 1914 distribution costs remained stable. Both authors are pioneering in an important and as yet neglected field in which many problems still remain. Why have distribution costs increased since the nineteenth century? What are the elements of an efficient distributing system? How can distribution be improved?

369

Does Distribution Cost Too Much?

PAUL W. STEWART AND J. FREDERICK DEWHURST

/939

THE PROBLEM

The idea that it costs too much to distribute goods and that modern methods of distribution are wasteful and inefficient has taken root in the public mind. Every day the consumer is exposed to sights and sounds which seem to confirm this impression—the spectacle of four gasoline stations, one on each corner of a crossroads, the constant bombardment of costly radio programs selling everything from cigarettes to pianos, and the frequent complaint of the farmer who gets only four or five cents of the fifteen cents we pay for a quart of milk.

Quite naturally the automobile driver and the cigarette smoker and the housewife begin to wonder if all the costs of placing goods at their disposal are necessary and warranted. And since they themselves have to pay all these costs, they question so great a toll on their purchasing power. Added to this is the general belief that while invention and scientific management have increased the efficiency and lowered the costs of making goods, the cost of distributing them has remained high.

It is the purpose of this [piece] to describe and measure these costs of distribution and to find out, if possible, the reasons for the spread between the cost of production and the price the consumer pays.

Efficiency Drive Came First in Production

A presumption that distribution is less efficient than production is raised by the fact that the field of distribution appears to have been neglected at the very time that the problems of production were being attacked with such vigor and success. For decades the inventive genius of American business has been chiefly dedicated to the lowering of production costs through mechanization and scientific management and to the elimination of inefficiencies in making goods. The results have astonished the world. It is equally true that the same inventive genius has hardly begun to be applied to the reduction of distribution costs. Originality and inventiveness have not been lacking in distribution but in this field they have been used all too often to persuade people to buy more goods rather than to reduce their price.

As early as the eighties of the last century Frederick W. Taylor commenced his epoch-making experiments in time and motion study and laid the foundations of the scientific management movement. In the years that

Reprinted from Paul W. Stewart and J. Frederick Dewhurst, *Does Distribution Cost Too Much?* (New York, 1939), pp. 3–8, 333–349. By permission of The Twentieth Century Fund.

followed, the work of Taylor and his successors brought revolutionary improvements in production technique which were widely adopted by American industry during the World War.

The attack on wastes in production culminated in the work of the famous Committee on Waste in Industry appointed by Herbert Hoover in 1921. The report of this Committee unquestionably made a deep impression on American industrial leadership. The series of concrete findings and recommendations brought out by the Committee resulted in widespread adoption of improved methods and further lowering of production costs.

Organized efforts to attack mounting distribution costs, however, did not begin on an important scale until about fifteen years ago. It was not until 1924 that the federal government recognized the need for further knowledge of distribution by the establishment of the Domestic Commerce Division in the Department of Commerce. At about the same time a series of domestic distribution conferences were held by the United States Chamber of Commerce. Since then there has been a rapid expansion of interest. The Boston Conference on Distribution, attended by businessmen and educators, has worked for the past decade on the problems that beset distribution. The American Marketing Association has brought about the exchange of ideas and experience on educational and research problems. Schools of business and research bureaus connected with the universities have made notable contributions. Also many trade associations in the distribution field have done valuable work through exchange of information, conferences and educational programs.

Not until 1929 was the first Census of Distribution taken. Before that time only sample studies were available and wide areas of distribution had never been described and measured. Further data on American distribution were collected by the Census Bureau in 1933 and again in 1935. From these studies the first picture of quantitative changes in distribution over a period of time is now available. A rising tide of other literature measures the attention which distribution is now attracting from individual businessmen, trade associations, schools of business, and government departments. . . .

CHANGING ROLES OF PRODUCTION AND DISTRIBUTION

In this connection, distribution is often compared unfavorably with production. Production costs have been reduced steadily, and in some cases sensationally, over the past several decades, while there is good reason to believe that distribution costs have been rising.

Since 1870, for example, the number of persons engaged in the production industries—farming, mining, manufacturing, etc.—in the United States has much less than trebled, while the number of persons engaged in distribution has increased nearly nine times. The whole process of producing and distributing goods is, of course, vastly more efficient today than in 1870. We are now producing and consuming more than nine times as large a physical volume of goods as we were seventy years ago, with a population only three times as large. Taking these figures at their face value, it appears that there has been more than a threefold increase in the output of goods produced per worker, while the amount of goods distributed per worker in the distribution industries has increased only slightly. This comparison is often regarded as a mark of the failure of distribution to improve its methods and reduce its costs. But it is questionable whether this impeachment is a sound one.

Producers, distributors and consumers all played different roles in 1870 than they do today. Every household was to some extent a factory, baking bread, making clothes, canning fruits and vegetables, and doing a multitude of other things which today the consumer expects the factory and retail store to do for him. Distributing goods was a simpler task than it is today, partly because the consumer bought more bulk goods and fewer specialized products—piece goods instead of women's dresses, sugar by the barrel instead of in pound packages, etc.—and performed more services for himself; and partly because specialized distribution agencies have had to assume more of what was formerly the responsibility of the manufacturer. Large-scale production, which is necessarily specialized production, has lengthened the path between producer and consumer.

Before the days of large-scale factory production the producer carried on a larger part of the entire task of getting raw materials first into fabricated form and then into the hands of the consumer than he does today, while the role the organized distributor is called upon to perform is vastly larger. The development of shoemaking from the village shoemaker's shop to the mass production factory of today illustrates what has happened. The shoemaker made shoes by hand in an inefficient way, but he had limited problems of distribution, because the consumer usually came to his shop, was measured for a pair of shoes and when they were ready carried them home on his feet, probably leaving his old shoes to be repaired. To the extent that the village shoemaker did expend his time and energy in selling, rather than making, shoes he failed to distinguish between the two functions. Though a single individual, he played the combined role of entrepreneur, worker, and distributor.

Today the functions of production and distribution are sharply separated. Shoes are *made* in a far more efficient way than they were by the village shoemaker. But in order to gain this greater efficiency, production has to be concentrated in a few centers separated by hundreds or thousands of miles and by weeks and months and even years between production and consumption. Distribution has to fill this gap in space and time and supply the personal service of fitting a pair of shoes to the feet of each customer. And without the system of distribution we have built up to do these things, modern efficiency in making shoes would be impossible. In other words, the spectacular development of modern mass production methods in *making* things is due just as much to the creation of an elaborate and necessarily costly distribution system as it is to the invention of labor-saving machinery. . . .

The consumer himself can properly be charged with a part of the responsibility for the higher distribution costs which have resulted from competition for his favor. The buyer expects—or has been led to expect —from the distributor a multitude of costly privileges and services which cannot be dispensed with until the buyer's attitude itself has been changed.

To say that consumers expect and demand increased services from distributors, however, is not the same thing as saying that the consumer is responsible for the higher costs they involve. To a very large extent the consumer expects more because he has been led by modern advertising and promotional efforts to expect more. He is the victim as well as the beneficiary of modern merchandising.

Moreover, not all of the higher costs of distribution result from increased services. A large part of what is paid for modern distribution goes for selling expense, for educating the consumer, for inducing him to buy one product instead of another, or sometimes for encouraging him to buy something which on sober second thought he decides he did not want to buy in the first place. All of these—as well as the very real services offered by distributors—are reflected in the costs of distribution.

The Costs of Variety and Convenience

Among the costs of modern distribution is that paid by the consumer for the privilege of free choice and variety. So long as tastes vary it will be impossible to standardize consumer goods in the same way as paving-bricks or steel rails can be standardized. It would be far more efficient in the narrow meaning of the term to dress all the men of the country in a uniform of olive drab and all the women in a standardized costume of navy blue. But this economy cannot be gained under our present system. This means that the retailer or wholesaler is denied one of the privileges which has made many modern factories so efficient in production—that of concentrating efforts on a single article or a limited range of standardized products. Unless the distributor offers a wide range of choice among a variety of brands and sizes and shapes and kinds of goods his customers will go elsewhere.

Another cost which is inevitable so long as human beings remain what they are today is the cost of immediacy. Not only does the consumer want what he wants but he also wants it when he wants it, which is usually now. If a million consumers were willing to place their orders and pay their money today for hats or shoes of a particular design and size, to be delivered next spring or next fall, the cost of distributing these products from the factory through wholesale and retail channels could be greatly reduced. Since consumers are not willing to do this the cost of immediacy means that manufacturers and distributors must assume the risks and incur the costs of forecasting what consumers will buy six months or a year hence. All of this means possible losses to distributors and greater costs to the consumer.

Another privilege—and another cost—is that of convenience. Consumers want to be able to supply at least some of their needs by running around the corner to the drugstore or grocery store. So long as they indulge this desire we shall have hundreds of thousands more retail outlets than we would need under a different system of living. Again, retail customers do not like to wait too long to be served. Hence, the retailer must maintain a working force to care for capacity demand rather than average demand. . . .

IS DISTRIBUTION TOO COSTLY? *yes*

Even with all the reservations and assumptions which have been made, the answer to the question posed in the title of this book—"does distribution cost too much?"—is "yes." The research findings prove this in two ways. First they show many features of the distribution process which reveal opportunities for savings: duplication of sales efforts, multiplicity of sales outlets, excessive services, multitudes of brands, and unnecessary advertising—all caused by competitive conditions; unreasonable demands and misinformed buying on the part of consumers; and, among distributors themselves, lack of a proper knowledge of costs, too great zeal for volume, poor management and planning, and unwise price policies. Second, the research findings show how newer distribution agencies, through economies of standardized and large-scale operation, have proven the inefficiency of those which they have displaced; and how other distributors have improved methods and lowered costs through a better understanding of their problems.

Taking the field of distribution as a whole the process undoubtedly costs too much. But how much too much is impossible to say. In other words we can say with confidence that there is waste in distribution, but we cannot reduce it to a percentage figure—as a whole, or in any of its parts. Nor can we say that distribution is more or less wasteful than production.

We can, however—even with the limited statistics that we have—point out specifically many ways in which the costs of distribution can be reduced or its efficiency increased through improvements in the design and operation of the present mechanism. The following . . . summarize the suggestions of the Committee.

RECOMMENDATIONS

Turning now to possibilities of improvement in distribution, there are three general areas where the problems of distribution costs should be attacked: first, consumer knowledge; second, efficient performance; third, legislative restrictions and regulations.

Distribution's Place in the American Economy Since 1869

HAROLD BARGER

The topic of this study is the changing place of distribution in the nation's economy. Has its output, i.e., the services it renders to the consumer, kept pace with the growth of the economy? What of the draft it makes upon the nation's labor force? Has distribution cost increased or diminished with the years? How have the relative importance of wholesale and retail trade, and the kind of merchant engaged in each, altered with time?

Until recently the field of distribution was seriously neglected by statisticians. The first careful surveys of distribution cost were made no earlier than World War I. Nor did the Bureau of the Census attempt to cover this sector of the economy prior to 1929, while the Bureau of Labor Statistics first took an interest in retail and wholesale trade at an even later date. On many aspects of distribution, therefore, we possess comprehensive and readily accessible information only for the two or three most recent decades. Although much scattered data for earlier years can be found, the contrast between the wealth of information available today and the sparsity of material prior to World War I is so marked that we were seriously tempted to confine the inquiry to recent developments in the field. We soon found, however, that what we were able to learn about distribution in recent times was so novel and surprising that we could not restrain our curiosity concerning an earlier era. Which of the trends disclosed for recent years by our relatively reliable modern data, we asked ourselves, also were present during that earlier period?

Reprinted from Harold Barger, *Distribution's Place in the American Economy Since 1869*, (Princeton, 1955), pp. ix–xi. By permission of the National Bureau of Economic Research.

Consider the three leading findings of the present study: (1) Between
1930 and 1950 the fraction of the labor force engaged in commodity
distribution (i.e. retail and wholesale trade) rose from one worker in
eight to one worker in six; between the same dates, persons engaged in
commodity production (i.e. agriculture, mining, and manufacturing)
underwent a relative decline from one-half of the labor force to two
workers in five. (2) Despite uncertainties in measuring output in trade,
we may say that output per man-hour rose by about one-fifth between
1929 and 1949; in agriculture, mining, and manufacturing combined, it
rose by two-thirds. (3) Distribution cost, measured as a fraction of the
retail value of commodities, remained remarkably stable. Since World
War I, for all finished goods and construction materials sold at retail,
retailers and wholesalers have together obtained with remarkable regularity around 37 cents of each dollar of retail value. Of course there were
some variations between branches of trade, and some movement from one
year to another, but no trend is discernible during the past three decades
in the merchant's share of the retail sales dollar.

To summarize: Since the 1920's the fraction of the labor force engaged in distributing commodities has increased sharply, while the fraction engaged in producing commodities has declined, though not so
sharply. Output per man-hour in distributing commodities increased, although much less rapidly than in their production. Finally, the distributor's share of the retail sales dollar showed neither an upward nor a downward trend.

These three findings rest upon census data and similarly solid foundations, and their reliability does not appear to be in question. What can we
discover about similar trends in the period before World War I?

We have ransacked the record. We have pieced together every available scrap of information. And this is our conclusion: The first and
second findings are just as applicable to the period between the Civil War
and World War I as they are to the period since World War I. The
third finding, by contrast, requires modification.

That is to say, the fraction of the labor force engaged in distributing
commodities has shown an upward trend, and the fraction engaged in
producing commodities a downward trend, ever since the Civil War.
Again, output per man-hour, in both distribution and production, has
tended to rise throughout the eight decades; but it has tended to rise
much more rapidly in agriculture, mining, and manufacturing than in
retail and wholesale trade. Finally, the distributor's share of the retail
sales dollar, decidedly stable since World War I, apparently experienced
a definite but very slow expansion between the Civil War and World
War I.

We believe that, stated thus broadly, our findings for the period prior
to World War I cannot well be assailed. However, the individual figures

upon which the above broad conclusions are based ... clearly are much less precise and reliable than those for the period since World War I. Let us see why.

The first finding—on the distribution of the labor force—rests upon the decennial population census, in using which, prior to 1930, the industrial must be approximated from the occupational tabulation. That is to say, the aggregate number of persons engaged in retail and wholesale trade has to be estimated from the numbers in certain "characteristic occupations," e.g. "dealers" and "clerks in stores." We have checked the figures, experimented with extreme assumptions about possible errors, and find that the broad conclusion is still warranted.

The second finding—the contrast in rates of change in man-hour output—rests upon the first, together with estimates for (1) trends in hours worked per year by persons engaged in commodity distribution and in commodity production, respectively, and (2) trends in the output of commodity distribution and of commodity production. Estimates for hours worked in commodity production have long been available, but for hours worked in retail and wholesale trade we found it necessary to digest numerous reports from statistical bureaus of individual states and other sources; hence the final figures are only approximate. Output estimates for the three commodity-producing industries rest upon decennial census data. Estimates of the net output of distribution are derived in turn from commodity output, adjusted to allow for changes in the volume of output that enters the distribution system and also for the volume of distributive services rendered per unit; but prior to 1929 the derivation rests upon a mass of partial and scattered data described in the report. Here too we experimented with extreme assumptions regarding the possibility of error; but, as will be seen from the quoted results of alternative calculations, our broad conclusions are not disturbed.

The third finding—a slow rise in the distributor's share of the retail sales dollar during the period prior to World War I—is largely independent of the foregoing sources and rests upon three distinctive types of data: (1) censuses of distribution taken in Massachusetts and Indiana prior to 1900; (2) surveys and opinions published in trade publications; and (3) the historical records of certain individual merchandising firms. The logical relationship between the first two findings and the third is investigated in the body of the report, and the latter found to be broadly consistent with the former.

In conclusion, it should be emphasized that the results offered in this volume for the period before World War I are in no sense merely extrapolations to earlier years of results already obtained for recent decades. The earlier figures represent the clearest picture of that period that can now be, or perhaps ever will be, assembled for the particular field to which they relate. The pre-World War I figures are included here both because the author believes they are adequately, though not overgenerously, supported by contemporary source materials and because they show that certain broad trends observable since World War I were continuations of tendencies already in operation in the late nineteenth century.

FOR FURTHER READING: Laudatory of distribution channels are George B. Hotchkiss, *Milestones of Marketing* (New York, 1938), Ralph Borsodi, *The Distribution Age* (New York, 1927), and Boris Emmett and John E. Jeuck, *Catalogues and Counters: A History of Sears, Roebuck and Company* (Chicago, 1950). A critical approach is in Stuart Chase, *The Tragedy of Waste* (New York, 1926). General orientation in this field can be gleaned from Ralph Cassady and W. C. Waite, *The Consumer and the Economic Order* (New York, 1949).

22. *Finance After 1865*

PROBLEM: *What were some patterns of economic growth after 1865?*

Only in the last few decades have economists and historians developed analytical techniques with which to identify and measure economic fluctuations. Many of their efforts have gone into studies to delineate business cycles derived from extensive compilations of statistics concerning important select indicators of economic activity like income, manufacturing output, and capital investment outlays. On the basis of such figures economists have devised indices which have enabled them to plot fluctuations in business activity in short and also long term or secular trends. Students of economics find such patterns useful in predicting future developments, while historians derive new insights from them in studying the past. In such a relatively new and difficult field it is not surprising that controversies have arisen over the particular form which economic cycles have taken in the past. One of the disputes has developed over analysis of the Panics of 1873, 1893, and 1907. Were all of these related to select long term trends, or was each a separate and unique fluctuation? An early student of business economics, Arthur Adams, found that cyclical swings between 1860 and 1925 did not reflect any continuity, but only constituted exceptions to long periods of stable equilibrium. As evidence he cited the crises of 1893 and 1907. A very different view on this problem was taken by Wesley Clair Mitchell, the outstanding pioneer in developing the concept of business cycles. Mitchell formulated new techniques of describing economic changes by utilizing statistical data in business reports and by a comparative analysis of existing theories of business behavior, especially bank operations. He also studied the volume of savings, investments, and retail purchases, as well as changes in the weather, to secure data which would make it possible to

plot cyclical trends. Utilizing such methods Mitchell concluded that the crises during the later nineteenth century
were related cyclical manifestations of a continuous pattern
of economic activity which never reached a state of equilibrium, contrary to Adams. For the tyro, both of these authors
raise useful questions about historical patterns of economic
activity. What seem to be the dominant trends in American
economic activity in the nineteenth and twentieth centuries?
What relationships exist between periods of depression, as in
1873, 1893, and 1907, and intervening periods of prosperity?
Is there regularity and continuity in economic trends?

Economics of Business Cycles

ARTHUR B. ADAMS

Recovery begins in depression with the beginning of the reestablishment
of price harmonies and harmony between the level of prices and cost of
production. With the gradual exhaustion of surplus stocks of goods in
the different fields, price harmonies gradually come about. As this is happening the prices of many commodities rise and the general level of
prices tends to rise slightly. Even while many factories are still closed
down the general level of prices may rise perceptibly higher than the
lowest point reached in depression.

Recovery ends when factories and shops resume normal capacity operation to supply goods currently demanded in the market. When such a
pitch of industrial activity is reached prices are measurably higher than
at the lowest point of depression, costs of production are low as compared with costs of production in prosperity, profits are not high but
reasonable, bank reserves are high and interest rates are low, but credit
is used cautiously. Retail trade is large in volume but will not sustain
price raises. At such times there is little optimism among business men but
they accept the situation with evident complacency. There is a balance
between the sum total of money incomes of consumers and the physical
quantity of consumers' goods flowing into the market.

Under such conditions there may be oscillating movements of the general level of prices within a narrow margin, and credit may contract and
expand, but the physical volume of business changes very little, and
profits in most lines remain reasonable. There may be intense spurts of

activity, first in this industry, then in another, and prices of individual commodities may rise and fall rapidly, but there is no development of a cumulative upward movement of prices, credit, and volume of output, or other movements which may reasonably be designated as a period of prosperity. When such a state of business follows a period of recovery, the business trend may gently oscillate up and down for several years, or until a war, a favorable balance of trade (caused by good crops), or the discovery of new sources of large prospective profits (due to inventions or discoveries), or a combination of two or more of these forces produces a general and rapid expansion of capital equipment.

Following several periods of recovery in this country there have been prolonged periods of oscillating equilibrium of business and industry. There were no physical forces superimposed upon the business system following recovery strong enough to produce high enough prospective profits to bring about a sufficient expansion of industry to produce prosperity. Such was the condition following the recovery from the Panic of 1893. The depression in 1896 was not due to technical business conditions, but to the threatening of the standard of value of money. No period of prosperity developed from 1893 until the industrial expansion of 1905–1907. Again, following the Panic of 1907 no period of prosperity developed until the World War expansion of 1915–1920. And following the crisis of 1920 recovery was fairly complete by January, 1923, and up to July, 1924, no period of prosperity had developed. In the meantime there has been some oscillation of prices, credit and profits, but these slight movements occurring within a few months were far too inconsequential to be designated as cyclical fluctuations. They represent nothing more than unrealized business efforts which would occur in any balanced business and industrial system.

A period of prosperity has often immediately followed a period of recovery. Such sequences, however, were not due to the fact that the business system, because of its nature, generates prosperity out of recovery. They were due largely to the fact that the dynamic physical forces which produce prosperity are more likely to be superimposed upon the business and industrial system during recovery than at other times, or that these forces when brought into play at that time have more influence in producing prosperity than they would have if introduced in other periods of the cycle. If, however, when recovery has completed itself and no large crops are produced, few profitable natural resources are made available for exploitation, and few new efficient mechanical contrivances and few new types of consumers' goods are introduced, the business world will not immediately enter upon a period of prosperity. Expanding consumers' demand and the old and common sources of prospective profits will not be sufficiently inviting to induce business men to enter upon a program of borrowing money and expanding industry.

The business and industrial world, then, is not always going through some phase of a business cycle. There are times when the whole economic system is in a state of an approximate equilibrium. It is not a static equilibrium but an oscillating one. This state of oscillating equilibrium may continue over a period of several years. Whenever it is established it will continue until one or more of the dynamic physical forces (good crops, exploitation of natural resources, inventions, or wars) are brought to bear upon the business world to produce larger money incomes. When this happens with sufficient magnitude, the oscillating equilibrium will be destroyed and economic society will enter upon a cyclical period of prosperity.

It would, therefore, be conducive to clear thinking in reference to business cycles to divide the space of time from the first business cycle to the present date into periods of time covered by business cycles and periods of time covered by oscillating business equilibria. It is a mistake to assume that cyclical movements are continuous or everlasting.

Business Cycles: The Problem and Its Setting

WESLEY C. MITCHELL

A WORKING CONCEPT OF BUSINESS CYCLES

To find out what business cycles are, we have looked at them through the eyes of economic theorists, through the eyes of economic statisticians, and through the eyes of business reporters. Each group of workers helps us to appreciate features of the common object which the other groups take for granted, or fail to see. It is by combining the three sets of observations that we can form the mental picture of business cycles most useful in the constructive work which lies before us.

(1) Elements Derived from Business Reports

Treated in one way, business reports give a most confusing view of business fluctuations; but treated in another way, they give the simplest view. When we wade through the commercial histories printed in financial papers or consular documents, we may get no general impression except that of infinite detail. But by careful planning and hard work, we can put these records in such form that they afford a view over wide areas and through decades. Then the details fade, and the broad features

Reprinted from *Business Cycles: The Problem and Its Setting* by Wesley C. Mitchell (New York, 1930), pp. 455–467. By permission of the National Bureau of Economic Research.

of commercial history become clear. Among these broad features, one of the most prominent is a pattern in the changes taking place in time—a pattern common to all countries which can be said to have a business history. Again and again in many lands, a period of active trade ends in a relapse; then dull times prevail; afterwards comes a quickening, and presently trade is active once more. This frequently recurring sequence, of which there are so many examples in the record slowly built up by the coöperation of numberless business reporters, is what men have in mind when they speak of the business cycle.

But business annals give us much more than this bare skeleton of a concept.

(1) Current commercial histories usually take nations as their units, but they make it clear that a given wave of prosperity or depression does not always sweep over all parts of a country, and that such a wave sometimes sweeps over the commercial world. So unequal are the areas affected by different waves that we cannot associate business cycles with any given geographical or political unit. For convenient discussion it seems wise to abide by the convention of our sources, and think of (say) Japanese cycles, Swedish cycles and Brazilian cycles. There is the more reason for this practice in that the record of business cycles in every country has its own peculiarities. But we must conceive of the phenomena as international, not only in the sense that they occur in many countries, but also in the sense that the state of trade prevailing in any country at any time actively promotes the development of a similar condition in all other countries with which the first has important business relations. On the other hand, we must recognize that in a large country whose economic organization is not highly integrated different sections sometimes have cyclical fluctuations more divergent than those of neighboring nations.

(2) The conception of prosperity or depression within a given country has the character of an average. Seldom does a detailed survey show that all branches of business are active, or all dull, at the same time. As a rule, the reporters are clear and unanimous concerning the "prevailing tone"; but sometimes they picture conditions as so mixed that it is hard to discover the trend. And sometimes when reporters agree concerning the prevailing tone, they agree also that certain industries present striking exceptions. In other words, a reader of commercial histories conceives of business cycles as a sequence of phases each of which is a highly complex aggregate of conditions in different industries—conditions which are never strictly uniform, and which are at times markedly divergent.

(3) Another characteristic of business cycles as pictured by commercial histories is that they vary in intensity. The writers tell of wild panics and of quiet recessions, of sensational booms and of mild prosperity, of complete prostration and of mere dullness, of dramatic revivals and of long-drawn-out recuperations. These descriptive terms and their

hundred variants cannot be interpreted with precision. We cannot even rank successive or contemporary cycles in the order of their intensities,— to say nothing of measuring degrees of intensity. But neither can we doubt the fact that cycles run the gamut from violent fluctuations to moderate swings. And if we follow these sources faithfully, we must drop crises from our conception of business cycles, for in the moderate swings no phase occurs which is fitly designated by that word.

(4) Concerning the wave-length of business cycles, commercial histories give us more definite impressions. We can measure approximately the intervals between successive recessions. There are doubtful cases, because the industrial complexity just referred to sometimes makes it hard to say whether a given set of difficulties was general enough to be called a recession; but these cases are not sufficiently numerous to cut much figure in the results.

Some cycles are found in the record which appear to have been nearer one year than two years in length. At the other extreme, we find a few cycles lasting 11 or 12 years. But the bulk of the cases fall within the three- to six-year range. And when a goodly number of observations are put together the measurements distribute themselves about their central tendency in a fairly regular, though not symmetrical, fashion.

Further, it appears that the phases of revival and recession, as reported in the sources from which business annals are compiled, are brief in comparison with the phases of prosperity and depression; that on the average, prosperity lasts a little longer than depression; that this relation of prosperity to depression is accentuated when wholesale prices have a rising secular trend, and reversed when that trend declines; that the very long cycles are due more to the prolongation of depression than to the prolongation of prosperity.

(5) On reading the business records of any country year after year, one is impressed by the continuity of cyclical changes. In the sequence of prosperity, recession, depression and revival, any stage can be treated as the end of one cycle and the beginning of another. Yet it seems wiser to say that there is no beginning and no end; or better still, that there is a continuous movement which passes through certain phases in an established order, but at a pace which varies from time to time and country to country.

(6) Current business commentators say many hasty things about the causes of changes in conditions which we cannot incorporate into a working conception of business cycles. But for one generalization along this line we have use: business cycles are highly sensitive phenomena, influenced by a host of factors not of business origin. Among such factors, wars, civil disturbances, inequalities in harvests, and epidemics play prominent rôles.

(7) Finally, a survey of business annals of countries at different stages

of development, and of the business annals of the same country through successive stages, suggests that business cycles are associated with a certain form of economic organization. This suggestion is confirmed by a longer-range study of economic history. While commercial and financial crises can be traced back a long time in England, the Netherlands, France, Southern Germany, and northern Italy, these early modern and late medieval crises appear to have been due far more largely to non-business factors than are modern recessions, and to have been less general in their incidence. Business cycles which affect the fortunes of the mass of people in a country, which succeed each other continuously, and which attain a semblance of regularity, do not become prominent in the economic history of a country until a large proportion of its people are living mainly by making and spending money incomes. Also, there is evidence that business cycles keep changing character as economic organization develops. The most violent manifestations are brought under control. Panics subside into crises, and crises into recessions. It seems probable that the average length of cycles grows shorter at one stage of institutional development, and at a later stage grows longer again. In fine, we must think of the recurrence of prosperity, recession, depression and revival as characteristic of economic activity only when economic activity is organized on the basis of what is here called "business economy."

Thus the conception of business cycles obtained from a survey of contemporary reports starts with the fundamental fact of rhythmical fluctuations in activity, and adds that these fluctuations are peculiar to countries organized on a business basis, that they appear in all such countries, that they tend to develop the same phase at nearly the same time in different countries, that they follow each other without intermissions, that they are affected by all sorts of nonbusiness factors, that they represent predominant rather than universal changes in trend, and that, while they vary in intensity and duration, the variations are not so wide as to prevent our identifying different cases as belonging to a single class of phenomena.

(2) Elements Derived from Theories of Business Cycles

What alterations in this concept are suggested by studying the theories of business cycles?

Read one after another in full detail, these theories are scarcely less confusing than are commercial reviews. It is feasible, however, to deal with the theories in much the same way as we have dealt with the business reports, ... theoretical accounts ... against ... historical accounts. ...

Treating one collection as we did the other, we can ask, What do the
theories as a whole tell us about the phenomena?

First, the theories put fresh emphasis upon the exceeding complexity of
cyclical fluctuations. But the complexity revealed by the theories is complexity of an order different from that revealed by commercial reports.
While the latter deal with business conditions in different areas and different industries, the theories deal with different processes—processes which
are supposed to run their course in, or to affect, all industries and all
communities organized upon a business basis.

Among the processes so intimately involved in cyclical fluctuations that
they have been made to yield explanations of business cycles, we noted
the following:

Banking operations—particularly the processes of expanding or contracting bank loans, with their effects in enlarging or reducing the volume
of credit currency; fluctuations in discount rates, and the fluctuations of
bank reserves which result from changes in the public's use of coin and
paper money, and from the banks' efforts to maintain solvency.

Saving and investing in their relation to the amount of construction
work undertaken, the supply of consumers' goods sent to market, and the
volume of retail buying.

The process of adjusting the current supply of goods of all sorts to the
demand for them, as that process affects business commitments, or is
affected by (1) the uncertainties incident to all business planning, (2)
changes in the marginal utilities of consumers' goods and the marginal
utility of money, on the one hand, and, on the other hand, by changes
in the demand for and in the operation of industrial equipment.

Disbursing money incomes to consumers and spending money by consumers, in relation to the processes of making and selling goods—relations which may be treated with reference to the influence of price
fluctuations upon the incomes and purchasing power of different classes,
with reference to the effect of saving by corporations and individuals
upon the demand for consumers' goods, or with reference to the difficulty of providing liquid capital for business enterprises without reducing
the demand for goods in general below the volume sent to market.

Making profits out of industrial operations—a process which is held to
breed illusions concerning the volume of demand, to magnify the moderate fluctuations of retail buying into violent oscillations in production,
or to cause the alternate marking up and writing down of the capital
values at which business enterprises are rated and upon which loan credits
are based.

Promoting new business ventures, or making revolutionary changes in
business methods.

"Progress" at large, a characteristic of the age which makes it impossible to keep the rates at which different factors grow properly adjusted to each other.

In addition to these economic processes our attention has been called to:

Waves of optimism and pessimism, which are held by one writer to "give birth to one another in an endless chain," and by another writer to result from fluctuations in birth-, death-, and morbidity-rates.

Cyclical changes in weather, which affect business on one line of analysis because they affect crop yields, on a second line of analysis because they affect health and mental attitudes, and on a third line because they give the industries using organic materials a rhythm different from that of the industries using inorganic materials.

Of course not all of these theories of business cycles can be valid in the sense of their authors. Indeed, if any one theory really shows the chief cause of cyclical fluctuations, none of the rival theories shows the chief cause. But we can take all of the theories into our working conception of business cycles in the sense that we can conceive of the recurrent sequences of prosperity, recession, depression and revival as involving cyclical fluctuations in each of the economic processes listed, and as affected by emotional and climatic conditions. Nor can we limit our view to the processes and conditions on which theories of business cycles have been erected. In working, we must be prepared to study any feature of modern life which appears to be intimately related to business fluctuations. But with every factor in the complex, whether suggested by others or discovered in our inquiry, we must deal critically. Among other things, this means that our conception of a multiplicity of processes involved in business cycles does not commit us in advance to any conclusion about the number of causes at work. If the evidence we find points in that direction, we can conclude that some single cause produces, directly and indirectly, the cyclical fluctuations in an uncounted list of processes.

While adding a significant feature to our conception of business cycles, the survey of theories sheds little light upon the suggestions derived from the survey of business annals. For the cycles explained by economic theorists are not the cycles recorded by business historians. Interested in establishing generalizations, a theorist passes lightly over the differences among successive cycles in the same country and synchronous cycles in different countries. He contemplates an ideal, or a typical, case, supposedly modeled on real cases and summing up all their really essential features. Nor is that procedure open to criticism, provided the theorist takes care to test his ideal construction for conformity to fact. Some modern theorists do so explicitly and at length; doubtless others believe that they have made adequate tests privately, though they spare their readers the heavy task of assessing their evidence. In any case, concentration upon an ideal case by a theorist does not mean that he denies the variability of the phenomena, but that he sets the variations aside in order to get a clearer view of what seem to him fundamentals.

On two points, however, most of the theories of business cycles are at variance with the concept derived from commercial reviews. These points were discussed in Chapter IV, and noted in the preceding section; but they must be mentioned in the present connection. (1) Most theorists take crises to be one of the phases of all business cycles, though a few writers define "crisis" in a way which makes it equivalent to "recession." (2) By taking cycles as the intervals between crises, and not counting mild recessions as crises, most theorists make the duration typical of business cycles roughly twice the length we deduce as typical. On both these points, the conception suggested by business annals, confirmed as it is by statistical analysis, is more useful in constructive work than its rival.

Nor can the idea presented in many theories that business cycles represent an alternate rupture and restoration of economic equilibrium be included in our working conception. Men who take as their point of departure the theorem that economic forces tend to establish a stable equilibrium may conceive the main problem to be, how this fundamental tendency is overcome at times and how it presently reasserts itself. I have not chosen that point of departure. Hence it is no part of my task to determine how the fact of cyclical oscillations in economic activity can be reconciled with the general theory of equilibrium, or how that theory can be reconciled with facts.

Yet this does not dispose of the matter. Whatever his methodological assumptions, anyone who deals with crises is likely to think of a balance of forces, particularly if his explanation centers in some single process. "Over-saving," "over-production," "under-consumption," "a rate of interest higher than that economically justified," "optimistic error," "excess capacity,"—all such phrases imply the idea of an equilibrium which has been disturbed. They may or may not be conscious applications of a general economic theorem. But when we enlarge our problem to include numerous processes and all phases of the cycle, the idea of equilibrium becomes less helpful in conceiving the whole movement than in dealing with details. Provided we interpret equilibrium, not in the mechanical, but in the bookkeeping sense, . . . we may compare one set of factors or forces with an opposing set, note which set exceeds the other for the time being, and inquire what consequences that excess produces. But in what useful way can we conceive of the equilibrium of the whole system we must contemplate, when that system includes factors which cannot be combined into two opposing totals—quantities of goods in physical terms, prices, pecuniary aggregates? If we could reduce every factor to its money value, the feat might be accomplished; but in the process we should bury qualitative distinctions of great moment. While we can relate all the qualitatively unlike factors in the problem to each other through their bearing upon prospective profits, we cannot add them all together and get results which are illuminating.

(3) *Elements Derived from Statistical Analysis*

Our collection of statistics is like our collection of business annals, and unlike our collection of theories, in that it deals with the cycles of history —fluctuations which have occurred in certain countries between certain dates. Hence the statistics can be used to test elements in our concept which are derived from commercial reviews. The tests confirm, with a welcome increase of definiteness, the view that business cycles run a continuous round; that they vary, but vary after the fashion characteristic of most social phenomena, in intensity, in duration and in the intensity and duration of their constituent phases; that the synchronous fluctuations in countries having business relations with one another tend to have a common pattern, and that the course of business changes is frequently altered by factors not of business origin.

On the other hand, our collection of statistics resembles our collection of theories, and differs from our collection of business annals, in that it deals with economic processes rather than with the fortunes of different industries. Hence, the impression derived from the theories, that a business cycle is a highly complex congeries of fluctuations in different processes, can be made clearer by appeal to statistics. And though statistics deal with historical cycles, to a limited extent we can combine the different cases they present in such a way as to test theoretical conceptions of what features of the historical cycles are typical, and what are exceptional.

Besides confirming certain elements in the concept derived from our other sources, the collection of statistics brings forcibly to our attention two elements which are traceable, rather than prominent, in business annals and in certain theories.

Time series show that the cyclical fluctuations characteristic of various economic processes differ in amplitude and timing; they show approximately how much these fluctuations differ in amplitude, and what order they follow in time.

Time series also show that the cyclical fluctuations of most (not all) economic processes occur in combination with fluctuations of several other sorts:—secular trends, primary and secondary, seasonal variations, and irregular fluctuations.

By developing special methods for segregating secular trends and seasonal variations, statisticians have enabled us to get a clearer view of cyclical fluctuations, though they have accomplished little toward isolating the irregular changes in their series. Thus we are forced to deal with materials, which, at best, show cyclical-irregular fluctuations in combination. Even so, we can sort the series into groups, based upon the regularity and the measure of agreement among their movements. There are some time series whose fluctuations, mild or violent, show slight traces of any rhythm. But there are enough series which show tolerably regular cyclical fluctuations, agreeing with one another and with our business annals in tenor, to give us confidence in the basic element of our conception—the recurrence of the prosperity-recession-depression-revival sequence.

TWO CRITICISMS CONSIDERED

One element in our working concept has been rejected by Dean Arthur B. Adams, who holds:

It is a mistake to think that cyclical movements are continuous. . . . Each business cycle is, in a large measure, separate and distinct from the one preceding it and the other succeeding it. Considerable time may elapse between the ending of one cycle and the beginning of another.

Adams illustrates this contention by reference to American experience:

No period of prosperity developed from 1893 until the industrial expansion of 1905–07. Again, following the Panic of 1907 no period of prosperity developed until the World War expansion of 1915–20.

Our annals, on the contrary, and the business indexes with which we have compared them, show between 1893 and 1907 a "submerged cycle" terminated by a recession early in 1896, a second period of somewhat greater activity terminated by a very mild reaction in 1900, and a third movement of expansion ending in the "rich man's panic" of 1903. Between 1907 and 1920, also, our annals and indexes show three cycles, marked off by recessions in 1910, 1913 and 1918.

Yet the difference between Dean Adams' view and the one taken here is more a difference in the use of terms than a difference concerning facts. For Adams recognizes that between 1893 and 1905, and again between 1907 and 1915, there was "some oscillation of prices, credit and profits." He thinks, however, that

these slight movements occurring within a few months were far too inconsequential to be designated as cyclical fluctuations.

What are here called business cycles of small amplitude, Dean Adams calls "periods of time covered by oscillating business equilibria." In his terminology, no fluctuation is a business cycle unless the prosperous phase develops into a "boom."

Perhaps it does not matter greatly which of these contrasting usages is adopted, so long as the facts are kept in mind. On either view, one must face the problem why some revivals grow into intense and prolonged prosperity, and why in other cases prosperity is mild and brief. But one who takes the trouble to measure the amplitudes of successive fluctuations in many time series throughout considerable periods, finds his observations so distributed about their central tendency that he has no basis for contrasting business cycles and what Dean Adams calls "oscillating business equilibria." Our inquiry will be more orderly if we treat all cyclical oscillations as belonging to one species of phenomena, and inquire into the variations characteristic of the species in respect to amplitudes, duration, and other measurable features.

Professor Irving Fisher doubts the validity of the whole conception with which we are concerned, and asks whether "the" business cycle is not a myth. His chief argument runs as follows:

if by the business cycle is meant merely the statistical fact that business does *fluctuate* above and below its average trend, there is no denying the existence of a cycle—and not only in business but in any statistical series whatsoever! If we draw any smooth curve to represent the general trend of population, the actual population figures must necessarily rise sometimes above and sometimes below this mean trend line. . . . In the same way weather conditions necessarily fluctuate about their own means; so does the luck at Monte Carlo. Must we then speak of "the population cycle," "the weather cycle" and "the Monte Carlo cycle"?

I see no more reason to believe in "the" business cycle. It is simply the fluctuation about its own mean. And yet the cycle idea is supposed to have more content than mere variability. It implies a regular succession of *similar* fluctuations, constituting some sort of *recurrence*, so that, as in the case of the phases of the moon, the tides of the sea, wave motion, or pendulum swing, we can forecast the future on the basis of a pattern worked out from past experience, and which we have reason to think will be copied in the future. We certainly cannot do that in predicting the weather, or Monte Carlo luck. Can we do so as to business? Not so long as business is dominated by changes in the price level!

Professor Fisher has rendered a wholesome service to students of business cycles by challenging their basic concept in this vigorous fashion. To discuss the issue in full would involve repeating once again many of the facts set forth in the preceding chapters and summarized in the preceding sections. That is not feasible; but it is well to recall what groups of facts the challenge must face.

Even when economic time series are reduced to percentage deviations from their secular trends adjusted for seasonal variations, the fluctuations in some cases still seem as irregular as the fluctuations of the weather, or of "Monte Carlo luck." But there are many series of which this cannot be said. When charted, the fluctuations of pig-iron production, unemployment percentages, bank clearings, and building permits, to cite but a few examples, prove to be decidedly less irregular than the fluctuations of a weather chart, a chart of net gold shipments, or of potato crops. In no case are the fluctuations highly regular; but in many cases they are far from haphazard, despite the inability of statisticians to free what they call "cyclical" changes from what they call "irregular" perturbations. Further, the cyclical-irregular fluctuations of the series which individually show semblance of regularity are found to have tolerably regular relations with one another in respect to time, duration, and amplitude of movement—relations many of which have been suggested by economic theory. Finally, in timing and direction these inter-correlated fluctuations agree closely with the evidence given by business annals concerning a long-continued and wide-spread recurrence of prosperity, recession, depression and revival.

To ascertain how regularly this sequence recurs, to learn all they can about its characteristics, causes, and consequences, is the problem upon which students of business cycles are working. They speak of cyclical fluctuations, instead of periodic fluctuations, just because the first term does not imply strict regularity of recurrence. To them "the cycle idea" does "have more content than mere variability"; but it does not have the content of periodicity. Anyone who makes business forecasts on the basis of a fixed time schedule is not applying their concept, but violating it. What they know about the recurrence does not yet enable them to make consistently successful business forecasts. But in that fact they see reason, not for giving up their work, but for pressing it further.

No competent judge questions the desirability of studying economic fluctuations in an objective fashion. Professor Fisher himself is one of the distinguished workers in the field. But he thinks that the subdivision of this broad problem which is called "business cycles" in America and "trade cycles" in England would flourish better under some other name. Perhaps a new name can be found which is equally apt and less subject to misconstruction. If so, it should be adopted. But no such blanket term as "economic undulations," "industrial fluctuations," "business oscillations," or "theory of conjunctures" will meet the needs of current research. For we have seen that various investigators believe they have discovered several different types of fluctuations in time series—secular trends, "long waves," secondary trends, generating cycles, commercial cycles (the commonest name for inter-crisis changes), business cycles, seasonal variations, irregular perturbations. Probably each of these types which withstands critical examination will become the object of intensive study by economic statisticians and by economic theorists, or better by men who unite these too-often separated interests. As knowledge grows, there will be increasing need of specific names to characterize each type of fluctuation and to differentiate each from the other types. To drop the name now widely used for one of the best established of these types, before a better substitute has been supplied, might cause more confusion than is now caused by misunderstanding of the word "cycles." Meanwhile, the general adoption of this word in other sciences to designate recurrent, but non-periodic, phenomena is familiarizing the intelligent public with its meaning.

FOR FURTHER READING: Emphasizing cyclical variations in business activity during the post-Civil War decades are Rendig Fels, *American Business Cycles, 1865–1879* (Chapel Hill, 1959), Samuel Rezneck, "Distress, Relief, and Discontent during the Depression of 1873–78," *Journal of Political Economy*, LVIII (December, 1950), pp. 494–512, O. V. Wells, "The Depression of 1873–79," *Agricultural History*, XI (July, 1937), pp. 237–249, W. M. Persons, "Index of General Business Conditions, 1875–1913," *Review of Economic Statistics*, IX (January, 1927), pp. 20–29. Less positive is Otto C. Lightner, *The History of Business Depressions* (New York, 1922).

23. *Labor After 1865*

PROBLEM: *What factors led to the growth of labor organizations after 1865?*

One of the outstanding characteristics of American economic development after 1865 was the growth of an organized labor movement. Workingmen formed the Knights of Labor, the American Federation of Labor, and also railroad and craft unions in response to many new problems arising from industrial expansion. But controversy soon arose between the advocates of craft organizations, seeking a restricted membership of skilled workers only, and the proponents of industrial unionism who sought to include all unskilled workers. In seeking to explain the rise of a labor movement during this period historians thus found conflicting views about factors which explain the success of craft unions. Was the narrow job-conscious program of the craft unions responsible for their success? The "Wisconsin School" of labor history, led by John R. Commons and Selig Perlman of the state university, as well as Philip Taft, whose selection is included below, answered this question in the affirmative. It interpreted the growth of labor in the light of the craft union experience. Taft attributed the rise of labor groups, especially the American Federation of Labor, to limited objectives, lack of broad social aims, abstention from politics, and the exclusion of intellectuals. Until recently this was the dominant interpretation of American labor history and rarely challenged. But with the formation of industrial, or all-inclusive, unions after 1933, perspectives changed. As J. B. S. Hardman, long a writer on labor problems, notes, the interests of many workers outside the Federation transcended mere job-consciousness and embraced broader social goals. Moreover, despite disclaimers, labor participation in politics has been more common than withdrawal and helps to explain workingmen's gains. Both writers raise vital issues that need to be considered in examining reasons for the growth of Labor in the United States. What factors explain the successes and failures of labor groups after 1865? Does the historical experience of labor after 1865 bear out the arguments of Taft or Hardman? Is there agreement among the authors concerning some underlying factors to explain the rise of labor organizations?

A Theory of the American Labor Movement

PHILIP TAFT   "Wisconsin School" of labor history

A theory of labor, or for that matter a theory about anything, is valid to the extent that it is capable of revealing significant relations in its universe of reference or it can be used to forecast conduct or consequences of policies or actions. The views developed by Professors Commons and Perlman must be examined in the light of their usefulness towards reaching meaningful explanations of the conduct and attitudes of labor.

Professor Commons first began his work in the field when the position of organized labor was much weaker than it is today, and when the community was much less hospitable to union organization and less tolerant of the pressures exerted by labor upon industry through the boycott and strike. American society and its major social institutions were wedded to the view that maximum welfare is more effectively obtained by the free play of the market and that labor unions were monopolies which interfered with the optimum allocation of resources. In some quarters a belief existed that the unions represented an alien and revolutionary force, and their activities should at least be circumscribed, if not completely suppressed.

Rejecting the notion of market equilibrium resulting from the competition of atomistic units, Commons attempted to show that modern economic life can best be explained, and even promoted, by allowing large and powerful aggregates to compete, negotiate, and work out a viable relationship. His view of the market is not atomistic, but pluralistic. "Instead of the traditional equilibrium between equal individuals of economic theory, the alternatives today are between an economic government based on (a) balance of power between self-governing corporations and unions, and a suppression of both organizations, or their leaders, by military power."

Reprinted from *Industrial Relations Research Association Proceedings*, III (Urbana, 1950), pp. 140–145. By permission of Philip Taft and the Industrial Relations Research Association.

Instead of regarding the labor union as a bearer of tyranny and monopoly, Commons viewed it as a liberating force, one that establishes constitutional government in industry and defines and limits the power of one of the parties over the other. To him, labor organization, because of its inherent democratic nature, was not antipathetic to the spirit or tradition of American democracy. Moreover, examining the realities of American life convinced him that the market mechanism is far less perfect in protecting the individual worker against exploitation by powerful economic groups than was assumed in traditional economic and political theories. Commons knew the American industrialism of the century at first hand, and early realized that the equality of bargaining assumed by the traditional view was a theoretical mirage. He refused to turn to socialism as the answer. He was in fact suspicious of too much dependence upon government, and for him, the more desirable solution was a well-organized, independent labor force dealing on terms of equality with its employers, and assuring the worker not only a fair wage but improved status directly flowing from a more equal distribution of power. Well organized groups were not necessarily evil, as long as they recognized the right of other parties to exist. Once each side recognized the other, an equilibrium would be found that would be not only socially bearable, but would assure the greatest amount of welfare. Commons knew the actual economic world too well to have much faith in the market mechanism as a protector of the individual worker's rights or position. He himself had seen in practice that even in the small shop, where the employer operates under conditions of competition in the product market, the individual worker was exposed to favoritism and discrimination. Commons' emphasis was on the desirability of industrial government, the necessity for curbing absolute power in industry if democracy was to survive. Not only did unions fail to weaken capitalism, but they served as a new source of strength, for they helped to democratize the system.

Commons sought to demonstrate that unions were not only compatible with a system of private enterprise, but were actually essential to it. His arguments are geared in the main as replies to those who believe that the unions are interfering with the most effective operation of the economic system or that they lead to unfair or undesirable allocation of resources. Professor Commons' arguments and views were directed mainly at the traditional attitudes found among economists and among other groups. Professor Perlman's views supplement, broaden, and strengthen the foundation laid by Commons. While in the main Commons' work might be regarded as an effort to convince the holders of traditional economic views that unions were desirable institutions, Professor Perlman attempted to defend the unions from the criticism, explicit or implied, of the left.

Trade-unionism has not been too highly regarded by those who saw the cure for social and economic injustices in the reorganization of society and its economic institutions. The Marxists, who were the largest and most influential group among the radical reformers, gave the trade-unions a subordinate place in the struggle of labor for a greater share of the national product, greater protection against the losses of income, and greater security against discrimination. At best, the socialists were inclined to look upon the union as an auxiliary, an institution inferior to the political party, and one which should take direction from it. In Germany, the trade-unions began to insist upon their independence in the 1890's, but not until 1906 did the leaders of the Social Democratic Party explicitly recognize the parity of the trade-unions. In France, the Marxist socialists took the same position, but even moderates like the Swede Hjalmar Branting, at the beginning underestimated the importance of trade-unions. The very facts which Commons emphasized as the most significant aspects of trade-unionism were in fact derided by these schools. The trade-unions, it was claimed, did not represent the basic and historical interests of labor. This conclusion was attractive not only to radical reformers, but to many other social reformers who sympathized with labor in general. To them the aspirations of the trade-unions seemed puny and of no great significance. The solution of the labor problem called for a more heroic program and action, and the labor movement was endowed with an historical mission which the trade-union leadership ignored.

The proponents of this view had no mandate from masses of workers, but this minor fact did not deter many of them from insisting that the trade-unions were derelict in recognizing and carrying out their mission. In the United States and in western European countries where the trade-unions could develop independent organization and leadership, the criticisms were, in the main, implied; although even in those countries, there were many who were skeptical about the usefulness of traditional trade-unionism. It was Lenin who put the case most cogently, when he argued that labor left to its devices would only achieve trade-union consciousness. This is undoubtedly true, but for Lenin this constituted a fatal defect or limitation in trade-unionism. In contrast to Commons and Professor Perlman, who see in the capacity of labor to develop its own institutions one of the significant factors for the extension of democratic and constitutional rule in industry, Lenin regards this fact as proof that labor needs the tutelage of the "intelligentsia." "The history of all countries shows that the working class, exclusively by its own effort, is able to develop only trade union consciousness, i.e., it may itself realize the necessity for combining in unions, to fight against employers and to strive to compel the government to pass necessary labor legislation, etc."

Professor Perlman approaches the problem quite differently. The union is not an institution that has been fashioned by inferior intelligence. This type of snobbery, which is by inference a justification for totalitarianism, is rejected, and the union is recognized as the result of conscious effort by workers to solve important problems. The worker is not concerned with a new society; he is interested in devising a system of economic government that will protect his status as a human being, and enable him to cope with the economic problems that besiege him. This type of institution is primarily concerned with the worker's job interests and the sharing of opportunities among the members. Professor Perlman argues that workers are conscious of scarcity of opportunity, and that their bargaining institutions are designed to make it easier for them to operate in these surroundings. The worker's primary interest is thus directed towards the job, and this is the central arena for the worker's feeling and thinking. If we examine trade-unions, which are labor's institution *par excellent*, its concentration upon job interest is almost, but not quite, its sole activity. Frequently when labor engages in political activity—repeal of the Taft-Hartley law—it is concerned primarily with the effect of legislation upon its ability to control the job. But the term, job interest, cannot be interpreted too narrowly. The worker does not operate in a social and economic vacuum. His position in the shop is influenced not only by the political climate in the community, but also by government and social policy. Nevertheless, the job interest is central to the worker's attitude, and institution-building which is the concern of other groups may or may not attract the interest of the worker, but his reaction is likely to be influenced by his job interest.

The Commons-Perlman theory has been fully developed for about a quarter of a century, and it is proper to examine its ability to aid us to understand the attitude and conduct of labor. Moreover, this period has witnessed an unprecedented growth of the labor movement, a growth not only of existing and well-established unions, but the virtual creation of a new labor empire. Yet once we allow for differences in the structure and the problems of the organizations, their basic approach is the same. Once the new organizations, those mainly affiliated with the Congress of Industrial Organizations, secured their positions against attack and were confident of their ability to survive, they developed policies of conserving and protecting their job territory similar to those devised by the older unions. Of course, the mass production industries are different in many significant respects from the artisan trades. Yet, the aim is generally the same and the C. I. O. unions, wherever they could exclude outsiders, as in the maritime trades, were not averse to limiting entry. A policy of "narrow" job monopoly is not feasible in the mass production industries, and in this area virtue is perhaps due more to necessity than to choice. As one examines the seniority and other types of protection slowly introduced, one recognizes that despite differences in union structure and even in the experiences of workers in many branches of modern industry, the focal point of interest remains the job.

Does this view necessarily imply that the labor movement will or should pursue certain specific policies? Only in a very broad sense. The Commons-Perlman view is that the worker is mainly concerned with improving his job interest, and while the exponents of certain social doctrines have sometimes pinned the word "labor" upon their views, these ideas do not have a strong hold upon the mind of the masses of workers. If the Commons-Perlman view is correct, it means that it is possible to work out compromises and that a wide area of adjustment is available which makes possible the avoidance of catastrophic changes.

The Commons-Perlman view limits itself to the possibilities of working out a "system of harmony" in the shop; it does not go beyond that point to inquire whether there is sufficient "dynamism" in the economy to provide a high enough level of employment to make possible the steady gain in standards of life and conduct which has characterized the American economy. Trade-unionism, with its slow adaptation to change, with its emphasis upon the protection and sharing of jobs, depends upon a society which offers opportunities for employment for the great majority of the labor force. It loses its effectiveness in a society with millions idle, as in pre-Nazi Germany. There the trade-unions persisted in their age-old attitudes, but the millions virtually locked out of the labor market were in no mood to listen to such a moderate, and at the time, a meaningless gospel. It might have been better for Germany and the world that they had, but desperation is not the begetter of sweet reasonableness. One can therefore conclude that the continued acceptance by large masses of the thesis of the predominance of job interest depends upon a high-employment economy. Given these conditions, the workers are likely to pursue the limited objectives envisaged in the Commons-Perlman view. This means social compromise. At one time this would have been regarded as a form of severe criticism, and certain observers still regard social compromise as a grave error if not sin. The argument made by a recent writer who was dissatisfied with the moderateness of the program of the English government is an example of this view. He argued that the English had not solved their problems. One might add neither had the Russians, if solving problems means overcoming sloth, inefficiency, low productivity, concentration of power, and injustice. Those of us who are living one-third of a century after the October Revolution have learned the difference between the theoretically attractive program and the frequently brutal reality. Social compromise has a great deal more to recommend it than the dogmatist bewitched by his vision assumes.

This view, which might be described as a theory of labor expectations, casts some light upon union wage policy. It tells us that workers are likely to be predominantly influenced by short-run considerations because of the feeling of scarcity which pervades their thinking, and that a general wage policy is not easy to impose for the worker's chief aim is the effect of change upon his own immediate position. It means that sectional bargaining is likely to be the more acceptable, and that workers are likely to pursue any special advantage they possess. These conclusions are implied in the theory of job interest, and while such a policy may be open to criticism, it follows from the worker's attitude towards his job and his union.

A social theory is neither democratic nor non-democratic. It is, however, influenced by the environment in which it arises. The Commons-Perlman view arose in a democratic society where the emphasis was on independent, self-governing groups, cooperating together to eliminate conflict and find a basis for mutual survival. It calls attention to basic attitudes which, if fostered and allowed full and free development, will make society more resistant to totalitarian attack.

From "Job-Consciousness" to Power Accumulation

J. B. S. HARDMAN

The merits or demerits of the theory we have come together to reappraise are not determinable by the "good work" which some of its upholders maintain it has done, i.e. helped develop popular acceptance of and friendship for organized labor in the United States. A theory is right or wrong regardless of the uses it may be put to and the consequent results. The test of the adequacy of any theory of the labor movement lies in what that theory may add to our understanding of what the labor movement is, what makes it what it is, and the nature and the operation of the interrelationship between labor and the national community. To be fruitful, our re-appraisal should rest first upon a restatement of the basic tenets of that theory, and second, upon a recitation of those American socio-economic, political, and intellectual developments in the last two decades that may clearly bear upon the theory under consideration. Alternative conclusions, then, might be: (1) that the theory stands; no revision is called for; (2) that only certain aspects of the theory need adjusting—and which aspects, and what kind of adjustment; and (3) that the theory was not tenable in the first place, and if so, why.

How valid is the Commons-Perlman theory of the labor movement today? The fact that we have come to discuss the matter is an indication that there is a growing uncertainty as to the total validity of that theory.

Reprinted from *Industrial Relations Research Association Proceedings*, III (Urbana, 1950), pp. 146–157. By permission of J. B. S. Hardman and the Industrial Relations Research Association.

Thus, Professor John T. Dunlop anteceded the present effort, quite competently too, when he published, in 1948, a thoughtful essay, "The Development of Labor Organization," as a chapter in *Insights into Labor Issues*, the interesting little volume edited by Richard A. Lester and Joseph Shister.

"Despite all the epoch-making developments in the field of labor organization in the past fifteen years," wrote Mr. Dunlop, "there has been virtually no contribution to the theory [of labor organization] and scarcely a reputable narrative of this period exists." (pp. 163–4)

What, in essence, is the Commons-Perlman, or Wisconsin theory? To the extent that an elaborate theoretic system is reducible to several single-paragraphed propositions, what follows represents fairly, I believe, Mr. Perlman's position.

At this point I will note that I am not at all of the opinion that the Commons-Perlman axis is really of one piece. A case in point is the oft repeated assertion by Professor John R. Commons—made by him again as late as 1932 in the Encyclopedia of the Social Sciences, in his carefully prepared statement on the labor movement—that "the labor movement always is a protest against capitalism," which does not quite jibe with Professor Selig Perlman's general position. Nor does Mr. Perlman, it seems to me, fully underwrite Mr. Commons' position with regard to the inescapable interaction between the labor movement and the social, economic and political milieu. So I propose from this point on to refer to Mr. Perlman's or the Wisconsin theory. I should include Professor Philip Taft, not one of the original, Mayflower pilgrims, but one who later joined them on the Rock.

These, then, are the cardinal propositions in the Wisconsin theoretic orientation.

1. *Labor Not Concerned with Social Order*. "Most American wage earners do not start with any general theory of industrial society. . . . Trade unionism . . . is a conservative social force. . . . The gains of trade unionism are to the worker on a par with private property to its owner. . . . When his trade union has had the time and the opportunity to win for him decent wages and living conditions, a reasonable security on the job and a partial voice in shop management, he will . . . be chary to raze the existing system to the ground. . . ."

As to this, while it is unquestionably true that American labor has at no time demonstrated such institution-wrecking intentions, as "razing the existing system to the ground," it is not reasonable to mistake the prevailing adherence to free private enterprise for a strong devotion to capitalism as a way of carrying on the nation's business. That particular way rated very low in 1932, and history has been known to repeat itself without advance notice to college history departments.

2. *Labor Not Interested in Management Control*. ". . . Workers will

. . . submit to an almost military union discipline in their struggle against an employer . . . will be guided by the union working rules, in seeking and holding jobs; but they will mistrust and obstruct their union leaders who have become shop-bosses under whatever scheme of workers' control. . . . The typical worker seldom dreams of shouldering the risks of management. . . . The province of the union is to assert labor's collective mastery over job opportunities and employment bargains, leaving the ownership of the business to the employer, and creating for its members an ever-increasing sphere of economic security and opportunity."

The sole basis for this claim is the good judgment of Mr. Perlman, and that stands rather high with me. Yet, to be considered final, the testimony of experience is wanted. If we may refer to the experience of our cousins in the United Kingdom, it is too soon to determine that a worker would rather die than work in a plant under management other than that representing stockholders. That a worker may not like, whether wisely or otherwise, to be "bossed" by his erstwhile shopmate does not prove that he would rise up in arms against any system of remote control that was not a bankers' reorganization committee or the three per cent stock control of the chairman of the board. If, on the other hand, the TVA Administration, and the management of the state-owned University of Wisconsin do not exactly represent capitalist enterprises, there is no proof that the employes of either feel unduly enslaved or pine for a return to the fleshpots of Egypt.

3. *Trade-Unionism Rooted in the Fact of Scarcity of Job Opportunity*. "The trade unionism of the American Federation of Labor . . . was a shift from an optimistic psychology, reflecting the abundance of opportunity in a partly settled continent, to the more pessimistic trade union psychology built upon the premise that the wage earner is faced by a scarcity of opportunity."

The consideration of "scarcity of job opportunity" occupies a significant position in Mr. Perlman's theory. It is an important point. Yet what appeared to be a permanent feature of the economy when that theory was fashioned 25 years ago, on the basis of observations and considerations of the preceding 25 years or more, no longer has the old validity. The statistical record of our national production and productivity since the mid-thirties leaves little doubt that manpower shortages, rather than job scarcity, are the prospect ahead, and, with what is happening in the world, likely to continue for a good many more years. I say this not to dispose of the "job-consciousness" argument but only to indicate the changed status of the point in the prevailing unionist psychology.

4. *Politics Is Labor's Undoing*. "The unionism of the A F of L was born . . . of the American branch of the International Workingmen's Association . . . so hardy that it survived even depression—mainly because it knew how to resist the lure of politics."

The position here expressed would have been of solider quality if the word *wrong* had preceded the word politics. However, more than mere negation or affirmation of politics is involved in the old AFL injunction: "no politics in the union"—which no one in the AFL, beginning with Samuel Gompers himself, ever took seriously, except as a means to oppose the brand of politics they didn't choose to play. The issue of opposition to "politics" involves the problem of what Mr. Perlman wants the unionists to think of the relations between the state and the community, including labor. American workers and their organizations and leaders, having gravitated toward politics all through their years—and always with good reason, although at times in bad form and/or insufficiently prepared —are now in political activity for keeps, and for what it is worth. They seem to consider it worth a good deal when done efficiently. . . .

Considering the extraordinary upsets that the events of this second quarter of the century have caused in nearly every phase of socio-political and intellectual life, it is, of course, inescapable that the major assumptions of the theory under discussion should no longer fully hold their ground. Totally new are the social power relations and the very structure of power in our power-blocs-propelled national and local communities. Let us take note of some of the elements in the altered situation.

1. *Crafts Ain't What They Used to Be*. Industrial and service mechanization has played havoc with craft practices and craft-consciousness. What we have witnessed in the expanding union areas is a rising "consciousness of kind" as the labor-cementing force, rather than craft-consciousness. This newer and inclusive consciousness is proving to be the base for ever-growing union power accumulation and utilization— which is a cadillac of another color and a greater speed than the restrictive fear of job scarcity. Power accumulation has become the overall meaning and the major urge of unionism. Consciousness of kind is not synonymous with class consciousness; it is inclusive and does not impede community integration.

2. *Yes, the People Are Workers.* The "labor people," the wage-earning and wage-dependent contingent of the labor force, have become the preponderant part of our cities and communities. The social impact of this fact of our demography upon national life goes beyond simple arithmetical significance. That not more than one-third to two-fifths of the wage-earning labor force is unionized affects the situation relatively little. We need not concern ourselves here with the wider implications of the suggestion by Professor Sumner H. Slichter that "a community in which employes are the principal influence will have its own ways of looking at things, its own scale of values, its own ideas on public policies, and, to some extent, its own jurisprudence." The relevantly significant fact is that the unions have not hesitated to mobilize the developing consciousness of kind into a political community leverage directed toward objectives be-

yond the restricted perimeter of job-consciousness. They have clearly
and avowedly stepped into the theoretically *verboten* realm of political
commingling with the diverse social components of American society
in the pursuit of aims wider than the traditional "core substance" of
T, D, and H's strictly "union aspiration." Also the leaders of the unions
have become sufficiently cosmopolitan to cross the lines separating the
AFL from the CIO and both from the Independents, and labor from the
"middle class," the intellectuals included. The workers never cease to be
people.

3. *"Voluntarism" in Suspended Animation*. Mark Twain's "exaggeration" does not apply to the story of the death or "withering away" of
that time-sainted "principle of voluntarism" which the late Samuel Gompers used to express so readily, so voluminously, and so reverently. That
principle, interpreted as uncontrollable proletarian fear of and unflinch-
ing unionist opposition to state action in economic relations, was accepted,
in the Wisconsin theory, as labor's second nature. Unionists of a vintage
beyond 1933 know little of the old shining armor that used to be on view
at 901 Massachusetts Ave., N.W., Washington, D. C., except that on
special occasions it is brought up from the basement and polished up a
bit—such an occasion as was recently noted with especial solemnity. The
mailing address is still the same, but the glorious symbol is now nothing
more than an industrial museum relic.

4. *No Government in Business, Really*. Every so often labor leaders,
labor-management experts, and professors of industrial relations, as a
matter of good taste, piously declare that collective bargaining should
be kept free of interference by federal, state, or city agencies. That is
as convincing and as real as that other bit of folklore about "such government being best which governs least." Just let the government try
to check out of "meddling" in industry-labor relations, and Messrs. Green
and Murray, yes, and even Mr. Lewis and Mr. George Harrison would
make the Boston Tea Party look small and pale by comparison with
what they would stage. Of course, each of the "parties at interest" want
the government to do the "meddling" the right way, their way.

I suggest that the notion that workers are distrustful of the state be
closely re-examined. They do not, as workers, distrust the state; they may
trust or distrust those in charge of the state—and that is why they prefer
that authority be vested in themselves, or in those whom they approve
for office. American labor is and always has been power-minded. . . .

My misgivings about the Wisconsin theory derive from its sustained
effort in lecturing to death the pre-A. F. of L. half-century of militant
labor unionism because it had been characterized by a consciousness of
almost every problem on the American scene; in fact, the theory condemned workers' organizations for putting their hearts into that other
mischievous dream: life, liberty, and the pursuit of happiness. It would

seem but reasonable to assume that those who reject the factual validity of working-class-consciousness in the exceptional circumstances of American history, economy, and popular characteristics, would not urge upon labor unionism permanent tenancy in a circumscribed socio-political doghouse, in an economic "isolation ward." I wonder whether some summer night Mr. Perlman's sleep may not have been disturbed by the apparition of some laborite Patrick Henry—named Powderly, or Gompers, or Lewis, or Murray—demanding:

Is American economic life so limited, is the struggle of labor so hopeless, as to confine the union's outlook and motivation to no more and no better than a fair distribution of scarce jobs, and a life of self-containment in economic misery? As for me, give unionism the sway of full-fledged American capacity for living, or write my movement off as dead!

I doubt whether the labor failures of the pre-A. F. of L. period prove any theoretic generalizations, except that in the course of human events some efforts are successful, others are not. If complete success be made the criterion of judgment, the verdict upon the subsequent A. F. of L. period up to 1932 should be negative: by 1932 the American labor movement was more dead than alive. Of course, attentive reading of all phases of the history of labor movement progress justifies the assertion that the earlier relative failures of the pre-A. F. of L. movements laid the groundwork for the subsequent progress of the A. F. of L. even as the failures and faults of the A. F. of L. itself went into the making of the success of unionism in the late thirties by the CIO, with the A. F. of L. joining and sharing in the end-result.

I suggest that the Wisconsin labor philosophy is, in effect, the synthesis of the experience of the A. F. of L. in the years between 1886 and 1932, largely as that experience was represented in the A. F. of L. center —and that was by no means all that there was to the American union movement of the period, or even within the A. F. of L. as a whole. There were leaders in the associated unions, and outside the Federation, with great talent, carrying on wise policies, and waging significant industrial and political contests. Yet, not they, but the fountainhead of the organization is the basis of the Wisconsin theory. The wisdom of that theory is the wisdom of the Gompers type of generalship, that won out in the intensive, widespread contests for hegemony, and having consolidated its hold, held on to offices and power forever after—within the limitations that no mortal can evade. This leadership in all too many instances was not remarkable for great initiative or daring, nor even for a capacity for sustained union building.

How well did that leadership and its practices merit the distinction of being made the standard of excellence and the foundation of a theory? In the last paragraph of the chapter: *Conclusions*, of the fourth and final volume of the *Labor History*, the authors, Professors Selig Perlman and

Philip Taft, sum up: "If historians are empowered to render verdicts on those who are making history, the verdict is that the general plan of labor's campaign through the forty years (Volume IV deals with the years 1896–1932) shows an appreciation of realities, but that several critical defeats came from lack of mutual co-ordination of labor's fighting armies."

But a command that makes "critical defeats" possible because of failure to achieve "mutual co-ordination of [its] fighting armies" is hardly classifiable as "those who are making history." Co-ordination of fighting armies is not something that labor can dispense with. The "command" did worse than fail to co-ordinate "labor's fighting armies." It was badly deficient in "appreciating realities." It either did not know how, or it did not care enough, to link labor's forces with the vital dynamism of American life. The consequences were disastrous to the movement, as well as to the nation. The most charitable view that can be taken is that labor's inability to contribute active thinking and thoughtful action toward the solution of the crisis was a failure no greater than that of the nation's industrial captaincy.

There came a change in the mid-thirties, but it cannot be said that it came "according to plan." There was little planning, if any. The turn of the very course of national history saved the nation from the depths into which the captains of industry and a government that would follow rather than lead had plunged it. And, in consequence of the historic national shift, the labor movement recovered, and has since been advancing. The leaders? "The gods led the wise ones and pushed the stubborn ones."

It is a decade-and-a-half since labor leadership, that part of it that was willing to move ahead when the road was sighted, began to fill its logical role. These leaders have been building union power, on economic, political, and social fronts, and endeavoring to reach the place labor merits as a most vital functional unit in the dynamic equilibrium of forces which is American organized society. The union leaders left behind the theory that had rationalized the movement's earlier behavior—licking its wounds. They cannot be expected to regret it. Must we continue "sitting by the waters of Babylon and weeping?"

I submit, in sum, that a realistic understanding of the labor movement can be achieved only if, first, we free ourselves of certain predispositions regarding American labor, and second, we take cognizance of the interplay of forces in American society. Ours is a power-conscious world. Groups contend for power. Within each group, individuals, singly or in coalitions, contend for mastery. Social power energy, like other forms of energy, centers upon peaks, and individual leaders appear as the carriers of condensated social-power energy. But though cloaked in personalities, and emphasizing special aims, the "core-substance" of unionism is an ever-evolving contest for a satisfying share in carrying on the business of living within the reach or the outlook of the nation and the time.

Recognizing the vital place of "job-consciousness" in union thinking, and the pressures of "scarcity of job opportunity," cognizance is to be taken of the fact that the thinking of union leaders, in the running of organizations and the shaping of long range policies, is primarily concerned with the building of power in industry. That power is sought in various ways: via control of manpower, and of industrial competence; through the exercise of political influence; and by the creation of a favorable public opinion.

Leadership is a major force in union building. Workers have always wanted and have readily followed strong leadership, and have more often than not been inclined to disregard generally undesirable concentration of power in their leaders if there seemed to be an adequate return. The role of leadership in American labor is paramount.

These traits of labor behavior in the United States have their roots in the undramatic yet irrefutable fact that the American workers are the American people and live in the American environment. To the extent that the earlier history of the American union and labor movements at times abounds in diversities rather than similarities of conduct, it is profitable to bear in mind that the trend toward an essential oneness of labor behavior parallels the development of a cohered American people and nation out of scattered and diffused communities; 1950 is the sequence, not the overturn, of 1850—in labor as well as in the nation.

These are propositions, I submit, which are cardinal materials for the construction of a labor movement theory.

FOR FURTHER READING: The Commons theory is defended by Philip Taft, "A Rereading of Selig Perlman's Theory of the Labor Movement," *Industrial and Labor Relations Review*, IV (1949), pp. 70–77. Critical appraisals include Adolf Sturmthal, "Comments on Selig Perlman's 'A Theory of the Labor Movement,'" *Industrial and Labor Relations Review*, IV (1950), pp. 483–496, and Charles A. Gulick and Melvin K. Bers, "Insight and Illusion in Perlman's Theory of the Labor Movement," *Industrial and Labor Relations Review*, VI (1952), pp. 510–531. A good survey is Mark Perlman, "Labor Movement Theories: Past, Present and Future," *Industrial and Labor Relations Review*, XIII (1959), pp. 338–348. See also L. S. Reed, *The Labor Philosophy of Samuel Gompers* (New York: 1930), and Leo Wolman, *Growth of American Trade Unions* (New York: 1924).

24. *World War I*

PROBLEM: *Did business groups desire American entrance into World War I?*

Since the causes for the entrance of the United States into World War I are complex, historians have deliberated over the emphasis to be accorded economic factors which hastened the end of American neutrality. Soon after 1919 a group of Revisionists arose who attributed the participation of the United States in World War I to the machinations of businessmen who had extended financial aid to the British. In this manner some Americans acquired a direct interest in an Allied victory. Such an interpretation "revised" the official explanation, as enunciated by Woodrow Wilson, that the United States entered the war to maintain its neutral rights and to make the world safe for democracy. Thus, an issue arose among historians over the motives for American participation. In the selection below, moderate Revisionist Richard Van Alstyne seeks to show that big business interests, especially those who made private American loans to the Allies, such as the J. P. Morgan syndicate, prejudiced American neutrality. This interpretation was increasingly challenged after the rise of European totalitarian regimes during the 1930's. Harold Syrett spoke for many of the new generation when he showed clearly that the business community, if judged by opinions reflected in its press, certainly was not united in its views toward the belligerents. Like others, business attitudes shifted with the war and were affected by patriotic and ethnic factors. Both authors help to unravel some of the complexities of economic motivations on the eve of United States entrance into World War I. How did business groups express their approval of the Allied cause? How many different views toward the war were reflected in the business press? Did businessmen lead public opinion or follow it? Why would businessmen favor peace?

Private American Loans to the Allies, 1914–1916

RICHARD W. VAN ALSTYNE *1933*

When on April 6, 1917, the United States declared war on the German Empire, the American people already held a "stake" in the war which, in round numbers, amounted to more than $2,300,000,000. Approximately $27,000,000 of this total represented investment in the cause of Germany. The remainder comprised advances made to the Allies, and consisted of a wide variety of private investments—credits extended by banks, short-term commercial notes taken by business houses in payment for war material, and loans with longer maturities, which were in large part absorbed by the general public.

Between the fall of 1914 and the summer of 1915 a revolution took place in the investment position of the United States. We ceased to be primarily a borrower of capital, and we suddenly became a lender on a large scale. Without the great struggle in Europe this startling reversal would have been impossible. The needs of the warring nations for the products of the American mine, field, and factory multiplied rapidly. Their means of immediate payment, on the contrary, steadily diminished. Their exports inevitably shrank. Attempts to pay in gold proved totally inadequate, and it became apparent that, if purchases were to continue, all thought of conducting business according to groceteria principles must be abandoned.

Wall Street indeed anticipated the need for accommodation. As early as the third week of the war rumors were noised abroad that certain French bankers had approached J. P. Morgan & Company on a loan. No difficulty from a legal or a moral standpoint was expected, since it was well understood that the rules of international law permitted the private citizens of a neutral nation to make loans to belligerent governments for war purposes. "Christianity listens to Sunday prayers for peace," remarked the *Wall Street Journal* ironically, "and the next day sends out representatives to the powers to see if anything more can be sold them to prolong the war." "In the judgment of this Government," countered President Wilson in a formal *obiter dictum* on August 15, "loans by American bankers to any foreign nation which is at war are inconsistent with the true spirit of neutrality." In his *Memoirs* William Jennings Bryan relates how sensitive the President and he were to the situation. They feared that if loans were sought by the belligerent governments, "the country would be divided into groups, each group engaged

Reprinted by permission from *Pacific Historical Review*, II, No. 2 (1933), pp. 180–193.

in negotiating loans to the belligerent countries with which it sympathized. . . ." Great numbers of the American people, Bryan believed, would get to have a material interest in the success of the country whose bonds they held, and their partisanship would increase accordingly. In short, the war hates of the Old World would be transferred to our shores, and civil strife might even occur.

The administration was destined to be faced with a serious dilemma, however. Its standards of international morality might be one thing; the precedents of international law and the demands of commerce were another. Loans to belligerents by private American citizens could not be prevented without damming up the channels of trade. Nor was there either any legal or any practicable method by which they could be confined to mere credit operations arranged by banks, and loans raised by popular subscription excluded, if the Allies chose to resort to the latter method.

In October, 1914, the administration was forced to modify its position. Omitting all reference this time to loans as "inconsistent with the true spirit of neutrality," it acknowledged freely that they could not be isolated from general trade and that it was not unneutral for Americans to grant them to either side. Bank credit was soon thereafter extended to the belligerents. The National City Bank made the first loan, consisting of a $10,000,000 advance to France in October, and during the winter months of 1914–15, similar modest advances were made to France, Russia, and Germany by other banking institutions. Rather significantly, the German loan was the first loan of a nation at war to be offered for *public* sale in this country.

These small transactions scarcely met the credit needs of Europe, however. Orders arrived in the United States so fast that in the three months from April to June, 1915, American exports to Europe more than doubled over the corresponding period in 1914. The influence of this movement was reflected in the foreign exchanges. Sterling began falling in June, reached $4.62½ on August 29, and then suddenly dipped to $4.50 on September 1, which was the low for the year. In the meantime secret efforts by Great Britain and France to obtain a large loan had proved unavailing, and it was finally decided in August to send a joint commission to America to negotiate.

The Anglo-French commission arrived in New York on September 10, and opened deliberations at once with a group of American financiers headed by J. P. Morgan & Company. Out of these early meetings the following facts emerged:

1. The Allied commission expected a credit of $1,000,000,000, upon which it desired to draw without restriction for the purchase of supplies in this country.

2. The bankers doubted that a $1,000,000,000 loan could be raised, and some, at least, of them expressed a desire for collateral.

3. The commission was not prepared to furnish collateral, and urged that the general credit of the two governments ought to be adequate.

4. As in the case of any large loan, a syndicate with broad membership must be arranged to underwrite this loan, and efforts would be made to obtain popular subscription.

5. The loan was to be treated as a national problem in foreign exchange. The Allies desired to buy munitions, but they were also interested in general purchases of bread-stuffs, meats, cotton, wool and woolen goods, leather and leather goods, etc., which would affect the prosperity of all sections of the country. Viewed in this light the loan was an undertaking of national importance. The problem of the bankers therefore was two-fold: to "educate" the nation to the benefits of financing the Allies, and to determine the amount and terms of the loan in such a way that it would attract not only financial institutions outside of New York, but small individual investors as well.

The project had no opposition from the administration. Indeed there were indications that it viewed the matter in a favorable light. The Comptroller of the Currency openly urged the banks to use their swollen cash reserves by lending to the Allies. The Federal Reserve Board let it be known that commercial paper connected with transactions arising out of the loan would be eligible for rediscount in the ordinary way. And from the State Department reassurance was obtained that the loan would not be considered unneutral. . . .

Definite and accurate information is here given as to the membership of the syndicate. The total subscribers, comprising banks, trust companies, insurance companies, private banking firms, dealers, manufacturers, and private individuals, aggregated 1567, and were distributed among forty-one states. One thousand four hundred forty-five of these were located in fourteen eastern states (including Ohio and Maryland). New York headed the list with 665 members (465 in New York City), Pennsylvania came second with 223, and Massachusetts third with 217. Thus the industrial and shipping center of the country was overwhelmingly represented. Thirteen Middle Western and Rocky Mountain states, representing the grain, meat, and mining interests, accounted for eighty-three members. The South came next with twenty-seven members, located in eleven states. And finally, the three states of the Pacific Coast, representing fruit and other agricultural interests, yielded twelve members.

Among the subscribers were 207 individuals, in addition to private manufacturing concerns, who apparently entered the syndicate as investors, and not with the intention of reselling their holdings. The newspapers indulged in much merry guessing as to who were the big subscribers. The first $100,000,000 of the offering was reported taken by six subscribers. In addition, many subscriptions ranging from $1,000,000 to $10,000,000 were alleged to have been received. Both John D. and William Rockefeller were said to be heavy investors, the Guggenheim brothers, Otto H. Kahn, James J. Hill, Charles W. Nash, president of General Motors, Irving T. Bush, president of the Bush Terminal Company, and John N. Willys, president of the Willys Knight Company of Toledo. This list, if authentic, indicates that the captains of industry —the munitions makers, steel men, automobile manufacturers, railroad and shipping men—whose interests were directly and very closely tied up with the cause of the Allies, invested heavily. Still another imposing list of known subscribers included Daniel Catlin of St. Louis, Joseph H. Choate of New York, Robert T. Lincoln of Washington, D. C., Charles W. Eliot of Cambridge, Massachusetts, and E. P. Ripley, president of the Santa Fe Railroad. A statement signed by these men and commending the loan to small investors appeared in the Chicago *Herald*, October 18, 1915, a step which must have borne some weight as a "talking point" in the sales campaign.

It is difficult, if not impossible, to obtain an accurate picture of the number of small investors. The writer has ascertained by direct inquiry from J. P. Morgan & Company and from one of the large banks in Chicago that no records have been kept of the number or distribution of the sales. Certain deductions may be made, however. The American Bank Note Company, at the time of the original issue, engraved the following pieces: 493,000 @ $1000 each; 25,000 @ $500 each; 48,000 @ $100 each. It seems reasonable to assume that there were almost as many individual subscribers to the issue of amounts of $500 and less as there were separate pieces printed. How many more subscribers bought bonds of $1000 denomination cannot be determined. It is clear that the dispersal of small sales was nationwide, however. . . .

On the other hand, the writer is greatly impressed by the cordial response with which American "big business" greeted the transaction. The loan reflected the close intimacy into which the industry of the country had already been drawn with the Allied cause. Subscription to it was not confined to corporations whose directors might be suspected of pro-Ally sentiment. Banks and other institutions with German affiliations subscribed to it, or, if they did not, they adopted a benevolently neutral attitude. The German Savings Bank of New York kept a strictly neutral attitude, despite pressure exerted on it by hostile propaganda. Kuhn, Loeb & Company abstained from joining the syndicate, but was reported to be in favor of the loan as a necessary protection for American business interests, and at least two members of the firm were said to have subscribed as individiduals. Realization that the loan was "good for business," belief that it was essential if the rising volume of exports was to continue, were hence the principal factors in determining its success. Probably the greater part was purchased by individuals or concerns whose business prosperity had come to be more or less directly dependent upon a continuation of the Allies' purchases. But all investors were convinced of the gilt edge quality of their investment, and believed unquestioningly in the financial integrity of the Allies. That they believed also in their military success, goes without saying.

Nevertheless, though the exigencies of American business demanded that the loan be absorbed, its consequences ran deep. The British and French governments acknowledged that it was "a measurable factor in the final outcome of the war." In England there was some grumbling over the rate of interest, but the loan was speedily ratified by Parliament and hailed as a "valuable financial stroke, with political value, in the widest sense, into the bargain."

The great Anglo-French loan proved indeed only a first step in a long series of American advances to the Allied Powers. It was the largest single advance and the only unsecured loan offered to the public. Beginning in July, 1916, and ending on April 1, 1917, it was followed by five additional loans to the British and French governments, ranging from $94,500,000 to $300,000,000 each. All of these later loans were secured by collateral, handled by syndicates, and sold to the public.

Of these manifold advances by far the most significant was the joint loan of October, 1915. Few private financial operations have received so much attention from the American people as did this transaction. It sharpened the division between "pro-Ally" and "pro-German," to the discomfiture of the latter. It buttressed the credit of the Allies at a crucial time, and buoyed up American exports of all kinds. It strengthened the tie between American business interests and the Allied governments, and, with the additional loans, saturated the American people with the consciousness that their material interests were bound up overwhelmingly with the cause of the Allies.

The Business Press and American Neutrality, 1914–1917

HAROLD C. SYRETT   *1945*

Few problems in recent American history have attracted more attention than the businessman's attitude toward the United States' role as a neutral during the First World War. Throughout the twenties and thirties many historians maintained that the American businessman consciously helped

Reprinted from *The Mississippi Valley Historical Review*, XXXII (September, 1945), pp. 215–230.

to maneuver this country into war. Charles and Mary Beard, Harry Elmer Barnes, and C. Hartley Grattan have all asserted that one of the reasons that the United States went to war was the businessman's desire to have the United States government underwrite his financial interests in the Allies. While these authors emphasized such other factors as British propaganda, inept American diplomacy, and German submarine warfare, they also made it clear that in their estimate the machinations of the American businessman could not be overlooked in any study of the United States decision to abandon neutrality. To Americans who sympathized with these views, the hearings before the Nye Committee in 1934–1935 seemed to provide documentary proof that the United States had been forced into war in 1917 by selfish business interests.

In recent years there has been a reaction against the tendency to ascribe our entrance into the war to the stratagems of the businessman. No major book has yet appeared to exonerate the businessman, but more than one historian has protested against the earlier interpretation. Professors Morison and Commager in their American history textbook have stated: "That the American financial stake in an Allied victory may have influenced some people is possible. But the financial community as a whole, it was well known at the time, favored American neutrality rather than American participation; for neutrality afforded Wall Street all the profits of war without the compensating sacrifices and taxation."

In marshalling their facts for both sides of this controversy, historians have generally overlooked one invaluable source—the business press. While business publications may not reveal the behind-the-scenes activities of the businessman, they do offer an insight into his reasoning. By their very nature, these papers cannot provide the final answer to the question of the businessman's responsibility for American participation in the World War. They do, however, contain a fund of information which cannot be ignored by anyone who wishes to understand the attitude of American financiers, merchants, and industrialists during this period.

A review of trade and financial papers from 1914 to 1917 shows that the businessman was interested primarily in his own economic welfare; but it does not show that he was any more desirous of war than the majority of Americans. Before the German announcement of unrestricted submarine warfare on January 31, 1917, the businessman viewed problems arising from the war as business questions which had to be settled on their economic merits. After that date, he became a nationalist as well as a businessman. . . .

The businessman's attitude toward loans to the belligerents shifted with the course of the war. Bryan's announcement on August 15, 1914 that the State Department disapproved of, but could not prevent, "loans by American bankers to any foreign nation which is at war," was endorsed by most business publications. On August 22, 1914, *Bradstreet's* wrote ". . . the consensus of opinion in financial circles is adverse to borrowing operations at present by foreign nations in the American markets. In fact, the ruling by our own government produced a feeling of relief in such quarters. The proposed establishment by foreign countries of large credits here at a juncture when it is important that renewed exports of our food-stuffs shall create a balance of trade in our favor could hardly fail to meet with opposition." In subsequent months, financial papers pointed out that the belligerents were poor risks and that American investors would object "to taking European bonds on the ground that the borrowers are every day destroying portions of the security therefor." As late as July, 1915, the *Journal of Commerce and Commercial Bulletin* was saying that the United States could not "afford to permit American resources to become so deeply pledged to the war as to leave us in a crippled or inflated state at the close of hostilities with a long period of comparative depression before us and only a perhaps doubtful investment in European securities as compensation."

By the fall of 1915 negotiations for the first large Anglo-French loan were in progress. It was good business to maintain American foreign trade, and this was the only way it could be done. The same papers which had criticized loans a few months earlier overcame their objections. The *Chicago Banker* now considered loans "pro-America in the strictest sense." The *Wall Street Journal* complained that opposition to the loan "assumes that we are lending money for war. We are not. We are financing American trade." The *Journal of Commerce and Commercial Bulletin* declared that there was "nothing unneutral about acceding to such a banking proposal as the visiting Commission is expected to make, and it is unfortunate to have it treated as if it were intended especially to help one party to the conflict in Europe." The *Commercial and Financial Chronicle* faced the issue without equivocation. It bluntly asserted that without the loan, the "inevitable effect would be to bring our merchandise export trade to a standstill, and this in turn might mean—it is no use mincing words—little short of national disaster." After September, 1915, only the *Bankers Magazine* remained in opposition to loans to the Allies. Under the title, "Lending For Destructive Purposes," it asked in its November, 1916 issue, ". . . is it not becoming apparent that these loans may have the effect of an indefinite prolongation of the war?" But there was an equally important question: "Is not our ability to supply loans to South America and perhaps to China for purposes of construction somewhat lessened by the large loans we are making to the Entente Allies for purposes of destruction?"

The businessman's attitude toward foreign loans was obviously determined by economic considerations. But even in his trade journals, he buttressed his stand with references to patriotism and morality. For this he should not necessarily be condemned. Like a lawyer pleading a case, the businessman could not afford to overlook any arguments which might contribute to the strength of the position which he had taken. . . .

Before February 1, 1917, only a few business publications were consistent supporters of the President's foreign policy. Writing on November 9, 1916, when the outcome of the election was still in doubt, the *Journal of Commerce and Commercial Bulletin* said that regardless of the result, the "course to be pursued in our foreign relations cannot safely be essentially different from that already adopted." But the *Journal of Commerce* was an exception. Most trade and financial papers were openly hostile to the administration's foreign policy. The *Bankers Magazine* thought that American policy should "be shaped more by practical common sense and less by that sickly sentimentalism of which William J. Bryan is perhaps the most conspicuous advocate." The *Economist* condemned "the spirit of vacillation in which Wilson has dealt with our relations to Germany." Although the business press freely criticized Wilson before 1917, it never proposed American belligerency as an alternative policy.

After the announcement on January 31, 1917 of Germany's campaign of unrestricted submarine warfare, few business publications had anything but praise for the administration. As April 2, 1917 approached, more and more papers came out for active participation in the war. Many editors, believing that they would be condemned for urging intervention, insisted that they were motivated only by patriotism. On March 29, 1917, *Iron Age* wrote: "Now is the golden opportunity [for iron and steel manufacturers] to take a decided stand, and take it promptly, in showing that they favor war, not for the sake of any financial or personal gain, but because the highest interests of liberty throughout the world, and especially in the American hemisphere, demand that the United States shall take its side and support the forces of the Entente Powers." On March 17, the *Dry Goods Economist* declared: "The question of whether this country is going to take steps right now to protect itself is not a political question; it is a business question. And it demands a businesslike and patriotic answer. It is for the merchants and manufacturers of this country . . . to enlighten their fellow citizens." It may or may not be significant that not one paper mentioned our loans to the Allies as a reason for American participation. . . .

Instead of wishing to send American troops abroad to preserve his loans, the American businessman—at least, in his trade publications— hoped to uphold his country's honor with a mere token war. This may have been part of the businessman's propaganda to conceal his real motives by painting a comparatively pleasant picture of this country's role in the conflict. On the other hand, it is also possible to conclude that the businessman did not realize that his financial stake in the war was threatened by a German victory. If he had known the precarious condition of the countries which had borrowed his money, he would in all likelihood have demanded an all-out effort. If the latter interpretation is correct, the businessman did not want a war to save his loans, but desired only a patriotic gesture which would provide the least possible interference with the *status quo*. As always, the businessman feared change more than any other factor.

The usual generalizations cannot explain the variations in the business press during the period of neutrality. The traditional isolationism of the Midwest does not apply in this case, for trade and financial papers in that section were as bellicose as those along the Atlantic seaboard. The only paper which opposed an American declaration of war was published in the canyons of downtown New York, and the ostensible reasons for its stand were those which had been cherished by westerners since the days of Jefferson. Nor can German origins be used to explain deviations from the norm. Business publications were probably more opposed to German-American groups than were any other portion of American opinion. Legal and moral arguments do not offer a much better guide to the business-man's attitude. Numerous references were made to international law and morality, but they were frequently termed irrelevant when they could not be used to reenforce economic views.

In general, the American businessman made up his mind for business reasons. When trade and financial papers differed over a particular issue, they were not reflecting conflicting sectional, national, moral, or legal opinions, but had reached their conclusions because of different economic interpretations. The only exception may be those papers which urged war, but warned against its economic effects.

Judged by his trade papers, the businessman cannot be charged with war mongering before 1917. His principal interest was profits. Business leaders may or may not be accused of shortsightedness in not realizing that their constant demand for higher profits might result in war, but this is not the same as asserting that American businessmen consciously maneuvered this country into war. After February 1, 1917, businessmen became "war mongers"; but so did most other Americans.

FOR FURTHER READING: Stressing American financial involvements as a factor for American participation in the war are C. C. Tansill, *America Goes to War* (New York, 1938), J. V. Fuller, "The Genesis of the Munitions Traffic," *Journal of Modern History*, VI (September, 1934), pp. 280–293, and Paul Birdsall, "Neutrality and Economic Pressures," *Science and Society*, III (Spring, 1939), pp. 217–228. Emphasizing non-economic forces are Charles Seymour, *American Diplomacy During the World War* (Baltimore, 1934), Walter Millis, *The Road to War* (Cambridge, 1935), Ernest R. May, *World War and American Isolation, 1914–1917* (Cambridge, 1959), and Hanson Baldwin, *World War I—An Outline History* (New York, 1962).

25. *Business in the 1920's*

PROBLEM: *Did advertising promote economic expansion?*

Of the various twentieth century economic trends which first assumed large scale proportions after World War I, mass consumption was one of the most important. After 1919, increased distribution of goods was fostered by numerous techniques, but none was more striking than the phenomenal development of advertising. To be sure, American businessmen had utilized it in earlier years but never on such an extensive scale. No wonder that with its maturation, students of the American economy sought to assess its impact. Its critics, represented by economists like Collis A. Stocking, charged that it disrupted natural functions of the economic system by creating artificial wants, frequently by misleading statements. In addition to creating unnecessary expenses, it also disrupted the normal functions of the market. A very different and more favorable approach was formulated by Neil H. Borden of the Harvard Business School, who claimed that advertising did not create new demands. It only accelerated expansion or contraction of those already in existence. But Borden also pointed to certain of its constructive, positive functions, such as the promotion of new investments and of technological change which increased real national income and fostered economic growth. Both authors raise some fundamental questions concerning advertising. How does advertising benefit the consumer? Can the advantages of advertising be retained without some of its negative characteristics? Does advertising create a conflict between moral and economic ends?

Modern Advertising and Economic Theory

COLLIS A. STOCKING

During the past few years there has been a veritable flood of articles, monographs and books about advertising. The bulk of this literature has come from the pens of the laity, professional advertisers, and teachers of advertising in our business colleges. The layman's criticisms have been written in an understandable and interesting style for popular appeal and have been heavily discounted in the field of "serious thought." The advertisers' pronouncements concerning their profession have been similarly discredited, possibly because they are assumed to be biased and not "scientific." The teachers of advertising seem to be essentially interested in the technique of advertising and have not been looked to for any penetrating analysis. It is not quite clear, however, how the economist can justify having continually ignored this amazingly powerful force which has entered his own arena. Can it be that he has been so generous with his explanations of the effect of other forces in our economic organization that, like Epimetheus of old, he has nothing left to bestow upon this perhaps the most noble of all economic handiwork?

It is interesting to note that in almost all of the older standard texts and treatises on economics only incidental mention of advertising occurs. Some of the more recent writers, in their meticulous desire to be all inclusive, give an account of the phenomenon; but, with two or three notable exceptions, the discussion is tacked on awkwardly like a vermiform appendix and has little or no connection with their basic presumptions. This observation will be readily accepted if the contentions of this article are tenable. The writer maintains it is impossible to admit fully the effect of advertising and at the same time regard orthodox theory as an adequate explanation of the marketing and distributive process. . . .

Economic theory is used here in the sense of an explanation of the direction of industry under a régime of free enterprise and free exchange. This is the sense in which the term economic theory is employed by Cournot, Jevons, Pareto, J. B. Clark, Schumpeter and others. This economic theory has generally concluded that under conditions of free enterprise each agent of production will be rewarded automatically according to its contribution in satisfying wants. F. H. Knight states the case as follows:

Modern society (on the economic side) is organized on the theory that the owners of productive resources will find their best use and place them in it, because in that way they can procure the largest returns for themselves. This

Reprinted by permission from the author and *American Economic Review,* XXI (March, 1931), pp. 43–55.

system, therefore, involves the assumption that even in a complex organization the separate contribution of each separate productive agency can be identified, and that free competitive relations tend to impute to each agency its specific contribution as its reward for participation in productive activity. And to the extent that the system works at all, that we have an economic order instead of chaos, this assumption must be justified.

It is to be maintained in this article that the effect of modern advertising is to render inadequate current economic theory as an explanation of modern commercial processes. Since this is the case, it might be recorded here that Knight conceives the purpose of economic theory to be the justification of the assumption he sets forth in the above quotation.[1]

Value is generally supposed to be determined as the result of dual forces of competition. We have, on the one hand, competition among various producers to rid themselves of products at the highest price possible, and on the other, competition among consumers to secure these products in which are incorporated want-satisfying qualities. The producers are thus motivated by the possibility of securing a profit, and the consumers are motivated by the desire to satisfy their wants. Under such conditions, if some product appears that can command a conspicuously profitable price for its producer, his competitors, it is presumed, will transfer their equipment to the creation of this product in order that they also may share in the extraordinary gains. When they transfer their equipment in this way, the supply of the product will be increased and the competition will force the price down. At the same time the supply of the commodities of which the production has been discontinued, will be lessened and consequently, to some degree, their prices will be raised. In this fashion the maximum physical production is identified with maximum net returns. There is a tendency, in other words, for the margin of net return which is identified with physical product to be equal in all lines of production.

Some such reasoning as this is basic in the so-called marginal theories of value. Of course it is freely admitted that certain lags, frictions and changes enter into the situation to prevent these forces from working perfectly. Legal restraints like patents, franchises, trade marks, etc., are obvious, and technological difficulties like immobility of some of the fac-

---

[1] In theory like H. J. Davenport's where production and distribution are synonymous terms, one cannot justify distribution on the basis that the shares of distribution depend upon the efficiency of production, because by his own analysis the amount of production is measurable only by the proceeds. It is significant that Davenport denies all ethical implications of his theory. But it is also significant that such a denial robs economic theory of the principal purpose for which it was developed.

It has been argued that Veblen's treatises are on economic theory, but more exactly they are explanations of the development of institutions. They are perhaps regarded as economics because the institutions are intimately connected with our economic practices.

The implications of classical and neo-classical economic theory are well demonstrated in L. A. Morrison's critical treatise on economic theory (yet in manuscript form); and the writer wishes to acknowledge Professor Morrison's influence.

tors are qualifying considerations. However, the tendency of economic forces toward maximum physical production and service in response to the tastes of the members of society, is presumed to be, to a large extent, inexorable.

The tastes which are the fundamental determinants of the alignments which productive agents will make are always presumed to be independent of the person catering to them. That such preferences are independent of the producers of goods who are to profit by their existence and that no enterprise can be held responsible for the desirability of consumptive habits, are important presumptions, for it is by such reasoning that the economist has been able to avoid the necessity of evaluating wants. The ethical question is specifically denied, the wants may be good or bad; but it is not necessary for the economist to pass judgment on them, for the pursuit of profit which directs economic activity is not responsible for their quality. "Economic wants may be serious, frivolous, or even positively pernicious, but the objects of these wants all alike possess utility in the economic sense." . . .

The opinion that there is something inherent in our system which automatically guides the instruments of production into those fields or pursuits which yield maximum satisfaction is reflected in the field of marketing and advertising in the rather popular shibboleth: "The consumer is King." It is assumed that the consumer executes a royal prerogative of thumbs down on the producer that contravenes His Majesty's peculiar tastes and thus metes out just punishment to the impudent or careless. Likewise the consumer is supposed to reward abundantly, by rich patronage, the courtier who caters most faithfully to his whims. As a corollary of this, it is presumed that the consumer knows best what he wants; and, since the ultimate end of production is the satisfaction of human wants the *summum bonum* of economic activity is achieved by the rather simple expedient of leaving it all to the consumer to decide.

Such conclusions emphasize the importance of remembering that traditional economic theory assumes of necessity that wants of the consumer of goods are independent of the enterpriser who is to furnish the goods. Imagine the confusion that would follow if J. B. Clark and Marshall and other votaries were forced to concede that the tastes of the consumer were manipulated by those who supplied the goods. Is it not true, however, that by modern advertising wants are often successfully directed so that an ambitious enterpriser is without the necessity of scrupulously abiding by the consumer's choices because he possesses the machinery for modifying and changing the consumer's wants to his own end of greater profits?

Here it must be recalled that, since the fundamental concepts of economic theory were first formulated, a great change has taken place in our methods of production. This may well account for the lack of adjustment between theory and the present-day economic system. The situation is suggestive of one of Veblen's observations to the effect that the habits of thought change more slowly than do the material circumstances of life. The current views concerning things, the common sense apprehensions of what are the proper limits, rights and responsibilities, are the outgrowth of traditions, experiences and speculations of past generations. Possibly advertising is too modern to be properly understood, although some commentators have held that modern advertising is a direct outgrowth of practices of antiquity. Perhaps some analogy can be made from carefully selected data; but such comparisons can be made only by neglecting important developments that give modern advertising its chief characteristics. . . .

It is maintained here that the fundamental aims of advertising are: the creation of wants, the shaping of tastes, the determination of values.[2] This thesis has been generally denied by teachers of advertising and advertising agencies, even though they will admit that manufacturers "have used advertising when their plants have necessitated a *readjustment* or *control* of the demand for their product." They do not admit "that the primary economic function of advertising is to stimulate or control consumption," that is, to create wants, but do declare that the demand for articles "is being awakened, intensified, directed and made articulate." Be this as it may, if we admit the infinite potentialities of tastes of individuals, the insistence that advertising awakens, intensifies, and directs desires and does not create them becomes inconsequential.

In elaboration of the views of teachers of advertising, and some economists, one writer insists that the chief function of advertising is education and calls attention to an analysis of a typical issue of one of our well-known women's magazines. The analysis indicated to him:

. . . that over 40 per cent of the advertisements contained information of such service that it might have been placed in the editorial columns. It told her how to prepare better meals, how to arrange her kitchen, how to decorate her home, how to preserve her personal appearance, and how to protect the health of herself and her family. In many instances she could make use of the information without buying the advertiser's product. When she is educated to a better knowledge of health and diet, or a keener appreciation of decorative arts in the home, she has benefited immediately. Later the advertiser may profit also, if and when she buys his article.

It is just such undue emphasis upon the incidental educational qualities of advertising that beclouds the whole issue from the standpoint of the

[2] This position is sometimes admitted by the advertisers and economists, though it seems that in their analysis, dissent is more frequent. Admission makes it easy to demonstrate that the accepted economic theory is deficient. If the producer has power to produce tastes, how can it be said that his energies will be expended in catering to the existing wants? The beneficence of such a system is perforce identified with the beneficence of the individuals who are to secure a reward for successfully warping the community's desires.

traditional economic analysis. It would be amazing if the advertisers were able to "put over" an idea without encroaching at all upon the field of general knowledge. It is surprising, indeed, that there is not a great deal more than 40 per cent of advertisements which contain information of such service that it might be placed in the editorial columns, when we recall that the modern magazine is essentially a product of advertising.

From the viewpoint of economic analysis it is unimportant whether the information disseminated by the advertiser be beneficial or pernicious; though it is granted that such questions of goodness or badness might be of interest in an ethical evaluation of advertising. It is admitted, in fact insisted by the writer, that any significant evaluation of advertising must proceed along such lines. It is necessary here only to emphasize that there is nothing in economic theory by which its goodness or badness can be tested. It may be profitable to the manufacturer, and the critic may deem it desirable that it be impressed upon the minds of the consumer that Lucky Strike cigarettes possess some magic quality for soothing the throat of the smoker, or that the socially élite sleep in Simmons beds, and so on. But in so far as he is not immune to the calculated and subtle influence of the advertiser, the critic's evaluations are the results of attitudes instilled in him by advertising. . . .

For the purpose of our analysis, it is not important that certain goods satisfy certain wants, but it is important that advertising has created the wants which the advertised goods will satisfy. Even if one is prepared to admit the contention which seems to be a great consolation to the advertiser, that in the major changes the consumer does largely select the trends of consumption, the thesis of this article remains untouched. Whoever heard of an advertising campaign failing because it was trying to create favor for something for which the people had no liking? Advertising fails only when it fails to make people want particular things. It is true that a few long-standing customs, the few that remain, may show a remarkable stubbornness before the advertiser's relentless attack. A few years ago we witnessed the "emancipation" of women from cumbersome styles. The long skirts were abandoned and with them went the constraining corsets. Everyone joined in the chorus sung in praise of the new sanity in dress. Today we witness the spectacle of the reverse. The style czars acting in collusion with the textile makers, it is alleged, have demanded the return of the long silhouette designs which require the wearing of the torturing corset in the achieving of a proper foundation. It is not surprising that women are adopting the new fashions, though some advertisers have been a little surprised at the slowness with which they were succeeding in putting the idea across.

Admitting for the sake of argument that the consumer enjoys some power of selecting trends of consumption, one is forced to note that the whole environmental scheme is colored by advertising practices. The

media by which the environment exerts its influence on the individual
have been redesigned or reconstructed to meet the needs of advertising.
In turning to the changes wrought by the aggregate of advertising campaigns, contemplate the less subtle changes in our scenery, both urban
and rural, attributable to the works of the outdoor advertisers. The
gaudy achievements in revamping the interiors of our street cars, suburban and interurban trains, busses, etc., are too conspicuous to need mention here. The same is true, to a less obvious degree, of the changes
wrought in the field of literature. The magazines of the early nineteenth
century were edited for a circulation that would now be unprofitable.
Most of them in the light of present-day standards would be regarded as
austere and dry. They were before the advent of advertising and the jazz
age of change. The gaudy, mad colors that make our corner news stands
resemble a drunken rainbow had not appeared upon the scene. The day
had not yet come when they could afford to give the magazine away. It
has been described as an age of crusades. Homely virtues were deter-
minedly cherished before the columns were to be sold to the god of
change who could afford to pay. Poe received four dollars a page for the
"Murders in the Rue Morgue." Hawthorne was offered five dollars a page
in 1842. Could it be that these men were unworthy amateurs? Probably
not, but advertising has changed the whole appearance of journalism.
The format, brilliant colors and contents of the modern magazine are
determined by advertising. The best writers are those who are most easily
incorporated in business purpose. Compare Poe, Hawthorne, Whittier,
Whitman, Cooper, Lowell, and Longfellow with Edgar Guest, the late
Dr. Frank Crane, Zane Grey, and Harold Bell Wright. The unusual success of the latter group is undoubtedly due to their easy adaptability to
the rather popular and profitable tastes of advertising.

It may be insisted that all these cultural developments are good. It
must, however, be reiterated that it makes no difference from the viewpoint of this analysis. It is of no consequence here whether the precepts
that advertising engenders are as impeccable as the beatitudes. If demand
can be created, how can we assume that productive energies are to flow
into those fields in which, because of small supplies and large demands,
prices are high above costs? Are we justified in assuming that there is a
tendency in that direction? Frequently we see just the opposite taking
place. "In some industries—the California Raisin Growers, for example—
increased consumption has resulted in great benefits by making demand
balance supply. Advertising was an important instrumentality without
which this purpose could not have been attained so easily and cheaply."

An important consideration of enterprise today is not the catering to
wants, but the creation, modification and direction of wants. In so far as
the returns depend on advertising, they are not derived from catering to
wants, but from cultivating tastes for commodities, the supply of which

the individual producer controls. Often in the business world the primary consideration is the success with which an enterprise can control taste and is not, as is commonly supposed, the ability to cater to wants that exist independent of the advertising activities of the producer. Imagine one reformulating J. B. Clark's specific productivity theory of value in a situation in which the wants he is talking about are wants created by the producer! By the same test, would not Marshall's net value product theory also come tumbling down; likewise all other conventional marginal distributive analyses that are based upon the concept of physical production? And if it is admitted that the greatest returns go to those who are most successful in manipulating our tastes for a profit, can any defense be made of our property system on the grounds that there is something inherent in our economic organization which safeguards society by forcing the individual who seeks to profit most to use his property to the advantage of others?

The Economic Effects of Advertising

NEIL H. BORDEN

Advertising is under fire. Its adverse critics come from many camps and their complaints tend to become increasingly vehement. Certain economists complain that its extensive use involves undue costs and is a bar to free competition, with a resultant adverse effect on the operation of the free price system. Home economics teachers charge it with being a poor guide to consumption. Students of ethics accuse it of showing frequent display of poor taste and misrepresentation. Businessmen themselves have not infrequently doubted its effectiveness for business purposes.

Proponents of advertising claim that it represents an economical means of effecting exchange; that it helps to lower costs because it makes possible large-scale operations in industries operating under decreasing costs; that it is an essential source of product information in an advanced economy; that it encourages product development and technological improvement by inducing consumers to want the new and improved things offered; in short, that it contributes to a high standard of living.

The discussions on both sides have often been characterized by sweeping generalization, by paucity of fact, and by lack of closely-knit, logical reasoning. There has been much wishful thinking and rationalization, because the issues involved have frequently turned upon questions of basic philosophies toward life that have a high emotional content, or because advertising has been a calling and a source of livelihood to those who have spoken out.

The adverse criticism has reached such proportions that neither businessmen nor the public can dismiss it as they have so often done in the past. Neither will unsupported counterclaim suffice. Either these criticisms are sound or they are not sound. Either they can be supported by evidence or they cannot be so supported. If advertising performs a useful economic function, it should be possible to demonstrate that fact. If, as opponents aver, costs are vastly out of proportion to benefits realized, that conclusion should be demonstrable. . . .

THE SIZE OF THE ADVERTISING EXPENDITURE

The size and importance of the economic problem of advertising is shown by the fact that in the 1920 decade, advertising expenditures averaged in excess of $2,000,000,000 a year, during the 1930 decade somewhat less than this figure, or 3% of the national income. The sum is 7% of the total amount spent for the distribution of goods and services. The figure of $2,000,000,000 is a gross expenditure, however, and is offset in part by the contribution which advertising makes to the publication of newspapers and magazines, which are sold at low cost to consumers, and to radio broadcasting, which provides free consumer entertainment. It was estimated that the contribution of advertising to publishing and broadcasting, based on a survey of the year 1935, was roughly one-fifth of total advertising expenditure.

It is evident that the potentialities for waste are great when such large sums are involved. But the possible economic significance of advertising is not limited to the potential wastes arising from ineffective employment of the men and resources represented by the large annual expenditure. Advertising has important effects upon the functioning of the economic system, and about these effects there has been much controversy.

PRINCIPAL CRITICISMS OF ADVERTISING

The more significant criticisms of advertising arising from this controversy may be grouped under three main heads: ideological, ethical, and economic. Persons who have criticized advertising on ideological grounds have basic objections of one kind or another to the functioning of our free, capitalistic system. Some object because they feel that an economic system which is directed and driven by free individuals impelled by a desire for profit is socially undesirable. They would substitute therefor some system whereby the production and distribution of goods are directed and controlled by government or socially controlled agencies. To such critics, advertising, which is one of the most evident of the tools used for gaining profit, is naturally objectionable. Other persons who object on ideological grounds condemn advertising along with many other activities of our economy because these activities encourage desire for material things. These critics speak out against advertising particularly because it is one of the most apparent of the forces leading to what they deem an undesirable materialism.

This study has made no effort to find the answers to these ideological criticisms, partly because there is no logical, scientific way of determining the answers, and partly because the task laid out for this study was an analysis of the facts regarding advertising within the framework of the existing free, capitalistic society. Such a society is one which relies on private initiative to supply desired goods and services; permits individuals to seek happiness in material welfare, if they so desire; and recognizes that in all social intercourse individuals may use influence to attain their ends, so long as they observe the ethical rules established by the social group.

The criticisms of advertising on ethical grounds arise primarily from three practices of advertisers: (1) the use of advertising to sell certain products which the critics hold to be undesirable and hence immoral and unethical; (2) the employment in some advertising of false and misleading statements which violate accepted ethical standards; (3) the employment of illustrations and statements which offend the critics' ideas of good taste. The criticisms of this sort are numerous because different individuals have different ideas as to what is ethical and in good taste. Some critics would practically rule out advertising because they look upon use of influence as dishonest and unethical, at least its use by the profit-seeker.

The adverse criticisms of advertising on economic grounds which have been made by various writers are numerous; the more significant are the following: (1) that much advertising represents wasteful expenditure because sellers compete in advertising, with the result that their efforts and resources go into reputation making, which, it is alleged, is of doubtful social value; (2) that through building a strong brand following, advertisers avoid price competition and consequently often secure high prices, and that the wide margins between price and production costs have been taken as profits by the sellers or have been used for wasteful advertising expenditure; (3) that advertising has contributed to the concentration of supply among a small number of producers and that this has tended to prevent a free play of price competition; (4) that advertising has encouraged meaningless product differentiation, thereby adding to the cost of goods and tending to make the consumers' buying problem unnecessarily complex and confusing; (5) that through its persuasive methods advertising has led consumers to make incorrect valuations of merchandise, and has induced them to divert their expenditures to advertisable products to the neglect of possibly more socially desirable products;

(6) that advertising has contributed to the violence of cyclical fluctuations through its encouragement of price rigidity and its excessive use in boom times and under-use in depressions. . . .

DOES ADVERTISING INCREASE DEMAND FOR TYPES OF PRODUCTS AS A WHOLE?

Study of demand for a wide range of products leads to the conclusion that basic trends of demand for products are determined primarily by underlying social and environmental conditions, and that advertising by itself serves not so much to increase demand for a product as to speed up the expansion of a demand that would come from favoring conditions, or to retard adverse demand trends due to unfavorable conditions. The demands for some products, for example, lettuce, sugar, green vegetables, and professional services, have grown even though the products are little advertised, for underlying social and environmental conditions have been favorable to expansion of their demand. Other industries for which there have been underlying conditions favorable to demand expansion have had their demand more rapidly expanded through use of advertising than would have occurred without such advertising. Among the products studied, this quickening of expansion has occurred in the case of cigarettes, dentifrices, oranges, automatic refrigerators, and other mechanical products such as automobiles, radios, and electric washers. On the other hand, for certain products for which underlying conditions caused adverse demand trends, demand was found to continue to contract in spite of considerable expenditures for advertising and promotion. Such was the situation with cigars, smoking tobacco, furniture, wheat flour, and men's shoes. In these instances advertising was powerless to reverse underlying declining trends, although it probably served to retard the declines. In other instances, certain products have had relatively constant per capita consumption over a period of years, even though substantial advertising was devoted to them. In short, such contrasting demand situations as mentioned above led to the conclusion that consumers' wants for products are determined by the character of consumers and their existing environment. Advertising has not changed people's characteristics; it has changed environment only as it has contributed indirectly over a long period in helping to bring a mobile society and a dynamic economy. In speeding up demand for new products it has contributed to the dynamic character of the economy.

DOES ADVERTISING INCREASE DEMAND FOR INDIVIDUAL CONCERNS?

Advertising can and does increase the demand for the products of many individual companies, but the extent to which it does so varies widely and depends upon the circumstances under which an enterprise operates. An individual company can use advertising profitably to increase sales only when it serves to stimulate a volume of sales at prices which more than cover all costs including the advertising outlay. Advertising's effectiveness in profitably stimulating sales for a concern depends upon the presence of a combination of conditions, of which the following are important.

First, advertising is likely to be more effective if a company is operating with a favorable primary demand trend than if it is operating with an adverse trend. With the industry's sales expanding, each concern has opportunity to strive for part of an increasing whole. Thus in the tobacco industry some companies in recent decades have put much of their advertising and promotional effort on cigarettes, because the demand for cigarettes has been expanding and promotional effort given to them has been particularly promising of results in the form of increased volume of sales. On the other hand, their advertising of cigars, smoking tobacco, and chewing tobacco has not been carried on with such favorable trends; and although advertising has been profitably used, each producer has been seeking to get a share of a contracting total demand.

Secondly, advertising is particularly helpful to individual companies in stimulating demand when their products provide large chance for differentiation. Conversely, advertising is of smaller help when there is a marked tendency for the products of various producers to become closely similar. Product differentiation provides the opportunity for influencing consumers to prefer one brand to another brand. Advertising provides the means for pointing out to consumers the significance of differentiating qualities. Moreover, when differentiations of significance to consumers are found, the seller often can secure wider gross margins than when such differentiations are absent, for when significant differentiations are effectively advertised, consumer valuations are affected. Wide margins, in turn, provide funds with which to support advertising. Among the products studied, smoking tobacco, cosmetics, dentifrices, soaps, electric refrigerators, and automobiles are products which have provided opportunities for product differentiations, and these individualizing points have been advertised. Conversely, sugar, salt, canned fruits, and sheeting are illustrative of products which have tended to be closely similar, with consequent limitations upon the use of advertising to increase the demand of individual companies. . . .

The study of demand shows that the opportunity for the use of advertising to increase demand varies markedly among different products. Although advertising for some products can be a very important means of increasing sales for the advertiser, yet, contrary to the view of many laymen, advertising does not always pay. Moreover, the use of advertising, like other business expenditures, involves risk for businessmen.

The study of demand shows further that even in product fields for which advertising may be used effectively by some concerns to increase their demand, other producers find opportunity to gain sales volume by other means. For example, by eliminating or greatly reducing the advertising and promotional functions, some manufacturers gain desired business by selling at a low price. Moreover, some sellers elect to use larger proportions of personal selling or other forms of promotion and less of advertising. . . .

DOES ADVERTISING TEND TO INCREASE OR DECREASE
THE REAL NATIONAL INCOME?

Advertising and aggressive selling as integral parts of the free competitive system have been a significant force in increasing the investment in productive facilities and in advancing the technology of production, two developments which have largely accounted for the four-fold increase of real national income per capita during the past 100 years. The tremendous advance in material welfare which has come since the Middle Ages would have been impossible without the building of a large-scale productive machine employing improved technology and management skills. But such an improved productive machine was called into being only as the result of strong social forces. On the one hand, there were forces to increase the willingness and desire of people to consume at a high quantitative level, for this willingness is not inherent in a population. On the other hand, there were forces leading to investment in productive facilities and to improvement in technology.

The willingness and desire of peoples in western countries to support a high level of consumption is basically attributable to social changes that have given these countries a mobile society in which individuals have been free to rise from the lowest to the highest class and have been able to aspire to the consumption of all types of products in the market. With the development of social mobility, the introduction of new wants and an increase in consumption were possible. Such changes were essential to the growth of industrialism and a dynamic economy.

From a long-range point of view, aggressive selling and advertising probably have played a considerable but indeterminable part in the formation of mental attitudes necessary for a high level of consumption. The study of demand in this volume has indicated that what people want is determined largely by their social backgrounds and habits. New products have been accepted by people, but the demand for them has grown relatively slowly. Once new products have been accepted by a few consumers, however, consumption usually has expanded through much of the social group. By helping to expand the use of products, advertising and selling have permitted the strong buying motives of emulation and imitation to come into play relatively quickly. They have played a particularly important part in bringing first sales, upon which emulative consumption depends. The new wants and new products which they have helped to bring in turn have become a part of environment influencing the further expansion of wants and desires of consumers.

While changes in social conditions and the forces of selling provide an explanation of growth of wants and willingness of the population to consume, this willingness could not have been satisfied had not the productive machine been called into existence. The productive machine which makes the products available provides the consumer income with which to purchase products. The existence of both the products and the income of consumers depends upon risk-taking by businessmen who see an opportunity for profit through making and selling goods which they think consumers will want. Their risk-taking activities bring the investment in factory and production facilities, which not only produce goods for consumption but employ labor and pay the wages and the return on capital upon which consumer income depends. In short, the activities of entrepreneurs create the markets for their own products.

Advertising and aggressive selling have an influence upon investment because they are important, integral parts of the system which leads to investment. Advertising and aggressive selling in themselves have not been the causes of the launching of new enterprises, or of the expansion of old, but they have been important elements whereby the new or enlarged enterprises might hope to gain a profitable demand. They frequently have been helpful in speeding up a demand which has called for increasing investment. They have promised the stability of demand and of profit to an enterprise which is attractive to investment. By such means have factories been built, men employed, and the products and incomes for increasing consumer satisfactions been established.

While advertising and aggressive selling have probably had greatest influence upon investment in new industries, they have also played a part in helping to increase the demand of established industries, which has called for investment to expand productive facilities. Even in the case of declining industries, the selling force has been employed to try to hold demand and thus to protect the investment in those industries against the inroads of the new industries. In some instances selling has also served to stimulate demand for new improvements in the products of declining industries and thus has served to give to the industry a new life cycle calling for investment.

Advertising and aggressive selling have also had a close relationship to the improvement in technology, which is one of the important explanations of the increase in national income. Technological improvements have come in considerable degree as the result of the activities of the producers of industrial goods. The spur to such producers to bring out improved machines has come from the opportunity to profit from meeting the desires of industrial buyers for more economical and efficient machines and materials. In turn, in the industrial goods field advertising and aggressive selling have played a part in promising to the enterpriser a profitable demand and thus have attracted investment. . . .

THE PLACE OF ADVERTISING IN A CAPITALISTIC ECONOMY—

A FINAL STATEMENT

In the end, what role of social significance does advertising play in our capitalistic economy? On the whole, does it add to consumer welfare? The discussion has shown that its use is accompanied by certain dangers, particularly those attending the tendency of businessmen to compete in advertising and thus to bring into prices a large amount of selling costs. On the other side of the ledger, what is advertising's offsetting contribution, if any?

Advertising's outstanding contribution to consumer welfare comes from its part in promoting a dynamic, expanding economy. Advertising's chief task from a social standpoint is that of encouraging the development of new products. It offers a means whereby the enterpriser may hope to build a profitable demand for his new and differentiated merchandise which will justify investment. From growing investment has come the increasing flow of income which has raised man's material welfare to a level unknown in previous centuries.

In a static economy there is little need of advertising. Only that minimum is necessary which will provide information regarding sources of merchandise required to facilitate exchange between buyers and sellers who are separated from each other. Clearly in a static economy it would be advisable to keep informational costs at a minimum, just as it would be wise to keep all costs at a minimum.

In a dynamic economy, however, advertising plays a different role. It is an integral part of a business system in which entrepreneurs are striving constantly to find new products and new product differentiations which consumers will want. Without opportunity to profit relatively quickly from the new products which they develop, entrepreneurs would not be inclined either to search for them or to risk investment in putting them on the market. Advertising and aggressive selling provide tools which give prospect of profitable demand. . . .

Since advertising has in large part been associated with the promotion of new and differentiated merchandise, a substantial part of advertising costs should be looked upon economically as growth costs. They are the costs incurred in raising the economy from one level to another. From the standpoint of social welfare these costs have been far more than offset by the rise in national income which they have made possible. Such costs should not be prevented or decried. In the future if man's material welfare is to be raised to higher levels in our free economy, the spark of enterprise must be kept glowing brightly; the chance to profit from the new should continue to exist. So long as individual enterprise flourishes and a dynamic economy continues, advertising and aggressive selling will play a significant social role.

FOR FURTHER READING: Critical accounts include Max A. Geller, *Advertising at the Crossroads—Federal Regulation vs. Voluntary Controls* (New York, 1952), Otis A. Pease, *The Responsibilities of American Advertising, 1920–1940* (New Haven, 1958), and James Rorty, *Our Master's Voice* (New York, 1934). More favorable in interpretation are F. A. Burt, *American Advertising Agencies* (New York, 1940), Edgar R. Jones, *Those Were the Good Old Days: A Happy Look at American Advertising, 1880–1930* (New York, 1959), and Frank Presley, *History and Development of Advertising* (New York, 1929).

26. *Origins of the Great Depression*

PROBLEM: *What factors led to the Crash of 1929?*

Few episodes in American history attracted as much attention from economists and historians as the great stock market Crash of 1929. Analyses of its causes have ranged within wide extremes, so that the issue has continued to exist. Contemporary writers, of whom the economist Irving Fisher of Yale was one of the most popular and most distinguished, tended to stress short-run factors. Fisher believed that a business recession and the overpricing of common stocks were important reasons, along with disturbances in the international balance of trade, a boom psychology, and close, unhealthy relationships between commercial and investment banks. A generation later another widely read economist, John Kenneth Galbraith of Harvard, also sought to assess the reasons for the crash, but placed great stress on long-term dislocations. Galbraith emphasized the maldistribution of wealth in the United States as well as weaknesses of the corporate structure. Both men offer concise and provocative appraisals which lead their readers into a broad array of problems relating to the origins of the great depression. Were the antecedents of the crash national or international? Was the great crash inevitable? Is there a common ground of agreement among these authors?

434

The Great Stock Market Crash of 1929

IRVING FISHER

What were the causes of the panic of 1929?

That the stock market crash was "primarily precipitated by foreign liquidation" is the view expressed by John S. Sinclair in the *New York Times* of October 27th. This liquidation accompanied the so-called Hatry Panic on the London Stock Exchange, which resulted in a deeper fall of the London stock price level—45.4 per cent from August 30th to December 27th, according to the British index—than occurred on the New York Stock Exchange between the high point on September 7th and the bottom of November 13th. Few realize today that the greatest fall of stocks in British history, comparable only with the Baring Panic of 1890, preceded and was an actuating cause of the American panic, and that a coincident fall in Paris and Berlin accompanied the British liquidation. It began with the failure of the banking house of Clarence Hatry in August, followed by his arrest in September and subsequent conviction for a gigantic forgery of stock certificates. This started the British liquidation in London and in New York. *Barron's Weekly* of December 9th notes that Britons were extremely active in "distributing" stocks at the high level in New York during September, as seen by the movement in sterling exchange. . . .

LINKING OF COMMERCIAL AND INVESTMENT BANKS

Mr. H. Parker Willis, editor of the New York *Journal of Commerce*, ascribes to the big commercial banks, which had organized speculative pools in the form of investment companies, a causal relation to the crash. I am informed by a country banker in Connecticut that there was a tendency among small banks to copy the big banks in the organization of these investment pools which helped swell the wave of speculation through the country. The big banks, of course, used the funds of their stockholders in speculation under intelligent guidance; the little banks could have no such expert guidance. But in either case there was abuse. The commercial banks are supposed to conduct their operations under close public regulation, but by means of affiliated investment companies, joined as closely as Siamese twins, they have been enabled to act irresponsibly, as is evidenced by the fact that these companies publish no statements and are held to accounting by no public body.

Reprinted from *The Stock Market Crash—and After*, pp. 32–55, by Irving Fisher (New York, 1930). Copyright renewed 1958 by Irving Norton Fisher and used with his permission.

OVERVALUATION OF COMMON STOCKS

That the prime cause was serious overvaluation of common stocks that had previously been undervalued is the opinion of Mr. Carl Snyder, of the Federal Reserve Bank of New York. In correspondence with me Mr. Snyder says, referring to the war inflation of commodity prices:

The long-sustained rise in the level of commodity prices necessarily brought a huge increase in the earnings of common shares, and this naturally forced a valorization of these shares in terms of something like a 57-cent dollar.

On the basis of this higher price level, stocks, through, say, the 1919–1924 period, were, as now seems clear, seriously undervalued. As soon as public confidence in the rate of earnings was established, there began a movement of revalorization that naturally swung to wild extremes, as stock markets always do. With this came a recurrence of the familiar 'new era' theory, which seems to blossom about once in a generation with unfailing regularity. All this brought what appears to have been as serious an overvaluation of common stocks as they had previously been undervalued—overvalued, I should say, because it is clear that we have as yet seen no readjustment of long-term interest rates and bond yields to what look like permanently lower levels. And would not this be inevitable if the high prices attained by the average of stocks were to continue? . . .

There is a measure of truth, also, in the judgment pronounced by another financial expert, who contributes this statement:

BUSINESS RECESSION

In my opinion the basic change was in the business curve and outlook. After nearly two and one-half years of advance at the rate of 1 per cent per month, in July of 1929 business turned downward, and it became evident that a business recession was in prospect. When prices were as high relative to earnings as they were in 1929, the recession outlook pulls the props from the stock market. The profit outlook had changed fundamentally. There were other causes that had been present for a year or more, but these had not broken the market. This downward turn in the business trend was the one new factor in the picture.

With this view the following statement by Mr. Lindsay Bradford, Vice President of the City Bank Farmers Trust Company of New York, is accordant:

Since early in 1929 considerable liquidation and distribution of stocks of various industries had been going on, and but little notice of it was taken due to the fact that the strength in certain other groups, such as the utilities, and certain outstanding industrials gave the whole market the appearance of such strength. This feature of the market was indicated during the Fall by the fact that when certain stocks were daily making new highs other groups were daily making new lows in the weeks before the panic ensued. The reason, it seems to me, that these groups, such as notably the automobile group, were weak was because as early as last June it was apparent that automobile buying was falling off and that the automobile companies as a whole were running into over-production. Similar weaknesses in the building situation were apparent in the early summer and it is such fundamentals as these which, in my opinion, were the real reasons for the decline in prices. . . .

FEDERAL RESERVE POLICY

The *Commercial and Financial Chronicle* also suggested that the market had been sent on a new upward journey by Federal Reserve action during the early part of August, 1929, in sanctioning an increase in the New York Federal Reserve discount rate from 5 per cent to 6 per cent, with simultaneous lowering of the buying rate for bankers' acceptances and the concurrent purchase of acceptances on a large scale. This, the *Chronicle* says, "meant the forcing out of reserve credit by the act of the Reserve System itself, and involved Federal Reserve inflation of a peculiarly objectionable type." . . .

"BOOM" ENTHUSIASM

Senator Robinson of Arkansas declared, and with some real basis in fact, in a formal statement on October 30, 1929, that if the foundation of the belief of ruined investors was faith in the strong position of American industry, it was also true that "no less personalities than a former President of the United States, the Secretary of the Treasury, and the former Secretary of Commerce, now President, contributed by unduly and repeated optimistic statements to the creation of enthusiastic if not frenzied ventures in stocks."

No doubt the "Coolidge boom" and the "Hoover boom" engendered such public enthusiasm, accompanied as they were by repeated statements of the country's prosperity and expected increases in prosperity. These statements led thousands of investors into undue borrowings in order to realize the benefits of this prosperity for themselves. But I cannot entirely agree with Professor Jacob H. Hollander, of Johns Hopkins University, in his view, expressed before the Academy of Political Science in New York on November 22, 1929, that the public by bidding up the price of securities, "ignored yield and earnings in the belief that the country's growth would increase the equity and boost the price" of shares of sound enterprises. No doubt their enthusiasm led them, as Professor Hollander asserts, to make no allowance for business recession, for speculative manipulation, or foreign disturbance.

My own impression has been and still is that the market went up principally because of sound, justified expectations of earnings, and only partly because of unreasoning and unintelligent mania for buying. . . .

The Great Crash, 1929

JOHN KENNETH GALBRAITH

There seems little question that in 1929, modifying a famous cliché, the economy was fundamentally unsound. This is a circumstance of first-rate importance. Many things were wrong, but five weaknesses seem to have had an especially intimate bearing on the ensuing disaster. They are:

1) The bad distribution of income. In 1929 the rich were indubitably rich. The figures are not entirely satisfactory, but it seems certain that the 5 per cent of the population with the highest incomes in that year received approximately one third of all personal income. The proportion of personal income received in the form of interest, dividends, and rent—the income, broadly speaking, of the well-to-do—was about twice as great as in the years following the Second World War.

This highly unequal income distribution meant that the economy was dependent on a high level of investment or a high level of luxury consumer spending or both. The rich cannot buy great quantities of bread. If they are to dispose of what they receive it must be on luxuries or by way of investment in new plants and new projects. Both investment and luxury spending are subject, inevitably, to more erratic influences and to wider fluctuations than the bread and rent outlays of the $25-a-week workman. This high-bracket spending and investment was especially susceptible, one may assume, to the crushing news from the stock market in October of 1929.

2) The bad corporate structure. In November 1929, a few weeks after the crash, the Harvard Economic Society gave as a principal reason why a depression need not be feared its reasoned judgment that "business in most lines has been conducted with prudence and conservatism." The fact was that American enterprise in the twenties had opened its hospitable arms to an exceptional number of promoters, grafters, swindlers, impostors, and frauds. This, in the long history of such activities, was a kind of flood tide of corporate larceny.

The most important corporate weakness was inherent in the vast new structure of holding companies and investment trusts. The holding companies controlled large segments of the utility, railroad, and entertainment business. Here, as with the investment trusts, was the constant danger of devastation by reverse leverage. In particular, dividends from the operating companies paid the interest on the bonds of upstream holding companies. The interruption of the dividends meant default on the bonds, bankruptcy, and the collapse of the structure. Under these circumstances, the temptation to curtail investment in operating plant in order to continue dividends was obviously strong. This added to deflationary pressures. The latter, in turn, curtailed earnings and helped bring down the corporate pyramids. When this happened, even more retrenchment was inevitable. Income was earmarked for debt repayment. Borrowing for new investment became impossible. It would be hard to imagine a corporate system better designed to continue and accentuate a deflationary spiral.

3) The bad banking structure. Since the early thirties, a generation of Americans has been told, sometimes with amusement, sometimes with indignation, often with outrage, of the banking practices of the late twenties. In fact, many of these practices were made ludicrous only by the depression. Loans which would have been perfectly good were made perfectly foolish by the collapse of the borrower's prices or the markets for his goods or the value of the collateral he had posted. The most responsible bankers—those who saw that their debtors were victims of circumstances far beyond their control and sought to help—were often made to look the worst. The bankers yielded, as did others, to the blithe, optimistic, and immoral mood of the times but probably not more so. A depression such as that of 1929–32, were it to begin as this is written, would also be damaging to many currently impeccable banking reputations.

However, although the bankers were not unusually foolish in 1929, the banking structure was inherently weak. The weakness was implicit in the large numbers of independent units. When one bank failed, the assets of others were frozen while depositors elsewhere had a pregnant warning to go and ask for their money. Thus one failure led to other failures, and these spread with a domino effect. Even in the best of times local misfortune or isolated mismanagement could start such a chain reaction. (In the first six months of 1929, 346 banks failed in various parts of the country with aggregate deposits of nearly $115 million.) When income, employment, and values fell as the result of a depression bank failures could quickly become epidemic. This happened after 1929. Again it would be hard to imagine a better arrangement for magnifying the effects of fear. The weak destroyed not only the other weak, but weakened the strong. People everywhere, rich and poor, were made aware of the disaster by the persuasive intelligence that their savings had been destroyed.

Needless to say, such a banking system, once in the convulsions of failure, had a uniquely repressive effect on the spending of its depositors and the investment of its clients.

4) The dubious state of the foreign balance. This is a familiar story. During the First World War, the United States became a creditor on international account. In the decade following, the surplus of exports over imports which once had paid the interest and principal on loans

from Europe continued. The high tariffs, which restricted imports and helped to create this surplus of exports remained. However, history and traditional trading habits also accounted for the persistence of the favorable balance, so called.

Before, payments on interest and principal had in effect been deducted from the trade balance. Now that the United States was a creditor, they were added to this balance. The latter, it should be said, was not huge. In only one year (1928) did the excess of exports over imports come to as much as a billion dollars; in 1923 and 1926 it was only about $375,000,-000. However, large or small, this difference had to be covered. Other countries which were buying more than they sold, and had debt payments to make in addition, had somehow to find the means for making up the deficit in their transactions with the United States.

During most of the twenties the difference was covered by cash—i.e., gold payments to the United States—and by new private loans by the United States to other countries. Most of the loans were to governments —national, state, or municipal bodies—and a large proportion were to Germany and Central and South America. The underwriters' margins in handling these loans were generous; the public took them up with enthusiasm; competition for the business was keen. If unfortunately corruption and bribery were required as competitive instruments, these were used. In late 1927 Juan Leguia, the son of the President of Peru, was paid $450,000 by J. and W. Seligman and Company and the National City Company (the security affiliate of the National City Bank) for his services in connection with a $50,000,000 loan which these houses marketed for Peru. Juan's services, according to later testimony, were of a rather negative sort. He was paid for not blocking the deal. The Chase extended President Machado of Cuba, a dictator with a marked predisposition toward murder, a generous personal line of credit which at one time reached $200,000. Machado's son-in-law was employed by the Chase. The bank did a large business in Cuban bonds. In contemplating these loans, there was a tendency to pass quickly over anything that might appear to the disadvantage of the creditor. Mr. Victor Schoepperle, a vice-president of the National City Company with the responsibility for Latin American loans, made the following appraisal of Peru as a credit prospect:

Peru: Bad debt record, adverse moral and political risk, bad internal debt situation, trade situation about as satisfactory as that of Chile in the past three years. Natural resources more varied. On economic showing Peru should go ahead rapidly in the next 10 years.

On such showing the National City Company floated a $15,000,000 loan for Peru, followed a few months later by a $50,000,000 loan, and some ten months thereafter by a $25,000,000 issue. (Peru did prove a highly adverse political risk. President Leguia, who negotiated the loans, was thrown violently out of office, and the loans went into default.)

In all respects these operations were as much a part of the New Era as Shenandoah and Blue Ridge. They were also just as fragile, and once the illusions of the New Era were dissipated they came as abruptly to an end. This, in turn, forced a fundamental revision in the foreign economic position of the United States. Countries could not cover their adverse trade balance with the United States with increased payments of gold, at least not for long. This meant that they had either to increase their exports to the United States or reduce their imports or default on their past loans. President Hoover and the Congress moved promptly to eliminate the first possibility—that the accounts would be balanced by larger imports—by sharply increasing the tariff. Accordingly, debts, including war debts, went into default and there was a precipitate fall in American exports. The reduction was not vast in relation to total output of the American economy, but it contributed to the general distress and was especially hard on farmers.

5) The poor state of economic intelligence. To regard the people of any time as particularly obtuse seems vaguely improper, and it also establishes a precedent which members of this generation might regret. Yet it seems certain that the economists and those who offered economic counsel in the late twenties and early thirties were almost uniquely perverse. In the months and years following the stock market crash, the burden of reputable economic advice was invariably on the side of measures that would make things worse. In November of 1929, Mr. Hoover announced a cut in taxes; in the great no-business conferences that followed he asked business firms to keep up their capital investment and to maintain wages. Both of these measures were on the side of increasing spendable income, though unfortunately they were largely without effect. The tax reductions were negligible except in the higher income brackets; businessmen who promised to maintain investment and wages, in accordance with a well-understood convention, considered the promise binding only for the period within which it was not financially disadvantageous to do so. As a result investment outlays and wages were not reduced until circumstances would in any case have brought their reduction.

Still, the effort was in the right direction. Thereafter policy was almost entirely on the side of making things worse. Asked how the government could best advance recovery, the sound and responsible adviser urged that the budget be balanced. Both parties agreed on this. For Republicans the balanced budget was, as ever, high doctrine. But the Democratic Party platform of 1932, with an explicitness which politicians rarely advise, also called for a "federal budget annually balanced on the basis of accurate executive estimates within revenues . . ."

A commitment to a balanced budget is always comprehensive. It then meant there could be no increase in government outlays to expand purchasing power and relieve distress. It meant there could be no further tax reductions. But taken literally it meant much more. From 1930 on the budget was far out of balance, and balance, therefore, meant an increase in taxes, a reduction in spending, or both. The Democratic platform in 1932 called for an "immediate and drastic reduction of governmental expenditures" to accomplish at least a 25 per cent decrease in the cost of government.

The balanced budget was not a subject of thought. Nor was it, as often asserted, precisely a matter of faith. Rather it was a formula. For centuries avoidance of borrowing had protected people from slovenly or reckless public housekeeping. Slovenly or reckless keepers of the public purse had often composed complicated arguments to show why balance of income and outlay was not a mark of virtue. Experience had shown that however convenient this belief might seem in the short run, discomfort or disaster followed in the long run. Those simple precepts of a simple world did not hold amid the growing complexities of the early thirties. Mass unemployment in particular had altered the rules. Events had played a very bad trick on people, but almost no one tried to think out the problem anew.

The balanced budget was not the only strait jacket on policy. There was also the bogey of "going off" the gold standard and, most surprisingly, of risking inflation. Until 1932 the United States added formidably to its gold reserves, and instead of inflation the country was experiencing the most violent deflation in the nation's history. Yet every sober adviser saw dangers here, including the danger of runaway price increases. Americans, though in years now well in the past, had shown a penchant for tinkering with the money supply and enjoying the brief but heady joys of a boom in prices. In 1931 or 1932, the danger or even the feasibility of such a boom was nil. The advisers and counselors were not, however, analyzing the danger or even the possibility. They were serving only as the custodians of bad memories.

The fear of inflation reinforced the demand for the balanced budget. It also limited efforts to make interest rates low, credit plentiful (or at least redundant) and borrowing as easy as possible under the circumstances. Devaluation of the dollar was, of course, flatly ruled out. This directly violated the gold standard rules. At best, in such depression times, monetary policy is a feeble reed on which to lean. The current economic clichés did not allow even the use of that frail weapon. And again, these attitudes were above party. Though himself singularly open-minded, Roosevelt was careful not to offend or disturb his followers. In a speech in Brooklyn toward the close of the 1932 campaign, he said:

The Democratic platform specifically declares, "We advocate a sound currency to be preserved at all hazards." That is plain English. In discussing this platform on July 30, I said, "Sound money is an international necessity, not a domestic consideration for one nation alone." Far up in the Northwest, at Butte, I repeated the pledge . . . In Seattle I reaffirmed my attitude . . .

The following February, Mr. Hoover set forth his view, as often before, in a famous letter to the President-elect:

It would steady the country greatly if there could be prompt assurance that there will be no tampering or inflation of the currency; that the budget will be unquestionably balanced even if further taxation is necessary; that the Government credit will be maintained by refusal to exhaust it in the issue of securities.

The rejection of both fiscal (tax and expenditure) and monetary policy amounted precisely to a rejection of all affirmative government economic policy. The economic advisers of the day had both the unanimity and the authority to force the leaders of both parties to disavow all the available steps to check deflation and depression. In its own way this was a marked achievement—a triumph of dogma over thought. The consequences were profound. . . .

FOR FURTHER READING: Also emphasizing ineffectiveness of government policies is Lauchlin Currie, "The Failure of Monetary Policy to Prevent the Depression of 1929–1932," *Journal of Political Economy*, XLII (April, 1934), pp. 145–177, and Arthur B. Adams, *Our Economic Revolution* (New York, 1933). Very readable summaries of depression causes are Frederick Lewis Allen, *Only Yesterday* (New York, 1931), and Harold G. Moulton, *The Recovery Problem in the United States* (Washington, 1936).

27. *The New Deal*

PROBLEM: *Did New Deal policies revive the economy?*

Whether the economic policies of the New Deal actually fostered a revival of business activity is still a debatable issue among economists as well as historians. Of the financial proposals that President Franklin D. Roosevelt advocated during the first eight years of his Administration, particularly the fiscal measures have been subjected to criticism. These included the manipulation of interest rates, and the creation of budget deficits through the financing of large-scale public works programs. In addition they embraced federal loans to banks, railroads, and home owners. Arthur Smithies, a former official of the United States Bureau of the Budget and an economics professor at Harvard University, argues that federal fiscal policies under the New Deal did not attain an optimum degree of effectiveness, primarily because the very high rate of investment in the 1920's had created a surfeit. This surfeit depressed plant expenditures, residential construction, business inventories and foreign investments in the Roosevelt era, and offset any stimulatory effects which such fiscal manipulation might have had otherwise. Yet the depression would have been much worse, Smithies argues, if the President had not undertaken such large-scale expenditures as he did. From this experience Smithies concludes that the federal government should use fiscal measures as a major tool to combat depressions. However, one of America's most distinguished economists, Gardiner C. Means, takes issue with this view, for he believes that monetary, rather than fiscal, measures were more important in stimulating recovery during the 1930's. Monetary policies included the manipulation of the quantity of money in circulation, as by alteration of the gold standard and the price of gold, by the purchase of silver, and by modification of the Treasury's borrowing procedures. These measures, rather than fiscal policies, Means argues, stabilized prices. Each of these writers presents persuasive evidence that bears on public policies during times of depression. What were alternatives to the New Deal's fiscal and monetary policies? How do political considerations affect the application of large scale fiscal or monetary experiments by government? What standards can be used to measure the effectiveness of the New Deal's economic recovery programs?

The American Economy in the Thirties

ARTHUR SMITHIES

I. INTRODUCTION

Any discussion of the United States economy in the thirties almost inevitably resolves itself into either a general discussion of the business cycle or a discussion of the role of government in economic life. In this paper I am going to place primary emphasis on the role of government, although it will of course be necessary to advert to the nature of the economic problem with which the government had to deal and that will raise the general business cycle issue.

I choose this course because the thirties was the first peacetime period in United States history where the government took positive action, on a wide scale, to control the general level of economic activity. The history of that period must therefore be in the forefront of the minds of those concerned with government policies to forestall depressions in the future.

The policy of the Hoover Administration was to follow the path of orthodoxy and to assume that the situation demanded nothing more than the encouragement and rehabilitation of business. Interest rates were lowered and governmental economies introduced, and the Hawley-Smoot Tariff was enacted. The pressure of events led to the establishment of the RFC, but the President only very reluctantly agreed to extension of RFC loans to small businesses, to individuals, and to the states for relief purposes. The agricultural policy of the Administration was not so much a product of the depression as a continuation of the policies which had been previously adopted to relieve rural distress, which had continued throughout the whole period of the twenties. Beyond that the President offered good advice and exhortation to business to maintain business and employment. Business responded to an extraordinary degree, but the

Reprinted by permission from the *American Economic Review*, Supplement, XXXVI (May, 1946), pp. 11–27.

pressure of events was too strong. The Administration resisted to the end any proposals for direct federal unemployment relief.

It is evident from the political history of the thirties that the United States was no longer prepared to tolerate the privations of a serious depression in the traditional and "capitalist" way. The verdict of the electorate in 1932 testifies to this and the election of 1936 even more so. For the qualified recovery which had been achieved by 1936 can hardly explain the unqualified verdict of approval which was given to the Administration—especially since the great New Deal instrument of recovery —the NRA—had proved a dismal failure and had been pronounced unconstitutional.

But more than relief and recovery were at issue. Social and economic reform—in particular, social security, recognition of the rising political power of labor, and of redistribution of income and economic power— could no longer be delayed. Professor Schumpeter contends that such reforms are inherently anticapitalist in the sense that they impair the effective operation of the capitalist system—and did in fact impair it in the second half of the decade of the thirties. One of my aims here is to examine the force of his contention.

I have said that politically the Administration had no alternative but to do something about the depression. While this cannot be denied, critics have argued that economically it would have been preferable to let nature take its course. My major purpose in this paper is to examine the need for a recovery policy and to evaluate the effectiveness of the recovery policies which were pursued.

II. THE EVOLUTION OF A POLICY

I want now to sketch very briefly the policy objectives of the Administration and the measures taken to reach them.

The First Phase. The President's first inaugural address did not contain many indications of the movement for reform that the New Deal was to be in its heyday, and neither did the legislation of the first "100 days." The first message to Congress requested banking legislation, the second, drastic economies in government, and the third the agricultural adjustment legislation. Recommendations for home and farm mortgage relief, for unemployment relief, for securities and exchange legislation, for emergency railroad legislation, and for TVA followed in quick succession. On May 17 the President transmitted his famous message which requested the Congress to enact legislation to deal with the question of industrial wages, prices, and labor conditions on a nationwide scale and to provide for a comprehensive public works program. This message led to the establishment of NRA and PWA.

Towards the end of 1933 the gold purchase scheme was adopted and this led to the devaluation of the dollar and the Gold Reserve Act of 1934. The Trade Agreements Act of 1934 laid the foundation for future United States co-operation in the international economic sphere.

The Administration, or rather the Federal Reserve Board, continued the policy of cheap money inaugurated during the Hoover Administration. The gold inflow which was partially stimulated by the devaluation of the dollar enabled low interest rates to be maintained throughout the decade and to become a permanent feature of the American economy.

The revenue measures of the first New Deal period consisted of increased liquor taxes following the repeal of prohibition, emergency taxes on corporations and capital stock to provide for interest and amortization on the money borrowed to finance the public works program, the processing taxes to finance AAA, and finally the general but moderate increases in income, estate, and gift taxes incorporated in the Revenue Act of 1934.

That very briefly was the basis for the economic policy of the Administration during its first two years. The most striking characteristic of that program was that it attempted on a national scale to cure the depression by removing specific abuses and dealing with specific maladjustments. Relief was provided to the chief sufferers from the depression, agriculture was dealt with as a special problem, and the main weapon of industrial recovery was to attempt to introduce order in industry and to increase purchasing power by reducing the margin between prices and wages through the operation of NRA. The impression I get from the President's statements on public works is that his motivation in urging the programs was to improve natural resources and to absorb unemployed labor into productive public employment in the absence of private employment rather than to use public works as a pump-priming device.

The point I want to emphasize is that an expansionary fiscal policy played a very minor role in the policy decisions of the period. Reductions of government salaries and veterans' benefits were recommended by the President on grounds of equity and economy. The processing taxes and the liquor taxes can only be described as deflationary. In fact, at a press conference on April 7, 1933, the President said: "So much of the legislation we have had this spring is of deflationary character . . . that we are faced with the problem of offsetting it in some way."

There can be no question in my mind that, despite large deficits, the Administration at this stage genuinely wanted to balance the budget, that it regarded its deflationary fiscal policies as contributions to recovery, that it hoped to achieve reflation through price policy rather than fiscal policy, and that it regarded reliance on public works as a last rather than a first resort.

The Second Phase. The year 1935 saw the symptoms of a pronounced change in the political orientation of the Administration. The meagre success of NRA and its ultimate invalidation by the Supreme Court meant that active co-operation of government and business in the process of recovery was at an end; and the mounting opposition from the Right to the New Deal as a whole meant that the Administration would have to enlist its support in other quarters. Moreover, the demand for reform which may have been numbed by the rigors of full depression was excited by the mildness of recovery. While the policies of the first New Deal aimed at relief and recovery those of the second were directed to recovery and reform.

The President refused to separate reform from recovery. In the State of the Union Message for 1935 he said: "The attempt to make a distinction between recovery and reform is a narrowly conceived effort to substitute the appearance of reality for reality itself." He announced his threefold security program: the security of a livelihood through the better use of the natural resources of the land in which we live; the security against the major hazards and vicissitudes of life; and the security of decent homes.

In the State of the Union Message of 1936 the President stepped up the tempo of his attack on "the royalists of the economic order [who] have conceded that political freedom was the business of the government, but . . . have maintained that economic slavery should be nobody's business." The year 1936 was the one and possibly the only year in which the government of the United States could be described as being definitely of the Left.

The second inaugural in 1937 was full of ebullient satisfaction at the progress of recovery, but the President significantly said that "prosperity already tests the persistence of our progressive purpose," and issued his dramatic reminder that one-third of the nation was still ill-clad, ill-housed, and ill-nourished. But that was practically the end of the second New Deal; the onset of depression in the fall of 1937, the changing complexion of the Congress, and the growing preoccupation with international matters barred the further progress of reform.

The legislative and executive action of the second New Deal falls into three main groups: First, measures to give effect to the President's security program and to establish the status of organized labor; second, measures to attack the position of the "economic royalists"; and third, measures to rescue the first New Deal from the shambles created by the Supreme Court.

The great permanent monument to the President's security program is of course the Social Security Act of 1935 which took preliminary steps to free families from poverty in old age and from the hardships of unemployment. Whether or not the principles of the other main security measures of the Administration—WPA and NYA—have become firmly established still remains to be seen. In his 1935 Message, the President had said: "The federal government must and shall quit this business of relief. I am not willing that the vitality of our people be further sapped by the giving of cash, of market baskets, of a few hours of weekly work cutting grass, raking leaves or picking up papers in the public parks."

The third item in the security program—decent homes—ran into legislative and judicial obstacles. FHA insurance contributed to middle-class housing; but it was not until 1937 that provision for low rent housing for slum dwellers was made and that was but a modest attempt.

Labor won its charter under the second New Deal. The National Labor Relations Act of 1935 firmly established the right of collective bargaining and assured that the bargaining would be conducted by representatives of the majority of the workers involved—an assurance which was not provided under Section 7A of the National Industrial Recovery Act. The other great labor measure—the Fair Labor Standards Act—was not passed until 1938, and finally legislated the principles of minimum wages, penalty overtime pay, and the prohibition of child labor.

The "antiroyalist" legislation included the public utilities legislation, but the measures that are of most importance, especially for present purposes, are the tax legislations of 1935 and 1936. The President recommended to Congress imposition of increased estate and gift taxes, increased individual surtaxes, and graduated corporation income tax, and requesting study of other taxes including those "to discourage unwieldy and unnecessary corporate surpluses." With the invalidation of AAA and the consequent loss of processing tax revenues, he recommended an undistributed profits tax in March, 1936.

The 1935 Message was based not on the need for more revenue but on the need for redistributing wealth, plugging evasion loopholes, and reducing concentrations of economic power. Although the 1936 recommendation was based on revenue needs, the particular form of tax chosen was determined on grounds of equity rather than economics. The tax laws of 1935 and 1936 thus differed markedly in their motivation from their New Deal predecessors whose primary objectives had been to increase the receipts of the Treasury. But neither were they motivated by the need for an expansionary fiscal policy.

The Supreme Court decisions removed the processing taxes of AAA and relieved the Administration of the embarrassing necessity of trying to make NRA succeed. The crop control features of AAA were salvaged by the Soil Conservation Act, but NRA had no major successor so far as its prices and wage features were concerned. In fact, the whole spirit of the second New Deal was inconsistent with "self-government in industry" which was the essence of NRA.

As a result of the Supreme Court's surgery and also of the enactment of the Bonus over the President's veto, the government's contribution to recovery after 1935 depended almost entirely on the fiscal effects of its policy; that is, efforts to create purchasing power by attempts to adjust the price-wage structure disappeared and the stimulus to economic activity given by the government was the income-creating effect of the budget deficit. But the deficit was not the result of fiscal plans laid by the government to achieve economic goals. It was rather the net result of the budgetary requirements of relief and reform measures and the political infeasibility of increasing taxation *pari passu* with expenditures. Expenditures depended on the amounts required to provide WPA employment for the unemployed and the new taxes were based largely on the Administration's program to redistribute wealth and income. It was thus a matter of accident rather than design if the fiscal policy actually pursued did in fact promote recovery at the desired rate.

The Third Phase. The third phase of the New Deal period opened with the depression in the second half of 1937. That depression took everyone by surprise—government and public alike. The year 1937 had opened with serene economic optimism. The 1938 budget was to be balanced and the economic instruments of government were to be directed to curbing a boom. The portents in the fall of 1937 were not heeded and it was only in the spring of 1938 that the Administration was convinced that it had a serious depression to contend with.

In April, 1938, the President sent to the Congress his "Recommendations Designed to Stimulate Further Recovery." This document is remarkable in that it was the first outright recommendation by the President designed to achieve recovery through fiscal policy. Increased appropriation for WPA, NYA, Farm Security, and CCC were urged with the frank objective of increasing national income. The government credit agencies were to make cheap credit available to business, and the President recommended a large expansion of the general public works program. The message is noteworthy for the omission of any recommendations for increased taxation. The Treasury had evidently been appeased by recommendations for the elimination of tax-exempt bonds and for federal and state taxation of all government salaries. The goal was a national income of 80 billion dollars, and the President asserted that that goal could be achieved only if private funds were put to work "and all of us recognize that such funds are entitled to a fair profit."

Beyond acting on the President's recommendations, the chief contribution of the Congress to the recovery program was to enact the Revenue Act of 1938 which repealed all but a token remnant of the excess profits tax and substituted a corporation income tax on firms earning more than $25,000.

The other main legislative achievements of the third phase were the Fair Labor Standards Act to which I have already referred and the new Agricultural Adjustment Act of 1938. The latter act instituted the present method of assistance to agriculture through voluntary acreage control and Commodity Credit Corporation price support.

The other noteworthy feature of the third phase was the antimonopoly campaign which found its expression in an aggressive application of the antitrust laws and aggressive investigation through the Temporary National Economic Committee. The NRA policy of recovery through agreement was finally and completely reversed.

Thus through a process of trial and error and of ordeal by Congress and the Supreme Court the Administration wound up its peacetime record and concluded the decade with a clear-cut recovery program of fiscal policy and cheap money. The agricultural policy was the most effective method yet devised to achieve the objective of a floor under agricultural prices. The reforms of the banking and financial system and social security were accepted as permanent, and labor had won its place in the sun. The main unfinished piece of business was the monopoly program. The onset of war postponed the formulation of a comprehensive antimonopoly policy.

III. EFFECTS ON THE ECONOMY

I shall now attempt to analyze the effects of the government's policies on the American economy during the thirties. To do this I shall first consider the behavior of the main determinants of private economic activity —the factors that influence private decisions to invest and to consume. Such a discussion should enable us to decide what effect the government's policy had on the structure of the American economy, and separate the sheep from the goats among the plethora of policies which were pursued.

Let me turn first to the vexed question of private investment. I shall discuss it in terms of the usual division into producers' plant and equipment, residential construction, net additions to inventories, and foreign investment.

Plant and Equipment. Both friendly critics and active opponents have argued that the New Deal policies—at any rate before 1938—were seriously detrimental to private investment in plant and equipment. It has been argued with cogency that the tax policy—the progressive individual income tax, corporation taxes, and especially the undistributed profits tax—diminished the incentives of individuals and corporations to risk their money in venturesome enterprises. It is possible that the antispeculation reforms, while increasing the soundness of investment, diminished its quantity. There is considerable agreement with Professor Schumpeter's argument that anticapitalist attitudes provided a chilly climate for innovation. Finally, there was the all-embracing charge that the mutual distrust of government and business produced a "strike of capital." These arguments lose none of their appeal since something is required to explain why plant and equipment expenditures in the thirties never approached their peak level in the twenties.

On the favorable side, it can be argued that the cheap money policy and the federal loan policy encouraged investment in the traditional way by reducing the cost of borrowing. Also, somewhat to my surprise, I find that Professor Schumpeter includes NRA as a positive recovery factor. He argued that it "pegged weak spots in industries, stopped spirals in many places, mended disorganized markets" and "even Blue Eagles do count for something when, objective conditions for revival being given, it is broken morale that is the matter." While I am quoting Professor Schumpeter, I should like to record his views on the contention that government deficits per se impede business expansion. He says: "Some of the arguments adduced for this possibility fully merit the shrugging of shoulders with which they are usually met; for instance, the argument that the unbalanced budget destroyed confidence."

These arguments are I believe all sound in principle, but, in order to assess their impact on the economy, we need some quantitative measure of their effects. The way for such measurement has been paved by Tinbergen's epoch-making work, but his own study does not extend to the period we are investigating. Tinbergen's work is now being revised, extended, and improved at the Cowles Commission and has resulted so far in a preliminary manuscript by Mr. Lawrence Klein. The Commission and Mr. Klein have generously given me permission to use their results with the caution that they must be regarded only as first approximations. This reservation applies not only to Mr. Klein's results but also to other conclusions based on correlation analysis to which I shall refer.

Mr. Klein has obtained a relation from the data over the period 1921–41 which satisfactorily "explains" the demand for net additions to plant and equipment in terms of the private net output of the economy in the recent past as a positive factor and the existing stock of capital equipment and the price level of capital goods as negative factors. The unexplained residuals are randomly distributed, and, so far as I can see, none of these residuals can be identified as disturbances of the relation due to government policy. For instance, in relation to the values yielded by the formula, investment was abnormally high in 1929, but still higher in 1937. The plausibility of the relation is increased by the satisfactory results which the same method yields for particular individual groups such as public utilities and mining and manufacturing.

I am not satisfied that this relation reveals the whole truth about investment demand in all circumstances. I believe an adequate theory requires the inclusion of net profits after taxes as an explanatory variable. It has not emerged as such in Mr. Klein's results because net corporate profits (excluding inventory revaluations) have remained very highly correlated with private output. Profits before taxes retained throughout

the thirties the same relation to private output, with practically no disturbance, as existed during the twenties. The tax changes of the thirties
were not sufficient to disturb greatly the relation between profits after
taxes and output. I therefore interpret Mr. Klein's results to mean not that
tax changes are irrelevant but that those which in fact did occur had no
significant effect.

Mr. Klein's demand function also does not include the rate of interest
as an explanatory variable. Although interest rates can be demonstrated
to be determining influences in other countries, they are apparently
dwarfed by other influences in the United States. Tinbergen reaches the
same conclusion and demonstrates that the determinants of investment
differ widely from country to country.

The results lead to the conclusion that the underlying factors determining investment in plant and equipment were the same in the twenties
and the thirties and that government policy affected investment only
insofar as it affected the explanatory variables of the relation.

The large stock of capital which played an important role in depressing
investment in the first half of the decade was the inheritance of the
twenties and not a product of the thirties. Government policy affected the
rate of investment insofar as it influenced national output and capital
goods prices. Its influence on output depends on the expansionary effects
of all the government policies. Prices of capital goods, and especially
construction costs, did rise abruptly and disproportionately between 1936
and 1937. This may be ascribed to wage increases and to increases of
world prices of raw materials.

I cannot regard these statistical conclusions as in any way final or
definitive, and I am sure the Cowles Commission takes the same point
of view. However, until evidence to the contrary appears, I am prepared
to enter a verdict of "not proven" to the charge that the political and
economic environment of the thirties affected the incentive to invest in
plant and equipment through its effect on business confidence.

Residential Construction. The low rate of investment in residential
building in the thirties has given rise to explanations involving lack of
confidence of the same type I have described in relation to plant and
equipment investment. I therefore need not repeat them here, but turn
at once to the statistical evidence.

There is a growing volume of reasonably satisfactory attempts—all on
the same lines—to explain statistically fluctuations in residential building,
and I feel I am here on less treacherous ground than that which I have
just left. I refer to the work of Roos, Chawner, Tinbergen and Derksen.
Mr. Klein has re-examined the whole question for the period 1921–41 in
the light of later statistics than were available to the other writers. He
explains expenditure on nonfarm residential building in terms of disposable
income, the rent level, construction costs, and net increases in families

in the recent past. But the rent level itself depends on conditions in the housing market. Mr. Derksen has given the most satisfactory explanation of rent in terms of the vacancy ratio two years before and nonfarm family income.

These studies give a satisfactory explanation of residential building over the twenties and the thirties, and lead to the conclusion that the major factor accounting for the low level of housing in the thirties was the high rate of construction in the twenties. Higher construction costs also reduced total housing expenditures in the later years of the decade. This was probably reflected, at least partially, in a reduction in the size rather than the number of dwelling units constructed.

Here again I can find little evidence that taxation or lack of confidence in the government was an important explanatory factor. Had it been, surely 1937 and 1938 would have been years of markedly subnormal activity, which they were not. Furthermore, I believe that these factors are less likely to have an adverse effect on residential building than on business plant and equipment expenditures. The main factors which account for the low level of residential construction shown in the thirties appear to be a relatively large supply of housing in relation to the number of families, especially in the first half of the decade, high construction costs, especially in the second half, and a low level of income throughout.

Business Inventories. The behavior of inventories over the thirties requires no particular comment except for two episodes. Inventories were liquidated under the impact of declining production after the onset of the depression and were built up as recovery got under way. The two exceptions to this regular behavior I want to notice are the short-lived inventory spurt in the second half of 1933 and the abnormal accumulations of inventories in the latter half of 1936 and 1937. The 1933 incident must be explained by the prospects of higher costs, especially wages, under NRA, while the accumulations in 1936 and 1937 were largely in response to the expectations of higher prices aroused by the sharp general increases in wage rates at that time—although the prospects for higher world prices for raw materials probably also had significant effects. The 1933 flurry was followed by a mild liquidation. The liquidation of the accumulations of 1936 and 1937 was a major factor in explaining the sharpness of the downswing in 1937 and 1938. These episodes were, I believe, the most important effects of the general behavior of wage rates in the period.

Foreign Investment. Foreign investment as represented by "net exports" reached an average annual rate of about 1 billion dollars in the latter half of the twenties. It did not regain this rate until European war demands expanded American exports at the end of the thirties. What then was the effect of the devaluation of the dollar and the trade agreements negotiated after 1934? It is impossible to isolate the effects of these measures since conditions in the outside world remained by no means static. I believe, however, that devaluation did accomplish some increase in the positive balance of payments in the year or two after it was undertaken, but that restrictive measures taken by other countries, whether in retaliation or for other reasons, very soon offset this effect. It is also an almost impossible problem to isolate the effects of the trade agreements. My own opinion is that the trade agreements negotiated in the thirties laid the foundations of a policy of freer trade in the future and did not have a marked impact on the operation of the economy of the thirties. I must hasten to add that this opinion does not belittle the achievement of those who succeeded in reversing the policy exemplified by the Hawley-Smoot tariff.

I conclude that the net effects of United States economic foreign policy were reflected in the domestic economy rather than in foreign trade. Chiefly by reducing confidence in other currencies, devaluation probably accelerated the gold inflow into the United States and thus facilitated the cheap money policy. Secondly, by raising the world dollar prices of agricultural products, the burden of aid to agriculture on the federal budget was somewhat reduced—and after all, was not the real objective of devaluation to raise agricultural prices?

Consumers' Expenditures. It has been widely argued that the government's policies of the thirties, whether designed for the purpose or not, did derive economic justification from their effect in increasing consumption in relation to national income.

NRA was intended by the President to raise wages by more than prices and thereby redistribute income and increase consumption. The antimonopoly policy of the latter part of the decade was intended to achieve the same result. There was a widespread belief that higher money wages, unassociated with any price policy, would increase mass purchasing power. One of the objectives of agricultural policy was to increase total consumption by improving the lot of agriculture. More progressive income taxes were held to redistribute income after taxes in favor of those more likely to spend on consumption. One of the main economic arguments for the undistributed profits tax was that it would reduce corporate savings and thereby increase income payments to consumers.

Here again the only way to assess the quantitative validity of these contentions is to test the matter statistically. Their quantitative effects would be reflected in the propensities of individuals to spend out of their disposable incomes and of corporations to distribute their incomes as dividends. This evidence can also be reinforced by such evidence as there is on the distribution of incomes.

There is widespread agreement among economists that consumers' expenditures throughout the whole interwar period can be explained as a function of disposable income with a rising time trend representing progress towards higher living standards. Disagreement only exists as to the form the relation should take. Some economists use deflated series, others the money data. Some contend that the regression shifts as between prosperity and depression years. My own belief is that the relation which satisfies both theoretical and statistical requirements best is to relate per capita real consumption to per capita real income for the whole period. But whatever the correct law is, there is no evidence that it changed during the thirties. Thus whatever changes in the distribution of individual incomes after taxes did occur, they had no perceptible influence on consumer spending in relation to disposable income in the aggregate.

The behavior of corporations in distributing their dividends has so far defied systematic explanation, but the figures do enable us to answer the question with which we are mainly concerned. Mr. Hoover's policy of exhortation probably did have some effect in inducing corporations to distribute more than they earned in 1930. But corporations as a whole continued this practice through 1938—though on a smaller scale. Unless it can be argued that Mr. Hoover's advice was still being adhered to it is difficult to explain the behavior of corporate savings except in terms of the depression itself.

The paucity of official data on the distribution of individual incomes does not permit any definitive conclusions. I am impressed, however, with the remarkable stability of the relation between private wages and salaries to private gross product. Throughout the twenties and thirties wages and salaries remained extraordinarily close to 50 per cent of the total. This relation is a dominant factor in determining the distribution of individual incomes. There is some indication that in 1937 labor did succeed in increasing its share of the total product, but these gains were rapidly wiped out by subsequent price adjustments. I am unable to find any identifiable influence of the antimonopoly policies. I infer, therefore, that the redistributive policies of the thirties either did not have their anticipated effects on consumption or were not carried as far as has sometimes been thought.

My survey of the determinants of investment and consumption thus leads to the conclusion that, by and large, during the thirties both businesses and consumers were influenced in making their expenditure decisions by the same factors in the same way as in the twenties. I submit this conclusion with some diffidence since the statistical relations on which it is based are admittedly tentative. But that evidence all leads in the same direction. On the other side there is only a priori opinion however well informed and experienced.

The analysis also enables us to identify the factors which did affect the data on which the decisions of investors and consumers were based. They are as follows:

1. The high rate of construction of business plant and equipment and

residential building during the twenties increased the stock of capital to a high level and thus made for abnormally low investment in the thirties.

2. Declining population growth contributed to the relative abundance of the supply of housing. I should add that I am speaking here of abundance from the point of view of the operation of the private ecomomy and not from any welfare point of view.

3. Increases in construction costs and the prices of capital equipment in relation to the general price level, particularly from 1937 on, contributed to the low rate of long-term investment, as compared with the twenties.

4. The rapid increases in wages contributed to the inventory speculation in 1936 and 1937.

5. The net foreign balance remained at a low level until European re-armament increased United States exports.

These are all factors tending to depress the level of national income. The single factor operating in the opposite direction was the expansionary fiscal policy of the federal government, which considerably more than offset the contraction in the construction programs of state and local governments which occurred after 1929, and afforded a strong positive stimulus to national income and thereby increased the rates of private consumption and private investment.

IV. EVALUATION OF POLICY

I can now attempt to answer the questions which I raised at the beginning of this paper: Was a positive government policy required if full recovery was to be achieved? What were the effects of the policy actually pursued? Did reform conflict with recovery?

We can answer the first question with some confidence. Even if all the disturbing influences that occurred during the thirties had been absent, the high rate of accumulation of capital during the twenties would have made for a low rate of investment and consequently a low rate of income during the thirties. If nature had been left to take its course, there would presumably have been a prolonged period of disinvestment and depression before it would have again become profitable for businesses to undertake the rate of investment expenditures required for full recovery. Our analysis leads to the conclusion that recovery would have arrived eventually, although there is no reason to believe that the "speculative" influences which made 1929 an exceptional year would have recurred. The contentions advanced in the heat of controversy that but for the New Deal full recovery would have been achieved by, say 1935, merit no attention. In fact, I know of no economist who would now argue that if "orthodox" policies had been continued, recovery up to 1937 would have been more rapid than it was.

Whatever the legitimate doubts about the statistical explanations of investment, I do believe the negative correlation between investment and the existing stock of capital is firmly established on both theoretical and statistical grounds. It follows that government action which mitigates depressions by policies which increase the rate of private investment tend to diminish its rate in the following boom. I make this observation, not as an argument against stabilization policies, but merely as a word of warning against the assumption that an effective countercyclical policy will achieve prosperity. Such a policy would tend to eliminate the peaks as well as the troughs. For full employment more is required.

From the point of view of recovery our analysis has shown that the only policies which need to be considered are fiscal policy and wage policy. I have ruled out the vast array of measures such as NRA, AAA, and devaluation, except insofar as they were reflected in fiscal policy and the behavior of wages. For any other effects would have been reflected in changes in the behavior of consumers and investors, which remained substantially unchanged.

I have nothing further to add on wage policy. I am not concerned to debate the extent to which the actual behavior of wages can be regarded as the consequence of the government's policy. I would like, however, to remove one possible misunderstanding. Wage behavior proved disruptive in the thirties, first, because changes were abrupt and, second, because they contributed to an increase in construction costs in relation to other costs. To acknowledge this must not be interpreted as criticism of a wage policy which requires increases in money wages consistent with increased productivity of labor and stability of prices.

I have shown that before 1938 the fiscal policy of the government was a matter of accident and, in detail, was a mass of contradictions. Expansionary expenditure programs were the occasion for the introduction of regressive tax measures. I feel quite convinced that in the early days of the New Deal it was political infeasibility alone that prevented further measures of taxation. We have seen that the tax measures undertaken did not in fact have the desired results on the relation of consumption to income or the feared results on investment. The results of the new taxes must be judged by their over-all effects. These were to reduce private net output in relation to the total. By the end of the thirties it was necessary to rely on a greater rate of government production of goods and services to attain any given national income goal than at the beginning of the decade. On the other hand, the deficit required to attain that goal was smaller as a result of the New Deal taxes. Sometime the United States may have to make up its mind whether it wants to keep private enterprise or hold down the national debt.

The expenditure side of the government's policy was also contradictory. Expenditures were cut to help balance the "regular budget" while the "emergency budget" increased. Expenditures were determined by the need to relieve distress rather than by any consideration of the relation of fiscal policy to economic expansion. Nevertheless, the rate of expansion between 1933 and 1936 was remarkable. But in the light of what was accomplished in 1941, I am inclined to think that rate of expansion could have been greater had the fiscal policy been more ambitious. There were few bottlenecks in 1933, and if they appeared later it was due to the slowness rather than the rapidity of recovery. For instance, prolonged depression in the building industry did impair the skilled labor supply.

It has been alleged that the inflationary situation in 1937 was the consequence of the expansionary fiscal policy. But the expansion from 1938 to 1941 was attended with no phenomena which could be described as inflationary. I therefore cannot accept the explanation for 1937, especially since that inflation can be accounted for on other grounds—particularly the inventory boom which I have already discussed.

The 1937 experience has been used as an argument that an expansionary fiscal policy cannot be tapered off without creating a depression. The year 1937, however, is hardly a fair test since, as we have seen, it contained the seeds of a highly unstable situation not themselves the result of the fiscal policy. But I do agree that tapering off may cause difficulties. I am to some extent reassured on this point by the remarkable way in which the economy has withstood the "tapering off" of war expenditures in the last few months. The government did face a difficult situation in 1937. Full employment had not been achieved but inflation had. Hindsight leads me to the view that it would have been preferable to let the inflation run its course rather than to contribute to a serious depression.

After 1938 fiscal policy again made its full contribution to an unspectacular recovery through 1940. Rearmament and war produced full recovery, but postponed for a later depression the conclusion of the peacetime experiment.

My analysis of investment has led me to disagree with Professor Schumpeter's contention that reforms are per se anticapitalist and therefore depressive. But I do agree that in other ways reform impeded recovery. In the first place the abruptness of the wage increases in 1936 and 1937 can be to some extent attributed to the government's labor policy. In the second place, reform measures gave rise to some of the contradictions of fiscal policy. From the national income point of view, social security meant a highly deflationary tax which was offset to only a trivial extent by disbursement of benefits. But the consequences were accidental and not necessary incidents of reform. My conclusion from the thirties—to say nothing of the forties—is that the American economy can stand a lot of buffeting and that immediate profits can do wonders for business confidence.

V. CONCLUSION

My main conclusion on government policy from the experience of the thirties is that fiscal policy did prove to be an effective and indeed the only effective means to recovery. This conclusion does not, of course, imply that other methods could not have been effective; merely that these would have had to be applied much more drastically and vigorously than they were in the thirties. For instance, if the government were to assume complete control over wages and prices, it might prove possible to achieve recovery by that means alone. If the government were to push far enough the policy of monetary expansion which will be discussed by Mr. Means, I have little doubt that that too would lead to recovery. My own opinion, however, is that a flexible fiscal policy, which pays due attention to flexibility on both the expenditure and revenue sides, would provide the most conservative solution.

I do not mean by this that direct controls have no place in stabilization policy. On the contrary I do believe that a vigorous antimonopoly policy is necessary to prevent abuse of fiscal policy. But I doubt whether such a policy can be relied on to effect major redistributions of income. The evidence of the thirties suggests that the redistributions that did occur in that decade were the direct consequence of fiscal policy.

The thirties have demonstrated that fiscal policy can promote expansion without disturbing the structure of the economy, but as I have said, the last chapter remains to be written; and meanwhile I am left with the impression that the road from depression to enduring recovery is not an easy one.

I am convinced that it is much easier economically to avert depressions than to cure them. My argument leads to the conclusion that the thirties can be explained in terms of the cyclical process and were very largely the product of what had gone before. And that means that a depression of the same order can and probably will recur unless it is arrested by government action. One very eminent observer has described the New Deal as "the price we paid for time to think." At present I am afraid there is danger that we may become impervious to thought in the forties as we were in the twenties.

A Critique of Professor Smithies

GARDINER C. MEANS

We are all familiar with the "economic interpretation of history." I want to speak of Dr. Smithies' paper as a fiscal interpretation of history, for it suffers from the same kind of defect. It leaves out of account what does not fit the theory.

The biggest single omission is the lack of discussion of monetary policy (other than devaluation) and the effects of changes in the stock of money outstanding. Yet there was important action in this field. The government pursued monetary policies between 1929 and 1933 which brought about a reduction of the money stock of 8 billion dollars, or more than 25 per cent. In contrast the New Deal adopted a policy of monetary expansion, bringing about an increase in the stock of money of 14 billion dollars, or over 50 per cent. In our economy, which functions on the basis of money, you cannot increase the money supply by over 50 per cent and have no significant effect. Yet Dr. Smithies has neither mentioned these major changes in his analysis of the thirties nor shown that they are irrelevant.

Actually it would be about as easy to "explain" the level of employment statistically by changes in the stock of money and in the demand for money as by fiscal changes. A decline in the rate of money expansion just preceded the start of the big depression and actually contraction and declining activity went together. Likewise, in recovery, monetary expansion and increased activity went hand in hand with certain exceptions which are consistent with our knowledge of changes in the demand to hold cash. Statistically, as good a case can be made for a monetary as for a fiscal explanation. Or rather, the fiscal explanation is no better *and no worse* than the monetary.

Of course I do not believe that a monetary interpretation of history would be more valid than a fiscal interpretation. The problem is larger then either though I suspect that the monetary has a great deal to do with it. What I am immediately concerned with saying is that Dr. Smithies has given no weight to the major changes in monetary policy and money stocks and that I believe this omission invalidates both Dr. Smithies' major conclusion and much of his analysis. I do not believe he has established "that fiscal policy is the one major instrument for recovery or stabilization in a free society." Nor do I believe that "the United States will have to make up its mind whether it wants to keep private enterprise or hold down the national debt." Theoretically, I believe either fiscal policy or monetary policy alone could produce stability; but in practice we need

Reprinted by permission of the *American Economic Review*, Supplement, XXXVI (May, 1946), pp. 32–35.

to use both, with major emphasis on monetary policy. Through the proper emphasis on monetary policy, we can avoid a policy of cumulative government deficits and yet maintain an economy of full employment. And I believe that the evidence of the thirties if properly interpreted would give support to this thesis. But my immediate object is simply to point out that the evidence Dr. Smithies presents is subject to quite a different interpretation than that which he gives. Let us look at his evidence.

The evidence which he presents is to the effect "that, by and large, during the thirties both businesses and consumers were influenced in making their expenditure decisions by the same factor in the same way as in the twenties." But can you say this if you look at money? In the twenties, businesses and consumers in the aggregate were willing to spend on consumption and investment the whole of the money they received as income provided their "cash on hand" amounted to about 30 per cent of their current income. In the thirties the business and consumer community was unwilling to spend the whole of its current money income even though it held cash on hand equal to half its current income. I submit that this was a major shift and that until it is properly explained, one has not established that businesses and consumers were influenced by the same factors in the same way as in the twenties. And though a part of the difference can be explained by lower interest rates in the thirties the bulk cannot be so explained. So far as I have been able to discover, there was a fundamental shift in the preference of the community to hold money as compared with spending it on consumption or investment goods. If this is true, it means we must examine Dr. Smithies' statistical reasoning more carefully for the two conclusions do not appear to be consistent.

The two main elements in his reasoning are based on evidence (1) that the behavior of businesses with respect to investment in the thirties fitted the same formula which it fitted in the twenties and (2) that the expenditure on consumption in the thirties bore the same relation to disposable income that it did in the twenties. In neither case do I question the evidence involved. I question only the reasoning which leads to the conclusion that the propensities to invest and to consume were stable because of this formula fitting.

I can make the illogic of this position clear most easily in the case of consumption. Dr. Smithies' reasoning assumes, like that of so many other economists, that the regression of consumption on disposable income represents the propensity to consume. Yet it would be perfectly possible to have a propensity to consume which fluctuated from time to time and still have the observations in the time series fall on a smooth regression line. This would be true, for example, if the propensity to invest were a constant. It would also be true if some third factor, say the stock of money outstanding, or the demand for money influenced the propensity to consume and the propensity to invest so that when the stock of money outstanding was high the propensity to invest and consume would be high and when low both propensities would be low. Until these possibilities have been eliminated we cannot accept the time series regression of consumption on disposable income (whether in the aggregate or per capita) as representing the propensity to consume. Some analyses which I have made suggest that if either the investment propensity or the consumption propensity is stable, it is *more* likely to be the investment function. But probably neither is stable. And if the regression of consumption on income does not represent the consumption function then much of Dr. Smithies' evidence to support his exclusive fiscal theory falls by the wayside.

Two recent developments give added weight to the skeptical attitude I am displaying toward this fiscal theory, one in the field of statistical analysis and the other in the field of forecasting. Recent efforts to construct statistical statements of the investment function have produced formulae which give unacceptably high multipliers if the regression of consumption on disposable income is accepted as representing the propensity to consume. One worker whose analysis of investment produced an extravagant multiplier concluded that his statistical analysis must be wrong. He did not even consider the possibility that his theory was wrong.

The other development, that in the area of forecasting, involves the gross underestimates of employment after the war which have been made by many of the protagonists of the exclusive fiscal theory. The forecast of only 46 million employed in the last quarter of 1945 is belied by the actual figures of 51, 52, and 52 employed in October, November, and December. The error in the forecast arose primarily from adherence to the Keynesian assumption that consumer expenditure is a relatively stable function of disposable income. Actually it turned out that while disposable income went down somewhat consumer expenditure on nondurable goods went up by over 10 per cent.

It can be argued that this major departure from the prewar relation of nondurable goods demand to disposable income is a temporary matter resulting from the peculiarities of the transition. It is clear that returned veterans have to restock their wardrobes. The reduction of war tension and war restraint can produce a temporary splurge of spending. Certainly some of the increase in the demand for nondurables comes from this source and must be considered temporary. But is it all temporary? It seems to me likely that an important part is not. Indeed, last summer it was my opinion, as many in Washington can testify, that nondurable demand would increase considerably, relative to disposable income, when the war came to an end, partly because of the temporary factors already mentioned and partly because the huge cash balances and other liquid assets held by the community would have the more or less permanent effect of increasing the propensity to consume. The possession of large cash balances would lead to the spending of a larger proportion of current income on consumption, including the consumption of nondurable goods. This is an effect which is independent of the heavy backlog of demand for durable goods. Since I have taken this position, I naturally interpret the increased propensity to consume as being more than temporary. Indeed I do not think the full rise in the propensity to consume has yet expressed itself. Many nondurable goods are not available in the quantity or in the quality which is wanted. If there were not serious limits on the supply of nondurables at present prices, I believe that nondurable sales would increase considerably relative to disposable income and only a part of the increase would be of a temporary character.

We will have to wait—perhaps a number of years—before we can be sure that there has been a significant and continuing upward shift in the propensity to consume. It is my prediction that events will show such an increase. If this prediction is vindicated it would seem to me pretty clear evidence that the propensity to consume is not fixed but is affected by the volume of money outstanding and can be increased or decreased by increasing or decreasing the total stock.

I have gone into this matter of the employment forecasts in some detail because a very basic issue appears to be involved. If the propensity to consume can be increased by an increase in the real money supply, the Keynesian theory of employment *cannot* be valid and the contribution which monetary policy can make to a program of economic stability is very much greater than the Keynesian theory would indicate. Even a secular tendency to oversave could be overcome without a continuing government deficit. In this case, a fiscal interpretation of history might have to give way to a monetary interpretation or a blend of the two in which monetary elements were dominant.

FOR FURTHER READING: An excellent survey stressing fiscal policy is Clay Anderson, "The Development of the Pump-Priming Theory," *Journal of Political Economy*, LII (June, 1944), pp. 14–59. The various monetary panaceas are discussed in Joseph E. Reeve, *Monetary Reform Movements: A Survey of Recent Plans and Panaceas* (Washington, 1943). See also Albert G. Hart, *Debts and Recovery, 1929–1937* (New York, 1938). For studies emphasizing the impact of monetary policies see C. G. Johnson, *The Treasury and Monetary Policy, 1933–1938* (New York, 1939), James D. Paris, *Monetary Policies of the United States, 1932–1938* (New York, 1938), and Kenneth D. Roos, "The Recession of 1937–38," *Journal of Political Economy*, LVI (June, 1948), pp. 239–248.

28. *Economic Effects of World War II*

PROBLEM: *Have wars stimulated American economic growth?*

Sweeping generalizations, affirmative and negative, and usually lacking supporting empirical evidence, have characterized efforts to assess the economic impact of America's wars. Only after 1942 did economists and historians subject this problem to more precise analysis. Seeking to define the issue in more specific terms, they examined the impact of war upon national wealth, on population, on fiscal policy and price behavior, and on industry and agriculture. Nevertheless, differences of opinion concerning general effects continue to persist. Professor Chester W. Wright, a leading economic historian from the University of Chicago, concluded as a result of his studies that the economic effects of America's wars have usually been slight, and have not significantly altered long-term trends. A somewhat different conclusion was reached by N. J. Silberling of Stanford University, who examined some of the same evidence but believed that wars have tended to retard economic expansion. Many more empirical studies of specific trends need to be made before the issue can be delineated with greater certainty. But these two authors have pioneered courageously in unfolding a vital and persistent problem which affects the interpretation of past and future economic development. What sectors of the American economy were most profoundly affected by World War II? How does the economic impact of the war in 1941–45 compare with the effects of previous conflicts? What factors need to be considered in an assessment of the economic results of wars?

The More Enduring Economic Consequences of American Wars

CHESTER W. WRIGHT

I

Only in recent years have the economic problems involved in the conduct of war begun to receive much attention from scholars. As a result of sad experience we now also have substantial groups engaged in studying the problems of postwar readjustment, but I know of no attempt to present a summary generalization of the more enduring reactions of American wars upon the economic life of the country. By the more enduring reactions I mean those which are felt after the postwar period of readjustment and which may be due either directly to the war or to the depression caused by the war.

It is to this very broad and intangible topic—since it is impossible to measure or sharply to separate most of the reactions due to war from those due to the infinitely complex group of other factors which shape the course of economic development—that I venture to address myself. My purpose is two-fold: First, I will try to suggest the manner and the extent to which our serious wars have tended to alter or to warp for a relatively enduring period the economic life and development of the country, hoping thus to secure some idea of the relative importance of war in shaping our economic progress. Second, by indicating both the desirable and the undesirable reactions I will seek to suggest certain problems that should be kept in view in any planning for the postwar generations. In what follows I shall confine myself to the reactions of the more serious wars—the Revolution, the War of 1812, the Civil War, and the First World War with occasional comments on possible reactions of the present war. It must be understood that what follows only attempts to suggest the more general *tendencies*. These tendencies may be either accentuated or counteracted by numerous other factors. Obviously, also, no two wars are alike and the rapid mechanization of warfare, especially in the twentieth century, has both altered and enormously magnified war's economic reactions.

The more enduring economic reactions of war—that is, those felt by the generations following the postwar readjustment—may take many forms, but they are primarily important economically as they affect (1) the productive capacity of the nation or the national income, (2) the per capita

Reprinted by permission from *The Journal of Economic History*, Supplement, III (December, 1943), pp. 9–26.

real income, (3) the distribution of wealth and income. What follows is chiefly concerned with these three things.

II

I turn first to the reaction on certain factors affecting the long-run productive capacity of the nation. In the case of population, the basic factor in the labor supply, it is well known that war brings a marked rise in the death rate and a decline in the birth rate which are followed by the reverse tendencies for a period after the return of peace. In the United States another important factor has been the effect of war on immigration. The loss of life attributable to war includes not only that among the military forces due to battle casualties and disease but that among the civilian population due to undermined vitality and epidemics caused by war, to which we now have to add that due to aerial warfare. It is said that during the great European wars of the nineteenth century the increase in mortality among the civilian population was several times that among the military forces. Fortunately, in the history of the United States, except for the influenza epidemic in 1918–1919, the loss from this cause seems to have been negligible.

Turning to specific wars in the United States, we find that lack of data makes it impossible to be definite about the effects of the Revolution on the growth of population. The small size of the fighting forces and the infrequency of actual conflict must have made the number of deaths among the armed forces relatively small and we have no evidence of an appreciable increase in mortality among the civilian population. Undoubtedly the chief reaction arose from the cutting down of immigration, which may have averaged 4,000 to 5,000 a year just before the war and probably did not regain this figure until about 1790. In addition the imports of slaves ceased and some were carried off by the British. The census estimates of the rate of growth of the population show a decided drop for the decade 1770–1780 but an abnormally high rate for the following decade, yet the average for the two is but a trifle below the rates prevailing both before and after these two decades. During the War of 1812 also the chief loss must have been due to the cutting off of immigration since the military losses could not have been large. If it is assumed that but for the war the rate of growth for the decade 1810–1820 would have been midway between the rates for the preceding and the following decades, the actual increase is found to be only about 131,000 less than would have occurred otherwise.

Applying the same crude formula to the Civil War decade of 1860–1870 gives an increase of some 1,300,000 less than might have been expected. This war, fought between our own people, is the only one in our history where the number of deaths among the armed forces was appreciable. On the Union side, including the 249,458 who died of disease or accident, the figure was 359,528; the Confederate losses are uncertain but have been estimated at 94,000 battle casualties and twice that from disease, which would bring the total for both sides to some 635,000. The loss in growth from the reduction in immigration during the decade may be roughly estimated at not over 500,000—thus making it the sole case where this was not the chief cause of loss—and most of the remainder can be attributed to a lower birth rate.

For the World War decade 1910–1920 the same formula indicates an increase of population about 3,300,000 less than might have been expected. The losses of the American forces from battle and disease were only some 122,500 up to May, 1919 and were greatly exceeded by the civilian deaths from the influenza epidemic of 1918–1919, variously estimated at between 400,000 and 600,000. The crude birth rate fell every year after 1914, when it was 28.1, to 25.1 in 1919, but after two years of recovery it sank to a still lower level, averaging 23.5 for the period 1922–1929. In view of this continued downward trend the war must be considered as a minor factor in the losses from the lowered birth rate. The age distribution of the population of the United States in 1930 shows no such "hollow classes" as were produced in the chief countries of Europe by this war. For the six years 1914–1919 the net immigration was about 2,500,000 less than it had totaled during the six preceding years. Clearly in this war too the drop in net immigration was the chief factor in the loss of potential population growth. Also it should be noted that the war greatly hastened and accentuated the shift to a policy of severe restriction on immigration which marked the following decade.

In this country in the past, therefore, the chief effect of war upon population growth has been due, except in the case of the Civil War, to the resulting reduction in the inflow of immigrants. In the case of the present war, obviously, immigration having previously been so severely restricted, any loss from this cause will be negligible, and we have the opportunity of making up for other losses by letting down the bars if we wish to. On the other hand, although the proportion of deaths due to disease has declined from twice that due to battle casualties at the time of the Civil War to a substantially equal proportion in the World War," we face the prospect of a loss from deaths among the armed forces which will doubtless exceed that of any previous war except the Civil War and conceivably may even surpass that record. Even in the latter eventuality the loss relative to the population would be much smaller.

As to the significance of such losses in population growth only a word is necessary. They are chiefly important economically as they may reduce the productive capacity of the country and the national income; just how important I shall try to suggest in my conclusion. The extent to which they may react upon the per capita real income and the standard of living is impossible of determination, but it must be very slight.

III

Turning to the enduring effects of war upon national wealth and capital accumulation, we face a broad problem with endless complications concerning which I can make only a few points. The complexity of the problem is well illustrated by J. M. Clark's excellent study of *The Costs of the World War to the American People* and the conclusion reached in this careful analysis is significant for our purposes. Writing in 1931 concerning the whole period 1914 to 1929 he said: "The United States showed no clearly demonstrable excess or shortage of production due to the War, over the entire period to 1929, so that our estimate of war costs might fairly be confined to the goods and services actually diverted to war uses, if the story had ended there." How much of the losses in national income during the depression after 1929 should be charged to the war will be largely a matter of opinion, though I cannot but believe it would be a very large proportion. While most of this loss, like that during the years of conflict, falls on the existing generation there is still a long-run loss to the extent that the succeeding generation inherits a smaller supply of capital goods or of the most durable consumer goods than would have been the case had peace prevailed.

Any attempt to estimate what this loss may amount to is beset with great difficulties. We have fairly definite figures on the government's outlay directly for war, but a part of this outlay, such as the greater disbursement for food and clothing, takes the place of some necessary civilian expenditure, while another part represents goods that may be salvaged for peacetime uses. The chief uncertainty arises in estimating what proportion of the loss in national income during the postwar depression can reasonably be attributed to the war, especially as this is likely to prove the greatest source of loss. The final question, how much of the civilian income lost because of the war would have been saved and converted into capital goods, we have a better basis for estimating, at least for more recent times, and we can be reasonably certain that for any period it would be only a small proportion.

The trend toward the mechanization of warfare has naturally greatly increased the possible losses of this character, partly because of the greater war outlay involved and partly because this greater outlay so aggravates the difficulties and costs of peace-time readjustment. It is most unlikely that the Revolution or the War of 1812 caused serious enduring losses of this type. In the Revolution the direct outlay, Continental and state, was probably not over $150,000,000 specie value and the postwar reaction was relatively brief. Government outlay during the War of

1812 was under $90,000,000, but the postwar depression, while slower in appearing, was more serious; yet some of this should be attributed to the abnormal stimulus given the country's economy before 1812 by the European wars. The Civil War losses must have attained much greater proportions. The direct government outlay in the Union alone was over five billion dollars and the process of readjustment was not completed before 1878. Yet it remained for the World War to give the country the first hint as to the cost of modern mechanized warfare. Relatively brief as our participation was, the direct government outlay, excluding loans, was about twenty-two billion dollars and the unprecedentedly long period of readjustment had not ended when the present war broke out. How great the resulting long-run losses of capital goods might be I shall attempt to suggest in my conclusion. Here it remains to note that whatever such losses may be they have significance for their reaction on both the productive capacity of the country and the per capita real income.

The depletion of the country's supply of exhaustible natural resources because of war can probably be ignored so far as any appreciable reactions are concerned almost up to date, but the nation has now reached a stage where the potential results should not be overlooked. Though much of the material used in the present war represents not a net increase in consumption but only a shift from civilian consumption, still the rapid growth in the use of these natural resources and the fact that certain of them have been depleted to the point where resort to higher-cost domestic or foreign sources of supply has become necessary, as with copper and forest products, or seems imminent, as with iron and possibly oil, are significant for the future. Just how significant will depend on various factors, such as discovery of new sources of supply, technological progress, and international commercial policies.

The question how far war stimulates or retards invention and technological progress is difficult to answer. The most definite measurable evidence available is the number of applications for patents and it is certainly significant that this underwent a distinct decline in 1861–1864 and again in 1918. War doubtless stimulates research and invention along a limited number of lines and these have been greatly broadened in scope with the mechanization of warfare, but it is not clear that it promotes general technological progress for peace-time purposes.

The partially or wholly incapacitated veterans, who because of their injuries are unable to earn as much as they might have otherwise, represent an enduring loss in national income while the cost of their care and of the pensions granted their dependents is made a public charge. To this charge there has to be added the pensions given the veterans who emerged from the war unscathed or to the dependents of deceased service men. The sum total of the public outlay for these purposes is one of the important enduring reactions of war; how large an item it amounts to in the course of time relative to the direct cost of war is seldom realized. For the Revolution the records are inadequate, but since the War of 1812 the federal government has spent for pensions to its veterans and their dependents a sum more than half as great as the direct cost of that war. In the case of the Mexican War the ratio is about two-thirds, for the Civil War it is one and one-half, and for the Spanish-American War it jumps to five and one-half. The rate at which this ratio has risen is a matter for serious contemplation. The ratio for the World War to the close of fiscal 1942, including the baby bond bonus, is one-third. This, however, covers a period of only twenty-four years and it must be noted that the peak annual outlay for Civil War pensions was not reached until 1921, fifty-six years after the end of the war, and that for the Spanish-American War, apparently, in 1940. We are still paying one pension for the War of 1812, one hundred and twenty-seven years later. Certainly few of war's economic reactions are more enduring! However, the effect of all this on national wealth and income must be very slight; it is primarily important as it reacts upon the distribution of that income.

War obviously may have a very stimulating or a retarding effect upon the growth of various branches of industry, but how much of that endures beyond the period of postwar readjustment is not easy to determine. The general field where this stimulus has been most marked in our history is manufacturing. Before the Civil War the stimulus from war needs was augmented by the cutting off of imported goods to supply the civilian needs; subsequently the declining importance of this latter factor was offset by the greater demands arising from the mechanization of warfare. Despite the difficulties faced in expanding output the Revolution stimulated various lines of manufacturing, though it is impossible to say how much, and it is probable more of the gain was lost on the return of peace than after most wars, the conditions between 1793 and 1808 being abnormally favorable to agriculture and commerce rather than to manufacturing. The rapid expansion of industry during the War of 1812 is well known though the rise started with the Embargo Act. Despite the unusual difficulties faced in the decade following the return of peace, much of the war-time gain seems to have been retained, thanks in part to the adoption of a policy of protection. For the Civil War period census figures are available, but these show a lower rate of growth (measured by the value added in manufacturing corrected for changes in the price level) for the decade 1859–1869 than for any decade covered by the census. Differences in business conditions during census years cannot explain much of this low rate of growth, but the ease with which manufactured goods could be imported into the North, as contrasted with the situation in 1776 and in 1812, doubtless substantially lessened the war stimulus. In the decade of the World War also the rate of growth, measured in the same way, was very moderate. Considering the record as a whole it is doubtful that wars, with the probable exception of that of 1812, gave an appreciable enduring impetus to the growth of manufacturing in this country.

Most of such impetus as was given came from the marked increase in protective tariff duties that followed all of these wars except the Revolution. In that case such increased duties as were imposed by the states were designed more to force commercial concessions than to protect manufactures. But ever since 1816 the protective duties on manufactured goods have been kept on a level substantially higher than would have been the case but for war's reactions. The industries granted protection on the ground that their maintenance was vital for defense, such as the dyestuffs industry, make up only an insignificant proportion of our total manufactures, but the practice of granting everyone a share whenever any upward revision was under consideration tended to spread protection to nearly every industry that asked for it. To what extent manufacturing as a whole has been maintained at a higher level because of duties arising from the impact of war would be impossible to determine, though we should beware of the common tendency to exaggerate the effects of protection in this country. Obviously whatever effect it had is significant for its undesirable reaction on the protective efficiency of the nation and on the per capita real income, though there were minor repercussions on the distribution of wealth and income.

The enduring reactions of our wars on the nation's agriculture have, I believe, been less marked than those on manufacturing, even though the immediate impact of war and its aftermath on the financial condition of farmers has commonly been very great. Also, more than in the case of manufacturing, these reactions have been influenced by the way in which each war affected foreign trade. During both the Revolution and the War of 1812 the country was largely cut off from its important foreign markets for farm products, and military demands only slightly offset this loss, but subsequently these markets were either recovered or replaced by new outlets and agriculture went on much as before. Possibly some enduring impetus to greater diversification of products remained. During the Civil War the blockade cut off the export of southern staples and led to efforts at diversification, but northern foodstuffs benefited from an unusual European demand as well as from the needs of the army. The most significant enduring reaction was on the organization of southern agriculture following the abolition of slavery, though in the North the introduction of farm machinery was hastened. The abnormal foreign demands of the World War simply reversed temporarily the downward trend in the export of farm products, while the postwar conditions accentuated it. It seems probable the more enduring reactions will be those that are the outgrowth of various measures of the 1930's which look more to the maintenance of the *status quo* than to readjustment to altered world conditions—a trend which in the long run would injure the national economy.

In agriculture, as in manufacturing, the effort to secure relief in periods of postwar depression led to increases in tariff duties that were relatively enduring; the Wool and Woolens Tariff of 1867 and the Emergency Tariff of 1921 and its successors are conspicuous examples. The effects, however, were generally much less serious than in the case of manufacturing, for the simple reason that, until very recently at least, so few of the great farm staples were in a position to benefit from the duties.

In the field of transportation, so far as inland transport is concerned, the most that can be said is that war slightly hastened the provision of certain limited facilities. How much was done during the Revolution is not clear, but the difficulties faced in overland transport when the coastwise water route was blockaded during the War of 1812 hastened the current movement to improve the roads. During the Civil War new construction of railroads was checked temporarily, though some connecting roads were built and an impetus was given to the adoption of the standard gauge and the extension of aid to the transcontinental lines. The World War taught some lessons as to the more efficient use of railroad facilities and hastened the introduction of the airplane, the spread in the use of which is likely to be the most enduring result in this field of the present war.

Far more striking, so far as immediate reactions are concerned, has been the effect of war on the nation's ocean shipping, though I hardly think it can be claimed that the long-run trend of development has been appreciably altered by our wars. Both the Revolution and the War of 1812 were disastrous for shipping, except as it turned to privateering, but recovery was reasonably prompt. The Civil War only hastened the decline of tonnage engaged in the foreign trade and what slight check upon that decline can be credited to the mail subsidies was due more to commercial objectives and interests than to those of defense. The World War was the first that caught the country with a supply of shipping totally inadequate for its needs, and that experience seemed likely to produce fairly enduring results, though not until the passage of the Merchant Marine Act of 1936.

IV

One of the most unfortunate features of our economic history is the way in which the fiscal needs of war have always been allowed and, despite all sad experience, are even today being allowed, to react upon our monetary and banking systems. Most of the resulting damage occurs during the war and the consequent depression, but some more enduring reactions can be traced, many of which proved advantageous. In the field of banking the Revolution led to the organization of the first modern bank in the country and the value of the services it was able to render doubtless hastened the founding of others, including the First Bank of the United States. The chaos in state banking during the War of 1812 and the lack of the advantages provided by a large central bank helped to overcome the widespread dislike of such an institution and hastened the chartering of the Second Bank. Similarly the Civil War hastened the adoption of the national banking system. Here the fiscal needs of the government were partly responsible for the requirement that notes be secured by government bonds. This requirement had an unfortunate reaction on the elasticity of the issue and the defect was not corrected for nearly half a century. The World War caused various modifications of the Federal Reserve System that had unfortunate consequences in the 1920's.

The reactions of war on the country's circulating medium, though momentous temporarily, were not very marked in the long run. In every serious war but the last, specie was driven from general circulation in most if not all of the country, but in time it returned. The chief enduring alterations were the injection of the greenbacks and the elimination of state bank notes in connection with the Civil War, to which might be added the recent retirement of gold from general use.

The tremendous impact of war on the fiscal system of the country leaves its chief enduring effect in the public debt piled up at such times together with the subsequent outlays required to pay the interest and retire the debt, to which should be added the outlay for defense in times of peace and, as previously noted, that for pensions. As is well known, until 1933 the total federal outlay for such purposes has commonly far exceeded that for all other purposes, even in times of peace. Federal taxes, therefore, have for the most part been one of the most lasting products of war. Until the Civil War, customs duties, first chosen chiefly with a view to their revenue-producing capacity and after 1815 with a view to protection, yielded by far the greater portion of federal income, while internal revenue taxes were only resorted to for brief periods when war expenditures were heavy. The great legacy of debt from the Civil War led to the adoption of internal revenue taxes as a permanent and substantial element in the federal tax system, though it was not until 1911, following the higher taxes chiefly required to meet the greatly increased military expenditures after the Spanish-American War, that the receipts from internal revenue regularly exceeded those from customs duties. The enormous World War debt had a similar reaction and internal revenue receipts, chiefly derived from the new income taxes, became by far the most important source of federal income. The significance of this war-caused burden of federal taxes arises, not from any appreciable effect upon the productive capacity or the per capita real income of the country, but rather from the reaction of the tax system upon the distribution of the national income. Down to the World War the federal system of taxation, with its chief reliance on customs duties and, after the Civil War, upon liquor and tobacco taxes among internal revenue duties, was decidedly regressive in character and tended to place an unjust proportion of the tax burden arising from war upon the masses. Since the World War, under the progressive income and estate taxes, most of this burden has been shifted to the more well-to-do, though of course this shift is in part a product of a growing sense of social justice quite independent of war's reactions.

V

While many of the reactions previously noted have been partly or entirely a product of the postwar period of readjustment, specific attention should be called to some of the lasting consequences of prolonged periods of depression. The role of the depression as a factor in retarding or stimulating long-run economic progress is a topic that deserves more notice than it has received. Moreover, the four periods of extreme inflation, deflation and depression which mark American history were all the product of our four serious wars and there are but two instances of prolonged depression, those following the panics of 1837 and 1893, that were not preceded by war. In the enumeration that follows it should be understood that in many cases the depression simply gave an impetus to trends of development which were supported, and often chiefly caused, by other forces.

A very substantial and enduring increase in real wage rates was a most important result of the greater drop in wholesale prices than in money wage rates after both the Civil War and the World War. Lack of adequate data makes it impossible to say what happened after the earlier wars, though I suspect there was only a very modest gain after the War of 1812 and probably little if any between the Revolution and the outbreak of the European wars. Since the beginning of the labor movement, war-time inflation has given a strong impetus to the organization of labor, while more recently the enormous demand for labor created by mechanized warfare has greatly strengthened its bargaining position. Though the succeeding depression always weakens the movement temporarily, I am confident that the net long-run outcome is a decided gain in strength; by 1880 the unions had a firmer basis than in 1861 and the power finally gained as a result of the World War was conspicuous.

While the economic order of the time was not such that the Revolution or the War of 1812 and their aftermaths gave any enduring impetus to the combination movement it is clear this was quite marked in the cases of the Civil and the World Wars. Small concerns lost ground to large concerns in both instances; the modern trust movement dates from the post-Civil War depression; the needs of the World War halted trust prosecutions and forced the organization of many trade associations while the subsequent depression was notable for the government's grant of exemptions from the anti-trust laws and its efforts to restrain competition.

Every depression has led to changes in our monetary and banking systems, some of which have already been noted, and, while not all were advantageous, not a few brought enduring reforms. After the Revolution the significant fact was not the return to the relief of more paper-money issues on the part of some of the states but rather the refusal of others to resort to this device and the safeguards against it which it was supposed were provided in the Constitution. After the War of 1812 some sections at least showed a lasting improvement in banking methods. The decade following the depression of the 1870's brought a much more effective regulation of state banks. The World War was followed by efforts—none too successful—to secure greater control over the use of bank credit and to expand the powers and influence of the Federal Reserve System.

The combination of war and its succeeding depression has always given an impetus to political and social reforms of an enduring character that were not without economic significance. The Revolution was accompanied by an appreciable broadening of franchise rights. Though the direct connection is less clear, Jacksonian democracy gained an impetus in the depressed 1820's following the War of 1812. The Civil War led to the enfranchisement of the Negroes and the World War hastened the grant of women's suffrage. The post-Revolution depression gave strength to the effort to obtain the Constitution and to the movements for prison reform and the abolition of slavery. The depressed 1820's added momentum to the demands for ending imprisonment for debt, easier access to the public lands, free schools, and better provision for relief of the poor. Efforts to protect and aid the freedmen were the most conspicuous of the social reforms arising from the Civil War, but that postwar period was not distinguished by its public spiritedness. The great impetus given to numerous measures of reform by the depression that ushered in the New Deal is sufficiently recent to need no elaboration. In general, as war and depression plus a growing social conscience have forced greater governmental interference in economic life they have hastened a trend which has been one of the basic features of our economic evolution for a hundred and fifty years. In a slow and ponderously moving democracy, where the conditions and problems of different regions are so diverse and the powers of government are divided between the states and the federal authority, the arousing of the people to action incident to wars and to their suffering in postwar depressions, which are nationwide in their impact, becomes in important factor in social change.

VI

Most of the reactions previously noted have been significant because of their effects upon the national income and the per capita real income, yet all of them inevitably had at least some effect on the distribution of wealth and income, since no economic change can take place without such an effect. It is still desirable to comment separately upon the effects of war and postwar depression on the redistribution of wealth and income.

The chief means by which these effects are brought about are too well known to require elaboration here. First, there are the immediate changes arising from inflation and deflation, and it is to be remembered that by far the most rapid and extreme advances and declines in prices in our history have been directly due to war. Such periods bring unjust gains and losses to debtors and creditors and to those dependent on wages and salaries. In addition war conditions yield certain branches of business enormous profits while others face heavy losses, and the success with which the difficulties of the depression are met by different people varies greatly. Each war's crop of newly rich has aroused widespread contemporary comment but its crop of newly poor enjoys the silence shared by the annals of that group. Secondly, there are the immediate losses due to the destruction, confiscation, or other deprivation of property in the course of the war. Actual destruction has commonly been relatively light in this country, but probably there was never such a general shift of wealth among the propertied classes in our history as that incident to the Revolution and the losses of the Tories, though this may have been equalled by the losses among the slave-holding planters of the Confederacy.

By far the greater portion of the war-caused redistribution of wealth and income is due to these causes and takes place during the war and the subsequent depression, but the results may long be felt among the individuals who make up the following generations. These later generations, moreover, are subjected to additional shifts in wealth and income that have their origin in war. First, the taxes arising from the war debt, the peace-time outlay for defense, the provision for care of veterans, pensions, and extra expenses in years of depression all involve a redistribution of income among large groups. If we are to judge from the past, this redistribution is a process which continues forever. Second, all the other enduring changes mentioned will inevitably react in one way or another to alter the distribution of wealth and income, though in most cases the result is likely to be of minor importance. What lasting effects all this shifting of wealth may have had upon the economic life of the country I do not attempt to estimate.

VII

One might go on to list other reactions of minor importance or those still more difficult to trace with any confidence, but I trust I have at least suggested those of chief economic significance, and it is time to summarize my general conclusions.

In American history wars have reduced the long-run productive capacity of the nation chiefly (1) by checking the growth of population, mainly, except in the case of the Civil War, through reducing the net inflow of immigrants; (2) by reducing the quantity of capital goods passed on to the succeeding generation, chiefly because of postwar depression losses rather than direct war-time outlay; (3) by leading to the adoption of various economic policies, commonly more immediately due to efforts at relief in postwar depressions, such as protective duties or parts of the recent agricultural program, which diverted the allocation of economic resources from the most efficient uses. Offsetting this last effect to an extent that cannot be determined is the impetus wars have given to the adoption of reforms leading to a more efficiently functioning economic order. Thus far the effects on exhaustible natural resources have been negligible, though that may not be true of the future. I therefore infer that the main enduring reactions arise from the reduced volume of population and capital goods.

If we omit the check on population growth, the same list of factors can be used to indicate the more enduring reactions of war on the per capita real income of the people. This omission obviously simply tends to decrease, but to decrease very substantially, the net amount of the enduring reaction on per capita real income.

Since it is quite impossible to measure the long-run reaction of war on all these factors any conclusion must be highly impressionistic, but a few points can be suggested which will help to convey some idea of their relative importance. As regards the loss in national income arising from a lowered rate of growth in the population and the labor supply we can find a suggestive clue in the careful estimate of J. M. Clark that the net cost to this country of deaths and disabilities due to the World War would average some $260,000,000 for a period of about thirty years following the close of the war and then rapidly taper off. Since the actual national income as calculated by Kuznets averaged $66.7 billion for the years 1919–1928 the loss from this source would be less than four-tenths of one per cent, a rather insignificant amount. Incidentally, it may be noted that the deaths from both battle and disease during the World War did not greatly exceed the deaths from accident (93,000) in the country during 1942 and that the annual impairment of capacity to work due to accidents probably exceeds that caused by the war. However, as we pointed out earlier, the war casualties made up only a small proportion of the loss in population growth arising from the World War. Certainly a portion of the still greater number of civilian deaths from influenza should be included while the loss from the decline in net immigration was many times greater. For the sake of greater definiteness, and without explaining in detail, I venture the wild guess, and it is only a guess, that the total loss from the slower population growth attributable to this war could not have been over 8 per cent of the national income for the period 1919–1938 and is more likely to have been between 3 and 6 per cent. Even these lower figures constitute a loss which begins to attain significant proportions.

The second important factor tending to reduce the long-run productive capacity of the country and the per capita real income is the decreased quantity of capital goods passed on to the generation living after the depression. Previous to the Civil War and probably to the World War this cannot have been very large, but the mechanization of warfare with the subsequent greater costs of readjustment have enormously increased it, even though a growing proportion of the war outlay goes into durable goods that can be salvaged for the uses of peace. Any very definite calculation of what this loss may amount to is impossible but a highly simplified hypothetical case may prove suggestive. Assume that the World War and the resulting depression reduced the national income available for savings through diversion of war outlays, destruction, and depression losses by a total of $100 billion, which is quite conceivable. Assume that the annual rate of capital formation would have been 8 per cent of the national income (because the rate of savings increases with a larger income) instead of the rate of 6.2 per cent which Kuznets figures as the average for the years 1919–1938. Then without the war the nation might have possessed eight billion dollars more of capital goods. If these capital goods earned 6 per cent, then eventually the national income might have been $480,000,000 a year greater. Even assuming all of this available from the start, it would have added less than three-quarters of one per cent to the average obtained in the period 1919–1938. Such a loss does not impress me as very significant.

Having so recklessly attempted to give some impression of the relative importance of the losses of population and capital due to war in their long-run effect upon the national income, I shall pass over the third group of factors previously noted, some of which produced favorable and some unfavorable reactions, with the simple comment that their net effect was probably the least important of all. By far the most important was the lowered rate of population growth.

But when we turn to the long-run reaction of war upon the per capita real income and the resulting standard of living the influence of the lowered rate of population growth may be considered as practically eliminated, for it certainly is negligible. I therefore come to the conclusion that the enduring reaction of our wars on this income has been very slight. It will be seen that this conclusion is in line with the general belief that the generation which fights the war and endures the postwar era of depression is the generation upon which as a whole nearly all of the burden falls. Also my conclusion as to the enduring effects of war upon national income helps to explain why it may be possible for a nation, once the postwar depression period has passed, to recover its prewar strength so rapidly and so completely.

The preceding conclusions lead me to raise the question whether the redistribution of wealth and income has not been the most important of the more enduring economic reactions of war in the history of this country. That it was far more important than the long-run reaction on the per capita real income appears to me beyond doubt. It is more difficult to compare it with that on the country's productive capacity and national income. The latter is significant primarily for nationalistic or political reasons as it affects the power of the country to protect itself and its interests. The redistribution of wealth and income is immediately significant—for I have not attempted to suggest its broader social consequences—because of its effect on the efforts of each family to supply its daily wants. It reacts to a greater or less degree on every family in the nation. The greatest economic suffering is caused not so much by the absolute amount of the war burden, as by the inequitable manner in which so much of that burden is placed upon some while others largely escape or greatly profit. We may well believe that a better distribution of wealth and income is desirable, but it is largely pure chance if that which comes out of war's reactions is better rather than worse. It is true the great impact of the shift falls upon the war generation. How enduring the effects may be will depend upon many factors in the case of each family. But there are also the subsequent reactions from other long-run economic changes arising from the war that have previously been noted. Certainly this redistribution may make a great difference to a large group among the children born to the war generation and this may very easily extend to their children's children.

Finally, if my analysis of the enduring economic reactions of American wars be reasonably correct, it should suggest, even though no two wars are alike, certain of the problems which this country must take into consideration in its planning for the postwar years that lie ahead.

The Dynamics of Business

N. J. SILBERLING

Holding to the view that wars have a most important bearing upon distinctive patterns of long waves in prices and in business activity, we may now examine more closely the process whereby a major war brings about inflation of the price level and of money values generally, whereas, on the other hand, it introduces disturbances of varying patterns and proportions in the business system. It is already clear that periods of intense warfare—accelerating some lines of production and trade and discouraging or even destroying others—produce effects upon business that cannot be expressed in a simply defined pattern, repeating itself upon each occasion. What we are now primarily interested in is the question *why* wars are capable of apparently producing such marked aberrations and deviations from the general drift of progress or growth. Before we undertake a study of the minor or year-to-year fluctuations in business, usually referred to today as "business cycles," it is desirable to formulate more definitely some conclusions as to the nature of the forces producing the long-term tidal movements. We shall turn first to the major cycles, because they seem to be associated with political policy under conditions of acute emergency. In fact, it may prove to be essential to divide our study of business dynamics into two distinct phases: wartime conditions and peacetime conditions. This distinction has been inadequately observed in studies of business conditions, doubtless because of the absence of reliable statistics and measurements of trade conditions over periods long enough to reveal the full perspective of relationships.

Probably the most fundamental economic characteristic of a major war emergency is the existence of a sudden, extremely intense, and powerfully mobilized demand on the part of the Government for the materials and equipment needed for the fighting forces (or for actual or potential allies). In our own national experience, this public demand has expressed itself primarily in money payments flowing through commercial channels. The Government has entered the markets as an urgent purchaser, not as an authority exercising the power to commandeer or to operate directly all machinery of production. This aspect of war supply has indeed been changing to a significant degree in recent years; some governments have assumed such sweeping control over production, trade, and finance that the war experience means merely a stepping up and altered character of a regimented production, no important buying of what is needed, and no need for huge issues of new money or credit. But to take the wars that have involved the American people since the beginning of the eighteenth century, the transitions from a peacetime basis to wartime basis, and the diversion of productive activity called for by the emergency have been marked by serious dislocation and extraordinary strain upon the normal mechanism of commerce, finance, and exchange. In none of these wars was there any extended period of previous preparation, gradual and deliberate mobilization of resources or capital or man power. The relatively *sudden* recognition of an inescapable emergency crashed upon an economic system normally functioning with relatively little governmental control over productive, commercial, and financial processes. Under war conditions the fighting personnel is commandeered; but the specialized material requirements, in amounts virtually without limit, are obtained under conditions that very soon cause competition between the Government and civilian consumers for possession of essential goods. The Government enters the markets supplied with virtually unlimited funds and bids against the private consumer or business firm; the result is naturally a swift and more or less cumulative spiral of price advances.

Contrasting with this sweeping intensification of demand and the prospect of enormous spendings of new money, obtained by borrowing or paper issues, to supplement inadequate tax revenue, actual production of the many materials needed can seldom be expanded fast enough. The drafting of men for war service removes labor from farms, factories, mines, and transportation. Women take their places only gradually. The direct allocation of allowable supplies to civilians, although today accepted as a necessary step by all governments, was not so much relied upon in earlier wars. There comes about a substitution of less well-trained, less skillful and efficient workers; a faster depreciation of machinery and transportation equipment and inadequate replacement occur. There may be, depending upon circumstances, an abrupt curtailment of raw materials from foreign countries. This quickly develops into bottlenecks of supply, creating the possibility of further swift advances in prices, in part speculative; at the same time inability to secure strategic materials hampers production of equipment in which those materials are indispensable.

In the case of most agricultural production, expansion of output to serve war needs is a relatively slow process. It requires a year or more to obtain even a modest increase, weather conditions permitting, in the output of field crops, and expansion in production of animal products requires considerably longer periods and tree crops still longer. A similar "inelasticity of supply" characterizes many of the important industrial metals and minerals. Mining operations can be speeded up somewhat if it is essential, but the discovery of new sources that can be economically developed even under the stimulus of intense demand is by no means a simple routine matter. Foodstuffs and mineral products invariably are in urgent demand under wartime conditions, for the fighting forces consume more food per capita than the same number of persons would require under normal conditions. Certain metals and minerals, such as steel, iron ore, copper, lead, tin, zinc, and more recently, aluminum, manganese, and nickel, are absolutely indispensable raw materials, without which a war cannot be effectively carried on. Likewise, among chemical products, some are capable of rapid supply expansion, but others are subject to limitations in technique or to curtailment of imported ingredients, and the prices of all such things can rise perpendicularly during a war emergency unless political control is exercised promptly. As some strategically important articles are observed to rise several hundred per cent in price, there is an acute psychological effect. Speculators and individual consumers accumulate supplies in all directions, and a forward buying and more or less speculative hoarding movement occur in business firms. This adds fuel to the inflation flame, and as the prices mount higher, the Government, in order to continue its purchases and ensure adequate supplies in the shortest possible time, must either devise new ways of enlarging its monetary resources, even to the point of abandoning the principles of sane finance, or impose stringent dictatorial controls over prices and uses.[1]

In a simple economy, such as prevailed in eighteenth- and early nineteenth-century America, it was far less easy than today to develop substitute materials to replace those urgently needed for production of arms, explosives, ships, and clothing for the fighting forces. Today the drain upon the strategic commodities is somewhat reduced, although by no means eliminated, through the remarkable developments in the chemical and metallurgical industries capable of providing within a relatively

---

[1] In January, 1940, for example, the Army and Navy Munitions Board announced a list of commodities that were considered "strategically important," that is, goods essential to national defense, for the supply of which, during war conditions, dependence must be placed in whole or in substantial part on sources outside the continental limits of the United States and for which strict conservation and distribution control measures were thought necessary. The following list of these strategic materials is presented as an illustration of the things that in this particular emergency were in this classification: *abacá* (Manila fiber), antimony, activated carbon, chrome ore, ferromanganese, manganese ore, mercury, mica, nickel, quartz crystals, quinine sulfate, rubber, silk, tin, tungsten ore. In addition to these materials, still another list was announced and designated as containing "critical" materials, those considered essential to defense, involving less difficult procurement problems than the foregoing but nevertheless some degree of necessity for conservation and distribution control. These include aluminum, asbestos, cork, graphite, hides and skins, iodine, kapok, opium, phenol, platinum, tanning extracts, toluol, vanadium ore, and wool.

It is of interest to note that the prices of the strategic commodities rose, on the average, about 25 per cent from the end of August to the end of September, 1939, after the outbreak of World War II. In present-day warfare, in all major countries, a much more alert attitude on the part of even nondictator governments than ever before is directed toward accumulation of supplies of scarce materials and the application of equitable rationing or even prohibition of civilian use. The importance of exercising drastic control over normal consumption, over prices that are advancing too fast or under speculative or hoarding pressure, is much better recognized today by our Federal Government than in past wars.

short time alternative or supplementary materials, thus making it less difficult to sustain distribution of consumer goods and preventing skyrocket-
ing prices. Rapid inflation has proved in the past so disastrous in its ultimate results that there is almost universally in a world at war a grim
determination to control or avert it, even at the cost of despotic methods.
It is by no means beyond question that if ways and means of avoiding the
kind of universal conflict now existing are not found and made effective,
these elaborate political devices for authoritarian control of war operations will project themselves rather generally into a future pattern of
regimented society in which the difference between wartime and peace-
time may be rendered permanently inconsequential.

Enough has been said of the economic effect of war to show the difficulty of formulating precise principles capable of application to any and
every war period. Generalization is dangerous. But as we look back over
the historical record of price behavior and general business changes, not
only are the dislocating effects of war clearly evident but the effects appear to follow long after the event. Let us pursue the subject somewhat
further. Why does it seem to be true that despite a temporary stimulating effect of war upon some industries, wars are generally associated
with a long-term retarding of business growth, as was apparently true
following World War I, which did not fully reveal its distorting effects
on the economic system of the world and of the United States until the
1930's?

An adequate answer to such a question cannot be attempted until
some further aspects of business dynamics have been more fully analyzed
in later chapters. We can, however, supplement the preceding sketch of
the fundamental forces of war disturbance by noticing the impact of war
demands upon extractive industries, particularly agriculture and mineral
production. Again we must emphasize the pronounced inelasticity of
supply characteristic of these industries, dramatized by the fierce pressures of military necessity and the accelerated tempo of demand. As
prices of the products rise, an enlargement of output does somehow come
about. If a war lasts for several years and if it involves the transportation
of food, fuel, and metal goods to other countries, there is certain to be a
substantial expansion in farm acreage and in the working of mineral deposits. This is usually true also of transportation facilities; there is emergency demand for ships, railroad equipment, and, in recent times, for a
tremendous variety of military apparatus moving on wheels or through
the air.

This expansion of effort involves the use of capital, which under war
conditions has usually been provided under considerable difficulty. The
heavy war borrowing by governments, owing to the impracticability of
quickly increasing taxes or the reluctance of political leaders to resort to
ruthless taxation, depletes the capital market until the Government itself

has taken steps to liberalize credit creation by setting aside the usual reserve requirements recognized by sound banking practice or statutory law. Although the issue of private-capital securities is rarely easy under intense war conditions, banking systems come to the rescue of hard-pressed producers and offer loans at longer than usual terms and for essentially capital purposes. In the Civil War period, for example, the commercial banks greatly increased their loans secured by the obligations of manufacturers and farmers. In World War I, with the banking system fortified by the recently established Federal Reserve System, such loans were forthcoming in very substantial sums.

The case of the farmer under these conditions is of special interest and importance because of the temptation to borrow and expand that rapidly ascending prices create in the mind of the average grower of crops or breeder of livestock. It has been consistently true that farm indebtedness tends to multiply fast in periods of wartime inflation, and this means, in turn, that the elevated fixed charges on intermediate and long-term debt remain long after the war is over and the prices of the farmers' products have probably collapsed to much lower levels. Most farmers operate without the refinements of accounting or the principles of sound business judgment. The sudden windfall of high prices and corresponding larger earnings is not seen as the fleeting experience that it is. Land hunger and the speculative urge to secure profit from the appreciation in land values open up the road to financial ruin during the long years of price deflation.[2] When a large productive group is thus caught in the toils of inflation, the ultimate effects upon the total buying power and prosperity of the country should not escape the notice of those who would understand the dynamics of business. The effects have frequently been exaggerated, but there is no denying the fact that such abrupt rise and fall of farm income does serve as one of the many important distorting influences upon the flow of trade and industry following periods of war.

In the case of mineral products, there are somewhat similar results. Some mineral deposits are controlled by fairly substantial business organizations or interests controlling extensive capital. Expansion in holdings and the working of new or previously uneconomic deposits tend to be a concomitant of war conditions. The effects are broadly similar to those in agriculture, although impinging on a smaller social group. The prices of metals in wartime have been very volatile; demand is insistent, and supply is inelastic over short periods of time. But by the time the emergency is over we face a situation of expanded and excessive mineral production capacity. With war demand ended, huge amounts of scrap metal, war

[2] At the beginning of World War II, well-organized farm groups, through powerful representation in Congress, for a time effectively opposed efforts by the Federal Administration to set maximum or "ceiling" levels for basic agricultural prices, even at levels higher (in terms of relative purchasing power) than those prevailing prior to World War I. . . .

surpluses, or supplies from new foreign sources must be disposed of, and they cannot be fitted into the normal operations of industry fast enough to avert an acute surplus problem and hence a deep, sharp decline in prices. This may also leave behind it, as in agriculture and animal raising, inflated capital structures and fixed charges capable of impairing for a considerable time the solvency of the less conservative units in the industry. This, in turn, restricts their own demand for labor and the products of equipment industries. These are illustrations of but a few of the outstanding sources of price dislocation under wartime conditions and the tendency to expand the scale of extractive operations. These cases serve to depict, in a broad and general way, the manner in which great wars generate not only temporary economic or financial dislocation but disturbance of such magnitude that the broad course of industrial progress may be appreciably modified for several decades. . . .

FOR FURTHER READING: Seymour E. Harris, *Inflation and the American Economy* (New York, 1945). Lester V. Chandler, *Inflation in the United States, 1940–1948* (New York, 1951). Simon Kuznets, *National Product in Wartime* (New York, 1945). To follow specific results of war upon the economy see Witt Bowden, *War and Postwar Wages, Prices, and Hours, 1914–23 and 1939–44* in U.S. Bureau of Labor Statistics *Bulletin* #852 (Washington, 1946) and Harold G. Moulton, *Effects of the Defense Program on Prices, Wages, and Profits* (Washington, 1941).

29. *American Economic Expansion and the American Character*

PROBLEM: *How has American economic expansion affected the American character?*

Anyone who contemplates the whole sweep of American economic development from its first beginnings is compelled to speculate about its impact on the personality of Americans. Statistical or other measuring devices to gauge such effects have not as yet been created, and at present no more than subjective insights can be offered. Among the most challenging assessments are those of Russell Davenport, one-time editor of *Fortune* magazine, and of the Stanford historian David Potter, the former stressing the influence of ideals on American character, the latter concentrating on the effects of materialism. Among the outstanding traits of Americans, Davenport lists undue emphasis on competition, excessive concern with material goods, conformity and standardization, and also great diversity. But he believes that these characteristics reflect fundamental democratic ideals such as a belief in the perfectibility of man, equality, generosity, kindness, and individualism. Potter outlines many of the same characteristic traits of Americans, yet instead of attributing them to idealism he finds their origins in materialistic circumstances, especially the abundance of the American environment. Abundance has affected behavior through diets, housing, clothing, and consequent patterns of human association, as in the relation between parents and children. If the assertions of neither of these writers can be proven, each nevertheless offers stimulating suggestions. Is national character mainly dependent on economic factors? How have other economic influences shaped specific character traits? Are economic changes reflected in consequent alterations of national character?

The American Way of Life

RUSSELL DAVENPORT

When a Frenchman wants to explain his country he speaks simply of "*la belle France*." The Britisher says, "There'll always be an England." These and other nations of the earth can tell a lot about themselves just by the use of their proper names. But the citizen of the U.S. has a different problem. There lives in him a kind of unspoken assumption that his nation is something more than a nation; that it is an experiment, perpetually evolving into something new; that it embodies an ideal. In referring to his country, therefore, he feels the need of including an abstraction or a general principle; and this leads him on a quest for words. . . .

To the foreign visitor the most disturbing thing about the American way of life is its unabashed "materialism." The visitor is drenched with sights and sounds and smells emanating from a man-made environment to which almost all Americans appear to give almost all their energies. Pervading these sensory experiences there are the psychological ones— the insouciant way in which the radio combines "entertainment" with the most humiliating requirements of the human organism—the ubiquitous advertising, seeking to identify human happiness with bright teeth— the infantile movie heroes—the wasteful "abundance" protruding from every retail store. The visitor sees all this, and is impelled to somber speculations concerning the fate of humanity. What price "the American Way of Life"?

The somber speculations lead to two forms of criticism. The first . . . runs to the effect that American capital exists for the purpose of exploiting the people, who have thereby been degraded. This attack, however, is an easy one to meet. It may be a halfway adequate picture of what capitalism in America used to be like, or of what it is still like in some

Reprinted from *U.S.A.—The Permanent Revolution* by Russell Davenport (New York, 1951), pp. 3-10, 19-28. By permission of *Fortune* and Time, Inc.

places today. But it no more fits modern America than a description of the living habits of Caesar.

The U.S. Bureau of Labor Statistics maintains a Consumers' Price Index, which is intended to show changes in the current cost of living, and which is therefore composed of the index levels of all articles that enter into the cost of living in an important way. This index, which is compiled specifically for "moderate income families," has for years included radios, electric sewing machines, electric refrigerators, vacuum cleaners, automobiles, tires, gasoline, and insurance; medical, dental, surgical, and hospital care; drugs and beauty-shop services—all this, that is to say, over and above necessities like food, clothing, and shelter. But the BLS has felt for some time that this index was deficient; certain items, important enough materially to affect the cost of living, were not included. These, therefore, have been added. They include television sets, electric toasters, frozen foods, canned baby foods, home permanent-wave lotions, and group hospitalization contracts. As the New York *Herald Tribune* wryly remarked, "What, no caviar?"

Now to talk of the exploitation of human needs, in an economy where all these items have become so important to the standard of living that they must be figured into the cost of living, is to talk nonsense. The American capitalistic system still works injustices; but to think of it in terms of exploitation is to think in terms of a past century. It is perfectly evident from the above list that it is not the capitalists who are using the people, but the people who are using the capitalists. Capital has become, not the master of this society, but its servant. No better evidence could be adduced than the figures recently made public by the Federal Reserve Board, which show that four out of ten American families possess at least $5,000 of assets over liabilities; and that very nearly one family in ten has net assets of $25,000 or more. It is not just a capitalistic system. It is a capitalistic people.

But this raises the second form of criticism. If the trouble isn't with the capitalists, then it must be with the people. Men and women who insist on such a high standard of living, and are willing to expend so much energy to get it, must be hopeless materialists. Is it not true that the curse of this majestic continent is the drab uniformity of its products and the discouraging conformity of its mores? The itinerant lecturer is especially exposed to this dreary prospect. On his way from town to town he sees the same ads for the same products; he hears the same clichés; he is asked the same question by people who look and act and dress and entertain themselves, apparently, in exactly the same way as the people in the town he thought he had left behind him—the name of whose central thoroughfare, incidentally, was also Main Street. If this is "freedom," thinks the itinerant lecturer, then what is all the shouting and ballyhoo about? There are quicker ways to build an anthill.

Now the American admits that his society is materialistic; that standardization is an essential of the "way of life"; that conformity is a danger he must watch and learn to counteract. Nevertheless, this criticism from the itinerant lecturer baffles him on the whole, because it seems to overlook more than it takes into account. For example, it overlooks the great American love of *diversity*.

The American responds to diversity as to something good, absolutely. The presence in his society of a bewildering number of races and national origins, creeds and shibboleths, economic interests and explosive ideas, is to him no problem at all. On the contrary, it is a great asset. In his labyrinthine political system the same idea is carried out. The forty-eight states, each with its separate constitution and different set of laws, each requiring special examinations or licenses for its lawyers, its doctors, its civil servants, even its automobile drivers, confront the foreigner as an irrationally complicated structure calculated to produce nothing but chaos. But the American thinks it is good; he can even prove that it is good. If there is only one of something, he is suspicious of it—as for example his federal government. This is only partly because he dreads the power of monopoly, whether political or economic. It is also because he sees diversity as the expression of freedom, the living proof that men and women are given the opportunity to be true to themselves.

There is a practical side to this also, as there is to everything American. The tendency of industrial enterprise is to wind up into big units in the name of efficiency; but Americans have always been aware of another kind of efficiency, a more creative kind, that can be achieved through decentralization—that is to say, through a diversity of operations. Outsiders often boggle at the idea of competition. But they should remember that competition in America is not the dog-eat-dog affair that social planners and Russian propaganda have made it out to be. Competition has caused suffering in America; it still does hurt when your company is thrown out of business and your job is lost. And yet the essence of American competition is far less desperate than that. It involves the releasing of energies, primarily, for the development of new ideas, new modifications, new "slants," any one of which may end up by revolutionizing some segment of human affairs. That is what diversity means to an American. And that is why he welcomes the existence in his society of people, of beliefs, of ideas that are difficult if not impossible to reconcile.

Thus it will be found upon closer inspection that there is not just one American way of life. There are American *ways* of life, almost without number. For example, there are the great regional differentiations, where nature herself has conspired with American institutions to create ways of life as different from each other as those of two nations might be. It is true that these American "sub-nations" are bound together by many common ties, including the important tie of language; yet their temperamental characteristics, their customs, their values and views, their personal objectives differ so greatly that a man who is happy and effective in one might be miserable and frustrated in another. . . .

. . . The truth, which has thus far been difficult for the rest of the world to grasp, is that Americans live on two planes at once—the practical and the ideal. The conflicts created by this ambivalent existence, which worry other people so much that they often feel constrained to reject one plane or the other, bother the American scarcely at all. Take for example one of his leading national characteristics. "I wish to preach," said Theodore Roosevelt at the turn of the century, "not the doctrine of ignoble ease, but the doctrine of the strenuous life." And when he said that, he said something profoundly American. The strenuosity of American life simply appalls the European. Why go at things so hard? Why take these interminable gambles, follow these restive hunches, constantly uproot that which has been successfully established? Why not be content with that which is good enough?

Of course, lots of things have happened since T.R. made that remark. In terms of physical work—of *toil*—American life is far less strenuous. The forty-hour week is almost universal; Saturdays are for the most part holidays; the lunch break is getting longer. The ECA productivity teams that visited this country observed that Americans did not seem to work any harder than Europeans. However, they got more done, and that is perhaps the key to the matter. Increasingly, Americans are emphasizing *mind*. They have discovered that through the use of the mind, especially in the development of technology, life can be made strenuous in a different and pleasanter way. To the visitor, whose technology may not be so advanced, or whose powers of invention may be less well developed, the distinction may seem somewhat academic; American life remains too strenuous to emulate. But to the American the distinction is a real one. He has discovered ways to keep up the pace without the physical punishment that old T.R. very likely had in mind. What makes his modern life strenuous, therefore, is simply that he insists *that the pace be kept up.*

The outsider, to be sure, may wonder to what purpose. For Americans not only work hard, they play hard; simple gaiety, as the Italians know it, for example, seems not to be in their make-up. All the energy that the American saves from toil by the smart application of technology is freely expended on his most conspicuous passion, the great American outdoors. In every section of the country, even the industrial East, Americans pour out an incredible amount of energy whacking golf balls, playing tennis and baseball, hiking, camping, sailing, fishing, hunting—everything but just "walking." Most foreigners fail to understand—let alone enjoy—all this dashing around. The strenuous life is bad enough at the factory: why double it during leisure time? This reaction is a matter of temperament, and Americans must be prepared to accept the criticism that they are just too damn energetic.

However, there is a principle involved which foreigners ought not to overlook. In the view of the American, life is not just a matter of the conservation of energy. On the contrary, in his experience, energy creates energy; a good hard game of tennis, or a hike in the hills, will actually improve your mental faculties the next morning. Thus the pace of technological life is maintained, not through the cultivation of repose, but by building up a kind of counterforce through physical exertions—supported, to be sure, by abundant vitamins. Here is *mens sana in corpore sano,* but raised to a higher power—to the great advantage, incidentally, of the seven-billion-dollar sport and vacation industries.

The strenuous life, then, is an American characteristic. But it is interesting, not merely as a characteristic, but because it illustrates so aptly the ambivalent nature of the American. The strenuous life derives, on the one hand, from the practical necessities of a virginal continent on which there was much work to do. But it derives, on the other, from an *ideal:* the ideal of the perfectibility of man, of human improvement. Where this ideal came from is a matter for scholars to debate; it has in any case been accepted in one form or another by Americans from the very beginning. It has given rise to many American faults, such as over-optimism and a superficial concept of "progress." But above all, it has kept Americans working, risking, venturing, striving; it has sparked the strenuous life.

This same ambivalence manifests itself in many other American characteristics. For instance, take those characteristics having to do with the great ideal of Equality, the fundamental "tendency" of American life. . . . The confidence that he is the equal of any man gives the American a certain ease of manner, even a brashness, which can be extremely irritating to those who have not been bred to "equality." On the other hand, it helps the American to be a friendly fellow, a trait that almost every foreigner notices upon arriving on our shores—despite the seemingly deliberate inhospitality of the immigration service and the customs officials. The American does not recognize many social barriers. This is especially true of the West, where the man who is painting your house will probably call you by your first name before you have decided how to address him. One of the little shockers for American labor leaders who went to England some while ago to help with productivity was the sight of English workers tipping their hats to the boss. American workers consider themselves the equals of the boss in everything except the externals, so they don't tip their hats. In fact—and this is the key to an understanding of Americans—the boss wouldn't like it if they did; it would make him feel uncomfortable: for he too has the ideal of equality.

Equality thus has its positive side: it does not merely equate privileges, it asserts obligations. There is the other fellow, and he has just the same rights as you. This doesn't mean that Americans go around thinking of the "other fellow" all the time; in fact, they may be planning some competitive scheme to put him out of business. But they are oriented from their childhood to the idea of the rights of other people. The civil liberties are not merely constraining laws. They, too, are ideals, imperfectly realized, but entering into the life of every American in such a way as to encourage qualities or virtues, the best word for which is "democratic."

The American has an ideal of generosity, also. He doesn't live up to this one any better than—or even as well as—he lives up to the related ideals of the civil liberties; but generosity is bred into him, nevertheless, as a great democratic virtue. Sometimes the American's generosity is no more than an openhanded way of doing things, which at its worst leads to sheer waste. At its best, however, no other national characteristic exhibits more clearly the way the American can combine the ideal and the practical. For, aside from its ethical status, generosity appeals to the American as an eminently practical trait to encourage. Wouldn't it be a much better world if everybody were generous? Then nobody, including you yourself, would have to worry so much. That is the practical side of the matter. But, he would add, you should never carry it so far as to look like a "sucker."

Still another ideal related to the general ideal of equality is that of kindness. This too the American regards as a democratic virtue. The American is capable of being brutish and some people think of him as ruthless. He himself likes to parade as a "tough guy." But his armor is usually paper-thin, and there are apt to be vulnerable spots—for example, children. Americans love children to the point of being silly about them, as almost everyone who has known the G.I.'s has observed. In fact, they universally spoil their own.

Whether Americans have more or less of these democratic virtues, whether they are friendlier than other people, or more generous, or kinder, is not at all the point. Such generalizations can never be proved and only lead to resentful arguments. The point is that Americans, practical and pragmatic by temperament, have nevertheless taken very seriously certain ideals having to do in a general way with the ideal of democratic equality.

And perhaps, next to their Proposition itself, this is the most valuable contribution that Americans have to offer the world. It is wrong, at the present stage of our evolution, to expect some great "cultural" development in America, equivalent to the culture of Europe that extends back for twenty or twenty-five creative centuries. The intellectuals who castigate Americans on this score miss the point. In the first place, they overlook the fact that there is a great activity in the creative arts throughout the country, especially at the community level; and second, they too easily forget that American culture is of necessity a *popular* culture, and hence inherently different from that which we inherit from Europe. Yet even after these modifications have been made, the fact remains that high culture is not what Americans have primarily to give. The big American contribution to Western civilization has to do, rather, with certain qualities of the heart deriving from democratic ideals. These ideals, in the form of recognized democratic virtues, are constantly at work in American society, and have a great deal to do with what is meant by "the American way of life." In fact, if this were not so, if the ideals were to vanish, or if Americans were to abandon the hope that people would someday learn to practice them, then the American way of life, as Americans construe it today, would also disappear. It would become something quite different. It survives as it is only on the presumption that most of the people will try to realize the democratic virtues most of the time.

Yet these ideals that the American cherishes are not just hung up in the air. They have a reference point that walks and talks and is "real"—the individual human being. Everything in America, be it national, regional, subregional, or local, comes back somehow to the individual. And the American can live his life on two planes at once in such a strenuous way precisely because he recognizes that the human individual may have— must have—ideals. That is the inner secret of the American way of life. It is a way of life to permit and encourage the development of the human individual, by his own free will, toward his own ideals.

This fact is nowhere better illustrated than in the American attitude toward "standardization." To see "standardization" as the American sees it, one must bring it back to the individual. The intelligent American will agree that standardization represents a certain danger. But on the other hand he will point out that in his society—in the American way of life—the individual does have opportunity, does develop and grow. And in the light of this great, essential truth he can put standardization in a certain perspective, which Europeans have not yet learned. For what is being standardized in America? Not the individual human spirit, which the American way of life intends to hold inviolately free. But the things that the human spirit uses—these are being standardized: the houses and vehicles, the tools and machines, to some extent the clothing and even the food. But these are, after all, the shell. They are not the human being himself, and so long as American institutions are careful to distinguish between human beings and things, why not standardize the things? Nature herself, after all, has in a certain sense standardized the human body. We don't expect to find people with five arms or with eyes in the backs of their heads. But we don't say for that reason that the human spirit cannot be free. The body is just a vehicle.

Indeed, to say that standardization must be the death of freedom is to express a far more materialistic attitude than the American attitude. It is to define man in terms of things—in terms of his body. To the American, his machines and gadgets are *extensions* of man. They are extensions of his faculties and powers—wings to enable him to fly, wheels to enable him to run, antennae to enable him to hear and see at great distances. Americans, indeed, have taken on the task of extending man in this way with a certain positive attitude, as if it were their special cosmic assignment. They really believe and really feel that they are doing something important, not to enchain the human soul, but to increase its power and scope, and thus to help emancipate it from the merely physical, from the earth. That is the positive side of American "materialism."

As for "conformity," the danger here may be greater, because one is not dealing with things but with the standardization of people themselves. Yet here too the same principle can be applied to a certain extent. Much American conformity may be due to a kind of social compulsion that is highly undesirable; but much of it also is simply a matter of convenience. The reason why garden clubs are more or less alike is not that anyone compels them to be alike, but just because it is easier to organize them that way. Anyone who might try to *enforce* conformity upon an American would find out soon enough that where his convictions are concerned he is capable of non-conformity to the point of bloodshed. Here, too, the American feels, a little perspective is in order. Conformity has not yet engulfed him. And he doubts that it ever really will.

This central focus of the American way of life—the concept of the inviolability of the human individual—was born politically in the Age of Reason and implemented by the announcement of the American Proposition. . . . But spiritually, of course, this concept goes back to the founding of Christianity, whence the American derives his basic ideal of the individual. Christianity has had many versions in America, many strange and eccentric variants. Yet it has always been inherent in the American way of life, binding it together in subtle ways, even for Americans who do not actually profess it. The idea of the perfectibility of man, for example, which gives Americans so much drive, is a Christian ideal. And the democratic virtues, which have to do with the relation of one man to another, are essentially Christian virtues. The American's Christianity is, to be sure, somewhat one-sided; his idea of "perfectibility," for example, is theologically naive; his optimism leads him to overlook some of the profounder, more tragic depths of the human soul; he is apt to translate spiritual truths to facilely into practical terms. Nevertheless, his tremendous faith in the human spirit saves him, most of the time, from the consequences of his own errors—and may yet save the free world. . . .

Abundance and Formation of Character

DAVID POTTER

Ever since the time of Freud, behavioral scientists have steadily been broadening their conception of the range of external experience which goes into the formation of personality. Freud himself dealt heavily in biological drives and instinctual impulses which were inherent in the individual and did not have to be accounted for by any experience with the external world. Subsequently, however, psychoanalysts like Erich Fromm and Karen Horney recognized that many manifestations which Freud had regarded as universal were, in fact, limited to specific cultures. In the course of time, these revisionists fought and won the battle for recognition of the principle that culture determines personality. But even after this victory many seemed anxious to confine themselves to the narrowest possible segment of the culture. It was generally agreed that "the effects of environmental forces in moulding the personality are, in general, the more profound, the earlier in the life history of the individual they are brought to bear." This premise gave to investigators a sound basis for assigning a very high priority to parent-child relationships and the experiences of infancy, and this priority seems to be altogether valid. But there has been an especially marked tendency in very recent studies to accord more recognition to the broad range of the cultural experience. It was because of this tendency that Haring, in his comparison between the characters of the Japanese of Amami Oshima and the Japanese of Japan proper, makes such an emphatic point of the fact that police tyranny and not infant training seems to be the critical factor in causing the divergence. The same reason led T. W. Adorno, in 1950, to assert the necessity for taking general social and economic conditions into account: "The major influences upon personality development arise in the course of child training as carried forward in a setting of family life. What happens here is profoundly influenced by economic and social factors. It is not only that each family in trying to rear its children proceeds according

Reprinted from *People of Plenty*, pp. 190–208, by David Potter by permission of the University of Chicago Press. Copyright 1949 by the University of Chicago Press.

to the ways of the social, ethnic, and religious groups in which it has membership, but crude economic factors affect directly the parents' behavior toward the child. This means that broad changes in social conditions and institutions will have a direct bearing upon the kinds of personalities that develop within a society." . . .

In the same way, almost all public and general forces can be found operating in the private and individual sphere. Hence it is not at all farfetched to argue that even a discussion of the general aspect of one of these forces is full of implicit indications which touch the personal lives and the conditioning and response of individuals. . . . But, if the utility of the historical approach in an understanding of the factors of personality formation is to be adequately proved, something more than an indirect or implicit relationship must be established. The questions recur: What, if anything, does the factor of abundance have to do with the process of personality formation (in so far as this process is understood) in the United States? How does the process differ from that in countries where the measure of abundance is not so great?

To these questions, I believe, some highly explicit answers are possible. Let us therefore be entirely concrete. Let us consider the situation of a six-month-old American infant, who is not yet aware that he is a citizen, a taxpayer, and a consumer.

This individual is, to all appearances, just a very young specimen of *Homo sapiens*, with certain needs for protection, care, shelter, and nourishment which may be regarded as the universal biological needs of human infancy rather than specific cultural needs. It would be difficult to prove that the culture has as yet differentiated him from other infants, and, though he is an American, few would argue that he has acquired an American character. Yet abundance and the circumstances arising from abundance have already dictated a whole range of basic conditions which, from his birth, are constantly at work upon this child and which will contribute in the most intimate and basic way to the formation of his character.

To begin with, abundance has already revolutionized the typical mode of his nourishment by providing for him to be fed upon cow's milk rather than upon his mother's milk, taken from the bottle rather than from the breast. Abundance contributes vitally to this transformation, because bottle feeding requires fairly elaborate facilities of refrigeration, heating, sterilization, and temperature control, which only an advanced technology can offer and only an economy of abundance can make widely available. I will not attempt here to resolve the debated question as to the psychological effects, for both mother and child, of bottle feeding as contrasted with breast feeding in infant nurture. But it is clear that the changeover to bottle feeding has encroached somewhat upon the intimacy of the bond between mother and child. The nature of this bond

is, of course, one of the most crucial factors in the formation of character. Bottle feeding also must tend to emphasize the separateness of the
infant as an individual, and thus it makes, for the first time, a point which
the entire culture reiterates constantly throughout the life of the average
American. In addition to the psychic influences which may be involved
in the manner of taking the food, it is also a matter of capital importance
that the bottle-fed baby is, on the whole, better nourished than the breast-
fed infant and therefore likely to grow more rapidly, to be more vigorous, and to suffer fewer ailments, with whatever effects these physical
conditions may have upon his personality.

It may be argued also that abundance has provided a characteristic
mode of housing for the infant and that this mode further emphasizes his
separateness as an individual. In societies of scarcity, dwelling units are
few and hard to come by, with the result that high proportions of newly
married young people make their homes in the parental ménage, thus
forming part of an "extended" family, as it is called. Moreover, scarcity
provides a low ratio of rooms to individuals, with the consequence that
whole families may expect as a matter of course to have but one room for
sleeping, where children will go to bed in intimate propinquity to their
parents. But abundance prescribes a different regime. By making it economically possible for newly married couples to maintain separate households of their own, it has almost destroyed the extended family as an
institution in America and has ordained that the child shall be reared in a
"nuclear" family, so-called, where his only intimate associates are his parents and his siblings, with even the latter far fewer now than in families
of the past. The housing arrangements of this new-style family are suggested by census data for 1950. In that year there were 45,983,000 dwelling units to accommodate the 38,310,000 families in the United States,
and, though the median number of persons in the dwelling unit was 3.1,
the median number of rooms in the dwelling unit was 4.6. Eighty-four
per cent of all dwelling units reported less than one person per room. By
providing the ordinary family with more than one room for sleeping, the
economy thus produces a situation in which the child will sleep either in a
room alone or in a room shared with his brothers or sisters. Even without
allowing for the cases in which children may have separate rooms, these
conditions mean that a very substantial percentage of children now sleep
in a room alone, for, with the declining birth rate, we have reached a
point at which an increasing proportion of families have one child or
two children rather than the larger number which was at one time typical. For instance, in the most recent group of mothers who had completed their childbearing phase, according to the census, 19.5 per cent had
had one child and 23.4 had had two. Thus almost half of all families with
offspring did not have more than two children throughout their duration.
In the case of the first group, all the children were "only" children

throughout their childhood, and in the second group half of the children were "only" children until the second child was born. To state this in another, and perhaps a more forcible, way, it has been shown that among American women who arrived at age thirty-four during the year 1949 and who had borne children up to that time, 26.7 per cent had borne only one child, and 34.5 per cent had borne only two. If these tendencies persist, it would mean that, among families where there are children, hardly one in three will have more than two children. . . .

Thus the economy of plenty has influenced the feeding of the infant, his regime, and the physical setting within which he lives. These material conditions alone might be regarded as having some bearing upon the formation of his character, but the impact of abundance by no means ends at this point. In so far as it has an influence in determining what specific individuals shall initiate the infant into the ways of man and shall provide him with his formative impressions of the meaning of being a person, it must be regarded as even more vital. When it influences the nature of the relationships between these individuals and the infant, it must be recognized as reaching to the very essence of the process of character formation.

The central figures in the *dramatis personae* of the American infant's universe are still his parents, and in this respect, of course, there is nothing peculiar either to the American child or to the child of abundance. But abundance has at least provided him with parents who are in certain respects unlike the parents of children born in other countries or born fifty years ago. To begin with, it has given him young parents, for the median age of fathers at the birth of the first child in American marriages (as of 1940) was 25.3 years, and the median age of mothers was 22.6 years. This median age was substantially lower than it had been in the United States in 1890 for both fathers and mothers. Moreover, as the size of families has been reduced and the wife no longer continues to bear a succession of children throughout the period of her fertility, the median age of mothers at the birth of the last child has declined from 32 years (1890) to 27 years (1940). The age of the parents at the birth of both the first child and the last child is far lower than in the case of couples in most European countries. There can be little doubt that abundance has caused this differential, in the case of the first-born by making it economically possible for a high proportion of the population to meet the expenses of homemaking at a fairly early age. In the case of the last-born, it would also appear that one major reason for the earlier cessation of child-bearing is a determination by parents to enjoy a high standard of living themselves and to limit their offspring to a number for whom they can maintain a similar standard.

By the very fact of their youth, these parents are more likely to remain alive until the child reaches maturity, thus giving him a better prospect of being reared by his own mother and father. This prospect is further reinforced by increases in the life-span, so that probably no child in history has ever enjoyed so strong a likelihood that his parents will survive to rear him. Abundance has produced this situation by providing optimum conditions for prolonging life. But, on the other hand, abundance has also contributed much to produce an economy in which the mother is no longer markedly dependent upon the father, and this change in the economic relation between the sexes has probably done much to remove obstacles to divorce. The results are all too familiar. During the decade 1940–49 there were 25.8 divorces for every 100 marriages in the United States, which ratio, if projected over a longer period, would mean that one marriage out of four would end in divorce. But our concern here is with a six-month-old child, and the problem is to know whether this factor of divorce involves childless couples predominantly or whether it is likely to touch him. The answer is indicated by the fact that, of all divorces granted in 1948, no less than 42 per cent were to couples with children under eighteen, and a very large proportion of these children were of much younger ages. Hence one might say that the economy of abundance has provided the child with younger parents who chose their role of parenthood deliberately and who are more likely than parents in the past to live until he is grown, but who are substantially less likely to preserve the unbroken family as the environment within which he shall be reared. . . .

Abundance, then, has played a critical part in revolutionizing both the physical circumstances and the human associations which surround the American infant and child. These changes alone would warrant the hypothesis that abundance has profoundly affected the formation of character for such a child.

FOR FURTHER READING: A brief discussion on American character and capitalism can be found in the booklet by the Center for the Study of American Institutions, *The American Character* (Santa Barbara, 1962). Suggestive is Denis W. Brogan, *The American Character* (New York, 1944), who discusses the widespread support of Americans for economic growth. Geoffrey Gorer, *The American Character* (New York, 1948), seeks to relate widely held values and the economic system. Some of the most incisive discussions of American character and the economy have come from foreign observers, among whom Alexis de Tocqueville, *Democracy in America* (New York, 1956), is outstanding. James Bryce, *The American Commonwealth*, edited by Louis Hacker (New York, 1959), is also worth examining. The most recent traveler to record his impressions on this subject is R. L. Bruckberger, *Image of America*, translated from the French by C. G. Paulding and Virgilia Peterson (New York, 1959).

30. *Recent Economic Issues:*
Taxation

PROBLEM: *What limits on tax rates ensure a prosperous and expanding economy?*

As is well known, the increasing scope of governmental services during the last two decades has also led to a significant rise of taxes in the United States. Both federal as well as state agencies have spent increasing proportions of their resources for social welfare, housing, and education. Although such policies find widespread support among Americans, one of the most controversial issues among contemporary economists is whether there are limits to the amounts of income that governments can tax away to finance such programs before they begin to stifle individual initiative and general economic growth. An affirmative stand on this question is taken by Colin Clark, an Australian economist now at Oxford University. In a widely discussed article published in 1951 he argued that 25 per cent of the national income was the maximum that could be taxed away safely without harmful effects for the economy. If that limit were exceeded, industrial expansion would be retarded, shortages of goods would result, and consequent inflation would set in. As evidence, Clark pointed to post-World War II experience in France, Italy, and the United States. Wherever taxes rose above one-fourth of the national income, inflation was quick to follow. But this provocative hypothesis has been widely challenged. One of its most outspoken critics has been Walter Heller, a University of Minnesota economist and tax expert who in 1961 was appointed chairman of the President's Council of Economic Advisers. Heller noted that post-World War II experience did not necessarily substantiate Clark's thesis because deficits and trade dislocations, rather than high taxes, helped to bring on worldwide inflation. Moreover, Heller pointed to the lack of clear evidence to indicate that tax rates above 25 per cent stifle individual initiative and investment, or that the moneyed classes are then suddenly persuaded to favor price inflation rather than price stability. The issue broached by Clark and Heller is by no means settled, but both raise pertinent questions about a major problem. How do high tax rates promote or impede economic growth? Does historical experience before 1945 substantiate Clark's thesis? How can desirable tax limits be determined?

The Danger Point in Taxes

COLIN CLARK

How high can taxes rise without economic trouble? The question is timely. People have always grumbled about taxes, but during the past three or four decades—as a result of two hot wars and the high defense costs of the cold war, to say nothing of the gradually rising expense of government services of many sorts—most of us have watched our taxes climb to such unprecedented heights that we must have sincerely wondered what the effective limit was; and in the United States today, with new war costs mounting and new tax increases being debated, the question presses with special urgency. Is there a discoverable point where the burden of taxes becomes insupportable—or supportable only by such dubious means as inflation?

We have learned, from the experience of many countries, what happens when taxes mount too high. Many people don't find it worth their while to work hard and efficiently. Production doesn't expand as fast as it should. There is a shortage of goods, followed by an inflationary rise in prices. The government then usually makes a countermove—attempting by price controls, wage controls, and rationing to "suppress" the inflation that is developing, hoping that in due course production and the real national income will grow enough to carry the burden without controls. But this, experience shows, usually takes too long; and there is then a quick escape into uncontrolled inflation—which benefits some people, but does great harm to the great majority, including especially those

From Colin Clark, "The Danger Point in Taxes," *Harper's* (December, 1950), pp. 67–69. Copyright, 1950, by Harper & Brothers. Reprinted with permission of the author.

lower-paid wage-earners who generally keep their savings in the form of money rather than real property.

All this is familiar to us as a sequence of events that has been repeated over and over again in the experience of many countries. Yet the part that excessively high taxes play in causing inflation is still not fully appreciated. It is very widely understood that if a government incurs very heavy expenditures, and these are *not* covered by taxation, and the government runs at a deficit, the automatic result will be an inflationary trend. It is not so generally understood that if a government incurs very heavy expenditures, and these *are* covered by taxation, so that the budget is balanced, the trend—while it may be deflationary for a time—will in the long run be toward inflation if the rate of taxation is too high to be borne. "The long run," in this case, is probably a period of two or three years, though this may depend on the nature of the emergency; in wartime it may be longer.

The question I am raising is, *how high is too high?* What is the danger point? How much of the national income can be taken in taxes before this uncomfortable sequence of events gets under way? Can we, by reviewing the experience of various nations during the past quarter-century, fix the point where the danger signals begin to fly? I believe we can.

TAX LIMITS BEFORE WORLD WAR II

The foundations of our knowledge on this subject were laid by Lord Keynes in a flash of brilliant insight in 1922. In that year, it may be remembered, inflation was proceeding apace in France and the exchange rate of the franc was falling rapidly. French official opinion hoped to bring it back to its 1914 parity by "restoring the balance of trade," and the first step toward this objective was to have been the military occupation of the Ruhr coal field. Meanwhile the French press was claiming that British and American "speculation" was the cause of the falling exchange rate. Keynes' insight, however, told him that the French inflation would continue. In attempting to pay a high rate of interest on a huge mass of national debt (*rentes*), the Finance Minister was imposing an intolerable burden of public expenditure, amounting to 34 per cent of the current national income.

Keynes remarked, "The level of the franc is going to be settled in the long run, not by speculation or the balance of trade, or even the outcome of the Ruhr adventure, but by the proportion of his earned income which the French taxpayer will permit to be taken from him to pay the claims of the French *rentier* (bondholder)."

In other words, inflation was the only way out of the financial impasse. And the inflation continued rapidly. Prices increased much faster than government expenditure and by 1926 the latter was only a little over 20 per cent of the national income. Then the inflation was checked and a measure of deflation followed. From 1927 onward prices were stabilized. But the interesting thing is that this period of economic and political stability was reached *with the level of government expenditure almost exactly 25 per cent of the national income.* (Lord Keynes commented in 1928: "The French budget balances with the burden of the *rentes* on the taxpayer bearable at the present level.")

A second relevant prophecy in the period between World War I and World War II also concerned French finances. It was made in 1934 by the Swedish economist Professor Bertil Ohlin. He pointed out that French public expenditure by that date had again become such an excessive proportion of the national income (nearly 34 per cent) that further devaluation of the franc was unavoidable. The devaluation which he predicted actually occurred in 1936 and French prices went on rising until 1938, by which time the proportion of government expenditure to the national income had again been reduced almost exactly to 25 per cent.

During the nineteen-twenties there were moderate deflations in Britain and Italy and a severe deflation in Norway. Each was carried to the point where it raised the proportion of taxation to national income somewhere between 23 and 25 per cent, beyond which it was not carried further. This demonstrates my point in reverse, so to speak.

During the period 1934–35 I prepared a Fabian pamphlet which examined in detail all the taxes then in force in the United Kingdom, estimating by rough common-sense methods the maximum additional revenue which could be obtained from them. (In making this study, I assumed that the British economy was brought to full employment out of the heavy unemployment then prevailing.) The interesting thing is that the conclusion reached by this method was also that the maximum feasible taxation was almost exactly 25 per cent of the national income.

Although this evidence is far from conclusive it certainly suggests that *the critical level of taxation beyond which inflationary forces come into play (and deflationary forces suffer a political check) is around 25 per cent of the national income.*

TAX LIMITS SINCE WORLD WAR II

In 1944 I wrote for the *Economic Journal* an article—eventually published in December 1945—in which I put forward the figure of 25 per cent as the measure of taxable capacity. Lord Keynes, who was editing the *Journal*, wrote me in May 1944 that "in Great Britain after the war I should guess that your figure of 25 per cent as the maximum tolerable proportion of taxation may be exceedingly near to the truth," and added that he would not be at all surprised if postwar experience confirmed it.

Now what has been the actual history of the matter since the end of

World War II? In the United States, taxation did not pass the critical limit until 1943, and even in the worst years of the war it rose no higher than 29 per cent of the national income. Suppressed inflation (rationing and price controls) ended in 1946; whereupon inflation continued at a moderate rate until 1948, bringing taxes down to almost exactly the 25 per cent level.

In a number of countries open inflation was in full swing before the war actually ended. Belgium avoided excessive debt and other burdens on the budget and was fortunate in escaping serious damage to her productive capacity. Her price level by 1946 had risen three- or four-fold above prewar and this rise sufficed to reduce the burden of government expenditure to 22 per cent of the national income. At this point price stabilization became possible. In France at the same time, however, government expenditure was one third of the national income and inflation continued rapidly. It went on to the end of 1948, when a price level twenty times prewar was reached. At that point the budget could be balanced at some 25 per cent of the national income.

In Italy inflation proceeded more rapidly, to over fifty times the prewar price level in 1947, when it was suddenly checked. The budget is now balanced with public expenditure at 22 per cent of national income, plus 7 per cent of national income in social insurance charges (the incidence of which is uncertain).

In Japan there was a hundred-fold inflation up to 1949, when prices were stabilized. Taxation is now 30 per cent of the national income; but our rule is not violated, for some measure of rationing and price control has continued to be necessary. No doubt the authorities expect that in the next year or so a rapid rise in production, without any further rise in prices being necessary, will raise the national income and thereby lower the tax ratio considerably.

Countries suffering severe suppressed inflation are Britain, Norway, and perhaps the Netherlands. Sweden has moderate suppressed inflation. Australia and New Zealand have suppressed inflation now in the process of becoming open. What are the significant facts about them?

Britain started the war with a figure of 26 per cent (including social insurance) of national income going to taxes. The figure rose to 42 per cent in 1945. There was a slight reduction in the next two years and then the figure started rising again to the appalling level of 43.7 per cent for 1949, well above the highest wartime ratio. Although Britain has made a great show of decontrolling a certain number of minor items, the main mass of controls is as rigid as ever, particularly over housing and most articles of food. Last year's devaluation is unlikely to make much difference because it has not been allowed to raise British wages and prices except to a minor degree. It seems inevitable that Britain's suppressed inflation, after a longer or shorter interval, will break out into open inflation, probably on a catastrophic scale. (Incidentally Hugh Dalton who, when Chancellor of the Exchequer, had a lot to do with boosting British tax rates up to current levels, thought my proposed tax rate of 25 per cent of the national income was far too high when I put it forward in the prewar Fabian pamphlet mentioned above. It seemed to him a dangerously radical proposal. After the war he set a 40 per cent figure. When I criticized it, he accused me of being a dangerous reactionary!)

The Netherlands figure is now 30 per cent. In Norway, which also suffers suppressed inflation, a ratio of some 40 per cent prevails. Sweden, which has a mild form of suppressed inflation, has a ratio of just over 25 per cent. Australia and New Zealand are also at about the 25 per cent level and are today emerging from suppressed into open inflation.

All these facts seem to support the conclusion—which is further reinforced by the recent experience of Finland, Switzerland, and Denmark—that the safe political and economic limit of taxation is somewhere near 25 per cent of the national income. In this figure all forms of taxation are included: direct and indirect, federal, state, and local. The figure doesn't tell what proportion of your *individual* income can legitimately be taken in taxation; it simply indicates how large a proportion of the *national* income can safely be taken. If the experience of the nineteen-forties, on top of that of the twenties and thirties, doesn't convince you that the 25 per cent figure is pretty nearly correct, then I don't know what will.

The Myth of Tax Limits

WALTER W. HELLER

Mr. Heller. Mr. Chairman and members of the committee, I should like to restrict my comments this morning to the question of the economic limits to taxation. And in that connection, if I may, I should like to submit a longer statement for the record.

The Chairman. It will be received for the record and inserted at the end of your statement.

Mr. Heller. The question I should like to address myself specifically to is this, is taxation in the United States at or near limits beyond which further tax increases are self-defeating? That is, would higher tax rates defeat themselves by impairing production and causing inflation?

This is the nub of the question raised by Colin Clark, Australian economist, who suggests that the answer is "Yes" as soon as a nation's taxes rise above 25 percent of its national income.

The Chairman. May I interrupt you to say that if you are going to

Reprinted from U.S. 82 Cong. 2nd session, Joint Committee on the Economic Report, *Hearings*, 1952 (Washington, 1952) V, pp. 315–25; title supplied by editor.

discuss Mr. Colin Clark, it might be appropriate for me to read into the record a letter he has written to the staff director of this committee. . . .

Economic Services,
South Brisbane, January 18, 1952

Mr. Grover W. Ensley,

*Staff Director, Joint Committee on the Economic Report,
Washington, United States of America.*

Dear Mr. Ensley: In reply to your cable of January 9, I would advise that my proposition about the 25-percent limit was originally put forward in an article in *Economic Journal,* December 1945 (published in England) a copy of which is presumably available to you. The article in Harpers supplemented this and brought it up to date without printing the original information in full detail. I would say that all the reasoning and conclusions of my article in *Harper's* magazine, to the best of my knowledge, still stand. No information which has become available since that date will effect any important alteration.

There is, however, one point which I should like to emphasize further, and that is the undoubted effect of high marginal rates of income tax on businesses, encouraging them to spend money freely on all those fields of expenditure which are allowed as a deduction for income-tax purposes. To my mind it is significant that so careful and responsible a periodical as *Fortune* recently published an article by a highly qualified taxation counsel, advising businessmen how to spend what is called 18-cent dollars; i.e., that each dollar spent on maintenance and in certain other ways only made a difference of 18 cents to the firm's net profit after taxation.

It is true that the loss of 18 cents remains a loss of 18 cents, and no business will overmaintain or otherwise spend money on purely unnecessary objects, but when it is in doubt whether or not to spend, it will always be biased in the direction of spending of more rather than less. In many respects such as the payment of higher wages, salaries, and bonuses, the payments for advertisement, entertainments, and public relations, the business can obtain definite advantages for itself in the future at the expense of the United States Treasury in the present.

This now brings us to the question of whether there are any grounds for hope that the 25-percent limit could be safely exceeded, and if so, under what circumstances. As you will see from the original articles in *Economic Journal* and *Harper's* the 25 percent is a round figure rather than a precise limit and should certainly be written 24–26 if not 23–27. When, however, your figure is as high as 27 I should say myself, I would be willing to bet with a fairly high degree of probability on a further increase of money wages and consequent inflation to the national income as a whole.

If taxation of this order of magnitude appears unavoidable, you may then ask whether there is any form or forms of taxation least likely to cause an upward pressure on prices and incomes.

Under circumstances envisaged with an inescapable necessity of imposing taxation at a level of 27 percent or more, on national income, we can minimize the upward pressure by a system which, in general terms, keeps down marginal taxation with consequent necessary raising of average rates of taxation. Such a program, it need hardly be pointed out, would be extremely unpopular. It would mean removing, where possible, the progressive elements in the tax system, charging lower rates on the high incomes and higher rates on the low incomes, relying upon indirect rather than direct taxation, and making indirect taxation fall upon necessaries rather than upon amenities.

Recently I spent a month in Italy, followed by a short visit to Britain, and could not help being struck by the contrast in fiscal policies between the two countries. It is probably true that in these countries I picked extreme representatives of the two different schools of thought. In Britain the necessaries of life are not only undertaxed, they are strongly subsidized with subsequent need for additional taxation elsewhere.

But on everything else, both direct and indirect taxation fall with extraordinary severity. Most wage earners pay substantial income tax and in addition immense taxation is imposed upon the modest amenities of the English workingman's life, beer and tobacco. Prohibitive purchase tax falls on many classes of household goods which would be regarded as necessaries in any country, and therefore, as a consequence of all this, production is sluggish and there are constant demands for higher money wages. A high official of the British Treasury agreed with me that the only way to reverse the process was to make the necessaries of life much dearer and the amenities much cheaper. This is what Italy has done and her production is increasing with extraordinary rapidity, while prices are stationary or even falling. The Italian has to work hard to buy the necessaries of life, but a slight further effort will bring him some of the amenities which are almost unobtainable in Britain. Italy has virtually no income tax and relies upon a system of indirect taxation, which falls, quite shamelessly, upon the necessaries of life.

If therefore, you think that you can advocate such a policy for the United States, you may be able to go a few points beyond the 25-percent limit without causing prices and incomes to rise.

I do not know whether my old friend, Senator Douglas, is a member of your committee. I think he might be interested in this correspondence.

You will notice from this letter that I have resigned from my old post as Director of the State Government's Bureau of Industry and have commenced to practice as an independent economic consultant. The above is my temporary address.

Yours truly,

COLIN CLARK.

COLIN CLARK AND THE ECONOMIC LIMITS OF TAXATION IN THE UNITED STATES,
SUBMITTED BY WALTER W. HELLER

(Notes for panel discussion on fiscal policy before the congressional Joint Committee on the Economic Report, Jan. 31, 1952, Washington, D. C., submitted in accordance with the invitation of the chairman, Senator Joseph C. O'Mahoney.)

Is taxation in the United States at or near limits beyond which further tax increases are self-defeating? That is, would higher tax rates defeat themselves by impairing production and causing inflation? This is the nub of the question raised by Colin Clark, Australian economist, who suggests that the answer is "Yes," as soon as a nation's taxes rise above 25 percent of its national income.

Since total taxes in the United States now equal about 31 percent of national income, and since Clark's thesis has been endorsed by many influential opponents of higher taxes, its validity is an important issue in Federal tax policy today.

This statement will briefly examine Clark's 25-percent rule from two main points of view: (1) Whether the statistics he cites as evidence do, in fact, establish 25 percent as the critical level of taxation beyond which inflation takes hold; and (2) to what extent the basic ideas he develops—quite apart from any quibble about whether 25 percent is the exact critical level—apply to the United States tax situation today.

A. STATISTICAL SUPPORT FOR THE 25-PERCENT RULE

Mr. Clark relies heavily on a variety of tax, price, and national income figures for a number of countries to establish his proposition that 25 percent of national income is the tax threshold to inflation—that beyond 25 percent, leaders in business, financial, and political circles "transfer their allegiance" to inflation, employers' resistance to wage increases and wasteful expenditures weakens noticeably, and incentives to work and invest are badly impaired. If his statistics bear him out for a large number of countries and over a considerable period of time, his 25-percent rule gains much strength even if one disagrees with his reasoning.

1. Postwar data

Mr. Clark cites figures for both Europe and the United States since World War II to show that taxes exceeding 25 percent of national income result in inflation and that this inflation, in turn, is the instrument which brings the level of taxation back to 25 percent. It is quite true that inflation existed side by side with high taxes all over the world from 1945 to 1948. To muster support for his theory, however, Mr. Clark would have to show that inflation was worse in those countries where taxation exceeded 25 percent than in those where it did not, or that the higher the taxes the greater the inflation. Mr. Clark does not demonstrate this and, in fact, it appears that deficit financing, together with war dislocations, is the culprit—under conditions of full employment, the higher the taxes and the lower the deficit (at any given level of expenditures) the less the degree of inflation.

With specific reference to the United States, Clark associates excessively high taxes with the moderate inflation of 1946–48 (after the end of price control and rationing) which, in turn, had the effect of "bringing taxes down to almost exactly the 25 percent level." Leaving aside the fact that the immediate postwar inflation is correlated much more closely with the deficits of 1944–45 than with tax levels, did inflation bring down the ratio of taxes to national income as Clark asserts? The answer is "No."

From 1946 to 1947, the ratio rose at the same time that prices increased. From 1947 to 1949, to be sure, the ratio fell—not because prices rose (which they did from 1948 to 1949) but because Congress reduced taxes by over $5 billion in 1948 and because we suffered a business recession starting at the end of 1948. The evidence contradicts rather than supports Mr. Clark—inflation raises the ratio of tax revenue to national income (because we have, on balance, a progressive tax system) even when taxes exceed the 25-percent limit. Taxes and prices demonstrated his error again in calendar 1950: While prices were rising from less than 170 at the end of 1949 to 180 at the end of 1950, the ratio of tax liabilities to national income rose from 26.3 percent in 1949 to 29.0 percent (excluding tax-rate increases) in 1950 with the budget roughly in balance. Inflation clearly appears to have raised, not lowered, the ratio, even though taxes exceeded the 25-percent level.

2. Earlier data

Very briefly, it may be noted that the data Mr. Clark cites for the interwar period also fail to establish his 25-percent rule. In fact, the very figures he relies on most—those for France—prove on close examination to deny his thesis more than they support it. For example, using Clark's own figures one finds that prices rose more and average price levels were higher in the two periods when taxes plus deficits fell short of 25 percent (1925–27 and 1936–38) than they did in the two periods when taxes plus deficits were above 25 percent (1922–24 and 1928–35).

Although Clark cites data for several other countries, these are for the most part not directly revelant to his 25-percent hypothesis. On one hand, many of the cited levels of taxation (plus deficits) were well below 25 percent of national income. On the other, at these levels, both inflationary and deflationary movements occurred, and rising taxes (plus deficits) were sometimes associated with rising, sometimes with falling, prices and vice versa.

Clark's own data, then, fail in significant instances to support the proposition that taxes or expenditures above about 25 percent bring on inflation or that inflation reduces the ratio of taxes to additional income. In fact, some of his most important evidence is more consistent with exactly the reverse position.

It may be that Clark has not looked at the right variables at all. For example, the size of deficits and surpluses (in relation, of course, to levels of employment) may be more important than levels of taxation alone. It may be found—in fact, most economists would expect to find—that higher taxes are anti-inflationary, not inflationary, even above the 25-percent level. Another useful line of inquiry would be to compare price movements at low versus high balanced budgets (again, with employment levels taken into account).

Showing that Clark's data failed to establish his 25-percent rule removes one important prop from his position but does not necessarily invalidate the arguments underlying the rule. If the arguments prove valid, it may be that his general concept is right but that its application varies in different countries and at different periods of time. It is conceivable, for example, that his reasoning would apply in the United States today at about 31 percent of national income. Clearly, we need to go beyond Clark's quantitative data and examine his qualitative arguments.

1. "Transfer of allegiance" to inflation

Clark's major reliance in past writings has been on the "transfer of allegiance" argument. When taxes break over the 25-percent line, some representatives of government, business, finance, and labor switch their allegiance from price stability to price inflation, with the result that the balance tips toward inflation.

Quite apart from the difficulty of visualizing how this transfer of allegiance takes place in practice—and why the individuals concerned should respond to the national average of taxation rather than to their own tax liabilities—there is no reason to believe that the balance of personal or group advantage will shift from price stability to inflation at any particular level of taxes, whether it be 25, 35, or 45 percent.

With respect to Government representatives, Mr. Clark puts much emphasis on interest on the public debt as a basis for favoring inflation over deflation. But, one may ask, could this possibly be a major factor in the United States where interest constitutes only 2 percent of national income and 8 percent of Federal expenditures? And even if it were more, why would the Government switch its allegiance at or near 25 percent rather than long before this point?

It is equally difficult to make sense out of this point for other groups. To be sure, inflation favors some and penalizes others. Among those whom it penalizes are creditors and fixed-income groups in particular. Why, for example, would landlords, insurance companies, and other savings institutions, charitable and educational institutions, and local governments switch their allegiance to inflation because of high taxes? The vigorous anti-inflationary campaigns conducted by insurance companies and, even more strikingly, the excellent cooperation of the banking community with the "voluntary credit restraint program" all contradicted Mr. Clark's argument that allegiance is switching to inflation at rates of taxation averaging above 25 percent of the national income.

2. Free spending by business

The second argument, on which he has placed increasing emphasis, is that high-tax rates tend to loosen the purse strings of business. There is less resistance to wage increases and less vigilance in regard to wasteful spending. It is assumed that the businessman reasons somewhat as follows: "Since the Government taxes 82 cents (or 70 cents) out of each additional dollar of profit, each additional dollar I spend will cost me only 18 cents (or 30 cents) so why not spend more?"[1] To be sure, this is one possible response to high marginal tax rates. But an equally plausible response would be for him to reason as follows: "Since higher-tax rates are cutting down my total profits by leaving me only 18 cents (or 30 cents) out of each additional dollar of profit, I had better earn as many of those dollars as possible to maintain total profits after taxes at satisfactory levels." In the absence of clear-cut factual information one way or the other, it is not clear which of these two lines of reasoning will govern his action.

This is not to deny that high marginal tax rates provide some stimulus to increasing or speeding up expenditures. To the extent that the businessman can make outlays today that will cost him only 18 cents (or 30 cents) on the dollar but will increase his profits in the future when taxes leave him, say, 50 cents or 60 cents on the dollar, he will be stimulated to spend. In other words, to the extent that he can feather his nest for a lower-tax future by high-level maintenance and repairs, by advertising, and by capital outlays which benefit from accelerated amortization, he may increase his total current expenditures and thereby add to current inflationary pressures. Many of these nest-feathering outlays are of course not wasteful in the long run.

When it comes to the category of high living on expense accounts, wasteful use of materials and manpower and the like—a category one might call loose-living expenditures—it is hard to see how the employer's self-interest would lead him to indulge in these to any considerable extent. They do not promise higher profits in the future; in fact, they will bring him out of the defense period with a bloated cost structure that weakens his competitive position. To be sure, such expenditures cost him little now but they also gain him little, and they may bring him losses in the long run.

With respect to lowered resistance to wage increases, certainly this has been a characteristic of the full-employment periods of World War II and the early 1950's. However, higher wages may represent higher bids in the scramble for manpower rather than a response to high rates of taxation.

3. Weakening of productive incentives

Turning to Mr. Clark's third main point—the weakening of incentives to work and invest—we find considerably more substance than in his first

---

[1] For corporations subject to excess profits tax but not at the ceiling rate the combined marginal tax rate is 82 percent. Once the ceiling is reached, it is 70 percent from there on.

two. Of course, it cannot be couched in terms of average tax rates alone. Incentives refer to individuals, and individuals in their capacity as workers, savers, and investors react, not to national averages, but to the specific taxes that hit their work, their saving, and their investing. Mr. Clark has recognized this in his letter of January 18, 1952, to this committee which is part of the record of these hearings. In view of his recognition that it is the response to marginal rather than average tax rates which governs individual actions, it is surprising that he holds even to a range of 23 to 27 percent in place of 25 percent as the critical limit of taxation. Merely granting that marginal rates are significant ought to widen this range much further in view of the great differences in tax distribution—in relative reliance on progressive and regressive taxes—that may occur at any given average level of taxation.

Nevertheless the impact of high taxes on incentives, especially work incentives, deserves close scrutiny. Surely, there is some level beyond which further tax increases will reduce output more than they will reduce purchasing power and therefore will be inflationary rather than deflationary. Beyond some level, further taxes may so impair the willingness to work and the incentives to take risks that they will cut the supply of goods and services even more than the demand for them. But it seems highly doubtful that this would occur at or near 25 percent, and there is no acceptable evidence that it is occurring at 30 percent or would occur at, say, 35 percent. However, since it may at some time be a limiting factor to taxation, it is worth further consideration.

What is the individual's reaction to high rates of tax on his additional income? On one hand, he is stimulated to work less and enjoy more leisure and, perhaps more important, to substitute untaxed work for taxed work wherever possible. For example, it may pay him to do plumbing and electrical work, carpentry, and painting around his house or to grow a garden rather than to put in overtime on his job. The overtime is taxable, while his work for himself is not. Whether he substitutes leisure for work, or less efficient for more efficient work, in either case the economy suffers a loss in total output.

At the same time, it must be recognized that there may be good reason for doing just the reverse of this. If higher taxes cut down the income to which an individual has been accustomed or which he has set as his target, he may work that much harder to achieve it. He may convert some of his leisure into additional work on his job to make up the loss, or he may be stimulated to do for himself the things around the house for which he previously hired others. In either case, there is a gain in output in response to higher taxes.

What evidence is available to prove the strength of one set of motives or the other? Unfortunately, in spite of many assertions regarding absenteeism, unwillingness to work overtime, reluctance to change jobs and other adverse effects of taxes on work, no firm evidence has been developed to prove their relationship to high taxation.

With respect to the responses of executives to high taxes, we do have some relevant evidence from a study made at the Harvard Graduate School of Business Administration by Thomas H. Sanders. Basing his conclusions on intensive interviews, Dr. Sanders notes that executives are in considerable part driven by nonmonetary motives and that, although taxes may make them somewhat less willing to move from one job to another, "for the most part, with considerable exceptions, businessmen are currently working as hard under high tax rates as they did under low tax rates. . . ."

Also, it is important in this connection to know that the greater majority of income recipients are taxable today at marginal rates below 30 percent, even including State income taxes. With respect to the Federal tax alone, figures presented at the Ways and Means Committee hearings a year ago by the Treasury showed that only 6.8 million out of 51.7 million taxpayers would have incomes reaching beyond the first surtax bracket (now 22.2 percent) and only 2.5 million beyond the second bracket (now 24.6 percent). It does not seem likely that taxes which leave them more than 70 cents out of each additional dollar of earnings will significantly discourage their work. In fact, at these rates of taxation, income-tax increases probably constitute an incentive to work harder and replace lost income rather than work less in order to pay less tax.

All of this assumes that the taxpayer is very conscious of the relation between additional effort and additional taxes and assumes further that he responds mainly to monetary rewards. To the extent that he is not fully aware of the relationship and to the extent that he works for the joy of working or for prestige and recognition, such adverse effects as taxes might have are further reduced.

4. Conclusions

Our conclusions from this review of Mr. Clark's supporting arguments are the following:

(1) It is difficult to conceive why and how high taxes—whether at 25 percent or some higher level—should tip the balance of advantages between inflation and deflation so as to cause any significant group to switch its allegiance to inflation.

(2) The weakening of resistance to wage increases and wasteful expenditure which is alleged to result from high taxes is highly conjectural, though high-tax rates undoubtedly provide a stimulus to incur some additional business expenses currently in the interest of higher future profits.

(3) With respect to work incentives, taxes undoubtedly have adverse effects, though there are substantial offsetting favorable effects at current

rates of taxation. How far taxes would have to be pushed before the adverse effects became prohibitively great is a matter of judgment, although it appears that we are not yet close to such limits.

(4) Mr. Clark's major arguments provide even less support for his 25-percent thesis (even when cast into a range of 23–27 percent) than his statistics. They provide no basis for concluding that taxes which cross over this critical line will bring on inflation. In fact, they suggest that no conclusion can be reached at all in terms of an average or aggregate levels of taxation, but that the problem must be thought of in terms of the marginal rates of specific taxes.

C. OTHER CONSIDERATIONS REGARDING LIMITS TO TAXATION OF EXPENDITURES

Even if neither the available data nor Mr. Clark's arguments established 23 to 27 percent of national income as the critical level of taxation, it does not necessarily follow that Clark's conclusions are wrong or, perhaps one should say, it does not follow that there are no economic limits to taxation or that we may not be in the vicinity of those limits in the United States today.[2]

1. Taxation

We have already noted above certain conditions under which further taxation, at stable levels of government expenditure, would have inflationary consequences. In a word, if the tax reduces the total demand for goods and services less than it curtails their supply, its net effect will be inflationary. If $2 billion of new taxes were to reduce total private spending by $1 billion (and saving by $1 billion) but at the same time curtailed the supply of goods and services by $1½ billion, the net result would clearly be inflationary.

Although we are still far from any such point, it may be useful to consider how a result of this sort could be brought about. With respect to the impact on spending versus saving, it is conceivable that as taxes rise beyond a certain point and as individuals accumulate larger amounts of assets, they will be more and more reluctant to cut further into their spending and will prefer to sacrifice current saving or draw on accumulated assets in response to further taxation. If taxes on business reach such high rates that only 5 or 10 percent of the marginal dollar is retained, looser business spending might also result. On the production side, impairment of incentives as discussed above may eventually become serious enough to cause a significant reduction of output in response to additional taxes. In short, at extremely high rates of taxation, the two factors com-

[2] No attempt is made here to appraise administrative and equity boundaries to taxation, though any comprehensive assessment of the practical limits to taxation would have to do so.

bined might make further rate increases inflationary rather than deflationary.

2. Expenditures

If we turn from taxes to expenditures and suggest that beyond a given
level, tax-financed additions to expenditures are inflationary, the argument
shifts to new ground. By and large, any increase in Government expenditures is expansionary. Whether financed by taxation or not, it tends to
increase national income. Especially after full employment is reached, the
expansionary effect puts upward pressure on prices. These effects operate at whatever ratio of national income governmental expenditures happen to be—whether it be 15 or 50 percent.

Once full employment is reached, Government economic policy can no
longer rely on increases in output but must shift resources from private to
public use. No doubt this becomes harder as expenditures rise. As long
as heavily regressive taxes are avoided, each dollar of additional taxes
(*a*) tends to displace less and less private spending, and (*b*) may have increasingly detrimental effects on output. To shift the resources without
causing inflation calls for increasing amounts of taxation or other anti-
inflationary measures per dollar of Government spending.

Thus, while not granting the Clark thesis that additional taxes beyond
25 percent of national income become inflationary, one might formulate
the following sort of proposition: As Government expenditures rise, their
inflationary effects are increasingly difficult to overcome by additional
taxation. But, even here, three qualifying points must quickly be made:
(1) This is a gradual process, with no reason to believe that there is a
sharp breakover to inflation at some particular percent of national income; (2) additional taxes are still seen as anti-inflationary in net effect
until levels far above 25 percent are reached (the precise level depending
on many factors, including especially the marginal rates of taxation); and
(3) in a situation like the present where the level of expenditures is well
above 25 percent of national income—total Federal, State and local expenditures in the fiscal year 1953 are likely to be about one-third of the
national income—additional taxes to reduce the deficit will still reduce
inflationary pressures, not increase them. In addition to their short-run
effect, they will slow down the growth of the debt and thereby hold
down the volume of liquid assets which would increase the threat of
future inflation.

In short, there are economic limits to taxation in terms of adverse
effects on output and ineffectiveness in reducing inflationary pressure.
But these are not inexorably reached at or near 25 percent of national
income, nor do we appear to have reached them in the United States
today even at levels of taxation and expenditures exceeding 30 percent of
national income.

FOR FURTHER READING: A good introduction to the subject is in *Annals of the American Academy of Political and Social Science* (November, 1949), vol. 266. Useful also is Richard Goode, "An Economic Limit on Taxes: Some Recent Discussions," *National Tax Journal*, V (September, 1952), pp. 227–233. Support for tax limits is also found in Harley Lutz, *Guideposts to a Free Economy* (New York, 1945). Many economists believe that no rigid criteria can be developed, especially Josiah Stamp, *Wealth and Taxable Capacity* (London, 1930), and Hugh Dalton, *Principles of Public Finance* (London, 1948). Paul Douglas expresses similar views in *Federal Tax Policy for Economic Growth and Stability, Report of the Joint Committee on the Economic Report* (Washington, 1956). A functional view of taxes is developed by Abba P. Lerner, *The Economics of Control* (New York, 1944).

31. *Recent Economic Issues: Big Business and Efficiency*

PROBLEM: *Is big or small business more efficient?*

The steady multiplication of giant business enterprises in the United States during the twentieth century has led to much discussion about the relationship between size and efficiency. Have large industrial units prospered primarily because of the economic advantages which they bring? Economists have divided over the issue and have produced plausible arguments on both sides. In defense of bigness, one of America's outstanding economists, the late Sumner H. Slichter of Harvard University, stressed the economic superiority of large-scale business combinations. He thought their technological efficiency to be especially important. Consequently Slichter believed that federal restraints on corporate mergers should be relaxed to allow greater economies in production. Competition then would actually be increased as scientific research in industries dominated by a few large firms would lead them into more active rivalry. This prescription was viewed rather skeptically by George Stigler of the University of Chicago, another eminent economist. Stigler strenuously opposed the formation of powerful and highly centralized business units. In the first place, he questioned the assumption that Big Business is always more efficient than its smaller counterparts, for evidence reveals that at times just the reverse might be true. Moreover, he argued that the monopolistic behavior of great corporations led them to adopt policies that were socially undesirable, such as the suppression of small competitors. He decried, too, the disproportionately large political influence of Big Business which stimulated the growth of Big Labor and Big Government. For these reasons Stigler believed that mergers should be made

518

more difficult so that a highly competitive economy could be encouraged. Both of these writers provide concise summaries of arguments that are frequently used in the debate over this issue. Why is competition desirable? What are the advantages and disadvantages of Big Business? How can present trends toward greater business consolidation be altered?

The Case for Bigness in Business

SUMNER H. SLICHTER

The 1957 decision of the Supreme Court in the du Pont-General Motors case suggests the desirability of a review and an appraisal of American policy toward competition, monopoly, and bigness in business. The decision reveals the strong determination of the court to prevent competition from being weakened and the court's willingness to resort to controversial interpretations of the law in order to implement the public policy of preventing restraints on competition.

But the decision also reminds us that much thinking on the relation of bigness to competition is out of date and unrealistic. Hence, the adaptation of traditional American antitrust policy to the facts of modern industry requires that we take a fresh look at the role of large enterprises in American business—particularly the role of large enterprises as a source of vigorous and dynamic competition.

When one compares the economy of the United States with the economies of other advanced industrial countries, four characteristics stand out conspicuously.

1. The government of the United States endeavors through broad and drastic laws to prevent restraints on competition and to forestall the growth of monopoly. Most other advanced industrial countries either tolerate considerable restraint on competition or even encourage organizations of business men that are designed to control competition.

2. Competition in American industry is far more vigorous and pervasive than in the industries of any other advanced industrial country. Indeed, the vigor of competition in the United States almost invariably attracted comment from the European productivity teams that visited this country in the years following the war.

3. The United States has many more huge business enterprises than any

other country. Several years ago this country had more than 100 corporations (exclusive of purely financial ones) with assets of more than $250 million each. General Motors produces far more cars than the combined British, German and French automobile industries, and the United States Steel Corporation produces more steel than the entire British steel industry.

4. Production in many American industries (especially those requiring large capital investment) is highly concentrated in the hands of a few large concerns. As a general rule, the concentration of production in other industrial countries is far less than here.

These four characteristics of the American economy are not unrelated. It would be wrong to ascribe the widespread and intense competition in American industry *solely* to the strong public policy against restraint of trade, monopolization and interference with competition. Conditions in the United States—the absence of class lines, the abundance of opportunity, the weakness of tradition—have long made life here highly competitive in all its aspects, and competition in business is just one manifestation of this general competitive spirit. But America's unique and firm public policy against restraints on competition has undoubtedly helped greatly to keep industry here strongly competitive.

This strong policy, however, has paradoxically encouraged the development of giant industrial corporations and the concentration of production in many industries among a few large concerns. The growth of enterprises in Europe has been limited by the practice of forming cartels— a practice which governments have tolerated and even encouraged. The cartel or trade association divides markets among its members, limits the growth of the most efficient concerns, and assures the weak, high-cost concern a share of the market.

In the United States, where cartels are illegal, each concern is pretty completely exposed to competition from all other firms, and business goes to the firms that can get it. This means that in many industries production is gradually concentrated in the hands of a few industrial giants, and only a small part of the business is left for small firms.

The trend toward corporate bigness in industry has led many students of anti-monopoly policy to believe that the American policy of encouraging competition and discouraging monopoly is turning out to be a failure and to conclude that steps need to be taken to limit the influences of large enterprises in American industry. Of many proposals that have been made, two principal ones are of particular interest.

One proposal is that new restrictions be placed on mergers. Some have urged that no merger be permitted which cannot be justified by technological reasons. Some have proposed that mergers involving a corporation above a given size be prohibited unless found by the Federal Trade Commission to be in the public interest.

The second proposal deals with the concentration of production in various industries into a few enterprises. It is urged that the government undertake a comprehensive survey of American industry to determine whether enterprises exceed the size required by modern technology and that the government be authorized to break up firms that are unnecessarily large.

Both of these proposals are based on fallacy. They rest upon a mistaken conception of the role of large corporations in American business and particularly upon the relation of large corporations to competition. Each, if put into effect, would weaken rather than strengthen competition. In fact, in order to stimulate competition, existing restrictions on mergers should be relaxed, not tightened, and large enterprises, instead of being threatened with breakup, should be given a clear mandate to grow, provided they use fair means. Let us examine more completely each of these two proposals to restrict the growth of enterprises.

The proposal that new restrictions be placed on mergers arises from the fact that the United States in recent years has been experiencing a great wave of mergers. But recent mergers have not weakened competition. On the contrary, they have indirectly strengthened it because they have enabled managements to build more diversified and better-integrated enterprises—enterprises which are more capable of reaching all parts of the vast domestic market, of adapting themselves to market shifts and changes in technology, of riding out the ups and downs of business, and of supporting technological research and development. Many large firms and firms of moderate size have acquired small firms, but the acquisitions by the very largest firms have not been numerous.

The specific circumstances surrounding each merger are unique, but a case-by-case examination shows how mergers are helping to build stronger enterprises, better able to compete and to hold their own in competition.

Let us consider a few examples. A maker of cans bought a concern manufacturing plastic pipe in order to get a foothold in the plastic pipe business. A maker of railroad freight cars bought companies making electrical equipment, truck trailers and dairy supplies in order to shift from a declining business to expanding businesses. A food manufacturer bought a West Coast manufacturer of salad seasoning in order to give nation-wide distribution to its product. A maker of household ware bought a supplier in order to have a source of pressed wood handles for its appliances.

Unusually competent managements often buy other concerns so that they can spread good administrative methods to less efficiently operated enterprises.

The many advantages produced by mergers show that the proposal that mergers be prohibited unless they can be justified by technological reasons does not make sense. There are good reasons for mergers that have nothing to do with technology.

Moreover, it would be unwise to require government approval of all mergers involving an enterprise above a specified size. That would be substituting the decision of government officials for the decision of businessmen on matters that the businessmen are better able to understand. The public interest is amply protected by the present drastic provision of Section 7 of the Clayton Act.

Indeed, the fact that mergers often make for more vigorous competition by helping managements build stronger and more efficient business enterprises indicates the need for relaxing the present severe restrictions on mergers contained in Section 7 of the Clayton Act. This section prohibits any merger which is likely to lessen competition substantially in *any* line of commerce. The fact that the merger may increase the intensity of competition in *other* lines of commerce makes no difference. As Section 7 now reads, the *total effect* of the merger on competition is irrelevant. If it is likely to lessen competition substantially in any one line of commerce, it is illegal.

Obviously the section, as it now reads, conflicts with the national policy of encouraging competition. It should be rewritten to make the legality of mergers depend upon the *total* effect of competition, thus permitting any merger that has the net effect of increasing competition.

The second proposal—to remake the structure of American industry by breaking up the largest enterprises—rests upon the mistaken view that, where output is concentrated among a few concerns, effective competition does not occur. The error of this view is shown by the vigorous competition in various industries in which most of the output is made by a few firms—in such industries as the automobile, tire, refrigerator, soap, cigarette, paper products, television and many others.

There are two principal reasons why competition tends to be vigorous when production is concentrated among a few large concerns. One is that such enterprises keep close track of their rank in sales and fight hard to move ahead of rivals or to avoid being surpassed by rivals. The second reason, and one that is rapidly gaining in importance, is the fact that competition among large firms is being stimulated by the growth of technological research.

It is only within the last several decades that managements have generally discovered the big returns yielded by technological research. As a result, the outlays by private industry on research and development increased nearly six-fold between 1940 and 1953. In 1957, the total research and development expenditures of private industry, exclusive of the aircraft industry, which is a special case, are running about 71 per cent greater than they were in 1953. By 1960 outlays on research are expected to be 21 per cent above 1957.

No expenditures are more competitive than outlays on research, for the purpose of these expenditures is to improve products, develop new products and cut costs. More than 70 per cent of the outlays on research and development are made by firms with 5,000 or more employees because concerns with large sales can best afford this overhead expense. Hence the rapidly mounting outlays on research indicate both the growing competitiveness of American industry and the increasingly important role large enterprises are playing in making competition more intense.

Incidentally, competition among large firms is superior in quality to competition among small firms and serves consumers more effectively. This is because the greater research by the large firms gives the consumers a wider range of choice over a period of years than competition among a much larger number of small firms that can afford little or no research. In general, the wider the range of choice open to consumers, the more effectively is the welfare of consumers advanced.

In view of the growing importance of large enterprises as a source of competition and the superior quality of this competition, a move to break up large concerns would be a blunder. There is much to be said, however, in favor of incentives for enterprises to split themselves voluntarily, if the managements consider a split desirable. The resulting increase in the number of top managements with independent authority to make policies and to try experiments would be favorable to technological progress—provided the concerns are large enough to support extensive research. A good incentive for voluntary splits would be created by relieving stockholders from liability for the capital gains tax on the appreciation of their holdings from the time they purchased the stock up to the date of the split.

But enforced splitting of enterprises, except as a remedy for flagrant monopolizing of trade by unscrupulous methods, would be another matter. In fact, the present law needs to be clarified in order to encourage a few of the very largest concerns to strive harder for a bigger share of the market. The managements of a few very large and efficient concerns apparently feel that efforts to get more business by cutting prices will be held to be attempts to monopolize. There is need to make clear that efforts to win business by giving consumers the benefits of low costs will not be regarded as monopolistic.

Americans need to understand that a variety of conditions—rapidly changing technology, the growing importance of industrial research, the growing strength of trade unions—tend to increase in many industries the size of the enterprise that is able both to compete and to survive in competition. Hence, we are likely to see a spread of the tendency for production to be concentrated in a few large or fairly large firms.

But this trend, if it occurs, should not disturb us. It will simply represent an adaptation of industry to the conditions of the time.

The Case against Big Business

GEORGE J. STIGLER

. . . Bigness in business has two primary meanings. First, bigness may be defined in terms of the company's share of the industry in which it operates: a big company is one that has a big share of the market or industry. By this test Texas Gulf Sulphur is big because it produces more than half the sulfur in America, and Macy's (whose annual sales are much larger) is small because it sells only a very small fraction of the goods sold by New York City retail stores. By this definition, many companies that are small in absolute size are nevertheless big—the only brick company in a region, for example—and many companies that are big in absolute size (Inland Steel, for example) are small. Second, bigness may mean absolute size—the measure of size being assets, sales, or employment as a rule. Then General Motors and U.S. Steel are the prototypes of bigness.

These two meanings overlap because most companies that are big in absolute size are also big in relation to their industries. There are two types of cases, however, in which the two meanings conflict. On the one hand, many companies of small absolute size are dominant in small markets or industries. I shall not discuss them here (although they require attention in a well-rounded antitrust program) for two reasons: they seldom have anywhere near so much power as the companies that are big relative to large markets and industries; and they raise few political problems of the type I shall discuss below. On the other hand, there are a few companies that are big in absolute size but small relative to their markets—I have already given Macy's as an example. These companies are not very important in the total picture, and I shall also put them aside in the following discussion.

For my purposes, then, big businesses will mean businesses that are absolutely large in size and large also relative to the industries in which they operate. They are an impressive list: U.S. Steel, Bethlehem, and Republic in steel, General Electric and Westinghouse in electrical equipment, General Motors, Ford, and Chrysler in automobiles, du Pont, Union Carbide, and Allied Chemical among others in chemicals, Reynolds, Liggett & Myers, and American Tobacco in cigarettes.

What bigness does not mean is perhaps equally important. Bigness has no reference to the size of industries. I for one am tired of the charge that the critics of the steel industry vacillate between finding the output too large and too small: at various times the industry's output has been too small; for fifty years the largest firm has been too large. Concerted action

Reprinted from the May, 1952 issue of *Fortune* magazine by special permission; © 1952 Time Inc.

by many small companies often leads to over-capacity in an industry: it is the basic criticism of resale price maintenance, for example, that it encourages the proliferation of small units by fixing excessive retail margins. Industries dominated by one or a few firms—that is, big businesses—seldom err in this direction. Nor does bigness have any direct reference to the methods of production, and opposition to big business is usually compatible with a decent respect for the "economies of large-scale production," on which more later.

The fundamental objection to bigness stems from the fact that big companies have monopolistic power, and this fundamental objection is clearly applicable outside the realm of corporate business. In particular, big unions are open to all the criticisms (and possibly more) that can be levied against big business. I shall not discuss labor unions, but my silence should not be construed as a belief that we should have a less stringent code for unions than for business.

There are two fundamental criticisms to be made of big businesses: they act monopolistically, and they encourage and justify bigness in labor and government.

First, as to monopoly. When a small number of firms control most or all of the output of an industry, they can individually and collectively profit more by cooperation than by competition. This is fairly evident, since cooperatively they can do everything they can do individually, and other things (such as the charging of noncompetitive prices) besides. These few companies, therefore, will usually cooperate.

From this conclusion many reasonable men, including several Supreme Court justices, will dissent. Does not each brand of cigarettes spend huge sums in advertising to lure us away from some other brand? Do not the big companies—oligopolists, the economists call them—employ salesmen? Do not the big companies introduce constant innovations in their products?

The answer is that they do compete—but not enough, and not in all the socially desirable ways. Those tobacco companies did not act competitively, but with a view to extermination, against the 10-cent brands in the 1930's, nor have they engaged in price competition in decades (*American Tobacco vs. United States, 328 U.S. 781*). The steel companies, with all their salesmen, abandoned cartel pricing via basing-point prices only when this price system was judged a conspiracy in restraint of trade in cement (*Federal Trade Commission vs. Cement Institute, 333 U.S. 683*). The plain fact is that big businesses do not engage in continuous price competition.

Nor is price the only area of agreement. Patent licensing has frequently been used to deprive the licensees of any incentive to engage in research; General Electric used such agreements also to limit other companies' output and fix the prices of incandescent lamps (*U.S. vs. General Electric,*

82 F. Supp. 753). The hearings of the Bone Committee are adorned with numerous examples of the deliberate deterioration of goods in order to maintain sales. For example, Standard Oil Development (a subsidiary of the Jersey company) persuaded Socony-Vacuum to give up the sale of a higher-potency commodity (pour-point depressant) whose sale at the same price had been characterized as "merely price cutting."

Very well, big businesses often engage in monopolistic practices. It may still be objected that it has not been shown that all big businesses engage in monopolistic practices, or that they engage in such practices all, or even most of, the time. These things cannot be shown or even fully illustrated in a brief survey, and it is also not possible to summarize the many court decisions and the many academic studies of big business. But it is fair to say that these decisions and studies show that big businesses usually possess monopolistic power, and use it. And that is enough.

For economic policy must be contrived with a view to the typical rather than the exceptional, just as all other policies are contrived. That some drivers can safely proceed at eighty miles an hour is no objection to a maximum-speed law. So it is no objection to an anti-trust policy that some unexercised monopoly power is thereby abolished. (Should there be some big businesses that forgo the use of their dominant position, it is difficult to see what advantage accrues from private ownership, for the profit motive is already absent.)

Second, as to bigness in labor and government. Big companies have a large—I would say an utterly disproportionate—effect on public thinking. The great expansion of our labor unions has been due largely to favoring legislation and administration by the federal government. This policy of favoring unions rests fundamentally upon the popular belief that workers individually competing for jobs will be exploited by big-business employers —that U.S. Steel can in separate negotiation (a pretty picture!) over-whelm each of its hundreds of thousands of employees. In good part this is an absurd fear: U.S. Steel must compete with many other industries, and not merely other steel companies, for good workers.

Yet the fear may not be wholly absurd: there may be times and places where big businesses have "beaten down" wages, although I believe such cases are relatively infrequent. (In any event, the reaction to the fear has been unwise: for every case where big business has held down workers there are surely many cases where big unions have held up employers.) But it cannot be denied that this public attitude underlies our national labor policy, the policy of local governments of condoning violence in labor disputes, etc.

Big business has also made substantial contributions to the growth of big government. The whole agricultural program has been justified as necessary to equalize agriculture's bargaining power with "industry,"

meaning big business. The federally sponsored milkshed cartels are defended as necessary to deal with the giant dairy companies.

Big business is thus a fundamental excuse for big unions and big government. It is true that the scope and evils of big business are usually enormously exaggerated, especially with reference to labor and agriculture, and that more often than not these evils are merely a soapbox excuse for shoddy policies elsewhere. To this large extent, there is need for extensive education of the public on how small a part of the economy is controlled by big business. But in light of the widespread monopolistic practices—our first criticism of bigness—it is impossible to tell the public that its fears of big business are groundless. We have no right to ask public opinion to veer away from big unions and big government—and toward big business.

Are we dependent upon big businesses for efficient methods of production and rapid advances in production methods? If we are, the policy of breaking up big businesses would lower our future standard of living and many people would cast about for other ways than dissolution to meet the problems of bigness.

A company may be efficient because it produces and sells a given amount of product with relatively small amounts of material, capital, and labor, or it may be efficient because it acquires the power to buy its supplies at unusually low prices and sell its products at unusually high prices. Economists refer to these as the social and the private costs of production respectively. Big businesses may be efficient in the social sense, and usually they also possess, because of their monopoly position, private advantages. But the ability of a company to employ its dominant position to coerce unusually low prices from suppliers is not of any social advantage.

It follows that even if big companies had larger profit rates or smaller costs per unit of output than other companies, this would not prove that they were more efficient in socially desirable ways. Actually, big businesses are generally no more and no less efficient than medium-sized businesses even when the gains wrung by monopoly power are included in efficiency. This is the one general finding in comparative cost studies and comparative profitability studies. Indeed, if one reflects upon the persistence of small and medium-sized companies in the industries dominated by big businesses, it is apparent that there can be no great advantages to size. If size were a great advantage, the smaller companies would soon lose the unequal race and disappear.

When we recall that most big businesses have numerous complete plants at various points throughout the country, this finding is not surprising. Why should U.S. Steel be more efficient than Inland Steel, when U.S. Steel is simply a dozen or more Inland Steels strewn about the country? Why should G.M. be appreciably more efficient than, say, a once-again independent Buick Motors? A few years ago Peter Drucker reported:

> The divisional manager . . . is in complete charge of production and sales. He hires, fires and promotes; and it is up to him to decide how many men he needs, with what qualifications and in what salary range—except for top executives whose employment is subject to a central-management veto. The divisional manager decides the factory layout, the technical methods and equipment used. . . . He buys his supplies independently from suppliers of his own choice. He determines the distribution of production within the several plants under his jurisdiction, decides which lines to push and decides on the methods of sale and distribution. . . . In everything pertaining to operations he is as much the real head as if his division were indeed an independent business.

If big businesses are not more efficient as a rule, how did they get big? The answer is that most giant firms arose out of mergers of many competing firms, and were created to eliminate competition. Standard Oil, General Electric, Westinghouse, U.S. Steel, Bethlehem, the meat packers, Borden, National Dairy, American Can, etc.—the full list of merger-created big businesses is most of the list of big businesses. A few big businesses owe their position to an industrial genius like Ford, and of course future geniuses would be hampered by an effective antitrust law—but less so than by entrenched monopolies or by public regulatory commissions.

We do not know what share of improvements in technology has been contributed by big businesses. Big businesses have made some signal contributions, and so also have small businesses, universities, and private individuals. It can be said that manufacturing industries dominated by big businesses have had no larger increases in output per worker on average than other manufacturing industries. This fact is sufficient to undermine the easy identification of economic progress with the laboratories of big businesses, but it does not inform us of the net effect of monopolies on economic progress.

At present, then, no definite effect of big business on economic progress can be established. I personally believe that future study will confirm the traditional belief that big businesses, for all their resources, cannot rival the infinite resource and cold scrutiny of many independent and competing companies. If the real alternative to bigness is government regulation or ownership, as I am about to argue, then the long-run consequences of big business are going to be highly adverse to economic progress.

Let me restate the main points of the foregoing discussion in a less emphatic—and I think also a less accurate—manner:

1. Big businesses often possess and use monopoly power.
2. Big businesses weaken the political support for a private-enterprise system.
3. Big businesses are not appreciably more efficient or enterprising than medium-sized businesses.

Few disinterested people will deny these facts—where do they lead?

A considerable section of the big-business community seems to have taken the following position. The proper way to deal with monopolistic practices is to replace the general prohibitions of the Sherman Act by a specific list of prohibited practices, so businessmen may know in advance and avoid committing monopolistic practices. The proper way to deal with the declining political support for private enterprise is to advertise the merits of private enterprise, at the same time claiming many of its achievements for big business. Much of this advertising has taken literally that form, apparently in the belief that one can sell a social system in exactly the same way and with exactly the same copywriters and media that one sells a brand of cigarettes.

The request for a list of specifically prohibited monopolistic practices will be looked upon by many persons as a surreptitious attack upon the Sherman Act. I am among these cynics: the powerful drive in 1949 to pass a law legalizing basing-point price systems is sufficient evidence that large sectors of big business are wholly unreconciled to the law against conspiracies in restraint of trade. Even when the request for a specific list of prohibitions is made in all sincerity, however, it cannot be granted: No one can write down a full list of all the forms that objectionable monopoly power has taken and may someday take. Moreover, almost all uncertainties over the legality of conduct arise out of the Robinson-Patman Act, not the Sherman Act, and I would welcome the complete repeal of the former act.[1]

We must look elsewhere for the solution of the problems raised by big business, and a satisfactory solution must deal with the facts I listed at the head of this section. Our present policy is not a satisfactory solution. The Sherman Act is admirable in dealing with formal conspiracies of many firms, but—at least with the Supreme Court's present conception of competition and of the proper remedies for demonstrated restraint of trade in oligopolistic industries—it cannot cope effectively with the problem posed by big business. In industries dominated by a few firms there is no need for formal conspiracies, with their trappings of quotas, a price-fixing committee, and the like. The big companies know they must "live with" one another, and the phrase means much the same thing as in the relationship between man and woman. Any competitive action one big company takes will lead to retaliation by the others. An informal code of behavior gradually develops in the industry: Firm X announces the new price, and except in very unusual circumstances Y and Z can be relied

---

[1] The prohibition against price discrimination was partly designed to cope with a real evil: the use by a large company of its monopoly power to extort preferential terms from suppliers. This exercise of monopoly, however, constitutes a violation of the Sherman Act, and no additional legislation is necessary if this act can be made fully effective. The Robinson-Patman Act, and certain other parts of the so-called "antitrust" amendments, also have another and objectionable purpose: to supervise and regulate the routine operations of businesses in order to ensure that they will display the symptoms of competitive behavior.

upon to follow. So long as there are a few big businesses in an industry, we simply cannot expect more than the tokens of competitive behavior. Antitrust decrees that the big businesses should ignore each other's existence serve no important purpose.[2]

This conclusion, I must emphasize, is not merely that of "economic theorists," although most (academic) economists will subscribe to it. It is also the conclusion our generation is reaching, for our generation is not satisfied with the behavior of big business. More and more, big businesses are being asked to act in "the social interest," and more and more, government is interfering in their routine operation. The steel industry, for example, what with congressional review of prices and presidential coercion of wages, is drifting rapidly into a public-utility status. And the drift will not be stopped by slick advertising.

No such drastic and ominous remedy as the central direction of economic life is necessary to deal with the problems raised by big business. The obvious and economical solution, as I have already amply implied, is to break up the giant companies. This, I would emphasize, is the minimum program, and it is essentially a conservative program. Dissolution of big businesses is a once-for-all measure in each industry (if the recent antimerger amendment to the Clayton Act is adequately enforced), and no continuing interference in the private operation of business is required or desired. Dissolution involves relatively few companies; one dissolves three or four big steel companies, and leaves the many smaller companies completely alone. Dissolution does not even need to be invoked in a large part of the economy: some of our biggest industries, such as textiles, shoes, and most food industries, will require no antitrust action.

A policy of "trust busting" requires no grant of arbitrary powers to any administrative agency; the policy can be administered by the Antitrust Division acting through the courts. It is sufficient, and it is desirable, that the policy be directed against companies whose possession of monopoly power is demonstrated, and that dissolution be the basic remedy for the concentration of control in an industry that prevents or limits competition. Indeed, the policy requires new legislation only to the extent of

---

[2] In the National Lead case (*67 Sup. Ct. 1634, 1947*) this company and du Pont were convicted of violating the Sherman Act. The two companies produced about 90 percent of all titanium, but the Court refused to order divestiture of plants. The Court documented the "vigorous and effective competition between National Lead and du Pont" with the fact that "The general manager of the pigments department of du Pont characterized the competition with Zirconium and Virginia Chemical as 'tough' and that [with] National Lead as 'plenty tough.'" Economists will always find such testimony an inadequate demonstration of competition. Even more unfortunate was the refusal of the Court to order divestiture of foreign holdings of the Timken Roller Bearing Company, which had also been convicted under the Sherman Act (*71 Sup. Ct. 971, 1951*). Here Mr. Justice Reed, the Chief Justice concurring, argues that so "harsh" a remedy as divestiture should be invoked only in extreme cases, perhaps forgetting that inadequate remedies for monopoly are "harsh" treatment of the public interest.

convincing the courts that an industry which does not have a competitive structure will not have competitive behavior.

The dissolution of big businesses is only a part of the program necessary to increase the support for a private, competitive enterprise economy, and reverse the drift toward government control. But it is an essential part of this program, and the place for courage and imagination. Those conservatives who cling to the status quo do not realize that the status quo is a state of change, and the changes are coming fast. If these changes were to include the dissolution of a few score of our giant companies, however, we shall have done much to preserve private enterprise and the liberal-individualistic society of which it is an integral part.

FOR FURTHER READING: The advantages and disadvantages of Big Business are clearly discussed in Clair Wilcox, *Competition and Monopoly in American Industry*, Temporary National Economic Committee, Monograph #21 (Washington, 1940). Joe S. Bain, "Economies of Scale, Concentration, and Entry," *American Economic Review*, XLIV (March, 1954), pp. 15–39, finds that the evidence does not justify a clear stand on the issue. More positive are Joseph Schumpeter, the great Austrian economist, in *Capitalism, Socialism, and Democracy* (New York, 1942), David Lilienthal, *Big Business: A New Era* (New York, 1952), Adolph A. Berle, *The Twentieth Century Capitalist Revolution* (New York, 1958), and John Chamberlain, *The Roots of Capitalism* (Princeton, 1959). Opposed to the concentration of power are George W. Stocking and Myron Watkins, *Monopoly and Free Enterprise* (New York, 1951), and George W. Stocking, *Workable Competition and Anti-Trust Policy* (Nashville, 1961). Also useful in this connection is John K. Galbraith, *American Capitalism* (New York, 1952).

32. *Economic Development and the Future*

PROBLEM: *What are some future directions of economic development?*

The past is frequently studied not for its own sake only, but also for the guidance it can give the future. One of the main objectives of economists is to discern such trends. But just what these directions are is a controversial issue among scholars, especially between the advocates of Marxism and their critics. Of the latter, Professor W. W. Rostow of the Massachusetts Institute of Technology has been prominent, since he elaborated a non-Communist Manifesto. Rostow's historical theory of economic growth is characterized by discontinuity and sudden thrusts of progress, and embraces five major stages of development. First, he notes the appearance of traditional societies in which men have not as yet learned the uses of technology. But the gradual impact of science leads them to a pre-take-off phase, a period of transition to industrialism. The take-off constitutes the third stage, when diversified economic expansion finally takes place. The economy then gradually develops maturity during which it experiences sustained, if fluctuating, complex economic progress. The final phase in Rostow's scheme is mass consumption, as consumers' goods and services become dominant in the economy. Whether spiritual stagnation lies beyond this epoch Rostow leaves open to question. This stimulating explanation of economic growth, applicable also to the United States, has been subjected to severe criticism, especially by Professor Paul Baran, a well-known Marxist economist, and E. J. Hobshawm, a British labor expert. They question Rostow's theory as an explanation of the pattern of economic development, and his neglect of Marxist doctrines. They say that not only did Rostow fail to provide a clear explanation of the mechanisms that linked one stage to another; he also did not propose any acceptable alternatives for the catalyst of economic progress pinpointed by Marx-productive forces. Thus, Baran and Hobshawm anticipate future economic tendencies within a Marxian framework. Both sides in this controversy raise fundamental issues. Are there patterns in economic growth? How can the directions of economic change be predicted? What are some possible directions of economic expansion during the second half of the twentieth century?

The Stages of Economic Growth

W. W. ROSTOW

It is possible to identify all societies, in their economic dimensions, as lying within one of five categories: the traditional society, the preconditions for take-off, the take-off, the drive to maturity, and the age of high mass-consumption.

THE TRADITIONAL SOCIETY

First, the traditional society. A traditional society is one whose structure is developed within limited production functions, based on pre-Newtonian science and technology, and on pre-Newtonian attitudes towards the physical world. Newton is here used as a symbol for that watershed in history when men came widely to believe that the external world was subject to a few knowable laws, and was systematically capable of productive manipulation.

The conception of the traditional society is, however, in no sense static; and it would not exclude increases in output. Acreage could be expanded; some *ad hoc* technical innovations, often highly productive innovations, could be introduced in trade, industry and agriculture; productivity could rise with, for example, the improvement of irrigation works or the discovery and diffusion of a new crop. But the central fact about the traditional society was that a ceiling existed on the level of attainable output per head. This ceiling resulted from the fact that the potentialities which flow from modern science and technology were either not available or not regularly and systematically applied.

From *The Stages of Economic Growth,* by W. W. Rostow (London, 1960), pp. 4–12. Reprinted by permission of the publishers, Cambridge University Press.

Both in the longer past and in recent times the story of traditional societies was thus a story of endless change. The area and volume of trade within them and between them fluctuated, for example, with the degree of political and social turbulence, the efficiency of central rule, the upkeep of the roads. Population—and, within limits, the level of life—rose and fell not only with the sequence of the harvests, but with the incidence of war and of plague. Varying degrees of manufacture developed; but, as in agriculture, the level of productivity was limited by the inaccessibility of modern science, its applications, and its frame of mind.

Generally speaking, these societies, because of the limitation on productivity, had to devote a very high proportion of their resources to agriculture; and flowing from the agricultural system there was an hierarchical social structure, with relatively narrow scope—but some scope—for vertical mobility. Family and clan connexions played a large role in social organization. The value system of these societies was generally geared to what might be called a long-run fatalism; that is, the assumption that the range of possibilities open to one's grandchildren would be just about what it had been for one's grandparents. But this long-run fatalism by no means excluded the short-run option that, within a considerable range, it was possible and legitimate for the individual to strive to improve his lot, within his lifetime. In Chinese villages, for example, there was an endless struggle to acquire or to avoid losing land, yielding a situation where land rarely remained within the same family for a century.

Although central political rule—in one form or another—often existed in traditional societies, transcending the relatively self-sufficient regions, the centre of gravity of political power generally lay in the regions, in the hands of those who owned or controlled the land. The landowner maintained fluctuating but usually profound influence over such central political power as existed, backed by its entourage of civil servants and soldiers, imbued with attitudes and controlled by interests transcending the regions.

In terms of history then, with the phrase "traditional society" we are grouping the whole pre-Newtonian world: the dynasties in China; the civilization of the Middle East and the Mediterranean; the world of medieval Europe. And to them we add the post-Newtonian societies which, for a time, remained untouched or unmoved by man's new capability for regularly manipulating his environment to his economic advantage.

To place these infinitely various, changing societies in a single category, on the ground that they all shared a ceiling on the productivity of their economic techniques, is to say very little indeed. But we are, after all, merely clearing the way in order to get at the subject of this book; that is, the post-traditional societies, in which each of the major characteristics of the traditional society was altered in such ways as to permit regular growth: its politics, social structure, and (to a degree) its values, as well as its economy.

THE PRECONDITIONS FOR TAKE-OFF

The second stage of growth embraces societies in the process of transition; that is, the period when the preconditions for take-off are developed; for it takes time to transform a traditional society in the ways necessary for it to exploit the fruits of modern science, to fend off diminishing returns, and thus to enjoy the blessings and choices opened up by the march of compound interest.

The preconditions for take-off were initially developed, in a clearly marked way, in Western Europe of the late seventeenth and early eighteenth centuries as the insights of modern science began to be translated into new production functions in both agriculture and industry, in a setting given dynamism by the lateral expansion of world markets and the international competition for them. But all that lies behind the break-up of the Middle Ages is relevant to the creation of the preconditions for take-off in Western Europe. Among the Western European states, Britain, favoured by geography, natural resources, trading possibilities, social and political structure, was the first to develop fully the preconditions for take-off.

The more general case in modern history, however, saw the stage of preconditions arise not endogenously but from external intrusion by more advanced societies. These invasions—literal or figurative—shocked the traditional society and began or hastened its undoing; but they also set in motion ideas and sentiments which initiated the process by which a modern alternative to the traditional society was constructed out of the old culture.

The idea spreads not merely that economic progress is possible, but that economic progress is a necessary condition for some other purpose, judged to be good: be it national dignity, private profit, the general welfare, or a better life for the children. Education, for some at least, broadens and changes to suit the needs of modern economic activity. New types of enterprising men come forward—in the private economy, in government, or both—willing to mobilize savings and to take risks in pursuit of profit or modernization. Banks and other institutions for mobilizing capital appear. Investment increases, notably in transport, communications, and in raw materials in which other nations may have an economic interest. The scope of commerce, internal and external, widens. And, here and there, modern manufacturing enterprise appears, using the new methods. But all this activity proceeds at a limited pace within an economy and a society still mainly characterized by traditional low-productivity methods, by the old social structure and values, and by the regionally based political institutions that developed in conjunction with them.

In many recent cases, for example, the traditional society persisted side by side with modern economic activities, conducted for limited economic purposes by a colonial or quasi-colonial power.

Although the period of transition—between the traditional society and the take-off—saw major changes in both the economy itself and in the balance of social values, a decisive feature was often political. Politically, the building of an effective centralized national state—on the basis of coalitions touched with a new nationalism, in opposition to the traditional landed regional interests, the colonial power, or both, was a decisive aspect of the preconditions period; and it was, almost universally, a necessary condition for take-off. . . .

THE TAKE-OFF

We come now to the great watershed in the life of modern societies: the third stage in this sequence, the take-off. The take-off is the interval when the old blocks and resistances to steady growth are finally overcome. The forces making for economic progress, which yielded limited bursts and enclaves of modern activity, expand and come to dominate the society. Growth becomes its normal condition. Compound interest becomes built, as it were, into its habits and institutional structure.

In Britain and the well-endowed parts of the world populated substantially from Britain (the United States, Canada, etc.) the proximate stimulus for take-off was mainly (but not wholly) technological. In the more general case, the take-off awaited not only the build-up of social overhead capital and a surge of technological development in industry and agriculture, but also the emergence to political power of a group prepared to regard the modernization of the economy as serious, high-order political business.

During the take-off, the rate of effective investment and savings may rise from, say, 5% of the national income to 10% or more; although where heavy social overhead capital investment was required to create the technical preconditions for take-off the investment rate in the preconditions period could be higher than 5%, as, for example, in Canada before the 1890's and Argentina before 1914. In such cases capital imports usually formed a high proportion of total investment in the preconditions period and sometimes even during the take-off itself, as in Russia and Canada during their pre-1914 railway booms.

During the take-off new industries expand rapidly, yielding profits a large proportion of which are reinvested in new plant; and these new industries, in turn, stimulate, through their rapidly expanding requirement for factory workers, the services to support them, and for other manufactured goods, a further expansion in urban areas and in other modern industrial plants. The whole process of expansion in the modern sector yields an increase of income in the hands of those who not only save at high rates but place their savings at the disposal of those engaged in modern sector activities. The new class of entrepreneurs expands; and it directs the enlarging flows of investment in the private sector. The economy exploits hitherto unused natural resources and methods of production.

New techniques spread in agriculture as well as industry, as agriculture is commercialized, and increasing numbers of farmers are prepared to accept the new methods and the deep changes they bring to ways of life. The revolutionary changes in agricultural productivity are an essential condition for successful take-off; for modernization of a society increases radically its bill for agricultural products. In a decade or two both the basic structure of the economy and the social and political structure of the society are transformed in such a way that a steady rate of growth can be, thereafter, regularly sustained.

One can approximately allocate the take-off of Britain to the two decades after 1783; France and the United States to the several decades preceding 1860; Germany, the third quarter of the nineteenth century; Japan, the fourth quarter of the nineteenth century; Russia and Canada, the quarter-century or so preceding 1914; while during the 1950's India and China have, in quite different ways, launched their respective take-offs.

THE DRIVE TO MATURITY

After take-off there follows a long interval of sustained if fluctuating progress, as the now regularly growing economy drives to extend modern technology over the whole front of its economic activity. Some 10–20% of the national income is steadily invested, permitting output regularly to outstrip the increase in population. The make-up of the economy changes unceasingly as technique improves, new industries accelerate, older industries level off. The economy finds its place in the international economy: goods formerly imported are produced at home; new import requirements develop, and new export commodities to match them. The society makes such terms as it will with the requirements of modern efficient production, balancing off the new against the older values and institutions, or revising the latter in such ways as to support rather than to retard the growth process.

Some sixty years after take-off begins (say, forty years after the end of take-off) what may be called maturity is generally attained. The economy, focused during the take-off around a relatively narrow complex of industry and technology, has extended its range into more refined and technologically often more complex processes; for example, there may be a shift in focus from the coal, iron, and heavy engineering industries of the railway phase to machine-tools, chemicals, and electrical equipment. This, for example, was the transition through which Germany, Britain, France, and the United States had passed by the end of the nineteenth century or shortly thereafter. But there are other sectoral patterns which have been followed in the sequence from take-off to maturity. . . .

Formally, we can define maturity as the stage in which an economy demonstrates the capacity to move beyond the original industries which powered its take-off and to absorb and to apply efficiently over a very wide range of its resources—if not the whole range—the most advanced fruits of (then) modern technology. This is the stage in which an economy demonstrates that it has the technological and entrepreneurial skills to produce not everything, but anything that it chooses to produce. It may lack (like contemporary Sweden and Switzerland, for example) the raw materials or other supply conditions required to produce a given type of output economically; but its dependence is a matter of economic choice or political priority rather than a technological or institutional necessity.

Historically, it would appear that something like sixty years was required to move a society from the beginning of take-off to maturity. Analytically the explanation for some such interval may lie in the powerful arithmetic of compound interest applied to the capital stock, combined with the broader consequences for a society's ability to absorb modern technology of three successive generations living under a regime where growth is the normal condition. But, clearly, no dogmatism is justified about the exact length of the interval from take-off to maturity.

THE AGE OF HIGH MASS-CONSUMPTION

We come now to the age of high mass-consumption, where, in time, the leading sectors shift towards durable consumers' goods and services: a phase from which Americans are beginning to emerge; whose not unequivocal joys Western Europe and Japan are beginning energetically to probe; and with which Soviet society is engaged in an uneasy flirtation.

As societies achieved maturity in the twentieth century two things happened: real income per head rose to a point where a large number of persons gained a command over consumption which transcended basic food, shelter, and clothing; and the structure of the working force changed in ways which increased not only the proportion of urban to total population, but also the proportion of the population working in offices or in skilled factory jobs—aware of and anxious to acquire the consumption fruits of a mature economy.

In addition to these economic changes, the society ceased to accept the further extension of modern technology as an overriding objective. It is in this post-maturity stage, for example, that, through the political process, Western societies have chosen to allocate increased resources to social welfare and security. The emergence of the welfare state is one manifestation of a society's moving beyond technical maturity; but it is also at this stage that resources tend increasingly to be directed to the production of consumers' durables and to the diffusion of services on a mass basis, if consumers' sovereignty reigns. The sewing-machine, the bicycle, and then the various electric-powered household gadgets were gradually diffused. Historically, however, the decisive element has been the cheap mass automobile with its quite revolutionary effects—social as well as economic— on the life and expectations of society.

For the United States, the turning point was, perhaps, Henry Ford's moving assembly line of 1913–14; but it was in the 1920's, and again in the post-war decade, 1946–56, that this stage of growth was pressed to, vir-tually, its logical conclusion. In the 1950's Western Europe and Japan appear to have fully entered this phase, accounting substantially for a momentum in their economies quite unexpected in the immediate post-war years. The Soviet Union is technically ready for this stage, and, by every sign, its citizens hunger for it; but Communist leaders face difficult political and social problems of adjustment if this stage is launched.

BEYOND CONSUMPTION

Beyond, it is impossible to predict, except perhaps to observe that Americans, at least, have behaved in the past decade as if diminishing relative marginal utility sets in, after a point, for durable consumers' goods; and they have chosen, at the margin, larger families—behaviour in the pattern of Buddenbrooks dynamics.[1] Americans have behaved as if, having been born into a system that provided economic security and high mass-consumption, they placed a lower valuation on acquiring additional increments of real income in the conventional form as opposed to the advantages and values of an enlarged family. But even in this adventure in generalization it is a shade too soon to create—on the basis of one case— a new stage-of-growth, based on babies, in succession to the age of consumers' durables: as economists might say, the income-elasticity of demand for babies may well vary from society to society. But it is true that the implications of the baby boom along with the not wholly unrelated deficit in social overhead capital are likely to dominate the American economy over the next decade rather than the further diffusion of consumers' durables.

[1] In Thomas Mann's novel of three generations, the first sought money; the second, born to money, sought social and civil position; the third, born to comfort and family prestige, looked to the life of music. The phrase is designed to suggest, then, the changing aspirations of generations, as they place a low value on what they take for granted and seek new forms of satisfaction.

Here then, in an impressionistic rather than an analytic way, are the stages-of-growth which can be distinguished once a traditional society begins its modernization: the transitional period when the preconditions for take-off are created generally in response to the intrusion of a foreign power, converging with certain domestic forces making for modernization; the take-off itself; the sweep into maturity generally taking up the life of about two further generations; and then, finally, if the rise of income has matched the spread of technological virtuosity (which, as we shall see, it need not immediately do) the diversion of the fully mature economy to the provision of durable consumers' goods and services (as well as the welfare state) for its increasingly urban—and then suburban —population. Beyond lies the question of whether or not secular spiritual stagnation will arise, and, if it does, how man might fend it off. . . .

The Stages of Economic Growth: *A Review*

PAUL BARAN AND ERNEST HOBSHAWM

On the jacket of W. W. Rostow's *The Stages of Economic Growth: A Non-Communist Manifesto*, the publisher advertises the product in these terms: "This book is a generalization from the whole span of modern history. It gives an account of economic growth based on a dynamic theory of production and interpreted in terms of actual societies. It helps to explain historical changes and to predict major political and economic trends; and it provides the significant links between economic and noneconomic behavior which Karl Marx failed to discern." The author's own sales-pitch is equally strident: "The stages are not merely descriptions. They are not merely a way of generalizing certain factual observations about the sequence of development of modern societies. They have an inner logic and continuity. They have an analytical bone-structure rooted in a dynamic theory of production" (pp. 12f.). And the reason for this enthusiasm is not only the light which the new theory is supposed to shed upon the process of economic and social evolution but also its alleged power to dispose once and for all of the Marxian dragon with which so many others have done battle but failed to slay. The reader is urged to "note the similarities between his (Marx's) analysis and the stages of growth; and the differences between the two systems of thought, stage by stage."

We propose to accept this invitation and to carry out the comparison which Professor Rostow suggests. In what follows, the first section will

Reprinted by permission from *Kyklos*, XIV (1961), pp. 234–242.

deal with the stages-of-growth scheme's contribution to the theory of economic development. The second section will attempt to answer the question whether Marxian thought is capable of surviving this newest assault.

I

Such attention as Professor Rostow's writings have hitherto been able to command in the literature on economic development has been based upon some of his earlier empirical studies. His theoretical contributions have been meager—in fact, largely confined to various types of classification. Does his latest effort significantly change this picture?

Professor Rostow advances three propositions. First, he insists that the problem of growth is a historical one which must be considered within a framework of a historical periodization. Second, he emphasizes—and this is perhaps his most notable point—that economic growth is not a continuous and smooth but a discontinuous and dialectical process which pivots on a sudden revolutionary transformation, the "take-off into self-sustained growth." Third, he stresses a particular aspect of this discontinuity of economic growth: that it proceeds not by a balanced development of all sectors of the economy, but by successive leaps forward of the economy's "leading sectors."

These are undoubtedly valuable insights, although it can hardly be said that they are new or that they originate with Professor Rostow. That theories of growth must be historical was perhaps the first discovery of political economy; it has merely been forgotten in the century or so in which economic growth was almost wholly neglected in academic economics, except for the Marxists and those who, like the Germans and Schumpeter, accepted much of the Marxist *Fragestellung* [framework] on the subject. The "take-off" is merely another name for the "industrial revolution" which was the basic analytic concept of modern economic history. . . . The argument for uneven development is equally old. It was advanced by Marx, developed by Lenin, and underlies the Schumpeter-Kondratiev analysis of 19th century economic development. To be sure, the rediscovery of old truths is a most creditable accomplishment—particularly in contemporary "behavioral sciences" where apparently any nonsense goes as long as it has never been said before—though not one calling in itself for a major ovation.

But when we come to consider Professor Rostow's other achievements in the field of the theory of growth, the weaknesses are all too obvious. The first and most serious is that his theory of "stages" actually tells us nothing except that there are stages. The four other stages are implicit in the "take-off," and add nothing to it. Given a "take-off" there must obviously be a stage before it when the conditions for economic growth are not present, another when the pre-conditions for the "take-off" exist, and yet another following it when "an economy demonstrates that it has the technological and entrepreneurial skills to produce not everything, but anything it wants" (which is Rostow's definition of the stage of "maturity"), and yet another when it has acquired the capacity to produce everything it wants (p. 10). Indeed, there is no departure ("take-off") of any kind—in the history of nature, of societies or of individuals —which cannot be thought of as being preceded and followed by a number of "stages." If one has a penchant for symmetry one only has to make sure that the total number of stages—the "take-off" included— should be uneven.

Thus once we have one corner, we have the entire Pentagon. One weakness of this procedure is, of course, that analysis must remain confined to its area. Accordingly, the Rostovian stage theory, despite its comprehensive historic and sociological claims reduces economic growth to a single pattern. Any and every country, whatever its other characteristics, is classifiable only in respect to its position on the stepladder, the middle rung of which is the "take-off." This gives the Rostovian stages an air of spurious generality—they appear to apply to any and all economies, to the USSR as to the USA, to China as to Brazil—which, as we shall see, is not without its ideological implications, though it overlooks the obvious fact that, however universal the technical problems of economic growth may be, different social types of economic organization can, or must, solve them in very different ways.

Yet even within its extremely narrow limits the Rostovian theory can neither explain nor predict without introducing considerations that are completely irrelevant to the stage schema. It simply fails to specify any mechanism of evolution which links the different stages. There is no particular reason why the "traditional" society should turn into a society breeding the "preconditions" of the "take-off." Rostow's account merely summarizes what these preconditions must be, and repeats a version of that "classical answer" the inadequacy of which has long been evident: a combination of the "discovery and rediscovery of regions beyond Western Europe" and the "developing of modern scientific knowledge and attitudes" (p. 31). Here is the *deus cum machina*. Nor is there any reason within the Rostovian stages why the "preconditions" should lead to the "take-off" to maturity, as is indeed evidenced by Rostow's own difficulty in discovering, except long *ex post facto*, whether a "take-off" has taken place or not. In fact the Rostovian "take-off" concept has no predictive value. Similarly, when it comes to analyzing the "inner structure" (p. 46) of the take-off or of any other stage, the Rostovian theory subsides into statements of the type that "things can happen in any one of a very large number of different ways," which constitute a rather limited contribution to knowledge.

Such explanations and predictions as Rostow attempts are therefore little more than verbiage which has no connection with his stages theory or indeed with any theory of economic and social evolution, being generally based on what might be charitably called coffeehouse sociology and political speculation. The nearest he actually comes to an attempt at an explanation of *why* economic growth takes place is his emphasis on the importance of "reactive nationalism" and the crucial role of "an inherently competitive system of power" in which states are historically enmeshed. The explanation tends to be circular—when a country has economic growth it is evidence of reactive nationalism—as well as open-ended: when an obviously nationalist country does *not* initiate a take-off, it is because "nationalism can be turned in any one of several directions" (p. 29). Moreover, even this type of explanation is crippled by Rostow's refusal to admit the profit motive into his analysis, a refusal not concealed by an occasional parenthetical remark granting its existence. Still, weak as it is, the explanation of economic growth by nationalism and the logic of international rivalry is the closest Rostow comes to an analysis of economic development as distinct from relabelling and classifying it.

And this is not very close. For in addition to an incapacity to answer relevant questions, Professor Rostow shows an astonishing lack of ability for even recognizing their existence or their import. Thus one of the crucial problems which face both the theorist and would-be planner of economic development under capitalist conditions is that "the criteria for private profit-maximization do not necessarily converge with the criteria for an optimum rate and pattern of growth in various sectors" (p. 50), indeed, that under pre-industrial conditions or in underdeveloped areas it can be shown that they are more likely than not to diverge. The statesman or economic administrator of a backward country knows that a century of western capitalism has failed to transfer any country across the gap which separates the advanced from the backward economies. He also knows that profit-oriented private investment can be relied on to build his country's tourist hotels but not its steelworks. Consequently he has increasingly taken to imitating the Soviet method of achieving economic growth, which does not suffer from this disadvantage, rather than relying on the 19th-century European or American method which does. Rostow neither explains any of these facts which determine the actual problem of economic development in underdeveloped areas, nor does he even seem aware of them beyond the casual mention already quoted. Conversely, the historian must explain why, in spite of this divergence, or lack of convergence, a limited number of countries around the North Atlantic in the 18th and 19th centuries actually managed to industrialize on a capitalist basis. Rostow appears equally oblivious of this problem.

This obtuseness is not accidental. Indeed, the nature of Professor

Rostow's approach makes it impossible for him to solve such problems, and difficult even to realize their existence. For if we argue that the main motor of economic change was at no time "profit-maximization (in the sense of) economic advantage" (pp. 149 ff.), we can hardly deal with, let alone answer questions which arise from the fact that all economic development between the "traditional" society and the appearance of the USSR was actually *capitalist* development and which calls therefore for an analysis of the specific characteristics of *capitalism*. If we abstract from everything that separates "eighteenth century Britain and Khrushchev's Russia; Meiji Japan and Mao's China; Bismarck's Germany and Nasser's Egypt" (p. 1), we shall be unable to explain why Nasser's Egypt finds Khrushchev's Russia a more useful guide to economic development than eighteenth century Britain. If we are anxious to minimize the element of economic advantage in the relation between advanced and dependent (colonial) economies (pp. 108–112, 137/38, 156), we shall be unable to say anything useful about problems which arise out of the fact that dependent economies are dependent.

Why, it may be asked, should a man adopt a theoretical approach so obviously defective and indeed self-defeating? At least one plausible answer may be suggested. Professor Rostow is, on his own admission, primarily concerned not with arriving at a theory of economic development, but with writing a "non-communist manifesto." Unlike other and wiser—we shall not say abler—scholars with similar objectives, he has chosen to abandon not merely Marx's conclusions and his arguments, but even the basic posing of the problem of economic development as Marx saw it. It was, as we have tried to show, an unwise decision, for the Marxian questions are fundamental to any attempt at an understanding of the process of economic development. What is required is at least an *understanding* of Marx's questions. To that level Professor Rostow has yet to rise.

II

An examination of the principal tenets of Rostow's theory of economic growth—if it can be at all said that such a *theory* is advanced in his book —thus reveals nothing that can be considered an addition to our knowledge of the history of economic development or an enrichment of our understanding of the processes involved. But Rostow offers something much more ambitious than "merely" a new theory of economic growth. He also proposes "a comprehensive, realistic and soundly based alternative to Marx's theory of how societies evolve." Let us examine this latest effort to put Marx into the wastebasket. Since, however, it is neither possible nor would it be rewarding to trace all the misconceptions and misrepresentations of Marxian thought which Rostow has managed to compress in a few pages, we will have to limit ourselves to two problems which Rostow himself considers to be central to his Manifesto.

The first relates to the nature of the engine which propels economic, social, and political evolution in the course of history. To this fundamental question, historical materialism provides a comprehensive and sophisticated answer. Far be it from us to seek to emulate Rostow in the claim that this answer supplies pat solutions to all problems raised by the complex events and patterns of history. What historical materialism does claim is to have discovered an indispensable *approach* to the understanding of historical constellations and to have focused attention on the nature of the principal energies responsible for their emergence, transformation, and disappearance. To put it in a nutshell: these energies are to be traced back to the always present tension between the degree of development of the forces of production on one side, and the prevailing relations of production on the other. To be sure, neither "forces of production" nor "relations of production" are simple notions. The former encompasses the existing state or rationality, science, and technology, the mode of organization of production and the degree of development of man himself, that "most important productive force of all" (Marx). The latter refers to the mode of appropriation of the products of human labor, the social condition under which production takes place, the principles of distribution, the modes of thought, the ideology, the *Weltanschauung* which constitute the "general ether" (Marx) within which society functions at any given time. The conflict between the two —sometimes dormant and sometimes active—is due to a fundamental difference in the "laws of motion" of forces and relations of production respectively. The forces of production tend to be highly dynamic. Driven by man's quest for a better life, by the growth and expansion of human knowledge and rationality, by increasing population, the forces of production tend continually to gain in strength, in depth and in scope. The relations of production on the other hand tend to be sticky, conservative. Prevailing systems of appropriation and social organization, and political institutions favor some classes and discriminate against, frustrate, oppress other classes. They give rise to vested interests. Modes of thought freeze and display a tenacity and longevity giving rise to what is sometimes referred to as "cultural lags." When the forward movement of the forces of production becomes stymied by the deadweight of dominant interests and the shackles of dominant thought, one or the other has to yield. And since a dominant class never willingly relinquishes its time-honored privileges (partly for reasons of self-interest and partly because its own horizon is more or less narrowly circumscribed by the prevailing ideology sanctifying those very privileges), the clash tends to become violent. This is not to say that obsolete, retrograde relations of production are *always* burst asunder and swept away by revolutions. Depending on the circumstances prevailing in each individual case, the process unfolds in a wide variety of ways. Violent upheavals "from below" and relatively peaceful transformations "from above" are as much within the range of possibilities as periods of protracted stagnation in which the political, ideological, and social power of the ruling classes is strong enough to prevent the emergence of new forms of economic and social organization, to block or to slow a country's economic development.

Marx's historical materialism insists, however, that the development of the forces of production has thus far been *the* commanding aspect of the historical process. Whatever may have been its vicissitudes, whatever may have been the setbacks and interruptions that it has suffered in the course of history, in the long run it has tended to overcome all obstacles, and to conquer all political, social and ideological structures, subordinating them to its requirements. This struggle between the forces of production and the relations of production proceeds unevenly. Dramatic conquests are less frequent than long periods of siege in which victories remain elusive, imperfect, and impermanent. Different countries display different patterns which depend on their size, location, the strength and cohesion of their ruling classes, the courage, determination and leadership of the underprivileged; on the measure of foreign influence and support to which both or either are exposed; on the pervasiveness and power of the dominant ideologies (e.g. religion). Moreover, the course taken by this struggle and its outcome differ greatly from period to period. Under conditions of capitalism's competitive youth they were different from what they have become in the age of imperialism; in the presence of a powerful socialist sector of the world, they are not the same as they were or would have been in its absence. No bloodless schema of 5 (or 3 or 7) "stages" can do justice to the multitude and variety of economic, technological, political, and ideological configurations generated by this never-ceasing battle between the forces and relations of production. What Marx and Engels and Lenin taught those whose ambition it was to learn rather than to make careers by "refuting" is that these historical configurations cannot be dealt with by "a generalization from the whole span of modern history," but have to be studied *concretely*, with full account taken of the wealth of factors and forces that participate in the shaping of any particular historical case.

To forestall a possible misunderstanding: the foregoing is not intended to advocate renunciation of theory in favor of plodding empiricism. Rather it suggests the necessity of an interpenetration of theory and concrete observation, of empirical research illuminated by rational theory, of theoretical work which draws its life blood from historical study. Consider for instance any one of the many existing underdeveloped countries. Pigeonholing it in one of Rostow's "stages" does not bring us any closer to an understanding of the country's economic and social condition or give us a clue to the country's developmental possibilities and prospects. What is required for that is as accurate as possible an assessment of the social and political forces in the country pressing for change and for development (the economic condition and the stratification of the peasantry, its political traditions and its ideological make-up, the economic and social status, internal differentiation and political aspirations of the bourgeoisie, the extent of its tie-up with foreign interests and the degree of monopoly prevailing in its national business, the closeness of its connection with the landowning interests and the measure of its participation in the existing government; the living and working conditions and the level of class consciousness of labor and its political and organizational strength). Nor is this by any means the entire job. On the other side of the fence are the groups, institutions, relations, and ideologies seeking to preserve the *status quo*, obstructing efforts directed towards its overturn. There are wealthy land-owners and/or rich peasants; there is a segment of the capitalist class firmly entrenched in monopolistic positions and allied with other privileged groups in society; there is a government bureaucracy interwoven with and resting upon the military establishment; there are foreign investors supported by their respective national governments and working hand in hand with their native retainers. Only a thorough historical-materialist analysis, piercing the ideological fog maintained by the dominant coalition of interests and destroying the fetishes continually produced and reproduced by those concerned with the preservation of the *status quo*, only such historical-materialist analysis can hope to disentangle the snarl of tendencies and countertendencies, forces, influences, convictions and opinions, drives and resistances which account for the pattern of economic and social development. And it is to this *Marxist* undertaking that Professor Rostow offers us his alternative: to assign the country in question to one of his "stages," and then to speculate on the "two possibilities" with which that country is confronted: it will either move on to the next "stage"—or it won't. And if it should move to the next "stage," it will again face two possibilities: it will either stay there for a while, or it will slide back again.

We may now turn briefly to Professor Rostow's other sally against Marx by which he seeks to provide "significant links between economic and non-economic behavior which Karl Marx failed to discern." This enterprise, he apparently feels, will deliver the "coup de grâce" to Marxian thought, "for," he assures us "it is absolutely essential to Marxism that it is over property that men fight and die" (p. 151). What Karl Marx—"a lonely man, profoundly isolated from his fellows"—did not discern, but Professor Rostow does, is the following: "Man . . . seeks, not merely economic advantage, but also power, leisure, adventure, continuity of experience and security . . . in short, net human behavior is . . . not an act of maximization, but . . . an act of balancing alternative and often conflicting human objectives." "This notion of balance among alternatives," Professor Rostow observes "is, of course, more complex and difficult than a simple maximization proposition; and it does not lead to a series of rigid, inevitable stages of history." We submit that this "notion" may well be "complex and difficult" but that it is also singularly devoid of any ascertainable content. It is remarkable how Professor Rostow, after having constructed a strawman bearing no resemblance to Marxism finds it beyond his powers to vanquish even such a "hand-picked" enemy.

Indeed—to put it bluntly—the whole argument is too helpless to serve even as a starting point for a serious discussion. Even a passing acquaintance with the most important writings of Marx, Engels, and more recent Marxist writers is all that is required to realize the irrelevance of Rostow's caricature of Marxism. Far from asserting that "history is uniquely determined by economic forces," and far from ignoring the "significant links between economic and non-economic behavior," the theory of historical materialism advanced by Marx and his followers is nothing if not a powerful effort to explore the manifold, and historically changing connections between the development of the forces and relations of production and the evolution of the consciousness, emotions, and ideologies of men. So much so that the Marxian theory of ideology has served as the point of departure and as a guide to an entire discipline known under the name of "sociology of knowledge," with all analytical history of religion, literature, art and science deriving its inspiration for the same source. Marx's theory of alienation anticipating much of the subsequent development of social psychology, is in the center of modern study and criticism of culture. Marx's political theory has served as a conceptual basis for most that is valuable in modern European and American historical scholarship. And *The Eighteenth of Brumaire of Louis Bonaparte*—to name only one unsurpassed gem of historical and sociological study—still shines as a model of a comprehensive and penetrating analysis of the "significant links between economic and non-economic behavior" in one particular historical case.

But all this escapes Mr. Rostow who is not only incapable of contributing anything to the discussion of the relevant problems but even fails to comprehend the context within which they arise. For the problem of the "links between economic and non-economic behavior," or for that matter of the explanation of any human activity, economic or other, is not and never has been whether or not man "balances alternatives" or "adheres to the principle of maximization" (which terms, incidentally, if they mean anything at all, amount to exactly the same), no more than there is meaning to the question whether man does or does not have "freedom of will." No one in his right mind—Marxist, mechanical materialist, or idealist—has ever denied that men make choices, exercise their wills, balance alternatives, or, for that matter, move their legs when they walk.

The problem is and always has been to discover what determines the nature of the alternatives that are available to men, what accounts for the nature of the goals which they set themselves in different periods of historical development, what makes them will what they will in various societies at various times. To this fundamental question there have been several answers. The theologian's solution has been that all human acts and decisions are governed by the omnipotent and inscrutable will of God. The idealist who substituted the human spirit for the Deity arrives at a very similar position, unable as he is to explain what accounts for the actions and transactions of the spirit. The adherents of "psychologism" view human activity as an emanation of the human psyche itself an aspect of an eternally constant human nature. The historical materialist considers human actions and motivations to be complex results of a dialectical interaction of biotic and social processes, the latter continually propelled by the dynamism of the forces and relations of production as well as by the ideological evolutions deriving from them and influencing them in turn. Professor Rostow, however, has the simplest solution of all: he does not know what the answer is, nor does he appear to care. Anything can happen: man moves hither and thither, balancing alternatives, making choices, striving for power, engaged in maximization of who knows what. And this is the new, original, unprecedented "theory" which makes good what Karl Marx failed to discern.

We owe the reader an apology. Taken by itself Rostow's Manifesto does not call for a lengthy review. If we have undertaken to write one nevertheless, it is because of considerations from the realm of the sociology of knowledge. His is an important document. It demonstrates in a particularly striking way the low estate to which Western social thought has declined in the current era of the cold war.

FOR FURTHER READING: Professor Paul Baran makes a positive formulation of future economic trends within a Marxian scheme in *The Political Economy of Growth* (New York, 1957). Other efforts to peer into the future are by Colin Clark, *The Conditions of Economic Progress* (2d revised edit., London, 1951), W. Arthur Lewis, *The Theory of Economic Growth* (London, 1955), Committee for Economic Development, *Economic Growth in the United States: Its Past and Future* (New York, 1958), and Sumner H. Slichter, who sums up a lifetime of thought on the subject in *Economic Growth in the United States: Its History, Problems, and Prospects*, edited by John T. Dunlop (Baton Rouge, 1961). Specific problems in relation to economic growth are discussed in J. J. Spengler (ed.), *Natural Resources and Economic Growth* (Washington, 1961), Bert F. Hoselitz, *Sociological Aspects of Economic Growth* (Glencoe, 1960), and Moses Abramovitz (ed.), *Capital Formation and Economic Growth* (Princeton, 1955).

Index